THE
CONSTITUTION

A DOCUMENTARY AND NARRATIVE HISTORY

Also by Page Smith

THE CONSTITUTION

A DOCUMENTARY AND NARRATIVE HISTORY

by

PAGE SMITH

MORROW QUILL PAPERBACKS
New York   1980

Library of Congress Cataloging in Publication Data

Smith, Page.
    1. United States—Constitutional history.

    Includes index.
    1. United States—Constitutional history.
I. Title.
KF4541.S64   342'.73'029   78-17225
ISBN 0-688-03340-0
      0-688-08349-8 pbk.

BOOK DESIGN   CARL WEISS

Printed in the United States of America.

3 4 5 6 7 8 9 10

To John Dizikes,

Student, Colleague, Teacher,

Friend

I wish to express my thanks to Charlotte Cassidy and Frances Rydell for their devoted attentions to this work, to Charles Natanson for invaluable assistance, and to Norman O. Brown for a crucial phrase.

CONTENTS

THE
CONSTITUTION

A DOCUMENTARY AND
NARRATIVE HISTORY

INTRODUCTION

IT IS OFTEN SAID THAT THE FEDERAL CONSTITUTION IS A LIVING document. But we hardly appreciate, I think, the degree to which this is true; how pervasive the influence of the Constitution is in the lives of all Americans. From the suspected murderer who insists on his "constitutional rights" to the American Indian, Chicano, or black who fights for those rights he or she believes guaranteed under the Constitution, the Constitution is daily invoked. Prisoners in death row wait for the latest word from the Supreme Court on whether the death penalty is constitutional. High-school students resist the order to cut off their hair on the ground that the order is an infringement of their constitutional rights. In the name of free speech pornographic book-stores and movie houses grow like unsightly scabs in urban and sub-urban areas. In my own town last week an indignant street poet solicited my support. The poet had been reciting and selling his poems on the town mall. A policeman ordered him to cease and desist, citing a local ordinance. The poet believed his freedom of speech had been infringed. He called the district attorney of the county with his com-plaint. The district attorney supported the poet's right to read his poems. A week later I encountered the poet again, cheerfully selling his poems and asserting thereby what he believed to be his constitu-tional right. One is tempted to say, "Only in America." I am not sure that is true. Poets sell their poems elsewhere—on the streets of Dar es Salaam and Katmandu for all I know—but nowhere else in the world are people as conscious of their relationship to their "Constitu-tion." In the United States no congressional statute or municipal ordinance is passed without attention to the question of whether it is or will be "constitutional," in other words in accord with legal principles laid down almost two hundred years ago by a handful of provincial politicians who had in effect assumed responsibility for devising a government to guide the affairs of three or four million people (the vast majority of them farmers) in thirteen states. That is the Constitution of the United States.

I believe it is safe to say that no other political document in the history of the human race has had anything approaching the influence of the federal Constitution. It is not perhaps going too far to say that Americans invented the modern notion of "a constitution." We will take note of the fact that constitutions of one kind or another have had a history extending back to classical times and earlier, but for all practical purposes, the modern constitution as a coherent written document, at least theoretically expressing the will of the people, was invented by American politicians in the summer of 1787.

How it came to be "invented" is a story that can be told relatively clearly, allowing as always in historical narrative for certain obscurities and impenetrable secrets. How it came to perform the function that it has in the lives of several hundred million Americans living in a vast technological society and how its influence has been felt in every part of the world is infinitely more mysterious and difficult to comprehend. It is the basic assumption of this book that most Americans know far too little about the origins and subsequent history of the document that they so constantly and confidently invoke. The Constitution exists as a specific document made up of a number of pages containing articles and sections that can be read with some comprehension by any reasonably literate person. But it is clear that it also exists in a realm of consciousness, of imagination, of myth, of the quasi religious, that has often only a casual relationship to the words on the pages. If we try to imagine our lives without the Constitution, we may begin to get some sense of the degree to which it dominates our lives. Suppose, for example, that it was suddenly obliterated from our collective memories, what would life in America in the last quarter of the twentieth century be like?

The federal Constitution is, of course, a rather odd composite document. Leaving aside, for a moment, the historical processes by which a particular set of principles concerning the "machinery" of government evolved—principles that were then incorporated in the "Constitution proper"—there is a vastly more complicated story of the first ten amendments. These, far more than any of those that followed, have come to be thought of as an integral part of the Constitution itself, so that when we speak of our constitutional rights we most often have reference to the "rights" guaranteed us in the first ten amendments, which were not, strictly speaking, part of the original Constitution at all and were, to a degree, an afterthought. It was not that the framers of the Constitution were in any sense opposed to the principles contained in the so-called Bill of Rights—the first eight amendments. It was rather that they thought these principles preceded the Constitution and were already clearly affirmed in every state constitution. When asked why they had not included those precious "rights" in the Constitution, they said, in effect: "They're implicit; they're what it's all about. If you have any uneasiness about them, reaffirm them by all means."

The respective articles of the Bill of Rights have been those portions of or "amendments to" the Constitution that have been most controversial throughout our history, that have been most often strained or ignored or, one might say, selectively observed. Today it is clear that a vast number of Americans would like to do away with one or more of those first eight amendments or at least severely limit their interpretation in certain cases. It seems as safe as any generalization can be to say that Americans are hostile to amendments which irritate or inconvenience them and supportive of those which appear to be to their advantage or which conform to their particular prejudices. Thus some Americans would be quite content to have persons silenced whose political, philosophical, or moral views they consider dangerous or evil. Others who hold unpopular views and wish to be free to express them, but who have an antipathy to firearms, would prefer to throw out the second amendment giving Americans the constitutional right to "bear arms."

The Constitution proper, dealing specifically with the form of our government and the powers of the various branches, has been considerably less controversial than the first eight amendments. But one hears increasingly the argument advanced that we have outgrown the Constitution. That it was framed by men with a very different view of the world from our own. That it was intended to govern the affairs of a simple agricultural society and is inadequate to deal with the vastly more complex problems of today. That it is archaic and cumbersome, slow to respond to crises, and subject to manipulation by big business and big labor.

Since the bizarre drama of Watergate, one hears these arguments less frequently. More than any other event in this century, Watergate served as a sober reminder of the role of the federal Constitution. To institute impeachment proceedings against the most powerful national leader in the world—the president of the United States—was such a profound and awesome experience that the nation will never be quite the same again. Millions of Americans became aware for the first time of the strange potency of the document framed by the Founding Fathers. To many people it seemed evident that the Constitution was all that stood between democratic government and the arbitrary and illegal use of executive power. Certainly Watergate, whatever the final judgment on it may be, was the most dramatic single domestic event in this century. In the television era the daily confrontations, the charges and denials, the most subtle changes of expression, the perspiration on a witness's upper lip or forehead were visible to millions of viewers glued to their sets. It was as though a classic Greek drama, cast in modern terms, had been brought by electronic technology to an audience of tens of millions. (The Greeks, of course, were fascinated by the way in which—inevitably, it seemed —the rich and powerful were brought down by the gods. In this case the Constitution played the role of the "gods." In terms of American mythology the Constitution was itself a creation of the gods, i.e., the Founding Fathers.) Finally the solemn ceremony of the impeachment proceedings themselves constituted a unique episode. No one can say with confidence what the outcome of the Watergate affair would have been had the framers of the Constitution neglected to provide for the impeachment of a president who used the powers of his office improperly, but it is hard to avoid the feeling that the history of the United States in succeeding years would have been quite different. Put another way, the mystic chords of memory that Lincoln spoke of as constituting the essential character of the nation were stirred to new life; a president only recently elected by the second largest electoral majority in the country's history was brought down by a sometimes difficult and obscure document almost two hundred years old, a document considered by many political theorists to be to a substantial degree obsolete.

In any event, it is this writer's settled conviction that few more extraordinary spectacles have been vouchsafed the race. Little as the average American knew or remembered (since the rudiments had once been drilled into him or her in school) of the specific provisions of the Constitution, the popular veneration of that document as the essence of whatever it was that made up the nation proved to be remarkably deep-seated and tenacious. Although professors and pundits had to scurry to their studies to brush up on one of the least familiar and seldom used articles of the Constitution, there was never serious doubt, once the nature of executive malfeasance was known, that the processes of the law would run their course.

The outcome of the Watergate scandal—the resignation of the president under the pressure of inevitable impeachment—was given a heightened significance by the fact that millions of Americans, especially the young, had reached the conclusion that justice was a very expensive commodity in the United States. If it was a contradiction in terms to say that the rich could buy justice, it could be said at least that they often seemed to be able to buy exemption from it. The Vietnam War had poisoned the common well of American life with bitterness and suspicion. It was the settled conviction of a substantial portion of the population that the government was both corrupt and impotent, that money and privilege were in the driver's seat, that the suppression of dissent and the exploitation of the powerless was, if not the policy, the inclination of government. The rage and frustration of a portion of the population found symbolic expression in acts of lawless violence directed primarily against property. At the Democratic Convention in Chicago in 1968, the anger of alienated young people was vented in riots and demonstrations in some ways more troubling than any such events in our history. The rioters were not the dispossessed—Irish resisting the draft during the Civil War, or desperate workers fighting for decent wages and working conditions —but predominately the privileged sons and daughters of the upper middle class.

The almost unbearably prolonged travail of Watergate focused attention on the nature of constitutional law as no other event could conceivably have done. When the president resigned, thousands of young people celebrated in Lafayette Square and along Pennsylvania Avenue in front of the White House. More than any other segment of the population, the young people who had persistently protested against the Vietnam War with riots and demonstrations felt vindicated by the conclusion of Watergate. They had played a crucial role in the downfall of two presidents—Lyndon Johnson's withdrawal from the presidential race in 1968, and the resignation of Richard Nixon in 1974.

The problems that plagued the country in the Vietnam era have not, of course, been solved or banished by Watergate, but one has the sense that Watergate may have been a kind of turning point in recent American history. If many things are still in serious disarray, there is a new confidence, if not in politicians, at least in the processes of government and in the vitality of the Constitution itself. The changes in the national psyche occasioned by Watergate may be illusory or transient. The increased awareness on the part of the American people of the nature and function of the Constitution occasioned by Watergate may soon be dissipated, but it is my conviction that in addition to checking a trend toward excessive executive power, we did win an interval in which to tackle the most urgent problems in our society.

Current doctrine has it that scholars are supposed to approach the subject of their researches in a spirit free of the ideological bias presumed to follow from specific political commitments. Only so, we are advised, is it possible to maintain a detached and objective view of the issues under investigation. Needless to say, this is not the guiding assumption here. The idea for this work was conceived as a consequence of Watergate. The notion has been to collect a series of documents chosen with a view to illuminating, for the reader, the origins, nature, and subsequent history of the federal Constitution of the United States and to offer such commentary on those documents as may assist the reader in understanding their function in the life of this nation and in his/her own life (not, of course, to mention their influence in the wider world beyond our shores). This is a presumptuous and perilous task. As we observed at the beginning of this introduction, the Constitution is a "living" document. It is so central to our experience as an "almost chosen people" that it is difficult to touch it without becoming at once involved in controversy. To attempt to analyze and explain it is a little like trying to perform an autopsy on a living person. I am therefore obliged to warn the reader of what he or she will doubtless soon become aware—that this is *my* understanding of the Constitution. I have tried to counterbalance this bent, or slant, by including key documents. But my critics may reply: The Constitution aside, it still is, after all, *your* selection. I know of no way around that problem. I can only say there is substantial scholarly agreement about what statutes, decisions, and interpretations are of particular importance in the development of constitutional law, if there are often wide differences about their meaning.

The center and climax of this book are the debates in the Constitutional Convention convened in May, 1787, in Philadelphia. Everything leads up to this extraordinary meeting. Everything else in the book follows from it and refers back to it. It is the *ur* event, It is one of perhaps a dozen such occasions in the history of the race, and for the modern world it is *the* determinative event, one of those rare moments when intellect and experience combine to change the world. The Declaration of Independence declares the end of colonial dependence and a visionary prospect of the future. But the federal Constitution marks the true beginning of the United States. Strictly speaking, we did not exist before. So it should be treasured and remembered. If I had my way all students would participate during their schooling in a reenactment of that dialogue. Parts would be assigned—Hamilton, Madison, Washington, James Wilson, Pierce Butler, George Mason—and the *ur* event would be re created like the origin ceremony of any great historic culture. Fecund in history, full of allusions to the past and references to the future, it is drama, poetry, epic. It is enactment, incorporation, em-bodi-ment. Profoundly moving and profoundly mysterious, it recapitulates the inexhaustible drama of men's efforts to discover how they may live together in some degree of harmony in communities, states, and nations, and that of course is, and continues to be, the primary object of our attention under however many guises it may present itself: sociology, psychology, literature, poetry, philosophy, history, government, politics, economics—they in essence all deal with the same question.

Since, in the generations immediately following the framing of the Constitution, we sanctified it and deified the men who wrote it, we had to desanctify and dedeify it and them. That was done by early-twentieth-century reformers like Charles Beard who experienced the Constitution as a reactionary document standing in the way of social progress. Since then it has been a commonplace to remind ourselves that the framers of the Constitution were, after all, only men, much like ourselves; which, it seems to me, is only partly true. I hold to the view that the great forces of history are like some powerful electric current. At times of crisis certain persons stand at the center of those forces; the forces flow through them and they are, to some degree, transformed. They do indeed then become somewhat larger than life. They discover that unsuspected energies and powers are available to them. They become intoxicated or "enlarged" by history. They do better than we can quite explain in terms of what we know about human limitations. So we denominate them heroes, often quite deservedly in my opinion. Certainly in this case.

And yet I would emphasize that far from it being my intention to redeify or resanctify the framers or their document, my aim is to accompany the reader on a journey whose primary purpose is to understand the roots of our existence as a nation. Whether, as some thought then and many claimed later, God intervened in the process, I don't know. I am concerned only with the profoundly human aspects of the matter. (When one of the delegates suggested opening each session of the convention with a prayer for the Almighty's guidance, Alexander Hamilton irreverently replied that he did not believe the delegates needed outside assistance.)

So let us proceed.

CHAPTER

I

ORIGINS

THE ORIGINS OF THE UNITED STATES CONSTITUTION ARE TO BE found in the struggle carried on in England since the days of Magna Charta to limit the arbitrary power of the king. The feudal barons who exacted the Great Charter from King John at Runnymede in 1215 were not interested, it is safe to assume, in abstract notions such as justice for the common people of England. They were determined to check the tendency of kings—and this particular king, more specifically—to demand money and services from them without their consent. While the original Charter contained sixty-three clauses, the overriding issue was that of money. The crown could not arbitrarily, and without the consent of his lords, deprive them of their property. Certain clauses protected debtors from arbitrary seizure of their lands. Others covered the financial aid owing to the crown and the circumstances under which a grand council of feudal lords must be called if the king needed additional revenues.

One of the most important provisions of the Charter declared that the same rules which governed the relations of the king to his lords should, in turn, apply to their relation with those dependent on them. The king also promised to refrain from unlawful arrest or seizure: "no freeman shall be taken or imprisoned or disseised, or outlawed, or exiled, or in any way destroyed . . . except by the lawful judgment of his peers or by the law of the land." By the same token the king agreed that "to no one will we sell, deny, or delay right or justice." These principles have come down to us in our own Bill of Rights in the clauses guaranteeing all citizens the right "to be secure . . . against unreasonable searches and seizures . . ." (Article IV) and stating that no one "shall be held to answer for a capital, or otherwise infamous crime, unless on a presentment or indictment of a Grand Jury . . . nor be deprived of life, liberty, or property, without due process of law . . ." (Article V) and promising "the right to a speedy and public trial, by an impartial jury of the State and district wherein the crime shall have been committed . . ." (Article VI).

The Great Charter stated that punishments shall fit the crimes, and then followed a string of specific prohibitions against the king or his agents taking "corn or other chattels," "horses or carts," or "another's wood" "without the consent of the owner" and just compensation.

The Charter was a bitter pill for King John to swallow. He died the next year—perhaps he choked on it—and his successor, Henry III, anxious to secure the allegiance of the rebellious barons, reissued the Charter in a modified form (forty-two clauses, against sixty-three in the original). The matters omitted were largely those having to do with the lords' specific grievances against John. The rewritten clauses were, in turn, furthered clarified and refined in 1217 and 1225.

The Great Charter had subsequently two functions: one, the direct practical one of establishing a set of laws governing the relations of the ruler with his principal supporters, which a monarch could only defy at the risk of arousing strong opposition; beyond that, of demonstrating that there were limits to the authority of a king. Implicit in this position was the view that there was a higher law, a law to which the king himself must bend, and, more important, that this higher law could be discovered by the subjects of the king and imposed on him. In other words, a document intended to meet certain practical exigencies, to resolve a particular dispute between a particular king and his restive followers, very soon broke loose and soared splendidly above the merely practical to become a statement of principle, a charter of liberties, an inspiration and a referent for every Englishman who felt his rights imperiled by arbitrary action of those above him.

The Magna Charta became the cornerstone of what was spoken of as "the British constitution." Unlike modern constitutions, beginning indeed with that of the United States, the British constitution was simply a collection of laws passed by Parliament and governmental principles established by the accumulation of common-law precedents. When a judge of the common-law courts handed down a decision that affected a substantial portion of the population or more clearly defined a relationship between corporate bodies, between individuals, or between an individual or a corporation and an agency of government, such a decision might well come to constitute another element in the "unwritten" constitution. It was, in fact, often impossible to distinguish clearly what had simply become a customary way of doing things from what had been deliberately ordained by parliamentary statute, although to the diligent researcher the statute books would presumably in time yield up the answer. This made for considerable haziness in the matter of what in fact the British constitution did consist of, a haziness dear to the British heart since it discouraged strong and unequivocal positions on issues. The consequence was that the British constitution became what the British people or what, more specifically, the British ruling class in some kind of uneasy interaction with the reigning monarch wished it to be at a particular time.

It would of course be a mistake to suggest that this kind of *modus vivendi* was easily or quickly achieved. The lords of the realm, sometimes abetted by a coalition of country gentlemen, merchants, and yeoman farmers (and sometimes opposed by them), worked after hours to strengthen Parliament and circumscribe the powers of the king. With the ascension to the throne by the Stuarts of Scotland, a stubborn and aggressive line, matters came to a head. The efforts of the first James Stuart to browbeat Parliament brought a strong reaction from parliamentary leaders. When Charles I, successor to James, tried to bypass Parliament and raise money by direct taxation to carry on the French War, Parliament responded with the Petition of Right in March, 1629, reasserting the rights first guaranteed under Magna Charta. The king arrested several of the leaders of Parliament, one of whom died in the Tower of London, then dissolved the Parliament and ruled for eleven years without it. Finally, having exhausted all other means of raising a revenue, he summoned Parliament into session in 1640 and instructed its members to raise new taxes. When Parliament refused to do so until the king had redressed a long list of grievances, the king once more dismissed it. Unable to pay an army of Scotsmen that he had recruited, Charles called Parliament back into session once more. This time its leaders openly defied the king and sharpened the crisis by presenting him with demands to which it was impossible for him to accede and retain any vestige of royal authority. The king and his followers recruited an army of some twenty thousand royalist supporters, and Parliament raised an army of its own. In 1649, after years of bitter fighting, Charles was captured, tried, and beheaded. The so-called Commonwealth was formed, nominally under the direction of Parliament but increasingly dominated by the Puritan military genius, Oliver Cromwell. When England, reacting against twenty years of turmoil and yearning for the idea of order and continuity represented by the monarchy, restored Charles II to the throne of England in 1660, the restoration was accompanied by a bitter reaction against the Puritans who had dominated the country during the Interregnum, the period during which England had been without a king. But the fact remained that a king had been deposed and, grimmer still, executed for treason to the state. While the tension between Parliament and a succession of kings remained, focusing generally on the issue of taxation, there was never again any serious question of Parliament's control of the purse strings.

On the death of Charles in 1685, his brother James succeeded him. James, by his conversion to Catholicism and by his determined efforts to ease the repressive laws against Catholics in England, aroused such popular opposition that a plan was hatched to oust him and replace him by William of Orange, who had distant claim to the throne. William landed in England and summoned Parliament into session in January, 1689. Parliament issued a proclamation declaring that "King James II, having endeavored to subvert the constitution of the kingdom by breaking the original contract between king and people, and by the advice of Jesuits and other wicked persons having violated the fundamental laws, and having withdrawn himself out of the kingdom [James had fled the country in the face of the uprising against him], has abdicated the government, and that the throne is vacant." The crown of England was then formally offered to William and Mary of Orange jointly. The offer was accompanied by a Declaration of Rights, affirming the "true, ancient and indubitable rights of the people of this realm." The rights were then enumerated. Again the most important provision was perhaps the one which declared that it was unconstitutional for the king to attempt to levy taxes without the consent of Parliament. But the Declaration also guaranteed the right of Englishmen to bear arms, forbade excessive bail, and stated the right of an accused person to a jury trial. To put the matter simply, what Magna Charta had stated as a kind of working hypothesis directed primarily at limiting the power of King John vis-à-vis his feudal barons became in 1689, as a direct consequence of the English Civil War, the Restoration, the overthrow of James II, and the bestowing of the throne by Parliament on William and Mary, an integral and essential part of the British constitution, though there was nowhere a particular document that described the proper functions of the government and the rights of the people. Put another way, the relationship of the various branches to the government (there was, indeed, hardly a proper notion of "branches" in the sense in which the word came to be used) was nowhere specifically defined or described, so that where the most essential part of the Constitution of the United States came to be the description of those branches, their powers, and their relationship to each other, Englishmen considered the essence of their unwritten or at least uncodified constitution to be the rights that Parliament, as the representative of the people, had exacted from the crown—prohibitions against the exercise of arbitrary power. There were good reasons why the British constitution was "unwritten," the first being that no one understood quite how it worked since it was a mysterious accumulation of centuries-old procedures and customs and thus the task of writing it all down was (and remains) beyond doing; secondly, since it was constantly changing—and most factions hoped to profit from the changes, or, more precisely, make them—no one wished to freeze it into some immutable document. Thus the British constitution, which many of the Founding Fathers insisted they were taking as a model, was the antithesis of the Constitution composed in Philadelphia in 1787.

Having carried the story of English constitutional development in a very sketchy fashion up to the end of the seventeenth century, it is necessary to go back to the early years of English settlement in America, back to the Pilgrims' voyage to the lonely spot on the New England coast that they called Plymouth. The Pilgrims, or Separatists— so called because they insisted on separating from the Church of England, which they considered hopelessly corrupt, rather than attempting to reform the church as their Puritan brethren of the later Massachusetts Bay Company did—had abandoned England to practice their own religious beliefs in Holland and then left Holland for the New World because they felt that they, and more especially their children, were in danger of losing their Englishness.

They had a patent—a grant of land—of somewhat uncertain validity obtained from a trading and land development company, entitled, misleadingly, the Council for New England. The patent contained no provision for any form of government. Included in the small party aboard the *Mayflower* were a number of "strangers," persons not of the same religious persuasion as the Separatists (or, as they thought of themselves, the Saints). The Pilgrim leaders were thus uneasy about how the rudiments of self-government might be established once the party had landed in its new home. Their response to this dilemma was to draw up a compact or agreement and prevail on everyone aboard to sign it. It was an ingenuous solution. It was also illegal or, at best, extralegal. The British crown claimed most of the North American continent. The laws of England were the only laws governing English subjects on English lands and the duly appointed officials of the crown were the only proper administrators of those laws.

During the nineteenth century, when the Pilgrims were elevated to preeminent positions in the pantheon of American heroes and heroines, the Mayflower Compact was celebrated as the foundation stone of the federal Constitution and much scholarly effort was expended to prove that the document was the acorn from which grew the mighty oak of the federal Constitution. The connection was, it turned out, too tenuous. The argument could not be sustained. Historians turned their attention from the Separatists to the more complex and influential Puritans who established the Bay Company at Boston ten years after the Separatists landed at Plymouth. The Mayflower Compact, in consequence, suffered a partial eclipse, remaining of importance primarily to genealogists. Only the descendants of the *Mayflower* voyagers who considered themselves the *ur* Americans and had banded together in a society to celebrate the splendid antiquity of their origins, continued to revere it as the primary document in our history.

Since it is a paper of great directness, simplicity, and brevity, it might be well to quote it virtually verbatim:

> In the name of God, Amen. We whose names are under-written, the loyall subjects of our dread soveraigne Lord, King James . . . having undertaken, for the glorie of God, and advancement of the Christian faith, and honour of our king and countrie, a voyage to plant the first colonie in the Northerne parts of Virginia, doe by these presents solemnly and mutaly in the presence of God, and one of another, covenant and combine our selves togeather into a civill body politick, for our better ordering and preservation and furtherance of the ends aforesaid; and by vertue hearof to enacte, constitute, and frame such just and equall lawes, ordinances, acts, constitutions, and offices, from time to time, as shall be thought most meete and convenient for the generall good of the Colonie,

unto which we promise all due submission and obedience. In witness wherof we have hereunder subscribed our names at Cap-Codd the 11. of November. . . . Ano: Dom. 1620.

Whether or not any clear line can be traced from the Mayflower Compact to the federal Constitution, there are a number of interesting and important points to be made about this remarkable document. One is its astonishing presumption. However the Pilgrims may have protested their devotion to their "dread soveraigne," he considered them to be a contentious, disloyal, and heretical handful of farmers and artisans, people of the lower orders of society, whose religious views bordered on outright treason. Happily for his own equanimity, the king remained quite oblivious to the existence of this insolent document which declared its purpose to be that of establishing "a civill body politick." He had far more important things on his mind. What is of primary concern to us about the Compact is the frame of mind, or kind of consciousness, that could conceive of such a statement. Most of us are familiar with it as a kind of historical curiosity, a quaint artifact that we are enjoined by our teachers to respect as part of the fabric of our national edifice, part of the structure of ideas, documents, events, and miscellaneous memorabilia which constitute our sense of ourselves as a people. So it is difficult to get ourselves into a frame of mind that will enable us to understand just how radical and unprecedented an event the drafting and signing of the Mayflower Compact was. Prior to the Protestant Reformation most people had belonged to what we might call corporate bodies, classes, orders: they were priests, monks, nuns, lords, vassals, serfs, inhabiters of a commune, members of a guild, etc. It was in those classes or bodies that they found the meaning of their lives. All these arrangements were, in a sense, ratified by the church, which, in turn, was deeply involved in all worldly matters, owning enormous amounts of property and wielding great power.

The Protestant Reformation quite literally re-formed a substantial portion of that traditional, corporate society. It gave a new shape, new aspirations, a new character to those individuals who formed new voluntary, or as we say today, "intentional" communities. It created a different consciousness. The re-formed communities had a new kind of power because their members came together as a consequence of the intentions or conscious will of particular individuals. Suddenly "individuals," no longer subsumed under any corporate entity, joined with other "individuals." These did not have to be, and by and large seldom were, important, powerful people, leaders, decision makers, people trained to command. They were more often obscure individuals of modest circumstances. Yet they discovered in themselves the power to make the most momentous decisions, decisions which formerly had been made only by rulers or by a collectivity or corporate body in their behalf. This is what was momentous about the Mayflower Compact; the fact that a handful of people, most of them with little or no formal education, did not hesitate to perform one of the most mysterious, powerful, and dramatic acts known to the species, to "covenant and combine our selves togeather into a civill body politick."

So the nineteenth-century historians and their followers were in a sense quite right in being amazed and awed by an event that we today take for granted. It was an act bold to the point of recklessness, and in demonstrating this strange capacity to form new human combinations—new communities—and establish governments to guide and control them, it did indeed anticipate the federal Constitution. It *was* the acorn of the new consciousness oak.

When the Puritans, a group more prosperous, numerous, and cautious, ventured forth from England ten years later, their situation bore certain similarities to their Separatist predecessors as well as conspicuous differences. Like the Pilgrims, the Puritans had no charter from the crown authorizing them to govern themselves. They had, to be sure, a royal charter, but it was for a trading company with the title of the Governor and Company of Massachusetts Bay. The charter provided for the affairs of the company to be run by a Great and General Court of the stockholders. What the Puritans did, in effect, was to constitute themselves the stockholders and carry with them to the New World a set of rules and regulations drawn up for the management of a commercial company in London. Their charter as a corporation, they claimed, gave them the authority to manage their own affairs. Thus by a kind of political sleight-of-hand they turned a business venture into a civil government. At least this dodge gave some color of legality to the government of the Massachusetts Bay Colony, and if it did not evince the same boldness as that shown by the signers of the Mayflower Compact, it proved far more durable. The Puritans also displayed the same confidence in their capacity to manage their own affairs that we have taken note of in the case of the Plymouth Separatists.

Since the Puritans came to Massachusetts armed with a document that they believed conferred legitimacy on their enterprise, they did not, like the Separatists, have to assert their intention to govern themselves in some kind of compact or agreement. But it is interesting to note that their leader, John Winthrop, felt impelled to draw up a general statement about the purposes of the projected colony while crossing the ocean. His "Modell of Christian Charity" is the theological and philosophical charter of the great Puritan migration that began in 1630. The purpose of the migration from Old England to New England, according to Winthrop, was "to improve our lives to doe more service to the Lord the comforte and encrease of the body of christe whereof wee are members that our selves and posterity may be better preserved from the Common corrupcions of this evill world to serve the Lord and worke out our Salvacion under the power and purity of his holy Ordinances." This goal was to be achieved primarily by observing the principles of justice and mercy. There was, Winthrop reminded his fellow voyagers, "a double Lawe by which wee are regulated in our conversacion one towardes another: in both the former respects, the lawe of nature and the lawe of grace, or the morrall lawe or the lawe of the gospell. . . ." The most basic of the "morrall" laws and the laws of the gospel was "to love his neighbor as himself." All human codes of law should rest on this precept. The fundamental responsibility of the settlers was "to love the Lord our God, and to love one another to walke in his wayes and keepe his Commandments and his Ordinance, and his lawes, and the Articles of our Covenant with him that wee may live and be multiplied, and that the Lord our God may bless us in the land whether wee goe to possess it. . . ."

Many things might be said about John Winthrop's "Modell of Christian Charity." I will say only a few. Read in its entirety, it is an eloquent celebration of the nature of the true community, a condensed sociology. Every community has mundane laws to govern its daily life, but these are merely formal and often repressive unless they rest on the commandments of the Lord and the teachings of the gospel. Beneath them all lies the first and greatest law—love thy neighbor as thyself.

The Pilgrims on the *Mayflower* had stated their intention to establish "a civill body politick"; Winthrop described the moral basis for such a body. The Puritans, although they followed a more discreet path, obviously felt as competent and as "empowered" as the Separatists to establish their own civil government. Conversely, the Plymouth settlers could find in Winthrop's essay only a confirmation of their own view of the nature of the true community. The Mayflower Compact and Winthrop's "Modell," taken together, reveal the "government-making power" of the re-formed consciousness.

CHAPTER

II

THE NATURE OF LAW

IT MIGHT BE APPROPRIATE HERE TO SAY SOMETHING ABOUT THE prevailing concepts of law in seventeenth-century England and America. We have already taken note of the long struggle in England to establish the supremacy of law over the arbitrary power of the crown. The issues involved were intensely practical, but behind the conflict over specific rights, an earnest theological and philosophical discussion took place over the very nature of law. The sixteenth and seventeenth centuries inherited two traditions concerning law: the classical tradition of ancient Greece and Rome and the Christian tradition of the Holy Catholic Church. The ancient philosophers, most notably Plato and Aristotle, had been much preoccupied with the nature and the function of law, from those laws which governed the natural world to the laws governing the world of men. Human societies responded to eternal laws very much like those which governed the natural world. Thus, in the view of Plato and most Greek philosophers, government ran through a cycle. A legitimate monarchial government tended to become an aristocracy as the lords whittled away the powers of the monarch, usually in the name of securing the rights of all citizens. The aristocracy, in turn, became an oligarchy, the rule of a few pursuing their own selfish interests rather than the general good (an oligarchy was thus the decadent form of aristocracy). Finally, the people, indignant at their exploitation, would, invariably, rise, overthrow the corrupt oligarchy, and establish a democracy. But a democracy was too turbulent and unruly to survive long. Its corrupt form was anarchy, where there was no law or order but everything was determined by the volatile public will. Anarchy was followed by the rise of a dictator or despot whose principal qualification for ruling was that he could bring order. The dictator sought to secure himself as a legitimate monarch or was replaced by one and the cycle began again. All human societies were involved, like the trees and plants, in such cycles. There were variations among different philosophers in the description and analysis of the phases of the cycles, but there was general agreement on some form of a deterministic cyclical theory, allowing always, of course, for whimsical interruptions by the gods.

Within this cosmic order, Plato entertained himself and subsequent generations with reflections on an ideal republic. The *Republic* tells us a great deal about Plato's ideal philosophy and a good deal about the attitudes of the philosopher and his contemporaries toward the social and political problems of his own time. Plato wished to have his republic ruled by a wise philosopher-king whose concern would be the happiness and well-being of his subjects. "The legislator . . . did not aim at making any one class in the State happy above the rest; the happiness was to be in the whole State, and he held the citizens together by persuasion and necessity, making them benefactors of the State, and therefore benefactors of one another; to this end he created them, not to please themselves, but to be his instruments in binding up the State."

Plato, as the protagonist, explains to those who have been chosen to be the princely philosophers that they "have been brought . . . into the world to be rulers of the hive, kings of yourselves and of other citizens. . . ." It is understandable that Plato's republic has always had a special charm for professors and philosophers who can imagine themselves as the wise and virtuous rulers of their fellows, and a particular horror for nonprofessors. The point here is that Plato saw the individual citizen as existing primarily for the community or city-state, absorbed within it and carrying on his or her duties rather like a bee (hence his reference to ruling the "hive").

If Plato's answer to the chaos and disorder of human society was to introduce a less human but more orderly society, like that of the ants or the bees, his disciple Aristotle had quite a different notion. He saw happiness not as residing in the community but rather in the person. In his view the state existed for the citizen rather than vice versa. Aristotle, at the same time, had no notion of the modern individual. A genuinely human man was an active citizen, part of a social group. "The man who is unable to join in partnerships or does not need to because he is himself sufficient is not part of a state; he is either a beast or a god." A man at the height of his powers was, to Aristotle, "the best of all animals; but he is the worst of all when he is detached from customs and justice. Injustice, given weapons," he continues, "is the most oppressive thing there is; and man is given weapons at birth, which are meant to serve prudence and goodness but can easily be turned to the opposite ends. Man without goodness is the most wicked and savage of animals. . . . Justice, however, is part of the state, since it settles what is just; and political partnership is regulated by legal justice." (It is, perhaps, worth recalling here that for the Puritan the basis of the community was love rather than justice: justice is the servant of love.)

Aristotle's prescription for the state has a remarkably modern sound: "the right thing is for the state to be a plurality, as we said before, unified and integrated by education." Modern America! In a fascinating discussion about the nature of a "citizen" and his relation to constitutions, Aristotle reflects on the problems created by "the change to a democratic constitution from an oligarchy or a tyranny. . . . If a democratic constitution is imposed by force, we shall have to say that the acts of this regime are no more acts of the whole than were the 'acts of the oligarchy' and the 'acts of the tyranny.' . . ." Reading Aristotle we at once understand ourselves to be back in a time when constitutions were written and rewritten with every change in government, a far cry from the infinitely slow development of the "unwritten" British constitution that was discussed earlier. We can imagine the attentiveness with which the drafters of the federal Constitution studied Aristotle and the other classical philosophers.

But we have been talking about those larger "laws" of which human constitutions are only an imperfect reflection. As Charles McIlwain has put it: "This is Aristotle's formula for the universe—the growth of ideas from potency into actuality; and the formula applies to the state as well as to the productions of art or the works of physical nature." The fact that the process of growth from the potential to the actual is constantly interrupted or aborted was due, Aristotle believed, to an ingrained tendency in the mass of men toward the corruption and vulgarization of all things, toward the creation of "a city of pigs" where "*mere* life is the end." This principle of Aristotle's made him the natural ancestor—as indeed was Plato—of all those who hold an elitist view of the human situation. But it also comported almost too neatly with the Christian notion of original sin. And it clearly made Aristotle, as we shall see, an important source for the American politicians who framed the federal Constitution.

Common then to both Aristotle and Plato and, indeed, to most of the philosophers of the ancient world was the conviction that there was, however described or defined, a set of higher laws or ideas or ideals of which earthly laws were an imperfect imitation. Christianity, in its early centuries, did not much attend to the question of law, and where it did it was clearly influenced, to a degree, by classical philosophy. It thus remained for St. Thomas Aquinas in the thirteenth century in his great codification of Christian doctrine to deal in a comprehensive way with the law. In Book XIII of the *Summa Theologica*, Question 91, he addressed himself to the nature of "eternal law," "divine law," "natural law," and "human law" (also sometimes called municipal law). The only serious problem about eternal law was whether God, having once established it, subjected himself to it. Aquinas described natural law as that law related to or derived from eternal or divine law. Human law is like science, or the laws of nature, in that it is the consequence of the efforts of human reason to comprehend the imperatives of divine law: "These particular determinations, devised by human reason, are called human laws." Aquinas then proceeds to a rather subtle discussion of the relation of natural law to divine law, the essence of which is that natural law "directs man by way of certain general precepts, common to both the perfect and the imperfect. . . ." But the divine law covers those matters that go beyond the natural law and affect primarily the saints on earth and those in heaven. It is nowhere stated by Aquinas— though it seems to me implicit in his discussion—that human laws are progressively refined to the end that they better reflect man's understanding of God's intentions. Since the thirteenth century had no notion of progress in the modern sense, it is not surprising that we find no such explicit formulation in Aquinas.

In any event, in the centuries following the appearance of *Summa Theologica* much of the discussion of the nature of higher law derived from Aquinas and used his terminology. Celestial law (law for the angels and souls made perfect) was sometimes added to or substituted for divine law, and the "law of nature" was introduced to cover laws dealing with the natural world as opposed to the human one. The next major discussion of the relation of higher law to mundane law came with Calvin's vast *Institutes of the Christian Religion,* the *Summa* of the Protesting Reformation. In Chapter XX, at the end of the *Institutes,* Calvin takes up the question of civil government. While it may appear to be remote from such explicitly theological matters as predestination, justification, and the priesthood of believers, it is, he tells his readers, a crucial issue for all Christians. In addition to the dangers posed by false doctrine, the faith is threatened by "the flatterers of princes, extolling their power beyond all just bounds." Some fanatics view "the whole system of civil government as a polluted thing, which has nothing to do with Christian men," but such men err. They fail to understand that "civil government is designed, as long as we live in this world, to cherish and support the external worship of God, to preserve the pure doctrine of religion, to defend the constitution of the Church, to regulate our lives in a manner requisite for the society of men, to form our manners to civil justice, to promote our concord with each other, and to establish general peace and tranquillity." All this would be superfluous, Calvin confesses, if the kingdom of God truly presided in the hearts of men. But the truth of the matter is that it is God's will "that while we are aspiring towards our true country, we be pilgrams on earth, and if such aids are necessary to our pilgrimage, they who take them away from man deprive him of his human nature. . . . They foolishly imagine a perfection which can never be found in any community of men." From all this it follows that "civil polity" is "equally as necessary to mankind as bread and water, light and air, and far more excellent." Government is necessary "that every person may enjoy his property without molestation; that men may transact their business together without fraud or injustice; that integrity and modesty may be cultivated among them; in short, that there may be a public form of religion among Christians, and that humanity may be maintained among men." While Calvin will not accept the notion that the state can make laws respecting religion, it can ensure an atmosphere in which religion flourishes.

Calvin then proceeds to a discussion of the nature of "civil administration." It has three branches: "The magistrate who is the guardian and conservator of the laws; The laws, according to which he governs; The people, who are governed by the laws, and obey the magistrate."

The magistrates "execute a Divine commission" in that their function is ordained of God. Calvin follows the classical permutations of government into monarchy, aristocracy, and democracy, with their three corrupt forms—tyranny, oligarchy, and anarchy—and expresses it as his opinion that "either aristocracy, or a mixture of aristocracy and democracy, far excels all others . . . because it very rarely happens that kings regulate themselves so that their will is never at variance with justice and rectitude. . . . The vice or imperfection of men therefore renders it safer and more tolerable for the government to be in the hands of the many, that they may afford each other mutual assistance and admonition, and that if any one arrogate to himself more than is right, the many may act as censors and masters to restrain his ambition."

Plato's gloomy view of human nature led him to place his hopes for the good society in a specially trained caste of philosopher-kings with the power to, in effect, coerce the people into happiness. Aristotle, on the other hand, put his faith in education as the means whereby man's propensity to wickedness might be restrained. Neither Plato nor Aristotle had any confidence in the capacity of the people in general to govern themselves wisely, though Aristotle is lacking Plato's authoritarian bent. Calvin, by contrast, has no truck with any utopian notions of a perfect earthly society. The perfect society is the heavenly kingdom; it would be blasphemous to believe that it could be achieved on earth. Yet civil government is ordained by God and obliged, so far as human perfections permit, to model itself on that other kingdom toward which the earthly pilgrim faithfully travels. Therefore the Christian must be actively involved in the affairs of what the Mayflower Compact called "the civill body politick." Perhaps most notably, Calvin rejected monarchial government because it concentrated too much power in the hands of a fallible man, and came down on the side of a mixed aristocracy and democracy where "the many" retained the means to check any improper (i.e., unconstitutional) exercise of power by the governors. There is another sentence in the *Institutes* to which we should be especially attentive. If a mixed form of aristocracy and democracy is the government which best guarantees the liberties of the people, it then follows that "if [the people] exert their strenuous and constant efforts for its preservation and retention . . . they act in perfect consistence with their duty." This sentence, perhaps more than any other, provided the

American colonists, inheritors of Calvin, with their rationale for resisting what they considered the unconstitutional encroachments of the British government on the liberties of Englishmen living in America.

On the subject of laws, Calvin is equally emphatic. Laws are, in Cicero's words, "the *souls of states*," and by the same token, "the law is a silent magistrate, and a magistrate a speaking law." Laws must be just and equitable. Different nations and different municipalities may have different laws "provided that they be framed according to the perpetual rule of love. . . ." It is worth noting here that Calvin, like Winthrop (who of course derived his doctrines from Calvin), states that the regulating principle in framing all laws is love (rather than justice).

In the Western world, the makers and enforcers of the law—those that Calvin calls the magistrates—have recognized that the most carefully and wisely drafted laws may not comprehend all the demands of justice or love. There has, therefore, been a dimension of the law called equity, perhaps best translated as "justice," to which cases can be appealed in which a plaintiff requires relief not adequately covered by existing laws or where an existing law works an unfair and unanticipated hardship. Thus in England there were common-law courts and equity courts, the latter where cases not covered by the common law can be tried.

Calvin is particularly concerned with the matter of "equity." "Equity, being natural," he writes, "is the same to all mankind; and consequently all laws, on every subject, ought to have the same equity for their end. . . . Now, as it is certain that the law of God, which we call the moral law, is no other than a declaration of natural law, and of that conscience which has been engraven by God on the minds of men, the whole rule of equity . . . is prescribed in it. This equity therefore, must alone be the scope, and rule, and end, of all laws."

Although Calvin applied the principle of equity primarily to those human laws giving effect to God's commandments to Moses, before many decades had passed the principle of equity as an effort to give effect to God's natural law was extended to include those rights that the English had struggled since the Magna Charta to establish as their natural, inherent, God-given rights.

On the one hand Calvin enjoined the faithful to respect the magistrates and the legitimate authority of government and to eschew revolution and rebelliousness. But if vengeance against "tyrannical domination" was the Lord's, Calvin was at pains to make clear that far from recommending acquiescence to tyranny, he affirmed "that if [the magistrates and representative bodies of the state] connive at kings in the oppression of their people, such forbearance involves the most nefarious perfidy, because they fraudulently betray the liberty of the people, of which they know that they have been appointed protectors by the ordination of God." It is, therefore, according to Calvin the Christian duty of all individuals or bodies representing the people at large to resist with the greatest resolution abuses of power by a ruler, secure in the knowledge that they are acting in the name of a higher law.

One or two more strands that were woven into the fabric of American constitutional theory remain to be described. The Jamestown colony, founded in 1607, thirteen years before the Pilgrims settled at Plymouth, was a very different kind of venture from Plymouth or Massachusetts Bay. Not without strong religious elements, it was primarily a commercial enterprise in which a group of "merchant adventurers" or investors in London, dispatched a company of "planters," or rather a motley assortment of individuals, to Virginia to make a profit for the London promoters. It was thus a far more conventional and legitimate undertaking than the two initial settlements in New England. The London Company was a properly chartered joint stock company whose shareholders hadn't the remotest notion of going to America or of establishing a self-governing colony there. They intended to run Jamestown like any proper trading post.

The London Company by the terms of its charter was given permission by the king "to nominate or appoint such officers as they shall think fit and requisite for the government, managing, ordering, and dispatching the affairs of the said company, and shall likewise have full power and authority to ordain and make such laws and ordinances for the good and welfare of the said plantation, as to them, from time to time, shall be thought requisite and meet: so always as the same shall not be contrary to the laws and statutes of this our realm of England." The last sentence is the determinative one. From the beginning of English settlement in America, the settlers in America were guaranteed, by the terms of the charters granted by the crown, the benefit of the same "laws and statutes" as their compatriots in the homeland. Since these laws and statutes were, by and large, the most liberal and benign yet conceived of, the colonists fell heir to laws far more liberal than those governing any other colonial people. Soon a familiar clause began to appear in all colonial charters conferring on the colonists "all privileges, franchises and liberties of this our kingdom of England."

The different colonies started, in most instances, with very different motivations by their founders and developed in very different ways, from the paternalistic, almost feudal pattern of life in the South to the democratic communities of New England. All, nonetheless, shared, as their common bond and heritage, these same precious "privileges, franchises and liberties." Moreover, all of them had "constitutions" or specific documents describing the manner in which their governments were to be established and how they were to function. Sometimes, as in the case of Massachusetts Bay, the government that evolved was a modification of a commercial company. In others, as in the "Fundamental Constitutions" of the Carolinas drafted by John Locke, the government was a mixture of liberal utopianism with feudal forms and ceremonies. Despite such wide variations, settlers in all the colonies came to view their rights as being both contained in the strange accumulation of "laws and stautes" and "privileges, franchises and immunities" which made up the British constitution, central to which were the rights collected, codified, and reaffirmed, so to speak, in the Declaration of Rights ratified by William and Mary upon their accepting the throne of England in 1689.

In addition, the colonists were very conscious of the fact that each colony had a document in which it was written down what the colonists' particular rights and duties were. All colonies had a governor, for example, although only Connecticut had the right to elect its governor (in Pennsylvania, the Penn family appointed a governor). Elsewhere by the time of the Revolution governors were appointed by the crown. All the colonies with the exception of Pennsylvania had bicameral, or two-house, legislatures, the lower house commonly called the Assembly (Virginia had a House of Burgesses and Massachusetts a Great and General Court), and the upper house, the Council. The Council was, typically, under the governor's thumb and the governor under the thumb of the British authorities to whom he owed his appointment. It followed that the assemblies were the centers of popular sentiment and, when the Revolutionary crisis developed, the locus of resistance to Parliament.

So, however the British may have viewed their largely unwritten constitution, Americans were early habituated to having things in writing.

It turned out, interestingly enough, to be a Frenchman, Baron Charles Louis de Secondat Montesquieu, who undertook to outline the nature of the British constitution. He described the British government, which, one might say, in the absence of a written document, *was* the constitution, as being composed of three branches—the executive, legislative, and judicial. Having discerned what many English themselves could not see, Montesquieu went on to praise the system of the British constitution in extravagant terms. In his *Spirit of the Laws* he enumerated the three now-classic forms of government with which we are familiar. He argued that in order for a government to ensure the happiness of its subjects it was necessary that the people be unafraid. "When the legislative and executive powers are united in the same person, or in the same body of magistrates there can be no liberty; because apprehensions may arise, lest the same monarch or senate should enact tyrannical laws to execute them in a tyrannical manner.

"Again, there is no liberty, if the power of judging be not separated from the legislative and executive powers. Were it joined with the legislative, the life and liberty of the subject would be exposed to arbitrary controul; for the judge would be then the legislator. Were it joined to the executive power, the judge might behave with all the violence of an oppressor.

"There would be an end of every thing, were the same man, or the same body whether of the nobles or of the people, to exercise those three powers, that of enacting the laws, that of executing the public resolutions, and that of judging the crimes or differences of individuals. By separating and keeping separate through the vigilance of the citizens, the three great branches of government, they would act as a check upon each other and so preserve the liberties of the people."

The Spirit of the Laws accomplished several important things: In the years following its publication it fixed the notion of the separation of powers—executive, legislative, and judicial—in the minds of all literate and liberal spirits; and it made the British government-constitution the archetype of this principle.

Whatever the British constitution was by the middle of the eighteenth century, it was not the result of any theory about the separation of powers. It was the result, as we have seen, of a centuries-long struggle to protect the people of England from the arbitrary acts of its kings. When this struggle was nearing its conclusion, Montesquieu examined its consequences and proclaimed his doctrine. Or, more likely, he formulated his doctrine and applied it to the existing political situation in England which, in practical fact, did not demonstrate the doctrine nearly as neatly as Montesquieu would have had us believe. But that was, in a sense, beside the point. It became true because Montesquieu persuaded us that it was true, or, at the very least, should be.

All of this brings us to the threshold of the American Revolutionary crisis so it is perhaps appropriate to recapitulate the main lines of our argument. What began as a contest of wills between King John and his feudal barons in the early years of the thirteenth century became, by a series of dramatic and often prolonged and bloody confrontations extending over the next four or five hundred years (more than twice as long as the United States has existed as a nation), cherished political principles. Indeed, they became more than that. They flowed as converging streams into and merged with the idea of natural law and divine law, with the idea of a system of higher law of which positive or mundane or municipal or human or civil law (whatever one called it) was no better than a blurred or dimly perceived copy. But that higher law, the divine law, gave the ultimate sanction to all dearly won "rights." It lifted them above the level of simply the "rights of Englishmen" and made them "the rights of man." And the government which had evolved, in a certain sense, in order to protect and enforce these rights—though it was often, to be sure, quite neglectful of them—became in turn a model for all nations that wished to establish such rights for themselves. Montesquieu's *Spirit of the Laws,* because it was written by the citizen of a country that had been England's principal rival for centuries, made that oddity (one stumbles constantly over calling it a "constitution," so firmly do we have fixed in our mind the image of a written document as the only proper constitution), the British constitution, available to the world for its admiration and emulation. Most important to us, he made it available to the American colonists who had already enjoyed its benefits and would soon make use of it in a way the Mother Country could hardly have anticipated.

One thing more might be added while we are still on the subject of higher law—eternal law, celestial law, divine law, and natural law.

A young professor of Trinity College, Cambridge, observed the fall of an apple and subsequently formulated the theory of gravity. When the results of Isaac Newton's experiments were published in *Principia Mathematica* in 1687, our notion of the structure of the natural world expanded dramatically. The concept of a system of higher law, divinely ordained, was strengthened. If Newton had been able to discern the particular laws that God had established to govern the movements of the planets in the heavens, how much more certain it was that God had ordained such laws for the direction of human societies. After Newton, the "mechanics" or "science" of politics came to be spoken of commonly as though the right social and political arrangements of men must have their own laws of gravitation. Montesquieu's *Spirit of the Laws* was not only the product of such a way of thinking, his separation and "balancing" of powers seemed encouragingly "mechanical."

Those two streams—the political struggle against arbitrary power and the idea of higher or "natural" laws—having merged were amalgamated with the Protesting System or the Re-formed Consciousness, which took it as a matter of course that ordinary individuals could form new communities and governments simply by agreeing to do so. And that these communities could at once claim all those laboriously accumulated rights of which we have spoken, confident that their ultimate guarantor was God himself. Needless to say, that proved a very potent amalgam.

CHAPTER
III

JAMES OTIS AND THE
BRITISH CONSTITUTION

THE CRISIS BETWEEN THE BRITISH COLONIES AND THE MOTHER
country was, in essence, a quarrel over the nature of authority. The
form in which that conflict presented itself was a contention over that
most basic "right," the right to the control of one's own property. As
the colonists were disposed to put it, no one had authority to take
money out of their pockets without their consent. While Parliament
had, as we have seen, fiercely resisted the right of the king to take
money out of *Parliament's* pockets, or, more accurately, out of the
pockets of the class of persons represented by the members of Parliament, they had no particular scruples about taking money out of the
pockets of their American cousins, or subjects. In fact, the objections
of the Americans, far from appearing to Parliament and its ministers
to be a proper concern for the rights of Englishmen not to be taxed
without representation, seemed captious and indeed little short of
treasonable. British constitutional theorists insisted that the colonists
were "virtually" represented in Parliament, a word that nowhere
appeared in the American political lexicon and that the colonists
suspected had been invented for the occasion. The argument that large
numbers of Englishmen in cities like Birmingham and Manchester
sent no representatives to Parliament and yet were obliged to pay
taxes levied by that body failed to impress the Americans. They could
not understand how two wrongs might make a right.

The American colonists, long accustomed to managing their own
affairs to a degree quite unprecedented in the history of any other

colonies, had no intention of giving ground. From their perspective across three thousand miles of ocean it seemed that Parliament was disposed to act frequently in an arbitrary manner and to do so with an ineffable self-righteousness. From the time of the passage of the Stamp Act in 1765, armed conflict between the colonies and the mother country was probably inevitable. In the view of the colonists the British government was acting in an unconstitutional manner and they had substantial support in that opinion from such English Whig leaders as William Pitt and Edmund Burke. The Americans cited Magna Charta, the Petition of Right from the era of the English Civil War, and the Proclamation of Rights that accompanied the Glorious Revolution and the ascent to the throne of William and Mary. They also cited the British constitution, which proved a demanding task since the constitution, being unwritten, was subject to an even wider range of interpretation than the later written constitutions, which, almost without exception, derived from it. After having fished in these murky waters for several years with uncertain results, the colonial political theorists began, with obvious reluctance, to shift their ground from arguments based on the British constitution to arguments based on the God-given immutable rights of man, of which the British constitution was only one manifestation.

Even before the Stamp Act in 1765, the passage the year before of the so-called Revenue Act, designed to raise revenue for the British treasury and tighten up the laws regulating colonial trade, had, in the words of James Otis, a Massachusetts politician and leader in the resistance to parliamentary taxation, "set people a-thinking, in six months more than they had in their lives before." James Otis wrote a tract entitled "The Rights of the British Colonies Asserted and Proved," in which he spelled out the essence of the colonial position in a way that was hardly improved on in the years prior to the Revolution. Otis began his essay with an account of the nature of authority, quoting "the incomparable" James Harrington's *Oceana*. Power was allied with property. The wealthy man had power although he might not have "much more wit than a mole or musquash." But it did not follow from this "that government is rightfully founded on property, alone." Nor is it "founded on grace. . . . Nor on force. . . . Nor on compact? Nor property?" Not altogether on any or all of these. Has it then, Otis asked his readers, "any solid foundation? and chief corner stone, but what accident, chance or confusion may lay one moment and destroy the next?"

In Otis's view it had "an everlasting foundation in the unchangeable will of God, the author of nature, whose laws never vary. The same omniscient, omnipotent, infinitely good and gracious Creator of the Universe, who has been pleased to make it necessary that what we call matter should gravitate, for the celestial bodies to roll round their axes, dance their orbits and perform their various revolutions in that beautiful order and concert, which we all admire, has made it equally necessary that . . . the different sexes should sweetly attract each other, form societies of single families of which larger bodies and communities are as naturally, mechanically and necessarily combined, as the dew of Heaven and the soft distilling rain is collected by all the enliv'ning heat of the sun." Government was thus founded "on the necessities of our nature. It is by no means an arbitrary thing, depending merely on compact or human will for its existence."

A few things must be said about this remarkable passage. First, it encapsulates two thousand years or more of Western history and political theory. Otis was thoroughly familiar with classical thought, with Plato and Aristotle, with the ancient historians Thucydides, Polybius, and Livy, and with the recent writings of John Locke, of Montesquieu, and a host of other political theorists. He was also clearly imbued with the Newtonian world view that saw the universe as one governed by inexorable (and discoverable) laws of nature. By analogy, human society was governed by similar laws. Just as "matter" must gravitate and the planets perform their revolutions, human communities must respond to the laws of their nature, often bafflingly obscure, to be sure, but reassuringly and eternally there.

The English philosopher-psychologist John Locke had offered the proposition that human society was founded on compact. Man in his original "state of nature," free and unfettered, equal one to another, had nonetheless suffered from a general state of lawlessness in which his own modest possessions were constantly threatened by others. He therefore had given up a degree of his freedom to form, for the sake of security, a kind of agreement or compact that constituted the first "governments." Government was thus founded on agreement. If those individuals who had been given certain powers in order to give effect to the compact of government violated its terms, the original agreement was dissolved and government must be constituted anew. The argument had been developed by Locke to counter the notion of "the divine right of kings"—that the authority of kings derived from God and that it was therefore blasphemy and sacrilege to question it (a doctrine that, not surprisingly, was especially congenial to kings). If power originated in an agreement among free individuals "in a state of nature," it could be revoked by those who had bestowed it. While Otis referred to this Lockean notion of compact, he plainly rejected it as inadequate. It did not meet the American situation. Moreover, Otis, with his Calvinistic background, was not especially enamored of the "natural man." Man in a state of nature was man after the fall, man tainted by original sin. And thus his compacts were tainted or compromised and must, like all human arrangements and contrivances, stand under the judgments of God. The shift was minor but of enormous potential consequence.

Otis, if he was wary of Locke's "man in a state of nature" as the ideal and original hypothetical founder of government, was as insistent as Locke that "the natural liberty of man is to be free from any superior power on earth, and not to be under the will or legislative authority of man, but only to have the law of nature for his rule." This, he added, "is the liberty of independent states . . . which liberty is only abridged in certain instances, not lost to those who are born in or voluntarily enter into society. . . ." And then, most decisively, "this gift of God cannot be annihilated."

Otis then went on to declare, somewhat surprisingly, "The power of Parliament is uncontroulable, but by themselves, and we must obey." What recourse then had the colonists against arbitrary and unconstitutional statutes of Parliament that deprived them of their rights as Englishmen? Otis's solution was not only ingenious, it was destined to become an essential and original element in the United States Constitution. Redress from unconstitutional laws passed by Parliament must come from "the executive courts." The judges of these courts will point out to Parliament, or "plainly demonstrate that [a particular statute] is against natural equity" (for "natural equity" read "natural law") and "will adjudge such Act void."

It was the sacred obligation of Parliament to "declare [i.e., enact] what is for the good of the whole." But it would be presumptuous of Parliament to assume that it, out of its own particular wisdom, could so declare or enact. "There must be," Otis continued, "in every instance a higher authority, viz. God. Should an Act of Parliament be against any of His natural laws, which are immutably true, their declaration would be contrary to eternal truth, equity, and justice, and consequently void; and so it would be adjudged by the Parliament itself, when convinced of their mistake. Upon this great principle, Parliaments repeal such acts, as soon as they find they have been mistaken, in having declared them to be for the public good, when in fact they were not so." Otis had included in the appendix of his essay examples of instances when "the executive courts have declared the Act 'of a whole Parliament void.' "

These cases, obscure and infrequent and virtually forgotten, were, for Otis, proof of the "grandeur of the British constitution" and "the wisdom of our ancestors!" The legislative and executive branches of the government were thus "a perpetual check and balance to each other. If the supreme executive errs, it is informed by the supreme legislative in Parliament: If the supreme legislative errs, it is informed by the supreme executive in the King's courts of law."

Otis's vivid presentation of the constitution would not have been recognized by any Englishman in England. He proved less that he was master of British constitutional theory, such as it was, than that he had been an assiduous reader of Montesquieu. Parliament hadn't the foggiest notion of repealing any of the statutes affecting the colonists unless forced to by bitter necessity. Certainly they were not disposed to do so on the basis of admonitions from the executive courts, suspected of being already too much instruments of crown policy. As for the executive branch, that is to say the king, encouraging the courts to pronounce parliamentary legislation intended to raise a revenue in America to be against "natural equity," unconstitutional, etc., that was quite unimaginable. The fact was that the king and his ministers were the originators of those statutes which had been passed by a compliant Parliament over the strong objections of some of its more liberal members. So to anyone with the vaguest notion of how the British government actually functioned, Otis's speculations must have appeared as the merest fantasy, a crude provincial interpretation of a Frenchman's fanciful account of the nature of the British constitution.

But Otis was not through. He recapitulated at the end of his essay. "The sum of my argument," he wrote, "is that civil government is of God: that the administrators of it were originally the whole people. . . ." The people had "devolved it on whom they pleased." In England it had been devolved on "the king, lords, and commons, the supreme, sacred and uncontroulable legislative power . . . that this constitution is the most free one, and by far the best, now existing on earth: that by this constitution, every man in the dominion is a free man: that no parts of his Majesty's dominions can be taxed without their consent. . . ."

History is determined not so much by what is true—which is often maddeningly difficult to determine, as any historian will attest—but rather by what people think is true. It did not much matter that Otis's confident description of the British constitution was largely fantasy; what mattered was that a substantial number of Americans believed it to be true, most of them quite independently of Otis's formulation. Thus if it was a poor reading of the constitution it was a close reading of the American mind, or temper, or consciousness—so close that it would be validated at every stage of the Revolutionary struggle and in the drafting of the Constitution itself. The remarkable power of Otis's version of the constitution (and the degree to which he articulated the attitudes and beliefs of his fellow colonists) is nowhere better demonstrated than in the establishment of the United States Supreme Court. If the Americans could not impose on the British government the colonists' own conception of how the executive courts should function in relation to Parliament, they could and did make it the most essential and integral and original element in their own Constitution when they sat down to draft it almost twenty-five years later.

Otis's essay is such a fascinating document because the author, under pressure to respond to a specific political event—the passage of the Revenue Act—brought together and collated a vast amount of history, much of it mythic, and injected it into a new body or carrier, so to speak. Or grafted this ancient limb on a new trunk. Whatever the appropriate metaphor, the essay is one of that rare class of documents which summarize a huge range of collective experience and define a wholly new application of that experience. History flowed through James Otis, as it does through all charismatic leaders in revolutionary times, like a current of high-voltage electricity. He was a kind of transformer who transferred and formed the current. Passionate speech or profound articulation always involves the mustering of historical forces and spirits and their deployment to meet a particular crisis in the affairs of particular men and women.

This is why I have given so much attention to a relatively obscure essay, written prior to the real crisis but in clear anticipation of it. Otis laid everything out plainly and simply enough. It then had to be enacted. His propositions had to become flesh and blood; had to inhabit real people; had to become history. All the problems confronted by the American in succeeding decades are there and at least some essential solutions. If there is not a final reference point—God—for human affairs, how do we in the long run avoid decadence and disintegration? If our "rights" are simply an accumulation of historical accidents, residues of obscure struggles that no longer stir us, indeed of which we are only dimly conscious, what is to prevent their being swept aside? It is manifestly absurd to cling to archaic myths in an age dominated by objective science. How can a bill of rights be derived from scientific inquiry? In that remorseless skepticism all "values" are dissolved, mere epiphenomena. I am not sure there are any universally satisfactory answers to such complex questions but I believe the questions should be constantly in our minds as we attempt to understand the way in which the idea of a constitution has shaped the reality of our history as a people.

CHAPTER

IV

JOHN ADAMS THINKS
ABOUT GOVERNMENT

IN THE YEARS BETWEEN THE APPEARANCE OF OTIS'S ESSAY AND THE outbreak of the Revolution, innumerable tracts and pamphlets were written by American patriots (or Whigs), by American Tories, and by their English counterparts. The great majority addressed themselves to the constitutional issue, trying to define the powers of Parliament and the rights of the colonists in such a way as to satisfy both parties to the dispute. Needless to say, the efforts were unsuccessful. The authors satisfied only their fellow partisans and not always them. At the very least, this prolonged and intense public debate raised the constitutional consciousness of the colonists and habituated them to thinking "constitutionally."

The most practical consequence of thinking "constitutionally" was that when it came time for the Americans to cast off the authority of king and Parliament they had a large store of theory to supplement a considerable accumulation of practical experience. Lexington and Concord were many months old before the various colonies could face up to the fearful task of framing instruments of governments— constitutions—which, in all probability, would make their rebellion against the crown irrevocable. In most colonies extralegal governing bodies, usually called Committees of Public Safety and Committees of Correspondence, had grown up within, or rather counter to, the legitimate governing agencies of the crown. The colonists were painfully aware that these revolutionary bodies lacked legitimacy. When colonists loyal to the crown resisted their edicts, they had no recourse but bullying and intimidation. Not until the royal governments had been replaced by patriot governments would these revolutionary, extralegal bodies be absorbed into some kind of orderly and legitimate government.

When the North Carolina delegates to Continental Congress came to Philadelphia in 1775 they came with instructions to bring back "every hint [they] could collect concerning government." They had heard John Adams, James Otis's young colleague from the Massachusetts delegation, "dilate" on the proper principles of constitution making, so they sought out Adams and asked him to put pen to paper. Adams found the notion irresistible. Borrowing "a little time from his sleep," he made two copies of his *Thoughts on Government*. George Wythe, dean of the Virginia bar and Thomas Jefferson's patron, saw one of the copies made for the North Carolinians and asked for one for himself. Soon there were half a dozen copies circulating among the delegates to Congress.

Adams prefaced his *Thoughts* with the reflection that "since the blessings of society depend entirely on . . . constitutions of government, there can be no employment more agreeable to a benevolent mind than a research after the best." The prerequisite to even sitting down to write a constitution was the conviction that "the blessings of society depend *entirely* [italics mine, as they say] on . . . constitutions of government." That was, by and large, a new notion, and the fact that Adams could state it as a truism indicates very clearly that, as a consequence of the historical developments we have described, Western man had come to focus his attention on the political question. We are so accustomed to the centrality of politics, of constitutions, charters, ordinances, and laws, that it is hard for us to imagine a period of history when such considerations were of decidedly minor importance, when custom, tradition, relationships between people and simple power were the essential elements in society. The American Revolution marked the emergence of politics as a subject of paramount importance. Previously, theological questions had predominated. The feudal world was a world dominated by customary relationships and hereditary loyalties, by divinely ordained institutions that were seldom examined or questioned. Now mankind was to experience "blessings" not primarily as a consequence of God's grace but as the result of properly framed constitutions. It would be going too far to say that John Adams and his coadjutors were undertaking to usurp the prerogatives of the Almighty but there is no doubt that they had the intoxicating sense that they stood at one of the crucial junctures of history and helped to tip the scale a bit in the direction of "blessings"; that they were, in short, contributing substantially to the future happiness of the human race. Some writers had gone so far as to suggest that the form of government did not matter as long as the government itself was well administered. This, to Adams, was absurd. To him nothing was more certain "from the history of nations and the nature of man, than that some forms of government are better fitted for being well administered than others." Again it is important to keep in mind that Adams' generation of American political activists was the first generation (with the possible exception of the ancient Greeks and Romans) that could have made such a confident declaration.

James Harrington, the most influential writer on politics of his age, and Thomas Hobbes, whose gloomy reflections on human nature were rebutted by Locke, had given special attention to the nature of government. European theorists like the German philosopher Pufendorf or the Frenchman Burlamaqui, and later Montesquieu, had also written extensively on government, and the notion that its proper end was the happiness of the governed was not new by any means. But the confident assertion of John Adams was that of a man who, with his fellow revolutionaries, was prepared to give practical effect to all the theoretical speculations of philosophers, to cut through them, select the best and soundest timbers, and erect them into the noblest constitution yet known to the race.

The best government would be a combination of a finely tuned mechanism, *à la* Newton's law of gravitation, and the secular manifestation of Christian teaching. Plato, despairing at the slothfulness and vulgarity of the ordinary man, had dreamed of an authoritarian state ruled by a superior breed of philosopher-kings; his pupil, Aristotle, agreeing that man was "the worst animal" of all "when detached from customs and justice," had relied on social constraints. Augustine had placed his faith in the Christian's yearning to emulate the City of God; St. Thomas Aquinas on the authority of the church; Calvin, contemptuous of those who yearned for earthly perfection, "which can never be found in any community of men," strongly supported "civil polity," or government, as necessary to man's well-being, to justice, and "integrity and modesty" in society during man's pilgrimage on earth. John Adams and his fellow patriots, as heirs of more than two thousand years of "Western" thought, saw in politics the means of social redemption. The highest expression of politics was clearly constitution making.

The best government, Adams argued in his preamble, was one that most effectively stimulated the virtue of its citizens and suppressed their vices. (We need only note here that Adams paid his respects to the Greek theorists by using their word "virtue.") Moreover, every government must rest on some principle or passion in the minds of the people. There had to be some common vision or, more commonly in the past, fear that united their sentiments. A government could only ratify or raise to a higher common denominator, feelings, emotions, and loyalties which already existed "in the minds of the people"; it could not create them.

But in drafting constitutions for the American states, "the noblest principles and most generous affections in our nature" must be called forth to create "the noblest and most generous models of government." It was clear that there was "no good government but what is republican . . . because the very definition of a republic is 'an empire of laws, and not of men.' " There would thus be a republic if all was secured by laws rather than by the arbitrary rule of a single person or group. As to the nature of this republican government, there were, admittedly, various models, but certain elements must be common to all. A true republic must have a representative assembly chosen by the owners of real property (land), or by electors otherwise qualified. The assembly should be, Adams continued, "in miniature an exact portrait of the people at large. It should feel, reason and act like them. . . . Equal interest among the people should have equal interests in it." But matters must not stop there. Since history demonstrated beyond doubt or argument that people as a whole were disposed to be governed more by popular prejudices than by reason, were often faulty in their judgments and given to transient passions and acts as arbitrary as those of any tyrant, there must be an upper house, smaller, more deliberative, a step removed from the changeable emotions of the populace at large. As Adams put it, "a people cannot be long free nor ever happy whose government is in one assembly," for "a single assembly is subject to all the vices, follies, and frailties of an individual, subject to fits of humor, starts of passion, flights of enthusiasm, partialities, or prejudice, and consequently productive of hasty results and absurd judgments."

It might be well to pause and consider this passage since Adams is articulating a view of human nature which, as we have seen, had been the predominant one since the time of the Greeks, but which, I believe it is correct to say, no longer pervades or is a conspicuous element in the thinking of modern men and women. We are, for example, much more conscious today of the laboriousness of the legislative process in bicameral (two-house) legislatures, like our federal Congress—House and Senate—and the great majority of our state legislatures, than we are of the dangers of hasty and ill-considered legislative acts (although it could be argued that examples of the latter are by no means unknown, a classic recent instance being the notorious Gulf of Tonkin Resolution passed by the Senate giving the late President Lyndon Johnson virtually a free hand in extending the American involvement in the Vietnam War). In any event it seems evident that one of our problems today is that we have no clear notion of human nature except a rather vague feeling that people are inherently good and only corrupted by bad institutions plus an accumulation of negative historical elements. In this we are children of the French Enlightenment, references to which are premature since that profoundly important development has not yet entered our story. Suffice it to say that the generation of Revolutionary politicians, for whom John Adams is here a spokesman, accepted the notion of man as a fallen creature with scarcely a dissent.

A single unchecked legislature, Adams declared, would lust after power, and in time "will not hesitate to vote itself perpetual." The legislative branch of a proper government should, therefore, consist of two branches, with the second house, or council, chosen by the first and the two together selecting a governor. The governor and the legislatures were to have a veto upon the actions of the others—hence checks and balances. All elections should be annual, for "where annual elections end, there slavery begins." Yearly elections would teach politicians "the great political virtues of humility, patience, and moderation, without which every man in power becomes a ravenous beast of prey."

Here we might add another word about the Revolutionary generation's view of power. If man was by nature inclined to evil, it followed that it was essential to distribute power as widely as possible. All concentrations of powers were dangerous because they were governed by a kind of mathematical law that went something like this: the opportunity to do evil increases by the square of the power exercised by an individual or class. The more power an individual or a group holds, the more grossly will that power be abused. Viewed in this light, government becomes a device for combating original sin. Such, indeed, was the notion of the framers of the various state constitutions and, eventually, the federal Constitution.

Annual elections were another of what we might call the "original sin provisions" in Adams' hypothetical constitution. (Whether elections were every year, every two years or every four years, the principle was the same, since all men were corruptible: limit all terms of office to as brief a time as was practical.) Adams had little to say on the operations of a court. It is interesting to note that he failed to follow up the notion of his idol, James Otis, that the judges of the executive courts should be charged with declaring whether or not a particular legislative enactment was constitutional.

If there were omissions in his plan, Adams was not aware of them. This system, if adopted, he wrote, could in the space of little more than a month, bring about "without the least convulsion, or even animosity . . . a total revolution in the government of a colony." By adopting some such plan "human nature would appear in its proper glory, asserting its own real dignity, pulling down tyrannies at a single exertion, and erecting such new fabrics as it thinks best calculated to promote its happiness." Adams was confident that a constitution based on such principles would bring with it "good humor, sociability, good manners and good morals. . . ." It would make the "common people brave and enterprising" and the sense of participating in government and so controlling their own future would make them "sober, industrious and frugal."

John Adams' euphoria at the notion that he stood at the gateway to a new epoch in history and was indeed himself an active agent of that new epoch burst out in a triumphant passage at the end of his *Thoughts*. "You and I, my dear friend," he wrote, "have been sent into life at a time when the greatest lawmakers of antiquity would have wished to live. How few of the human race have ever enjoyed an opportunity of making an election of government, more than of air, soil or climate, for themselves or their children! When, before the present epocha, had three millions of people full power and a fair opportunity to form and establish the wisest and happiest government that human wisdom can contrive?" That was the haunting refrain. The first time in history! To be the envy of political theorists, princes, and lawmakers from classical times to the present! Without keeping constantly in mind this conviction on the part of the politicians of the Revolutionary generation that they were inaugurating a new historical era, it is impossible to understand the significance of their achievement.

As we have indicated earlier, there were already plenty of functioning models of government in the respective states. In most instances it sufficed simply to incorporate the established agencies of government in a written document. What actually happened was perhaps not as revolutionary as Adams believed: a mistaken notion of how the British constitution functioned, derived primarily from Montesquieu, was imposed on the already quite satisfactory colonial governments that had developed in the somewhat more than a hundred years since the major period of British settlement in America.

But to put the matter thus vastly oversimplifies it. The men involved in framing the various state constitutions did not exactly start from scratch. They had before them a wide variety of options and, as we shall see, they explored a good many of them. Perhaps the most important and most complex task was to construct governments that would not be taken over by the more wealthy and powerful class in each state. From Virginia, Patrick Henry wrote John Adams of his uneasiness that "among most of our opulent families" there existed "a strong bias to aristocracy" that must be resisted. Adams wrote promptly to encourage his Virginia friend in his struggle against "the dons, the bashaws, the grandees, the patricians, the sachems, the nabobs, call them by what names you will." These fine gentlemen might "sigh and groan, and fret and sometimes stamp and curse," but all in vain. It was the will of the great body of the people and their leaders in every state "that a more equal liberty than has prevailed in other parts of the earth must be established in America." The "insolent domination" of "a few, a very few opulent, monopolizing families" would be "brought down nearer to the confines of reason and moderation."

It proved no easy task. The Bill of Rights, "as the basis and foundation of government," was the first portion of the Virginia Constitution and it was preceded by a preamble written by George Mason that declared that "all men are by nature equally free and independent. . . ." There were immediate objections. One of the members of the Virginia Convention wrote his brother: "A certain set of aristocrats—for we have such monsters here—finding that their miserable system cannot be raised on such foundations, have to this time kept us so at bay on the first line, which declares all men to be born free and independent. A number of absurd or unmeaning alterations have been proposed."

The preamble that aroused the opposition of the "aristocrats" was adopted by Jefferson in the Declaration of Independence with a few small but significant changes. Jefferson, incidentally, moved heaven and earth to get himself appointed to the Virginia Constitutional Convention at Richmond. That seemed to him a far more interesting and important task than remaining prisoner in Philadelphia while he labored over the Declaration of Independence.

The first six articles of the Virginia Bill of Rights incorporated propositions that were the direct consequence of the Revolutionary struggle and not derived from the Proclamation of Rights of 1689. Among these is the assertion that all power is derived directly from the people and that public officials are their servants; that any government which does not protect and advance the happiness and safety of the people may be altered or abolished by a majority of the community, that there can be no hereditary officers or titles, that the legislative and executive branches of the government must be "separate and distinct" from the judiciary, and that elective offices must be limited to short and specific terms so that the holders of office may be periodically "reduced to a private station."

The constitution proper, or "form of government," follows, the reader will note, the general outlines of John Adams' *Thoughts*, which is not to credit him with the Virginia Constitution but simply to emphasize the degree to which Adams was giving voice to common assumptions about the nature of government.

The terms "Senate" and "House" describing the upper and lower branches of the legislature were, of course, to reappear in the federal Constitution, as was the stipulation regarding the origin of all laws in the House.

THE VIRGINIA BILL OF RIGHTS
12 June 1776

At a General Convention of Delegates and Representatives, from the several counties and corporations of Virginia, held at the Capitol in the City of Williamsburg on Monday the 6th May 1776.

A Declaration of Rights made by the representatives of the good people of Virginia, assembled in full and free Convention; which rights do pertain to them and their posterity, as the basis and foundation of government.

1. That all men are by nature equally free and independent, and have certain inherent rights, of which, when they enter into a state of society, they cannot by any compact deprive or divest their posterity; namely, the enjoyment of life and liberty, with the means of acquiring and possessing property, and pursuing and obtaining happiness and safety.

2. That all power is vested in, and consequently derived from, the people; that magistrates are their trustees and servants, and at all times amenable to them.

3. That government is, or ought to be instituted for the common benefit, protection, and security of the people, nation, or community; of all the various modes and forms of government, that is best which is capable of producing the greatest degree of happiness and safety, and is most effectually secured against the danger of maladministration; and that when any government shall be found inadequate or contrary to these purposes, a majority of the community hath an indubitable, unalienable and indefeasible right to reform, alter or abolish it, in such manner as shall be judged most conducive to the public weal.

4. That no man, or set of men, are entitled to exclusive or separate emoluments or privileges from the community, but in consideration of publick services; which, not being descendible, neither ought the offices of magistrate, legislator or judge to be hereditary.

5. That the legislative and executive powers of the state should be separate and distinct from the judiciary; and that the members of the two first may be restrained from oppression, by feeling and participating the burthens of the people, they should, at fixed periods, be reduced to a private station, return into that body from which they were originally taken, and the vacancies be supplied by frequent, certain, and regular elections, in which all, or any part of the former members to be again eligible or ineligible, as the laws shall direct.

6. That elections of members to serve as representatives of the

people in assembly, ought to be free; and that all men having sufficient evidence of permanent common interest with, and attachment to the community, have the right of suffrage, and cannot be taxed or deprived of their property for publick uses, without their own consent, or that of their representatives so elected, nor bound by any law to which they have not, in like manner, assented for the public good.

7. That all power of suspending laws, or the execution of laws, by any authority without consent of the representatives of the people, is injurious to their rights, and ought not to be exercised.

8. That in all capital or criminal prosecution a man hath a right to demand the cause and nature of his accusation, to be confronted with the accusers and witnesses, to call for evidence in his favour, and to a speedy trial by an impartial jury of his vicinage, without whose unanimous consent he cannot be found guilty; nor can he be compelled to give evidence against himself; that no man be deprived of his liberty, except by the law of the land or the judgment of his peers.

9. That excessive bail ought not to be required, nor excessive fines imposed, nor cruel and unusual punishments inflicted.

10. That general warrants, whereby an officer or messenger may be commanded to search suspected places without evidence of an act committed, or to seize any person or persons not named, or whose offence is not particularly described and supported by evidence, are grievous and oppressive, and ought not to be granted.

11. That in controversies respecting property, and in suits between man and man, the ancient trial by jury is preferable to any other, and ought to be held sacred.

12. That the freedom of the press is one of the great bulwarks of liberty, and can never be restrained but by despotick governments.

13. That a well-regulated militia, composed of the body of the people trained to arms, is the proper, natural and safe defence of a free state; that standing armies in time of peace should be avoided as dangerous to liberty; and that in all cases the military should be under strict subordination to, and governed by, the civil power.

14. That the people have a right to uniform government; and, therefore, that no government separate from, or independent of the government of Virginia, ought to be erected or established within the limits thereof.

15. That no free government, or the blessings of liberty, can be preserved to any people, but by a firm adherence to justice, moderation, temperance, frugality and virtue, and by frequent recurrence to fundamental principles.

16. That religion, or the duty which we owe to our Creator, and the

manner of discharging it, can be directed only by reason and conviction, not by force or violence; and therefore all men are equally entitled to the free exercise of religion, according to the dictates of conscience; and that it is the mutual duty of all to practise Christian forbearance, love, and charity towards each other.

THE CONSTITUTION OF VIRGINIA
29 June 1776

The Constitution, or Form of Government, agreed to and resolved upon by the Delegates and Representatives of the several counties and corporations of Virginia.

1. Whereas George the third [a digest of the Declaration of Independence follows]. . . . By which several acts of misrule, the government of this country, as formerly exercised under the crown of Great Britain, is TOTALLY DISSOLVED.

2. We, the Delegates and Representatives of the good people of Virginia, having maturely considered the premises, and viewing with great concern the deplorable conditions to which this once happy country must be reduced, unless some regular adequate mode of civil polity is speedily adopted, and in compliance with a recommendation of the General Congress, do ordain and declare the future form of government of Virginia to be as followeth:

3. The legislative, executive, and judiciary departments shall be separate and distinct, so that neither exercise the powers properly belonging to the other: nor shall any person exercise the powers of more than one of them at the same time; except that the justices of the county courts shall be eligible to either House of Assembly.

4. The legislative shall be formed of two distinct branches, who, together, shall be a complete Legislature. They shall meet once, or oftener, every year, and shall be called the GENERAL ASSEMBLY OF VIRGINIA.

5. One of these shall be called the House of Delegates, and consist of two representatives, to be chosen for each county, and for the district of West-Augusta, annually, of such men as actually reside in, and are freeholders of the same, or duly qualified according to law, and also of one delegate or representative to be chosen annually for the city of Williamsburg, and one for the borough of Norfolk, and a representative for each of such other cities and boroughs, as may hereafter be allowed particular representation by the legislature; but when any city or borough shall so decrease as that the number of persons having right of suffrage therein shall have been for the space of seven years successively less than

half the number of voters in some one county in Virginia, such city or borough thenceforward shall cease to send a delegate or representative to the Assembly.

6. The other shall be called the Senate, and consist of twenty-four members, of whom thirteen shall constitute a House to proceed on business; for whose election the different counties shall be divided into twenty-four districts, and each county of the respective district, at the time of the election of its delegates, shall vote for one Senator, who is actually a resident and freeholder within the district, or duly qualified according to law, and is upwards of twenty-five years of age; and the Sheriffs of each county, within five days at farthest after the last county election in the district, shall meet at some convenient place, and from the poll so taken in their respective counties return as a Senator the man who shall have the greatest number of votes in the whole district. To keep up this Assembly by rotation, the districts shall be equally divided into four classes and numbered by lot. At the end of one year after the general election, the six members elected by the first division shall be displaced, and the vacancies thereby occasioned supplied from such class or division, by new election, in the manner aforesaid. This rotation shall be applied to each division, according to its number, and continued in due order annually.

7. The right of suffrage in the election of members for both Houses shall remain as exercised at present, and each House shall choose its own speaker, appoint its own officers, settle its own rules of proceeding, and direct writs of election, for the supplying intermediate vacancies.

8. All laws shall originate in the House of Delegates, to be approved or rejected by the Senate, or to be amended with consent of the House of Delegates; except money bills, which in no instance shall be altered by the Senate, but wholly approved or rejected.

9. A Governour, or chief magistrate, shall be chosen annually, by joint ballot of both Houses to be taken in each House respectively, deposited in the conference room, the boxes examined jointly by a committee of each House, and the numbers severally reported to them, that the appointments may be entered (which shall be the mode of taking the joint ballot of both Houses, in all cases) who shall not continue in that office longer than three years successively, nor be eligible until the expiration of four years after he shall have been out of that office. An adequate, but moderate salary shall be settled on him, during his continuance in office; and he shall, with the advice of a Council of State, exercise the executive powers of government according to the laws of this Commonwealth; and shall not, under any pretence, exercise any power

or prerogative by virtue of any law, statute or custom of England. But he shall, with the advice of the Council of State, have the power of granting reprieves or pardons, except where the prosecution shall have been carried on by the House of Delegates, or the law shall otherwise particularly direct; in which cases, no reprieve or pardon shall be granted, but by resolve of the House of Delegates.

10. Either House of the General Assembly may adjourn themselves respectively. The Governour shall not prorogue or adjourn the Assembly during their sitting, nor dissolve them at any time; but he shall, if necessary, either by advice of the Council of State, or on application of a majority of the House of Delegates, call them before the time to which they shall stand prorogued or adjourned.

11. A Privy Council, or Council of State, consisting of eight members, shall be chosen by joint ballot of both Houses of Assembly, either from their own members or the people at large, to assist in the administration of government. They shall annually choose, out of their own members, a president, who, in case of death, inability, or absence of the Governour from the government, shall act as Lieutenant-Governour. Four members shall be sufficient to act, and their advice and proceedings shall be entered on record, and signed by the members present (to any part whereof, any member may enter his dissent) to be laid before the General Assembly, when called for by them. This Council may appoint their own clerk, who shall have a salary settled by law, and take an oath of secrecy in such matters as he shall be directed by the board to conceal. A sum of money appropriated to that purpose shall be divided annually among the members, in proportion to their attendance; and they shall be incapable, during their continuance in office, of sitting in either House of Assembly. Two members shall be removed, by joint ballot of both Houses of Assembly, at the end of every three years, and be ineligible for the three next years. These vacancies, as well as those occasioned by death or incapacity, shall be supplied by new elections, in the same manner.

12. The Delegates for Virginia to the Continental Congress shall be chosen annually, or superseded in the meantime by joint ballot of both Houses of Assembly.

13. The present militia officers shall be continued, and vacancies supplied by appointment of the Governour, with the advice of the Privy Council, on recommendations from the respective county courts; but the Governour and Council shall have a power of suspending any officer, and ordering a court-martial, on complaint of misbehaviour or inability, or to supply vacancies of officers, happening when in actual

service. The Governour may embody the militia, with the advice of the Privy Council; and when embodied, shall alone have the direction of the militia, under the laws of the country.

14. The two Houses of Assembly shall, by joint ballot, appoint Judges of the Supreme Court of Appeals, and General Court, Judges in Chancery, Judges of Admiralty, Secretary, and the Attorney-General, to be commissioned by the Governour, and continue in office during good behaviour. In case of death, incapacity, or resignation, the Governour, with the advice of the Privy Council, shall appoint persons to succeed in office, to be approved or displaced by both Houses. These officers shall have fixed and adequate salaries, and, together with all others holding lucrative offices, and all ministers of the Gospel of every denomination, be incapable of being elected members of either House of Assembly or the Privy Council.

15. The Governour, with the advice of the Privy Council, shall appoint Justices of the Peace for the counties; and in case of vacancies, or a necessity of increasing the number hereafter, such appointments to be made upon the recommendation of the respective county courts. The present acting Secretary in Virginia, and clerks of all the county courts, shall continue in office. In case of vacancies, either by death, incapacity, or resignation, a Secretary shall be appointed as before directed, and the clerks by the respective courts. The present and future clerks shall hold their offices during good behaviour, to be judged of and determined in the General Court. The sheriffs and coroners shall be nominated by the respective courts, approved by the Governour, with the advice of the Privy Council, and commissioned by the Governour. The Justices shall appoint Constables; and all fees of the aforesaid officers be regulated by law.

16. The Governour, when he is out of office, and others offending against the State, either by mal-administration, corruption, or other means by which the safety of the State may be endangered, shall be impeachable by the House of Delegates. Such impeachment to be prosecuted by the Attorney-General, or such other person or persons as the House may appoint in the General Court, according to the laws of the land. If found guilty, he or they shall be either forever disabled to hold any office under government, or be removed from such office *pro tempore*, or subjected to such pains or penalties as the law shall direct.

17. If all or any of the Judges of the General Court should on good grounds (to be judged of by the House of Delegates) be accused of any of the crimes or offences before mentioned, such House of Delegates may, in like manner, impeach the Judge or Judges so accused; to be prosecuted in the Court of Appeals; and he or they, if found guilty, shall

be punished in the same manner as is prescribed in the preceding clause. . . .

22. In order to introduce this government, the representatives of the people met in Convention shall choose a Governour and Privy Council, also such other officers directed to be chosen by both Houses as may be judged necessary to be immediately appointed. The Senate to be first chosen by the people to continue until the last day of March next, and the other officers until the end of the succeeding session of Assembly. In case of vacancies, the speaker of either House shall issue writs for new elections.

Several further comments may be in order. The Virginia Constitution is included here, virtually in its entirety (Articles 18 through 21 are omitted as irrelevant to the main line of this book), because it was the second state constitution adopted (New Hampshire was first) and because it became a model for a number of other state constitutions. It also represented roughly the center or "right-center" of the state constitutions in terms of the conservative-radical political spectrum among the patriots. The attentive reader will have noted, in Article 11, provision for a "Privy Council, or Council of State." This was intended to function in part as a kind of cabinet and in part as a check upon the very limited powers of the governor, and it reflected Americans' deep-seated suspicion of executive power. They not unnaturally equated executive power with George III's dominance over Parliament, a dominance which they had come to feel was the source of all their woes. The consequence was that virtually no state constitution granted the governor (in Pennsylvania he was called "president") any substantial degree of power. The balance was invariably tilted very decisively toward the legislature. It took almost fifteen years of often painful experience to demonstrate that a weak executive could cause a "general debility" in government.

It is also worth noting that the Virginia Constitution, passed on June 12, 1776, preceded by almost a month the Declaration of Independence. Rhode Island and Connecticut, which had the most liberal royal charters, permitting them, among other things, to elect their own governors, found that they could produce satisfactory constitutions by doing little more than deleting from their charters all mention of the King of England.

There was a substantial measure of irony in the fact that North

Carolina, whose delegates had prompted John Adams to record his *Thoughts on Government,* was so sharply divided between conservatives and radicals that it was hard pressed to produce any constitution at all. One of the conservatives in the state constitutional convention noted glumly that "everyone who has the least pretentions to be a gentleman is borne down per ignobile vulgus—a set of men without reading, experience, or principles to govern them."

While the arrangement that John Adams had recommended for the election of a governor—a joint ballot of both houses—was hardly designed to produce an independent chief executive, Adams' theory of a balanced government required a strong executive to balance the legislative branch. The governor of North Carolina was the most powerless of all state governors. To a query as to the governor's powers under the new constitution one of the delegates replied that he had "Power to sign a receipt for his salary." Any adult freeman, resident in the state, could vote for members of the lower house, but a freehold of fifty acres was required to qualify to vote for a senator. This provision serves as a reminder that a commonplace of constitutional theory was that an upper house, while serving as a check upon the popular prejudices and enthusiasms that might compromise the deliberations of the lower house, was also the special guardian of the propertied interests. The rationale for this view of the function of an upper house went back to the days of ancient Rome. Even though suffrage, the right to vote for any public official or representative, was, as we have noted earlier, almost without exception tied to the ownership of real property—typically a house and the land it stood on—there was a concern that those with very modest properties might vote to expropriate the lands of wealthy individuals with extensive holdings.

Since the drafters of state constitutions were, in the main, well-to-do individuals, they had a natural inclination to protect their interests. Those who read ancient history (and most did) were well aware that in the Rome of the Gracchus brothers, the people having gained control of the assembly had passed laws with the support of Tiberius —the so-called Agrarian Laws—limiting the amount of land an individual could hold to 312 acres and distributing the land owned by the wealthy in excess of that amount to the landless poor. I suppose it is safe to say no law or statute from an earlier age, with the exception of the British Bill of Rights, worked so powerfully on the imaginations of the framers of the various American constitutions and finally of the federal Constitution as did the Agrarian Laws of the Gracchi. Few debates on the question of suffrage and the nature and function of an upper legislative branch took place without reference to the danger of Agrarian Laws. The fact is that in every historical age prior to our own, the predominant form of wealth has been land and since, as we have noted, the Founding Fathers, almost without exception, believed that man was innately greedy and selfish, it was hardly surprising that history often seemed to them little more than a record of the successful efforts of individuals, classes, and nations to collect, by force or guile, a disproportionate share of the land, i.e., the wealth of their country. Consequently the concern of the American constitution makers that the have-nots might at some day in the future be tempted to take from the haves is understandable. Two points must be made in fairness to them. First, that there were probably more property owners in colonial America in proportion to the general population than in any other post-tribal society of which history has a record and that property was, in addition, more equitably distributed, there being less distance between the richest and the poorest than in any modern nation. Moreover, if the framers of constitutions were anxious to protect the propertied class from the avarice of the people, they believed themselves to be equally concerned with protecting the people from the predatory and "self-aggrandizing" instincts of the rich, whose desire for wealth was theoretically insatiable. Or so history suggested. The protection of those of modest means against the exploitive inclinations of the rich was to be ensured by giving the former control of the finances of the state through their representation in the powerful "popular" house and their exclusive authority to initiate all bills appropriating money. This right, reinforced with fair and equitable laws, and administered by an executive zealous for the welfare of the people as a whole, would, the constitution makers hoped, protect those at the lower levels of society, who had been, traditionally, in greatest need of protection. In other words, the constitutions should guarantee power to the traditionally powerless.

Of course the best defense against Agrarian Laws was the wide diffusion of property. If every voter owned property and thus had a stake in its protection against arbitrary expropriation, then the modest property owner and the wealthy had a common bond. It was the threat of a landless proletariat that haunted the dreams of the framers of constitutions. Jefferson went so far as to declare that the land was a common heritage of the members of a society although it might be uncommonly divided. Agricultural land might be appropriated for industrial use, but in such instances jobs must be found for those displaced from the land. If not, right to the land reverted to the unemployed. Indeed, Jefferson went even further by advocating that land revert to the public after a generation or two and be redistributed among all the citizens. This was his solution to the apparently ineradicable impulse of human beings to exploit each other. If there was not some mechanism by means of which undue accumulations of property were broken up, the result must be increasing inequities in society and eventual revolutionary upheaval. It should be said that these notions came to Jefferson later in life when, as ambassador to France, he witnessed the opening phases of the French Revolution. But they had a solid foundation in American attitudes that dated from the early years of the Revolutionary crisis.

That it did not work out quite that way is hardly the fault of the framers. The spirit of natural human rapacity, wedded to modern industrial capitalist technology, proved too potent a force to be contained by any barricade of laws however ingeniously devised. Today in the United States huge corporations own millions of acres of land on the ground that only units of such vast size can be efficiently farmed.

In any event we shall continue to encounter this theme—how to protect the legitimate interests of different groups in society against exploitation on the one hand or expropriation on the other—throughout this book. It is, of course, the essence of government, and no government can succeed in the long run that does not embody what the eighteenth century called "natural equity" and what we might translate today as social, economic, and legal justice for all its citizens.

CHAPTER

V

THE RADICAL ALTERNATIVE

It is not the intention of this book to trace in detail the constitutions of the colonies turned states, though a detailed comparison of them is, in many ways, an illuminating exercise. We are looking rather for types and models. The Constitution of the Commonwealth of Pennsylvania is thus of special interest since it marked the high tide of radical idealism in constitution making. When the Pennsylvania delegates to the constitutional convention sat down to draw up a frame of government in the summer of 1776, a few weeks after the passage of the congressional resolution on independence, the state was securely in the hands of the more radical politicians. This was primarily because the conservative and moderate patriots had lost their credibility, as we say today, by their dogged opposition to independence. Popular feeling so far outran them that a number were voted out of the assembly and replaced by more ardent revolutionaries. Presided over by Benjamin Franklin and badly split along ideological lines, the delegates proceeded to their deliberations in a spirit of mutual recrimination.

Article VIII, which respected the rights of the Quakers to not bear arms, was unique to Pennsylvania. It is important also to note that the Pennsylvania Bill of Rights included the right of a citizen to emigrate from one state to another, or "to form a new State in vacant countries, or in such countries as they can purchase." This clause is a striking example of the manner in which self-interest can work to good purpose. The clause was intended to protect the interests of Pennsylvania investors, or land speculators, in the Vandalia Company, which was attempting to start a new settlement and, hopefully, state in the area of present-day Kentucky and Tennessee. Its positive effect was that it raised the whole issue of how new states might be added to the confederation and thus paved the way for such provisions in both the Articles of Confederation and later in the Constitution itself. Article XVI added to the Virginia Bill of Rights the right of free assembly and the right to petition for redress of grievances.

In the "Frame of Government" the most important aspects were the single-house legislature, the establishment of courts in every county so that justice was readily available to the ordinary citizen, the provision that militiamen should select their own officers, and the stipulation that suffrage should be exercised by every freeman over the age of twenty-one who had resided in the state for a year and paid taxes during that year (with the additional provision that the sons of freemen had the right to vote even though they had not paid taxes). The latter provision for what was, in effect, universal male suffrage was the most democratic such provision in any state constitution. The powers of the "President" were almost entirely submerged in those of the Council. He had little more weight than his North Carolina counterpart.

No man was to hold office for more than two years—two annual elections—after which he must lay out for three years before being eligible for reelection. The way in which the Pennsylvania constitution makers undertook to solve the problem of the notorious fickleness and hasty enthusiasms of the popular branch of the legislature —since there was no upper house to act as a check upon it—was by requiring that all proposed laws must, after an initial hearing, be printed and circulated among the people so that popular reaction might be gathered "and, except on occasions of sudden necessity, shall not be passed into laws until the next session of the assembly" (Article 15).

Every officer of the state was susceptible to impeachment for the improper conduct of his office. Nine articles (22–30) deal with the administration of justice, and here again the Constitution was notable for its efforts to lessen the weight of the judicial system on the poorer elements in the state, the most significant reform being the article that forbade imprisonment for debt except on presumption of fraud.

A strikingly original article in the Pennsylvania Constitution (Article 47) provided that a Council of Censors be elected every seven years "whose duty it shall be to enquire whether the Constitution has been preserved inviolate in every part; and whether the legislative and executive branches of government have performed their duty as guardians of the people, or assumed to themselves, or exercised other or greater powers than they are entitled to by the constitution."

Revolutionary movements are generally puritanical in nature and the Pennsylvania Constitution was no exception. It provides (Article 45) that "Laws for the encouragement of virtue, and prevention of vice and immorality, shall be made and constantly kept in force. . . ." The Council of Censors was borrowed from an institution of the Roman republic. It apparently was never convened, and it was omitted from the new Constitution drafted in 1790 when the conservatives had regained control of the state.

The opponents of the Constitution of 1776 were relentless in their attacks on the document and its framers. They described the majority of the delegates "as honest well meaning Countrymen . . . intirely unacquainted with such matters"; men "hardly equal to the Task to form a new plan of government." Another dismissed them as "numsculs." "Not sixth part of us ever read a word on the subject [of government]." One delegate wrote, "but I believe we might at least have prevented ourselves from being ridiculous in the eyes of the world were it not for a few enthusiastic members who are totally unacquainted with the principles of government. It is not only that their notions are original," he added, "but that they would go to the devil for popularity."

John Adams was especially offended by the unicameral legislature. "No country ever will be happy long, or ever entirely safe and free, which is thus governed," he wrote a friend, and to Abigail he observed, "We live in an age of political experiment. Among many that will fail some, I hope, will succeed. But Pennsylvania will be divided and weakened and rendered much less vigorous in the cause by the wretched ideas of government which prevail in the minds of many people in it."

The radical delegates were by no means as ill informed in matters of government as their enemies declared. Dr. Young, who was caustically referred to as "bawling Dr. Young," for his demagogic harangues, was widely read in government and he was aided by James Cannon, a Scotsman and professor of mathematics at the College of Philadelphia. Timothy Matlack, who was also in the forefront of the radical leaders, was as literate and learned as most of his rivals. That the framers of the Pennsylvania Constitution were well to the left of most American constitution makers is indisputable. That they were ignorant or ill informed is untrue. In a sense their handiwork never had a fair chance. The more conservative elements in the state—the Quakers and the proprietary interests—made war on it from its inception. Certainly it was an odd document, excessively long and rather overblown, dotted with what might be called "little democratic asides," but it remains nonetheless worthy of close attention. Dr. Young, who was apparently its principal architect, traveled on to Vermont, where he persuaded that frontier state to adopt a constitution that was almost identical after it joined the Confederation in July, 1777.

From the adoption of the New Hampshire Constitution in January, 1776, to the Vermont Constitution in June, 1777, covered a period of some eighteen months, certainly the most concentrated period of constitution making in history. Its importance can hardly be overestimated. The state constitutions were an indispensable prelude to the federal Constitution. There is hardly a single idea or article contained in the federal Constitution that was not proposed or essayed in a state constitution, with the exception, of course, of the role of the Supreme Court. In most of the state constitutions little more than lip service was given to the principle of separation of powers. The powers of the executive branch were, as we have seen, severely circumscribed while those of the legislature were extended and the judiciary was consigned to a decidedly subordinate role. Pennsylvania gave the Council of Censors, rather than the courts, the role of watchdog over the Constitution. It thereby at least acknowledged the problem. James Otis's rhapsodic description of the function of the executive courts under the British constitution fell on unheeding ears as far as the drafting of state constitutions was concerned. The reason was doubtless that, as we shall see, it was in the effort to establish some kind of judicial system for the confederated states during the course of the Revolution that the whole issue of courts of broad jurisdiction came to the fore.

CHAPTER

VI

THE ARTICLES
OF CONFEDERATION

JUST AS THE STATES THEMSELVES HAD, PRIOR TO THE ADOPTION OF constitutions, lived in a condition of uncertain legitimacy, the Continental Congress, which constituted no more than a kind of informal committee of the states without any clearly stated authority or rules to govern its own functions, was similarly ill defined. Even before the passage of the resolution on independence, Congress had formed a committee consisting of one delegate from each state to draw up a constitution. The task fell primarily to John Dickinson, and he, working with exemplary speed, had a draft ready for the consideration of the delegates soon after the resolution on independence, July 2.

One of the problems that had dogged the delegates from the moment they first assembled at Philadelphia in 1774 was the question of whether votes should be by delegates or by colonies. If the outcome was never seriously in doubt—it was by colonies—it left a bad taste in the mouths of the large states—Virginia, Pennsylvania, New York, and Massachusetts—who felt that their larger populations counted for nothing when weighed against tiny Delaware or Rhode Island. Thus when the delegates began to debate the Articles of Confederation, as the committee had decided to call them, they concentrated on Article V, which declared: "In determining questions, each state shall have one vote." Benjamin Franklin spoke for the large states when he declared: "Let the smaller colonies have equal money and equal men and then have an equal vote. . . . If they have an equal vote without bearing equal burdens, a confederation upon such an iniquitous base will never last long."

Dr. John Witherspoon, the president of the College of New Jersey at Princeton and a delegate to Congress, drew on history, as became a professor, to show that wherever large states had it in their power to oppress smaller ones they did—good Calvinist doctrine. If equal representation were abandoned on that principle, Witherspoon asked, would votes be allocated according to wealth, population, geographical size? He had discovered the large state's point of vulnerability. The Southern states, for example, were disposed to argue that slaves count twice, once as population and once as property. John Adams, as a large-state man, argued somewhat impractically before the age of computers that the interests represented in Congress "should be the mathematical representative of the interest without doors"—that is to say the different interest groups in the different states. Perhaps sensing the slipperiness of such a line of argument, Adams shifted his ground to the contention that what was really at issue was the formation of a new nation, "what America would be 'when our bargain shall be made,'" in other words, when the Confederated states were free from Great Britain and must become a nation. "The confederacy," he insisted, "is to make us one individual only, it is to form us, like separate parcels of metal, into one common mass. We shall no longer retain our separate individuality, but become a single individual." This was considerably further than most delegates were ready to go. Some still yearned for a reconciliation and a return to the arms of Mother England. Others believed that in any confederacy it was essential that the states retain that "separate individuality" that John Adams seemed so ready to abandon. On the issue of representation neither side was prepared to yield.

An almost equally thorny problem concerned the right of Congress to limit the boundaries of each state. Virginia, on the basis of its colonial charter, claimed a substantial part of North America from lower waters of the Chesapeake Bay to the Pacific Ocean. The other states were understandably uneasy at such extravagant ambitions. If Virginia, already one of the largest states, were to take in tens of thousands of additional square miles *and* proportional voting were to be accepted, would not Virginia in time dominate every other state?

Most of the delegates were speculators in Western lands and a number of states besides Virginia claimed substantial areas beyond their colonial borders. The initial discussion then did little more than demonstrate the very considerable differences between the delegates, most conspicuously, but not exclusively, the differences between the large and small states on the matter of representation, equal or proportional. It may thus have been with some sense of relief that the delegates put the matter of the Articles of Confederation aside and turned to more pressing problems. It was sixteen months later before they got back to the subject. Then, on November 15, 1777, the delegates adopted "Articles of Confederation and Perpetual Union" to be called "The United States of America."

ARTICLES OF CONFEDERATION
1777 (1781)

To all to whom these Presents shall come, we the undersigned Delegates of the States affixed to our Names, send greeting.

Whereas the Delegates of the United States of America, in Congress assembled, did, on the 15th day of November, in the year [1777] . . . agree to certain Articles of Confederation and perpetual Union between the States of . . . in the words following, viz.:

Articles of Confederation and perpetual Union between the states of New Hampshire, Massachusetts-Bay, Rhode Island and Providence Plantations, Connecticut, New-York, New-Jersey, Pennsylvania, Delaware, Maryland, Virginia, North-Carolina, South-Carolina, and Georgia.

I. The stile of this Confederacy shall be "The United States of America."

II. Each state retains its sovereignty, freedom, and independence, and every power, jurisdiction, and right, which is not by this Confederation expressly delegated to the United States, in Congress assembled.

III. The said states hereby severally enter into a firm league of friendship with each other, for their common defence, the security of their liberties, and their mutual and general welfare, binding themselves to assist each other, against all force offered to, or attacks made upon them, or any of them, on account of religion, sovereignty, trade, or any other pretence whatever.

IV. The better to secure and perpetuate mutual friendship and intercourse among the people of the different states in this union, the free inhabitants of each of these states, paupers, vagabonds, and fugitives from justice excepted, shall be entitled to all privileges and immunities of free citizens in the several states; and the people of each state shall have free ingress and regress to and from any other state, and shall enjoy therein all the privileges of trade and commerce, subject to the same duties, impositions and restrictions as the inhabitants thereof respectively, provided that such restriction shall not extend so far as to prevent the removal of property imported into any state, to any other state, of which the owner is an inhabitant; provided also that no imposition, duties or restriction shall be laid by any state, on the property of the United States, or either of them.

If any person guilty of, or charged with treason, felony, or other high misdemeanor in any state, shall flee from justice, and be found in any of the United States, he shall, upon demand of the Governor or executive power of the state from which he fled, be delivered up and removed to the state having jurisdiction of his offence.

Full faith and credit shall be given in each of these states to the records, acts, and judicial proceedings of the courts and magistrates of every other state.

V. For the more convenient management of the general interests of the United States, delegates shall be annually appointed in such manner as the legislature of each state shall direct, to meet in Congress on the first Monday in November, in every year, with a power reserved to each state to recall its delegates, or any of them, at any time within the year, and to send others in their stead for the remainder of the year.

No state shall be represented in Congress by less than two, nor by more than seven members; and no person shall be capable of being a delegate for more than three years in any term of six years; nor shall any person, being a delegate, be capable of holding any office under the United States, for which he, or another for his benefit receives any salary, fees, or emolument of any kind.

Each state shall maintain its own delegates in a meeting of the states, and while they act as members of the committee of the states.

In determining questions in the United States in Congress assembled, each state shall have one vote.

Freedom of speech and debate in Congress shall not be impeached or questioned in any court or place out of Congress, and the members of Congress shall be protected in their persons from arrests and imprisonments, during the time of their going to and from, and attendance on Congress, except for treason, felony, or breach of the peace.

VI. No state, without the consent of the United States in Congress assembled, shall send any embassy to, or receive any embassy from, or enter into any conference, agreement, alliance, or treaty with any king, prince, or state; nor shall any person holding any office of profit or trust under the United States, or any of them, accept of any present, emolument, office, or title of any kind whatever from any king, prince, or foreign state; nor shall the United States in Congress assembled, or any of them, grant any title of nobility.

No two or more states shall enter into any treaty, confederation or alliance whatever between them, without the consent of the United States in Congress assembled, specifying accurately the purposes for which the same is to be entered into, and how long it shall continue.

No state shall lay any imposts or duties, which may interfere with any stipulations in treaties, entered into by the United States in Congress assembled, with any king, prince, or state, in pursuance of any treaties already proposed by Congress, to the courts of France and Spain.

No vessels of war shall be kept up in time of peace by any state, except such number only, as shall be deemed necessary by the United States in Congress assembled, for the defence of such state, or its trade; nor shall any body of forces be kept up by any state in time of peace, except such number only, as in the judgment of the United States in Congress assembled, shall be deemed requisite to garrison the forts necessary for the defence of such state; but every state shall always keep up a well regulated and disciplined militia, sufficiently armed and accoutred, and shall provide and constantly have ready for use, in public stores, a due number of field pieces and tents, and a proper quantity of arms, ammunition, and camp equipage.

No state shall engage in any war without the consent of the United States in Congress assembled, unless such state be actually invaded by enemies, or shall have received certain advice of a resolution being formed by some nation of Indians to invade such state, and the danger is so imminent as not to admit of a delay till the United States in Congress assembled can be consulted: nor shall any state grant commissions to any ships or vessels of war, nor letters of marque or reprisal, except it be after a declaration of war by the United States in Congress assembled, and then only against the kingdom or state and the subjects thereof, against which war has been so declared, and under such regulations as shall be established by the United States in Congress assembled, unless such state be infested by pirates, in which case vessels of war may be fitted out for that occasion, and kept so long as the danger shall continue, or until the United States in Congress assembled, shall determine otherwise.

VII. When land-forces are raised by any state for the common defence, all officers of or under the rank of colonel, shall be appointed by the legislature of each state respectively, by whom such forces shall be raised, or in such manner as such state shall direct, and all vacancies shall be filled up by the state which first made the appointment.

VIII. All charges of war, and all other expences that shall be incurred for the common defence or general welfare, and allowed by the United States in Congress assembled, shall be defrayed out of a common treasury, which shall be supplied by the several states in proportion to the value of all land within each state, granted to or surveyed for any person, as such land and the buildings and improvements thereon shall be estimated according to such mode as the United States in Congress assembled, shall from time to time direct and appoint.

The taxes for paying that proportion shall be laid and levied by the authority and direction of the legislatures of the several states within the time agreed upon by the United States in Congress assembled.

IX. The United States in Congress assembled, shall have the sole and exclusive right and power of determining on peace and war, except in the cases mentioned in the sixth article—of sending and receiving ambassadors—entering into treaties and alliances, provided that no treaty of commerce shall be made whereby the legislative power of the respective states shall be restrained from imposing such imposts and duties on foreigners, as their own people are subjected to, or from prohibiting the exportation or importation of any species of goods or commodities whatsoever—of establishing rules for deciding in all cases, what captures on land or water shall be legal, and in what manner prizes taken by land or naval forces in the service of the United States shall be divided or appropriated—of granting letters of marque and reprisal in times of peace—appointing courts for the trial of piracies and felonies committed on the high seas and establishing courts for receiving and determining finally appeals in all cases of captures, provided that no member of Congress shall be appointed a judge of any of the said courts.

The United States in Congress assembled shall also be the last resort on appeal in all disputes and differences now subsisting or that hereafter may arise between two or more states concerning boundary, jurisdiction, or any other cause whatever; which authority shall always be exercised in the manner following. Whenever the legislative or executive authority or lawful agent of any state in controversy with another shall present a petition to Congress stating the matter in question and praying for a hearing, notice thereof shall be given by order of Congress to the legislative or executive authority of the other state in controversy, and a day assigned for the appearance of the parties by their lawful agents, who shall then be directed to appoint by joint consent, commissioners or judges to constitute a court for hearing and determining the matter in question: but if they cannot agree, Congress shall name three persons out of each of the United States, and from the list of such persons each party shall alternately strike out one, the petitioners beginning, until the number shall be reduced to thirteen; and from that number not less than seven, nor more than nine names as Congress shall direct, shall in the presence of Congress be drawn out by lot, and the persons whose names shall be so drawn or any five of them, shall be commissioners or judges, to hear and finally determine the controversy, so always as a major part of the judges who shall hear the cause shall agree in the determination: and if either party shall neglect to attend at the day appointed, without showing reasons, which Congress shall judge sufficient, or being present shall refuse to strike, the Congress shall proceed to nominate three persons out of each state, and the secretary of Congress shall strike in behalf of such party absent or refusing; and the judgment and sentence of the court to be appointed, in the manner before prescribed, shall be final and conclusive; and if any of the parties shall refuse to submit to the authority of such court, or to appear or defend their claim or cause, the court shall nevertheless proceed to pronounce sentence, or judgment, which shall in like manner be final and decisive, the judgment or sentence and other proceedings being in either case transmitted to Congress and lodged among the acts of Congress for the security of the parties concerned: provided that every commissioner, before he sits in judgment, shall take an oath to be administered by one of the judges of the supreme or superior court of the state, where the cause shall be tried, "well and truly to hear and determine the matter in question, according to the best of his judgment, without favour, affection, or hope of reward": provided also, that no state shall be deprived of territory for the benefit of the United States.

All controversies concerning the private right of soil claimed under different grants of two or more states, whose jurisdictions as they may respect such lands, and the states which passed such grants are adjusted, the said grants or either of them being at the same time claimed to have originated antecedent to such settlement of jurisdiction, shall on the petition of either party to the Congress of the United States, be finally determined as near as may be in the same manner as is before prescribed for deciding disputes respecting territorial jurisdiction between different states.

The United States in Congress assembled shall also have the sole and exclusive right and power of regulating the alloy and value of coin struck by their own authority, or by that of the respective states—fixing the standard of weights and measures throughout the United States—regulating the trade and managing all affairs with the Indians, not members of any of the states, provided that the legislative right of any state within its own limits be not infringed or violated—establishing or regulating post-offices from one state to another, throughout all the United States, and exacting such postage on the papers passing thro' the same as may be requisite to defray the expences of the said office—appointing all officers of the land forces, in the service of the United States, excepting regimental officers—appointing all the officers of the naval forces, and commissioning all officers whatever in the service of the United States—making rules for the government and regulation of the said land and naval forces, and directing their operations.

The United States in Congress assembled shall have authority to appoint a committee, to sit in the recess of Congress, to be denominated "A Committee of the States," and to consist of one delegate from each state; and to appoint such other committees and civil officers as may be necessary for managing the general affairs of the United States under their direction—to appoint one of their number to preside, provided that no person be allowed to serve in the office of president more than one year in any term of three years; to ascertain the necessary sums of money to be raised for the service of the United States, and to appropriate and apply the same for defraying the public expences—to borrow money, or emit bills on the credit of the United States, transmitting every half-year to the respective states an account of the sums of money so borrowed or emitted—to build and equip a navy—to agree upon the number of land forces, and to make requisitions from each state for its quota, in proportion to the number of white inhabitants in such state; which requisition shall be binding, and thereupon the legislature of each state shall appoint the regimental officers, raise the men and cloath, arm, and equip them in a soldier-like manner, at the expence of the United States; and the officers and men so cloathed, armed, and equipped shall march to the place appointed, and within the time agreed on by the United States in Congress assembled. But if the United States in Congress assembled shall, on consideration of circumstances, judge proper that any state should not raise men, or should raise a smaller number than its quota, and that any other state should raise a greater number of men than the quota thereof, such extra number shall be raised, officered, cloathed, armed, and equipped in the same manner as the quota of such state, unless the legislature of such state shall judge that such extra number cannot be safely spared out of the same, in which case they shall raise, officer, cloath, arm, and equip as many of such extra number as they judge can be safely spared. And the officers and men so cloathed, armed, and equipped, shall march to the place appointed, and within the time agreed on by the United States in Congress assembled.

The United States in Congress assembled shall never engage in a war, nor grant letters of marque and reprisal in time of peace, nor enter into any treaties or alliances, nor coin money, nor regulate the value thereof, nor ascertain the sums and expences necessary for the defence and welfare of the United States, or any of them, nor emit bills, nor borrow money on the credit of the United States, nor appropriate money, nor agree upon the number of vessels of war, to be built or purchased, or the number of land or sea forces to be raised, nor appoint a commander in chief of the army or navy, unless nine states assent to the same: nor shall a question on any other point, except for adjourning from day to day, be determined, unless by the votes of a majority of the United States in Congress assembled.

The Congress of the United States shall have power to adjourn to any time within the year, and to any place within the United States, so that no period of adjournment be for a longer duration than the space of six months, and shall publish the journal of their proceedings monthly, except such parts thereof relating to treaties, alliances or military operations, as in their judgment require secrecy; and the yeas and nays of the delegates of each state on any question shall be entered on the journal, when it is desired by any delegate; and the delegates of a state, or any of them, at his or their request shall be furnished with a transcript of the said journal, except such parts as are above excepted, to lay before the legislatures of the several states.

X. The Committee of the States, or any nine of them, shall be authorized to execute, in the recess of Congress, such of the powers of Congress as the United States in Congress assembled, by the consent of nine states, shall from time to time think expedient to vest them with; provided that no power be delegated to the said Committee, for the exercise of which, by the Articles of Confederation, the voice of nine states in the Congress of the United States assembled is requisite.

XI. Canada acceding to this confederation, and joining in the measures of the United States, shall be admitted into, and entitled to all the advantages of this union: but no other colony shall be admitted into the same, unless such admission be agreed to by nine states.

XII. All bills of credit emitted, monies borrowed, and debts contracted by, or under the authority of Congress, before the assembling of the United States, in pursuance of the present confederation, shall be deemed and considered as a charge against the United States, for payment and satisfaction whereof the said United States, and the public faith are hereby solemnly pledged.

XIII. Every state shall abide by the determination of the United States in Congress assembled, on all questions which by this confederation are submitted to them. And the Articles of this Confederation shall be inviolably observed by every state, and the union shall be perpetual;

nor shall any alteration at any time hereafter be made in any of them; unless such alteration be agreed to in a Congress of the United States, and be afterwards confirmed by the legislatures of every state.

And Whereas it hath pleased the Great Governor of the World to incline the hearts of the legislatures we respectively represent in Congress, to approve of, and to authorize us to ratify the said articles of confederation and perpetual union. Know Ye that we the undersigned delegates, by virtue of the power and authority to us given for that purpose, do by these presents, in the name and in behalf of our respective constituents, fully and entirely ratify and confirm each and every of the said articles of confederation and perpetual union, and all and singular the matters and things therein contained: And we do further solemnly plight and engage the faith of our respective constituents, that they shall abide by the determinations of the United States in Congress assembled, on all questions, which by the said confederation are submitted to them. And that the articles thereof shall be inviolably observed by the states we respectively represent, and that the union shall be perpetual. In Witness whereof we have hereunto set our hands in Congress. Done at Philadelphia in the state of Pennsylvania the ninth day of July, in the year of our Lord one Thousand seven Hundred and Seventy-eight, and in the third year of the independence of America.

I would call the reader's attention especially to Article II, which stipulates, "Each state retains its sovereignty, freedom, and independence, and every power, jurisdiction, and right, which is not by this Confederation expressly delegated to the United States, in Congress assembled." This was certainly a far cry from John Adams' statement that the confederacy should be formed into "one common mass." It simply described what was, in fact, the case: namely, that the Confederation Congress was virtually powerless. It could resolve anything but enforce nothing. It could requisition money and supplies from the states but it could only beg compliance. Few revolutionary bodies have had such limited powers. Yet it was not entirely a loss. It did establish the principle that citizens of one state were entitled to "all privileges and immunities of free citizens in the several states." It limited foreign negotiations to the agents of Congress. It forbade any state to wage war without the consent of Congress and reserved to itself the sole right to determine "war or peace."

Perhaps most important, it provided a cumbersome and virtually unworkable procedure for deciding disputes between states (copied from an English practice for the determination of disputed elections) and thus took a cautious, tentative step toward the notion of a "supreme" court. Moreover, the pressure for passage of the Articles (so that the United States might finally, after two and a half years of *de facto* war, have a constitution to guide it) was so great that those states with extensive claims to Western lands finally were forced to abandon them. Virginia's decision to waive her vast claims paved the way for the acceptance of the Articles by Congress.

It is not necessary to detail the particulars in which the Articles deviated from the ideal of a republican constitution. The reader can readily compare the Articles with the principles laid down in John Adams' *Thoughts* or with the Virginia Constitution itself. Not only was there no chief executive officer other than the president of Congress, but the executive functions of the government were to be exercised only between sessions of Congress, at which time they were the responsibility of a Committee of States to consist of one delegate from each state.

Weak as the Articles were, they had no legal status until they were ratified by the last state, Maryland, in March, 1781, a few months before Yorktown. In other words, a people obsessed with written constitutions fought a prolonged and demanding war without one, improvising as they went along, behaving, through the latter years of the war, as though the Articles had indeed been ratified and were to be observed as the supreme law of the land.

For one instance, congressional commissioners did hear several cases on appeal from particular states or disputes between states. In the case of Gideon Olmstead, involving the distribution of prize money resulting from the capture of a British merchant vessel, the *Active*, the congressional commissioners overthrew the judgment of the Pennsylvania court on appeal. The state officials refused to accept the judgment of the commissioners. In the case of a contest over land between Connecticut and Pennsylvania, the commissioners, meeting at Trenton, decided in favor of Pennsylvania. James Wilson, a prominent Philadelphia lawyer and sometime delegate to Congress, noted that the decision of the Trenton Court, as it was referred to, marked the first time that a dispute between particular states had been settled by a quasi-judicial body.

After the conclusion of the Treaty of Paris in 1783, which brought the Revolution officially to an end, the inadequacies of the Articles of Confederation became, if possible, more glaring. There were numerous times when there were not enough states present in Congress to constitute a quorum and, in consequence, virtually no business could be done. When Congress was adjourned and the Council of States summoned to serve in its stead, it proved equally difficult to assemble a quorum of the states. There was no order, no system, and no clear center of authority. Congress itself, on those occasions when attendance of at least a quorum of delegates enabled it to do business, was that *bête noire* of all sound political theorists, a unicameral legislature. The congressional commissioners handed down infrequent decisions that were usually ignored by the defeated party to the action. Reviewing the ineptitudes of Congress, John Fiske, a nineteenth-century historian, termed the era between the end of the war in 1783 and the establishment of the new federal government under the Constitution "the Critical Period."

Fiske argued that the problems of the nation grew progressively worse under the Articles. In Fiske's words, "It is not too much to say that the period of five years following the peace of 1783 was the most critical moment in all the history of the American people. The dangers from which we were saved [by the drafting of the federal Constitution] were even greater than the dangers from which we were saved in 1865." No longer under the pressure of an external enemy, the confederacy seemed destined to dissolve into "thirteen little republics, ripe for endless squabbling, like the republics of ancient Greece and medieval Italy." The enemies of America in England, of whom, not surprisingly, there were a substantial number, were inclined to agree with Josiah Tucker, dean of Glouchester Cathedral (who professed himself a friend of America), who declared, "As to the future grandeur of America, and its being a rising empire under one head, whether republican or monarchial, it is one of the idlest and most visionary notions that was ever conceived even by writers of romance. . . . The mutual antipathies and clashing interests of the Americans, their difference of government, habitudes, and manners, indicate that they will have no centre of union and no common interest. They never can be united into one compact empire under any species of government whatever; a disunited people till the end of time, suspicious and distrustful of each other, they will be divided and subdivided into little commonwealths, or principalities. . . ." There were Englishmen who anticipated the time when individual states might seek to return to their filial relationship with the mother country, to security and prosperity under her benign rule.

Political theorists, among them some Americans, pointed out that it was an irrevocable rule of political life, one of the Newtonian laws of human affairs, that a republican form of government could only prevail in a limited geographical area. The larger the physical extent of a country the more power must be concentrated at the center to keep the extremities from flying off into their own orbits. The thirteen original colonies covered so vast a range from Georgia to Maine that a traveler, employing the most rapid means of transportation, must take more than a month to traverse it.

Certainly it is true that Congress was unable to exert any control over foreign commerce and states were constantly tempted to take advantage of their neighbors in the matter of duties and restrictions on trade. Thus when Massachusetts, Rhode Island, and New Hampshire imposed restraints on British trade in the hope of exacting concessions from Parliament, Connecticut not only opened her ports to unrestricted trade with England but went so far as to lay duties on imports from Massachusetts. Serious men, alarmed at the state of confusion and disorder, discussed forming regional confederations. There was talk in New England of a separate confederation. James Monroe, the future president of the United States, alarmed by such rumors, proposed three confederacies, one of New England states, one of the middle states and one of the Southern states. Every effort, he noted, must be made to persuade Pennsylvania to cast its lot with the South.

George Washington was only one among many who expressed alarm over the state of the confederacy. He wrote to Madison that "without some alteration in our political creed, the superstructure we have been seven years raising at the expense of so much blood and treasure, must fall. We are fast verging to anarchy and confusion." David Ramsay, a Charlestown doctor and delegate to Congress, wrote to his friend Benjamin Rush, a Philadelphia physician, early in 1786: "There is a languor in the States that forebodes ruin. The present Congress for want of more States has not the power to coin a copper. In 1775 there was more patriotism in a village than there is now in the 13 states."

An uprising of angry farmers in Massachusetts (1786–87) led by Daniel Shays, a veteran of the Revolution, further alarmed politicians already apprehensive over the impotence of the Congress. John Jay wrote to Washington that "our affairs seem to lead to some crisis, some revolution—something that I cannot foresee or conjecture. I am uneasy and apprehensive; more so than during the war . . . we are going and doing wrong, and therefore I look forward to evils and calamities." Jay then added the almost conventional "original sin" sentence: "The mass of men are neither wise nor good, and the virtue like the resources of a country, can only be drawn to a point and exerted by strong circumstances ably managed, or a strong government ably administered." The fact was, as history had so often demonstrated, people had a limited tolerance for anarchy. Jay feared that the "orderly and industrious" portion of the population, dismayed at the general uncertainty and, above all, "by the insecurity of property," might consider "the charms of liberty as imaginary and delusive," and turn to a dictator or king—"any change that may promise them quiet and security."

Washington replied in an equally somber spirit. "We must take human nature as we find it," he replied. "Perfection falls not to the share of mortals. . . . We are apt to run from one extreme into another. . . . I am told that even respectable characters speak of a monarchical form of government without horror. . . . What a triumph for advocates of despotism to find that we are incapable of governing ourselves, and that systems founded on the basis of equal liberty are merely ideal and fallacious!"

In the face of such sentiments it is not surprising that sentiment for extensive changes in the Articles of Confederation or, as some preferred, a new constitution, gathered force. Virginia was involved in wrangles with Maryland about fishing rights on the Potomac River (a controversy which continues to the present day). A conference was proposed at Annapolis to try to resolve the dispute. The Virginia Assembly, under prodding from James Madison, passed a resolution calling for a meeting of representatives from all the states "to consider and recommend a Federal Plan for regulating commerce." The two issues might thus be combined. Five delegates from each state should be sent to Annapolis to adjudicate the Virginia-Maryland contention and at the same time consider some means of bringing order into foreign commerce.

There are several points to be made. One is that the individuals with mercantile interests were prominent among those seeking changes in the Articles since they suffered directly from the chaotic situation in foreign trade. Allied with them were those holding various forms of obligations from Congress incurred during the war which the Confederation Congress was powerless to honor. But the matter did not stop here. Congress was unable to carry out the provisions of the Treaty of Paris, which had concluded the war, especially those articles protecting the rights of the Tories. In retaliation the British retained the posts on the frontier that they held at the end of the conflict and their presence encouraged the Indians of the Northwest to continue their depredations against the frontier settlements.

There was a clear division of interest on the question of maintaining or replacing the Articles of Confederation. All those who were jealous of the sovereignty of the states were opposed to any move that would strengthen a national government. Those who owed prewar debts to English merchants, debts whose repayment was stipulated in the Treaty of Paris, were quite satisfied with a federal government too weak to enforce that provision. The advocates of reform had, therefore, to proceed as discreetly as possible for fear of arousing the suspicions and resistance of those who on the ground of self-interest or, in some instances, simply sentiment were determined to preserve the Articles of Confederation against any substantial modification.

The Annapolis Convention was the first step toward the extensive reform or complete redoing of the Articles. The French chargé d'affaires in New York, Louis-Guillaume Otto, reported to the French foreign minister in September and October of 1786 on its progress. After recounting American concern over the British forts, the anxiety about control of the Mississippi River and the Shays affair in Massachusetts, Otto declared that among the lower orders (*bas peuple*) there was a general disposition to have as little government as possible—"complete and limitless liberty," a phantom, in Otto's view, which could never be consistent with public tranquility. Only five states had responded to the appeal of Virginia to gather at Annapolis, but the delegates from these states had issued a call for a more formal convention to meet the following summer in Philadelphia to revise the Articles. The call to the convention was worded with a deliberate ambiguity, Otto reported, in order not to alarm the friends of the Articles. In translating he had indeed found it necessary to try to convey the "deliberate obscurity of the original, an obscurity which the ordinary citizens could not understand but which the powerful and enlightened portion of the population would have no difficulty understanding."

To Otto the wealthy merchants and the great landowners had formed a kind of conspiracy to gather into their hands a greater measure of control over the states, over foreign commerce, over the administration of justice, and over the taxing power. He saw the movement to strengthen the Constitution as a scheme to deprive the people of "that liberty of which they have made such bad use." One will give credence to the Frenchman's analysis according to his or her own reading of the deficiencies inherent in the Articles. But there is no reason to doubt that the report of the commissioners at Annapolis was, as Otto reported, characterized by "an infinite number of circumlocutions and ambiguous phrases designed to persuade their constituents that it had been impossible to take into consideration a general plan of commerce and the powers relative thereto without touching at the same time on other matters intimately connected with the prosperity and national importance of the United States."

In the early decades of the present century, when the Constitution and especially its most striking and novel feature, the Supreme Court, was under attack as regressive and reactionary, the issue was raised by scholars as to whether the Constitution was not, in fact, to be understood best as a document drawn up by a ruling class to retrieve the power that it had lost under the Articles of Confederation and therefore need be treated with no particular veneration or respect. To give this argument the greatest effect it was necessary or at least helpful to argue, as a corollary, that the Articles of Confederation were far more democratic, far more in accord with popular sentiment than the constitution that replaced them. I doubt if this is a fruitful way to approach the problem. While it is almost certainly the case that the anarchy and chaos that were described or anticipated by those who felt the Articles were inadequate was vastly exaggerated—Shays' Rebellion, which was cited as the most striking evidence of "anarchy," concerned the state of Massachusetts and it is hard to understand how the Federal Constitution, had it been in force, could have affected it one way or another—it seems to me indisputably true that the Articles could not have provided sufficient governmental structure to make possible the development of a modern commercial and, ultimately, industrial nation. Undoubtedly the advocates of a new constitution were primarily those individuals who experienced its inadequacies most directly: lawyers, merchants, and large-scale landowners engaged in or highly conscious of such matters as trade, taxation, the administration of the law, the relationships between the states, the need to meet financial obligations, and so on. Roughly 90 percent of the population were engaged in what today we would call subsistence farming, essentially providing food for themselves and some modest cash crop. Not unnaturally, it mattered very little to them what ships sailed out of the ports of Boston or New York or whether the terms of the Treaty of Paris in regard to the Tories were strictly observed or, indeed, whether Congress had weight with other nations. We must also keep in mind that those politicians who pressed hardest for a new constitution were, by and large, the same ones who had drafted and voted for the Articles of Confederation.

The fact of the matter is that if we consider how preoccupied most of the Revolutionary statesmen were with the importance of constitutions and how much in agreement about the basic form a constitution should take, the wonder is that as odd and misshapen a document as the Articles had ever emerged from Congress. The only explanation I can come up with is that the Revolutionary politicians thought of constitutions in terms of "states." A state was a political entity like Virginia or France, like Massachusetts or Great Britain. The Continental Congress, or the Confederation Congress, as it came to be called after ratification of the Articles, was not, in that sense a "state" at all; it was a loose alliance of states joined together to wage war against a common enemy. Therefore it did not require a constitution in the classic meaning of that word; a compact or agreement was more appropriate. Surprisingly, the question of constitution versus confederation was never really raised. No one, so far as I can ascertain, got up in Congress during the debates over the Articles and said clearly and unequivocally: "Stop! What are we doing? We are debating what is in effect a constitution and yet it is in defiance of every principle laid down by Montesquieu, whom we all revere as the highest authority on constitutions."

This interpretation of how the delegates to Congress came up with the Articles in the first place has the added advantage of reminding us how nugatory and tentative the idea of nationhood was during the Revolution and how jealous the individual states were of their independence or, as they put it, their sovereignty. We must bear in mind that one of the most critical questions debated in the pre-Revolutionary period was the question of whether sovereignty, or ultimate power, was divisible. The colonists argued that while Parliament and the crown held all final power (one recalls James Otis's essay on the "Rights of the Colonies"), certain subordinate powers had been devolved to the particular colonies and that these powers were irrevocable. To the colonists it followed that sovereignty was *divisible.* Certain powers could be granted to subordinate units which could not be recalled at will and which were, therefore, in their particular sphere as "absolute" as those powers retained by the original source of the power. This, to be sure, was the nub of the issue between the states and any federal, or, as it was sometimes called, "consolidated" national government. What the states were being asked to do was without modern precedent. They were being asked, or were asking themselves, to create a power superior to them, to which they would then, in carefully specified circumstances, defer. The whole drama was a fascinating reprise of the Lockean theory of the origin of human communities. The reader will recall that Locke postulated an original "state of nature" in which every individual was "equally free and independent." This condition, according to Locke, resulted in a situation where no man had any security in his life or property. Individuals in their free and unencumbered state of nature then banded together and gave up some of their unqualified freedom in order to have an essential degree of order or "civil polity," i.e., security.

In much the same way as this mythic Lockean hypothesis, the American states, completely sovereign and in "a state of nature," so to speak, were planning to surrender a substantial portion of their respective sovereignties in order to enjoy compensatory advantages. Perhaps the most important element in the whole equation was the fact that the Revolution had created a common set of experiences and memories which provided the moral and psychological preconditions for a united nation.

In 1776, impatient patriots had pressed Congress for a statement confirming the independence from Great Britain that the colonists had already experienced in more than a year of fighting. Perhaps it was the case in 1786—though it is a far more difficult case to prove— that the politicians of the various states who met at Annapolis and called for a constitutional convention to meet the following spring were responding, much as the delegates in Congress did in 1776, to a widespread feeling among the people of the various states that the

United States was indeed a nation, a state, a single if diverse people, and should have a constitution that made that fact clear to the world. We will certainly adduce some evidence in support of that supposition as we proceed with our story.

In any event, regardless of who intended to do what to whom, most of the states did, in fact, appoint delegates to the convention to be held in Philadelphia in May, though not, to be sure, without a good deal of wrangling and a substantial amount of suspicion and uneasiness. The feelings of Congress itself were expressed in a letter from Henry Lee, a Virginia delegate, to a friend in Virginia. The Annapolis commissioners had sent their call for a constitutional convention to Congress with a request that it be forwarded to the states, thus giving it the official imprimatur of that body. This proved no easy matter, as Lee noted: "With difficulty the friends to the system adopted by the convention induced Congress to commit your report, altho' all were truly sensible of the respect manifested by the convention to this body, and all zealous to accomplish the objects proposed by the authors of the commercial convention. Indeed their conviction of the inadequacy of the present federal government renders them particularly zealous to amend and strengthen it. But different opinions prevail as to the mode; some think with the Annapolis meeting, others consider Congress not only the constitutional but the most eligible [efficient] body to originate and propose necessary amendments to the confederation, and others prefer State conventions for the express purpose, and a congress of deputies, appointed by these conventions with plenipotentiary powers. . . ."

The letters written by delegates to Congress in the waning months of 1786 and the early ones of 1787 serve to underline its sense of its own impotence. Some delegates arrived in December and lingered on in New York until January waiting for a quorum of the states to assemble. Some waited for weeks and then returned home a few days prior to the arrival of delegates who would have constituted a quorum. At the end of January, a Connecticut delegate, Stephen Mitchell, wrote home that it was still not clear whether "we have a Congress or no." The terms of some of the delegates present were about to run out, and if they decamped for home all possibility of "making a congress" for this session would be lost. "The Scituation of Congress is truely deplorable," Mitchell added. "I cannot see there remains any necessity for keeping up a Representation in Congress, in our present

Scituation, all we can possibly do, is to recommend [to the states], which is an old stale device no better than the wish of a few individuals relative to publick Concerns."

The date for the convening of the constitutional convention had been set by Congress for the second Monday in May, the fourteenth. On that day only a discouraging handful of delegates gathered in the "long room" of the Pennsylvania State House. Some of them must have wondered if there was going to be a convention at all. Traveling was slow and difficult in the spring, roads were rutted and muddy and streams and rivers high. Gradually the delegates trickled in, but it was eleven days later before a majority of the states were represented and it was possible officially to convene the convention. Rhode Island, Vermont, New Hampshire, Connecticut, and Maryland were not represented. Rufus King was the only delegate from Massachusetts. Robert Yates and Alexander Hamilton were there from New York. Pennsylvania and Virginia had the largest and the ablest delegations. Gouverneur Morris, James Wilson, and Robert Morris, "the financier of the Revolution," represented the Quaker state (missing was Benjamin Franklin who was home ill), while George Washington, George Mason (drafter of the preamble to the Virginia Constitution and principal architect, the reader will recall, of that document), George Wythe, leader of the Virginia bar, Edmund Randolph, spokesman for the large states, and, most important of all, James Madison, who was not only one of the most influential members of the convention but whose painstaking notes provide the greater part of what we know about the actual discussions that took place in the convention, represented Virginia. North Carolina had an able but undistinguished delegation. South Carolina had an outstanding delegation in which the stars were the two Pinckney cousins, Charles and Charles Cotesworth, John Rutledge, a wartime governor, and Pierce Butler, one of the richest planters in the state. Georgia was represented by one delegate, William Few. There were several conspicuous absences, the most notable perhaps being those of Thomas Jefferson and John Adams. Jefferson was the congressional representative, or ambassador, to France and John Adams to England.

The deliberations of the convention were secret, a practice Madison defended by pointing out that only if the delegates were free of those pressures that must inevitably have followed from public attention to the debates could they speak with complete candor and approach all issues with an open mind. While an official journal which recorded the votes and resolutions of the delegates was kept, we are indebted to James Madison for the greater part of our knowledge of what the delegates said. The journal, kept by the secretary of the convention, William Jackson, and accompanying papers were turned over to Washington, the chairman, or "president," of the convention at the conclusion of its deliberations and Washington deposited them with the Department of State in 1796 when he left the office of president. They remained in the archives of the State Department until 1818, when Congress, by a joint resolution of both houses, ordered them to be printed. James Monroe, then President, instructed his Secretary of State, John Quincy Adams, to get the papers in order for publication. It was a task that might have defeated an editor less energetic and intelligent than Adams. He rounded up a number of additional papers and documents, many of them still in the hands of delegates, and published them in a large volume of more than five hundred pages, declaring, with understandable satisfaction, that "a correct and tolerably clear view of the proceedings of the Convention may be presented."

Madison retained his notes. In 1840, four years after his death, four volumes of his papers were published, his notes on the debates making up a major part of them. They were at once recognized as being by far the fullest and most complete record of the debates themselves and, while not without error, at every point where they could be checked against other notes or records, they proved remarkably accurate. Other delegates took less complete notes; among these the most important are those by Robert Yates of New York, Rufus King of Massachusetts, and James McHenry of Maryland, who attended the convention for two relatively brief periods.

In 1911, Max Farrand, professor of history at Yale, published a four-volume set of documents relating to the convention. Farrrand wove together, day by day, all the records of the journal and the various notes of delegates, Madison's, of course, providing by far the major portion. This impressive compilation was reprinted in 1937 with corrections and additions and is available to every serious student of the Constitution. It has been used here.

The plan followed in this work, intended for the use of the general reader rather than the constitutional scholar, is to reprint the most relevant portions of Madison's notes in order to give a sense of the way in which the Constitution took shape in the weeks between May 25 and September 17, a period of almost four months. There will be a minimum of explanatory comment confined largely to suggestions as to what points merit particular attention.

CHAPTER

VII

DEBATES IN THE FEDERAL
CONVENTION OF 1787
AS REPORTED
BY JAMES MADISON

Monday May 14th 1787 was the day fixed for the meeting of the deputies in Convention for revising the federal system of Government. On that day a small number only had assembled. Seven States were not convened till,

Friday 25 of May, when the following members appeared to wit:

viz, From *Massachusetts* Rufus King. *N. York* Robert Yates, Alexander Hamilton. *N. Jersey*, David Brearly, William Churchill Houston, William Patterson. *Pennsylvania*, Robert Morris, Thomas Fitzsimmons, James Wilson, Gouverneur Morris. *Delaware*, George Read, Richard Basset, Jacob Broome. *Virginia,* George Washington, Edmund Randolph, John Blair, James Madison, George Mason, George Wythe, James McClurg. *N. Carolina*, Alexander Martin, William Richardson Davie, Richard Dobbs Spaight, Hugh Williamson. *S. Carolina*, John Rutlidge, Charles Cotesworth Pinckney, Charles Pinckney, Pierce Butler. *Georgia*, William Few.

Mr. Robert Morris informed the members assembled that by the instruction & in behalf, of the deputation of Pennsylvania he proposed George Washington Esquire late Commander in chief for president of the Convention. . . .

General Washington was accordingly unanimously elected by ballot, and conducted to the Chair by Mr. R. Morris and Mr. Rutlidge; from which in a very emphatic manner he thanked the Convention for the honor they had conferred on him, reminded them of the novelty of the scene of business in which he was to act, lamented his want of better qualifications, and claimed the indulgence of the House towards the involuntary errors which his inexperience might occasion. . . .

Monday May 28 . . .

Mr. Wythe from the Committee for preparing rules made a report which employed the deliberations of this day.

Mr. King objected to one of the rules in the Report authorising any member to call for the yeas & nays and have them entered on the minutes. He urged that as the acts of the Convention were not to bind the Constituents, it was unnecessary to exhibit this evidence of the votes; and improper as changes of opinion would be frequent in the course of the business & would fill the minutes with contradictions.

Colonel Mason seconded the objection; adding that such a record of the opinions of members would be an obstacle to a change of them on conviction; and in case of its being hereafter promulged must furnish handles to the adversaries of the Result of the Meeting.

The proposed rule was rejected nem. contradicente. The standing rules agreed to were as follow:

[viz. A House to do business shall consist of the Deputies of not less than seven States; and all questions shall be decided by the greater number of these which shall be fully represented: but a less number than seven may adjourn from day to day.

Immediately after the President shall have taken the chair, and the members their seats, the minutes of the preceding day shall be read by the Secretary.

Every member, rising to speak, shall address the President; and whilst he shall be speaking, none shall pass between them, or hold discourse with another, or read a book, pamphlet or paper, printed or manuscript —and of two members rising at the same time, the President shall name him who shall be first heard.

A member shall not speak oftener than twice, without special leave, upon the same question; and not the second time, before every other, who had been silent, shall have been heard, if he choose to speak upon the subject. . . .]

Mr. Butler moved that the House provide against interruption of business by absence of members, and against licentious publications of their proceedings—to which was added by—Mr. Spaight—a motion to provide that on the one hand the House might not be precluded by a vote upon any question, from revising the subject matter of it when they see cause, nor, on the other hand, be led too hastily to rescind a decision, which was the result of mature discussion.—Whereupon it was ordered that these motions be referred to the consideration of the Committee appointed to draw up the standing rules and that the Committee make report thereon. . . .

Tuesday May 29 . . .

That members only be permitted to inspect the journal.

That nothing spoken in the House be printed, or otherwise published or communicated without leave. . . .

Mr. Randolph then opened the main business.

He expressed his regret, that it should fall to him, rather than those, who were of longer standing in life and political experience, to open the great subject of their mission. But, as the convention had originated from Virginia, and his colleagues supposed that some proposition was expected from them, they had imposed this task on him.

He then commented on the difficulty of the crisis, and the necessity of preventing the fulfilment of the prophecies of the American downfal.

He observed that in revising the foederal system we ought to inquire 1. into the properties, which such a government ought to possess, 2. the defects of the confederation, 3. the danger of our situation & 4. the remedy.

1. The Character of such a government ought to secure 1. against foreign invasion: 2. against dissentions between members of the Union, or seditions in particular states: 3. to procure to the several States, various blessings, of which an isolated situation was incapable: 4. to be able to defend itself against incroachment: & 5. to be paramount to the state constitutions.

2. In speaking of the defects of the confederation he professed a high respect for its authors, and considered them, as having done all that patriots could do, in the then infancy of the science, of constitutions, & of confederacies,—when the inefficiency of requisitions was unknown—no commercial discord had arisen among any states—no rebellion had appeared as in Massachusetts—foreign debts had not become urgent—the havoc of paper money had not been foreseen—treaties had not been violated—and perhaps nothing better could be obtained from the jealousy of the states with regard to their sovereignty.

He then proceeded to enumerate the defects: 1. that the confederation produced no security against foreign invasion; congress not being permitted to prevent a war nor to support it by their own authority—Of this he cited many examples; most of which tended to shew, that they could not cause infractions of treaties or of the law of nations, to be punished: that particular states might by their conduct provoke war without controul; and that neither militia nor draughts being fit for defence on such occasions, inlistments only could be successful, and these could not be executed without money.

2. that the foederal government could not check the quarrels between states, nor a rebellion in any, not having constitutional power nor means to interpose according to the exigency:

3. that there were many advantages, which the U.S. might acquire, which were not attainable under the confederation—such as a productive impost—counteraction of the commercial regulations of other nations—pushing of commerce ad libitum—&c &c.

4. that the foederal government could not defend itself against the incroachments from the states.

5. that it was not even paramount to the state constitutions, ratified, as it was in many of the states.

3. He next reviewed the danger of our situation, appealed to the sense of the best friends of the U.S.—the prospect of anarchy from the laxity of government every where; and to other considerations.

4. He then proceeded to the remedy; the basis of which he said must be the republican principle

He proposed as conformable to his ideas the following resolutions, which he explained one by one.

RESOLUTIONS PROPOSED BY MR. RANDOLPH IN CONVENTION MAY 29, 1787

1. Resolved that the Articles of Confederation ought to be so corrected & enlarged as to accomplish the objects proposed by their institution; namely, "common defence, security of liberty and general welfare."

2. Resolved therefore that the rights of suffrage in the National Legislature ought to be proportioned to the Quotas of contribution, or to the number of free inhabitants, as the one or the other rule may seem best in different cases.

3. Resolved that the National Legislature ought to consist of two branches.

4. Resolved that the members of the first branch of the National Legislature ought to be elected by the people of the several States every   for the term of   ; to be of the age of   years at least, to receive liberal stipends by which they may be compensated for the devotion of their time to public service; to be ineligible to any office

established by a particular State, or under the authority of the United States, except those peculiarly belonging to the functions of the first branch, during the term of service, and for the space of   after its expiration; to be incapable of reelection for the space of   after the expiration of their term of service, and to be subject to recall.

5. Resolved that the members of the second branch of the National Legislature ought to be elected by those of the first, out of a proper number of persons nominated by the individual Legislatures, to be of the age of   years at least; to hold offices for a term sufficient to ensure their independency; to receive liberal stipends, by which they may be compensated for the devotion of their time to public service; and to be ineligible to any office established by a particular State, or under the authority of the United States, except those peculiarly belonging to the functions of the second branch, during the term of service, and for the space of   after the expiration thereof.

6. Resolved that each branch ought to possess the right of originating Acts; that the National Legislature ought to be impowered to enjoy the Legislative Rights vested in Congress by the Confederation & moreover to legislate in all cases to which the separate States are incompetent, or in which the harmony of the United States may be interrupted by the exercise of individual Legislation; to negative all laws passed by the several States, contravening in the opinion of the National Legislature the articles of Union; and to call forth the force of the Union against any member of the Union failing to fulfill its duty under the articles thereof.

7. Resolved that a National Executive be instituted; to be chosen by the National Legislature for the term of   years, to receive punctually at stated times, a fixed compensation for the services rendered, in which no increase or diminution shall be made so as to affect the Magistracy, existing at the time of increase or diminution, and to be ineligible a second time; and that besides a general authority to execute the National laws, it ought to enjoy the Executive rights vested in Congress by the Confederation.

8. Resolved that the Executive and a convenient number of the National Judiciary, ought to compose a Council of revision with authority to examine every act of the National Legislature before it shall operate, & every act of a particular Legislature before a Negative thereon shall be final; and that the dissent of the said Council shall amount to a rejection, unless the Act of the National Legislature be again passed, or that of a particular Legislature be again negatived by   of the members of each branch.

9. Resolved that a National Judiciary be established to consist of

one or more supreme tribunals, and of inferior tribunals to be chosen by the National Legislature, to hold their offices during good behaviour; and to receive punctually at stated times fixed compensation for their services, in which no increase or diminution shall be made so as to affect the persons actually in office at the time of such increase or diminution. that the jurisdiction of the inferior tribunals shall be to hear & determine in the first instance, and of the supreme tribunal to hear and determine in the dernier resort, all piracies & felonies on the high seas, captures from an enemy; cases in which foreigners or citizens of other States applying to such jurisdictions may be interested, or which respect the collection of the National revenue; impeachments of any National officers, and questions which may involve the national peace and harmony.

10. Resolved that provision ought to be made for the admission of States lawfully arising within the limits of the United States, whether from a voluntary junction of Government & Territory or otherwise, with the consent of a number of voices in the National legislature less than the whole.

11. Resolved that a Republican Government & the territory of each State, except in the instance of a voluntary junction of Government & territory, ought to be guaranteed by the United States to each State

12. Resolved that provision ought to be made for the continuance of Congress and their authorities and privileges, until a given day after the reform of the articles of Union shall be adopted, and for the completion of all their engagements.

13. Resolved that provision ought to be made for the amendment of the Articles of Union whensoever it shall seem necessary, and that the assent of the National Legislature ought not to be required thereto.

14. Resolved that the Legislative Executive & Judiciary powers within the several States ought to be bound by oath to support the articles of Union

15. Resolved that the amendments which shall be offered to the Confederation, by the Convention ought at a proper time, or times, after the approbation of Congress to be submitted to an assembly or assemblies of Representatives, recommended by the several Legislatures to be expressly chosen by the people, to consider & decide thereon.

He concluded with an exhortation, not to suffer the present opportunity of establishing general peace, harmony, happiness and liberty in the U.S. to pass away unimproved.

It was then Resolved—That the House will tomorrow resolve itself into a Committee of the Whole House to consider of the state of the American Union.—and that the propositions moved by Mr. Randolph be referred to the said Committee.

Mr. Charles Pinkney laid before the house the draught of a federal Government which he had prepared, to be agreed upon between the free and independent States of America.—Mr. P. plan ordered that the same be referred to the Committee of the Whole appointed to consider the state of the American Union.

Adjourned

Some comment is appropriate on the Virginia Plan, delivered by Edmund Randolph, but obviously the work of several members of the Virginia delegation. First, it was a remarkably broad and comprehensive plan and represented a kind of quantum leap from the Articles (which, it had generally been put about, the delegates intended merely to revise and strengthen). Here we are, at the first instant, with a proposed constitution that incorporates most of those constitutional principles so patently missing from the Articles of Confederation. The Virginia Plan reveals two crucially important facts. First, the prime movers of the convention had made in their own minds the transition from the idea of a loose confederation of states to the idea of the United States as constituting a single state and as such requiring a constitution that followed certain accepted constitutional principles already represented in a somewhat diluted form in the state constitutions. A vast amount of talk and thought must have gone on among a number of state politicians in the months prior to the convening of the delegates in Philadelphia. A set of proposals as fully and thoughtfully developed as those presented by Randolph don't come off the top of anyone's head or off the top of any number of heads. The fact is, most of the provisions of the Virginia Plan appeared in the final version of the Constitution fourteen weeks and a great deal of talk later, among the most important of them the phrase "common defence, security of liberty, and general welfare," the notion of a two-branch legislature, the principle that the national legislature should have the power "to legislate in all cases to which the separate states are incompetent"; the principle that whenever conflicts arose between state and federal laws, federal laws should take precedence; that there be a national executive; that a national judiciary be established "to consist of one or more supreme tribunal, and of inferior tribunals . . . to hold their offices during good behaviour," such courts to have original jurisdiction in a wide range of cases affecting the national interest; that new states be admitted to the Union and guaranteed a republican form of government; that provision be made for amending the Constitution without the assent of the "National Legislature"; and, finally, that any "amendments" made to the Articles of Confederation should be submitted not to Congress but to special ratifying conventions called by the states. John Adams was in France, but the Virginia Resolves conformed to most of the constitutional principles that he had sketched out ten years earlier.

One point should be emphasized. The Virginia Plan was the initial move by the large states. Its most controversial provision was stated very promptly in the second resolution "that the rights of suffrage in the National Legislature ought to be proportioned to the Quotas of contribution, or to the number of free inhabitants. . . ." Here was the essential bone of contention that was to very nearly defeat the enterprise. The reader will recall that from the early days of the Continental Congress through the period of the Confederation, the issue of whether the states were to vote equally or proportionally had troubled the councils of the new and precariously united states.

A substantial portion of Madison's notes of the first two weeks, or, more precisely, the first seventeen days, is included here—a luxury we will not be able to afford for subsequent weeks—because they are, in my opinion, by far the most important period of the convention. There is such drama and excitement in these first efforts, so much is accomplished, so many issues defined, explored, and at least partially or tentatively resolved. We see the federal Constitution take shape in what seems to me a miraculously short time. Individual positions and attitudes are established and the prospectives and interests of the various states described. Personal and sectional alliances are formed, the characteristics and temperaments of the delegates emerge—the cautious and the judicious, the hasty and the impatient, the compromisers and the stonewallers.

Wednesday May 30

Roger Sherman (from Connecticut) took his seat.

The House went into Committee of the Whole on the State of the Union. Mr. Gorham was elected to the Chair by Ballot.

The propositions of Mr. Randolph which had been referred to the Committee being taken up. He moved on the suggestion of Mr. G. Morris, that the first of his propositions to wit "Resolved that the articles of Confederation ought to be so corrected & enlarged, as to accomplish the objects proposed by their institution; namely, common defence, security of liberty & general welfare:—should be postponed, in order to consider the 3 following:

1. that a Union of the States merely federal will not accomplish the objects proposed by the articles of Confederation, namely common defence, security of liberty, & general welfare.

2. that no treaty or treaties among the whole or part of the States, as individual Sovereignties, would be sufficient.

3. that a *national* Government ought to be established consisting of a *supreme* Legislative, Executive & Judiciary. . . .

Mr. Charles Pinkney wished to know of Mr. Randolph whether he meant to abolish the State Governments altogether. Mr. R. replied that he meant by these general propositions merely to introduce the particular ones which explained the outlincs of the system he had in view.

Mr. Butler said he had not made up his mind on the subject, and was open to the light which discussion might throw on it. After some general observations he concluded with saying that he had opposed the grant of powers to Congress heretofore, because the whole power was vested in one body. The proposed distribution of the powers into different bodies changed the case, and would induce him to go great lengths.

General Pinkney expressed a doubt whether the act of Congress recommending the Convention, or the Commissions of the Deputies to it, could authorise a discussion of a System founded on different principles from the federal Constitution.

Mr. Gerry seemed to entertain the same doubt.

Mr. Gouverneur Morris explained the distinction between a *federal* and *national, supreme,* Government; the former being a mere compact resting on the good faith of the parties; the latter having a compleat and *compulsive* operation. He contended that in all Communities there must be one supreme power, and one only.

Mr. Mason observed that the present confederation was not only deficient in not providing for coercion & punishment against delinquent States; but argued very cogently that punishment could not in the nature of things be executed on the States collectively, and therefore that such a Government was necessary as could directly operate on individuals, and would punish those only whose guilt required it.

Mr. Sherman who took his seat today, admitted that the Confederation had not given sufficient power to Congress and that additional powers were necessary; particularly that of raising money which he said would involve many other powers. He admitted also that the General & particular jurisdictions ought in no case to be concurrent. He seemed however not [to] be disposed to make too great inroads on the existing system; intimating as one reason that it would be wrong to lose every amendment, by inserting such as would not be agreed to by the States. . . .

On the question as moved by Mr. Butler, on the third proposition it was resolved in Committee of the whole that a national government ought to be established consisting of a supreme Legislative Executive & Judiciary. [Passed 6 to 1, New York divided.] . . .

The following Resolution being the 2nd of those proposed by Mr. Randolph was taken up, viz—"that the rights of suffrage in the National Legislature ought to be proportioned to the quotas of contribution, or to the number of free inhabitants, as the one or the other rule may seem best in different cases."

Mr. Madison observing that the words "*or to the number of free inhabitants*," might occasion debates which would divert the Committee from the general question whether the principle of representation should be changed, moved that they might be struck out.

Mr. King observed that the quotas of contribution which would alone remain as the measure of representation, would not answer, because waving every other view of the matter, the revenue might hereafter be so collected by the general Government that the sums respectively drawn from the States would not appear; and would besides be continually varying.

Mr. Madison admitted the propriety of the observation, and that some better rule ought to be found.

Mr. Madison, moved, in order to get over the difficulties, the following resolution—"that the equality of suffrage established by the articles of Confederation ought not to prevail in the national Legislature, and that an equitable ratio of representation ought to be substituted." This was seconded by Mr. Gouverneur Morris, and being generally relished, would have been agreed to; when,

Mr. Reed moved that the whole clause relating to the point of Representation be postponed; reminding the Committee that the deputies from Delaware were restrained by their commission from assenting to any change of the rule of suffrage, and in case such a change should be fixed on, it might become their duty to retire from the Convention.

Mr. Gouverneur Morris observed that the valuable assistance of those members could not be lost without real concern, and that so early a proof of discord in the Convention as a secession of a State, would add much to the regret; that the change proposed was however so fundamental an article in a national Government that it could not be dispensed with.

Mr. Madison observed that whatever reason might have existed for the equality of suffrage when the Union was a federal one among sovereign States, it must cease when a national Government should be put into the place. In the former case, the acts of Congress depended so much for their efficacy on the cooperation of the States, that these had a weight both within & without Congress, nearly in proportion to their extent and importance. In the latter case, as the acts of the General Government would take effect without the intervention of the State legislatures, a vote from a small State would have the same efficacy & importance as a vote from a large one, and there was the same reason for different numbers of representatives from different States, as from Counties of different extents within particular States. He suggested as an expedient for at once taking the sense of the members on this point and saving the Delaware deputies from embarrassment, that the question should be taken in Committee, and the clause on report to the House be postponed without a question there. This however did not appear to satisfy Mr. Read.

By several it was observed that no just construction of the Act of Delaware, could require or justify a secession of her deputies, even if the resolution were to be carried thro' the House as well as the Committee. It was finally agreed however that the clause should be postponed: it being understood that in the event the proposed change of representation would certainly be agreed to, no objection or difficulty being started from any other quarter than from Delaware. . . .

Thursday May 31 . . .

In Committee of the whole on Mr. Randolph's propositions.

The 3rd Resolution "that the national Legislature ought to consist of two branches" was agreed to without debate or dissent, except that of Pennsylvania, given probably from complaisance to Doctor Franklin who was understood to be partial to a single House of Legislation.

Resol: 4. first clause "that the members of the first branch of the National Legislature ought to be elected by the people of the several States" being taken up,

Mr. Sherman opposed the election by the people, insisting that it ought to be by the State Legislatures. The people he said, immediately should have as little to do as may be about the Government. They want information and are constantly liable to be misled.

Mr. Gerry. The evils we experience flow from the excess of democracy. The people do not want virtue, but are the dupes of pretended patriots. In Massachusetts it had been fully confirmed by experience that they are daily misled into the most baneful measures and opinions by the false reports circulated by designing men, and which no one on the spot can refute. One principal evil arises from the want of due provision for those employed in the administration of Government. It would seem to be a maxim of democracy to starve the public servants. He mentioned the popular clamour in Massachusetts for the reduction of salaries and the attack made on that of the Governor though secured by the spirit of the Constitution itself. He had he said been too republican heretofore; he was still however republican, but had been taught by experience the danger of the levilling spirit.

Mr. Mason, argued strongly for an election of the larger branch by the people. It was to be the grand depository of the democratic principle of the Government. It was, so to speak, to be our House of Commons— It ought to know & sympathise with every part of the community; and ought therefore to be taken not only from different parts of the whole republic, but also from different districts of the larger members of it, which had in several instances particularly in Virginia, different interests and views arising from difference of produce, of habits &c &c. He admitted that we had been too democratic but was afraid we should incautiously run into the opposite extreme. We ought to attend to the rights of every class of the people. He had often wondered at the indifference of the superior classes of society to this dictate of humanity & policy; considering that however affluent their circumstances, or elevated their situations, might be, the course of a few years, not only might but certainly would, distribute their posterity throughout the lowest classes of Society. Every selfish motive therefore, every family attachment, ought to recommend such a system of policy as would provide no less carefully for the rights and happiness of the lowest than of the highest orders of Citizens.

Mr. Wilson contended strenuously for drawing the most numerous branch of the Legislature immediately from the people. He was for raising the federal pyramid to a considerable altitude, and for that reason wished to give it as broad a basis as possible. No government could long subsist without the confidence of the people. In a republican Government this confidence was peculiarly essential. He also thought it wrong to increase the weight of the State Legislatures by making them the electors of the national Legislature. All interference between the general and local Governments should be obviated as much as possible. On examination it would be found that the opposition of States to federal measures had proceded much more from the officers of the States, than from the people at large.

Mr. Madison considered the popular election of one branch of the

National Legislature as essential to every plan of free Government. He observed that in some of the States one branch of the Legislature was composed of men already removed from the people by an intervening body of electors. That if the first branch of the general legislature should be elected by the State Legislatures, the second branch elected by the first—the Executive by the second together with the first; and other appointments again made for subordinate purposes by the Executive, the people would be lost sight of altogether; and the necessary sympathy between them and their rulers and officers, too little felt. He was an advocate for the policy of refining the popular appointments by successive filtrations, but thought it might be pushed too far. He wished the expedient to be resorted to only in the appointment of the second branch of the Legislature, and in the Executive & Judiciary branches of the Government. He thought too that the great fabric to be raised would be more stable and durable, if it should rest on the solid foundation of the people themselves, than if it should stand merely on the pillars of the Legislatures.

Mr. Gerry did not like the election by the people. The maxims taken from the British constitution were often fallacious when applied to our situation which was extremely different. Experience he said had shewn that the State legislatures drawn immediately from the people did not always possess their confidence. He had no objection however to an election by the people if it were so qualified that men of honor & character might not be unwilling to be joined in the appointments. He seemed to think the people might nominate a certain number out of which the State legislatures should be bound to choose.

Mr. Butler thought an election by the people an impracticable mode.

On the question for an election of the first branch of the national Legislature by the people. [Passed, 6 to 2, 2 divided.] . . .

The Committee proceeded to Resolution 5. "that the second, [or senatorial] branch of the National Legislature ought to be chosen by the first branch out of persons nominated by the State Legislatures."

Mr. Spaight contended that the 2nd branch ought to be chosen by the State Legislatures and moved an amendment to that effect.

Mr. Butler apprehended that the taking so many powers out of the hands of the States as was proposed, tended to destroy all that balance and security of interests among the States which it was necesary to preserve; and called on Mr. Randolph the mover of the propositions, to explain the extent of his ideas, and particularly the number of members he meant to assign to this second branch.

Mr. Randolph observed that he had at the time of offering his propositions stated his ideas as far as the nature of general propositions required; that details made no part of the plan, and could not perhaps with propriety have been introduced. If he was to give an opinion as to the number of the second branch, he should say that it ought to be much smaller than that of the first; so small as to be exempt from the passionate proceedings to which numerous assemblies are liable. He observed that the general object was to provide a cure for the evils under which the U.S. laboured; that in tracing these evils to their origin every man had found it in the turbulence and follies of democracy: that some check therefore was to be sought for against this tendency of our Governments: and that a good Senate seemed most likely to answer the purpose.

Mr. King reminded the Committee that the choice of the second branch as proposed (by Mr. Spaight) viz. by the State Legislatures would be impracticable, unless it was to be very numerous, or *the idea of proportion* among the States was to be disregarded. According to this *idea*, there must be 80 or 100 members to entitle Delaware to the choice of one of them.—Mr. Spaight withdrew his motion.

Mr. Wilson opposed both a nomination by the State Legislatures, and an election by the first branch of the national Legislature, because the second branch of the latter, ought to be independent of both. He thought both branches of the National Legislature ought to be chosen by the people, but was not prepared with a specific proposition. He suggested the mode of chusing the Senate of New York to wit of uniting several election districts, for one branch, in chusing members for the other branch, as a good model.

Mr. Madison observed that such a mode would destroy the influence of the smaller States associated with larger ones in the same district; as the latter would chuse from within themselves, altho' better men might be found in the former. The election of Senators in Virginia where large & small counties were often formed into one district for the purpose, had illustrated this consequence. Local partiality, would often prefer a resident within the County or State, to a candidate of superior merit residing out of it. Less merit also in a resident would be more known throughout his own State.

Mr. Sherman favored an election of one member by each of the State Legislatures.

Mr. Pinkney moved to strike out the "nomination by the State Legislatures." On this question. . . . [Lost: 9 nays, Delaware divided.]

On the whole question for electing by the first branch out of nominations by the State Legislatures. . . . [Lost: 7 nays, 2 ayes.]

So the clause was disagreed to & a chasm left in this part of the plan.

The sixth Resolution stating the cases in which the national Legislature ought to legislate was next taken into discussion: On the question whether each branch should originate laws, there was an unanimous affirmative without debate. On the question for transferring all the Legislative powers of the existing Congress to this Assembly, there was also a silent affirmative nem. con.

On the proposition for giving "Legislative power in all cases to which the State Legislatures were individually incompetent."

Mr. Pinkney and Mr. Rutledge objected to the vagueness of the term *incompetent*, and said they could not well decide how to vote until they should see an exact enumeration of the powers comprehended by this definition.

Mr. Butler repeated his fears that we were running into an extreme in taking away the powers of the States, and called on Mr. Randolph for the extent of his meaning.

Mr. Randolph disclaimed any intention to give indefinite powers to the national Legislature, declaring that he was entirely opposed to such an inroad on the State jurisdictions, and that he did not think any considerations whatever could ever change his determination. His opinion was fixed on this point.

Mr. Madison said that he had brought with him into the Convention a strong bias in favor of an enumeration and definition of the powers necessary to be exercised by the national Legislature; but had also brought doubts concerning its practicability. His wishes remained unaltered; but his doubts had become stronger. What his opinion might ultimately be he could not yet tell. But he should shrink from nothing which should be found essential to such a form of Government as would provide for the safety, liberty and happiness of the community. This being the end of all our deliberations, all the necessary means for attaining it must, however reluctantly, be submitted to.

On the question for giving powers, in cases to which the States are not competent. [Carried: 9 ayes, Connecticut divided.] . . .

The last clause of Resolution 6. authorizing an exertion of the force of the whole against a delinquent State came next into consideration.

Mr. Madison, observed that the more he reflected on the use of force, the more he doubted the practicability, the justice and the efficacy of it when applied to people collectively and not individually.—A union of the States containing such an ingredient seemed to provide for its own destruction. The use of force against a State, would look more like a declaration of war, than an infliction of punishment, and would probably be considered by the party attacked as a dissolution of all previous compacts by which it might be bound. He hoped that such a system would be framed as might render this recourse unnecessary, and moved that the clause be postponed. This motion was agreed to nem. con.

The Committee then rose & the House

Adjourned

Friday June 1st 1787 . . .

The Committee of the whole proceeded to Resolution 7. "that a national Executive be instituted, to be chosen by the national Legislature —for the term of   years &c to be ineligible thereafter, to possess the executive powers of Congress &c."

Mr. Pinkney was for a vigorous Executive but was afraid the Executive powers of the existing Congress might extend to peace & war &c., which would render the Executive a monarchy, of the worst kind, to wit an elective one.

Mr. Wilson moved that the Executive consist of a single person. Mr. C. Pinkney seconded the motion, so as to read "that a National Ex. to consist of a single person, be instituted."

A considerable pause ensuing and the Chairman asking if he should put the question, Doctor Franklin observed that it was a point of great importance and wished that the gentlemen would deliver their sentiments on it before the question was put.

Mr. Rutlidge animadverted on the shyness of gentlemen on this and other subjects. He said it looked as if they supposed themselves precluded by having frankly disclosed their opinions from afterwards changing them, which he did not take to be at all the case. He said he was for vesting the Executive power in a single person, tho' he was not for giving him the power of war and peace. A single man would feel the greatest responsibility and administer the public affairs best.

Mr. Sherman said he considered the Executive magistracy as nothing more than an institution for carrying the will of the Legislature into effect, that the person or persons ought to be appointed by and accountable to the Legislature only, which was the depositary of the supreme will of the Society. As they were the best judges of the business which ought to be done by the Executive department, and consequently of the number necessary from time to time for doing it, he wished the number might not be fixed but that the legislature should be at liberty to appoint one or more as experience might dictate.

Mr. Wilson preferred a single magistrate, as giving most energy dispatch and responsibility to the office. He did not consider the Prerogatives of the British Monarch as a proper guide in defining the Executive powers. Some of these prerogatives were of Legislative nature. Among others that of war & peace &c. The only power he conceived strictly Executive were those of executing the laws, and appointing officers, not appertaining to and appointed by the Legislature.

Mr. Gerry favored the policy of annexing a Council to the Executive in order to give weight & inspire confidence.

Mr. Randolph strenuously opposed a unity in the Executive magistracy. He regarded it as the foetus of monarchy. We had he said no motive to be governed by the British Government as our prototype. He did not mean however to throw censure on that Excellent fabric. If we were in a situation to copy it he did not know that he should be opposed to it; but the fixt genius of the people of America required a different form of Government. He could not see why the great requisites for the Executive department, vigor, despatch & responsibility could not be found in three men, as well as in one man. The Executive ought to be independent. It ought therefore in order to support its independence to consist of more than one.

Mr. Wilson said that unity in the Executive instead of being the fetus of monarchy would be the best safeguard against tyranny. He repeated that he was not governed by the British Model which was inapplicable to the situation of this Country; the extent of which was so great, and the manners so republican, that nothing but a great confederated Republic would do for it.

Mr. Wilson's motion for a single magistrate was postponed by common consent, the Committee seeming unprepared for any decision on it; and the first part of the clause agreed to, viz—"that a National Executive be instituted."

Mr. Madison thought it would be proper, before a choice should be made between a unity and a plurality in the Executive, to fix the extent of the Executive authority; that as certain powers were in their nature Executive, and must be given to that department whether administered by one or more persons, a definition of their extent would assist the judgment in determining how far they might be safely entrusted to a single officer. He accordingly moved that so much of the clause before the Committee as related to the powers of the Executive should be struck out & that after the words "that a national Executive ought to be instituted" there be inserted the words following viz. "with power to carry into effect the national laws, to appoint to offices in cases not otherwise provided for, and to execute such other powers 'not Legislative nor Judiciary in their nature,' as may from time to time be delegated by the national Legislature." The words "not legislative nor judiciary in their nature" were added to the proposed amendment in consequence of a suggestion by General Pinkney that improper powers might otherwise be delegated.

Mr. Wilson seconded this motion—

Mr. Pinkney moved to amend the amendment by striking out the last member of it; viz: "and to execute such other powers not Legislative nor Judiciary in their nature as may from time to time be delegated." He said they were unnecessary, the object of them being included in the "power to carry into effect the national laws."

Mr. Randolph seconded the motion.

Mr. Madison did not know that the words were absolutely necessary, or even the preceding words—"to appoint to offices &c. the whole being perhaps included in the first member of the proposition. He did not however see any inconveniency in retaining them, and cases might happen in which they might serve to prevent doubts and misconstructions.

In consequence of the motion of Mr. Pinkney, the question on Mr. Madison's motion was divided; and the words objected to by Mr. Pinkney struck out; by the votes of Connecticut, New York, New Jersey, Pennsylvania, Delaware, North Carolina & Georgia against Massachusetts, Virginia & South Carolina the preceding part of the motion being first agreed to; Connecticut divided, all the other States in the affirmative.

The next clause in Resolution 7, relating to the mode of appointing, & the duration of, the Executive being under consideration,

Mr. Wilson said he was almost unwilling to declare the mode which he wished to take place, being apprehensive that it might appear chimerical. He would say however at least that in theory he was for an election by the people. Experience, particularly in New York & Massachusetts, shewed that an election of the first magistrate by the people at large, was both a convenient & successful mode. The objects of choice in such cases must be persons whose merits have general notoriety.

Mr. Sherman was for the appointment by the Legislature, and for making him absolutely dependent on that body, as it was the will of that which was to be executed. An independence of the Executive on the supreme Legislature, was in his opinion the very essence of tyranny if there was any such thing.

Mr. Wilson moves that the blank for the term of duration should be filled with three years, observing at the same time that he preferred this short period, on the supposition that a re-eligibility would be provided for.

Mr. Pinkney moves for seven years.

Mr. Sherman was for three years, and against the doctrine of rotation as throwing out of office the men best qualifyed to execute its duties.

Mr. Mason was for seven years at least, and for prohibiting a re-eligibility as the best expedient both for preventing the effect of a false complaisance on the side of the Legislature towards unfit characters; and a temptation on the side of the Executive to intrigue with the Legislature for a re-appointment.

Mr. Bedford was strongly opposed to so long a term as seven years. He begged the committee to consider what the situation of the Country would be, in case the first magistrate should be saddled on it for such a period and it should be found on trial that he did not possess the qualifications ascribed to him, or should lose them after his appointment. An impeachment he said would be no cure for this evil, as an impeachment would reach misfeasance only, not incapacity. He was for a triennial election, and for an ineligibility after a period of nine years.

On the question of seven years . . . [Carried: 5 ayes, 4 noes, 1 divided.]

The *mode of appointing* the Executive was the next question.

Mr. Wilson renewed his declarations in favor of an appointment by the people. He wished to derive not only both branches of the Legislature from the people, without the intervention of the State Legislatures but the Executive also; in order to make them as independent as possible of each other, as well as of the States;

Col. Mason favors the idea, but thinks it impracticable. He wishes however that Mr. Wilson might have time to digest it into his own form.—the clause "to be chosen by the National Legislature"—was accordingly postponed.—

Mr. Rutlidge suggests an election of the Executive by the second branch only of the national Legislature.

The Committee then rose and the House

Adjourned

Saturday June 2nd In Committee of Whole . . .

Mr. Wilson made the following motion, to be substituted for the mode proposed by Mr. Randolph's resolution, "that the Executive Magistracy shall be elected in the following manner: That the States be divided into   districts: & that the persons qualified to vote in each district for members of the first branch of the national Legislature elect   members for their respective districts to be electors of the Executive magistracy, that the said Electors of the Executive magistracy meet at   and they or any   of them so met shall proceed to elect by ballot, but not out of their own body   person   in whom the Executive authority of the national Government shall be vested."

Mr. Wilson repeated his arguments in favor of an election without the intervention of the States. He supposed too that this mode would produce more confidence among the people in the first magistrate, than an election by the national Legislature.

Mr. Gerry, opposed the election by the national legislature. There would be a constant intrigue kept up for the appointment. The Legislature & the candidates would bargain & play into one another's hands, votes would be given by the former under promises or expectations from the latter, of recompensing them by services to members of the Legislature or to their friends. He liked the principle of Mr. Wilson's motion, but fears it would alarm and give a handle to the State partisans, as tending to supersede altogether the State authorities. He thought the Community not yet ripe for stripping the States of their powers, even such as might not be requisite for local purposes. He was for waiting till people should feel more the necessity of it. He seemed to prefer the taking the suffrages of the States instead of Electors, or letting the Legislatures nominate, and the electors appoint. He was not clear that the people ought to act directly even in the choice of electors, being too little informed of personal characters in large districts, and liable to deceptions.

Mr. Williamson could see no advantage in the introduction of Electors chosen by the people who would stand in the same relation to them as the State Legislatures, whilst the expedient would be attended with great trouble and expence.

On the question for agreeing to Mr. Wilson's substitute, it was negatived. . . .

On the question for electing the Executive by the national Legislature for the term of seven years, it was agreed to. . . .

Doctor Franklin moved that what related to the compensation for the services of the Executive be postponed, in order to substitute—"whose necessary expences shall be defrayed, but who shall receive no salary, stipend fee or reward whatsoever for their services"—He said that being very sensible of the effect of age on his memory, he had been unwilling to trust to that for the observations which seemed to support his motion, and had reduced them to writing, that he might with the permission of the Committee read instead of speaking them. Mr. Wilson made an offer to read the paper, which was accepted—The following is a literal copy of the paper.

Sir.

It is with reluctance that I rise to express a disapprobation of any one article of the plan for which we are so much obliged to the honorable gentlemen who laid it before us. From its first reading I have borne a good will to it, and in general wished it success. In this particular of salaries to the Executive branch I happen to differ; and as my opinion may appear new and chimerical, it is only from a persuasion that it is right, and from a sense of duty that I hazard it. The Committee will judge of my reasons when they have heard them, and their judgment may possibly change mine.—I think I see inconveniences in the appointment of salaries; I see none in refusing them, but on the contrary, great advantages.

Sir, there are two passions which have a powerful influence on the affairs of men. These are ambition and avarice; the love of power, and the love of money. Separately each of these has great force in prompting men to action; but when united in view of the same object, they have in many minds the most violent effects. Place before the eyes of such men, a post of *honour* that shall be at the same time a place of *profit*, and they will move heaven and earth to obtain it. The vast number of such places it is that renders the British Government so tempestuous. The struggles for them are the true sources of all those factions which are perpetually dividing the Nation, distracting its Councils, hurrying sometimes into fruitless & mischievous wars, and often compelling a submission to dishonorable terms of peace.

And of what kind are the men that will strive for this profitable pre-eminence, through all the bustle of cabal, the heat of contention, the infinite mutual abuse of parties, tearing to pieces the best of characters? It will not be the wise and moderate; the lovers of peace and good order, the men fittest for the trust. It will be the bold and the violent, the men of strong passions and indefatigable activity in their selfish pursuits. These will thrust themselves into your Government and be your rulers.—And these too will be mistaken in the expected happiness of their situation: For their vanquished competitors of the same spirit, and from the same motives will perpetually be endeavoring to distress their administration, thwart their measures, and render them odious to the people.

Besides these evils, Sir, tho' we may set out in the beginning with moderate salaries, we shall find that such will not be of long continuance. Reasons will never be wanting for proposed augmentations. And there will always be a party for giving more to the rulers, that the rulers may be able in return to give more to them.— Hence as all history informs us, there has been in every State & Kingdom a constant kind of warfare between the governing & governed: the one striving to obtain more for its support, and the other to pay less. And this has alone occasioned great convulsions, actual civil wars, ending either in dethroning of the Princes, or enslaving of the people. Generally indeed the ruling power carries its point, the revenues of princes constantly increasing, and we see that they are never satisfied, but always in want of more. The more the people are discontented with the oppression of taxes; the greater need the prince has of money to distribute among his partizans and pay the troops that are to suppress all resistance, and enable him to plunder at pleasure. There is scarce a king in a hundred who would not, if he could, follow the example of Pharoah, get first all the peoples money, then all their lands, and then make them and their children servants for ever. It will be said, that we don't propose to establish Kings. I know it. But there is a natural inclination in mankind to Kingly Government. It sometimes relieves them from Aristocratic domination. They had rather have one tyrant than five hundred. It gives more of the appearance of equality among Citizens, and that they like. I am apprehensive therefore, perhaps too apprehensive, that the Government of these States, may in future times, end in a Monarchy. But this Catastrophe I think may be long delayed, if in our proposed System we do not sow the seeds of contention, faction & tumult, by making our posts of honor, places of profit. If we do, I fear that tho' we do employ at first a number, and not a single person, the number will in time be set aside, it will only nourish the foetus of a King, as the honorable gentleman from Virginia very aptly expressed it, and a King will the sooner be set over us.

It may be imagined by some that this is an Utopian Idea, and that we can never find men to serve us in the Executive department, without paying them well for their services. I conceive this to be a mistake. Some existing facts present themselves to me, which incline me to a contrary opinion. The high Sheriff of a County in England is an honorable office, but it is not a profitable one. It is rather expensive and therefore not sought for. But yet, it is executed and well executed, and usually by some of the principal Gentlemen of the County. . . .

To bring the matter nearer home, have we not seen, the great and most important of our offices, that of General of our armies executed for eight years together without the smallest salary, by a Patriot whom I will not now offend by any other praise; and this through fatigues and distresses in common with the other brave men his military friends & Companions, and the constant anxieties peculiar to his station? And shall we doubt finding three or four men in all the U. States, with public spirit enough to bear sitting in peaceful Council for perhaps an equal term, merely to preside over our civil concerns, and see that our laws are duly executed. Sir, I have a better opinion of our Country. I think we shall never be without a sufficient number of wise and good men to undertake and execute well and faithfully the office in question.

Sir, The saving of the salaries that may at first be proposed is not an object with me. The subsequent mischiefs of proposing them are what I apprehend. And therefore it is, that I move the amendment. If it is not seconded or accepted I must be contented with the satisfaction of having delivered my opinion frankly and done my duty.

The motion was seconded by Col. Hamilton with the view he said merely of bringing so respectable a proposition before the Committee, and which was besides enforced by arguments that had a certain degree of weight. No debate ensued, and the proposition was postponed for the consideration of the members. It was treated with great respect, but rather for the author of it, than from any apparent conviction of its expediency or practicability.

Mr. Dickenson moved "that the Executive be made removeable by the National Legislature on the request of a majority of the Legislatures of individual States." It was necessary he said to place the power of removing somewhere. He did not like the plan of impeaching the Great officers of State. He did not know how provision could be made for removal of them in a better mode than that which he had proposed. He had no idea of abolishing the State Governments as some gentlemen seemed inclined to do. The happiness of this Country in his opinion required considerable powers to be left in the hands of the States.

Mr. Bedford seconded the motion.

Mr. Sherman contended that the National Legislature should have power to remove the Executive at pleasure.

Mr. Mason. Some mode of displacing an unfit magistrate is rendered indispensable by the fallibility of those who choose, as well as by the corruptibility of the man chosen. He opposed decidedly the making the Executive the mere creature of the Legislature as a violation of the fundamental principle of good Government.

Mr. Madison and Mr. Wilson observed that it would leave an equality of agency in the small with the great States; that it would enable a minority of the people to prevent ye removal of an officer who had rendered himself justly criminal in the eyes of a majority; that it would open a door for intrigues against him in States where his administration tho' just might be unpopular, and might tempt him to pay court to particular States whose leading partizans he might fear, or wish to engage as his partizans. They both thought it bad policy to introduce such a mixture of the State authorities, where their agency could be otherwise supplied.

Mr. Dickenson considered the business as so important that no man ought to be silent or reserved. He went into a discourse of some length, the sum of which was, that the Legislative, Executive, & Judiciary departments ought to be made as independent as possible; but that such an Executive as some seemed to have in contemplation was not consistent with a republic: that a firm Executive could only exist in a limited monarchy. In the British Government itself the weight of the Executive arises from the attachments which the Crown draws to itself, & not merely from the force of its prerogatives. In place of these attachments we must look out for something else. One source of stability is the double branch of the Legislature. The division of the Country into distinct States formed the other principal source of stability. This division ought therefore to be maintained, and considerable powers to be left with the States. This was the ground of his consolation for the future fate of his Country. Without this, and in case of a consolidation of the States into one great Republic, we might read its fate in the history of smaller ones. A limited Monarchy he considered as *one* of the best Governments in the world. It was not *certain* that the same blessings were derivable from any other form. It was certain that equal blessings had never yet been derived from any of the republican form. A limited Monarchy however was out of the question. The spirit of the times—the state of our affairs, forbade the experiment, if it were desireable. Was it possible moreover in the nature of things to introduce it even if these obstacles were less insuperable. A House of Nobles was essential to such a Government could these be created by a breath, or by a stroke of the pen? No. They were the growth of ages, and could only arise under a complication of circumstances none of which existed in this Country. But though a form the most perfect *perhaps* in itself be unattainable, we must not despair. If ancient republics have been found to flourish for a moment only & then vanish for ever, it only proves that they were badly constituted; and that we ought to seek for every remedy for their diseases. One of these remedies he conceived to be the accidental lucky division of this Country into distinct States; a division which some seemed desirous to abolish altogether. As to the point of representation in the national Legislature as it might affect States of different sizes, he said it must probably end in mutual concession. He hoped that each State would retain an equal voice at least in one branch of the National Legislature, and supposed the sums paid within each State would form a better ratio for the other branch than either the number of inhabitants or the quantum of property.

A motion being made to strike out "on request by a majority of the Legislature of the individual States" and rejected, Connecticut, South Carolina, & Georgia being ay, the rest no: the question was taken—

On Mr. Dickenson's motion for making Executive removeable by National Legislature at request of majority of State Legislatures was also rejected—all the States being in the negative Except Delaware which gave an affirmative vote. . . .

Mr. Rutlidge and Mr. C. Pinkney moved that the blank for the number of persons in the Executive be filled with the words "one person." He supposed the reasons to be so obvious & conclusive in favor of one that no member would oppose the motion.

Mr. Randolph opposed it with great earnestness, declaring that he should not do justice to the Country which sent him if he were silently to suffer the establishment of a Unity in the Executive department. He felt an opposition to it which he believed he should continue to feel as long as he lived. He urged 1. that the permanent temper of the people was adverse to the very semblance of Monarchy. 2. that a unity was unnecessary a plurality being equally competent to all the objects of the department. 3. that the necessary confidence would never be reposed in a single Magistrate. 4. that the appointments would generally be in favor of some inhabitant near the center of the Community, and consequently the remote parts would not be on an equal footing. He was in favor of three members of the Executive to be drawn from different portions of the Country. . . .

The motion was then postponed the Committee rose & the House

Adjourned

Monday, June 4. In Committee of the Whole

The Question was resumed on motion of Mr. Pinkney seconded by Wilson, "shall the blank for the number of the Executive be filled with a single person?"

Mr. Wilson was in favor of the motion. It had been opposed by the gentleman from Virginia [Mr. Randolph] but the arguments used had not convinced him. He observed that the objections of Mr. R. were levelled not so much against the measure itself, as against its unpopularity. If he could suppose that it would occasion a rejection of the plan of which it should form a part, though the part was an important one, yet he would give it up rather than lose the whole. On examination he could see no evidence of the alledged antipathy of the people. On the contrary he was persuaded that it does not exist. All know that a single magistrate is not a King. One fact has great weight with him. All the 13 States tho agreeing in scarce any other instance, agree in placing a single magistrate at the head of the Government. The idea of three heads has taken place in none. The degree of power is indeed different; but there are no co-ordinate heads. In addition to his former reasons for preferring a unity, he would mention another. The *tranquility* not less than the vigor of the Government he thought would be favored by it. Among three equal members, he foresaw nothing but uncontrouled, continued, & violent animosities; which would not only interrupt the public administration; but diffuse their poison thro' the other branches of Government, thro' the States, and at length thro' the people at large. If the members were to be unequal in power the principle of the opposition to the unity was given up. If equal, the making them an odd number would not be a remedy. In Courts of Justice there are two sides only to a question. In the Legislative & Executive departments questions have commonly many sides. Each member therefore might espouse a separate one & no two agree.

Mr. Sherman. This matter is of great importance and ought to be well considered before it is determined. Mr. Wilson he said had observed that in each State a single magistrate was placed at the head of the Government. It was so he admitted, and properly so, and he wished the same policy to prevail in the federal Government. But then it should be also remarked that in all the States there was a Council of advice, without which the first magistrate could not act. A council he thought necessary to make the establishment acceptable to the people. Even in G.B. the King has a Council; and though he appoints it himself, its advice has its weight with him, and attracts the Confidence of the people.

Mr. Williamson asks Mr. Wilson whether he means to annex a Council.

Mr. Wilson means to have no Council, which oftener serves to cover, than prevent malpractices.

Mr. Gerry was at a loss to discover the policy of three members for the Executive. It would be extremely inconvenient in many instances, particularly in military matters, whether relating to the militia, an army, or a navy. It would be a general with three heads.

On the question for a single Executive it was agreed to. . . . [7 to 3.]

First Clause of Proposition 8th relating *to a Council of Revision* taken into consideration.

Mr. Gerry doubts whether the Judiciary ought to form a part of it, as they will have a sufficient check against encroachments on their own department by their exposition of the laws, which involved a power of deciding on their Constitutionality. In some States the Judge had actually set aside laws as being against the Constitution. This was done too with general approbation. It was quite foreign from the nature of ye office to make them judges of the policy of public measures. He moves to postpone the clause in order to propose "that the National Executive shall have a right to negative any Legislative act which shall not be afterwards passed by   parts of each branch of the national Legislature."

Mr. King seconds the motion, observing that the Judges ought to be able to expound the law as it should come before them, free from the bias of having participated in its formation.

Mr. Wilson thinks neither the original proposition nor the amendment go far enough. If the Legislative Executive & Judiciary ought to be distinct & independent. The Executive ought to have an absolute negative. Without such a self-defense the Legislature can at any moment sink it into non-existence. He was for varying the proposition in such a manner as to give the Executive & Judiciary jointly an absolute negative.

On the question to postpone in order to take Mr. Gerry's proposition into consideration it was agreed to . . .

Mr. Gerry's proposition being now before Committee, Mr. Wilson & Mr. Hamilton move that the last part of it [viz., "which shall not be afterwards passed unless by   parts of each branch of the National legislature"] be struck out, so as to give the Executive an absolute negative on the laws. There was no danger they thought of such a power being too much exercised. It was mentioned by Col: Hamilton that the King of G.B. had not exerted his negative since the Revolution.

Mr. Gerry sees no necessity for so great a controul over the legislature as the best men in the Community would be comprised in the two branches of it. . . .

Mr. Sherman was against enabling any one man to stop the will of the whole. No one man could be found so far above all the rest in wisdom. He thought we ought to avail ourselves of his wisdom in revising the laws, but not permit him to overrule the decided and cool opinions of the Legislature.

Mr. Madison supposed that if a proper proportion of each branch should be required to overrule the objections of the Executive, it would answer the same purpose as an absolute negative. It would rarely if ever happen that the Executive constituted as ours is proposed to be would, have firmness eno' to resist the legislature, unless backed by a certain part of the body itself. The King of G.B. with all his splendid attributes would not be able to withstand ye unanimous and eager wishes of both houses of Parliament. To give such a prerogative would certainly be obnoxious to the temper of this Country; its present temper at least. . . .

Mr. Butler had been in favor of a single Executive Magistrate; but could he have entertained an idea that a compleat negative on the laws was to be given him he certainly should have acted very differently. It had been observed that in all countries the Executive power is in a constant course of increase. This was certainly the case in G.B. Gentlemen seemed to think that we had nothing to apprehend from an abuse of the Executive power. But why might not a Cataline or a Cromwell arise in this Country as well as in others. . . .

Col. Mason observed that a vote had already passed he found [he was out at the time] for vesting the executive powers in a single person. Among these powers was that of appointing to offices in certain cases. . . . The Executive may refuse its assent to necessary measures till new appointments shall be referred to him; and having by degrees engrossed all these into his own hands, the American Executive, like the British, will by bribery & influence, save himself the trouble & odium of exerting his negative afterwards. We are Mr. Chairman going very far in this business. We are not indeed constituting a British Government, but a more dangerous monarchy, an elective one. We are introducing a new principle into our system, and not necessary as in the British Government where the Executive has greater rights to defend. Do gentlemen mean to pave the way to hereditary Monarchy? Do they flatter themselves that the people will ever consent to such an innovation? If they do I venture to tell them, they are mistaken. The people never will consent. And do gentlemen consider the danger of delay, and the still greater danger of a rejection, not for a moment but forever, of the plan which shall be proposed to them. Notwithstanding the oppressions & injustice experienced among us from democracy; the genius of the people is in favor of it, and the genius of the people must be consulted. He could not but consider the federal system as in effect dissolved by the appointment of this Convention to devise a better one. And do gentlemen look forward to the dangerous interval between the extinction of an old, and the establishment of a new Government and to the scenes of confusion which may ensue. He hoped that nothing like a Monarchy would ever be attempted in this Country. A hatred to its oppressions had carried the people through the late Revolution. Will it not be eno' to enable the Executive to suspend offensive laws, till they shall be coolly revised, and the objections to them overruled by a greater majority than was required in the first instance. He never could agree to give up all the rights of the people to a single Magistrate. If more than one had been fixed on, greater powers might have been entrusted to the Executive. He hoped this attempt to give such powers would have its weight hereafter as an argument for increasing the number of the Executive. . . .

On the question for striking out so as to give Executive an absolute negative [unanimously in the negative]. . . .

On a question for enabling *two thirds* of each branch of the Legislature to overrule the revisionary check: it passed in the affirmative sub silentio; and was inserted in the blank of Mr. Gerry's motion. . . .

It was then moved & seconded to proceed to the consideration of the 9th resolution submitted by Mr. Randolph—when on motion to agree to the first clause namely "Resolved that a National Judiciary be established" It passed in the affirmative nem. con.

It was then moved & seconded to add these words to the first clause of the ninth resolution namely—"to consist of one supreme tribunal, and of one or more inferior tribunals" which passed in the affirmative—

The Committee then rose and the House

Adjourned

Tuesday June 5. In Committee of the Whole

The words, "one or more" were struck out before "inferior tribunals" as an amendment to the last clause of Resolution 9th. The Clause—"that the National Judiciary be chosen by the National Legislature," being under consideration.

Mr. Wilson opposed the appointment of Judges by the National Legislature: Experience shewed the impropriety of such appointments by numerous bodies. Intrigue, partiality, and concealment were the necessary consequences. A principal reason for unity in the Executive was that officers might be appointed by a single, responsible person.

Mr. Rutlidge was by no means disposed to grant so great a power to any single person. The people will think we are leaning too much towards Monarchy. He was against establishing any national tribunal except a single supreme one. The State tribunals are most proper to decide in all cases in the first instance. . . .

Mr. Madison disliked the election of the Judges by the Legislature or any numerous body. Besides, the danger of intrigue and partiality, many of the members were not judges of the requisite qualifications. The Legislative talents which were very different from those of a Judge, commonly recommended men to the favor of Legislative Assemblies. It was known too that the accidental circumstances of presence and absence, of being a member or not a member, had a very undue influence on the appointment. On the other hand he was not satisfied with referring the appointment to the Executive. He rather inclined to give it to the Senatorial branch, as numerous eno' to be confided in—as not so numerous as to be governed by the motives of the other branch; and as being sufficiently stable and independent to follow their deliberate judgments. He hinted this only and moved that the *appointment by the Legislature* might be struck out, & a blank left to be hereafter filled on maturer reflection. Mr. Wilson seconds it. On the question for striking out. [Passed 8 to 2.] . . .

The following clauses of Resol: 9. were agreed to viz "to hold their offices during good behaviour, and to receive punctually at stated times, a fixed compensation for their services, in which no increase or diminution shall be made so as to affect the persons actually in office at the time of such increase or diminution."

The remaining clause of Resolution 9. was postponed.

Resolution 10 was agreed to—viz—that provision ought to be made for the admission of States lawfully arising within the limits of the U. States, whether from a voluntary junction of Government & Territory, or otherwise, with the consent of a number of voices in the National Legislature less than the whole. . . .

Propos: 13. "*that provision ought to be made for hereafter amending the system now to be established, without requiring the assent of the National Legislature,*" being taken up.

Mr. Pinkney doubted the propriety or necessity of it.

Mr. Gerry favored it. The novelty & difficulty of the experiment requires periodical revision. The prospect of such a revision would also give intermediate stability to the Government. Nothing had yet happened in the States where this provision existed to prove its impropriety. The proposition was postponed for further consideration. . . .

Propos. 14. "*requiring oath from the State officers to support National Government*" was postponed after a short uninteresting conversation. . . .

Propos. 15 for "*recommending Conventions under appointment of the people to ratify the new Constitution*" &c. being taken up.

Mr. Sharman thought such a popular ratification unnecessary: the articles of Confederation providing for changes and alterations with the assent of Congress and ratification of State Legislatures.

Mr. Madison thought this provision essential. The articles of Confederation themselves were defective in this respect, resting in many of the States on the Legislative sanction only. Hence in conflicts between acts of the States, and of Congress especially where the former are of posterior date, and the decision is to be made by State tribunals, an uncertainty must necessarily prevail, or rather perhaps a certain decision in favor of the State authority. He suggested also that as far as the articles of Union were to be considered as a Treaty only of a particular sort, among the Governments of Independent States, the doctrine might be set up that a breach of any one article, by any of the parties, absolved the other parties from the whole obligation. For these reasons as well as others he thought it indispensable that the new Constitution should be ratified in the most unexceptionable form, and by the supreme authority of the people themselves.

Mr. Gerry observed that in the Eastern States the Confederation had been sanctioned by the people themselves. He seemed afraid of referring the new system to them. The people in that quarter have at this time the wildest ideas of Government in the world. They were for abolishing the Senate in Massachusetts and giving all the other powers of Government to the other branch of the Legislature.

Mr. King supposed that the last article of the Confederation rendered the legislature competent to the ratification. The people of the Southern States where the federal articles had been ratified by the Legislatures only, had since *impliedly* given their sanction to it. He thought notwithstanding that there might be policy in varying the mode. A Convention being a single house, the adoption may more easily be carried thro' it, than thro' the Legislatures where there are several branches. The Legislatures also being to lose power, will be most likely to raise objections. The people having already parted with the necessary powers it is immaterial to them, by which Government they are possessed, provided they be well employed.

Mr. Wilson took this occasion to lead the Committee by a train of observations to the idea of not suffering a disposition in the plurality of States to confederate anew on better principles, to be defeated by the inconsiderate or selfish opposition of a few States. He hoped the provision for ratifying would be put on such a footing as to admit of such a partial union, with a door open for the accession of the rest.

Mr. Pinkney hoped that in case the experiment should not unanimously take place, nine States might be authorized to unite under the same Government. . . .

Mr. Rutlidge having obtained a rule for reconsideration of the clause for establishing *inferior* tribunals under the national authority, now moved that that part of the clause in propos. 9 should be expunged: arguing that the State Tribunals might and ought to be left in all cases to decide in the first instance the right of appeal to the supreme national tribunal being sufficient to secure the national rights & uniformity of Judgments: that it was making an unnecessary encroachment on the jurisdiction of the States and creating unnecessary obstacles to their adoption of the new system.—Mr. Sherman seconded the motion.

Mr. Madison observed that unless inferior tribunals were dispersed throughout the Republic with *final* jurisdiction in *many* cases, appeals would be multiplied to a most oppressive degree; that besides, an appeal would not in many cases be a remedy. What was to be done after improper Verdicts in State tribunals obtained under the biassed directions of a dependent Judge, or the local prejudices of an undirected jury? To remand the cause for a new trial would answer no purpose. To order a new trial at the Supreme bar would oblige the parties to bring up their witnesses, tho' ever so distant from the seat of the Court. An effective Judiciary establishment commensurate to the legislative authority, was essential. A Government without a proper Executive & Judiciary would be the mere trunk of a body, without arms or legs to act or move.

Mr. Wilson opposed the motion on like grounds. He said the admiralty jurisdiction ought to be given wholly to the national Government, as it related to cases not within the jurisdiction of particular states, & to a scene in which controversies with foreigners would be most likely to happen.

Mr. Sherman was in favor of the motion. He dwelt chiefly on the supposed expensiveness of having a new set of Courts, when the existing State Courts would answer the same purpose.

Mr. Dickinson contended strongly that if there was to be a National Legislature, there ought to be a national Judiciary, and that the former ought to have authority to institute the latter.

On the question for Mr. Rutlidge's motion to strike out "inferior tribunals" . . . [passed 5 to 4.]

Mr. Wilson & Mr. Madison then moved, in pursuance of the idea expressed above by Mr. Dickinson, to add to Resol: 9. the words following "that the National Legislature be empowered to institute inferior tribunals." They observed that there was a distinction between establishing such tribunals absolutely, and giving a discretion to the Legislature to establish or not establish them. They repeated the necessity of some such provision.

Mr. Butler. The people will not bear such innovations. The States will revolt at such encroachments. Supposing such an establishment to be useful, we must not venture on it. We must follow the example of Solon who gave the Athenians not the best Government he could devise; but the best they would receive.

Mr. King remarked as to the comparative expence that the establishment of inferior tribunals would cost infinitely less than the appeals that would be prevented by them.

On this question as moved by Mr. Wilson & Mr. Madison. . . . [Passed 8 to 1.]

The Committee then rose & the House adjourned to 11 o'clock tomorrow.

Wednesday June 6. In Committee of the Whole

Mr. Pinkney according to previous notice & rule obtained, moved "that the first branch of the national Legislature be elected by the State Legislatures, and not by the people." contending that the people were less fit Judges in such a case, and that the Legislatures would be less likely to promote the adoption of the new Government, if they were to be excluded from all share in it.

Mr. Rutlidge seconded the motion.

Mr. Gerry. Much depends on the mode of election. In England, the people will probably lose their liberty from the smallness of the proportion having a right of suffrage. Our danger arises from the opposite extreme: hence in Massachusetts the worst men get into the Legislature. Several members of that Body had lately been convicted of infamous crimes. Men of indigence, ignorance & baseness, spare no pains, however dirty to carry their point against men who are superior to the artifices practised. He was not disposed to run into extremes. He was as much principled as ever against aristocracy and monarchy. It was necessary on the one hand that the people should appoint one branch of the Government in order to inspire them with the necessary confidence. But he wished the election on the other to be so modified as to secure more effectually a just preference of merit. His idea was that the people should nominate certain persons in certain districts, out of whom the State Legislatures should make the appointment.

Mr. Wilson. He wished for vigor in the Government, but he wished that vigorous authority to flow immediately from the legitimate source of all authority. The Government ought to possess not only first the *force*, but secondly the *mind or sense* of the people at large. The Legislature ought to be the most exact transcript of the whole Society. Representation is made necessary only because it is impossible for the people to act collectively. The opposition was to be expected he said from the *Governments*, not from the Citizens of the States. The latter had parted as was observed [by Mr. King] with all the necessary powers; and it was immaterial to them, by whom they were exercised, if well exercised. The State officers were to be the losers of power. The people he supposed would be rather more attached to the national Government than to the State Governments as being more important in itself, and more flattering to their pride. There is no danger of improper elections if made by *large* districts. Bad elections proceed from the smallness of the districts which give an opportunity to bad men to intrigue themselves into office.

Mr. Sherman. If it were in view to abolish the State Governments the elections ought to be by the people. If the State Governments are to be continued, it is necessary in order to preserve harmony between the National & State Governments that the elections to the former should be made by the latter. The right of participating in the National Government would be sufficiently secured to the people by their election of the State Legislatures. The objects of the Union, he thought were few. 1. defence against foreign danger. 2. against internal disputes & a resort to force. 3. Treaties with foreign nations. 4. regulating foreign commerce, & drawing revenue from it. These & perhaps a few lesser objects alone rendered a Confederation of the States necessary. All other matters civil & criminal would be much better in the hands of the States. The people are more happy in small than large States. States may indeed be too small as Rhode Island, & thereby be too subject to faction. Some others were perhaps too large, the powers of Government not being able to pervade them. He was for giving the General Government power to legislate and execute within a defined province.

Col. Mason. Under the existing Confederacy, Congress represent the *States* not the *people* of the States: their acts operate on the *States*, not on the individuals. The case will be changed in the new plan of Government. The people will be represented; they ought therefore to choose the Representatives. The requisites in actual representation are that the Representatives should sympathize with their constituents; should think as they think, & feel as they feel; and that for these purposes should even be residents among them. Much he said had been alleged against democratic elections. He admitted that much might be said; but it was to be considered that no Government was free from imperfections & evils; and that improper elections in many instances, were inseparable from Republican Governments. But compare these with the advantage of this Form in favor of the rights of the people, in favor of human nature. He was persuaded there was a better chance for proper elections by the people if divided into large districts, than by the State Legislatures. Paper money had been issued by the latter when the former were against it. Was it to be supposed that the State Legislatures then would not send to the National legislature patrons of such projects, if the choice depended on them.

Mr. Madison considered an election of one branch at least of the Legislature by the people immediately, as a clear principle of free Government and that this mode under proper regulations had the additional advantage of securing better representatives, as well as of avoiding too great an agency of the State Governments in the General one.— He differed from the member from Connecticut [Mr. Sharman] in thinking the objects mentioned to be all the principal ones that required a

National Government. Those were certainly important and necessary objects; but he combined with them the necessity of providing more effectually for the security of private rights, and the steady dispensation of Justice. Interferences with these were evils which had more perhaps than any thing else, produced this convention. Was it to be supposed that republican liberty could long exist under the abuses of it practised in some of the States. The gentleman [Mr. Sharman] had admitted that in a very small State, faction & oppression would prevail. It was to be inferred then that wherever these prevailed the State was too small. Had they not prevailed in the largest as well as the smallest tho' less than in the smallest; and were we not thence admonished to enlarge the sphere as far as the nature of the Government would admit. This was the only defence against the inconveniences of democracy consistent with the democratic form of Government. All civilized Societies would be divided into different Sects, Factions, & interests, as they happened to consist of rich & poor, debtors & creditors, the landed, the manufacturing, the commercial interests, the inhabitants of this district or that district, the followers of this political leader or that political leader or that political leader, the disciples of this religious Sect or that religious Sect. In all cases where a majority are united by a common interest or passion, the rights of the minority are in danger. What motives are to restrain them? A prudent regard to the maxim that honesty is the best policy is found by experience to be as little regarded by bodies of men as by individuals. Respect for character is always diminished in proportion to the number among whom the blame or praise is to be divided. Conscience, the only remaining tie, is known to be inadequate in individuals: In large numbers, little is to be expected from it. Besides, Religion itself may become a motive to persecution & oppression.—These observations are verified by the Histories of every Country ancient & modern. In Greece & Rome the rich & poor, the creditors & debtors, as well as the patricians & plebians alternately oppressed each other with equal unmercifulness. What a source of oppression was the relation between the parent cities of Rome, Athens & Carthage, & their respective provinces: the former possessing the power, & the latter being sufficiently distinguished to be separate objects of it? Why was America so justly apprehensive of Parliamentary injustice? Because G. Britain had a separate interest real or supposed, & if her authority had been admitted, could have pursued that interest at our expence. We have seen the mere distinction of colour made in the most enlightened period of time, a ground of the most oppressive dominion ever exercised by man over man. What has been the source of those unjust laws complained of among ourselves? Has it not been the real or supposed interest of the major number? Debtors have defrauded their creditors. The landed interest has borne hard on the mercantile interest. The Holders of one species of property have thrown a disproportion of taxes on the holders of another species. The lesson we are to draw from the whole is that where a majority are united by a common sentiment, and have an opportunity, the rights of the minor party become insecure. In a Republican Government the Majority if united have always an opportunity. The only remedy is to enlarge the sphere, & thereby divide the community into so great a number of interests & parties, that in the first place a majority will not be likely at the same moment to have a common interest separate from that of the whole or of the minority; and in the second place, that in case they should have such an interest, they may not be apt to unite in the pursuit of it. It was incumbent on us then to try this remedy, and with that view to frame a republican system on such a scale & in such a form as will controul all the evils which have been experienced.

Mr. Dickenson considered it as essential that one branch of the Legislature should be drawn immediately from the people; and as expedient that the other should be chosen by the Legislatures of the States. This combination of the State Governments with the national Government was as politic as it was unavoidable. In the formation of the Senate we ought to carry it through such a refining process as will assimilate it as near as may be to the House of Lords in England. He repeated his warm eulogiums on the British Constitution. He was for a strong National Government but for leaving the States a considerable agency in the System. The objection against making the former dependent on the latter might be obviated by giving to the Senate an authority permanent & irrevocable for three, five or seven years. Being thus independent they will speak & decide with becoming freedom.

Mr. Read. Too much attachment is betrayed to the State Governments. We must look beyond their continuance. A national Government must soon of necessity swallow all of them up. They will soon be reduced to the mere office of electing the National Senate. He was against patching up the old federal System: he hoped the idea would be dismissed. It would be like putting new cloth on an old garment. The confederation was founded on temporary principles. It cannot last: it cannot be amended. If we do not establish a good Government on new principles, we must either go to ruin, or have the work to do over again. The people at large are wrongly suspected of being averse to a General Government. The aversion lies among interested men who possess their confidence.

Mr. Pierce was for an election by the people as to the first branch & by the States as to the second branch; by which means the Citizens of the States would be represented both *individually & collectively*.

General Pinkney wished to have a good National Government & at the same time to leave a considerable share of power in the States. An election of either branch by the people scattered as they are in many States, particularly in S. Carolina was totally impracticable. He differed from gentlemen who thought that a choice by the people would be a better guard against bad measures, than by the Legislatures. A majority of the people in S. Carolina were notoriously for paper money as a legal tender; the Legislature had refused to make it a legal tender. The reason was that the latter had some sense of character and were restrained by that consideration. The State Legislatures also he said would be more jealous, & more ready to thwart the National Government, if excluded from a participation in it. The Idea of abolishing these Legislatures would never go down.

Mr. Wilson, would not have spoken again, but for what had fallen from Mr. Read; namely, that the idea of preserving the State Government ought to be abandoned. He saw no incompatibility between the National & State Governments provided the latter were restrained to certain local purposes; nor any probability of their being devoured by the former. In all confederated Systems ancient & modern the reverse had happened; the Generality being destroyed gradually by the usurpations of the parts composing it.

On the question for electing the first branch by the State Legislatures as moved by Mr. Pinkney: it was negatived. . . .

Mr. Wilson moved to reconsider the vote excluding the Judiciary from a share in the revision of the laws, and to add after "National Executive" the words "with a convenient number of the national Judiciary"; remarking the expediency of reinforcing the Executive with the influence of that Department.

Mr. Madison seconded the motion. He observed that the great difficulty in rendering the Executive competent to its own defence arose from the nature of Republican Government which could not give to an individual citizen that settled pre-eminence in the eyes of the rest, that weight of property, that personal interest against betraying the national interest, which appertain to an hereditary magistrate. In a Republic personal merit alone could be the ground of political exaltation, but it would rarely happen that this merit would be so pre-eminent as to produce universal acquiescence. The Executive Magistrate would be envied & assailed by disappointed competitors: His firmness therefore would need support. He would not possess those great emoluments from his station, nor that permanent stake in the public interest which would place him out of the reach of foreign corruption: He would stand in need therefore of being controuled as well as supported. An association of the

Judges in his revisionary function would both double the advantage and diminish the danger. It would also enable the Judiciary Department the better to defend itself against Legislative encroachments. Two objections had been made first that the Judges ought not to be subject to the bias which a participation in the making of laws might give in the exposition of them. Secondly that the Judiciary Department ought to be separate & distinct from the other great Departments. The first objection had some weight; but it was much diminished by reflecting that a small proportion of the laws coming in question before a Judge would be such wherein he had been consulted; that a small part of this proportion would be so ambiguous as to leave room for his prepossessions; and that but a few cases would probably arise in the life of a Judge under such ambiguous passages. How much good on the other hand would proceed from the perspicuity, the conciseness, and the systematic character which the Code of laws would receive from the Judiciary talents. As to the second objection, it either had no weight, or it applied with equal weight to the Executive & to the Judiciary revision of the laws. The maxim on which the objection was founded required a separation of the Executive as well as of the Judiciary from the Legislature & from each other. There would in truth however be no improper mixture of these distinct powers in the present case. In England, whence the maxim itself had been drawn, the Executive had an absolute negative on the laws; and the supreme tribunal of Justice [the House of Lords] formed one of the other branches of the Legislature. In short whether the object of the revisionary power was to restrain the Legislature from encroaching on the other coordinate Departments, or on the rights of the people at large; or from passing laws unwise in their principle, or incorrect in their form, the utility of annexing the wisdom and weight of the Judiciary to the Executive seemed incontestable.

Mr. Gerry thought the Executive, whilst standing alone would be more impartial than when he could be covered by the sanction & seduced by the sophistry of the Judges.

Mr. King. If the Unity of the Executive was preferred for the sake of responsibility, the policy of it is as applicable to the revisionary as to the Executive power.

Mr. Pinkney had been at first in favor of joining the heads of the principal departments the Secretary of War, of foreign affairs &—in the council of revision. He had however relinquished the idea from a consideration that these could be called in by the Executive Magistrate whenever he pleased to consult them. He was opposed to an introduction of the Judges into the business.

Col. Mason was for giving all possible weight to the revisionary institution. The Executive power ought to be well secured against Legislative usurpations on it. The purse & the sword ought never to get into the same hands whether Legislative or Executive.

On the question for joining the Judges to the Executive in the revisionary business. . . . [Lost 8 to 3.] . . .

The Committee rose & the House adjourned to 11 o'clock tomorrow.

Madison's speculations on June 6th are worth some special attention. Speaking in support of popular election to the lower house, he declared it to be "the only defence against the inconveniences of democracy consistent with the democratic form of Government." He then added a cardinal tenet of his fellow revolutionaries: "All civilized Societies would be divided into different Sects, Factions, & interests, as they happened to consist of rich & poor, debtors & creditors, the landed, the manufacturing, the commercial interests, the inhabitants of this district or that district, the followers of this political leader or that political leader, the disciples of this religious Sect or that religious Sect. In all cases where a majority are united by a common interest or passion, the rights of the minority are in danger." If you had to choose a half dozen or so statements by the Founding Fathers that indicated the basic assumptions that lay behind the particular political forms that they created, these sentences should certainly be included. We have encountered the arguments before and will certainly encounter them again but perhaps never more directly or trenchantly stated. Our old friend original sin is back again.

Thursday June 7, 1787—In Committee of the Whole

Mr. Pinkney according to notice moved to reconsider the clause respecting the negative on State laws, which was agreed to and tomorrow for fixed [fixed for] the purpose.

The Clause providing for the appointment of the second branch of the national Legislature, having lain blank since the last vote on the mode of electing it, to wit, by the first branch, Mr. Dickenson now moved "that the members of the second branch ought to be chosen by the individual Legislatures."

Mr. Sharman seconded the motion; observing that the particular States would thus become interested in supporting the national Government and that a due harmony between the two Governments would be maintained. He admitted that the two ought to have separate and distinct jurisdictions, but that they ought to have a mutual interest in supporting each other.

Mr. Wilson. . . . He wished the Senate to be elected by the people as well as the other branch, and the people might be divided into proper districts for the purpose & moved to postpone the motion of Mr. Dickenson, in order to take up one of that import.

Mr. Morris seconded him.

Mr. Madison, if the motion [of Mr. Dickenson] should be agreed to, we must either depart from the doctrine of proportional representation; or admit into the Senate a very large number of members. The first is inadmissible, being evidently unjust. The second is inexpedient. The use of the Senate is to consist in its proceeding with more coolness, with more system, & with more wisdom, than the popular branch. Enlarge their number and you communicate to them the vices which they are meant to correct. He differed from Mr. Dickenson who thought that the additional number would give additional weight to the body. On the contrary it appeared to him that their weight would be in an inverse ratio to their number. The example of the Roman Tribunes was applicable. They lost their influence and power, in proportion as their number was augmented. The reason seemed to be obvious: They were appointed to take care of the popular interests & pretensions at Rome, because the people by reason of their numbers could not act in concert; were liable to fall into factions among themselves, and to become a prey to their aristocratic adversaries. The more the representatives of the people were multiplied, the more they partook of the infirmities of their constituents, the more liable they became to be divided among themselves either from their own indiscretions or the artifices of the opposite faction, and of course the less capable of fulfilling their trust. When the weight of a set of men depends merely on their personal characters; the greater the number the greater the weight. When it depends on the degree of political authority lodged in them the smaller the number the greater the weight. These considerations might perhaps be combined in the intended Senate; but the latter was the material one.

Mr. Gerry. 4 modes of appointing the Senate have been mentioned. 1. by the first branch of the National Legislature. This would create a dependence contrary to the end proposed. 2. by the National Executive. This is a stride towards monarchy that few will think of. 3. by the people. The people have two great interests, the landed interest, and the commercial including the stockholders. To draw both branches from the people will leave no security to the latter interest; the people being chiefly composed of the landed interest, and erroneously supposing, that the other interests are adverse to it. 4. by the Individual Legislatures. The elections being carried thro' this refinement, will be most likely to provide some check in favor of the commercial interest against the landed; without which oppression will take place, and no free Government can last long where that is the case. He was therefore in favor of this last.

Mr. Dickenson. The preservation of the States in a certain degree of agency is indispensable. It will produce that collision between the different authorities which should be wished for in order to check each other. To attempt to abolish the States altogether, would degrade the Councils of our Country, would be impracticable, would be ruinous. He compared the proposed National System to the Solar System, in which the States were the planets, and ought to be left to move freely in their proper orbits. The Gentleman from Pennsylvania [Mr. Wilson] wished he said to extinguish these planets. If the State Government were excluded from all agency in the national one, and all power drawn from the people at large, the consequence would be that the national Government would move in the same direction as the State Governments now do, and would run into all the same mischiefs. The reform would only unite the 13 small streams into one great current pursuing the same course without any opposition whatever. He adhered to the opinion that the Senate ought to be composed of a large number, and that their influence from family weight & other causes would be increased thereby. He did not admit that the Tribunes lost their weight in proportion as there number was augmented and gave a historical sketch of this institution. If the reasoning of [Mr. Madison] was good it would prove that the number of the Senate ought to be reduced below ten, the highest number of the Tribunitial corps.

Mr. Wilson. The subject it must be owned is surrounded with doubts and difficulties. But we must surmount them. The British Government cannot be our model. We have no materials for a similar one. Our manners, our laws, the abolition of entails and of primogeniture, the whole genius of the people, are opposed to it. He did not see the danger of the States being devoured by the National Government. On the contrary, he wished to keep them from devouring the national Government. He was not however for extinguishing these planets as was supposed by Mr. Dickenson—neither did he on the other hand, believe that they would warm or enlighten the Sun. Within their proper orbits they must still be suffered to act for subordinate purposes for which their existence is made essential by the great extent of our Country. He could not comprehend in what manner the landed interest would be rendered less predominant in the Senate, by an election through the medium of the Legislatures than by the people themselves. If the Legislatures, as was now complained, sacrificed the commercial to the landed interest, what reason was there to expect such a choice from them as would defeat their own views. He was for an election by the people in large districts which would be most likely to obtain men of intelligence & uprightness; subdividing the districts only for the accomodation of voters. . . .

Mr. Pinkney thought the second branch ought to be permanent & independent, & that the members of it would be rendered more so by receiving their appointment from the State Legislatures. This mode would avoid the rivalships & discontents incident to the election by districts. He was for dividing the States into three classes according to their respective sizes, & for allowing to the first class three members—to the second, two, & to the third, one. . . .

Col. Mason. Whatever power may be necessary for the National Government a certain portion must necessarily be left in the States. It is impossible for one power to pervade the extreme parts of the U.S. so as to carry equal justice to them. The State Legislatures also ought to have some means of defending themselves against encroachments of the National Government. In every other department we have studiously endeavored to provide for its self-defence. Shall we leave the States alone unprovided with the means for this purpose? And what better means can we provide than the giving them some share in, or rather to make them a constituent part of, the National Establishment. There is danger on both sides no doubt; but we have only seen the evils arising on the side of the State Governments. Those on the other side remain to be displayed. The example of Congress does not apply. Congress had no power to carry their acts into execution as the National Government will have.

On Mr. Dickinson's motion for an appointment of the Senate by the State Legislatures. . . . [Passed unanimously.]

The Committee rose & The House

Adjourned

Friday June 8. In Committee of the Whole

On a reconsideration of the clause giving the National Legislature a negative on such laws of the States as might be contrary to the articles of Union, or Treaties with foreign nations,

Mr. Pinkney moved "that the National Legislature should have authority to negative all laws which they should judge to be improper." He urged that such a universality of the power was indispensably necessary to render it effectual; that the States must be kept in due subordination to the nation; that if the States were left to act of themselves in any case, it would be impossible to defend the national prerogatives, however extensive they might be on paper; that the acts of Congress had been defeated by this means; nor had foreign treaties escaped repeated violations; that this universal negative was in fact the corner stone of an efficient national Government; that under the British Government the negative of the Crown had been found beneficial, and the *States* are more one nation now, than the *Colonies* were then.

Mr. Madison seconded the motion. He could not but regard an indefinite power to negative legislative acts of the States as absolutely necessary to a perfect system. Experience had evinced a constant tendency in the States to encroach on the federal authority; to violate national Treaties; to infringe the rights & interests of each other; to oppress the weaker party within their respective jurisdictions. A negative was the mildest expedient that could be devised for preventing these mischiefs. The existence of such a check would prevent attempts to commit them. Should no such precaution be engrafted, the only remedy would lie in an appeal to coercion. Was such a remedy eligible? was it practicable? Could the national resources, if exerted to the utmost enforce a national decree against Massachusetts abetted perhaps by several of her neighbours? It would not be possible. A small proportion of the Community, in a compact situation, acting on the defensive, and at one of its extremities might at any time bid defiance to the National authority. Any Government for the U. States formed on the supposed practicability of using force against the unconstitutional proceedings of the States, would prove as visionary & fallacious as the Government of Congress. The negative would render the use of force unnecessary. The States could of themselves then pass no operative act, any more than one branch of a Legislature where there are two branches, can proceed without the other. But in order to give the negative this efficacy, it must extend to all cases. A discrimination would only be a fresh source of contention between the two authorities. In a word, to recur to the illustrations borrowed from the planetary system. This prerogative of the General Government is the great pervading principle that must controul the centrifugal tendency of the States; which, without it, will continually fly out of their proper orbits and destroy the order & harmony of the political System.

Mr. Williamson was against giving a power that might restrain the States from regulating their internal police.

Mr. Gerry could not see the extent of such a power, and was against every power that was not necessary. He thought a remonstrance against unreasonable acts of the States would reclaim them. If it should not force might be resorted to. He had no objection to authorize a negative to paper money and similar measures. When the confederation was depending before Congress, Massachusetts was then for inserting the power of emitting paper money among the exclusive powers of Congress. He observed that the proposed negative would extend to the regulations of the Militia, a matter on which the existence of a State might depend. The National Legislature with such a power may enslave the States. Such an idea as this will never be acceded to. It has never been suggested or conceived among the people. No speculative projector, and there are enough of that character among us, in politics as well as in other things, has in any pamphlet or newspaper thrown out the idea. The States too have different interests and are ignorant of each other's interests. The negative therefore will be abused. New States too having separate views from the old States will never come into the Union. They may even be under some foreign influence; are they in such case to participate in the negative on the will of the other States?

Mr. Sherman thought the cases in which the negative ought to be exercised, might be defined. He wished the point might not be decided till a trial at least should be made for that purpose.

Mr. Wilson would not say what modifications of the proposed power might be practicable or expedient. But however novel it might appear the principle of it when viewed with a close & steady eye, is right. There is no instance in which the laws say that the individual should be bound in one case, & at liberty to judge whether he will obey or disobey in another. The cases are parallel. Abuses of the power over the individual person may happen as well as over the individual States. Federal liberty is to States, what civil liberty, is to private individuals. And States are not more unwilling to purchase it, by the necessary concession of their political sovereignty, [than] the savage is to purchase civil liberty by the surrender of his personal sovereignty, which he enjoys in a State of nature. A definition of the cases in which the Negative should be exercised, is impracticable. A discretion must be left on one side or the other? will it not be most safely lodged on the side of the National Government? Among the first sentiments expressed in the first Congress one was that Virginia is no more, that Massachusetts is no [more], that Pennsylvania is no more &c. We are now one nation of brethren. We must bury all local interests & distinctions. This language continued for some time. The tables at length began to turn. No sooner were the State Governments formed than their jealousy & ambition began to display themselves. Each endeavoured to cut a slice from the common loaf, to add to its own morsel, till at length the confederation became frittered down to the impotent condition in which it now stands. Review the progress of the articles of Confederation thro' Congress & compare the first and last draught of it. To correct its vices is the business of this convention. One of its vices is the want of an effectual controul in the whole over its parts. What danger is there that the whole will unnecessarily sacrifice a part? But reverse the case, and leave the whole at the mercy of each part, and will not the general interest be continually sacrificed to local interests?

Mr. Dickenson deemed it impossible to draw a line between the cases proper & improper for the exercise of the negative. We must take our choice of two things. We must either subject the States to the danger of being injured by the power of the National Government or the latter to the danger of being injured by that of the States. He thought the danger greater from the States. To leave the power doubtful, would be opening another spring of discord, and he was for shutting as many of them as possible. . . .

Mr. Madison observed that the difficulties which had been started were worthy of attention and ought to be answered before the question was put. The case of laws of urgent necessity must be provided for by some emanation of the power from the National Government into each State so far as to give a temporary assent at least. This was the practice in Royal Colonies before the Revolution and would not have been inconvenient, if the supreme power of negativing had been faithful to the American interest, and had possessed the necessary information. He supposed that the negative might be very properly lodged in the senate alone, and that the more numerous & expensive branch therefore might not be obliged to sit constantly.—He asked Mr. Butler what would be the consequence to the small States of a dissolution of the Union which seemed likely to happen if no effectual substitute was made for the defective System existing, and he did not conceive any effectual system could be substituted on any other basis than that of a proportional suffrage? If the large States possessed the avarice & ambition with which they were charged, would the small ones in their neighbourhood, be more secure when all controul of a General Government was withdrawn.

Mr. Butler was vehement against the Negative in the proposed extent, as cutting off all hope of equal justice to the distant States. The people there would not he was sure give it a hearing.

On the question for extending the negative power to all cases as proposed by [Mr. Pinkney & Mr. M—]. . . . [Lost 8 to 4.] . . .

Attention is directed to Madison's comment in the debates of June 8 in which, borrowing from "the planetary system," he compares a

"General Government" to a center of gravity "that must controul the centrifugal tendency of the States; which, without it, will continually fly out of their proper orbits and destroy the order and harmony of the political System." The reader will recall James Otis's comparison of government to "the planetary system" in his 1764 essay on the "Rights of the Colonists. . . ."

Also of particular interest are the remarks of James Wilson on the same day, recalling to the delegates how, in the first flush of revolutionary enthusiasm, they had declared twelve years earlier "that Virginia is no more, that Massachusetts is no [more], that Pennsylvania is no more &c. We are now one nation of brethren. We must bury all local interests & distinctions." How far the states had moved in the direction of faction and particularism from that noble vision! The convention, Wilson argued, was an effort to recapture that earlier vision of a truly united people.

Saturday June 9. . . . In Committee of the Whole

Mr. Patterson moves that the Committee resume the clause relating to the rule of suffrage in the National Legislature.

Mr. Brearly seconds him. He was sorry he said that any question on this point was brought into view. It had been much agitated in Congress at the time of forming the Confederation, and was then rightly settled by allowing to each sovereign State an equal vote. Otherwise the smaller States must have been destroyed instead of being saved. The substitution of a ratio, he admitted carried fairness on the face of it; but on a deeper examination was unfair and unjust. Judging of the disparity of the States by the quota of Congress Virginia would have 16 votes, and Georgia but one. A like proportion to the others will make the whole number ninety. There will be 3 large states, and 10 small ones. The large States by which he meant Massachusetts, Pennsylvania, and Virginia will carry every thing before them. It had been admitted, and was known to him from facts within N. Jersey that where large & small counties were united into a district for electing representatives for the district, the large counties always carried their point, and Consequently that the large States would do so. Virginia with her sixteen votes will be a solid column indeed, a formidable phalanx. While Georgia with her Solitary vote, and the other little States will be obliged to throw themselves constantly into the scale of some large one, in order to have any weight at all. He had come to the convention with a view of being as useful as he could in giving energy and stability to the federal Government. When the proposition for destroying the equality of votes came forward, he was astonished, he was alarmed. Is it fair then it will be asked that Georgia should have an equal vote with Virginia? He would not say it was. What remedy then? One only, that a map of the U.S. be spread out, that all the existing boundaries be erased, and that a new partition of the whole be made into 13 equal parts.

Mr. Patterson considered the proposition for a proportional representation as striking at the existence of the lesser States. He would premise however to an investigation of this question some remarks on the nature, structure, and powers of the Convention. The Convention he said was formed in pursuance of an Act of Congress that this act was recited in several of the Commissions, particularly that of Massachusetts which he required to be read: that the amendment of the confederacy was the object of all the laws and commissions on the subject; that the articles of the Confederation were therefore the proper basis of all the proceedings of the Convention. We ought to keep within its limits, or we should be charged by our Constituents with usurpation, that the people of America were sharp-sighted and not to be deceived. But the Commissions under which we acted were not only the measure of our power, they denoted also the sentiments of the States on the subject of our deliberation. The idea of a national Government as contradistinguished from a federal one, never entered into the mind of any of them, and to the public mind we must accommodate ourselves. We have no power to go beyond the federal scheme, and if we had the people are not ripe for any other. We must follow the people; the people will not follow us. —The *proposition* could not be maintained whether considered in reference to us as a nation, or as a confederacy. A confederacy supposes sovereignty in the members composing it & sovereignty supposes equality. If we are to be considered as a nation, all State distinctions must be abolished, the whole must be thrown into hotchpot, and when an equal division is made, then there may be fairly an equality of representation. . . . Give the large States an influence in proportion to their magnitude, and what will be the consequence? Their ambition will be proportionally increased, and the small States will have every thing to fear. It was once proposed by Galloway & some others that America should be represented in the British Parliament and then be bound by its laws. America could not have been entitled to more than 1/3 of the number of Representatives which would fall to the share of G.B. Would American rights & interests have been safe under an authority thus constituted? . . . He was attached strongly to the plan of the existing confederacy, in which the people choose their Legislative representatives; and the Legislatures their federal representatives. No other amendments were wanting than to mark the orbits of the States with due precision, and provide for the use of coercion, which was the great point. He alluded to the hint thrown out heretofore by Mr. Wilson of the necessity to which the large States might be reduced of confederating among themselves, by a refusal of the others to concur. Let them unite if they please, but let them remember that they have no authority to compel the others to unite. N. Jersey will never confederate on the plan before the Committee. She would be swallowed up. He had rather submit to a monarch, to a despot, than to such a fate. He would not only oppose the plan here but on his return home do every thing in his power to defeat it there.

Mr. Wilson hoped if the Confederacy should be dissolved, that a *majority*, that a *minority* of the States would unite for their safety. He entered elaborately into the defence of a proportional representation, stating for his first position that as all authority was derived from the people, equal numbers of people ought to have an equal number of representatives, and different numbers of people different numbers of representatives. This principle had been improperly violated in the Confederation, owing to the urgent circumstances of the time. . . . Are not the Citizens of Pennsylvania equal to those of N. Jersey? does it require 150 of the former to balance 50 of the latter? Representatives of different districts ought clearly to hold the same proportion to each other, as their respective Constituents hold to each other. If the small States will not confederate on this plan, Pennsylvania & he presumed some other States, would not confederate on any other. We have been told that each State being sovereign, all are equal. So each man is naturally a sovereign over himself, and all men are therefore naturally equal. Can he retain this equality when he becomes a member of Civil Government? He can not. As little can a Sovereign State, when it becomes a member of a federal Government. If N.J. will not part with her Sovereignty it is in vain to talk of Government. A new partition of the States is desireable, but evidently and totally impracticable. . . .

The Committee rose & the House

Adjourned

Monday. June 11. . . . In Committee of the Whole

The clause concerning the rule of suffrage in the national Legislature postponed on Saturday was resumed.

Mr. Sharman proposed that the proportion of suffrage in the first branch should be according to the respective numbers of free inhabitants; and that in the second branch or Senate, each State should have one vote and no more. He said as the States would remain possessed of certain individual rights, each State ought to be able to protect itself: otherwise a few large States will rule the rest. The House of Lords in England he observed had certain particular rights under the Constitution, and hence they have an equal vote with the House of Commons that they may be able to defend their rights.

Mr. Rutlidge proposed that the proportion of suffrage in the first branch should be according to the quotas of contribution. The justice of this rule he said could not be contested. Mr. Butler urged the same idea: adding that money was power; and that the States ought to have weight in the Government in proportion to their wealth.

Mr. King & Mr. Wilson, in order to bring the question to a point moved "that the right of suffrage in the first branch of the national Legislature ought not to be according [to] the rule established in the articles of Confederation, but according to some equitable ratio of representation." The clause so far as it related to suffrage in the first branch was postponed in order to consider this motion.

Mr. Dickenson contended for the *actual* contributions of the States as the rule of their representation & suffrage in the first branch. By thus connecting the interest of the States with their duty, the latter would be sure to be performed.

Mr. King remarked that it was uncertain what mode might be used in levying a national revenue; but that it was probable, imposts would be one source of it. If the *actual* contributions were to be the rule the non-importing States, as Connecticut and N. Jersey, would be in a bad situation indeed. It might so happen that they would have no representation. This situation of particular States had been always one powerful argument in favor of the 5 Per Cent impost. . . .

On the question for agreeing to Mr. King's and Mr. Wilson's motion it passed in the affirmative. . . .

It was then moved by Mr. Rutlidge, seconded by Mr. Butler to add to the words "equitable ratio of representation" at the end of the motion just agreed to, the words "according to the quotas of contribution." On motion of Mr. Wilson, seconded by Mr. C. Pinckney, this was postponed; in order to add, after, after the words "equitable ratio of representation" the words following "in proportion to the whole number of white & other free Citizens & inhabitants of every age, sex, & condition including those bound to servitude for a term of years and three-fifths of all other persons not comprehended in the foregoing description, except Indians not paying taxes, in each State," this being the rule in the Act of Congress agreed to by eleven States, for apportioning quotas of revenue on the States, and requiring a Census only every 5–7, or 10 years.

Mr. Gerry thought property not the rule of representation. Why then should the blacks, who were property in the South, be in the rule of representation more than the Cattle & horses of the North. [Passed 9 to 2.] . . .

Mr. Sharman moved that a question be taken whether each State shall have one vote in the second branch. Every thing he said depended on this. The smaller States would never agree to the plan on any other principle than an equality of suffrage in this branch. Mr. Elsworth seconded the motion. On the question for allowing each State one vote in the second branch. [Lost 6 to 5.] . . .

Mr. Wilson & Mr. Hamilton moved that the right of suffrage in the second branch ought to be according to the same rule as in the first branch. On this question for making the ratio of representation the same in the second as in the first branch it passed in the affirmative. . . .

Resol: 11, for guarantying Republican Government & territory to each State being considered: the words "or partition" were, on motion of Mr. Madison, added, after the words "voluntary junction": [passed 7 to 4]. . . .

Mr. Read disliked the idea of guarantying territory. It abetted the idea of distinct States which would be a perpetual source of discord. There can be no cure for this evil but in doing away States altogether and uniting them all into one great Society.

Alterations having been made in the Resolution, making it read "that a republican Constitution & its existing laws ought to be guaranteed to each State by the U. States" the whole was agreed to nem. con.

Resolution 13, for amending the national Constitution hereafter without consent of [the] National Legislature being considered, several members did not see the necessity of the Resolution at all, nor the propriety of making the consent of the National Legislature unnecessary.

Col. Mason urged the necessity of such a provision. The plan now to be formed will certainly be defective, as the Confederation has been found on trial to be. Amendments therefore will be necessary, and it will be better to provide for them, in an easy, regular and Constitutional way than to trust to chance and violence. It would be improper to require the consent of the National Legislature, because they may abuse their power, and refuse their consent on that very account. The opportunity for such an abuse, may be the fault of the Constitution calling for amendment.

Mr. Randolph enforced these arguments.

The words, "without requiring the consent of the National Legislature"

were postponed. The other provision in the clause passed nem. con. . . . .
Committee rose & House

Adjourned

Tuesday June 12. In Committee of Whole

The Question taken on Resolution 15, to wit, referring the new system to the people of the States for ratification it passed in the affirmative. . . .

Mr. Sharman & Mr. Elseworth moved to fill the blank left in the 4th Resolution for the periods of electing the members of the first branch with the words, "every year." Mr. Sharman observing that he did it in order to bring on some question.

Mr. Rutlidge proposed "every two years."

Mr. Jennifer proposed "every three years," observing that the too great frequency of elections rendered the people indifferent to them, and made the best men unwilling to engage in so precarious a service.

Mr. Madison seconded the motion for three years. Instability is one of the great vices of our republics, to be remedied. Three years will be necessary, in a Government so extensive, for members to form any knowledge of the various interests of the States to which they do not belong, and of which they can know but little from the situation and affairs of their own. One year will be almost consumed in preparing for and travelling to & from the seat of national business.

Mr. Gerry. The people of New England will never give up the point of annual elections, they know of the transition made in England from triennial to septennial elections, and will consider such an innovation here as the prelude to a like usurpation. He considered annual elections as the only defence of the people against tyranny. He was as much against a triennial House as against a hereditary Executive.

Mr. Madison, observed that if the opinions of the people were to be our guide, it would be difficult to say what course we ought to take. No member of the Convention could say what the opinions of his Constituents were at this time; much less could he say what they would think if possessed of the information & lights possessed by the members here; & still less what would be their way of thinking 6 or 12 months hence. We ought to consider what was right & necessary in itself for the attainment of a proper Government. A plan adjusted to this idea will recommend itself—The respectability of this convention will give weight to their recommendation of it. Experience will be constantly urging the adoption of it, and all the most enlightened & respectable citizens will be its advocates. Should we fall short of the necessary & proper point, this influential class of Citizens will be turned against the plan, and little support in opposition to them can be gained to it from the unreflecting multitude.

Mr. Gerry repeated his opinion that it was necessary to consider what the people would approve. This had been the policy of all Legislators. If the reasoning of Mr. Madison were just, and we supposed a limited Monarchy the best form in itself, we ought to recommend it, tho' the genius of the people was decidedly adverse to it, and having no hereditary distinctions among us, we were destitute of the essential materials for such an innovation.

On the question for triennial election of the first branch [Passed]. . . .

Mr. Spaight moved to fill the blank for the duration of the appointment to the second branch of the National Legislature with the words "7 years."

Mr. Sherman, thought 7 years too long. He grounded his opposition he said on the principle that if they did their duty well, they would be reelected. And if they acted amiss, an earlier opportunity should be allowed for getting rid of them. He preferred 5 years which would be between the terms of [the] branch & of the executive.

Mr. Pierce proposed 3 years. 7 years would raise an alarm. Great mischiefs had arisen in England from their septennial act which was reprobated by most of their patriotic Statesmen.

Mr. Randolph was for the term of 7 years. The democratic licentiousness of the State Legislatures proved the necessity of a firm Senate. The object of this second branch is to controul the democratic branch of the National Legislature. If it be not a firm body, the other branch being more numerous, and coming immediately from the people, will overwhelm it. The Senate of Maryland constituted on like principles had been scarcely able to stem the popular torrent. No mischief can be apprehended, as the concurrence of the other branch, and in some measure, of the Executive, will in all cases be necessary. A firmness & independence may be the more necessary also in this branch, as it ought to guard the Constitution against encroachments of the Executive who will be apt to form combinations with the demagogues of the popular branch.

Mr. Madison, considered 7 years as a term by no means too long. What we wished was to give to the Government that stability which was every where called for, and which the Enemies of the Republican form alledged to be inconsistent with its nature. He was not afraid of giving too much stability by the term of Seven years. His fear was that the popular branch would still be too great an overmatch for it. It was to be much lamented that we had so little direct experience to guide us. The Constitution of Maryland was the only one that bore any analogy to this part of the plan. In no instance had the Senate of Maryland created just suspicions of danger from it. In some instances perhaps it may have erred by yielding to the House of Delegates. In every instance of their opposition to the measures of the H. of D. they had had with them the suffrages of the most enlightened and impartial people of the other States as well as of their own. In the States where the Senates were chosen in the same manner as the other branches, of the Legislature, and held their seats for 4 years, the institution was found to be no check whatever against the instabilities of the other branches. He conceived it to be of great importance that a stable & firm Government organized in the republican form should be held out to the people. If this be not done, and the people be left to judge of this species of Government by the operations of the defective systems under which they now live, it is much to be feared the time is not distant when, in universal disgust, they will renounce the blessing which they have purchased at so dear a rate, and be ready for any change that may be proposed to them.

On the question for "seven years" as the term for the second branch [passed 8 to 1, 2 states divided.] . . .

Mr. Butler & Mr. Rutlidge proposed that the members of the second branch should be entitled to no salary or compensation for their services. On the question, [lost 7 to 3]. . . .

Wednesday June 13. In Committee of the Whole

REPORT OF THE COMMITTEE OF WHOLE ON MR. RANDOLPH'S PROPOSITIONS

1. Resolved that it is the opinion of this Committee that a National Government ought to be established, consisting of a Supreme Legislative, Executive & Judiciary.

2. Resolved that the National Legislature ought to consist of two branches.

3. Resolved that the members of the first branch of the National Legislature ought to be elected by the people of the several States for the term of three years, to receive fixed Stipends by which they may be compensated for the devotion of their time to public service, to be paid out of the National Treasury: to be ineligible to any office established by a particular State, or under the authority of the U. States, (except those peculiarly belonging to the functions of the first branch), during the term of service, and under the national Government for the space of one year after its expiration.

4. Resolved that the members of the second branch of the National Legislature ought to be chosen by the individual Legislatures, to be of the age of 30 years at least, to hold their offices for a term sufficient to

ensure their independency, namely, seven years, to receive fixed stipends by which they may be compensated for the devotion of their time to public service to be paid out of the National Treasury; to be ineligible to any office established by a particular State, or under the authority of the U. States, (except those peculiarly belonging to the functions of the second branch) during the term of service, and under the National Government for the space of one year after its expiration.

5. Resolved that each branch ought to possess the right of originating Acts.

6. Resolved that the National Legislature ought to be empowered to enjoy the Legislative rights vested in Congress by the Confederation, and moreover to legislate in all cases to which the separate States are incompetent; or in which the harmony of the U.S. may be interrupted by the exercise of individual legislation; to negative all laws passed by the several States contravening in the opinion of the National Legislature the articles of Union, or any treaties subsisting under the authority of the Union.

7. Resolved that the rights of suffrage in the first branch of the National Legislature, ought not to be according to the rule established in the articles of confederation but according to some equitable ratio of representation, namely, in proportion to the whole number of white & other free citizens & inhabitants, of every age, sex, and condition, including those bound to servitude for a term of years, & three-fifths of all other persons, not comprehended in the foregoing description, except Indians not paying taxes in each State:

8. Resolved that the right of suffrage in the second branch of the National Legislature ought to be according to the rule established for the first.

9. Resolved that a National Executive be instituted to consist of a single person, to be chosen by the National Legislature for the term of seven years, with power to carry into execution the national laws, to appoint to offices in cases not otherwise provided for—to be ineligible a second time, & to be removeable on impeachment and conviction of malpractices or neglect of duty—to receive a fixed stipend by which he may be compensated for the devotion of his time to public service to be paid out of the national Treasury.

10. Resolved that the National Executive shall have a right to negative any Legislative Act, which shall not be afterwards passed unless by two-thirds of each branch of the National Legislature.

11. Resolved that a National Judiciary be established, to consist of one supreme tribunal, the Judges of which [shall] be appointed by the second branch of the National Legislature, to hold their offices during

good behaviour, & to receive punctually at stated times a fixed compensation for their services, in which no increase or diminution shall be made, so as to affect the persons actually in office at the time of such increase or diminution.

12. Resolved that the National Legislature be empowered to appoint inferior Tribunals.

13. Resolved that the jurisdiction of the National Judiciary shall extend to all cases which respect the collection of the National revenue, impeachments of any National Officers, and questions which involve the national peace & harmony.

14. Resolved that provision ought to be made for the admission of States lawfully arising within the limits of the U. States, whether from a voluntary junction of Government & territory or otherwise, with the consent of a number of voices in the National Legislature less than the whole.

15. Resolved that provision ought to be made for the continuance of Congress and their authorities and privileges until a given day after the reform of the articles of Union shall be adopted and for the completion of all their engagements.

16. Resolved that a Republican Constitution & its existing laws ought to be guaranteed to each State by the U. States.

17. Resolved that provision ought to be made for the amendment of the Articles of Union whensoever it shall seem necessary.

18. Resolved that the Legislative, Executive & Judiciary powers within the several States ought to be bound by oath to support the articles of Union.

19. Resolved that the amendments which shall be offered to the confederation by the Convention ought at a proper time or times after the approbation of Congress to be submitted to an Assembly or Assemblies recommended by the several Legislatures to be expressly chosen by the people to consider and decide thereon.

At the end of session on June 13, when Nathaniel Gorham, one of the Massachusetts delegates, brought in a report on the specific resolutions or articles that the convention had agreed upon, based on the Virginia Plan, it seemed that the principal timbers of the new Constitution had been put firmly in place. But things were not to be so simple. There had been, on the issue of representation, a series of disturbingly close votes, six states to five. Moreover, voting almost invariably with the large states were the Southern states, the Carolinas and Georgia, all "small states" in terms of wealth and population.

Thus the large states—Massachusetts, Pennsylvania, and Virginia—
were only able to maintain their majority by virtue of the fact that
the Southern states voted as a bloc with Virginia. That was, beyond
question, a shaky foundation for the new Constitution. William Paterson of New Jersey underlined the point when he reminded the
delegates that their commission was to strengthen the Articles of
Confederation not draft a new constitution and threatened to lead
a small-state secession from Philadelphia unless the small states got
equal representation.

Roger Sherman had suggested the solution of proportional representation in the lower house, equal representation for the states in
the upper house, or senate, but this had been brushed aside by the
large-state delegates, confident that they had a majority of the votes.

Now, on the 14th of June, Paterson asked for an early adjournment
to allow New Jersey and several other "deputations" to review the
Gorham report and to prepare a "purely federal" scheme in response
to it. When the "New Jersey Plan" was presented to the delegates
the next day its initial resolution began ominously (for the advocates
of the Virginia Plan at least).

The delegates, being human, squabbled, repeated themselves, went
back again over ground trod many times before, lost their tempers.
Madison and Wilson as the spokesmen for the large-state faction
were especially tenacious. One has the feeling that weeks of debate
could have been avoided if these two had been willing to compromise.
For a time it seemed as though the remarkable accomplishments of
the first two weeks would be lost in the increasingly acrimonious debate over equal versus proportional representation. The weakness in
the position of the large-state men was revealed by their inability
to deal with the issue of how the upper house, i.e., the body which
theoretically should be the smaller, more deliberative body, was to
be chosen in such a way as to represent the propertied interests *and*
be substantially smaller in numbers than the lower house.

Thursday June 14. In Convention

Mr. Patterson, observed to the Convention that it was the wish of
several deputations, particularly that of N. Jersey, that further time
might be allowed them to contemplate the plan reported from the Committee of the Whole, and to digest one purely federal, and contradistinguished from the reported plan. He said they hoped to have such an

one ready by tomorrow to be laid before the Convention: And the Convention adjourned that leisure might be given for the purpose.

Friday, June 15, 1787

Mr. Patterson, laid before the Convention the plan which he said several of the deputations wished to be substituted in place of that proposed by Mr. Randolph. After some little discussion of the most proper mode of giving it a fair deliberation it was agreed that it should be referred to a Committee of the whole, and that in order to place the two plans in due comparison, the other should be recommitted. At the earnest desire of Mr. Lansing & some other gentlemen, it was also agreed that the Convention should not go into Committee of the whole on the subject till tomorrow, by which delay the friends of the plan proposed by Mr. Patterson would be better prepared to explain & support it, and all would have an opportunity of taking copies.

The propositions from N. Jersey moved by Mr. Patterson were in the words following.

1. Resolved that the articles of Confederation ought to be so revised, corrected & enlarged, as to render the federal Constitution adequate to the exigencies of Government, & the preservation of the Union.

2. Resolved that in addition to the powers vested in the U. States in Congress, by the present existing articles of Confederation, they be authorized to pass acts for raising a revenue, by levying a duty or duties on all goods or merchandizes of foreign growth or manufacture, imported into any part of the U. States, by Stamps on paper, vellum or parchment, and by a postage on all letters or packages passing through the general post-office, to be applied to such federal purposes as they shall deem proper & expedient; to make rules & regulations for the collection thereof; and the same from time to time, to alter & amend in such manner as they shall think proper: to pass Acts for the regulation of trade & commerce as well with foreign nations as with each other: provided that all punishments, fines, forfeitures & penalties to be incurred for contravening such acts rules and regulations shall be adjudged by the Common law Judiciaries of the State in which any offence contrary to the true intent & meaning of such Acts, rules & regulations shall have been committed or perpetrated, with liberty of commencing in the first instance all suits & prosecutions for that purpose in the superior common law Judiciary in such State, subject nevertheless, for the correction of all errors, both in law & fact in rendering Judgment, to an appeal to the Judiciary of the U. States.

3. Resolved that whenever requisitions shall be necessary, instead of the rule for making requisitions mentioned in the articles of Confedera-

tion, the United States in Congress be authorized to make such requisitions in proportion to the whole number of white & other free citizens & inhabitants of every age sex and condition including those bound to servitude for a term of years & three-fifths of all other persons not comprehended in the foregoing description, except Indians not paying taxes; that if such requisitions be not complied with, in the time specified therein, to direct the collection thereof in the non-complying States & for that purpose to devise and pass acts directing & authorizing the same; provided that none of the powers hereby vested in the U. States in Congress shall be exercised without the consent of at least   States, and in that proportion if the number of Confederated States should hereafter be increased or diminished.

4. Resolved that the U. States in Congress be authorized to elect a federal Executive to consist of   persons, to continue in office for the term of   years, to receive punctually at stated times a fixed compensation for their services, in which no increase or diminution shall be made so as to affect the persons composing the Executive at the time of such increase or diminution, to be paid out of the federal treasury; to be incapable of holding any other office or appointment during their time of service and for   years thereafter; to be ineligible a second time, & removeable by Congress on application by a majority of the Executives of the several States; that the Executives besides their general authority to execute the federal acts ought to appoint all federal officers not otherwise provided for, & to direct all military operations; provided that none of the persons composing the federal Executive shall on any occasion take command of any troops, so as personally to conduct any [military] enterprise as General or in other capacity.

5. Resolved that a federal Judiciary be established to consist of a supreme Tribunal the Judges of which to be appointed by the Executive, & to hold their offices during good behaviour, to receive punctually at stated times a fixed compensation for their services in which no increase or diminution shall be made, so as to affect the persons actually in office at the time of such increase or diminution; that the Judiciary so established shall have authority to hear & determine in the first instance on all impeachments of federal officers, & by way of appeal in the dernier resort in all cases touching the rights of Ambassadors, in all cases of captures from an enemy, in all cases of piracies & felonies on the high Seas, in all cases in which foreigners may be interested, in the construction of any treaty or treaties, or which may arise on any of the Acts for regulation of trade, or the collection of the federal Revenue: that none of the Judiciary shall during the time they remain in office be capable of

receiving or holding any other office or appointment during their time of service, or for   thereafter.

6. Resolved that all Acts of the U. States in Congress made by virtue & in pursuance of the powers hereby & by the articles of Confederation vested in them, and all Treaties made & ratified under the authority of the U. States shall be the supreme law of the respective States so far forth as those Acts or Treaties shall relate to the said States or their Citizens, and that the Judiciary of the several States shall be bound thereby in their decisions, any thing in the respective laws of the Individual States to the contrary notwithstanding; and that if any State, or any body of men in any State shall oppose or prevent the carrying into execution such acts or treaties, the federal Executive shall be authorized to call forth the power of the Confederated States, or so much thereof as may be necessary to enforce and compel an obedience to such Acts, or an observance of such Treaties.

7. Resolved that provision be made for the admission of new States into the Union.

8. Resolved the rule for naturalization ought to be the same in every State.

9. Resolved that a Citizen of one State committing an offense in another State of the Union, shall be deemed guilty of the same offense as if it had been committed by a Citizen of the State in which the offense was committed.

Adjourned

Saturday June 16. In Committee of the Whole on Resolutions Proposed by Mr. Patterson & Mr. Randolph

Mr. Lansing called for the reading of the first resolution of each plan, which he considered as involving principles directly in contrast; that of Mr. Patterson says he sustains the sovereignty of the respective States, that of Mr. Randolph destroys it: the latter requires a negative on all the laws of the particular States; the former, only certain general powers for the general good. The plan of Mr. Randolph in short absorbs all power except what may be exercised in the little local matters of the States which are not objects worthy of the supreme cognizance. He grounded his preference of Mr. Patterson's plan, chiefly on two objections against that of Mr. Randolph. 1. want of power in the Convention to discuss & propose it. 2. the improbability of its being adopted. 1. He was decidedly of opinion that the power of the Convention was restrained to amendments of a federal nature, and having for their basis the Confederacy in being. The Act of Congress The tenor of the Acts of the States, the Commissions produced by the several deputations all proved this. And this limitation of the power to an amendment of the Confederacy, marked the opinion of the States, that it was unnecessary & improper to go farther. He was sure that this was the case with his State. New York would never have concurred in sending deputies to the convention, if she had supposed the deliberations were to turn on a consolidation of the States, and a National Government.

2. Was it probable that the States would adopt & ratify a scheme, which they had never authorized us to propose? and which so far exceeded what they regarded as sufficient? We see by their several Acts particularly in relation to the plan of revenue proposed by Congress in 1783, not authorized by the Articles of Confederation, what were the ideas they then entertained. Can so great a change be supposed to have already taken place. To rely on any change which is hereafter to take place in the sentiments of the people would be trusting to too great an uncertainty. We know only what their present sentiments are. And it is in vain to propose what will not accord with these. The States will never feel a sufficient confidence in a general Government to give it a negative on their laws. The Scheme is itself totally novel. There is no parallel to it to be found. The authority of Congress is familiar to the people, and an augmentation of the powers of Congress will be readily approved by them.

Mr. Patterson, said as he had on a former occasion given his sentiments on the plan proposed by Mr. Randolph he would now, avoiding repetition as much as possible, give his reasons in favor of that proposed by himself. He preferred it because it accorded 1. with the powers of the Convention, 2. with the sentiments of the people. If the confederacy was radically wrong, let us return to our States, and obtain larger powers, not assume them of ourselves. I came here not to speak my own sentiments, but the sentiments of those who sent me. Our object is not such a Government as may be best in itself, but such a one as our Constituents have authorized us to prepare, and as they will approve. If we argue the matter on the supposition that no Confederacy at present exists, it can not be denied that all the States stand on the footing of equal sovereignty. All therefore must concur before any can be bound. If a proportional representation be right, why do we not vote so here? If we argue on the fact that a federal compact actually exists, and consult the articles of it we still find an equal Sovereignty to be the basis of it. He reads the 5th art: of Confederation giving each State a vote—& the 13th declaring that no alteration shall be made without unanimous consent. This is the nature of all treaties. What is unanimously done, must be unanimously undone. It was observed [by Mr. Wilson] that the larger States gave up the point, not because it was right, but because the circumstances of the moment urged the concession. Be it so. Are they for that reason at liberty to take it back. Can the donor resume his gift without the consent of the donee. This doctrine may be convenient, but it is a doctrine that will sacrifice the lesser States. The large States acceded readily to the confederacy. It was the small ones that came in reluctantly and slowly. N. Jersey & Maryland were the two last, the former objecting to the want of power in Congress over trade: both of them to the want of power to appropriate the vacant territory to the benefit of the whole. —If the sovereignty of the States is to be maintained, the Representatives must be drawn immediately from the States, not from the people: and we have no power to vary the idea of equal sovereignty. The only expedient that will cure the difficulty, is that of throwing the States into Hotchpot. To say that this is impracticable, will not make it so. Let it be tried, and we shall see whether the Citizens of Massachusetts, Pennsylvania, & Virginia accede to it. It will be objected that Coercion will be impracticable. But will it be more so in one plan than the other? Its efficacy will depend on the quantum of power collected, not on its being drawn from the States, or from the individuals; and according to his plan it may be exerted on individuals as well as according [to] that of Mr. Randolph. A distinct executive & Judiciary also were equally provided by this plan. It is urged that two branches in the Legislature are necessary. Why? for the purpose of a check. But the reason of the precaution is not applicable to this case. Within a particular State, where party heats prevail, such a check may be necessary. In such a body as Congress it is less necessary, and besides, the delegations of the different States are checks on each other. Do the people at large complain of Congress? No, what they wish is that Congress may have more power. If the power now proposed be not enough, the people hereafter will make additions to it. With proper powers Congress will act with more energy and wisdom than the proposed National Legislature; being fewer in number, and more secreted & refined by the mode of election. The plan of Mr. Randolph will also be enormously expensive. Allowing Georgia & Delaware two representatives each in the popular branch the aggregate number of that branch will be 180. Add to it half as many for the other branch and you have 270, members coming once at least a year from the most distant as well as the most central parts of the republic. In the present deranged state of our finances can so expensive a system be seriously thought of? By enlarging the powers of Congress the greatest part of this expense will be saved, and all purposes will be answered. At least a trial ought to be made.

Mr. Wilson entered into a contrast of the principal points of the two plans so far he said as there had been time to examine the one last proposed. These points were 1. in the Virginia plan there are 2 & in some degree 3 branches in the Legislature: in the plan from N.J. there is to be a *single* legislature only—2. Representation of the people at large is the basis of the one:—the State Legislatures, the pillars of the other— 3. proportional representation prevails in one:—equality of suffrage in the other—4. A single Executive Magistrate is at the head of the one:— a plurality is held out in the other.—5. in the one the majority of the people of the U.S. must prevail:—in the other a minority may prevail. 6. the National Legislature is to make laws in all cases to which the separate States are incompetent &–:—in place of this Congress are to have additional power in a few cases only—7. A negative on the laws of the States:—in place of this coercion to be substituted—8. The Executive to be removeable on impeachment & conviction;—in one plan: in the other to be removeable at the instance of a majority of the Executives of the States—9. Revision of the laws provided for in one:—no such check in the other—10. inferior national tribunals in one:—none such in the other. 11. In the one jurisdiction of National tribunals to extend &c—; an appellate jurisdiction only allowed in the other. 12. Here the jurisdiction is to extend to all cases affecting the National peace & harmony: there, a few cases only are marked out. 13. finally the ratification is in this to be by the people themselves:—in that by the legislative authorities according to the 13 art: of Confederation.

With regard to the *power of the Convention,* he conceived himself authorized to *conclude nothing,* but to be at liberty to *propose any thing.* In this particular he felt himself perfectly indifferent to the two plans.

With *regard to the sentiments of the people,* he conceived it difficult to know precisely what they are. Those of the particular circle in which one moved, were commonly mistaken for the general voice. He could not persuade himself that the State Governments & Sovereignties were so much the idols of the people, nor a National Government so obnoxious to them, as some supposed. Why should a National Government be unpopular? Has it less dignity? will each Citizen enjoy under it less liberty or protection? Will a Citizen of *Delaware* be degraded by becoming a Citizen of the *United States?* Where do the people look at present for relief from the evils of which they complain? Is it from an internal reform of their Governments? no, Sir. It is from the National Councils that relief is expected. For these reasons he did not fear, that the people would not follow us into a national Government and it will be a further recommendation of Mr. Randolph's plan that it is to be submitted to *them,* and not to the *Legislatures,* for ratification.

Proceeding now to the first point on which he had contrasted the two plans, he observed that anxious as he was for some augmentation of the federal powers, it would be with extreme reluctance indeed that he could ever consent to give powers to Congress. He had two reasons either of which was sufficient. 1. Congress as a Legislative body does not stand on the people. 2. it is a *single* body. 1. He would not repeat the remarks he had formerly made on the principles of Representation. He would only say that an inequality in it, has ever been a poison contaminating every branch of Government. In G. Britain where this poison has had a full operation, the security of private rights is owing entirely to the purity of Her tribunals of Justice, the Judges of which are neither appointed nor paid, by a venal Parliament. The political liberty of that Nation, owing to the inequality of representation is at the mercy of its rulers. He means not to insinuate that there is any parallel between the situation of that Country & ours at present. But it is a lesson we ought not to disregard, that the smallest bodies in G.B. are notoriously the most corrupt. Every other source of influence must also be stronger in small than large bodies of men. When Lord Chesterfield had told us that one of the Dutch provinces had been seduced into the views of France, he need not have added, that it was not Holland, but one of the *smallest* of them. There are facts among ourselves which are known to all. Passing over others, he will only remark that the *Impost*, so anxiously wished for by the public was defeated not by any of the *larger* States in the Union. 2. *Congress is a single Legislature.* Despotism comes on Mankind in different Shapes, sometimes in an Executive, sometimes in a Military, one. Is there no danger of a Legislative despotism? Theory & practice both proclaim it. If the Legislative authority be not restrained, there can be neither liberty nor stability; and it can only be restrained by dividing it within itself, into distinct and independent branches. In a single House there is no check, but the inadequate one, of the virtue & good sense of those who compose it.

On another great point, the contrast was equally favorable to the plan reported by the Committee of the whole. It vested the Executive powers in a single Magistrate. The plan of N. Jersey, vested them in a plurality. In order to controul the Legislative authority, you must divide it. In order to controul the Executive you must unite it. One man will be more responsible than three. Three will contend among themselves till one becomes the master of his colleagues. In the triumvirates of Rome first Caesar, then Augustus, are witnesses of this truth. The Kings of Sparta, & the Consuls of Rome prove also the factious consequences of dividing the Executive Magistracy. Having already taken up so much time he would not, he said, proceed to any of the other points. Those on which he had dwelt, are sufficient of themselves: and on a decision of them, the fate of the others will depend.

Mr. Pinkney, the whole comes to this, as he conceived. Give N. Jersey an equal vote, and she will dismiss her scruples, and concur in the National system. He thought the Convention authorized to go any length in recommending, which they found necessary to remedy the evils which produced this Convention.

Mr. Elseworth proposed as a more distinctive form of collecting the mind of the Committee on the subject, "that the Legislative power of the U.S. should remain in Congress." This was not seconded though it seemed better calculated for the purpose than the first proposition of Mr. Patterson in place of which Mr. Elseworth wished to substitute it.

Mr. Randolph, was not scrupulous on the point of power. When the salvation of the Republic was at stake, it would be treason to our trust, not to propose what we found necessary. He painted in strong colours, the imbecility of the existing Confederacy, & the danger of delaying a substantial reform. In answer to the objection drawn from the sense of our Constituents as denoted by their acts relating to the Convention and the objects of their deliberation, he observed that as each State acted separately in the case, it would have been indecent for it to have charged the existing Constitution with all the vices which it might have perceived in it. The first State that set on foot this experiment would not have been justified in going so far, ignorant as it was of the opinion of others, and sensible as it must have been of the uncertainty of a successful issue to the experiment. There are certainly seasons of a peculiar nature where the ordinary cautions must be dispensed with; and this is certainly one of them. He would not as far as depended on him leave any thing that seemed necessary, undone. The present moment is favorable, and is probably the last that will offer.

The true question is whether we shall adhere to the federal plan, or introduce the national plan. The insufficiency of the former has been fully displayed by the trial already made. There are but two modes, by which the end of a General Government can be attained: the first is by coercion as proposed by Mr. Patterson's plan; 2. by real legislation as proposed by the other plan. Coercion he pronounced to be *impracticable, expensive, cruel to individuals.* It tended also to habituate the instruments of it to shed the blood & riot in the spoils of their fellow Citizens, and consequently trained them up for the service of ambition. We must resort therefor to a National *Legislation over individuals,* for which Congress are unfit. To vest such power in them, would be blending the Legislative with the Executive, contrary to the recorded maxim on this subject: If the Union of these powers heretofore in Congress has been safe, it has been owing to the general impotency of that body. Congress are moreover not elected by the people, but by the Legislatures who retain even a power of recall. They have therefore no will of their own, they are a mere diplomatic body, and are always obsequious to the views of the States, who are always encroaching on the authority of the U. States. A provision for harmony among the States, as in trade, naturalization &c.— for crushing rebellion whenever it may rear its crest—and for certain other general benefits, must be made. The powers for these purposes, can never be given to a body, inadequate as Congress are in point of representation, elected in the mode in which they are, and possessing no more confidence than they do: for notwithstanding what has been said to the contrary, his own experience satisfied him that a rooted distrust of Congress pretty generally prevailed. A National Government alone, properly constituted, will answer the purpose; and he begged it to be considered that the present is the last moment for establishing one. After this select experiment, the people will yield to despair.

The Committee rose & the House

Adjourned

Monday June 18. In Committee of the Whole on the Propositions of Mr. Patterson & Mr. Randolph

. . . Mr. Hamilton, had been hitherto silent on the business before the Convention, partly from respect to others whose superior abilities, age & experience rendered him unwilling to bring forward ideas dissimilar to theirs, and partly from his delicate situation with respect to his own State, to whose sentiments as expressed by his Colleagues, he could by no means accede. The crisis however which now marked our affairs, was too serious to permit any scruples whatever to prevail over the duty imposed on every man to contribute his efforts for the public safety & happiness. He was obliged therefore to declare himself unfriendly to both plans. He was particularly opposed to that from N. Jersey, being fully convinced, that no amendment of the Confederation, leaving the States in possession of their Sovereignty could possibly answer the purpose. On the other hand he confessed he was much discouraged by the amazing extent of Country in expecting the desired blessings from any general sovereignty that could be substituted.—As to the powers of the Convention, he thought the doubts started on that subject had arisen from distinctions & reasonings too subtle. A *federal* Government he conceived to mean an association of independent Communities into one. Different Confederacies have different powers, and exercise them in different ways. In some instances the powers are exercised over collective bodies; in others over individuals, as in the German Diet—& among ourselves in cases of piracy. Great latitude therefore must be given to the signification of the term. The plan last proposed departs itself from the *federal* idea, as understood by some, since it is to operate eventually on individuals. He agreed moreover with the Honorable gentleman from Virginia [Mr. Randolph] that we owed it to our Country, to do on this emergency whatever we should deem essential to its happiness. The States sent us here to provide for the exigencies of the Union. To rely on & propose any plan not adequate to these exigencies, merely because it was not clearly within our powers, would be to sacrifice the means to the end. . . .

The great question is what provision shall we make for the happiness of our Country? He would first make a comparative examination of the two plans—prove that there were essential defects in both—and point out such changes as might render a *national one*, efficacious.—The great & essential principles necessary for the support of Government are 1. an active & constant interest in supporting it. This principle does not exist in the States in favor of the federal Government. They have evidently in a high degree, the esprit de corps. They constantly pursue internal interests adverse to those of the whole. They have their particular debts— their particular plans of finance &c. All these when opposed to, invariably prevail over the requisitions & plans of Congress. . . . 2. The love of power. Men love power. The same remarks are applicable to this principle. The States have constantly shewn a disposition rather to regain the powers delegated by them than to part with more, or to give effect to what they had parted with. The ambition of their demagogues is known to hate the controul of the General Government. . . . All the passions then we see, of avarice, ambition, interest, which govern most individuals, and all public bodies, fall into the current of the States, and do not flow in the stream of the General Government. The former therefore will generally be an overmatch for the General Government and render any confederacy, in its very nature precarious. Theory is in this case fully confirmed by experience. The Amphyctionic Council had it would seem ample powers for general purposes. It had in particular the power of fining and using force against delinquent members. What was the consequence. Their decrees were mere signals of war. . . . The German Confederacy affords another lesson. The authority of Charlemagne seemed to be as great as could be necessary. The great feudal chiefs however, exercising their local sovereignties, soon felt the spirit & found the means of, encroachments, which reduced the imperial authority to a nominal sovereignty. . . . Other examples instruct us in the same truth. The Swiss cantons have scarce any Union at all, and have been more than once at war with one another—How then are all these evils to be avoided? only by such a compleat sovereignty in the general Government as will turn all the strong principles & passions above mentioned on its side. Does the scheme of N. Jersey produce this effect? does it afford any substantial remedy whatever? On the contrary it labors under great defects, and the defect of some of its provisions will destroy the efficacy of others. It gives a direct revenue to Congress but this will not be sufficient. The balance can only be supplied by requisitions: which experience proves can not be relied on. If States are to deliberate on the mode, they will also deliberate on the object of the supplies, and will grant or not grant as they approve or disapprove of it. The delinquency of one will invite and countenance it in others. Quotas too must in the nature of things be so unequal as to produce the same evil. To what standard will you resort? . . . Take numbers of inhabitants for the rule and make like comparison of different countries, and you will find it to be equally unjust. The different degrees of industry and improvement in different Countries render the first objct a precarious measure of wealth. . . . Whence then is the national revenue to be drawn? from Commerce? even from exports which notwithstanding the common opinion are fit objects of moderate taxation, from excise, &c &c. These though not equal, are less uncqual than quotas. Another destructive ingredient in the plan, is that equality of suffrage which is so much desired by the small States. It is not in human nature that Virginia & the large States should consent to it, or if they did that they should long abide by it. It shocks too much the ideas of Justice, and every human feeling. Bad principles in a Government though slow arc sure in their operation and will gradually destroy it. . . . The members of Congress being chosen by the States & subject to recall, represent all the local prejudices. . . . It is against all the principles of a good Government to vest the requisite powers in such a body as Congress. Two Sovereignties can not co-exist within the same limits. Giving powers to Congress must eventuate in a bad Government or in no Government. The plan of N. Jersey therefore will not do. What then is to be done? Here he was embarrassed. The extent of the Country to be governed, discouraged him. The expence of a general Government was also formidable; unless there were such a diminution of expence on the side of the State Governments as the case would admit. If they were extinguished, he was persuaded that great economy might be obtained by substituting a general Government. He did not mean however to shock the public opinion by proposing such a measure. On the other hand he saw no *other* necessity for declining it. They are not necessary for any of the great purposes of commerce, revenue, or agriculture. Subordinate authorities he was aware would be necessary. There must be district tribunals: corporations for local purposes. But cui bono, the vast & expensive apparatus now appertaining to the States. . . . The moderate wages for the first branch would only be a bait to little demagogues. Three dollars or thereabouts he supposed would be the utmost. The Senate he feared from a similar cause, would be filled by certain undertakers who wish for particular offices under the Government. This view of the subject almost led him to despair that a Republican Government could be established over so great an extent. He was sensible at the same time that it would be unwise to propose one of any other form. In his private opinion he had no scruple in declaring, supported as he was by the opinions of so many of the wise & good, that the British Government was the best in the world: and that he doubted much whether any thing short of it would do in America. He hoped Gentlemen of different opinions would bear with him in this, and begged them to recollect the change of opinion on this subject which had taken place and was still going on. It was once thought that the power of Congress was amply sufficient to secure the end of their institution. The error was now seen by every one. The members most tenacious of republicanism, he observed, were as loud as any in declaiming against the vices of democracy. This progress of the public mind led him to anticipate the time, when others as well as himself would join in the praise bestowed by Mr. Neckar on the British Constitution, namely, that it is the only Government in the world "which unites public strength with individual security."—In every community where industry is encouraged, there will be a division of it into the few & the many. Hence separate interests will arise. There will be debtors & creditors &c. Give all power to the many, they will oppress the few. Give all power to the few, they will oppress the many. Both therefore ought to have power, that each may defend itself against the other. To the want of this check we owe our paper money, instalment laws &c. To the proper adjustment of it the British owe the excellence of their Constitution. Their house of Lords is a most noble institution. Having nothing to hope for by a change, and a sufficient interest by means of their property, in being faithful to the national interest, they form a permanent barrier against every pernicious innovation, whether attempted on the part of the Crown or of the Commons. No temporary Senate will have firmness enough to answer the purpose. The Senate [of Maryland] which seems to be so much appealed to, has not yet been sufficiently tried. Had the people been unanimous & eager, in the late appeal to them on the subject of a paper emission they would have yielded to the torrent. Their acquiescing in such an appeal is a proof of it.—Gentlemen differ in their opinions concerning the necessary checks, from the different estimates they form of the human passions. They suppose seven years a sufficient period to give the senate an adequate firmness, from not duly considering the amazing violence & turbulence of the democratic spirit. When a great object of Government is pursued, which seizes the popular passions, they spread like wild fire, and become irresistable. He appealed to the gentlemen from the New England States whether experience had not there verified the remark.—As to the Executive, it seemed to be admitted that no good one could be established on Republican principles. Was not this giving up the merits of the question: for can there be a good Government without a good Executive. The English model was the only good one on this subject. . . . One of the weak sides of Republics was their being liable to foreign influence & corruption. Men of little character, acquiring great power become easily the tools of intermedling Neibours. . . .—What is the inference from all these observations? That we ought to go as far in order to attain stability and permanency, as republican principles will admit. Let one branch of the Legislature hold their places for life or at least during good behaviour. Let the Executive also be for life. He appealed to the feelings of the members present whether a term of seven years, would induce the sacrifices of private affairs which an acceptance of public trust would require, so as to ensure the services of the best Citizens. On this plan we should have in the Senate a permanent will, a weighty interest, which would answer essential purposes. But is this a Republican Government, it will be asked? Yes if all the Magistrates are appointed, and vacancies are filled, by the people, or a process of election originating with the people. He was sensible that an Executive constituted as he proposed would have in fact but little of the power and independence that might be necessary. . . . Having made these observations he would read to the Committee a sketch of a plan which he should prefer to either of those under consideration. He was aware that it went beyond the ideas of most members. But will such a plan be adopted out of doors? In return he would ask will the people adopt the other plan? At present they will adopt neither. But he sees the Union dissolving or already dissolved—he sees evils operating in the States which must soon cure the people of their fondness for democracies—he sees that a great progress has been already made & is still going on in the public mind. He thinks therefore that the people will in time be unshackled from their prejudices; and whenever that happens, they will themselves not be satisfied at stopping where the plan of Mr. Randolph would place them, but be ready to go as far at least as he proposes. He did not mean to offer the paper he had sketched as a proposition to the

Committee. It was meant only to give a more correct view of his ideas, and to suggest the amendments which he should probably propose to the plan of Mr. Randolph in the proper stages of its future discussion. . . .

[Hamilton's plan featured an Assembly elected for three years and Senators and a Governor elected to serve for life or "good behavior." All state militia were to be under the direct control of the national government and the Governor had an absolute veto on those laws "about to be passed" as well as on those passed.]

Tuesday June 19. In Committee of Whole on the Propositions of Mr. Patterson

The substitute offered yesterday by Mr. Dickenson being rejected by a vote now taken on it; Connecticut, New York, New Jersey, Delaware ay. Massachusetts, Pennsylvania, Virginia, North Carolina, South Carolina, Georgia no. Maryland divided. Mr. Patterson's plan was again at large before the Committee.

[Mr. Madison] begged [the advocates of equal representation] to consider the situation in which they would remain in case their pertinacious adherence to an inadmissible plan, should prevent the adoption of any plan. The contemplation of such an event was painful; but it would be prudent to submit to the task of examining it at a distance, that the means of escaping it might be the more readily embraced. Let the Union of the States be dissolved, and one of two consequences must happen. Either the States must remain individually independent & sovereign; or two or more Confederacies must be formed among them. In the first event would the small States be more secure against the ambition & power of their larger neighbours, than they would be under a general Government pervading with equal energy every part of the Empire, and having an equal interest in protecting every part against every other part? In the second, can the smaller expect that their larger neighbours would confederate with them on the principle of the present confederacy, which gives to each member, an equal suffrage; or that they would exact less severe concessions from the smaller States, than are proposed in the scheme of Mr. Randolph . . . ?

Mr. Wilson observed that by a National Government he did not mean one that would swallow up the State Governments as seemed to be wished by some gentlemen. He was tenacious of the idea of preserving the latter. He thought, contrary to the opinion of [Col. Hamilton] that they might not only subsist but subsist on friendly terms with the former. They were absolutely necessary for certain purposes which the former could not reach. All large Governments must be subdivided into lesser jurisdictions. As Examples he mentioned Persia, Rome, and particularly the divisions and subdivisions of England by Alfred.

Col. Hamilton coincided with the proposition as it stood in the Report. He had not been understood yesterday. By an abolition of the States, he meant that no boundary could be drawn between the National & State Legislatures; that the former must therefore have indefinite authority. If it were limited at all, the rivalship of the States would gradually subvert it. Even as corporations of extent of some of them as Virginia, Massachusetts &c. would be formidable. As *States*, he thought they ought to be abolished. But he admitted the necessity of leaving in them, subordinate jurisdictions. The examples of Persia & the Roman Empire, cited by [Mr. Wilson] were he thought in favor of his doctrine: the great powers delegated to the Satraps & proconsuls, having frequently produced revolts, and schemes of independence.

Mr. King, wished as every thing depended on this proposition, that no objections might be improperly indulged against the phraseology of it. He conceived that the import of the terms "States" "Sovereignty" "*national*" "federal," had been often used & applied in the discussions inaccurately & delusively. The States were not "Sovereigns" in the sense contended for by some. They did not possess the peculiar features of sovereignty, they could not make war, nor peace, nor alliances nor treaties. Considering them as political Beings, they were dumb, for they could not speak to any foreign Sovereign whatever. They were deaf, for they could not hear any propositions from such Sovereign. They had not even the organs or faculties of defence or offence, for they could not of themselves raise troops, or equip vessels, for war. On the other side, if the Union of the States comprises the idea of a confederation, it comprises that also of consolidation. A Union of the States is a Union of the men composing them, from whence a *national* character results to the whole. Congress can act alone without the States—they can act & their acts will be binding against the Instructions of the States. If they declare war: war is de jure declared—captures made in pursuance of it are lawful—No acts of the States can vary the situation, or prevent the judicial consequences. If the States therefore retained some portion of their sovereignty, they had certainly divested themselves of essential portions of it. If they formed a confederacy in some respects—they formed a Nation in others—The Convention could clearly deliberate on & propose any alterations that Congress could have done under the federal articles, and could not Congress propose by virtue of the last article, a change in any article whatever: and as well that relating to the equality of suffrage, as any other. He made these remarks to obviate some scruples which had been expressed. He doubted much the practicability of annihilating the States; but thought that much of their power ought to be taken from them.

Mr. Martin, said he considered that the separation from G.B. placed the 13 States in a state of Nature towards each other; that they would have remained in that state till this time, but for the confederation; that they entered into the confederation on the footing of equality; that they met now to amend it on the same footing; and that he could never accede to a plan that would introduce an inequality and lay 10 States at the mercy of Virginia, Massachusetts, and Pennsylvania.

Mr. Wilson, could not admit the doctrine that when the Colonies became independent of G. Britain, they became independent also of each other. He read the declaration of Independence, observing thereon that the *United Colonies* were declared to be free & independent States; and inferring that they were independent, not *individually* but *Unitedly* and that they were confederated as they were independent, States.

Col. Hamilton, assented to the doctrine of Mr. Wilson. He denied the doctrine that the States were thrown into a State of Nature. He was not yet prepared to admit the doctrine that the Confederacy, could be dissolved by partial infractions of it. He admitted that the States met now on an equal footing but could see no inference from that against concerting a change of the system in this particular. He took this occasion of observing for the purpose of appeasing the fears of the small States, that two circumstances would render them secure under a National Government in which they might lose the equality of rank they now held: one was the local situation of the 3 largest States, Virginia, Massachusetts, & Pennsylvania. They were separated from each other by distance of place, and equally so, by all the pecularities which distinguish the interests of one State from those of another. No combination therefore could be dreaded. In the second place, as there was a gradation in the States from Virginia the largest down to Delaware the smallest, it would always happen that ambitious combinations among a few States might & would be counteracted by defensive combinations of greater extent among the rest. No combination has been seen among large Counties merely as such, against lesser Counties. The more close the Union of the States, and the more compleat the authority of the whole: the less opportunity will be allowed the stronger States to injure the weaker.

Adjourned

Wednesday June 20, 1787. In Convention . . .

In the long and bitter argument over equal versus proportional representation a number of the delegates undertook to challenge the notion that two branches of the national legislature were required. One, they contended, would be quite enough. Two must be redundant. The possibility that the delegates might swing to a unicameral legislature unnerved the nationalists.

Mr. Wilson, urged the necessity of two branches; observed that if a proper model were not to be found in other Confederacies it was not to be wondered at. The number of them was small & the duration of some at least short. The Amphyctionic & Achaean were formed in the infancy of political Science; and appear by their History & fate, to have contained radical defects. The Swiss & Belgic Confederacies were held together not by any vital principle of energy but by the incumbent pressure of formidable neighbouring nations. The German owed its continuance to the influence of the Hapsburgs of Austria. He appealed to our own experience for the defects of our Confederacy. He had been 6 years in the 12 since the commencement of the Revolution, a member of Congress, and had felt all its weaknesses. He appealed to the recollection of others whether on many important occasions, the public interest had not been obstructed by the small members of the Union. The success of the Revolution was owing to other causes, than the Constitution of Congress. In many instances it went on even against the difficulties arising from Congress themselves. He admitted that the large States did accede as had been stated, to the Confederation in its present form. But it was the effect of necessity not of choice. There are other instances of their yielding from the same motive to the unreasonable measures of the small States. The situation of things is now a little altered. He insisted that a jealousy would exist between the State Legislatures & the General Legislature: observing that the members of the former would have views & feelings very distinct in this respect from their constituents. A private Citizen of a State is indifferent whether power be exercised by the General or State Legislatures, provided it be exercised most for his happiness. His representative has an interest in its being exercised by the body to which he belongs. He will therefore view the National Legislature with the eye of a jealous rival. He observed that the addresses of Congress to the people at large, had always been better received & produced greater effect, than those made to the Legislatures.

On the question for postponing in order to take up Mr. Lansing's proposition "to vest the powers of Legislation in [a single] Congress." [Lost 6 to 4, Maryland divided.] . . .

Adjourned

Thursday, June 21, was spent in retracing familiar ground, specifically the powers of the States vis-à-vis the national government and the proper terms for the members of the lower house.

June 22 was spent discussing the provision of salaries for legislators and the minimum age for election to the lower house.

Saturday, June 23, was devoted to discussing the eligibility of legislators for other offices and the right of appointment in general.

Monday. June 25. In Convention

Resolution 4. being taken up [the method of election, terms, etc., of the Senate].

Mr. Pinkney spoke as follows— The efficacy of the System will depend on this article. In order to form a right judgment in the case, it will be proper to examine the situation of this Country more accurately than it has yet been done. The people of the U. States are perhaps the most singular of any we are acquainted with. Among them there are fewer distinctions of fortune & less of rank, than among the inhabitants of any other nation. Every freeman has a right to the same protection & security; and a very moderate share of property entitles them to the possession of all the honors and privileges the public can bestow: hence arises a greater equality, than is to be found among the people of any other country, and an equality which is more likely to continue—I say this equality is likely to continue, because in a new Country, possessing immense tracts of uncultivated lands, where every temptation is offered to emigration & where industry must be rewarded with competency, there will be few poor, and few dependent—Every member of the Society almost, will enjoy an equal power of arriving at the supreme offices & consequently of directing the strength & sentiments of the whole Community. None will be excluded by birth, & few by fortune, from voting for proper persons to fill the offices of Government—the whole community will enjoy in the fullest sense that kind of political liberty which consists in the power the members of the State reserve to themselves, of arriving at the public offices, or at least, of having votes in the nomination of those who fill them.

If this State of things is true & the prospect of its continuing probable, it is perhaps not politic to endeavour too close an imitation of a Government calculated for a people whose situation is, & whose views ought to be extremely different.

Much has been said of the Constitution of G. Britain. I will confess that I believe it to be the best Constitution in existence; but at the same time I am confident it is one that will not or can not be introduced into this Country, for many centuries.—If it were proper to go here into a historical dissertation on the British Constitution, it might easily be shewn that the peculiar excellence, the distinguishing feature of that Government can not possibly be introduced into our System—that its balance between the Crown & the people can not be made a part of our Constitution.—that we neither have [n]or can have the members to compose it, nor the rights, privileges & properties of so distinct a class of Citizens to guard.—that the materials for forming this balance or check do not exist, nor is there a necessity for having so permanent a part of our Legislative, until the Executive power is so constituted as to have something fixed & dangerous in its principle—By this I mean a sole, hereditary, though limited Executive. . . .

I have said that such a body [as Parliament] cannot exist in this Country for ages, and that untill the situation of our people is exceedingly changed no necessity will exist for so permanent a part of the Legislature. To illustrate this I have remarked that the people of the United States are more equal in their circumstances than the people of any other Country—that they have very few rich men among them,—by rich men I mean those whose riches may have a dangerous influence, or such as are esteemed rich in Europe—perhaps there are not one hundred such on the Continent; that it is not probable this number will be greatly increased: that the genius of the people, their mediocrity of situation & the prospects which are afforded their industry in a Country which must be a new one for centuries are unfavorable to the rapid distinction of ranks. The destruction of the right of primogeniture & the equal division of the property of Intestates will also have an effect to preserve this mediocrity; for laws invariably affect the manners of a people. On the other hand that vast extent of unpeopled territory which opens to the frugal & industrious a sure road to competency & independence will effectually prevent for a considerable time the increase of the poor or discontented, and be the means of preserving that equality of condition which so eminently distinguishes us.

If equality is as I contend the leading feature of the U. States, where then are the riches & wealth whose representation & protection is the peculiar province of this permanent body. Are they in the hands of the few who may be called rich; in the possession of less than a hundred citizens? certainly not. They are in the great body of the people, among whom there are no men of wealth, and very few of real poverty.—Is it probable that a change will be created, and that a new order of men will arise? If under the British Government, for a century no such change was probable, I think it may be fairly concluded it will not take place while even the semblance of Republicanism remains.—How is this change to be effected? Where are the sources from whence it is to flow? From the landed interest? No. That is too unproductive & too much divided in most of the States. From the Monied interest? If such exists at present, little is to be apprehended from that source. Is it to spring from commerce? I believe it would be the first instance in which a nobility sprang from merchants. Besides, Sir, I apprehend that on this point the policy of the U. States has been much mistaken. We have unwisely considered ourselves as the inhabitants of an old instead of a new country. We have adopted the maxims of a State full of people & manufactures & established in credit. We have deserted our true interest, and instead of applying closely to those improvements in domestic policy which would have ensured the future importance of our commerce, we have rashly & prematurely engaged in schemes as extensive as they are imprudent. This however is an error which daily corrects itself & I have no doubt that a few more severe trials will convince us, that very different commercial principles ought to govern the conduct of these States.

The people of this country are not only very different from the inhabitants of any State we are acquainted with in the modern world; but I assert that their situation is distinct from either the people of Greece or Rome, or of any State we are acquainted with among the ancients.—Can the orders introduced by the institution of Solon, can they be found in the United States? Can the military habits & manners of Sparta be resembled to our habits & manners? Are the distinctions of Patrician & Plebeian known among us? Can the Helvetic or Belgic confederacies, or can the unwieldy, unmeaning body called the Germanic Empire, can they be said to possess either the same or a situation like ours? I apprehend not.—They are perfectly different, in their distinctions of rank, their Constitutions, their manner & their policy.

Our true situation appears to me to be this.—a new extensive Country containing within itself the materials for forming a Government capable of extending to its citizens all the blessings of civil & religious liberty— capable of making them happy at home. This is the great end of Republican Establishments. We mistake the object of our Government, if we hope or wish that it is to make us respectable abroad. Conquest or superiority among other powers is not or ought not ever to be the object of republican systems. If they are sufficently active & energetic to rescue us from contempt & preserve our domestic happiness & security, it is all we can expect from them,—it is more than almost any other Government ensures to its citizens.

I believe this observation will be found generally true:—that no two people are so exactly alike in their situation or circumstances as to admit the exercise of the same Government with equal benefit: that a system must be suited to the habits & genius of the people it is to govern, and must grow out of them.

The people of the U.S. may be divided into three classes—*Professional men* who must from their particular pursuits always have a considerable weight in the Government while it remains popular—*Commercial men,* who may or may not have weight as a wise or injudicious commercial policy is pursued.—If that commercial policy is pursued which I conceive to be the true one, the merchants of this Country will not or ought not for a considerable time to have much weight in the political scale.— The third is the *landed interest*, the owners and cultivators of the soil, who are and ought ever to be the governing spring in the system.—These three classes, however distinct in their pursuits are individually equal in the political scale, and may be easily proved to have but one interest. The dependence of each on the other is mutual. The merchant depends on the planter. Both must in private as well as public affairs be connected with the professional men; who in their turn must in some measure depend upon them. Hence it is clear from this manifest connection, & the equality which I before stated exists, & must for the reasons then assigned, continue, that after all there is one, but one great & equal body of citizens composing the inhabitants of this Country among whom there are no distinctions of rank, and very few or none of fortune.

For a people thus circumstanced are we then to form a government & the question is what kind of Government is best suited to them.

Will it be the British Government? No. Why? Because G. Britain contains three orders of people distinct in their situation, their possessions & their principles.—These orders combined form the great body of the Nation, and as in national expences the wealth of the whole community must contribute, so ought each component part to be properly & duly represented—No other combination of power could form this due representation, but the one that exists.—Neither the peers or the people could represent the royalty, nor could the Royalty & the people form a proper representation for the Peers.—Each therefore must of necessity be represented by itself, or the sign of itself; and this accidental mixture has certainly formed a Government admirably well balanced.

But the U. States contain but one order that can be assimilated to the British Nation,—this is the order of Commons. They will not surely then attempt to form a Government consisting of three branches, two of which shall have nothing to represent. They will not have an Executive & Senate [hereditary] because the Kings & Lords of England are so. The same reasons do not exist and therefore the same provisions are not necessary.

We must as has been observed suit our Government to the people it is to direct. These are I believe as active, intelligent & susceptible of good

Government as any people in the world. The Confusion which has produced the present relaxed State is not owing to them. It is owing to the weakness & [defects] of a Government incapable of combining the various interests it is intended to unite, and destitute of energy.—All that we have to do then is to distribute the powers of Government in such a manner, and for such limited periods, as while it gives a proper degree of permanency to the Magistrate, will reserve to the people, the right of election they will not or ought not frequently to part with.—I am of opinion that this may be easily done; and that with some amendments the propositions before the Committee will fully answer this end.

No position appears to me more true than this; that the General Government can not effectually exist without reserving to the States the possession of their local rights. They are the instruments upon which the Union must frequently depend for the support & execution of their powers, however immediately operating upon the people, and not upon the States. . . .

The mode of constituting the 2nd branch being under consideration. . . .

Mr. Wilson. the question is shall the members of the 2nd branch be chosen by the Legislatures of the States? When he considered the amazing extent of Country—the immense population which is to fill it, the influence which the Government we are to form will have, not only on the present generation of our people & their multiplied posterity, but on the whole Globe, he was lost in the magnitude of the object. The project of Henry the 4th & his Statesmen was but the picture in miniature of the great portrait to be exhibited. He was opposed to an election by the State Legislatures. In explaining his reasons it was necessary to observe the twofold relation to which the people would stand. 1. as Citizens of the General Government. 2. as Citizens of their particular State. The General Government was meant for them in the first capacity: the State Governments in the second. Both Governments were derived from the people—both meant for the people—both therefore ought to be regulated on the same principles. The same train of ideas which belonged to the relation of the Citizens to their State Governments were applicable to their relation to the General Government and in forming the latter, we ought to proceed, by abstracting as much as possible from the idea of State Governments. With respect to the province & objects of the General Government they should be considered as having no existence. The election of the 2nd branch by the Legislatures, will introduce & cherish local interests & local prejudices. The General Government is not an assemblage of States, but of individuals for certain political purposes—it is not meant for the States, but for the individuals composing them; the *individ-*

uals therefore not the *States*, ought to be represented in it: A proportion in this representation can be preserved in the 2nd as well as in the 1st branch; and the election can be made by electors chosen by the people for that purpose. He moved an amendment to that effect which was not seconded. . . .

The balance of the Monday, June 25, session and much of the following day were given over to a debate of the terms of the senators. Four, five, six, seven, nine years and life were all proposed and voted down. Madison's comments during the debate follow:

In order to judge of the form to be given to this institution, it will be proper to take a view of the ends to be served by it. These were first to protect the people against their rulers: secondly to protect the people against the transient impressions into which they themselves might be led. A people deliberating in a temperate moment, and with the experience of other nations before them, on the plan of Government most likely to secure their happiness, would first be aware, that those charged with the public happiness, might betray their trust. An obvious precaution against this danger would be to divide the trust between different bodies of men, who might watch & check each other. In this they would be governed by the same prudence which has prevailed in organizing the subordinate departments of Government, where all business liable to abuses is made to pass through separate hands, the one being a check on the other. It would next occur to such a people, that they themselves were liable to temporary errors, thro' want of information as to their true interest, and that men chosen for a short term, & employed but a small portion of that in public affairs, might err from the same cause. This reflection would naturally suggest that the Government be so constituted, as that one of its branches might have an opportunity of acquiring a competent knowledge of the public interests. Another reflection equally becoming a people on such an occasion, would be that they themselves, as well as a numerous body of Representatives, were liable to err also, from fickleness and passion. A necessary fence against this danger would be to select a portion of enlightened citizens, whose limited number, and firmness might seasonably interpose against impetuous councils. It ought finally to occur to a people deliberating on a Government for themselves, that as different interests necessarily result from the liberty meant to be secured, the major interest might under sudden impulses be tempted to commit injustices on the minority. In all civilized Countries the people fall into different classes having a real or supposed difference of interests. There will be creditors & debtors, farmers, merchants &

manufacturers. There will be particularly the distinction of rich & poor. It was true as had been observed [by Mr. Pinkney] we had not among us those hereditary distinctions, of rank which were a great source of the contests in the ancient Governments as well as the modern States of Europe, nor those extremes of wealth or poverty which characterize the latter. We cannot however be regarded even at this time, as one homogeneous mass, in which every thing that affects a part will affect in the same manner the whole. In framing a system which we wish to last for ages, we should not lose sight of the changes which ages will produce. An increase of population will of necessity increase the proportion of those who will labour under all the hardships of life, & secretly sigh for a more equal distribution of its blessings. These may in time outnumber those who are placed above the feelings of indigence. According to the equal laws of suffrage, the power will slide into the hands of the former. No agrarian attempts have yet been made in this Country, but symptoms, of a leveling spirit, as we have understood, have sufficiently appeared in a certain quarters to give notice of the future danger. How is this danger to be guarded against on republican principles? How is the danger in all cases of interested coalitions to oppress the minority to be guarded against? Among other means by the establishment of a body in the Government sufficiently respectable for its wisdom & virtue, to aid on such emergences, the preponderance of justice by throwing its weight into that scale. Such being the objects of the second branch in the proposed Government he thought a considerable duration ought to be given to it. He did not conceive that the term of nine years could threaten any real danger; but in pursuing his particular ideas on the subject, he should require that the long term allowed to the 2nd branch should not commence till such a period of life, as would render a perpetual disqualification to be re-elected little inconvenient either in a public or private view. He observed that as it was more than probable we were now digesting a plan which in its operation would decide for ever the fate of Republican Government we ought not only to provide every guard to liberty that its preservation could require, but be equally careful to supply the defects which our own experience had particularly pointed out.

Mr. Sherman. Government is instituted for those who live under it. It ought therefore to be so constituted as not to be dangerous to their liberties. The more permanency it has the worse if it be a bad Government. Frequent elections are necessary to preserve the good behavior of rulers. They also tend to give permanency to the Government by preserving that good behavior, because it ensures their re-election. In Connecticut elections have been very frequent, yet great stability &

uniformity both as to persons & measures have been experienced from its original establishment to the present time; a period of more than 130 years. He wished to have provision made for steadiness & wisdom in the system to be adopted; but he thought six or four years would be sufficient. He should be content with either. . . .

On the question for 6 years 1/3 to go out biennially [passed 7 to 4]. . . .

The 5. Resol: "that each branch have the right of originating acts" was agreed to nem: con:

Adjourned

On Wednesday, June 27, Luther Martin of Maryland talked for three hours on the importance of equal representation. Madison noted wryly: "He was too much exhausted he said to finish his remarks, and reminded the House that he should tomorrow, resume them."

Thursday June 28. In Convention

"Mr. L. Martin resumed his discourse," Madison wrote, adding after several pages of résumé: "This was the substance of the residue of his discourse which was delivered with much diffuseness & considerable vehemence."

[At this stage, with the delegates apparently hopelessly deadlocked, Franklin made his famous plea for divine intervention.]

Mr. President

The small progress we have made after 4 or five weeks close attendance & continual reasonings with each other—our different sentiments on almost every question, several of the last producing as many noes as ays, is methinks a melancholy proof of the imperfection of the Human Understanding. We indeed seem to feel our own want of political wisdom, since we have been running about in search of it. We have gone back to ancient history for models of Government, and examined the different forms of those Republics which having been formed with the seeds of their own dissolution now no longer exist. And we have viewed Modern States all round Europe, but find none of their Constitutions suitable to our circumstances.

In this situation of this Assembly, groping as it were in the dark to find political truth, and scarce able to distinguish it when presented to us, how has it happened, Sir, that we have not hitherto once thought of humbly applying to the Father of lights to illuminate our understandings? In the beginning of the Contest with G. Britain, when we were sensible of danger we had daily prayer in this room for the divine protection.—Our prayers, Sir, were heard, & they were graciously answered. All of us who were engaged in the struggle must have observed frequent instances of a superintending providence in our favor. To that kind providence we owe this happy opportunity of consulting in peace on the means of establishing our future national felicity. And have we now forgotten that powerful friend? or do we imagine that we no longer need his assistance? I have lived, Sir, a long time, and the longer I live, the more convincing proofs I see of this truth—*that God Governs in the affairs of men*. And if a sparrow cannot fall to the ground without his notice, is it probable that an empire can rise without his aid? We have been assured, Sir, in the sacred writings, that "except the Lord build the House they labour in vain that build it." I firmly believe this; and I also believe that without his concurring aid we shall succeed in this political building no better, than the Builders of Babel: We shall be divided by our little partial local interests; our projects will be confounded, and we ourselves shall become a reproach and bye word down to future ages. And what is worse, mankind may hereafter from this unfortunate instance, despair of establishing Governments by Human wisdom and leave it to chance, war and conquest.

I therefore beg leave to move—that henceforth prayers imploring the assistance of Heaven, and its blessings on our deliberations, be held in this Assembly every morning before we proceed to business, and that one or more of the Clergy of this City be requested to officiate in that Service—

Mr. Sharman seconded the motion.

Mr. Hamilton & several others expressed their apprehensions that however proper such a resolution might have been at the beginning of the convention, it might at this late day, 1. bring on it some disagreeable animadversions. & 2. lead the public to believe that the embarrassments and dissensions within the Convention, had suggested this measure. It was answered by Doctor Franklin, Mr. Sherman & others, that the past omission of a duty could not justify a further omission—that the rejection of such a proposition would expose the Convention to more unpleasant animadversions than the adoption of it: and that the alarm out of doors that might be excited for the state of things within, would at least be as likely to do good as ill.

Mr. Williamson, observed that the true cause of the omission could not be mistaken. The Convention had no funds.

Mr. Randolph proposed in order to give a favorable aspect to the measure, that a sermon be preached at the request of the convention on the 4th of July, the anniversary of Independence; & thenceforward prayers be used in the Convention every morning. Dr. Franklin seconded this motion. After several unsuccessful attempts for silently postponing the matter by adjourning the adjournment was at length carried, without any vote on the motion.

Friday June 29th. In Convention

Doctor Johnson. The controversy must be endless whilst Gentlemen differ in the grounds of their arguments; Those on one side considering the States as districts of people composing one political Society; those on the other considering them as so many political societies. The fact is that the States do exist as political Societies, and a Government is to be formed for them in their political capacity, as well as for the individuals composing them. Does it not seem to follow, that if the States as such are to exist they must be armed with some power of self-defence. This is the idea of [Colonel Mason] who appears to have looked to the bottom of this matter. Besides the Aristocratic and other interests, which ought to have the means of defending themselves, the States have their interests as such, and are equally entitled to like means. On the whole he thought that as in some respects the States are to be considered in their political capacity, and in others as districts of individual citizens, the two ideas embraced on different sides, instead of being opposed to each other, ought to be combined; that in *one* branch the *people*, ought to be represented; in the *other* the *States*. . . .

Johnson's suggestion, offered earlier by Sherman, was not at first followed up. Read retrieved Hamilton's authoritarian scheme urging that that plan, however imperfect, was better than nothing and might, in time, be amended, but Hamilton objected.

Mr. Hamilton. . . . Some of the consequences of a dissolution of the Union, and the establishment of partial confederacies, had been pointed out. He would add another of a most serious nature. Alliances will immediately be formed with different rival & hostile nations of Europes, who will foment disturbances among ourselves, and make us parties to all their own quarrels. Foreign Nations having American dominions are & must be jealous of us. Their representatives betray the utmost anxiety for our fate, & for the result of this meeting, which must have an essential influence on it.—It had been said that respectability in the eyes of foreign Nations was not the object at which we aimed; that the proper object of republican Government was domestic tranquility & happiness. This was an ideal distinction. No Government could give us tranquility & happiness at home, which did not possess sufficient stability and strength to make us respectable abroad. This was the critical moment for forming such a Government. We should run every risk in trusting to future amendments. As yet we retain the habits of union. We are weak & sensible of our weakness. Henceforward the motives will become feebler, and the difficulties greater. It is a miracle that we [are] now here exercising our tranquil & free deliberations on the subject. It would be madness to trust to future miracles. A thousand causes must obstruct a reproduction of them.

Mr. Elseworth moved that the rule of suffrage in the 2nd branch be the same with that established by the articles of confederation. . . . He hoped it would become a ground of compromise with regard to the 2nd branch. We were partly national; partly federal. The proportional representation in the first branch was comformable to the national principle & would secure the large States against the small. An equality of voices was conformable to the federal principle and was necessary to secure the Small states against the large. He trusted that on this middle ground a compromise would take place. He did not see that it could on any other. And if no compromise should take place, our meeting would not only be in vain but worse than in vain. To the Eastward he was sure Massachusetts was the only State that would listen to a proposition for excluding the States as equal political Societies, from an equal voice in both branches. The others would risk every consequence rather than part with so dear a right. An attempt to deprive them of it, was at once cutting the body of America in two, and as he supposed would be the case, somewhere about this part of it. The large States he conceived would notwithstanding the equality of votes, have an influence that would maintain their superiority. Holland, as had been admitted [by Mr. Madison] had, notwithstanding a like equality in the Dutch Confederacy, a prevailing influence in the public measures. The power of self-defence was essential to the small States. Nature had given it to the smallest insect of the creation. He could never admit that there was no danger of combinations among the large States. They will like individuals find out and avail themselves of the advantage to be gained by it. It was true the danger would be greater, if they were contiguous and had a more immediate common interest. A defensive combination of the small States was rendered more difficult by their greater number. He would mention another consideration of great weight. The existing confederation was founded on the equality of the States in the article of suffrage: was it meant to pay no regard to this antecedent plighted faith. Let a strong Executive, a Judiciary & Legislative power be created; but Let not too much be attempted; by which all may be lost. He was not in general a half-way man, yet he preferred doing half the good we could, rather than do nothing at all. The other half may be added, when the necessity shall be more fully experienced. . . .

Adjourned

Saturday June 30, 1787. In Convention

. . . Mr. King observed that the simple question was whether each State should have an equal vote in the 2nd branch; that it must be apparent to those gentlemen who liked neither the motion for this equality, nor the report as it stood, that the report was as susceptible of melioration as the motion; that a reform would be nugatory & nominal only if we should make another Congress of the proposed Senate: that if the adherence to an equality of votes was fixed & unalterable, there could not be less obstinacy on the other side, & that we were in fact cut asunder already, and it was in vain to shut our eyes against it: that he was however filled with astonishment that if we were convinced that every *man* in America was secured in all his rights, we should be ready to sacrifice this substantial good to the phantom of *State* sovereignty: that his feelings were more harrowed & his fears more agitated for his Country than he could express, that he conceived this to be the last opportunity of providing for its liberty & happiness: that he could not therefore but repeat his amazement that when a just Government founded on a fair representation of the *people* of America was within our reach, we should renounce the blessing, from an attachment to the ideal freedom & importance of *States*: that should this wonderful illusion continue to prevail, his mind was prepared for every event, rather than to sit down under a Government founded on a vicious principle of representation, and which must be as short lived as it would be unjust. . . . He never could listen to an equality of votes as proposed in the motion.

Mr. Dayton. When assertion is given for proof, and terror substituted for argument, he presumed they would have no effect however eloquently spoken. It should have been shewn that the evils we have experienced have proceeded from the equality now objected to: and that the seeds of dissolution for the State Governments are not sown in the General Government. He considered the system on the table as a novelty, an amphibious monster; and was persuaded that it never would be received by the people.

Mr. Martin, would never confederate if it could not be done on just principles. . . .

Mr. Bedford, contended that there was no middle way between a perfect consolidation and a mere confederacy of the States. The first is out of the question, and in the latter they must continue if not perfectly, yet equally sovereign. If political Societies possess ambition, avarice, and all the other passions which render them formidable to each other, ought we not to view them in this light here? Will not the same motives operate in America as elsewhere? If any gentleman doubt it let him look at the votes. Have they not been dictated by interest, by ambition? Are not the large States evidently seeking to agggrandize themselves at the expense of the small? They think no doubt that they have right on their side, but interest had blinded their eyes. Look at Georgia. Though a small State at present, she is actuated by the prospect of soon being a great one. South Carolina is actuated both by present interest and future prospects. She hopes too to see the other States cut down to her own dimensions. North Carolina has the same motives of present & future interest. Virginia follows. Maryland is not on that side of the Question. Pennsylvania has a direct and future interest. Massachusetts has a decided and palpable interest in the part she takes. Can it be expected that the small States will act from pure disinterestedness. Look at G. Britain. Is the Representation there less unequal? But we shall be told again that that is the rotten part of the Constitution. Have not the boroughs however held fast their constitutional rights? and are we to act with greater purity than the rest of mankind. An exact proportion in the Representation is not preserved in any one of the States. Will it be said that an inequality of power will not result from an inequality of votes. Give the opportunity, and ambition will not fail to abuse it. The whole History of mankind proves it. The three large States have a common interest to bind them together in commerce. But whether a combination as we suppose, or a competition as others suppose, shall take place among them, in either case, the smaller States must be ruined. We must like Solon make such a Government as the people will approve. Will the smaller States ever agree to the proposed degradation of them. It is not true that the people will not agree to enlarge the powers of the present Congress. The Language of the people has been that Congress ought to have the power of collecting an impost, and of coercing the States where it may be necessary. On the first point they have been explicit &, in a manner, unanimous in their declarations. And must they not agree to this & similar measures if they ever mean to discharge their engagements. The little States are willing to observe their engagements, but will meet the large ones on no ground but that of the Confederation. We have been told with a dictatorial air that this is the last moment for a fair trial in favor of a good Government. It will be the last indeed if the propositions reported from the Committee go forth to the people. He was under no apprehensions. The Large States dare not dissolve the Confederation. If they do the small ones will find some foreign ally of more honor and good faith, who will take them by the hand and do them justice. He did not mean by this to intimidate or alarm. It was a natural consequence; which ought to be avoided by enlarging the federal powers not annihilating the federal system. This is what the people expect. All agree in the necessity of a more efficient Government and why not make such an one; as they desire. . . .

Adjourned

Monday July 2nd. In Convention . . .

Mr. Pinkney thought an equality of votes in the 2nd branch inadmissible. At the same time candor obliged him to admit that the large States would feel a partiality for their own Citizens & give them a preference, in appointments: that they might also find some common points in their commercial interests, and promote treaties favorable to them. There is a real distinction between the Northern & Southern interests. North Carolina, South Carolina, & Georgia in their Rice & Indigo had a peculiar interest which might be sacrificed. How then shall the larger States be prevented from administering the General Government as they please, without being themselves unduly subjected to the will of the smaller? By allowing them some but not a full proportion. He was extremely anxious that something should be done, considering this as the last appeal to a regular experiment. Congress have failed in almost every effort for an amendment of the federal System. Nothing has prevented a dissolution of it, but the appointment of this Convention; & he could not express his alarms for the consequences of such an event. . . .

Mr. Sharman. We are now at a full stop, and nobody he supposed meant that we should break up without doing something. A committee he thought most likely to hit on some expedient.

Mr. Gouverneur Morris. thought a Committee advisable as the Convention had been equally divided. He had a stronger reason also. The mode of appointing the 2nd branch tended he was sure to defeat the object of it. What is this object? to check the precipitation, changeableness, and excesses of the first branch. Every man of observation had seen in the democratic branches of the State Legislatures, precipitation— in Congress changeableness, in every department excesses against personal liberty, private property & personal safety. What qualities are necessary to constitute a check in this case? *Abilities* and *virtue*, are equally necessary in both branches. Something more then is now wanted. 1. the checking branch must have a personal interest in checking the other branch, one interest must be opposed to another interest. Vices as they exist, must be turned against each other. 2. It must have great personal property, it must have the aristocratic spirit; it must love to lord it through pride, pride is indeed the great principle that actuates both the poor & the rich. It is this principle which in the former resists, in the latter abuses authority. 3. It should be independent. In Religion the Creature is apt to forget its Creator. That it is otherwise in political affairs, the late debates here are an unhappy proof. The aristocratic body, should be as independent & as firm as the democratic. If the members of it are to revert to a dependence on the democratic choice, the democratic scale will preponderate. All the guards contrived by America have not restrained the Senatorial branches of the Legislature from a servile complaisance to the democratic. If the 2nd branch is to be dependent we are better without it. To make it independent, it should be for life. It will then do wrong, it will be said. He believed so: He hoped so. The Rich will strive to establish their dominion & enslave the rest. They always did. They always will. The proper security against them is to form them into a separate interest. The two forces will then control each other. Let the rich mix with the poor and in a Commercial Country, they will establish an oligarchy. Take away commerce, and the democracy will triumph. Thus it has been all the world over. So it will be among us. Reason tells us we are but men: and we are not to expect any particular interference of Heaven in our favor. By thus combining & setting apart, the aristocratic interest, the popular interest will be combined against it. There will be a mutual check and mutual security. . . . He hoped there was strength of mind enough in this House to look truth in the face. He did not hesitate therefore to say that loaves & fishes must bribe the Demagogues. They must be made to expect higher offices under the general than the State Governments. A Senate for life will be a noble bait. Without such captivating prospects, the popular leaders will oppose & defeat the plan. He perceived that the 1st branch was to be chosen by the people of the States: the 2nd by those chosen by the people. Is not here a Government by the States. A Government by Compact between Virginia in the 1st & 2nd branch; Massachusetts in the 1st & 2nd branch &c. This is going back to mere treaty. It is no Government at all. It is altogether dependent on the States, and will act over again the part which Congress has acted. A firm Government alone can protect our liberties. He fears the influence of the rich. They will have the same effect here as elsewhere if we do not by such a Government keep them within their proper sphere. We should remember that the people never act from reason alone. The Rich will take advantage of their passions & make these the instruments for oppressing them. The Result of the Contest will be a violent aristocracy, or a more violent despotism. The schemes of the Rich will be favored by the extent of the Country. The people in such distant parts can not communicate & act in concert. They will be the dupes of those who have more knowledge & intercourse. The only security against encroachments will be a select & sagacious body of men, instituted to watch against them on all sides. He meant only to hint these observations, without grounding any motion on them.

Mr. Randolph favored the commitment though he did not expect much benefit from the expedient. He animadverted on the warm & rash language of Mr. Bedford on Saturday; reminded the small States that if the large States should combine some danger of which he did not deny there would be a check in the revisionary power of the Executive, and intimated that in order to render this still more effectual, he would agree that in the choice of the Executive each State should have an equal vote. He was persuaded that two such opposite bodies as Mr. Morris had planned, could never long co-exist. Dissensions would arise as has been seen even between the Senate and H. of Delegates in Maryland, appeals would be made to the people; and in a little time, commotions would be the result —He was far from thinking the large States could subsist of themselves any more than the small; an avulsion would involve the whole in ruin, and he was determined to pursue such a scheme of Government as would secure us against such a calamity. . . .

Doctor Williamson. If we do not concede on both sides, our business must soon be at an end. . . .

Mr. Gerry was for [appointing a committee to propose a compromise]. Something must be done, or we shall disappoint not only America, but the whole world. He suggested a consideration of the State we should be thrown into by the failure of the Union. We should be without an Umpire to decide controversies and must be at the mercy of events. What too is to become of our treaties—what of our foreign debts, what of our domestic? We must make concessions on both sides. Without these the Constitutions of the several States would never have been formed. . . .

The Committee elected by ballot, were Mr. Gerry, Mr. Elseworth, Mr. Yates, Mr. Patterson, Dr. Franklin, Mr. Bedford, Mr. Martin, Mr. Mason, Mr. Davy, Mr. Rutlidge, Mr. Baldwin.

That time might be given to the Committee, and to such as chose to attend to the celebrations on the anniversary of Independence, the Convention adjourned till Thursday.

Thursday July 5th. In Convention

Mr. Gerry delivered in from the Committee appointed on Monday last the following Report.

> The Committee to whom was referred the 8th Resol. of the Report from the Committee of the whole House, and so much of the 7th as has not been decided on, submit the following Report: That the subsequent propositions be recommended to the Convention on condition that both shall be generally adopted. I. that in the 1st branch of the Legislature each of the States now in the Union shall be allowed 1 member for every 40,000 inhabitants of the description reported in the 7th Resolution of the Committee of the whole House: that each State not containing that number shall be allowed 1 member: that all bills for raising or appropriating money, and for fixing the Salaries of the officers of the Government of the U. States shall originate in the 1st branch of the Legislature, and shall not be altered or amended by the 2nd branch: and that no money shall be drawn from the public Treasury, but in pursuance of appropriations to be originated in the 1st branch. II. That in the 2nd branch each State shall have an equal vote.

Mr. Gouverneur Morris. thought the form as well as the matter of the Report objectionable. It seemed in the first place to render amendments impracticable. In the next place, it seemed to involve a pledge to agree to the 2nd part if the 1st should be agreed to. He conceived the whole aspect of it to be wrong. He came here as a Representative of America; he flattered himself he came here in some degree as a Representative of the whole human race; for the whole human race will be affected by the proceedings of this Convention. He wished gentlemen to extend their views beyond the present moment of time; beyond the narrow limits of place from which they derive their political origin. If he were to believe some things which he had heard, he should suppose that we were assembled to truck and bargain for our particular States. He can-not descend to think that any gentlemen are really actuated by these views. We must look forward to the effects of what we do. These alone ought to guide us. Much has been said of the sentiments of the people. They were unknown. They could not be known. All that we can infer is that if the plan we recommend be reasonable & right; all who have reasonable minds and sound intentions will embrace it, notwithstanding what had been said by some gentlemen. Let us suppose that the larger States shall agree; and that the smaller refuse: and let us trace the consequences. The opponents of the system in the smaller States will no doubt make a party, and a noise for a time, but the ties of interest, of kindred & of common habits which connect them with the other States will be too strong to be easily broken. In New Jersey particularly he was sure a great many would follow the sentiments of Pennsylvania & New York. This Country must be united. If persuasion does not unite it, the sword will. He begged that this consideration might have its due weight. The scenes of horror attending civil commotion can not be described, and the conclusion of them will be worse than the term of their continuance. The stronger party will then make traitors of the weaker; and the Gallows & Halter will finish the work of the sword. How far foreign powers would be ready to take part in the confusions he would not say. Threats that they will be invited have it seems been thrown out. He drew the melancholy picture of foreign intrusions as exhibited in the History of Germany, & urged it as a standing lesson to other nations. He trusted that the Gentlemen who may have hazarded such expressions, did not entertain them till they reached their own lips. But returning to the Report he could not think it in any respect calculated for the public good. As the 2nd branch is now constituted, there will be constant disputes & appeals to the States which will undermine the General Government & control & annihilate the 1st branch. Suppose that the delegates from Massachusetts & Rhode Island in the Upper House disagree, and that the former are outvoted. What Results? they will immediately declare that their State will not abide by the decision, and make such representations as will produce that effect. The same may happen as to Virginia & other States. Of what avail then will be what is on paper. State attachments, and State importance have been the bane of this Country. We can not annihilate; but we may perhaps take out the teeth of the serpents. He wished our ideas to be enlarged to the true interest of man, instead of being circumscribed within the narrow compass of a particular Spot. And after all how little can be the motive yielded by selfishness for such a policy. Who can say whether he himself, much less whether his children, will the next year be an inhabitant of this or that State. . . .

Mr. Elseworth said he had not attended the proceedings of the Committee, but was ready to accede to the compromise they had reported. Some compromise was necessary; and he saw none more convenient or reasonable.

Mr. Gerry. Though he had assented to the Report in the Committee, he had very material objections to it. We were however in a peculiar situation. We were neither the same Nation nor different Nations. We ought not therefore to pursue the one or the other of these ideas too closely. If no compromise should take place what will be the consequence. A secession he foresaw would take place; for some gentlemen seem decided on it; two different plans will be proposed; and the result no man could foresee. If we do not come to some agreement among ourselves some foreign sword will probably do the work for us.

Mr. Mason. The Report was meant not as specific propositions to be adopted; but merely as a general ground of accommodation. There must be some accommodation on this point, or we shall make little further progress in the work. Accommodation was the object of the House in the appointment of the Committee; and of the Committee in the Report they had made. And however liable the Report might be to objections, he thought it preferable to an appeal to the world by the different sides, as had been talked of by some Gentlemen. It could not be more inconvenient to any gentleman to remain absent from his private affairs, than it was for him: but he would bury his bones in this City rather than expose his Country to the Consequences of a dissolution of the Convention without any thing being done. . . .

Friday and Saturday, July 6 and 7, were given over to discussion of the number of inhabitants of a state that would entitle it to a representative in the lower house and to the provision of the Committee that all money bills should originate in the lower house.

Monday July 9th. In Convention . . .

Mr. Gouverneur Morris delivered a report from the Committee of 5 members to whom was committed the clause in the Report of the Committee consisting of a member from each State, stating the proper ratio of Representatives in the 1st branch, to be as 1 to every 40,000 inhabitants, as follows viz

> The Committee to whom was referred the 1st clause of the 1st proposition reported from the grand Committee, beg leave to report
> I. that in the 1st meeting of the Legislature the 1st branch thereof consist of 56. members of which Number, New Hampshire shall have 2. Massachusetts 7. Rhode Island 1. Connecticut 4. New York 5. New Jersey 3. Pennsylvania 8. Delaware 1. Maryland 4. Virginia 9. North Carolina 5. South Carolina 5. Georgia 2.—
> II. But as the present situation of the States may probably alter as well in point of wealth as in the number of their inhabitants, that the Legislature be authorized from time to time to augment the number of Representatives. And in case any of the States shall hereafter be divided, or any two or more States united, or any new States

created within the limits of the United States, the Legislature shall possess authority to regulate the number of Representatives in any of the foregoing cases, upon the principles of their wealth and number of inhabitants.

Mr. Sherman wished to know on what principles or calculations the Report was founded. It did not appear to correspond with any rule of numbers, or of any requisition hitherto adopted by Congress.

Mr. Gorham. Some provision of this sort was necessary in the outset. The number of blacks & whites with some regard to supposed wealth was the general guide. Fractions could not be observed. The Legislature is to make alterations from time to time as justice & propriety may require. Two objections prevailed against the rate of 1 member for every 40,000 inhabitants. The 1st was that the Representation would soon be too numerous: the 2nd that the Western States who may have a different interest, might if admitted on that principle by degrees, outvote the Atlantic. Both these objections are removed. The number will be small in the first instance and may be continued so; and the Atlantic States having the Government in their own hands, may take care of their own interest, by dealing out the right of Representation in safe proportions to the Western States. These were the views of the Committee. . . .

Mr. Patterson considered the proposed estimate for the future according to the Combined rule of numbers and wealth, as too vague. For this reason New Jersey was against it. He could regard negroe slaves in no light but as property. They are no free agents, have no personal liberty, no faculty of acquiring property, but on the contrary are themselves property, & like other property entirely at the will of the Master. Has a man in Virginia a number of votes in proportion to the number of his slaves? And if Negroes are not represented in the States to which they belong, why should they be represented in the General Government. What is the true principle of Representation? It is an expedient by which an assembly of certain individuals chosen by the people is substituted in place of the inconvenient meeting of the people themselves. If such a meeting of the people was actually to take place, would the slaves vote? They would not. Why then should they be represented. He was also against such an indirect encouragement of the slave trade; observing that Congress in their act relating to the change of the 8 art: of Confederation had been ashamed to use the term "slaves" & had substituted a description. . . .

Mr. King had always expected that as the Southern States are the richest, they would not league themselves with the Northern unless some respect were paid to their superior wealth. If the latter expect those preferential distinctions in Commerce & other advantages which they will derive from the connection they must not expect to receive them without allowing some advantages in return. Eleven out of 13 of the States had agreed to consider Slaves in the apportionment of taxation; and taxation and Representation ought to go together. . . .

Tuesday. July 10. In Convention

Mr. King reported from the Committee yesterday appointed that the States at the 1st meeting of the General Legislature, should be represented by 65 members in the following proportions, to wit. New Hampshire by 3. Massachusetts 8. Rhode Island 1. Connecticut 5. New York 6. New Jersey 4. Pennsylvania 8. Delaware 1. Maryland 6. Virginia 10. North Carolina 5. South Carolina 5. Georgia 3.

Mr. Rutlidge moved that New Hampshire be reduced from 3 to 2. members. Her numbers did not entitled her to 3 and it was a poor State.

General Pinkney seconds the motion.

Mr. King. New Hampshire has probably more than 120,000 Inhabitants and has an extensive Country of tolerable fertility. Its inhabitants therefore may be expected to increase fast. He remarked that the four Eastern States having 800,000 souls, have 1/3 fewer representatives than the four Southern States, having not more than 700,000 souls rating the blacks, as 5 for 3. The Eastern people will advert to these circumstances, and be dissatisfied. He believed them to be very desirous of uniting with their Southern bretheren, but did not think it prudent to rely so far on that disposition as to subject them to any gross inequality. He was fully convinced that the question concerning a difference of interests did not lie where it had hitherto been discussed, between the great & small States; but between the Southern & Eastern. For this reason he had been ready to yield something in the proportion of representatives for the security of the Southern. No principle would justify the giving them a majority. They were brought as near an equality as was possible. He was not averse to giving them a still greater security, but did not see how it could be done.

General Pinkney. The Report before it was committed was more favorable to the Southern States than as it now stands. If they are to form so considerable a minority, and the regulation of trade is to be given to the General Government, they will be nothing more than overseers for the Northern States. He did not expect the Southern States to be raised to a majority of representatives, but wished them to have something like an equality. At present by the alterations of the Committee in favor of the Northern States they are removed farther from it than they were before. One member had indeed been added to Virginia which he was glad of as he considered her as a Southern State. He was glad also that the members of Georgia were increased.

Mr. Williamson was not for reducing New Hampshire from 3 to 2. but for reducing some others. The Southern Interest must be extremely endangered by the present arrangement. The Northern States are to have a majority in the first instance and the means of perpetuating it.

Mr. Dayton observed that the line between the Northern & Southern interest had been improperly drawn: that Pennsylvania was the dividing State, there being six on each side of her.

General Pinkney urged the reduction, dwelt on the superior wealth of the Southern States, and insisted on its having its due weight in the Government.

Mr. Gouverneur Morris regretted the turn of the debate. The States he found had many Representatives on the floor. Few he feared were to be deemed the Representatives of America. He thought the Southern States have by the report more than their share of representation. Property ought to have its weight, but not all the weight. If the Southern States are to supply money. The Northern States are to spill their blood. Besides, the probable Revenue to be expected from the Southern States has been greatly overrated. He was against reducing New Hampshire. . . .

Adjourned

Wednesday July 11. In Convention

Mr. Randolph's motion requiring the Legislature to take a periodical census for the purpose of redressing inequalities in the Representation, was resumed.

Mr. Sherman was against shackling the Legislature too much. We ought to choose wise & good men, and then confide in them.

Mr. Mason. The greater the difficulty we find in fixing a proper rule of Representation, the more unwilling ought we to be, to throw the task from ourselves, on the General Legislature. He did not object to the conjectural ratio which was to prevail in the outset; but considered a Revision from time to time according to some permanent & precise standard as essential to the fair representation required in the 1st branch. According to the present population of America, the Northern part of it had a right to preponderate, and he could not deny it. But he wished it not to preponderate hereafter when the reason no longer continued. From the nature of man we may be sure, that those who have power in their hands will not give it up while they can retain it. On the contrary we know they will always when they can rather increase it. If the

Southern States therefore should have 3/4 of the people of America within their limits, the Northern will hold fast the majority of Representatives. 1/4 will govern the 3/4. The Southern States will complain: but they may complain from generation to generation without redress. Unless some principle therefore which will do justice to them hereafter shall be inserted in the Constitution, disagreeable as the declaration was to him, he must declare he could neither vote for the system here, nor support it, in his State. Strong objections had been drawn from the danger to the Atlantic interests from new Western States. Ought we to sacrifice what we know to be right in itself, lest it should prove favorable to States which are not yet in existence. If the Western States are to be admitted into the Union, as they arise, they must, he would repeat, be treated as equals, and subjected to no degrading discriminations. They will have the same pride & other passions which we have, and will either not unite with or will speedily revolt from the Union, if they are not in all respects placed on an equal footing with their brethren. It has been said they will be poor, and unable to make equal contributions to the general Treasury. He did not know but that in time they would be both more numerous & more wealthy than their Atlantic brethren. The extent & fertility of their soil, made this probable; and though Spain might for a time deprive them of the natural outlet for their productions, yet she will, because she must, finally yield to their demands. He urged that numbers of inhabitants; though not always a precise standard of wealth was sufficiently so for every substantial purpose.

Mr. Williamson was for making it the duty of the Legislature to do what was right & not leaving it at liberty to do or not to do it. He moved that Mr. Randolph's proposition be postponed in order to consider the following "that in order to ascertain the alterations that may happen in the population & wealth of the several States, a census shall be taken of the free white inhabitants and 3/5ths of those of other descriptions on the 1st year after this Government shall have been adopted and every   year thereafter; and that the Representation be regulated accordingly."

Mr. Randolph agreed that Mr. Williamson's proposition should stand in the place of his. He observed that the ratio fixt for the 1st meeting was a mere conjecture, that it placed the power in the hands of that part of America, which could not always be entitled to it, that this power would not be voluntarily renounced; and that it was consequently the duty of the Convention to secure its renunciation when justice might so require; by some constitutional provisions. If equality between great & small States be inadmissible, because in that case unequal numbers of Constituents would be represented by equal numbers of votes; was it not equally inadmissible that a larger & more populous district of America should hereafter have less representation, than a smaller & less populous district. If a fair representation of the people be not secured, the injustice of the Government will shake it to its foundations. What relates to suffrage is justly stated by the celebrated Montesquieu, as a fundamental article in Republican Governments. If the danger suggested by Mr. Gouverneur Morris be real, of advantage being taken of the Legislature in pressing moments, it was an additional reason, for tying their hands in such a manner that they could not sacrifice their trust to momentary considerations. Congress have pledged the public faith to New States, that they shall be admitted on equal terms. They never would nor ought to accede on any other. The census must be taken under the direction of the General Legislature. The States will be too much interested to take an impartial one for themselves.

Mr. Butler and General Pinkney insisted that blacks be included in the rule of Representation, *equally* with the Whites: and for that purpose moved that the words "three-fifths" be struck out.

Mr. Gerry thought that 3/5 of them was to say the least the full proportion that could be admitted.

Mr. Ghorum. This ratio was fixed by Congress as a rule of taxation. Then it was urged by the Delegates representing the States having slaves that the blacks were still more inferior to freemen. At present when the ratio of representation is to be established, we are assured that they are equal to freemen. The arguments on the former occasion had convinced him that 3/5 was pretty near the just proportion and he should vote according to the same opinion now.

Mr. Butler insisted that the labour of a slave in South Carolina was as productive & valuable as that of a freeman in Massachusetts, that as wealth was the great means of defence and utility to the Nation they were equally valuable to it with freemen; and that consequently an equal representation ought to be allowed for them in a Government which was instituted principally for the protection of property, and was itself to be supported by property.

Mr. Mason, could not agree to the motion, notwithstanding it was favorable to Virginia because he thought it unjust. It was certain that the slaves were valuable, as they raised the value of land, increased the exports & imports, and of course the revenue, would supply the means of feeding & supporting an army, and might in cases of emergency become themselves soldiers. As in these important respects they were useful to the community at large, they ought not to be excluded from the estimate of Representation. He could not however regard them as equal to freemen and could not vote for them as such. He added as worthy of remark, that the Southern States have this peculiar species of property, over & above the other species of property common to all the States.

Mr. Williamson reminded Mr. Ghorum that if the Southern States contended for the inferiority of blacks to whites when taxation was in view, the Eastern States on the same occasion contended for their equality. He did not however either then or now, concur in either extreme, but approved of the ratio of 3/5.

On Mr. Butler's motion for considering blacks as equal to Whites in the apportionment of Representation. [Lost 7 to 3.] . . .

Mr. Gouverneur Morris. . . . He could not persuade himself that numbers would be a just rule at any time. The remarks of [Mr. Mason] relative to the Western Country had not changed his opinion on that head. Among other objections it must be apparent they would not be able to furnish men equally enlightened, to share in the administration of our common interests. The Busy haunts of men not the remote wilderness, was the proper school of political Talents. If the Western people get the power into their hands they will ruin the Atlantic interests. The Back members are always most averse to the best measures. He mentioned the case of Pennsylvania formerly. The lower part of the State had the power in the first instance. They kept it in your own hands & the Country was the better for it. Another objection with him against admitting the blacks into the census, was that the people of Pennsylvania would revolt at the idea of being put on a footing with slaves. They would reject any plan that was to have such an effect. Two objections had been raised against leaving the adjustment of the Representation from time, to time, to the discretion of the Legislature. The first was they would be unwilling to revise it at all. The second that by referring to *wealth* they would be bound by a rule which if willing, they would be unable to execute. The 1st objection distrusts their fidelity. But if their duty, their honor & their oaths will not bind them, let us not put into their hands our liberty, and all our other great interests: let us have no Government at all. In the second place, if these ties will bind them, we need not distrust the practicability of the rule. It was followed in part by the Committee in the apportionment of Representatives yesterday reported to the House. The best course that could be taken would be to leave the interests of the people to the Representatives of the people.

Mr. Madison, was not a little surprised to hear this implicit confidence urged by a member who on all ocasions, had inculcated so strongly, the political depravity of men, and the necessity of checking one vice and interest by opposing to them another vice & interest. If the Representatives of the people would be bound by the ties he had mentioned, what need was there of a Senate? What of a Revisionary power? But his reasoning was not only inconsistent with his former reasoning, but with itself. At the same time that he recommended this implicit confidence to the Southern States in the Northern Majority, he was still more zealous in exhorting all to a jealousy of Western Majority. To reconcile the gentleman with himself, it must be imagined that he determined the human character by the points of the compass. The truth was that all men having power ought to be distrusted to a certain degree. The case of Pennsylvania had been mentioned where it was admitted that those who were possessed of the power in the original settlement, never admitted the new settlements to a due share of it. England was a still more striking example. The power there had long been in the hands of the boroughs, of the minority; who had opposed & defeated every reform which had been attempted. Virginia was in a lesser degree another example. With regard to the Western States, he was clear & firm in opinion, that no unfavorable distinctions were admissible either in point of justice or policy. He thought also that the hope of contributions to the Treasury from them had been much underrated. Future contributions it seemed to be understood on all hands would be principally levied on imports & exports. The extent and fertility of the Western Soil would for a long time give to agriculture a preference over manufactures. Trials would be repeated till some articles could be raised from it that would bear a transportation to places where they could be exchanged for imported manufactures. Whenever the Mississippi should be opened to them, which would of necessity be the case, as soon as their population would subject them to any considerable share of the public burden, imposts on their trade could be collected with less expense & greater certainty, than on that of the Atlantic States. In the mean time, as their supplies must pass through the *Atlantic States*, their contributions would be levied in the same manner with those of the Atlantic States. . . . He would admit that in no situation, numbers of inhabitants were an accurate measure of wealth. . . . The value of labour, might be considered as the principal criterion of wealth and ability to support taxes; and this would find its level in different places where the intercourse should be easy & free, with as much certainty as the value of money or any other thing. Wherever labour would yield most, people would resort, till the competition should destroy the inequality. Hence it is that the people are constantly swarming from the more to the less populous places—from Europe to America, from the Northern & Middle parts of the U.S. to the Southern & Western. They go where land is cheaper, because there labour is dearer. If it be true that the same quantity of produce raised on the banks of the Ohio is of less value, than on the Delaware, it is also true that the same labor will raise twice or thrice, the quantity in the former, that it will raise in the latter situation. . . .

Mr. Gouverneur Morris was compelled to declare himself reduced to the dilemma of doing injustice to the Southern States or to human nature, and he must therefore do it to the former. For he could never agree to give such encouragement to the slave trade as would be given by allowing them a representation for their negroes, and he did not believe those States would ever confederate on terms that would deprive them of that trade. . . .

July 12 was taken up with a discussion of the basis for taxation. The debates centered around the proposal that "taxation shall be in proportion to Representation" in the lower house. Here once more the discussion over how slaves were to be counted came to the fore and produced considerable bitterness. The following day Gouverneur Morris spoke again to this issue.

Mr. Gouverneur Morris. If Negroes were to be viewed as inhabitants, and the revision was to proceed on the principle of numbers of inhabitants they ought to be added in their entire number, and not in the proportion of 3/5. If as property, the word wealth was right, and striking it out, would produce the very inconsistency which it was meant to get rid of.—The train of business & the late turn which it had taken, had led him he said, into deep meditation on it, and He would candidly state the result. A distinction had been set up & urged, between the Northern & Southern States. He had hitherto considered this doctrine as heretical. He still thought the distinction groundless. He sees however that it is persisted in, and that the Southern Gentlemen will not be satisfied unless they see the way open to their gaining a majority in the public Councils. The consequence of such a transfer of power from the maritime to the interior & landed interest will he foresees be such an oppression of commerce, that he shall be obliged to vote for the vicious principle of equality in the 2nd branch in order to provide some defence for the Northern States against it. But to come more to the point: either this distinction is fictitious or real; if fictitious let it be dismissed & let us proceed with due confidence. If it be real, instead of attempting to blend incompatible things, let us at once take a friendly leave of each other. There can be no end of demands for security if every particular interest is to be entitled to it. The Eastern States may claim it for their fishery, and for other objects, as the Southern States claim it for their peculiar objects. In this struggle between the two ends of the Union, what part ought the middle States in point of policy to take: to join their Eastern brethren according to his ideas. If the Southern States get the power into their hands, and be joined as they will be with the interior Country, they will inevitably bring on a war with Spain for the Mississippi. This language is already held. The interior Country having no property nor interest exposed on the sea, will be little affected by such a war. He wished to know what security the Northern & middle States will have against this danger. It has been said that North Carolina, South Carolina, and Georgia only will in a little time have a majority of the people of America. They must in that case include the great interior Country, and every thing was to be apprehended from their getting the power into their hands.

Mr. Butler. The security the Southern States want is that their negroes may not be taken from them, which some gentlemen within or without doors, have a very good mind to do. It was not supposed that North Carolina, South Carolina, & Georgia would have more people than all the other States, but many more relatively to the other States than they now have. The people & strength of America are evidently bearing Southwardly & South westwardly.

Mr. Wilson. If a general declaration would satisfy any gentleman he had no indisposition to declare his sentiments. Conceiving that all men wherever placed have equal rights and are equally entitled to confidence, he viewed without apprehension the period when a few States should contain the superior number of people. The majority of people wherever found ought in all questions to govern the minority. If the interior Country should acquire this majority, it will not only have the right, but will avail themselves of it whether we will or no. This jealousy misled the policy of G. Britain with regard to America. The fatal maxims espoused by her were that the Colonies were growing too fast, and that their growth must be stinted in time. What were the consequences? first, enmity on our part, then actual separation. Like consequences will result on the part of the interior settlements, if like jealousy & policy be pursued on ours. Further, if numbers be not a proper rule, why is not some better rule pointed out. No one has yet ventured to attempt it. Congress have never been able to discover a better. No State as far as he had heard, has suggested any other. In 1783, after elaborate discussion of a measure of wealth all were satisfied then as they are now that the rule of numbers, does not differ much from the combined rule of numbers & wealth. Again he could not agree that property was the sole or the primary object of Government & society. The cultivation & improvement of the human mind was the most noble object. With respect to this object, as well as to other *personal* rights, numbers were surely the natural & precise measure of Representation. And with respect to property, they could not vary much from the precise measure. In no point of view however could the establishment of numbers as the rule of representation in the 1st branch vary his opinion as to the impropriety of letting a vicious principle into the 2nd branch. . . .

Adjourned

Saturday. July 14. In Convention

Mr. L. Martin called for the question on the whole report, including the parts relating to the origination of money bills, and the equality of votes in the 2nd branch.

Mr. Gerry. wished before the question should be put, that the attention of the House might be turned to the dangers apprehended from Western States. He was for admitting them on liberal terms, but not for putting ourselves into their hands. They will if they acquire power like all men, abuse it. They will oppress commerce, and drain our wealth into the Western Country. To guard against these consequences, he thought it necessary to limit the number of new States to be admitted into the Union, in such a manner, that they should never be able to outnumber the Atlantic States. He accordingly moved "that in order to secure the liberties of the States already confederated, the number of Representatives in the 1st branch, of the States which shall hereafter be established, shall never exceed in number, the Representatives from such of the States as shall accede to this confederation.

Mr. King. seconded the motion.

Mr. Sherman, thought there was no probability that the number of future States would exceed that of the Existing States. If the event should ever happen, it was too remote to be taken into consideration at this time. Besides We are providing for our posterity, for our children & our grand Children, who would be as likely to be citizens of new Western States, as of the old States. On this consideration alone, we ought to make no such discrimination as was proposed by the motion.

Mr. Gerry. If some of our children should remove, others will stay behind, and he thought it incumbent on us to provide for their interests. There was a rage for emigration from the Eastern States to the Western Country, and he did not wish those remaining behind to be at the mercy of the Emigrants. Besides foreigners are resorting to that country, and it is uncertain what turn things may take there.—On the question for agreeing to the Motion of Mr. Gerry, it passed in the negative. . . .

Mr. Rutlidge proposed to reconsider the two propositions touching the originating of money bills in the first & the equality of votes in the second branch.

Mr. Sherman was for the question on the whole at once. It was he said a conciliatory plan, it had been considered in all its parts, a great deal of time had been spent on it, and if any part should now be altered, it would be necessary to go over the whole ground again. . . .

Still the large states remained adamant. Outmaneuvered and out-voted, they returned time and again to the attack, refusing to compromise what they felt was an essential principle.

Adjourned

Monday. July 16. In Convention

On the question for agreeing to the whole Report as amended & including the equality of votes in the 2nd branch, it passed in the Affirmative. . . .

The whole, thus passed is in the words following viz

Resolved that in the original formation of the Legislature of the U.S. the first branch thereof shall consist of sixty-five members, of which number New Hampshire shall send 3. Massachusetts 8. Rhode Island 1. Connecticut 5. New York 6. New Jersey 4. Pennsylvania 8. Delaware 1. Maryland 6. Virginia 10. North Carolina 5. South Carolina 5. Georgia 3.—But as the present situation of the States may probably alter in the number of their inhabitants, the Legislature of the U.S. shall be authorized from time to time to apportion the number of Representatives; and in case any of the States shall hereafter be divided, or enlarged by, addition of territory, or any two or more States united, or any new States created within the limits of the U.S. the Legislature of the U.S. shall possess authority to regulate the number of Representatives in any of the foregoing cases, upon the principle of their number of inhabitants, according to the provisions hereafter mentioned, namely—provided always that representation ought to be proportioned according to direct taxation; and in order to ascertain the alteration in the direct taxation, which may be required from time to time by the changes in the relative circumstances of the States—

Resolved, that a Census be taken within six years from the 1st meeting of the Legislature of the U.S. and once within the term of every 10 years afterwards of all the inhabitants of the U.S. in the manner and according to the ratio recommended by Congress in their Resolution of April 18, 1783, and that the Legislature of the U.S. shall proportion the direct taxation accordingly—

Resolved, that all bills for raising or appropriating money, and for fixing the salaries of officers of the Government of the U.S. shall originate in the first branch of the Legislature of the U.S. and shall not be altered or amended in the 2nd branch: and that no money shall be drawn from the public Treasury, but in pursuance of appropriations to be originated in the 1st branch.

Resolved that in the 2nd branch of the Legislature of the U.S. each State shall have an equal vote. . . .

Mr. Randolph. The vote of this morning [involving an equality of suffrage in 2nd branch] had embarrassed the business extremely. All the powers given in the Report from the Committee of the whole, were founded on the supposition that a Proportional representation was to prevail in both branches of the Legislature. When he came here this morning his purpose was to have offered some propositions that might if possible have united a great majority of votes, and particularly might provide against the danger suspected on the part of the smaller States, by enumerating the cases in which it might lie, and allowing an equality of votes in such cases. But finding from the preceding vote that they persist in demanding an equal vote in all cases, that they have succeeded in obtaining it, and that New York if present would probably be on the same side, he could not but think we were unprepared to discuss this subject further. It will probably be in vain to come to any final decision with a bare majority on either side. For these reasons he wished the Convention might adjourn, that the large States might consider the steps proper to be taken in the present solemn crisis of the business, and that the small States might also deliberate on the means of conciliation.

Mr. Patterson, thought with Mr. Randolph that it was high time for the Convention to adjourn that the rule of secrecy ought to be rescinded, and that our Constituents should be consulted. No conciliation could be admissible on the part of the smaller States on any other ground than that of an equality of votes in the 2nd branch. If Mr. Randolph would reduce to form his motion for an adjournment sine die, he would second it with all his heart.

General Pinkney wished to know of Mr. Randolph whether he meant an adjournment sine die, or only an adjournment for the day. If the former was meant, it differed much from his idea. He could not think of going to South Carolina and returning again to this place. Besides it was chimerical to suppose that the States if consulted would ever accord separately, and beforehand.

Mr. Randolph, had never entertained an idea of an adjournment sine die; & was sorry that his meaning had been so readily & strangely mis-interpreted. He had in view merely an adjournment till tomorrow, in order that some conciliatory experiment might if possible be devised, and that in case the smaller States should continue to hold back, the larger might then take such measures, he would not say what, as might be necessary.

Mr. Patterson seconded the adjournment till tomorrow, as an oppor-tunity seemed to be wished by the larger States to deliberate further on conciliatory expedients.

On the question for adjourning till tomorrow, the States were equally divided. . . . So it was lost.

Mr. Broome thought it his duty to declare his opinion against an ad-journment sine die, as had been urged by Mr. Patterson. Such a measure he thought would be fatal. Something must be done by the Convention, though it should be by a bare majority.

Mr. Gerry observed that Massachusetts was opposed to an adjourn-ment, because they saw no new ground of compromise. But as it seemed to be the opinion of so many States that a trial should be made, the State would now concur in the adjournment.

Mr. Rutlidge could see no need of an adjournment because he could see no chance of a compromise. The little States were fixt. They had repeatedly & solemnly declared themselves to be so. All that the large States then had to do, was to decide whether they would yield or not. For his part he conceived that although we could not do what we thought best, in itself, we ought to do something. Had we not better keep the Government up a little longer, hoping that another Convention will supply our omissions, than abandon every thing to hazard. Our Con-stituents will be very little satisfied with us if we take the latter course.

Mr. Randolph & Mr. King renewed the motion to adjourn till to-morrow.

On the question. Massachusetts ay. Connecticut no. New Jersey ay. Pennsylvania ay. Delaware no. Maryland ay. Virginia ay. North Caro-lina ay. South Carolina ay. Georgia divided.

Adjourned

On the morning following before the hour of the convention a number of the members from the larger States, by common agreement met for the purpose of consulting on the proper steps to be taken in consequence of the vote in favor of an equal Representation in the 2nd branch, and the apparent inflexibility of the smaller States on that point. Several members from the latter States also attended. The time was wasted in vague conversation on the subject, without any specific proposition or agreement. It appeared indeed that the opinions of the members who disliked the equality of votes differed so much as to the importance of that point, and as to the policy of risking a failure of any general act of the Convention, by inflexibly opposing it. Several of them supposing that no good Government could or would be built on that foundation, and that as a division of the Convention into two opinions was unavoidable; it would be better that the side comprising the principal States, and a majority of the people of America, should propose a scheme of Government to the States, than that a scheme should be proposed on the other side, would have concurred in a firm opposition to the smaller States, and in a separate recommendation, if eventually necessary. Others seemed inclined to yield to the smaller States, and to concur in such an act however imperfect & exceptionable, as might be agreed on by the Convention as a body, though decided by a bare majority of States and by a minority of the people of the U. States. It is probable that the result of this consultation satisfied the smaller States that they had nothing to apprehend from a union of the larger, in any plan whatever against the equality of votes in the 2nd branch.

The most critical day in the debates was July 16, when William Paterson, doubtless quite consciously, interpreted Randolph's call for adjournment to mean a dissolution of the convention. Randolph, it will have been observed, immediately denied such an intention, chagrined that "his meaning had been so readily & strangely misinterpreted."

When the delegates reconvened the next day, the large-state faction was plainly a defeated party. It was clear that it was equal representation in the upper house or no Constitution. From this point, the delegates concentrated their attention on what were, in effect, the practical details to fill out the grand outlines of the Constitution. We will therefore give much less space to the subsequent debates.

It is worth noting, in passing, that one of the most important features of the Constitution, proportional representation in the House and equal representation in the Senate, was a compromise of the most excruciating kind, accepted only with the greatest reluctance by both parties. Put another way, after an opening act of great buoyancy and brilliance, Act Two seemed to move inexorably toward a tragic conclusion. At the end tragedy was averted by the narrowest of margins and the way prepared for a final and concluding act, which, absorbing as it is, follows a rather intricate path to the proverbial happy ending.

On the seventeenth the delegates came back to the question of the chief executive's term of office and method of appointment. The vote to have the "Executive Magistrate" appointed by the National Legislature was unanimous.

On Wednesday, July 18, the Convention turned its attention to the judiciary, agreeing unanimously that "a National Judiciary be established to consist of one supreme tribunal." The question of how judges would be appointed proved a much more controversial question, the delegates being almost equally divided in preferring the executive or the legislative branch. Unable to resolve this issue, they took up the almost equally controversial problem of the chief magistrate's term of office. The debate continued the next day.

Thursday. July 19. In Convention . . .

Mr. Patterson . . . proposed that the Executive should be appointed by Electors to be chosen by the States in a ratio that would allow one elector to the smallest and three to the largest States.

Mr. Wilson. It seems to be the unanimous sense that the Executive should not be appointed by the Legislature, unless he be rendered ineligible a second time: he perceived with pleasure that the idea was gaining ground, of an election mediately or immediately by the people.

Mr. Madison. If it be a fundamental principle of free Government that the Legislative, Executive & Judiciary powers should be *separately* exercised, it is equally so that they be *independently* exercised. There is the same & perhaps greater reason why the Executive should be independent of the Legislature, than why the Judiciary should: A coalition of the two former powers would be more immediately & certainly dangerous to public liberty. It is essential then that the appointment of the Executive should either be drawn from some source, or held by some tenure, that will give him a free agency with regard to the Legislature. This could not be if he was to be appointable from time to time by the Legislature. It was not clear that an appointment in the first instance even with an eligibility afterwards would not establish an improper connection between the two departments. Certain it was that the appointment would be attended with intrigues and contentions that ought not to be unnecessarily admitted. He was disposed for these reasons to refer the appointment to some other source. The people at large was in his opinion the fittest in itself. It would be as likely as any that could be devised to produce an Executive Magistrate of distinguished Character. The people generally could only know & vote for some Citizen whose merits had rendered him an object of general attention & esteem. There was one difficulty however of a serious nature attending an immediate choice by the people. The right of suffrage was much more diffusive in the Northern than the Southern States; and the latter could have no influence in the election on the score of the Negroes. The substitution of electors obviated this difficulty and seemed on the whole to be liable to fewest objections. . . .

Mr. Butler was against a frequency of the elections. Georgia & South Carolina were too distant to send electors often.

Mr. Elseworth was for 6 years. If the elections be too frequent, the Executive will not be firm enough. There must be duties which will make him unpopular for the moment. There will be *outs* as well as *ins*. His administration therefore will be attacked and misrepresented.

Mr. Williamson was for 6 years. The expence will be considerable & ought not to be unnecessarily repeated. If the Elections are too frequent, the best men will not undertake the service and those of an inferior character will be liable to be corrupted.

On the question for 6 years? [Passed 9 to 1.]

On July 20 the delegates considered the question of how "electors" were to be chosen and failing to resolve that took up the matter of impeachment.

"to be removeable on impeachment and conviction for mal practice or neglect of duty." see Resol: 9.

Mr. Pinkney & Mr. Gouverneur Morris moved to strike out this part of the Resolution. Mr. Pinkney observed he ought not to be impeachable whilst in office

Mr. Davis. If he be not impeachable whilst in office, he will spare no efforts or means whatever to get himself re-elected. He considered this as an essential security for the good behaviour of the Executive.

Mr. Wilson concurred in the necessity of making the Executive impeachable whilst in office.

Mr. Gouverneur Morris. He can do no criminal act without Coadjutors who may be punished. In case he should be re-elected, that will be sufficient proof of his innocence. Besides who is to impeach? Is the impeachment to suspend his functions. If it is not the mischief will go on. If it is the impeachment will be nearly equivalent to a displacement, and will render the Executive dependent on those who are to impeach.

Col. Mason. No point is of more importance than that the right of impeachment should be continued. Shall any man be above Justice? Above all shall that man be above it, who can commit the most extensive injustice? When great crimes were committed he was for punishing the principal as well as the Coadjutors. There had been much debate & difficulty as to the mode of choosing the Executive. He approved of that which had been adopted at first, namely of referring the appointment to the National Legislature. One objection against Electors was the danger of their being corrupted by the Candidates; & this furnished a peculiar reason in favor of impeachments whilst in office. Shall the man who has practiced corruption & by that means procured his appointment in the first instance, be suffered to escape punishment, by repeating his guilt?

Doctor Franklin was for retaining the clause as favorable to the Executive. History furnishes one example only of a first Magistrate being formally brought to public Justice. Every body cried out against this as unconstitutional. What was the practice before this in cases where the chief Magistrate rendered himself obnoxious? Why recourse was had to assassination in which he was not only deprived of his life but of the opportunity of vindicating his character. It would be the best way therefore to provide in the Constitution for the regular punishment of the Executive where his misconduct should deserve it, and for his honorable acquittal when he should be unjustly accused.

Mr. Gouverneur Morris admits corruption & some few other offences to be such as ought to be impeachable; but thought the cases ought to be enumerated & defined:

Mr. Madison thought it indispensable that some provision should be made for defending the Community against the incapacity, negligence or perfidy of the chief Magistrate. The limitation of the period of his service, was not a sufficient security. He might lose his capacity after his appointment. He might pervert his administration into a scheme of peculation or oppression. He might betray his trust to foreign powers. The case of the Executive Magistracy was very distinguishable, from that of the Legislature or of any other public body, holding offices of limited duration. It could not be presumed that all or even a majority of the members of an Assembly would either lose their capacity for discharging, or be bribed to betray, their trust. Besides the restraints of their personal integrity & honor, the difficulty of acting in concert for purposes of corruption was a security to the public. And if one or a few members only should be seduced, the soundness of the remaining members, would maintain the integrity and fidelity of the body. In the case of the executive Magistracy which was to be administered by a single man, loss of capacity or corruption was more within the compass of probable events, and either of them might be fatal to the Republic.

Mr. Pinkney did not see the necessity of impeachments. He was sure they ought not to issue from the Legislature who would in that case hold them as a rod over the Executive and by that means effectually destroy his independence. His revisionary power in particular would be rendered altogether insignificant.

Mr. Gerry urged the necessity of impeachments. A good magistrate will not fear them. A bad one ought to be kept in fear of them. He hoped the maxim would never be adopted here that the chief magistrate could do no wrong. . . .

Mr. Randolph. The propriety of impeachments was a favorite principle with him. Guilt wherever found ought to be punished. The Executive will have great opportunities of abusing his power; particularly in time of war when the military force, and in some respects the public money will be in his hands. Should no regular punishment be provided, it will be irregularly inflicted by tumults & insurrections. He is aware of the necessity of proceeding with a cautious hand, and of excluding as much as possible the influence of the Legislature from the business. He suggested for consideration an idea which had fallen [from Col Hamilton] of composing a forum out of the Judges belonging to the States: and even of requiring some preliminary inquest whether just grounds of impeachment existed. . . .

Mr. Gouverneur Morris's opinion had been changed by the arguments used in the discussion. He was now sensible of the necessity of impeachments, if the Executive was to continue for any [length of] time in office. Our Executive was not like a Magistrate having a life interest, much less like one having an hereditary interest in his office. He may be bribed by a greater interest to betray his trust; and no one would say that we ought to expose ourselves to the danger of seeing the first Magistrate in foreign pay, without being able to guard against it by displacing him. One would think the King of England well secured against bribery. He has as it were a fee simple in the whole Kingdom. Yet Charles II was bribed by Louis XIV. The Executive ought therefore to be impeachable for treachery; Corrupting his electors, and incapacity were other causes of impeachment. For the latter he should be punished not as a man, but as an officer, and punished only by degradation from his office. This Magistrate is not the King but the prime-Minister. The people are the King. When we make him amenable to Justice however we should take care to provide some mode that will not make him dependent on the Legislature. . . .

On the Question, Shall the Executive be removeable on impeachments &c.? [Passed, 8 to 2.] . . .

On Saturday, July 21 (in convention), despite the objections of Elbridge Gerry, the delegates took up once more Wilson's and Madison's notion that the chief executive and the "supreme National Judiciary have a 'Revisionary power,'" the power to veto laws before they were put into effect. After much discussion, the motion lost.

Monday, July 23. In Convention . . .

Resol: 19. "referring the new Constitution to Assemblies to be chosen by the people for the express purpose of ratifying it" was . . . taken into consideration.

Mr. Elseworth moved that it be referred to the Legislatures of the States for ratification. Mr. Patterson seconded the motion.

Col. Mason considered a reference of the plan to the authority of the people as one of the most important and essential of the Resolutions. The Legislatures have no power to ratify it. They are the mere creatures of the State Constitutions, and can not be greater than their creators. And he knew of no power in any of the Constitutions, he knew there was no power in some of them, that could be competent to this object. Whither then must we resort? To the people with whom all power remains that has not been given up in the Constitutions derived from them. It was of great moment he observed that this doctrine should be cherished as the basis of free Government. Another strong reason was that admitting the Legislatures to have a competent authority, it would be wrong to refer the plan to them, because succeeding Legislatures having equal authority could undo the acts of their predecessors; and the National Government would stand in each State on the weak and tottering foundation of an Act of Assembly. There was a remaining consideration of some weight. In some of the States the Governments were not derived from the clear & undisputed authority of the people. This was the case in Virginia. Some of the best & wisest citizens considered the Constitution as established by an assumed authority. A National Constitution derived from such a source would be exposed to the severest criticisms. . . .

[Mr. Madison] considered the difference between a system founded on the Legislatures only, and one founded on the people, to be the true difference between a *league* or *treaty,* and a *Constitution.* The former in point of *moral obligation* might be as inviolable as the latter. In point of *political operation,* there were two important distinctions in favor of the latter. 1. A law violating a treaty ratified by a pre-existing law, might be respected by the Judges as a law, though an unwise or perfidious one.

A law violating a constitution established by the people themselves, would be considered by the Judges as null & void. 2. The doctrine laid down by the law of Nations in the case of treaties is that a breach of any one article by any of the parties, frees the other parties from their engagements. In the case of a union of people under one Constitution, the nature of the pact has always been understood to exclude such an interpretation. Comparing the two modes in point of expediency he thought all the considerations which recommended this Convention in preference to Congress for proposing the reform were in favor of State Conventions in preference to the Legislatures for examining and adopting it. . . .

On Tuesday, July 24 (in convention), Rutledge, Randolph, Gorham, Wilson, and Ellsworth were appointed to a committee "to report a Constitution conformable to the Resolutions passed by the Convention. . . ."

Thursday July 26. In Convention . . .

The proceedings since Monday last were referred unanimously to the Committee of detail, and the Convention then unanimously Adjourned till Monday, August 6. that the Committee of detail might have time to prepare & report the Constitution. . . .

The balance of the week of August 6 was occupied by going over each article of the proposed Constitution. There was a lengthy discussion of whether the times of the meeting of the National Legislature should be specified by the Constitution or left to that body to set their own meetings as necessary. The delegates then considered once more the requirements for the suffrage—how much property a voter should have in order to qualify, the minimum age, etc.

Tuesday August 7. In Convention . . .

Col. Mason. We all feel too strongly the remains of ancient prejudices, and view things too much through a British medium. A Freehold is the qualification in England, & hence it is imagined to be the only proper one. The true idea in his opinion was that every man having evidence of attachment to & permanent common interest with the Society ought to share in all its rights & privileges. Was this qualification restrained to freeholders? Does no other kind of property but land evidence a common interest in the proprietor? does nothing besides property mark a permanent attachment. Ought the merchant, the monied man, the parent of a number of children whose fortunes are to be pursued in his own Country, to be viewed as suspicious characters, and unworthy to be trusted with the common rights of their fellow Citizens?

Mr. Madison. the right of suffrage is certainly one of the fundamental articles of republican Government, and ought not to be left to be regulated by the Legislature. A gradual abridgment of this right has been the mode in which Aristocracies have been built on the ruins of popular forms. Whether the Constitutional qualification ought to be a freehold, would with him depend much on the probable reception such a change would meet with in the States where the right was now exercised by every description of people. In several of the States a freehold was now the qualification. Viewing the subject in its merits alone, the freeholders of the Country would be the safest depositories of Republican liberty. In future times a great majority of the people will not only be without landed, but any other sort of, property. These will either combine under the influence of their common situation; in which case, the rights of property & the public liberty, will not be secure in their hands: or which is more probable, they will become the tools of opulence & ambition, in which case there will be equal danger on another side. . . .

Doctor Franklin. It is of great consequence that we should not depress the virtue & public spirit of our common people; of which they displayed a great deal during the war, and which contributed principally to the favorable issue of it. He related the honorable refusal of the American seamen who were carried in great numbers into the British Prisons during the war, to redeem themselves from misery or to seek their fortunes, by entering on board the Ships of the Enemies to their Country; contrasting their patriotism with a contemporary instance in which the British seamen made prisoners by the Americans, readily entered on the ships of the latter on being promised a share of the prizes that might be made out of their own Country. This proceeded he said from the different manner in which the common people were treated in America & G. Britain. He did not think that the elected had any right in any case to narrow the privileges of the electors. He quoted as arbitrary the British Statute setting forth the danger of tumultuous meetings, and under that pretext narrowing the right of suffrage to persons having freeholds of a certain value; observing that this Statute was soon followed by another under the succeeding Parliament subjecting the people who had no votes to peculiar labors & hardships. He was persuaded also that such a restriction as was proposed would give great uneasiness in the populous States. The sons of a substantial farmer, not being themselves free-holders, would not be pleased at being disfranchised, and there are a great many persons of that description. . . .

Mr. Rutledge thought the idea of restraining the right of suffrage to the freeholders a very unadvised one. It would create division among the people & make enemies of all those who should be excluded. . . .

Wednesday August 8. In Convention

The delegates then turned to the term of residency required for immigrants before they could qualify as citizens. A motion was made by General Pinckney to increase the number of representatives allowed to South Carolina on the basis of a larger slave population. This brought indignant protests from Rufus King and Gouverneur Morris. The bitterness of their comments is an indication of how strongly the delegates felt about the slavery issue.

Mr. King wished to know what influence the vote just passed was meant to have on the succeeding part of the Report, concerning the admission of slaves into the rule of Representation. . . . The admission of slaves was a most grating circumstance to his mind, & he believed would be so to a great part of the people of America. He had not made a strenuous opposition to it heretofore because he had hoped that this concession would have produced a readiness which had not been manifested, to strengthen the General Government and to mark a full confidence in it. The Report under consideration had by the tenor of it, put an end to all those hopes. In two great points the hands of the Legislature were absolutely tied. The importation of slaves could not be prohibited—exports could not be taxed. Is this reasonable? What are the great objects of the General System? 1. defence against foreign invasion. 2. against internal sedition. Shall all the States then be bound to defend each; & shall each be at liberty to introduce a weakness which will render defence more difficult? Shall one part of the U.S. be bound to defend another part, and that other part be at liberty not only to increase its own danger, but to withhold the compensation for the burden? If slaves are to be imported shall not the exports produced by their labor, supply a revenue the better to enable the General Government to defend their masters?—There was so much inequality & unreasonableness in all this, that the people of the Northern States could never be reconciled to it. No candid man could undertake to justify it to them. He had hoped that some accommodation would have taken place on this subject; that at least a time would have been limited for the importation of slaves. He never could agree to let them be imported without limitation & then be represented in the National Legislature. Indeed he could so little persuade himself of the rectitude of such a practice, that he was not sure he could assent to it under any circumstances. At all events, either slaves should not be represented, or exports should be taxable.

Mr. Sherman regarded the slave trade as iniquitous; but the point of representation having been settled after much difficulty & deliberation, he did not think himself bound to make opposition; especially as the present article as amended did not preclude any arrangement whatever on that point in another place of the Report. . . .

Mr. Gouverneur Morris moved to insert "free" before the word inhabitants. Much he said would depend on this point. He never would concur in upholding domestic slavery. It was a nefarious institution. It was the curse of heaven on the States where it prevailed. Compare the free regions of the Middle States, where a rich & noble cultivation marks the prosperity & happiness of the people, with the misery & poverty which overspread the barren wastes of Virginia, Maryland & the other States having slaves. Travel through the whole Continent & you behold the prospect continually varying with the appearance & disappearance of slavery. The moment you leave the Eastern States & enter New York, the effects of the institution become visible, passing through the Jerseys & entering Pennsylvania every criterion of superior improvement witnesses the change. Proceed southwardly & every step you take through the great region of slaves presents a desert increasing, with the increasing proportion of these wretched beings. Upon what principle is it that the slaves shall be computed in the representation? Are they men? Then make them Citizens and let them vote. Are they property? Why then is no other property included? The Houses in this city [Philadelphia] are worth more than all the wretched slaves which cover the rice swamps of South Carolina. The admission of slaves into the Representation when fairly explained comes to this: that the inhabitant of Georgia and South Carolina who goes to the Coast of Africa, and in defiance of the most sacred laws of humanity tears away his fellow creatures from their dearest connections & damns them to the most cruel bondage, shall have more votes in a Government instituted for protection of the rights of mankind, than the Citizen of Pennsylvania or New Jersey who views with a laudable horror, so nefarious a practice. He would add that Domestic slavery is the most prominent feature in the aristocratic countenance of the proposed Constitution. The vassalage of the poor has ever been the favorite offspring of Aristocracy. And What is the proposed compensation to the Northern States for a sacrifice of every principle of right, of every impulse of humanity. They are to bind themselves to march their militia for the defence of the Southern States; for their defence against those very slaves of whom they complain. They must supply vessels & seamen in case of foreign Attack. The Legislature will have indefinite power to tax them by excises, and duties on imports: both of which will fall heavier on them than on the Southern inhabitants; for the bohea tea used by a Northern freeman, will pay more tax than the whole consumption of the miserable slave, which consists of nothing more than his physical subsistence and the rag that covers his nakedness. On the other side the Southern States are not to be restrained from importing fresh supplies of wretched Africans, at once to increase the danger of attack, and the difficulty of defence; nay they are to be encouraged to it by an assurance of having their votes in the National Government increased in proportion, and are at the same time to have their exports & their slaves exempt from all contributions for the public service. Let it not be said that direct taxation is to be proportioned to representation. It is idle to suppose that the General Government can stretch its hand directly into the pockets of the people scattered over so vast a Country. They can only do it through the medium of exports, imports & excises. For what then are all these sacrifices to be made? He would sooner submit himself to a tax for paying for all the negroes in the United States, than saddle posterity with such a Constitution. . . .

Adjourned

Thursday August 9. In Convention

The debate on the length of residence required before an immigrant to the United States could qualify as a candidate for the legislature also brought an interesting and important discussion. Gouverneur Morris proposed fourteen years' citizenship as the minimum time. Madison replied:

[He] was not averse to some restrictions on this subject; but could never agree to the proposed amendment. He thought any restriction however in the *Constitution* unnecessary, and improper. unnecessary; because the National Legislature is to have the right of regulating naturalization, and can by virtue thereof fix different periods of residence as conditions of enjoying different privileges of Citizenship: Improper; because it will give a tincture of illiberality to the Constitution: because it will put it out of the power of the National Legislature even by special acts of naturalization to confer the full rank of Citizens on meritorious strangers & because it will discourage the most desirable class of people from emigrating to the U.S. Should the proposed Constitution have the intended effect of giving stability & reputation to our Governments great numbers of respectable Europeans: men who love liberty and wish to partake its blessings, will be ready to transfer their fortunes hither. All such would feel the mortification of being marked with suspicious incapacitations though they should not covet the public honors. He was not apprehensive that any dangerous numbers of strangers would be appointed by the State Legislatures, if they were left at liberty to do so: nor that foreign powers would make use of strangers as instruments for their purposes. Their bribes would be expended on men whose circumstances would rather stifle than excite jealousy & watchfulness in the public.

Mr. Butler was decidedly opposed to the admission of foreigners without a long residence in the Country. They bring with them, not only attachments to other Countries; but ideas of Government so distinct from ours that in every point of view they are dangerous. He acknowledged that if he himself had been called into public life within a short time after his coming to America, his foreign habits, opinions & attachments would have rendered him an improper agent in public affairs. He mentioned the great strictness observed in Great Britain on this subject.

Doctor Franklin was not against a reasonable time, but should be very sorry to see any thing like illiberality inserted in the Constitution. The people in Europe are friendly to this Country. Even in the Country with which we have been lately at war, we have now & had during the war, a great many friends not only among the people at large but in both houses of Parliament. In every other Country in Europe all the people are our friends. We found in the course of the Revolution that many strangers served us faithfully—and that many natives took part against their Country. When foreigners after looking about for some other Country in which they can obtain more happiness, give a preference to ours it is a proof of attachment which ought to excite our confidence & affection.

Mr. Randolph did not know but it might be problematical whether emigrations to this Country were on the whole useful or not: but he could never agree to the motion for disabling them for 14 years to participate in the public honours. He reminded the Convention of the language held by our patriots during the Revolution, and the principles laid down in all our American Constitutions. Many foreigners may have fixed their fortunes among us under the faith of these invitations. All persons under this description, with all others who would be affected by such a regulation, would enlist themselves under the banners of hostility to the proposed System. He would go as far as seven years, but no farther.

Mr. Wilson said he rose with feelings which were perhaps peculiar; mentioning the circumstance of his not being a native, and the possibility, if the ideas of some gentlemen should be pursued, of his being incapacitated from holding a place under the very Constitution, which he had shared in the trust of making. He remarked the illiberal complexion which the motion would give to the System, & the effect which a good system would have in inviting meritorious foreigners among us, and the discouragement & mortification they must feel from the degrading discrimination, now proposed. He had himself experienced this mortification. On his removal into Maryland, he found himself, from defect of residence, under certain legal incapacities which never ceased to produce chagrin, though he assuredly did not desire & would not have accepted the offices to which they related. To be appointed to a place may be matter of indifference. To be incapable of being appointed, is a circumstance grating and mortifying.

Mr. Gouverneur Morris. The lesson we are taught is that we should be governed as much by our reason, and as little by our feelings as possible. What is the language of Reason on this subject? That we should not be polite at the expence of prudence. There was a moderation in all things. It is said that some tribes of Indians, carried their hospitality so far as to offer to strangers their wives & daughters. Was this a proper model for us? He would admit them to his house, he would invite them to his table, would provide for them comfortable lodgings; but would not carry the complaisance so far as, to bed them with his wife. He would let them worship at the same altar, but did not choose to make Priests of them. He ran over the privileges which emigrants would enjoy among us, though they should be deprived of that of being eligible to the great offices of Government; observing that they exceeded the privileges allowed to foreigners in any part of the world; and that as every Society from a great nation down to a club had the right of declaring the conditions on which new members should be admitted, there could be no room for complaint. As to those philosophical gentlemen, those Citizens of the World as they call themselves, He owned he did not wish to see any of them in our public Councils. He would not trust them. The men who can shake off their attachments to their own Country can never love any other. These attachments are the wholesome prejudices which uphold all Governments, Admit a Frenchman into your Senate, and he will study to increase the commerce of France: an Englishman, and he will feel an equal bias in favor of that of England. . . .

Question on the motion of Mr. Gouverneur Morris to insert 14 in place of 4 years [lost 7 to 4] . . .

Adjourned

Friday August 10. In Convention

In a tedious discussion of property qualifications for membership in the legislature, Franklin spoke for most liberal requirements:

Doctor Franklin expressed his dislike of every thing that tended to debase the spirit of the common people. If honesty was often the companion of wealth, and if poverty was exposed to peculiar temptation, it was not less true that the possession of property increased the desire of more property. Some of the greatest rogues he was ever acquainted with, were the richest rogues. We should remember the character which the Scripture requires in Rulers, that they should be men hating covetousness. This Constitution will be much read and attended to in Europe, and if it should betray a great partiality to the rich, will not only hurt us in the esteem of the most liberal and enlightened men there, but discourage the common people from removing into this Country. . . .

As the delegates reviewed their handiwork, they displayed that tendency known to all such bodies to fret and nitpick and to reopen issues already apparently resolved; in short, to waffle, procrastinate, and waste time. On Wednesday, August 15, when Madison brought up the issue of a revisionary council once more Rutledge expressed vigorous opposition to further discussion and "complained much of the tediousness of the proceedings." Ellsworth "held the same language. We grow more & more skeptical as we proceed. If we do not decide soon, we shall be unable to come to any decision."

The protests made little difference. The delegates were, in a sense, in a nitpicking phase of their deliberations and it is not surprising that all kinds of doubts and misgivings came to the surface as the Constitution hardened into what was to be its final form.

On the 18th of August, Rutledge proposed that the new government assume all the debts incurred by the states during the Revolution. "It was politic, as by disburdening the people of the State debts

it would conciliate them to the plan." King added the notion that
"all unlocated lands of particular States ought to be given up if State
debts were to be assumed." The issues of the assumption of state
debts and authority over the militia were referred to a committee
which reported to the convention on August 21:

> The Legislature of the U.S. shall have power to fulfil the engage-
> ments which have been entered into by Congress, and to discharge
> as well the debts of the U.S. as the debts incurred by the several
> States during the late war, for the common defence and general
> welfare
>
> To make laws for organizing arming and disciplining the militia,
> and for governing such part of them as may be employed in the
> service of the U.S. reserving to the States respectively, the appoint-
> ment of the officers, and the authority of training the Militia accord-
> ing to the discipline prescribed by the United States.

When the delegates took up the matter of import and export duties,
the issue of slavery once more asserted itself. On Wednesday, August
22, discussing Article VII, Section 4, forbidding any restraint by the
national legislature on "the importation of persons":

> [Roger Sherman] was for leaving the clause as it stands. He disap-
> proved of the slave trade; yet as the States were now possessed of the
> right to import slaves, as the public good did not require it to be taken
> from them, & as it was expedient to have as few objections as possible
> to the proposed scheme of Government, he thought it best to leave the
> matter as we find it. He observed that the abolition of Slavery seemed
> to be going on in the U.S. & that the good sense of the several States
> would probably by degrees complete it. He urged on the Convention the
> necessity of despatching its business.
>
> Col. Mason. This infernal traffic originated in the avarice of British
> Merchants. The British Government constantly checked the attempts of
> Virginia to put a stop to it. The present question concerns not the im-
> porting States alone but the whole Union. The evil of having slaves was
> experienced during the late war. Had slaves been treated as they might
> have been by the Enemy, they would have proved dangerous instru-
> ments in their hands. But their folly dealt by the slaves, as it did by the
> Tories. He mentioned the dangerous insurrections of the slaves in
> Greece and Sicily; and the instructions given by Cromwell to the Com-
> missioners sent to Virginia, to arm the servants & slaves, in case other

means of obtaining its submission should fail. Maryland & Virginia he said had already prohibited the importation of slaves expressly. North Carolina had done the same in substance. All this would be in vain if South Carolina and Georgia be at liberty to import. The Western people are already calling out for slaves for their new lands, and will fill that Country with slaves if they can be got through South Carolina & Georgia. Slavery discourages arts & manufactures. The poor despise labor when performed by slaves. They prevent the immigration of Whites, who really enrich & strengthen a Country. They produce the most pernicious effect on manners. Every master of slaves is born a petty tyrant. They bring the judgment of heaven on a Country. As nations can not be rewarded or punished in the next world they must be in this. By an inevitable chain of causes & effects providence punishes national sins, by national calamities. He lamented that some of our Eastern brethren had from a lust of gain embarked in this nefarious traffic. As to the States being in possession of the Right to import, this was the case with many other rights, now to be properly given up. He held it essential in every point of view that the General Government should have power to prevent the increase in slavery. . . .

Mr. Pinkney. If slavery be wrong, it is justified by the example of all the world. He cited the case of Greece, Rome & other ancient States; the sanction given by France, England, Holland & other modern States. In all ages one-half of mankind have been slaves. If the Southern States were let alone they will probably of themselves stop importations. He would himself as a Citizen of South Carolina vote for it. An attempt to take away the right as proposed will produce serious objections to the Constitution which he wished to see adopted. . . .

Mr. Dickenson considered it as inadmissible on every principle of honor & safety that the importation of slaves should be authorized to the States by the Constitution. The true question was whether the national happiness would be promoted or impeded by the importation, and this question ought to be left to the National Government not to the States particularly interested. If England & France permit slavery, slaves are at the same time excluded from both those Kingdoms. Greece and Rome were made unhappy by their slaves. He could not believe that the Southern States would refuse to confederate on the account apprehended; especially as the power was not likely to be immediately exercised by the General Government. . . .

Mr. Rutlidge. If the Convention thinks that North Carolina, South Carolina & Georgia will ever agree to the plan, unless their right to import slaves be untouched, the expectation is vain. The people of those States will never be such fools as to give up so important an interest. He was strenuous against striking out the Section, and seconded the motion of General Pinkney for a commitment. . . .

Mr. Sherman said it was better to let the Southern States import slaves than to part with them, if they made that a sine qua non. He was opposed to a tax on slaves imported as making the matter worse, because it implied they were *property*. He acknowledged that if the power of prohibiting the importation should be given to the General Government that it would be exercised. He thought it would be its duty to exercise the power. . . .

, Mr. Randolph was for committing in order that some middle ground might, if possible, be found. He could never agree to the clause as it stands. He would sooner risk the constitution. He dwelt on the dilemma to which the Convention was exposed. By agreeing to the clause, it would revolt the Quakers, the Methodists, and many others in the States having no slaves. On the other hand, two States might be lost to the Union. Let us then, he said, try the chance of a commitment. . . .

The resolution of the matter was found in a clause that prohibited the importation of slaves after 1808.

While the day-to-day revisions and emendations of the Constitution are too lengthy to reproduce here and difficult at best to follow without the closest attention, for anyone with even a modest acquaintance with the deliberative proceedings of public bodies they make fascinating reading and deepen the reader's respect for the rational faculties of the delegates. This was the most trying and tiresome period of the convention. To descend from the plateau of lofty political principles to the precise wording of sentences and clauses, aware always of the vast implications in many words and combinations of words is a singularly taxing enterprise. What is amazing is the tenacity with which they stuck to their task, reminding each other from time to time of how much rested on the outcome. Some of the delegates, Mason, Randolph, Gerry, and Luther Martin of Maryland, cast a shadow over the final weeks by hinting that they found the Constitution as it was taking shape hopelessly inadequate. Mason declared he would sooner chop off his hand than put his signature to the document and Gerry "represented the system as full of vices." Randolph voiced his misgivings and stated he intended to press for state conventions to propose amendments to the present document "to be submitted to another General Convention. . . ." Alexander Hamilton expressed his disillusionment with the course the deliberations had taken by virtually withdrawing from the debates. "He meant," he declared, "to support the plan to be recommended, as better than nothing."

Some of the most important work was now done in committee and submitted to the whole body. It was in this fashion that the proposal to have the president impeached by the Senate upon recommendation by the House made its way in as well as the notion of the electoral college, resolving an issue which had plagued the delegates from the earliest sessions. The office of vice-president appeared under similar auspices as did the troublesome issue of appointments—by the president with the concurrence of the Senate. The week of September 3 was largely taken up with the mode of selecting the president. One had the feeling that the delegates finally accepted the electoral method out of exhaustion rather than out of any strong conviction that it was a rational system.

On Saturday, September 8, the work of the convention to date was turned over to a committee on style to be put in the best literary form, a task which fell largely to Gouverneur Morris.

Wednesday September 12, 1787. In Convention

Doctor Johnson from the Committee of stile &c. reported a digest of the plan, of which printed copies were ordered to be furnished to the members. He also reported a letter to accompany the plan, to Congress. . . .

WE, THE PEOPLE OF THE UNITED STATES, IN ORDER TO FORM a more perfect union, to establish justice, insure domestic tranquility, provide for the common defence, promote the general welfare, and secure the blessings of liberty to ourselves and our posterity, do ordain and establish this Constitution for the United States of America.

ARTICLE 1

Sect. 1. ALL legislative powers herein granted shall be vested in a Congress of the United States, which shall consist of a Senate and House of Representatives.

Sect. 2. The House of Representatives shall be composed of members chosen every second year by the people of the several states, and the electors in each state shall have the qualifications requisite for electors of the most numerous branch of the state legislature.

No person shall be a representative who shall not have attained to the age of twenty-five years, and been seven years a citizen of the United States, and who shall not, when elected, be an inhabitant of that state in which he shall be chosen.

Representatives and direct taxes shall be apportioned among the several states which may be included within this Union, according to their respective numbers. which shall be determined by adding to the whole number of free persons, including those bound to servitude for a term of years, and excluding Indians not taxed, three-fifths of all other persons. The actual enumeration shall be made within three years after the first meeting of the Congress of the United States, and within every subsequent term of ten years, in such manner as they shall by law direct. The number of representatives shall not exceed one for every forty thousand, but each state shall have at least one representative: and until such enumeration shall be made, the state of New Hampshire shall be entitled to choose three, Massachusetts eight, Rhode Island and Providence Plantations one, Connecticut five, New York six, New Jersey four, Pennsylvania eight, Delaware one, Maryland six, Virginia ten, North Carolina five, South Carolina five, and Georgia three.

When vacancies happen in the representation from any state, the Executive authority thereof shall issue writs of election to fill such vacancies.

The House of Representatives shall choose their Speaker and other officers; and they shall have the sole power of impeachment.

Sect. 3. The Senate of the United States shall be composed of two senators from each state, chosen by the legislature thereof, for six years: and each senator shall have one vote.

Immediately after they shall be assembled in consequence of the first election, they shall be divided [by lot] as equally as may be into three classes. The seats of the senators of the first class shall be vacated at the expiration of the second year, of the second class at the expiration of the fourth year, and of the third class at the expiration of the sixth year, so that one-third may be chosen every second year: and if vacancies happen by resignation, or otherwise, during the recess of the Legislature of any state, the Executive thereof may make temporary appointments until the next meeting of the Legislature.

No person shall be a senator who shall not have attained to the age of thirty years, and been nine years a citizen of the United States, and who shall not, when elected, be an inhabitant of that state for which he shall be chosen.

The Vice-President of the United States shall be, ex officio President of the senate, but shall have no vote, unless they be equally divided.

The Senate shall choose their other officers, and also a President pro tempore, in the absence of the Vice-President, or when he shall exercise the office of President of the United States.

The Senate shall have the sole power to try all impeachments. When sitting for that purpose, they shall be on oath. When the President of the United States is tried, the Chief Justice shall preside: And no person shall be convicted without the concurrence of two-thirds of the members present.

Judgment in cases of impeachment shall not exceed further than to removal from office, and disqualification to hold and enjoy any office of honor, trust or profit under the United States: but the party convicted shall nevertheless be liable and subject to indictment, trial, judgment and punishment, according to law.

Sect. 4. The times, places and manner of holding elections for senators and representatives, shall be prescribed in each state by the legislature thereof: but the Congress may at any time by law make or alter such regulations.

The Congress shall assemble at least once in every year, and such meeting shall be on the first Monday in December, unless they shall by law appoint a different day.

Sect. 5. Each house shall be the judge of the elections, returns and qualifications of its own members, and a majority of each shall constitute a quorum to do business: but a smaller number may adjourn from day to day, and may be authorized to compel the attendance of absent members, in such manner, and under such penalties as each house may provide.

Each house may determine the rules of its proceedings; punish its members for disorderly behaviour, and, with the concurrence of two-thirds, expel a member.

Each house shall keep a journal of its proceedings, and from time to time publish the same, excepting such parts as may in their judgment require secrecy; and the yeas and nays of the members of either house on any question shall, at the desire of one-fifth of those present, be entered on the journal.

Neither house, during the session of Congress, shall, without the consent of the other, adjourn for more than three days, nor to any other place than that in which the two houses shall be sitting.

Sect. 6. The senators and representatives shall receive a compensation for their services, to be ascertained by law, and paid out of the treasury of the United States. They shall in all cases, except treason, felony and breach of the peace, be privileged from arrest during their attendance at the session of their respective houses, and in going to and returning from the same; and for any speech or debate in either house, they shall not be questioned in any other place.

No senator or representative shall, during the time for which he was elected, be appointed to any civil office under the authority of the United States, which shall have been created, or the emoluments whereof shall have been encreased during such time; and no person holding any office under the United States, shall be a member of either house during his continuance in office.

Sect. 7. The enacting stile of the laws shall be, "Be it enacted by the senators and representatives in Congress assembled."

All bills for raising revenue shall originate in the house of representatives: but the senate may propose or concur with amendments as on other bills.

Every bill which shall have passed the house of representatives and the senate, shall, before it become a law, be presented to the president of the United States. If he approve he shall sign it, but if not he shall return it, with his objections to that house in which it shall have originated, who shall enter the objections at large on their journal, and proceed to reconsider it. If after such reconsideration two-thirds of that house shall agree to pass the bill, it shall be sent, together with the objections, to the other house, by which it shall likewise be reconsidered, and if approved by two-thirds of that house, it shall become a law. But in all such cases the votes of both houses shall be determined by yeas and nays, and the names of the persons voting for and against the bill shall be entered on the journal of each house respectively. If any bill shall not be returned by the President within ten days (Sundays excepted) after it shall have been presented to him, the same shall be a law, in like manner as if he had signed it, unless the Congress by their adjournment prevent its return, in which case it shall not be a law.

Every order, resolution, or vote to which the concurrence of the Senate and House of Representatives may be necessary (except on a question of adjournment) shall be presented to the President of the United States; and before the same shall take effect, shall be approved by him, or, being disapproved by him, shall be repassed by three-fourths of the Senate and House of Representatives, according to the rules and limitations prescribed in the case of a bill.

Sect. 8. The Congress may by joint ballot appoint a treasurer. They shall have power

To lay and collect taxes, duties, imposts and excises; to pay the debts and provide for the common defence and general welfare of the United States.

To borrow money on the credit of the United States.

To regulate commerce with foreign nations, among the several states, and with the Indian tribes.

To establish an uniform rule of naturalization, and uniform law on the subject of bankruptcies throughout the United States.

To coin money, regulate the value thereof, and of foreign coin, and fix the standard of weights and measures.

To provide for the punishment of counterfeiting the securities and current coin of the United States.

To establish post offices and post roads.

To promote the progress of science and useful arts, by securing for limited times to authors and inventors the exclusive right to their respective writings and discoveries.

To constitute tribunals inferior to the supreme court.

To define and punish piracies and felonies committed on the high seas, and [punish] offences against the law of nations.

To declare war, grant letters of marque and reprisal, and make rules concerning captures on land and water.

To raise and support armies: but no appropriation of money to that use shall be for a longer term than two years.

To provide and maintain a navy.

To make rules for the government and regulation of the land and naval forces.

To provide for calling forth the militia to execute the laws of the union, suppress insurrections and repel invasions.

To provide for organizing, arming and disciplining the militia, and for governing such part of them as may be employed in the service of the United States, reserving to the States respectively, the appointment of the officers, and the authority of training the militia according to the discipline prescribed by Congress.

To exercise exclusive legislation in all cases whatsoever, over such district (not exceeding ten miles square) as may, by cession of particular States, and the acceptance of Congress, become the seat of the government of the United States, and to exercise like authority over all places purchased by the consent of the legislature of the state in which the same shall be, for the erection of forts, magazines, arsenals, dock-yards, and other needful buildings —And

To make all laws which shall be necessary and proper for carrying into execution the foregoing powers, and all other powers vested by this constitution in the government of the United States, or in any department or officer thereof.

Sect. 9. The migration or importation of such persons as the several states now existing shall think proper to admit, shall not be prohibited by the Congress prior to the year one thousand eight hundred and eight, but a tax or duty may be imposed on such importation, not exceeding ten dollars for each person.

The privilege of the writ of habeas corpus shall not be suspended, unless when in cases of rebellion or invasion the public safety may require it.

No bill of attainder shall be passed, nor any ex post facto law.

No capitation tax shall be laid, unless in proportion to the census herein before directed to be taken.

No tax or duty shall be laid on articles exported from any state.

No money shall be drawn from the treasury, but in consequence of appropriations made by law.

No title of nobility shall be granted by the United States. And no person holding any office of profit or trust under them, shall, without the consent of the Congress, accept of any present, emolument, office, or title, of any kind whatever, from any king, prince, or foreign state.

Sect. 10. No state shall coin money, or emit bills of credit, or make any thing but gold or silver coin a tender in payment of debts, or pass any bill of attainder, or ex post facto laws, or laws altering or impairing the obligation of contracts; or grant letters of marque and reprisal, or enter into any treaty, alliance, or confederation, or grant any title of nobility.

No state shall, without the consent of Congress, lay imposts or duties on imports or exports, or with such consent, but to the use of the treasury of the United States. Or keep troops or ships of war in time of peace, or enter into any agreement or compact with another state, or with any foreign power. Or engage in any war, unless it shall be actually invaded by enemies, or the danger of invasion be so imminent, as not to admit of delay until the Congress can be consulted.

II

Sect. 1. The executive power shall be vested in a president of the United States of America. He shall hold his office during the term of four years, and, together with the vice-president, chosen for the same term, be elected in the following manner:

Each state shall appoint, in such manner as the legislature thereof may direct, a number of electors, equal to the whole number of senators and representatives to which the state may be entitled in Congress: but no senator or representative shall be appointed an elector, nor any person holding an office of trust or profit under the United States.

The electors shall meet in their respective states, and vote by ballot for two persons, of whom one at least shall not be an inhabitant of the same state with themselves. And they shall make a list of all the persons voted for, and of the number of votes for each; which list they shall sign and certify, and transmit sealed to the seat of the general government, directed to the president of the senate. The president of the senate shall in the presence of the senate and house of representatives open all the certificates, and the votes shall then be counted. The person having the greatest number of votes shall be the president, if such number be a majority of the whole number of electors appointed; and if there be more than one who have such majority, and have an equal number of votes, then the house of representatives shall immediately choose by ballot one of them for president; and if no person have a majority, then from the five highest on the list the said house shall in like manner choose the president. But in choosing the president, the votes shall be taken by states and not per capita, the representation from each state having one vote. A quorum for this purpose shall consist of a member or members from two-thirds of the states, and a majority of all the states shall be necessary to a choice. In every case, after the choice of the president by the representatives, the person having the greatest number of votes of the electors shall be the vice-president. But if there should remain two or more who have equal votes, the senate shall choose from them by ballot the vice-president.

The Congress may determine the time of choosing the electors, and the time in which they shall give their votes; but the election shall be on the same day throughout the United States.

No person except a natural born citizen, or a citizen of the United States, at the time of the adoption of this constitution, shall be eligible to the office of president; neither shall any person be eligible to that office who shall not have attained to the age of thirty-five years, and been fourteen years a resident within the United States.

In case of the removal of the president from office, or of his death, resignation, or inability to discharge the powers and duties of the said office, the same shall devolve on the vice-president, and the Congress may by law provide for the case of removal, death, resignation or inability, both of the president and vice-president, declaring what officer shall then act as president, and such officer shall act accordingly, until the disability be removed, or the period for choosing another president arrive.

The president shall, at stated times, receive a fixed compensation for his services, which shall neither be encreased nor diminished during the period for which he shall have been elected.

Before he enter on the execution of his office, he shall take the following oath or affirmation: "I ———, do solemnly swear (or affirm) that I will faithfully execute the office of president of the United States, and will to the best of my judgment and power, preserve, protect and defend the constitution of the United States."

Sect. 2. The president shall be commander in chief of the army and navy of the United States, and of the militia of the several States: he may require the opinion, in writing, of the principal officer in each of the executive departments, upon any subject relating to the duties of their respective offices, when called into the actual service of the United States, and he shall have power to grant reprieves and pardons for offences against the United States, except in cases of impeachment.

He shall have power, by and with the advice and consent of the senate, to make treaties, provided two-thirds of the senators present concur; and he shall nominate, and by and with the advice and consent of the senate, shall appoint ambassadors, other public ministers and consuls, judges of the supreme court, and all other officers of the United States, whose appointments are not herein otherwise provided for.

The president shall have power to fill up all vacancies that may happen during the recess of the senate, by granting commissions which shall expire at the end of their next session.

Sect. 3. He shall from time to time give to the Congress information of the state of the union, and recommend to their consideration such measures as he shall judge necessary and expedient: he may, on extraordinary occasions, convene both houses, or either of them, and in case of disagreement between them, with respect to the time of adjournment, he may adjourn them to such time as he shall think proper: he shall receive ambassadors and other public ministers: he shall take care that the laws be faithfully executed, and shall commission all the officers of the United States.

Sect. 4. The president, vice-president and all civil officers of the United States, shall be removed from office on impeachment for, and conviction of treason, bribery, or other high crimes and misdemeanors.

III

Sect. 1. The judicial power of the United States, both in law and equity, shall be vested in one supreme court, and in such inferior courts as the Congress may from time to time ordain and establish. The judges, both of the supreme and inferior courts, shall hold their offices during good behaviour, and shall, at stated times, receive for their services, a compensation, which shall not be diminished during their continuance in office.

Sect. 2. The judicial power shall extend to all cases, both in law and equity, arising under this constitution, the laws of the United States, and treaties made, or which shall be made, under their authority. To all cases affecting ambassadors, other public ministers and consuls. To all cases of admiralty and maritime jurisdiction. To controversies to which the United States shall be a party. To controversies between two or more States; between a state and citizens of another state; between citizens of different States; between citizens of the same state claiming lands under grants of different States, and between a state, or the citizens thereof, and foreign States, citizens or subjects.

In cases affecting ambassadors, other public ministers and consuls, and those in which a state shall be party, the supreme court shall have original jurisdiction. In all the other cases before mentioned, the supreme court shall have appellate jurisdiction, both as to law and fact, with such exceptions, and under such regulations as the Congress shall make.

The trial of all crimes, except in cases of impeachment, shall be by jury; and such trial shall be held in the state where the said crimes shall have been committed; but when not committed within any state, the trial shall be at such place or places as the Congress may by law have directed.

Sect. 3. Treason against the United States, shall consist only in levying war against them, or in adhering to their enemies, giving them aid and comfort. No person shall be convicted of treason unless on the testimony of two witnesses to the same overt act, or on confession in open court.

The Congress shall have power to declare the punishment of treason, but no attainder of treason shall work corruption of blood nor forfeiture, except during the life of the person attainted.

IV

Sect. 1. Full faith and credit shall be given in each state to the public acts, records, and judicial proceedings of every other state. And the Congress may by general laws prescribe the manner in which such acts, records and proceedings shall be proved, and the effect thereof.

Sect. 2. The citizens of each state shall be entitled to all privileges and immunities of citizens in the several states.

A person charged in any state with treason, felony, or other crime, who shall flee from justice, and be found in another state, shall on demand of the executive authority of the state from which he fled be delivered up, and removed to the state having jurisdiction of the crime.

No person legally held to service or labour in one state, escaping into another, shall in consequence of regulations subsisting therein be discharged from such service or labour, but shall be delivered up on claim of the party to whom such service or labour may be due.

Sect. 3. New states may be admitted by the Congress into this union; but no new state shall be formed or erected within the jurisdiction of any other state; nor any state be formed by the junction of two or more states, or parts of states, without the consent of the legislatures of the states concerned as well as of the Congress.

The Congress shall have power to dispose of and make all needful rules and regulations respecting the territory or other property belonging to the United States: and nothing in this Constitution shall be so construed as to prejudice any claims of the United States, or of any particular state.

Sect. 4. The United States shall guarantee to every state in this union a Republican form of government, and shall protect each of them against invasion; and on application of the legislature or executive, against domestic violence.

V

The Congress, whenever two-thirds of both houses shall deem necessary, or on the application of two-thirds of the legislatures of the several states, shall propose amendments to this constitution, which shall be valid to all intents and purposes, as part thereof, when the same shall have been ratified by three-fourths at least of the legislatures of the several states, or by conventions in three-fourths thereof, as the one or the other mode of ratification may be proposed by the Congress: Provided, that no amendment which may be made prior to the year 1808 shall in any manner affect the and   section of the   article

VI

All debts contracted and engagements entered into before the adoption of this Constitution shall be as valid against the United States under this Constitution as under the confederation.

This constitution, and the laws of the United States which shall be made in pursuance thereof; and all treaties made, or which shall be made, under the authority of the United States, shall be the supreme law of the land; and the judges in every state shall be bound thereby, any thing in the constitution or laws of any state to the contrary notwithstanding.

The senators and representatives beforementioned, and the members of the several state legislatures, and all executive and judicial officers, both of the United States and of the several States, shall be bound by oath or affirmation, to support this constitution; but no religious test shall ever be required as a qualification to any office or public trust under the United States.

VII

The ratification of the conventions of nine States, shall be sufficient for the establishment of this constitution between the States so ratifying the same.

LETTER

We have now the honor to submit to the consideration of the United States in Congress assembled, that Constitution which as appeared to us the most advisable.

The friends of our country have long seen and desired, that the power of making war, peace and treaties, that of levying money and regulating commerce, and the correspondent executive and judicial authorities should be fully and effectually vested in the general government of the Union: but the impropriety of delegating such extensive trust to one body of men is evident—Hence results the necessity of a different organization.

It is obviously impracticable in the federal government of these States to secure all rights of independent sovereignty to each, and yet provide for the interest and safety of all—Individuals entering into society must give up a share of liberty to preserve the rest. The magnitude of the sacrifice must depend as well on situation and circumstance, as on the object to be obtained. It is at all times difficult to draw with precision the line between those rights which must be surrendered, and those which may be reserved; and on the present occasion this difficulty was encreased by a difference among the several States as to their situation, extent, habits, and particular interests.

In all our deliberations on this subject we kept steadily in our view, that which appears to us the greatest interest of every true American, the consolidation of our union, in which is involved our prosperity, felicity, safety, perhaps our national existence. This important consideration, seriously and deeply impressed on our minds, led each State in the Convention to be less rigid on points of inferior magnitude, than might have been otherwise expected; and thus the Constitution, which we now present, is the result of a spirit of amity, and of that mutual deference and concession which the peculiarity of our political situation rendered indispensable.

That it will meet the full and entire approbation of every State is not perhaps to be expected; but each will doubtless consider, that had her interest alone been consulted, the consequences might have been particularly disagreeable or injurious to others; that it is liable to as few exceptions as could reasonably have been expected, we hope and believe; that it may promote the lasting welfare of that country so dear to us all, and secure her freedom and happiness, is our most ardent wish.

Mr. Williamson moved to reconsider the clause requiring three-fourths of each House to overrule the negative of the President, in order to strike out ¾ and insert ⅔. He had he remarked himself proposed ¾ instead of ⅔, but he had since been convinced that the latter proportion was the best. The former puts too much in the power of the President.

Mr. Sherman was of the same opinion; adding that the States would not like to see so small a minority and the President, prevailing over the general voice. In making laws regard should be had to the sense of the people, who are to be bound by them, and it was more probable that a single man should mistake or betray this sense than the Legislature. . . .

The reconsideration being agreed to. On the question to insert ⅔ in place of ¾. [Passed 7 to 4.]

In one of the final sessions of the convention, George Mason brought up the issue of a Bill of Rights as part of the Constitution:

. . . He wished the plan had been prefaced with a Bill of Rights,

& would second a Motion if made for the purpose. It would give great quiet to the people; and with the aid of the State declarations, a bill might be prepared in a few hours.

Mr. Gerry concurred in the idea & moved for a Committee to prepare a Bill of Rights. Col. Mason seconded the motion.

Mr. Sherman, was for securing the rights of the people where requisite. The State Declarations of Rights are not repealed by this Constitution; and being in force are sufficient. There are many cases where juries are proper which can not be discriminated. The Legislature may be safely trusted.

Col. Mason. The Laws of the U.S. are to be paramount to State Bills of Rights.

On the question for a Committee to prepare a Bill of Rights [Failed, unanimously]

In view of the fact that a major objection to the Constitution in the state-ratifying conventions came to center on the absence of a Bill of Rights, it is surprising that no more discussion or attention was devoted to it. Sherman's argument that the states all had their own Bills of Rights was doubtless seized upon by a convention which, seeing the end of its deliberations in sight, could not bear to address itself to so substantial an issue in the waning days.

The Committee on Style and Arrangement came in with the recommendation on the thirteenth that the Constitution be sent to Congress with the request that it go from there to state conventions "chosen in each State by the people thereof . . . for their assent & ratification . . ."

On Saturday, September 15, with the Constitution completed and awaiting final approval and signing, Edmund Randolph, who had brought in at the beginning of the convention, almost three months earlier, a plan which in its main outlines had anticipated to a remarkable degree the final document, rose to express his dissatisfaction with the work of the convention. He was followed by Mason:

Mr. Randolph animadverting on the indefinite and dangerous power given by the Constitution to Congress, expressing the pain he felt at differing from the body of the Convention, on the close of the great & awful subject of their labours, and anxiously wishing for some accommodating expedient which would relieve him from his embarrassments, made a motion importing "that amendments to the plan might be offered by the State Conventions, which should be submitted to and finally decided on by another general Convention." Should this proposition be disregarded, it would he said be impossible for him to put his name to the instrument. Whether he should oppose it afterwards he would not then decide but he would not deprive himself of the freedom to do so in his own State, if that course should be prescribed by his final judgment.

Col. Mason seconded & followed Mr. Randolph in animadversions on the dangerous power and structure of the Government, concluding that it would end either in monarchy, or a tyrannical aristocracy; which, he was in doubt, but one or other, he was sure. This Constitution had been formed without the knowledge or idea of the people. A second Convention will know more of the sense of the people, and be able to provide a system more consonant to it. It was improper to say to the people, take this or nothing. As the Constitution now stands, he could neither give it his support nor vote in Virginia; and he could not sign here what he could not support there. With the expedient of another Convention as proposed, he could sign.

Mr. Pinkney. These declarations from members so respectable at the close of this important scene, give a peculiar solemnity to the present moment. He descanted on the consequences of calling forth the deliberations & amendments of the different States on the subject of Government at large. Nothing but confusion & contrariety will spring from the experiment. The States will never agree in their plans, and the Deputies to a second Convention coming together under the discordant impressions of their Constituents, will never agree. Conventions are serious things, and ought not to be repeated. He was not without objections as well as others to the plan. He objected to the contemptible weakness & dependence of the Executive. He objected to the power of a majority only of Congress over Commerce. But apprehending the danger of a general confusion, and an ultimate decision by the sword, he should give the plan his support.

Mr. Gerry, stated the objections which determined him to withhold his name from the Constitution. 1. the duration and re-eligibility of the Senate. 2. the power of the House of Representatives to conceal their journals. 3. the power of Congress over the places of election. 4. the unlimited power of Congress over their own compensations. 5. that Massachusetts has not a due share of Representatives allotted to her. 6. that 3/5 of the Blacks are to be represented as if they were freemen. 7. that under the power over commerce, monopolies may be established. 8. The vice president being made head of the Senate. He could however he said get over all these, if the rights of the Citizens were not rendered insecure 1. by the general power of the Legislature to make what laws they may please to call necessary and proper. 2. raise armies and money without limit. 3. to establish a tribunal without juries, which will be a Star-chamber as to Civil cases. Under such a view of the Constitution, the best that could be done he conceived was to provide for a second general Convention.

On the question on the proposition of Mr. Randolph. All the States answered—no

On the question to agree to the Constitution, as amended. All the States ay.

The Constitution was then ordered to be engrossed.

And the House adjourned.

On Monday, September 17, "the engrossed Constitution being read," Franklin rose to make a final plea for the reconciliation of all objectors to the finished document. James Wilson read it for him.

Mr. President

I confess that there are several parts of this constitution which I do not at present approve, but I am not sure I shall never approve them: For having lived long, I have experienced many instances of being obliged by better information, or fuller consideration, to change opinions even on important subjects, which I once thought right, but found to be otherwise. It is therefore that the older I grow, the more apt I am to doubt my own judgment, and to pay more respect to the judgment of others. Most men indeed as well as most sects in Religion, think themselves in possession of all truth, and that wherever others differ from them it is so far error. Steele a Protestant in a Dedication tells the Pope, that the only difference between our Churches in their opinions of the certainty of their doctrines is, the Church of Rome is infallible and the Church of England is never in the wrong. But though many private persons think almost as highly of their own infallibility as of that of their sect, few express it so naturally as a certain French lady, who in a dispute with her sister, said "I don't know how it happens, Sister but I meet with no body but myself, that's always in the right—*Il n'y a que moi qui a tourjours raison.*"

In these sentiments, Sir, I agree to this Constitution with all its faults, if they are such; because I think a general Government necessary for us, and there is no form of Government but what may be a blessing to the people if well administered, and believe farther that this is likely to be well administered for a course of years, and can only end in Despotism, as other forms have done before it, when the people shall become so corrupted as to need despotic Government, being incapable of any other. I doubt too whether any other Convention we can obtain, may be able to make a better Constitution. For when you assemble a number of men to have the advantage of their joint wisdom, you inevitably assemble with those men, all their prejudices, their passions, their errors of opinion, their local interests, and their selfish views. From such an assembly can a perfect production be expected? It therefore astonishes me, Sir, to find this system approaching so near to perfection as it does; and I think it will astonish our enemies, who are waiting with confidence to hear that our councils are confounded like those of the Builders of Babel; and that our States are on the point of separation, only to meet hereafter for the purpose of cutting one another's throats. Thus I consent, Sir, to this Constitution because I expect no better, and because I am not sure, that it is not the best. The opinions I have had of its errors, I sacrifice to the public good. I have never whispered a syllable of them abroad. Within these walls they were born, and here they shall die. If every one of us in returning to our Constituents were to report the objections he has had to it, and endeavor to gain partisans in support of them, we might prevent its being generally received, and thereby lose all the salutary effects & great advantages resulting naturally in our favor among foreign Nations as well as among ourselves, from our real or apparent unanimity. Much of the strength & efficiency of any Government in procuring and securing happiness to the people, depends, on opinion, on the general opinion of the goodness of the Government, as well as of the wisdom and integrity of its Governors. I hope therefore that for our own sakes as a part of the people, and for the sake of posterity, we shall act heartily and unanimously in recommending this Constitution (if approved by Congress & confirmed by the Conventions) wherever our influence may extend, and turn our future thoughts & endeavors to the means of having it well administered.

On the whole, Sir, I can not help expressing a wish that every member of the Convention who may still have objections to it, would with me, on this occasion doubt a little of his own infallibility, and to make manifest our unanimity, put his name to this instrument.—

He then moved that the Constitution be signed by the members and offered the following as a convenient form viz. "Done in Convention by the unanimous consent of *the States* present the 17th of September &c—In Witness whereof we have hereunto subscribed our names."

This ambiguous form had been drawn up by Mr. Gouverneur Morris in order to gain the dissenting members, and put into the hands of Doctor Franklin that it might have the better chance of success.

Mr. Gorham said if it was not too late he could wish, for the purpose of lessening objections to the Constitution, that the clause declaring "the number of Representatives shall not exceed one for every forty thousand" which had produced so much discussion, might be yet reconsidered, in order to strike out 40,000 & insert "thirty thousand." This would not he remarked establish that as an absolute rule, but only give Congress a greater latitude which could not be thought unreasonable.

Mr. King & Mr. Carrol seconded & supported the idea of Mr. Gorham.

When the President rose, for the purpose of putting the question, he said that although his situation had hitherto restrained him from offering his sentiments on questions depending in the House, and it might be thought, ought now to impose silence on him, yet he could not forbear expressing his wish that the alteration proposed might take place. It was much to be desired that the objections to the plan recommended might be made as few as possible. The smallness of the proportion of Representatives had been considered by many members of the Convention an insufficient security for the rights & interests of the people. He acknowledged that it had always appeared to himself among the exceptionable parts of the plan, and late as the present moment was for admitting amendments, he thought this of so much consequence that it would give him much satisfaction to see it adopted.

No opposition was made to the proposition of Mr. Gorham and it was agreed to unanimously.

On the question to agree to the Constitution enrolled in order to be signed. It was agreed to all the States answering ay.

Mr. Randolph then rose and with an allusion to the observations of Doctor Franklin apologized for his refusing to sign the Constitution notwithstanding the vast majority & venerable names that would give sanction to its wisdom and its worth. He said however that he did not mean by this refusal to decide that he should oppose the Constitution without doors. He meant only to keep himself free to be governed by his duty as it should be prescribed by his future judgment. He refused to sign, because he thought the object of the Convention would be frustrated by the alternative which it presented to the people. Nine States will fail to ratify the plan and confusion must ensue. With such a view of the subject he ought not, he could not, by pledging himself to support the plan, restrain himself from taking such steps as might appear to him most consistent with the public good.

Mr. Gouverneur Morris said that he too had objections, but considering the present plan as the best that was to be attained, he should take it with all its faults. The majority had determined in its favor and by that determination he should abide. The moment this plan goes forth all other considerations will be laid aside, and the great question will be, shall there be a national Government or not? and this must take place or a general anarchy will be the alternative. He remarked that the signing in the form proposed related only to the fact that *the States* present were unanimous.

Mr. Williamson suggested that the signing should be confined to the letter accompanying the Constitution to Congress, which might perhaps do nearly as well, and would he found be satisfactory to some members who disliked the Constitution. For himself he did not think a better plan was to be expected and had no scruples against putting his name to it.

Mr. Hamilton expressed his anxiety that every member should sign. A few characters of consequence, by opposing or even refusing to sign the Constitution, might do infinite mischief by kindling the latent sparks which lurk under an enthusiasm in favor of the Convention which may soon subside. No man's ideas were more remote from the plan than his own were known to be; but is it possible to deliberate between anarchy and Convulsion on one side, and the chance of good to be expected from the plan on the other.

Mr. Blount said he had declared that he would not sign, so as to pledge himself in support of the plan, but he was relieved by the form proposed and would without committing himself attest the fact that the plan was the unanimous act of the States in Convention.

Doctor Franklin expressed his fears from what Mr. Randolph had said, that he thought himself alluded to in the remarks offered this morning to the House. He declared that when drawing up that paper he did not know that any particular member would refuse to sign his name to the instrument, and hoped to be so understood. He professed a high sense of obligation to Mr. Randolph for having brought forward the plan in the first instance, and for the assistance he had given in its progress, and hoped that he would yet lay aside his objections, and by concurring with his brethren, prevent the great mischief which the refusal of his name might produce.

Mr. Randolph could not but regard the signing in the proposed form, as the same with signing the Constitution. The change of form therefore could make no different with him. He repeated that in refusing to sign the Constitution, he took a step which might be the most awful of his life, but it was dictated by his conscience, and it was not possible for him to hesitate, much less, to change. He repeated also his persuasion, that the holding out this plan with a final alternative to the people, of accepting or rejecting it in toto, would really produce the anarchy & civil convulsions which were apprehended from the refusal of individuals to sign it.

Mr. Gerry described the painful feelings of his situation, and the embarrassment under which he rose to offer any further observations on the subject which had been finally decided. Whilst the plan was depending, he had treated it with all the freedom he thought it deserved. He now felt himself bound as he was disposed to treat it with the respect due to the Act of the Convention. He hoped he should not violate that respect in declaring on this occasion his fears that a Civil war may result from the present crisis of the U.S. In Massachusetts, particularly he saw the danger of this calamitous event—In that State there are two parties, one devoted to Democracy, the worst he thought of all political evils, the other as violent in the opposite extreme. From the collision of these in opposing and resisting the Constitution, confusion was greatly to be feared. He had thought it necesary, for this & other reasons that the plan should have been proposed in a more mediating shape, in order to abate the heat and opposition of parties. As it has been passed by the Convention, he was persuaded it would have a contrary effect. He could not therefore by signing the Constitution pledge himself to abide by it at all events. The proposed form made no difference with him. But if it were not otherwise apparent, the refusals to sign should never be known from him. Alluding to the remarks of Doctor Franklin, he could not he said but view them as levelled at himself and the other gentlemen who meant not to sign;

General Pinkney. We are not likely to gain many converts by the ambiguity of the proposed form of signing. He thought it best to be candid and let the form speak the substance. If the meaning of the signers be left in doubt, his purpose would not be answered. He should sign the Constitution with a view to support it with all his influence, and wished to pledge himself accordingly.

Doctor Franklin. It is too soon to pledge ourselves before Congress and our Constituents shall have approved the plan.

Mr. Ingersol did not consider the signing, either as a mere attestation of the fact, or as pledging the signers to support the Constitution at all events; but as a recommendation, of what, all things considered, was the most eligible.

On the motion of Doctor Franklin

New Hampshire ay. Massachusetts ay. Connecticut ay. New Jersey ay. Pensylvania ay. Delaware ay. Maryland ay. Virginia ay. North Carolina ay. South Carolina divided. Georgia ay.

Mr. King suggested that the Journals of the Convention should be either destroyed, or deposited in the custody of the President. He thought if suffered to be made public, a bad use would be made of them by those who would wish to prevent the adoption of the Constitution.

Mr. Wilson preferred the second expedient, he had at one time liked the first best; but as false suggestions may be propagated it should not be made impossible to contradict them.

A question was then put on depositing the Journals and other papers of the Convention in the hands of the President, on which,

New Hampshire ay. Massachusetts ay. Connecticut ay. New Jersey ay. Pennsylvania ay. Delaware ay. Maryland no. Virginia ay. North Carolina ay. South Carolina ay. Georgia ay.

The President having asked what the Convention meant should be done with the Journals &c, whether copies were to be allowed to the members if applied for. It was Resolved nem: con "that he retain the Journal and other papers, subject to the order of the Congress, if ever formed under the Constitution.

The members then proceeded to sign the instrument.

Whilst the last members were signing it Doctor Franklin looking towards the President's Chair, at the back of which a rising sun happened to be painted, observed to a few members near him, that Painters had found it difficult to distinguish in their art a rising from a setting sun. I have said he, often and often in the course of the Session, and the vicissitudes of my hopes and fears as to its issue, looked at that behind the President without being able to tell whether it was rising or setting: But now at length I have the happiness to know that it is a rising and not a setting Sun.

The Constitution being signed by all the members except Mr. Randolph, Mr. Mason, and Mr. Gerry who declined giving it the sanction of their names, the Convention dissolved itself by an Adjournment sine die—

The few alterations and corrections made in these debates which are not in my hand writing, were dictated by me and made in my presence by John C. Payne.

JAMES MADISON.

CHAPTER

VIII

THE CONSTITUTION
AND THE STATES

THE GREAT WORK WAS ENDED. NOW THE NEWLY CONSTRUCTED SHIP of state must be launched on the uncertain waters of state politics. Those delegates who had drafted the Constitution and signed turned back to their home states to fight for its ratification. Hamilton, Madison, and John Jay of New York (who had not been present at the convention) sat down to write a detailed explanation and defense of the major principles of the Constitution. Printed in a number of newspapers throughout the states, it became at once the classic statement of the Constitution, the preeminent work of American political philosophy.

Even before the Constitution was printed and distributed its enemies were declaiming against it, denouncing it as the work of a secret cabal which wished to rivet the chains of servitude on the people of the states.

It was, its enemies said, the work of a "dark conclave." The delegates had decided, uneasily, to send the Constitution to Congress, asking for its approval and for Congress, in turn, to forward it to the states with the request that state conventions be called to discuss and, hopefully, ratify it. The leader of the opposition in Congress was the Virginian Richard Henry Lee. Opposed to him was his cousin Henry, or Light Horse Harry, Lee, the brilliant young cavalryman whose daring forays had contributed so much to the success of the Southern campaign of Nathanael Greene.

In addition to declaiming against the Constitution in Congress,

Richard Henry Lee wrote to his political allies in a number of states arguing the iniquities of the Constitution and urging them to muster their forces to defeat it. Edward Carrington, a Virginia delegate to Congress, wrote to Madison, warning him of Lee's maneuvers, adding, "The New York faction is rather active in spreading the seeds of opposition. This, however, has been expected [from the fact that John Lansing, one of the New York delegates to the convention, had left Philadelphia in disgust and gone home to rally opposition to the Constitution], and will not make an impression so injurious as the same circumstances would in some other states. Colonel Hamilton has boldly taken his ground in the public papers and, having truth and propriety on his side, it is to be hoped he will stem the tide of folly and iniquity."

Madison, worn out from his labors in Philadelphia, yearned for home, but he and several other members of the convention who were also delegates to Congress hurried on to New York to defend their handiwork and to try to prevail on Congress to endorse it.

Lee was the first to raise the question of the absence of a Bill of Rights in the Constitution. He promptly made up a list of proposed amendments, beginning with a Bill of Rights and adding to it provision for a "Privy Council" to provide a check on the powers of the president. Lee's joining of forces with George Mason promised special difficulties for the Constitution in Virginia. Patrick Henry, whose loyalty to the Articles of Confederation was unshakable, had refused to be a delegate to the convention and his opposition had, therefore, to be assumed. Lee, Mason, and Henry were three of the most popular and powerful politicians in the Old Dominion and their opposition clearly imperiled the Constitution there.

On October 1, Lee wrote Mason: "Your prediction of what would happen in Congress was exactly verified. It was with us, as with you, this or nothing: and this urged with the most extreme intemperance. The greatness of the powers given, the multitude of places to be created produce a coalition of monarchy men, military men, aristocrats and drones whose noise, impudence and zeal exceeds all belief. . . . In this state of things the patriot voice is raised in vain for such changes and securities as reason and experience prove to be necessary against the encroachments of power upon the indispensable rights of human nature."

The supporters of the Constitution had enough votes in Congress to get the Constitution sent forward to the states, but they had to send it without the endorsement of Congress. The friends of the Constitution employed an ingenious dodge. Since they could not get a unanimous *endorsement* from the Congress, they declared in their resolution that "Congress had voted *unanimously to transmit . . .* the resolves of the Convention," hoping that to the hasty reader it would appear that Congress had unanimously endorsed it. So it went forth to the states on September 28.

Knowing that the state Assembly was scheduled to adjourn in a day or so, and that the chance might thus be lost to call a convention promptly, one of the Pennsylvania delegates to Congress hurried back to the city with the resolution of Congress. Getting wind of what was up, the anti-Constitutional members of the assembly decided to return home, thus depriving that body of a quorum. Indignant Constitutionalists tracked to their quarters two of the delegates needed to constitute a quorum, dragged them through the streets to the state house, and there barred the doors while a vote was taken to call for a ratifying convention, elections to take place on the first Tuesday in November, the delegates to convene in Philadelphia two weeks later, on November 20.

The Pennsylvania newspapers were filled meanwhile with bitter attacks on the Constitution and articles in defense of the document by the Constitutionalists, or Federalists, as they preferred to call themselves. A Federalist offered "a Receipt for an Antifederal Essay." The ingredients were *"Well-born,* nine times—*Aristocracy,* eighteen times—*Liberty of Conscience,* once—*Negro slavery,* once mentioned —*Trial by Jury,* seven times—*Great Men,* six times repeated—MR. WILSON, forty times—and lastly, GEORGE MASON's *Right Hand in a Cutting-Box* nineteen times [a reference to Mason's saying he had rather cut off his hand than put his signature to the Constitution]— put them all together, and dish them up at pleasure. . . . These *words . . .* will bear being served, after being once used, a dozen times to the same table and palate." A Federalist poet characterized the anti-Constitutionalists as a wicked old woman:

> Thy cruel heart with rancour has its load,
> Natural to thee as poison to a toad . . .
> Old drunken pisspot, sink of filth and sin
> Plaister without, rottenness within . . .
> Repent, or know I'll double every curse;
> But no, thou canst not mend, nor e'er be worse.

When the returns from the election of delegates were in, the Federalists had a two-to-one majority in the Pennsylvania ratifying convention, yet it was important not to appear to be ramming the Constitution down the throats of those opposed to it. The document must be reviewed, article by article, its opponents heard out and their misgivings, so far as possible, allayed. This task fell primarily to James Wilson as one of the Pennsylvania delegates to the convention and, with Madison, perhaps its principal architect.

Diminutive Delaware, plainly pleased with the institution of the Senate giving the small states their equal representation, voted unanimously on December 7 to ratify the Constitution. Pennsylvania, after three weeks of heated debate, followed on December 12, by the anticipated two-to-one majority, 46 to 23. In his final plea for ratification Wilson declared, "By adopting this system we shall probably lay a foundation for erecting temples of liberty in every part of the earth. It has been thought by many, that on the success of the struggle America has made for freedom, will depend the exertions of the brave and enlightened of other nations." Not just America would profit from the success of the new government. "It will draw from Europe many worthy characters, who pant for the enjoyment of freedom. It will induce princes, in order to preserve their subjects, to restore to them a portion of that liberty of which they have for so many ages been deprived. It will be subservient to the great designs of providence, with regard to this globe; the multiplication of mankind, their improvement in knowledge, and their advancement in happiness."

New Jersey, whose delegates had been the authors of "the New Jersey Plan," followed suit on December 18, again unanimously. But the Federalists knew that the real struggles lay ahead. Connecticut, under the guidance of Oliver Ellsworth, seemed secure enough, but in three of the largest and most important states, the outcome was a toss-up. In Massachusetts, the wounds of Shays' Rebellion had still not healed. The opposition to the Constitution was loud and determined. In New York, divisions that had their roots in colonial times embittered all political issues. Maryland was a question mark. Luther Martin would do his best there to defeat the Constitution. Virginia would undoubtedly be the scene of one of the most closely contested encounters between the friends and enemies of the Constitution.

It was assumed that South Carolina and Georgia would approve by comfortable margins. Rhode Island, which had refused to participate in the convention, was out of the picture. Even if New Hampshire and Vermont joined the Federalist ranks, thus making up the nine states required for ratification and technically establishing the new government, it would be a truncated government from the first if it failed to include any one of the closely contested states, and a disaster if all three remained outside the federal fold. If the years under the Articles of Confederation, the years between the end of the Revolution in 1783 and the beginning of a new government with the inauguration of Washington in 1789, were the "critical years" in American history, the critical months were from December 7, 1787, when Delaware agreed to the Constitution, to July 26, 1788, when New York finally came aboard by the narrowest of margins.

In those states where the Constitution was heavily favored, the discussions of it were, on the whole, perfunctory, and little (in some instances, nothing) of the proceedings has been preserved. But in Massachusetts, which had the largest number of delegates, the record of the debates is almost as voluminous as those of the federal convention itself.

Much the same thing happened in New York and Virginia. Indeed, the Virginia debates occupy a volume of 663 pages in Jonathan Elliot's five-volume work on the *Debates on the Adoption of the Federal Constitution*. The state debates, while not so compelling as the debates in the federal convention, are nonetheless full of fascinating material. Repetitious and often acrimonious, they give a marvelously comprehensive picture of the dominant political and social ideas of the time and the characters of the men who enunciated them. In the debates that took place in the major states the opinions and sentiments of several hundred individuals from a wide geographical range both within particular states and regionally from Massachusetts to Virginia are recorded. Common to all the anti-Constitutional arguments is a concern for the absence of a Bill of Rights. The Constitutionalists soon realized that it had been a mistake to omit the enumeration of these rights and uniformly conceded that the first act of the new government should be to amend the Constitution to include them. Other common complaints were that the state governments would be obliterated by the federal government; that the president had been given too much power; that the convention had no authority to do more than strengthen the Articles of Confederation and that it had, illegally, undertaken to establish a new system. The authority of Congress to maintain an army in time of peace was frequently attacked, as were its taxing powers, the authority given to the Supreme Court, and the abandonment of annual for biennial elections. The fact is that virtually every provision of the Constitution was attacked at one time or another. As we have seen, an often-repeated charge was that the Constitution was the work of "aristocrats" and "great men" and thus anti-democratic, designed to strengthen the hold of a particular class on the reins of government. The defense by the Constitutionalists was based on endlessly reiterated assurance of the good faith and good intentions of the framers, of the total inadequacy of the Articles, and of the careful checks that the Constitution contained against abuses of power.

Running through all the opposition statements was a profound suspicion of human motives and an assumption that all power would be, in time, abused. *Underlying* virtually all the opposition rhetoric was a bone-deep provincialism, a devotion to state interests, and a deep hostility to any "consolidated" national government. Historians, in reviewing the fight for ratification, have sometimes been inclined to see the issue in the terms that the enemies of the Constitution cast it during the state debates—as a prosperous ruling class versus "the people," as "aristocracy" versus "democracy," but it seems to me that it is better understood as a struggle between those who had a vision of the United States as a great power in the world and those who feared that power meant corruption and thus clung to the image of a simple provincial society as the best bulwark against the inevitable corruptions of power and wealth.

The method followed here in dealing with the state ratifying conventions is to give excerpts from the state debates of Massachusetts, Virginia, and New York with the hope of suggesting the nature of these discussions.

In Massachusetts, as in New York (Lansing) and Virginia (Mason and Randolph), a delegate to the federal convention, Elbridge Gerry, had refused to sign the Constitution and returned home to oppose it. Gerry's effectiveness as an opponent of the Constitution was somewhat mitigated by the fact that while the most common argument of its enemies in Massachusetts was that it was undemocratic, Gerry's main objection was that it was *too* democratic. He could not, therefore, as Patrick Henry and George Mason were to do in Virginia, place himself at the head of the democratic faction. In Massachusetts the issues that received the most attention from the opposition were biennial elections, the failure to outlaw slavery, and the lack of a requirement that every holder of public office be a Christian. John Hancock was one of the most popular political figures in the state. Although ailing and weak, he was prevailed upon by the Federalists to preside over the debates and lend his considerable prestige to the constitutional cause. Samuel Adams, another Revolutionary hero, was inclined to the anti-Constitutional side and said little during the debates although he was finally persuaded to vote yea. Nathaniel Gorham and Rufus King, who had been delegates to the Philadelphia convention, carried the principal burden for the defense, patiently answering questions about various articles in the Constitution and rebutting attacks on it.

General William Thompson of Billerica made himself the spokesman for the partisans of annual elections, crying out, as the recorder noted, "in the following pathetic apostrophe: 'O my country, never give up your annual elections! young men, never give up your jewel!' "

The spirit of pastoral provincialism was expressed by a delegate from Plymouth County who declared, "I think that the operation of paper money, and the practice of privateering, have produced a gradual decay of morals; introduced pride, ambition, envy, lust of power; produced a decay of patriotism, and the love of commutative justice; and I am apprehensive these are the invariable concomitants of luxury in which we are unblessedly involved, almost to our total destruction. . . . As people become more luxurious, they become more incapacitated for governing themselves."

The deliberations of the convention were disturbed by headlines in the Boston *Gazette*, an avid anti-Federal paper which, under the headline "Bribery and Corruption!!!" charged that "The most diabolical plan is on foot to corrupt the members of the Convention, who oppose the adoption of the new Consttiution. Large sums of money have been brought in from a neighboring state for that purpose, contributed by the wealthy." After ordering an investigation of the allegation, the delegates resumed their deliberations. This time General Thompson pushed a go-slow policy. The delegates should adjourn for five or six months to see what the other states—Virginia and New York—would do. It was clearly a notion that appealed to many of the delegates. Some, indeed, had been sent with instructions to vote against the Constitution and thus felt themselves bound whatever their personal views might be. The Federalists did their best to scotch the idea.

On the afternoon of January 22, young William Symmes of Andover rose to attack the power of Congress to collect taxes from the states. "It is a power, sir, to burden us with a standing army of ravenous collectors—harpies, perhaps, from another state, but who, however, were never known to have bowels for any purpose, but to fatten on the life-blood of the people. In an age or two, this will be the case; and when the Congress shall become tyrannical, these vultures, their servants, will be the tyrants of the village, by whose presence all freedom of speech and action will be taken away."

Thompson, having failed to persuade the delegates to adjourn, pressed the notion of amending "the old Confederation." It had been said that without a strong central government the country was powerless against external enemies, but Thompson was convinced that "the balance of power in the old countries will not permit it; the other nations will protect us. Besides, we are a brave and happy people. . . . By uniting we stand, by dividing we fall. We are in our childhood yet: don't let us grow too fast, lest we grow out of shape. I have proved that we are a respectable people, in possession of liberty, property, and virtue, and none in a better situation to defend themselves. Why all this racket? . . . There are some parts of this Constitution which I cannot digest; and, sir, shall we swallow a large bone for the sake of a little meat? Some say, Swallow the whole now and pick out the bone afterwards. But I say, Let us pick off the meat, and throw the bone away."

Amos Singletary of Worcester County attacked the power of the federal legislature to raise money. It was such power, unconstitutionally exercised by Parliament, which had brought on the Revolution. "These lawyers, and men of learning, and moneyed men, that talk so finely, and gloss over matters so smoothly, to make us poor illiterate people swallow down the pill, expect to get into Congress themselves; they expect to be the managers of this Constitution, and get all the power and all the money into their own hands, and then they will swallow up all us little folks, like the great *Leviathan*, . . . yes, just as the whale swallowed up Jonah."

Singletary was answered by another farmer, Josiah Smith of Plymouth County, who declared himself as "a plain man" who got his living "by the plough." He was disposed to "say a few words to my brother ploughjoggers in this house. I have lived in a part of the country where I have known the worth of good government by the want of it. There was a black cloud that rose in the east last winter, and spread over the west." Here Mr. Widgery interrupted: "Mr. President, I wish to know what the gentleman means by the east." "I mean, sir, the county of Bristol [the origin of Shays' Rebellion]; the cloud rose there, and burst upon us, and produced a dreadful effect. It brought on a state of anarchy, and that led to tyranny. I say it brought anarchy. People that used to live peaceably, and were before good neighbors, got distracted, and took up arms against government. . . . People I say took up arms; and then, if you went to speak to them, you had the musket of death presented to your breast. They would rob you of your property; threaten to burn your houses; oblige you to be on your guard night and day. . . . Our distress was so great we should have been content to snatch at any thing that looked like a government . . . even if it had been a monarch; and that monarch might have proved a tyrant;—so that you see that anarchy leads to tyranny, and better have one tyrant than so many at once.

"Now, Mr. President, when I saw this Constitution, I found it was a cure for these disorders. It was just such a thing as we wanted. I got a copy of it and read it over and over. I have been a member of the Convention to form our own state constitution, and had learnt something of the checks and balances of power, and I found them all here. I did not go to any lawyer, to ask his opinion; we have no lawyer in our town, and we do well enough without. I formed my own opinion, and was pleased with this Constitution. My honorable old daddy there [pointing to Mr. Singletary] won't think that I expect to be a Congressman, and swallow up the liberties of the people. I never had any post, nor do I want one. But I don't think the worse of the Constitution because lawyers, and men of learning, and moneyed men, are fond of it. I don't suspect that they want to get into Congress and abuse their power. . . . I am not of such a jealous make. They that are honest men themselves are not apt to suspect other people. . . . I think those gentlemen, who are so very suspicious that as soon as a man gets into power he turns rogue, had better look at home. . . . Some gentlemen say, Don't be in a hurry; take time to consider, and don't take a leap in the dark. I say, Take things in time; gather fruit when it is ripe. There is a time to sow and a time to reap; we sowed our seed when we sent men to the federal Convention; now is the harvest, now is the time to reap the fruit of our labor; and if we don't do it now, I am afraid we shall never have another opportunity."

In the last week of the Massachusetts Convention the issue of slavery came up. The fact that the Constitution in any way recognized or condoned slavery was offensive. The Reverend James Neal of Kittery spoke the sentiments of many delegates. "His profession . . . obliged him to bear witness against any thing that should favor the making merchandise of the bodies of men, and, unless his objection was removed, he could not put his hand to the Constitution."

At which point, General Thompson exclaimed, "Mr. President, shall it be said that, after we have established our own independence and freedom, we make *slaves* of others. O! Washington, what a name he has had! How he has immortalized himself! But he holds those in slavery who have as good a right to be free as he has. He is still for self; and, in my opinion, his character has sunk fifty per cent."

General Heath, one of the veteran general officers of the Continental army, attempted to mollify the opponents of slavery. "No gentleman, within these walls," he declared, "detests every idea of slavery more than I do: it is generally detested by the people of this commonwealth; and I ardently hope that the time will soon come when our brethren in the Southern States will view it as we do, and put a stop to it; but to this we have no right to compel them. Two questions naturally arise: if we ratify the Constitution, shall we do any thing by our act to hold the blacks in slavery? or shall we become partakers of other men's sins? I think neither of them."

After the Constitution had been attacked by Colonel Jones of Bristol on the ground that it contained no requirement for a religious oath and that, in his view, "a person could not be a good man without being a good Christian," and defended by the Reverend Payson on the same ground (Payson declaring "had there been a religious test as a qualification for office, it would in my opinion, have been a great blemish upon the instrument"), General Heath rose to remind the delegates of how solemn an obligation they lay under.

It was, in truth, "a question as momentous as ever invited the attention of man. We are soon to decide on a system of government, digested, not for the people of the commonwealth of Massachusetts only—not for the present people of the United States only—but, in addition to these, for all those states which may hereafter rise into existence within the jurisdiction of the United States, and for millions of people yet unborn; a system of government, not for a nation of slaves, but for a people as free and virtuous as any on earth . . . who, under the smiles of Heaven, have established their independence and sovereignty, and have taken equal rank among the nations of the earth. . . . What can be more solemn? What can be more interesting? Every thing depends on our union. I know that some have supposed, that, although the union should be broken, particular states may retain their importance; but this cannot be. The strongest-nerved state, even [as] the right arm, if separated from the body must wither. If the great union be broken, our country, as a nation, perishes; and if our country so perishes; it will be as impossible to save a particular state as to preserve one of the fingers of a mortified hand."

It was perhaps appropriate that in a state which had begun its life as "the Bible Commonwealth," one of the last and most eloquent voices raised in behalf of the Constitution in the waning hours of the convention should have been that of a minister of the gospel, the Reverend Samuel Stillman. "I shall . . . cling to the Union as the rock of our salvation," he declared, "and urge Virginia to finish the salutary work which she hath begun. . . . May the God who has the hearts of all men under his control, inspire every member of Congress [with the disposition to accept the will of the majority]. Then shall we lay aside every opposite interest, and unite, as a band of brothers, in the ratification of this Constitution of national government."

After reviewing the various criticisms of the Constitution and attempting to meet them, Stillman declared, "I am ready . . . to submit my life, my liberty, my family, my property, and, as far as my vote will go, the interests of my constituents, to this general government."

Despite all the heavy artillery that the Federalists mustered for their cause, the vote itself was nerve-wrackingly close. The northern and western counties voted overwhelmingly against acceptance of the Constitution, the seacoast counties generally in its favor. Without the support of Suffolk and Essex counties (Boston and the heavily populated north coast) the Constitution must have been defeated. The final tally was yeas 187, nays 168—a difference of 19 votes out of 355 cast. In other words, in the most populous state in the Confederation ten votes decided the issue.

Had Massachusetts rejected the Constitution, it is certainly the case that the anti-Constitutionalists in Virginia and New York would have taken heart. The chances of those states ratifying would have been seriously diminished. New Hampshire, where the vote was also uncomfortably close, and assent accompanied by a long list of proposed amendments, would doubtless have gone along with her neighbor to the south.

One encouraging sign for the Federalists was that despite the closeness of the vote, many of the leading opponents of the Constitution rose to express their compliance with the will of the majority. That, indeed, was perhaps the principal accomplishment of the Massachusetts convention; that a spirit of conciliation marked the close of its long-extended and often bitter debates.

The Federalists in other states, especially in Pennsylvania, where the anti-Constitutionalists were threatening to resist the new government by force if necessary, made a great deal of the good spirit in which the Massachusetts anti-Constitutionalists took defeat. "Boston disagreed," a writer in the *Pennsylvania Mercury* observed, "but the opposition, perceiving that the Federalists were carrying the day, gave in with good grace and a feast was held in which *all* joined," the celebrants singing together:

> John Foster Williams in a ship
> Joined in the social band, sir,
> And made the lasses dance and skip
> To see him sail on land, sir.
>
> > Yankee Doodle, keep it up!
> > Yankee Doodle, dandy,
> > Mind the music and the step,
> > And with the girls be handy.
>
> Now politicians of all kinds
> Who are not yet decided;
> May see how Yankees speak their minds
> *And yet are not divided.*
>
> > Yankee Doodle, keep it up! etc.

The ratification by Massachusetts was followed by that of Maryland on April 2 (Georgia had ratified on January 2). South Carolina ratified May 23, and on June 2, the apprehensively anticipated Virginia convention met in Richmond. Refusal by that state would almost certainly tip the balance against the Constitution in New York, whose delegates were to assemble in two weeks' time, with consequences difficult to predict. Certainly it was not inconceivable that the whole laboriously built structure of assent might come tumbling down like a house of cards. Attention everywhere turned to Virginia.

No other state had such an array of forensic talent and political sagacity engaged on both sides of the issue. It counted heavily that Edmund Randolph and George Mason, both delegates to the convention, and privy to its innermost workings, had rejected the finished document. Richard Henry Lee, although not a delegate, was bitterly opposed to it, as was Patrick Henry, the famed veteran of innumerable political contests, a man whose name stirred the deepest memories of Revolutionary ardor.

The Constitutionalists had leaders almost as redoubtable: Madison, of course, and the incumbent governor, the widely respected Edmund Pendleton, John Marshall, and George Wythe, one of the most respected figures in the Virginia bar. There were dozens of other able and influential men on both sides of the issue, many cousins of one degree or another, since Virginians were notoriously inbred: Carters, Tylers, Burwells, Nicholases, Lees, Carringtons, Careys, Masons, Peachys, and Walkes.

But Patrick Henry dominated them all. He was fiery, passionate, "pathetic" ("stirring" in its eighteenth-century meaning), and maudlin by turns. Finally, one suspects, he wore everyone out and did his cause more ill than good. It was his last hurrah, in any event, and he made the most of it. Madison was his principal adversary and there could hardly have been a greater contrast in personalities. Where Henry was flamboyant, Madison was reserved. Where Henry was emotional, Madison was logical. Where Henry's extravagant phrases shook the rafters, Madison often was barely audible.

George Mason opened the debates with a plea for waiving formal rules so that freest and fullest discussion might take place. "The curse denounced by the divine vengeance will be small compared to what will justly fall upon us, if from any sinister views we obstruct the fullest inquiry." The Constitution must be reviewed, "clause by clause."

After Wilson Nicholas began the formal discussion with a long and learned defense of the Constitution which included references to the reigns of Edward I and II of England, Magna Charta, Henry IV and Louis XI of France and a good deal about the reign of Charles II and William and Mary as well as a lengthy quotation from Dr. Price's famous work on civil liberty, Patrick Henry sounded the note that would be his theme throughout the convention. "I consider myself," he declared, "as the servant of the people of this commonwealth, as sentinel over their rights, liberty, and happiness." When he had sought election as a delegate to the convention he had become "extremely agitated for the situation of public affairs. I conceived the republic to be in extreme danger. . . . Whence has arisen this fearful jeopardy? It arises from this fatal system; it arises from a proposal to change our government—a proposal that goes to the utter annihilation of the most solemn engagements of the states—a proposal of establishing nine states into a confederacy, to the eventual exclusion of four states. . . . If a wrong step be now made, the republic may be lost forever."

Henry was convinced that the delegates at Philadelphia were determined to establish "a great consolidated government, instead of a confederation. That this is a consolidated government is demonstrably clear; and the danger of such a government is . . . very striking. I have the highest veneration for those gentlemen; but, sir, give me leave to demand, What right had they to say, *We, the people*? My political curiosity, exclusive of my anxious solicitude for the public welfare, leads me to ask, Who authorized them to speak the language of, *We, the people*, instead of *We, the states*? . . . The people gave them no power to use their name. That they exceeded their power is perfectly clear."

When Henry finished, Edmund Randolph rose to answer him in what was one of the most dramatic moments of the debates. He agreed that the nation had "without war, or even the menace of the smallest force" been brought to a point where "an error . . . may blast their happiness." What was essential in this perilous moment was "a mutual toleration, and a persuasion that no man has a right to impose his opinions on others." Randolph wanted to make clear that the reason that he had been unwilling to sign the Constitution was not because he thought the delegates had exceeded their powers, as Patrick Henry had argued, but because he felt that it was in serious need of amendments and, above all, he wished to discover "the genius of America," in regard to the Constitution, i.e., the sentiments of the electorate in general. He was satisfied that the people of the state were, indeed, "prepared for the important change" from the Confederation to the new Constitution. His only concern now was for the necessary amendments. He was prepared to follow the lead of Massachusetts and accept the Constitution with recommended amendments.

Randolph's defection was of crucial importance. It divided the ranks of the anti-Constitutionalists and inevitably demoralized them. Even George Mason's reply and his charge that the Constitution was "calculated to annihilate totally the state governments" failed to erase the impression that Randolph's reply to Henry had made on the delegates. Mason insisted that "these two concurrent powers [the national and the state governments] cannot exist long together; the one will destroy the other." The national government must triumph. "Is it to be supposed," Mason asked the delegates, "that one national government will suit so extensive a country, embracing so many climates, and containing inhabitants so very different in manners, habits, and customs? It is ascertained, by history, that there never was a government over a very extensive country without destroying the liberties of the people: history also, supported by the opinions of the best writers, shows us that monarchy may suit a large territory, and despotic governments over so extensive a territory but that popular governments can only exist in small territories. Is there a single example, on the face of the earth, to support a contrary opinion?" After attacking the right of the national legislature to collect taxes, Mason concluded by warning that the most oppressive aspect of all was the power given to the national judiciary.

Edmund Pendleton followed with a detailed and able defense of the proposed government contrasting it with the generally admitted weaknesses of the Articles of Confederation, their "imbecility." He paid particular attention to the accusation that the Constitution would establish a "consolidated government." A consolidated government, Pendleton noted, would be one in which all powers were concentrated in it without limitation. But this was clearly not the case. Specific powers were apportioned to the states. Congress could by no means legislate for the state of Virginia.

Henry Lee—Light Horse Harry—denominated "of Westmoreland" to distinguish him from Henry Lee of Bourbon (a reference to his ancestral home, not his drinking habits), also turned his fire on Henry. "The *éclat* and brilliance which had distinguished that gentleman, the honors with which he has been dignified, and the brilliant talents which he has so often displayed, have attracted my attention and respect. On so important occasion, and before so respectable a body, I had expected a new display of his powers of oratory; but instead of proceeding to investigate the merits of the new plan of government, the worthy character informed us of the horrors he felt, of apprehensions to his mind, which made him tremblingly fearful of the fate of the commonwealth. Mr. Chairman, was it proper to appeal to the fears of this house? The question before us belongs to the judgment of this house. I trust he has come to judge, and not to alarm."

Henry rose promptly to his own defense. This time he concentrated his attack on the absence of a Bill of Rights. "The rights of conscience, trial by jury, liberty of the press, all your immunities and franchises, all pretensions to human rights and privileges are rendered insecure, if not lost, by this change, so loudly talked of by some, and inconsiderately by others. . . . It is said eight states have adopted this plan. I declare that if twelve and a half had adopted it, I would, with manly firmness, and in spite of an erring world, reject it. . . . Will the abandonment of your most sacred rights tend to the security of your liberty? Liberty, the greatest of all earthly blessings—give us that precious jewel, and you may take every thing else! But I am fearful I have lived long enough to become an old-fashioned fellow. Perhaps an invincible attachment to the dearest rights of man may, in these refined, enlightened days, be deemed old-fashioned; if so, I am content to be so. . . . We are come hither to preserve the poor commonwealth of Virginia, if it can be possibly done: something must be done to preserve your liberty and mine. The Confederation, this same despised government, merits, in my opinion, the highest encomium. . . ."

In Henry, perhaps more than any of his fellow anti-Constitutionalists in Virginia and in the other states, the accents of an idyllic rural America could be heard, a fear of involvement in a harsh and often cruel world; fear of power; the dream of purity and isolation. It was clear to Henry that "most of the human race" were presently groaning under tyrannical and oppressive governments, "and those nations who have gone in search of grandeur, power, and splendor, have also fallen a sacrifice, and been the victims of their own folly. While they have acquired those visionary blessings, they lost their freedom."

The supporters of the Constitution had argued that there was no turning back now. Eight states had ratified the Constitution. The Confederation was, in effect, defunct. For Virginia to reject the Constitution at this point would be to create a situation verging on anarchy. Henry was unimpressed with the argument. "Is there any revolution in Virginia?" he asked. "Whither is the spirit of America gone? Whither is the genius of America fled? It was but yesterday, when our enemies marched in triumph through our country. Yet the people of this country could not be appalled by their pompous armaments: they stopped their career, and victoriously captured them. Where is the peril, now, compared to that?"

Hour after hour Henry held forth until finally the weary transcriber simply noted parenthetically "(Here Mr. HENRY strongly and pathetically expatiated on the probability of the President's enslaving America, and the horrid consequences that must result.)." Observing the impatience of many members, Henry came at last to an end. He had, he feared, fatigued his listeners, yet he had "not said one hundred thousandth part of what I have on my mind, and wish to impart." That, certainly, was chilling news to many of the delegates.

Randolph rebuked him. "If we go on in this irregular manner . . . instead of three to six weeks, it will take us six months to decide this question." Randolph then undertook to demonstrate both the "inefficacy" of the Confederation and the "necessity of establishing a national government." He commenced by declaring: "Mr. Chairman, I am a child of the revolution." In elucidating the Constitution and attempting to refute the various charges which, Randolph complained, Henry had discharged in a blunderbuss fashion, he came back repeatedly to the argument that rejection of the Constitution would result in dissolution of the Union and place every state in peril.

Randolph proved himself no mean rival to Henry for forensic honors as he closed by exhorting the delegates: "I have labored for the continuance of the Union—the rock of our salvation [had he read the Reverend Stillman's speech in the Massachusetts convention?]. I believe that, as sure as there is a God in heaven, our safety, our political happiness and existence, depend on the union of the states; and that without this union, the people of this and the other states will undergo the unspeakable calamities which discord, faction, turbulence, war, and bloodshed, have produced in other countries. The American spirit ought to be mixed with American pride, to see the Union magnificently triumphant. Let that glorious pride, which once defied the British thunder, reanimate you again. Let it not be recorded of Americans, that, after having overcome the most astonishing difficulties, and after having gained the admiration of the world by their incomparable valor and policy, they lost their acquired reputation, their national consequence and happiness, by their own indiscretion. . . . Catch the present moment—seize it with avidity and eagerness—for it may be lost, never to be regained! If the Union be now lost, I fear it will remain so forever."

Mr. Madison then arose (but he spoke so low that his exordium could not be heard distinctly): "I shall not attempt to make impressions by any ardent professions of zeal for the public welfare. We know the principles of every man will, and ought to be, judged, not by his professions and declarations, but by his conduct. . . . We ought, sir, to examine the Constitution on its own merits solely: we are to inquire whether it will promote the public happiness: its aptitude to produce this desirable object ought to be the exclusive subject of our present researches. In this pursuit, we ought not to address our arguments to the feelings and passions, but to those understandings and judgments which were selected by the people of this country, to decide this great question by a calm and rational investigation. . . . If powers be necessary, apparent danger is not sufficient reason against conceding them."

Then it was Henry again, master of the turn of phrase, not at all chastened by Madison's appeal for reason rather than emotion. Rehearsing all his by now well-tried arguments, talking, talking, talking. Gradually the debates turned into an endurance contest—Patrick Henry against Madison and Randolph with occasional relief by others. Henry reserved his special contempt for the notion that the Constitution contained any of those checks and balances conceded by every authority to be essential to good government. The Constitution, in his opinion, was "the most fatal plan that could possibly be conceived to enslave a free people."

Randolph indicated the degree to which the general tone of the debates had deteriorated by charging Henry with having attacked him "in the most illiberal manner. . . . I disdain his aspersions and his insinuations. His asperity is warranted by no principle of parliamentary decency, nor compatible with the least shadow of friendship; and if our friendship must fall, *let it fall, like Lucifer, never to rise again!*"

Young James Monroe, a future president of the United States, could not forbear to "express the great anxiety which I feel upon the present occasion. . . . When we contemplate the fate that has befallen other nations, whether we cast our eyes back into the remotest ages of antiquity, or derive instruction from those examples which modern times have presented to our view, and observe how prone all human institutions have been to decay; how subject the best-formed and most wisely organized governments have been to lose their checks and totally dissolve; how difficult it has been for mankind, in all ages and countries, to preserve their dearest rights and best privileges, impelled as it were by an irresistible fate of despotism;— if we look forward to those prospects that sooner or later await our country, unless we shall be exempt from the fate of other nations, even to a mind the most sanguine and benevolent some gloomy apprehensions must necessarily crowd upon it. This consideration is sufficient to teach us the limited capacity of the human mind—how subject the wisest men have been to error."

Monroe declared that he came not as a partisan but "to hear with candor the explanation of others." (In the end he voted with Henry and Mason not to ratify the Constitution.) He then went on to praise democracies as the ideal form of government, reviewing their history from ancient Thebes to the Swiss cantons. From his examination of "those leagues" he had concluded "that nothing be adduced from any of them, to warrant departure from a confederacy to a consolidation." The state governments were all "perfectly democratic. The freedom of mankind has found an asylum here which it could find nowhere else. . . . Why, then, this haste—this wild precipitation?"

William Grayson was one of the anti-Constitutional stalwarts. He entertained himself, and doubtless those of a similar disposition, by ridiculing the notion that the United States needed an army and navy to provide for the country's defense in time of war. Are we to assume, he asked, that "Pennsylvania and Maryland are to fall upon us from the north, like the Goths and Vandals of old; the Algerines, whose flat-sided vessels never came further than Madeira, are to fill up the Chesapeake with mighty fleets, and to attack us on our front; the Indians to invade us with numerous armies on our rear, in order to convert our cleared lands into hunting grounds; and the Carolinians, from the south (mounted on alligators, I presume) are to come and destroy our cornfields, and eat up our little children! These, sir, are the mighty dangers which await us if we reject [the Constitution]."

One of the principal bones of contention among the delegates was the determination of the anti-Constitutionalists to attack the Constitution in the most general terms, denouncing it *in toto*, so to speak, while its defenders wished to proceed one article at a time, explaining and defending each in turn. So adamant and impassioned were the opponents of the Constitution that it was not until the latter part of the convention that they could be brought to pay attention to particulars. At this point, as they may have suspected would be the case, divisions in the ranks of the anti-Constitutionalists became evident. This was perhaps most striking on the issue of slavery. George Mason rose to denounce the "fatal section" which permitted the slave trade to continue for twenty years. Picking up the theme he had sounded so eloquently in the federal convention, he declared, "The augmentation of slaves weakens the states; and such a trade is diabolical in itself, and disgraceful to mankind. . . . As much as I value a union of all the states, I would not admit the Southern States into the Union unless they agree to the discontinuance of this disgraceful trade, because it would bring weakness, and not strength, to the Union." And then the bitter irony. "And, though this infamous tariff be continued, we have no security for the property of that kind [black slaves] which we have already." The more liberal spirits of the South were haunted by two nightmares. In the first, slavery, with all its degrading effects on masters and slaves alike, remained the incubus of the region. In the second, the Northern states, dominating the new union and strongly opposed to slavery, took their slaves away or turned them loose to murder their former owners in their beds.

John Tyler "warmly enlarged on the impolicy, iniquity, and disgracefulness of this wicked trade. . . . He thought nothing could justify it." Henry also squirmed on the horns of the dilemma. He was especially alarmed by the provision in the Constitution which permitted Congress to pass laws for "the general welfare." Would this not mean that a majority of nonslaveholding states might "call for the abolition of slavery? May they not pronounce all slaves free, and will they not be warranted by that power? . . . They have the power in clear inequivocal terms, and will clearly and certainly exercise it. . . . The majority of Congress are to the north, and the slaves are to the south. . . . I repeat again, that it would rejoice my very soul that every one of my fellow-beings was emancipated. As we ought with gratitude to admire that decree of Heaven which has numbered us among the free, we ought to lament and deplore the necessity of holding our fellow-men in bondage. But is it practicable, by any human means, to liberate them without producing the most dreadful and ruinous consequences?"

In his denunciations of the federal Constitution Henry eulogized the British constitution, quoting Montesquieu and comparing the two "systems" much to the advantage of the British. By Henry's logic the unwritten British constitution was infinitely superior to the written American one because it restrained the "self-love" of those responsible for governing. For the claim that the federal Constitution had such restraints built into it he had only scorn: "There will be no checks, no real balances, in this government. What can avail your specious, imaginary ideal checks and contrivances?"

And yet again in Henry's words: "We are not feared by foreigners; we do not make nations tremble. Would this, sir, constitute happiness, or secure liberty? I trust, sir, our political hemisphere will ever direct their operations to the security of those objects, liberty and happiness."

When the discussion passed on to the matter of the Supreme Court, John Marshall rose to answer George Mason's criticisms. In view of Marshall's role in the development of the Supreme Court, it seems appropriate to include his comments extensively, calling particular attention to his assurance that "no state will be called to the bar of the federal court."

> Mr. John Marshall. Mr. Chairman, this part of the plan before us is a great improvement on that system from which we are now departing. . . . Gentlemen have gone on an idea that the federal courts will not determine the causes which may come before them with the same fairness and impartiality with which other courts decide. . . .
> . . . If this committee will consider it fully they will find it has no foundation, and that we are as secure there as anywhere else. What mischief results from some causes being tried there? Is there not the utmost reason to conclude that judges, wisely appointed, and independent in their office, will never countenance any unfair trial? What are the subjects of its jurisdiction? Let us examine them with an expectation that causes will be as candidly tried there as elsewhere, and then determine. . . . I had an apprehension that those gentlemen who placed

no confidence in Congress would object that there might be no inferior courts. I own that I thought that those gentlemen would think there would be no inferior courts, as it depended on the will of Congress, but that we should be dragged to the centre of the Union. But I did not conceive that the power of increasing the number of courts could be objected to by any gentleman, as it would remove the inconvenience of being dragged to the centre of the United States. I own that the power of creating a number of courts is, in my estimation, so far from being a defect that it seems necessary to the perfection of this system. . . . With respect to its cognizance in all cases arising under the Constitution and the laws of the United States, he [Mason] says that the laws of the United States being paramount to the laws of the particular States, there is no case but what this will extend to. Has the government of the United States power to make laws on every subject? Does he understand it so? Can they make laws affecting the mode of transferring property, or contracts, or claims, between citizens of the same State? Can they go beyond the delegated powers? If they were to make a law not warranted by any of the powers enumerated, it would be considered by the judges as an infringement of the Constitution which they are to guard. They would not consider such a law as coming under their jurisdiction. They would declare it void. . . .

To what quarter will you look for protection from an infringement on the Constitution, if you will not give the power to the judiciary? There is no other body that can afford such a protection. But the honorable member objects to it, because he says that the officers of the government will be screened from merited punishment by the federal judiciary. The federal sheriff, says he, will go into a poor man's house and beat him, or abuse his family, and the federal court will protect him. Does any gentleman believe this? Is it necessary that the officers will commit a trespass on the property or persons of those with whom they are to transact business? Will such great insults on the people of this country be allowable? Were a law made to authorize them, it would be void. The injured man would trust to a tribunal in his neighborhood. To such a tribunal he would apply for redress, and get it. There is no reason to fear that he would not meet that justice there which his country will be ever willing to maintain. But, on appeal, says the honorable gentleman, what chance is there to obtain justice? This is founded on an idea that they will not be impartial. There is no clause in the Constitution which bars the individual member injured from applying to the State courts to give him redress. He says that there is no instance of appeals as to fact in common law cases. The contrary is well known to you, Mr. Chairman, to be the case in this Commonwealth. With respect to mills, roads, and other cases, appeals lye from the inferior to the superior court, as to fact as well as law. Is it a clear case, that there can be no case in common law in which an appeal as to fact might be proper and necessary? Can you not conceive a case where it would be productive of advantages to the people at large to submit to that tribunal the final determination, involving facts as well as law? Suppose it should be deemed for the convenience of the citizens that those things which concerned foreign ministers should be tried in the inferior courts, if justice would be done, the decision would satisfy all. But if an appeal in matters of fact could not be carried to the superior court, then it would result that such cases could not be tried before the inferior courts, for fear of injurious and partial decisions. . . .

With respect to disputes between a State and the citizens of another State, [the Constitution's] jurisdiction has been decried with unusual vehemence. I hope that no gentleman will think that a State will be called at the bar of the federal court. Is there no such case at present? Are there not many cases in which the legislature of Virginia is a party, and yet the State is not sued? Is it rational to suppose that the sovereign power shall be dragged before a court? The intent is, to enable States to recover claims of individuals residing in other States. I contend this construction is warranted by the words. But, say they, there will be partiality in it if a State cannot be defendant—if an individual cannot proceed to obtain judgment against a State, though he may be sued by a State. It is necessary to be so, and cannot be avoided. I see a difficulty in making a State defendant, which does not prevent its being plaintiff. If this be only what cannot be avoided, why object to the system on that account? If an individual has a just claim against any particular State, is it to be presumed that, on application to its Legislature, he will not obtain satisfaction? But how could a State recover any claim from a citizen of another State, without the establishment of these tribunals?

The honorable member objects to suits being instituted in the federal courts, by the citizens of one State, against the citizens of another State. . . . It may be necessary with respect to the laws and regulations of commerce, which Congress may make. It may be necessary in cases of debt, and some other controversies. In claims for land, it is not necessary, but it is not dangerous. In the court of which State will it be instituted? said the honorable gentleman. It will be instituted in the court of the State where the defendant resides, where the law can come at him, and nowhere else. By the laws of which State will it be determined? said he. By the laws of the State where the contract was made. According to those laws, and those only, can it be decided. . . . Let us consider that, when citizens of one State carry on trade in another State, much must be due to the one from the other, as is the case between North Carolina and Virginia. Would not the refusal of justice to our citizens, from the courts of North Carolina, produce disputes between the States? Should the federal judiciary swerve from their duty in order to give partial and unjust decisions? . . .

He objects, in the next place, to its jurisdiction in controversies between a State and a foreign State. Suppose, says he, in such a suit, a foreign State is cast; will she be bound by the decision? If a foreign State brought a suit against the Commonwealth of Virginia, would she not be barred from the claim if the federal judiciary thought it unjust? The previous consent of the parties is necessary; and, as the federal judiciary will decide, each party will acquiesce. It will be the means of preventing disputes with foreign nations. On an attentive consideration of these points, I trust every part will appear satisfactory to the committee.

The exclusion of trial by jury, in this case, he urged to prostrate our rights. Does the word *court* only mean the judges? Does not the determination of a jury necessarily lead to the judgment of the court? Is there anything here which gives the judges exclusive jurisdiction of matters of fact? What is the object of a jury trial? To inform the court of the facts. When a court has cognizance of facts does it not follow that they can make inquiry by a jury? It is impossible to be otherwise. I hope that in this country, where impartiality is so much admired, the laws will direct facts to be ascertained by a jury. But, says the honorable gentleman, the juries in the ten miles square will be mere tools of parties, with which he would not trust his person or property; which, he says, he would rather leave to the court. Because the government may have a district of ten miles square, will no man stay there but the tools and officers of the government? Will nobody else be found there? Is it so in any other part of the world, where a government has legislative power? Are there none but officers, and tools of the government of Virginia in Richmond? Will there not be independent merchants and respectable gentlemen of fortune within the ten miles square? Will there not be worthy farmers and mechanics? Will not a good jury be found there, as well as anywhere else? . . .

The honorable gentleman says that unjust claims will be made, and the defendant had better pay them than go to the Supreme Court. Can you suppose such a disposition in one of your citizens, as that, to oppress another man, he will incur great expenses? What will he gain by an unjust demand? Does a claim establish a right? He must bring his witnesses to prove his claim. If he does not bring his witnesses, the expenses must fall upon him. Will he go on a calculation that the defendant will not defend it, or cannot produce a witness? Will he incur a great deal of expense, from a dependence on such a chance? Those who know human nature, black as it is, must know that mankind are too well attached to their interest to run such a risk. I conceive that this power is absolutely necessary, and not dangerous; that, should it be attended by little inconveniences, they will be altered, and that they can have no interest in not altering them. Is there any real danger? When I compare it to the exercise of the same power in the government of Virginia, I am persuaded there is not. The federal government has no other motive, and has every reason for doing right which the members of our State Legislature have. Will a man on the Eastern Shore be sent to be tried in Kentucky, or a man from Kentucky be brought to the Eastern Shore to have his trial? A government, by doing this, would destroy itself. I am convinced the trial by jury will be regulated in the manner most advantageous to the community.

George Nicholas had a good point when he noted, toward the end of the debates, that while Patrick Henry had come around to declaring that he was for the Constitution with certain amendments, "if the delegates when they retire from these walls . . . take the Constitution and strike out such parts as the honorable gentleman (Mr. Henry) has given his approbation to . . . they will find what a curious kind of government he would make it. It appears to me, sir, that he has objected to the whole; and that no part of it, if he had his way, would be agreed to."

In the closing days of the convention tempers flared. Henry and Mason seemed to be saying that if the Constitution was ratified prior to extensive amending, they would resist it with every means at their disposal. When Mason spoke of fearing "popular resistance to its operations . . . and the *dreadful effects* which must ensue, should the people resist," Henry Lee could not refrain from denouncing such sentiments. "I respect the honorable gentleman," he declared, "and never believed I should live to have heard fall from his lips opinions so injurious to our country, and so opposite to the dignity of this assembly. If the dreadful picture which he has drawn be so abhorrent to his mind as he has declared, let me ask . . . if he has not pursued the very means to bring into action the horrors which he deprecates. Such speeches, within these walls, from a character so venerable and estimable, easily progress into overt acts, among the less thinking and the vicious. . . . But if the madness of some, and the vice of others, should risk the awful appeal, I trust that the friends to the paper on your table, conscious of the justice of their cause . . . will meet the afflicting call with that firmness and fortitude which become men summoned to defend what they conceive to be the true interest of their country. . . ."

The theme was reiterated by partisans of both sides. Henry declared that if the amendments were not agreed to, "every movement and operation of government will cease; and how long that baneful thing, civil discord, will stay from this country, God only knows. When men are free from restraint, how long will you suspend their fury? The interval between this and bloodshed is but a moment."

As the debates approached their conclusion, a delegate very similar in temperament to our friend Josiah Smith of the Massachusetts Convention, Zachariah Johnson, rose to rebut Henry. "It is my lot," he declared, "to be among the poor people. The most that I can claim or flatter myself with, is to be of the middle rank. I wish no more, for I am contented. But I shall give my opinion unbiased and uninfluenced, without erudition or eloquence, but with firmness and candor; and in doing so I will satisfy my conscience. If this Constitution be bad, it will bear equally as hard on me as on any other member of the society. It will bear hard on my children, who are as dear to me as any man's children can be to him."

The delegates were being called upon "to decide the greatest of all questions—a question which may involve the felicity or misery of myself and posterity. I have hitherto listened to both sides, and attended to hear the discussion of the most complicated parts of the system by gentlemen of great abilities. . . . When I view the necessity of government among mankind, and its happy operation when judiciously constructed; and when I view the principles of this Constitution, and the satisfactory and liberal manner in which they have been developed by the gentleman in the chair, and several other gentlemen; and when I view, on the other hand, the strained construction which has been put, by the gentlemen on the other side, on every word and syllable, in endeavoring to prove oppressions which can never possibly happen,—my judgment is convinced of the safety and propriety of this system. This conviction does not rise from a blind acquiescence or dependence on the assertions and opinions of others, but from a full persuasion of its rectitude, after an attentive and mature consideration of the subjects; the arguments of the other gentlemen having only confirmed the opinion which I have previously formed, and which I was determined to abandon, should I find it to be ill founded. . . . This Constitution may have defects. There can be no human institution without defects. We must go out of this world to find it otherwise. The annals of mankind do not show one example of a perfect constitution." Johnson then went on to compare the present situation with the period in English history when "the Parliament of England beheaded King Charles I., conquered their enemies, obtained liberty, and established a kind of republic." With such fair prospects before them, they faltered and "for want of an efficient and judicious system of republican government, confusion and anarchy took place. Men became so lawless, so destitute of principle, and so utterly ungovernable, that, to avoid greater calamities, they were driven to the expedient of sending for the son of that monarch whom they had beheaded, that he might become their master. This is like our situation in some degree. . . . Shall we lose our blood and treasure, which we lost in the revolution, and permit anarchy and misery to complete the ruin of the country? Under these impressions, and for these reasons, I am for adopting the constitution without previous amendments. I will go to any length afterwards, to reconcile it to the gentlemen, by proposing subsequent amendments. The great and wise state of Massachusetts has taken this step. The great and wise state of Virginia might safely do the same. I am content to rest my happiness on that footing."

It is agreeable to speculate that Zachariah Johnson's speech turned the tide finally in favor of the Constitution among those delegates, if any, who still wavered. But that is speculation. What can be said confidently was that it was the final statement by a member of the pro-Constitution side. When Patrick Henry got up to reply to it, he may have known or sensed that he had lost the day for he concluded by saying: "I beg pardon to this house for having taken up more time than came to my share, and I thank them for the patience and polite attention with which I have been heard. If I shall be in the minority, I shall have those painful sensations which arise from a conviction of *being overpowered in a good cause.* Yet I will be a peaceable citizen. My head, my hand, and my heart shall be at liberty to retrieve the loss of liberty, and remove the defects of this system in a constitutional way. I wish not to go to violence, but will wait with hopes that the spirit which predominated in the revolution is not yet gone, nor the cause of those who are attached to the revolution yet lost. I shall therefore patiently wait in expectation of seeing that government changed, so as to be compatible with the safety, liberty, and happiness of the people."

The first resolution that the delegates were to vote on stated that a Bill of Rights must be drawn up prior to Virginia's ratification of the Constitution "together with amendments to the most exceptionable parts of the said Constitution. . . ." It was defeated 88 to 80, in other words by 5 votes. On the vote to ratify the Constitution as it stood, ayes 89; noes 79. Again a shift of six votes would have carried the day for the opponents of the Constitution.

The Virginia debates are a puzzle. For one thing, one is not entirely sure what lies behind them. For instance, did Patrick Henry really believe in all the calamities he declared must follow from the adoption of the Constitution? Barring other evidence we must, I think, take him at his word. But what state of mind did his perfervid utterances reveal? Did they, in fact, go beyond a narrow parochialism? It was always *Virginia's* rights and liberties that Henry dwelt on; the danger to Virginia from exploitation by the commercial states of the North. Was it his wish to kill the Constitution by one means or another primarily because he distrusted the New England states? From praising the Articles of Confederation in the early days of the convention he came to join in the general denunciation of the Articles. From excoriating the new plan of government unmercifully he passed on to calling simply for prior amendments rather than subsequent ones. It seems clear that he and Mason understood that their relentless strictures against the Constitution had failed to win support in the convention and that it was expedient to shift their ground.

The modern reader can hardly fail to be impressed by the general level of the discussion as well as by a growing sense of frustration as arguments on both sides were repeated and repeated. It is understandable that Madison, never robust, was at times too exhausted to continue. Then there are the simple mechanics: John Beckley's skill (if it was he) in transcription and the fact that virtually all the speakers spoke prose. One might assume that they had written out their speeches beforehand (as was certainly the case in many instances during the federal convention) were it not for the fact that succeeding speakers replied to each other in a manner that would not have been possible if their speeches had been written.

In addition, of course, the secretary noted from time to time that a delegate's voice sank so low that it could not be heard distinctly. The fact that most remarks were apparently extemporaneous makes it all the more remarkable that a succession of speakers could, in speeches extending over a substantial period of time keep clearly in their minds the points they wished to make in rebuttal of an opponent's arguments. All of which serves perhaps to remind us that we are dealing with what was doubtless the most articulate generation in our history and with men whose gifts in public discourse are probably without parallel, unless it be in the greatest days of British parliamentary debate.

It is worth noting that in the extensive discussions over the role of the Supreme Court, little was said about the Court's right to declare laws passed by Congress unconstitutional. Undoubtedly this was, in large part, because the defenders of the Constitution were so busy refuting claims that the Supreme Court would exercise excessive power or dominate the state courts. Under such circumstances it would have been folly to add to the paranoia of the champions of state sovereignty by suggesting the wider range of powers for the Court.

With the issue decided in Virginia, attention turned to New York. During the Virginia debates, New Hampshire had, as we have noted, ratified the Constitution by a narrow margin. Virginia was thus the tenth state to ratify. Technically the Constitution could be said to have been approved by the states, but it was hard to believe that the Union could be solid or enduring without New York, the keystone state, wealthy, populous, and strategically located between the New England and the Middle and Southern states.

New York, in fact, had only assembled in convention a week before the end of the Virginia debates. The anti-Constitutionalists in Virginia plainly staked their hopes for the defeat of the Constitution on the determined opposition of their northern ally.

In New York the most notable event had been the publication of the *Federalist Papers*, addressed "To the People of the State of New York." These essays had appeared initially in the *Independent Journal*. For all conscientious students of the Constitution the *Federalist Papers* are an essential text. Written by Madison, John Jay, and Hamilton, they constitute the most thorough and most brilliant explication of the federal Constitution (or any other constitution) ever written. There is insufficient space in this work to reprint the *Federalist Papers* in their entirety. Moreover, the reader is by now acquainted, through the federal and state debates, with the main propositions in the Federalist argument. For example, one of the most famous essays is the Tenth Paper, written by James Madison. In it Madison argues that one of the most conspicuous advantages of the new government is its "tendency to break and control the violence of faction." Madison then goes on to describe the different "interests" in a country and the importance of preventing a combination of such interests—"an overbearing majority"—from riding roughshod over the interests of the minority. We are already familiar, of course, with Madison's development, somewhat more eloquently in my view, of the same notion in the federal debates themselves. Indeed, splendid as the *Federalist Papers* are, if one had to choose between them and the debates, the preference must clearly go to the debates, which have a drama and immediacy, as well as a candor about them, that is necessarily missing from the *Papers*.

The exception must be the concluding essays on the national judiciary, for two reasons. First, the discussions of the judiciary in the convention itself were somewhat sparse. Second, a main focus of this work is of course the Supreme Court and its decisions, and the whole concept of the role and function of the Court was substantially influenced by Hamilton's description of it; thus papers 78 to 82 are included here, 79 excepted. In the 78th Paper, Hamilton gives special attention to the argument that giving the Court authority to declare acts of the legislative branch void will give the Court "superiority" over the legislature rather than simply serving as a "balance." In the argument for the appointment of judges "during good behavior" rather than by election. Hamilton makes the point that the judges of the Supreme Court will require "an uncommon portion of fortitude . . . to do their duty as faithful guardians of the Constitution, where legislative invasions of it have been instigated by the major voice of the community."

It was important that the explicator of the powers of the judiciary should be a person with a predilection for a strong central government, a prominent feature of which must clearly be a Court with extensive powers.

CHAPTER

IX

THE FEDERALIST PAPERS

We proceed now to an examination of the judiciary department of the proposed government.

In unfolding the defects of the existing Confederation, the utility and necessity of a federal judicature have been clearly pointed out. It is the less necessary to recapitulate the considerations there urged as the propriety of the institution in the abstract is not disputed; the only questions which have been raised being relative to the manner of constituting it, and to its extent. To these points, therefore, our observations shall be confined.

The manner of constituting it seems to embrace these several objects: 1st. The mode of appointing the judges. 2nd. The tenure by which they are to hold their places. 3rd. The partition of the judiciary authority between different courts and their relations to each other.

First. As to the mode of appointing the judges: this is the same with that of appointing the officers of the Union in general and has been so fully discussed in the two last numbers that nothing can be said here which would not be useless repetition.

Second. As to the tenure by which the judges are to hold their places: this chiefly concerns their duration in office, the provisions for their support, the precautions for their responsibility.

According to the plan of the convention, all judges who may be appointed by the United States are to hold their offices *during good behavior;* which is conformable to the most approved of the State constitutions, and among the rest, to that of this State. Its propriety having been drawn into question by the adversaries of that plan is no light symptom of the rage for objection which disorders their imaginations and judgments. The standard of good behavior for the continuance in office of the judicial magistracy is certainly one of the most valuable of the modern improvements in the practice of government. In a monarchy it is an excellent barrier to the despotism of the prince; in a republic it is a no less excellent barrier to the encroachments and oppressions of the representative body. And it is the best expedient which can be devised in any government to secure a steady, upright, and impartial administration of the laws.

Whoever attentively considers the different departments of power must perceive that, in a government in which they are separated from each other, the judiciary, from the nature of its functions, will always be the least dangerous to the political rights of the Constitution; because it will be least in a capacity to annoy or injure them. The executive not only dispenses the honors but holds the sword of the community. The legislature not only commands the purse but prescribes the rules by which the duties and rights of every citizen are to be regulated. The judiciary, on the contrary, has no influence over either the sword or the purse; no direction either of the strength or of the wealth of the society, and can take no active resolution whatever. It may truly be said to have neither FORCE nor WILL but merely judgment; and must ultimately depend upon the aid of the executive arm even for the efficacy of its judgments.

This simple view of the matter suggests several important consequences. It proves incontestably that the judiciary is beyond comparison the weakest of the three departments of power; that it can never attack with success either of the other two; and that all possible care is requisite to enable it to defend itself against their attacks. It equally proves that though individual oppression may now and then proceed from the courts of justice, the general liberty of the people can never be endangered from that quarter; I mean so long as the judiciary remains truly distinct from both the legislature and the executive. For I agree that "there is no liberty if the power of judging be not separated from the legislative and executive powers." And it proves, in the last place, that as liberty can have nothing to fear from the judiciary alone, but would have everything to fear from its union with either of the other departments; that as all the effects of such a union must ensue from a dependence of the former on the latter, notwithstanding a nominal and apparent separation; that as, from the natural feebleness of the judiciary, it is in continual jeopardy of being overpowered, awed, or influenced by its co-ordinate branches; and that as nothing can contribute so much to its firmness and independence as permanency in office, this quality may therefore be justly regarded as an indispensable ingredient in its constitution, and, in a great measure, as the citadel of the public justice and the public security.

The complete independence of the courts of justice is peculiarly essential in a limited Constitution. By a limited Constitution, I understand one which contains certain specified exceptions to the legislative authority; such, for instance, as that it shall pass no bills of attainder, no *ex post facto* laws, and the like. Limitations of this kind can be preserved in practice no other way than through the medium of courts of justice, whose duty it must be to declare all acts contrary to the manifest tenor of the Constitution void. Without this, all the reservations of particular rights or privileges would amount to nothing.

Some perplexity respecting the rights of the courts to pronounce legislative acts void, because contrary to the Constitution, has arisen from an imagination that the doctrine would imply a superiority of the judiciary to the legislative power. It is urged that the authority which can declare the acts of another void must necessarily be superior to the one whose acts may be declared void. As this doctrine is of great importance in all the American constitutions, a brief discussion of the grounds on which it rests cannot be unacceptable.

There is no position which depends on clearer principles than that every act of a delegated authority, contrary to the tenor of the commission under which it is exercised, is void. No legislative act, therefore, contrary to the Constitution, can be valid. To deny this would be to affirm that the deputy is greater than his principal; that the servant is above his master; that the representatives of the people are superior to the people themselves; that men acting by virtue of powers may do not only what their powers do not authorize, but what they forbid.

If it be said that the legislative body are themselves the constitutional judges of their own powers and that the construction they put upon them is conclusive upon the other departments it may be answered that this cannot be the natural presumption where it is not to be collected from any particular provisions in the Constitution. It is not otherwise to be supposed that the Constitution could intend to enable the representatives of the people to substitute their *will* to that of their constituents. It is far more rational to suppose that the courts were designed to be an intermediate body between the people and the legislature in order, among other things, to keep the latter within the limits assigned to their authority. The interpretation of the laws is the proper and peculiar province of the courts. A constitution is, in fact, and must be regarded by the judges as, a fundamental law. It therefore belongs to them to ascertain its meaning as well as the meaning of any particular act proceeding from the legislative body. If there should happen to be an irreconcilable variance between the two, that which has the superior obligation and validity ought, of course, to be preferred; or, in other words, the Constitution ought to be preferred to the statute, the intention of the people to the intention of their agents.

Nor does his conclusion by any means suppose a superiority of the judicial to the legislative power. It only supposes that the power of the people is superior to both, and that where the will of the legislature, declared in its statutes, stands in opposition to that of the people, declared in the Constitution, the judges ought to be governed by the latter rather than the former. They ought to regulate their decisions by the fundamental laws rather than by those which are not fundamental.

This exercise of judicial discretion in determining between two contradictory laws is exemplified in a familiar instance. It not uncommonly happens that there are two statutes existing at one time, clashing in whole or in part with each other and neither of them containing any repealing clause or expression. In such a case, it is the province of the courts to liquidate and fix their meaning and operation. So far as they can, by any fair construction, be reconciled to each other, reason and law conspire to dictate that this should be done; where this is impracticable, it becomes a matter of necessity to give effect to one in exclusion of the other. The rule which has obtained in the courts for determining their relative validity is that the last in order of time shall be preferred to the first. But this is a mere rule of construction, not derived from any positive law but from the nature and reason of the thing. It is a rule not enjoined upon the courts by legislative provision but adopted by themselves, as consonant to truth and propriety, for the direction of their conduct as interpreters of the law. They thought it reasonable that between the interfering acts of an *equal* authority that which was the last indication of its will should have the preference.

But in regard to the interfering acts of a superior and subordinate authority of an original and derivative power, the nature and reason of the thing indicate the converse of that rule as proper to be followed. They teach us that the prior act of a superior ought to be preferred to the subsequent act of an inferior and subordinate authority; and that accordingly, whenever a particular statute contravenes the Constitution, it will be the duty of the judicial tribunals to adhere to the latter and disregard the former.

It can be of no weight to say that the courts, on the pretense of a repugnancy, may substitute their own pleasure to the constitutional intentions of the legislature. This might as well happen in the case of two contradictory statutes; or it might as well happen in every adjudication upon any single statute. The courts must declare the sense of the law; and if they should be disposed to exercise WILL instead of JUDG-

MENT, the consequence would equally be the substitution of their pleasure to that of the legislative body. The observation, if it proved anything, would prove that there ought to be no judges distinct from that body.

If, then, the courts of justice are to be considered as the bulwarks of a limited Constitution against legislative encroachments, this consideration will afford a strong argument for the permanent tenure of judicial offices, since nothing will contribute so much as this to that independent spirit in the judges which must be essential to the faithful performance of so arduous a duty.

This independence of the judges is equally requisite to guard the Constitution and the rights of individuals from the effects of those ill humors which the arts of designing men, or the influence of particular conjunctures, sometimes disseminate among the people themselves, and which, though they speedily give place to better information, and more deliberate reflection, have a tendency, in the meantime, to occasion dangerous innovations in the government, and serious oppressions of the minor party in the community. Though I trust the friends of the proposed Constitution will never concur with its enemies in questioning that fundamental principle of republican government which admits the right of the people to alter or abolish the established Constitution whenever they find it inconsistent with their happiness; yet it is not to be inferred from this principle that the representatives of the people, whenever a momentary inclination happens to lay hold of a majority of their constituents incompatible with the provisions in the existing Constitution would, on that account, be justifiable in a violation of those provisions; or that the courts would be under a greater obligation to connive at infractions in this shape than when they had proceeded wholly from the cabals of the representative body. Until the people have, by some solemn and authoritative act, annulled or changed the established form, it is binding upon themselves collectively, as well as individually; and no presumption, or even knowledge of their sentiments, can warrant their representatives in a departure from it prior to such an act. But it is easy to see that it would require an uncommon portion of fortitude in the judges to do their duty as faithful guardians of the Constitution, where legislative invasions of it had been instigated by the major voice of the community.

But it is not with a view to infractions of the Constitution only that the independence of the judges may be an essential safeguard against the effects of occasional ill humors in the society. These sometimes extend no farther than to the injury of the private rights of particular classes of citizens, by unjust and partial laws. Here also the firmness of the judicial magistracy is of vast importance in mitigating the severity and confining the operation of such laws. It not only serves to moderate the immediate mischiefs of those which may have been passed but it operates as a check upon the legislative body in passing them; who, perceiving that obstacles to the success of an iniquitous intention are to be expected from the scruples of the courts, are in a manner compelled, by the very motives of the injustice they meditate, to qualify their attempts. This is a circumstance calculated to have more influence upon the character of our governments than but few may be aware of. The benefits of the integrity and moderation of the judiciary have already been felt in more States than one; and though they may have displeased those whose sinister expectations they may have disappointed, they must have commanded the esteem and applause of all the virtuous and disinterested. Considerate men of every description ought to prize whatever will tend to beget or fortify that temper in the courts; as no man can be sure that he may not be tomorrow the victim of a spirit of injustice, by which he may be a gainer today. And every man must now feel that the inevitable tendency of such a spirit is to sap the foundations of public and private confidence and to introduce in its stead universal distrust and distress.

That inflexible and uniform adherence to the rights of the Constitution, and of individuals, which we perceive to be indispensable in the courts of justice, can certainly not be expected from judges who hold their offices by a temporary commission. Periodical appointments, however regulated, or by whomsoever made, would, in some way or other, be fatal to their necessary independence. If the power of making them was committed either to the executive or legislature there would be danger of an improper complaisance to the branch which possessed it; if to both, there would be an unwillingness to hazard the displeasure of either; if to the people, or to persons chosen by them for the special purpose, there would be too great a disposition to consult popularity to justify a reliance that nothing would be consulted but the Constitution and the laws. . . .

Upon the whole, there can be no room to doubt that the convention acted wisely in copying from the models of those constitutions which have established *good behavior* as the tenure of their judicial offices, in point of duration; and that so far from being blamable on this account, their plan would have been inexcusably defective if it had wanted this important feature of good government. The experience of Great Britain affords an illustrious comment on the excellence of the institution.

No. 80: Hamilton

To judge with accuracy of the proper extent of the federal judicature it will be necessary to consider, in the first place, what are its proper objects.

It seems scarcely to admit of controversy that the judiciary authority of the Union ought to extend to these several descriptions of cases: 1st, to all those which arise out of the laws of the United States, passed in pursuance of their just and constitutional powers of legislation; 2nd, to all those which concern the execution of the provisions expressly contained in the articles of Union; 3rd, to all those in which the United States are a party; 4th, to all those which involve the PEACE of the CONFEDERACY, whether they relate to the intercourse between the United States and foreign nations or to that between the States themselves; 5th, to all those which originate on the high seas, and are of admiralty or maritime jurisdiction; and lastly, to all those in which the State tribunals cannot be supposed to be impartial and unbiased.

The first point depends upon this obvious consideration, that there ought always to be a constitutional method of giving efficacy to constitutional provisions. What, for instance, would avail restrictions on the authority of the State legislatures, without some constitutional mode of enforcing the observance of them? The States, by the plan of the convention, are prohibited from doing a variety of things, some of which are incompatible with the interests of the Union and others with the principles of good government. The imposition of duties on imported articles and the emission of paper money are specimens of each kind. No man of sense will believe that such prohibitions would be scrupulously regarded without some effectual power in the government to restrain or correct the infractions of them. This power must either be a direct negative on the State laws, or an authority in the federal courts to overrule such as might be in manifest contravention of the articles of Union. There is no third course that I can imagine. The latter appears to have been thought by the convention preferable to the former, and I presume will be most agreeable to the States.

As to the second point, it is impossible, by any argument or comment, to make it clearer than it is in itself. If there are such things as political axioms, the propriety of the judicial power of a government being coextensive with its legislative may be ranked among the number. The mere necessity of uniformity in the interpretation of the national laws decides the question. Thirteen independent courts of final jurisdiction over the same causes, arising upon the same laws, is a hydra in government from which nothing but contradiction and confusion can proceed.

Still less need said in regard to the third point. Controversies between the nation and its members or citizens can only be properly referred to the national tribunals. Any other plan would be contrary to reason, to precedent, and to decorum.

The fourth point rests on this plain proposition, that the peace of the WHOLE ought not to be left at the disposal of a PART. The Union will undoubtedly be answerable to foreign powers for the conduct of its members. And the responsibility for an injury ought ever to be accompanied with the faculty of preventing it. As the denial or perversion of justice by the sentences of courts, as well as in any other manner, is with reason classed among the just causes of war, it will follow that the federal judiciary ought to have cognizance of all causes in which the citizens of other countries are concerned. This is not less essential to the preservation of the public faith than to the security of the public tranquillity. . . .

The power of determining causes between two States, between one State and the citizens of another, and between the citizens of different States, is perhaps not less essential to the peace of the Union than that which has been just examined. . . .

A method of terminating territorial disputes between the States, under the authority of the federal head, was not unattended to, even in the imperfect system by which they have been hitherto held together. But there are many other sources, besides interfering claims of boundary, from which bickerings and animosities may spring up among the members of the Union. To some of these we have been witnesses in the course of our past experience. It will readily be conjectured that I allude to the fraudulent laws which have been passed in too many of the States. And though the proposed Constitution establishes particular guards against the repetition of those instances which have heretofore made their appearance, yet it is warrantable to apprehend that the spirit which produced them will assume new shapes that could not be foreseen nor specifically provided against. Whatever practices may have a tendency to disturb the harmony between the States are proper objects of federal superintendence and control.

It may be esteemed the basis of the Union that "the citizens of each State shall be entitled to all the privileges and immunities of citizens of the several States." And if it be a just principle that every government *ought to possess the means of executing its own provisions by its own authority* it will follow that in order to the inviolable maintenance of that equality of privileges and immunities to which the citizens of the

Union will be entitled, the national judiciary ought to preside in all cases in which one State or its citizens are opposed to another State or its citizens. To secure the full effect of so fundamental a provision against all evasion and subterfuge, it is necessary that its construction should be committed to that tribunal which, having no local attachments, will be likely to be impartial between the different States and their citizens and which, owing its official existence to the Union, will never be likely to feel any bias inauspicious to the principles on which it is founded.

The fifth point will demand little animadversion. The most bigoted idolizers of State authority have not thus far shown a disposition to deny the national judiciary the cognizance of maritime causes. These so generally depend on the laws of nations and so commonly affect the rights of foreigners that they fall within the considerations which are relative to the public peace. The most important part of them are, by the present Confederation, submitted to federal jurisdiction.

The reasonableness of the agency of the national courts in cases in which the State tribunals cannot be supposed to be impartial speaks for itself. No man ought certainly to be a judge in his own cause, or in any cause in respect to which he has the least interest or bias. This principle has no inconsiderable weight in designating the federal courts as the proper tribunals for the determination of controversies between different States and their citizens. And it ought to have the same operation in regard to some cases between the citizens of the same State. Claims to land under grants of different States, founded upon adverse pretensions of boundary, are of this description. The courts of neither of the granting States could be expected to be unbiased. The laws may have even prejudged the question and tied the courts down to decisions in favor of the grants of the State to which they belonged. And even where this had not been done, it would be natural that the judges, as men, should feel a strong predilection to the claims of their own government.

Having thus laid down and discussed the principles which ought to regulate the constitution of the federal judiciary we will . . . review it in detail. It is, then, to extend:

First. To all cases in law and equity, *arising under the Constitution* and *the laws of the United States.* This corresponds to the two first classes of causes which have been enumerated, as proper for the jurisdiction of the United States. It has been asked what is meant by "cases arising under the Constitution," in contradistinction from those "arising under the laws of the United States"? The difference has been already explained. All the restrictions upon the authority of the State legislatures furnish examples of it. They are not, for instance, to emit paper money; but the interdiction results from the Constitution and will have no connection with any law of the United States. Should paper money, notwithstanding, be emitted, the controversies concerning it would be cases arising under the Constitution and not the laws of the United States, in the ordinary signification of the terms. This may serve as a sample of the whole. . . .

From this review of the particular powers of the federal judiciary, as marked out in the Constitution, it appears that they are all conformable to the principles which ought to have governed the structure of that department and which were necessary to the perfection of the system. If some partial inconveniences should appear to be connected with the incorporation of any of them into the plan it ought to be recollected that the national legislature will have ample authority to make such *exceptions* and to prescribe such regulations as will be calculated to obviate or remove these inconveniences. The possibility of particular mischiefs can never be viewed, by a well-informed mind, as a solid objection to a general principle which is calculated to avoid general mischiefs and to obtain general advantages.

No. 81: Hamilton

Let us now return to the partition of the judiciary authority between different courts and their relations to each other. . . .

It is not true [as has been alleged] that the parliament of Great Britain, or the legislatures of the particular States, can rectify the exceptionable decisions of their respective courts, in any other sense than might be done by a future legislature of the United States. The theory, neither of the British, nor the State constitutions, authorizes the revisal of a judicial sentence by a legislative act. Nor is there anything in the proposed Constitution, more than in either of them, by which it is forbidden. In the former, as well as in the latter, the impropriety of the thing, on the general principles of law and reason, is the sole obstacle. A legislature, without exceeding its province, cannot reverse a determination once made in a particular case; though it may prescribe a new rule for future cases. This is the principle and it applies in all its consequences, exactly in the same manner and extent, to the State governments, as to the national government now under consideration. Not the least difference can be pointed out in any view of the subject.

It may in the last place be observed that the supposed danger of judiciary encroachments on the legislative authority which has been upon many occasions reiterated is in reality a phantom. Particular misconstructions and contraventions of the will of the legislature may now and then happen; but they can never be so extensive as to amount to an inconvenience, or in any sensible degree to affect the order of the political system. This may be inferred with certainty from the general nature of the judicial power, from the objects to which it relates, from the manner in which it is exercised, from its comparative weakness, and from its total incapacity to support its usurpations by force. And the inference is greatly fortified by the consideration of the important constitutional check which the power of instituting impeachments in one part of the legislative body, and of determining upon them in the other, would give to that body upon the members of the judicial department. This is alone a complete security. There never can be danger that the judges, by a series of deliberate usurpations on the authority of the legislature, would hazard the united resentment of the body intrusted with it, while this body was possessed of the means of punishing their presumption by degrading them from their stations. While this ought to remove all apprehensions on the subject it affords, at the same time, a cogent argument for constituting the Senate a court for the trial of impeachments.

Having now examined, and, I trust, removed the objections to the distinct and independent organization of the Supreme Court, I proceed to consider the propriety of the power of constituting inferior courts, and the relations which will subsist between these and the former.

The power of constituting inferior courts is evidently calculated to obviate the necessity of having recourse to the Supreme Court in every case of federal cognizance. It is intended to enable the national government to institute or *authorize*, in each State or district of the United States, a tribunal competent to the determination of matters of national jurisdiction within its limits. . . .

I am not sure but that it will be found highly expedient and useful to divide the United States into four or five or half a dozen districts, and to institute a federal court in each district in lieu of one in every State. The judges of these courts, with the aid of the State judges, may hold circuits for the trial of causes in the several parts of the respective districts. Justice through them may be administered with ease and dispatch and appeals may be safely circumscribed within a narrow compass. This plan appears to me at present the most eligible of any that could be adopted; and in order to [accomplish] it, it is necessary that the power of constituting inferior courts should exist in the full extent in which it is to be found in the proposed Constitution.

These reasons seem sufficient to satisfy a candid mind, that the want of such a power would have been a great defect in the plan. Let us now examine in what manner the judicial authority is to be distributed between the supreme and the inferior courts of the Union.

The Supreme Court is to be invested with original jurisdiction only "in cases affecting ambassadors, other public ministers, and consuls, and those in which a STATE shall be a party." Public ministers of every class are the immediate representatives of their sovereigns. All questions in which they are concerned are so directly connected with the public peace, that, as well for the preservation of this as out of respect to the sovereignties they represent, it is both expedient and proper that such questions should be submitted in the first instance to the highest judicatory of the nation. Though consuls have not in strictness a diplomatic character, yet, as they are the public agents of the nations to which they belong, the same observation is in a great measure applicable to them. In cases in which a State might happen to be a party, it would ill suit its dignity to be turned over to an inferior tribunal.

Though it may rather be a digression from the immediate subject of this paper, I shall take occasion to mention here a supposition which has excited some alarm upon very mistaken grounds. It has been suggested that an assignment of the public securities of one State to the citizens of another would enable them to prosecute that State in the federal courts for the amount of those securities; a suggestion which the following considerations prove to be without foundation.

It is inherent in the nature of sovereignty not to be amenable to the suit of an individual *without its consent*. This is the general sense and the general practice of mankind; and the exemption, as one of the attributes of sovereignty, is now enjoyed by the government of every State in the Union. Unless, therefore, there is a surrender of this immunity in the plan of the convention, it will remain with the States and the danger intimated must be merely ideal. The circumstances which are necessary to produce an alienation of State sovereignty were discussed in considering the article of taxation and need not be repeated here. A recurrence to the principles there established will satisfy us that there is no color to pretend that the State governments would by the adoption of that plan, be divested of the privilege of paying their own debts in their own way, free from every constraint but that which flows from the obligations of good faith. The contracts between a nation and individuals are only binding on the conscience of the sovereign, and have no pretensions to a compulsive force. They confer no right of action independent of the sovereign will. To what purpose would it be to authorize suits against States for the debts they owe? How could recoveries be enforced? It is evident that it could not be done without waging war against the contracting State; and to ascribe to the federal courts, by mere implication, and in destruction of a preexisting right of the State governments, a power which would involve such a consequence, would be altogether forced and unwarrantable.

Let us resume the train of our observations. We have seen that the original jurisdiction of the Supreme Court would be confined to two classes of cases, and those of a nature rarely to occur. In all other cases of federal cognizance the original jurisdiction would appertain to the inferior tribunals; and the Supreme Court would have nothing more than an appellate jurisdiction "with such *exceptions* and under such *regulations* as the Congress shall make."

The propriety of this appellate jurisdiction has been scarcely called in question in regard to matters of law; but the clamors have been loud against it as applied to matters of fact. Some well-intentioned men in this State, deriving their notions from the language and forms which obtain in our courts, have been induced to consider it as an implied supersedure of the trial by jury, in favor of the civil-law mode of trial, which prevails in our courts of admiralty, probate, and chancery. . . .

But it does not follow that the re-examination of a fact once ascertained by a jury will be permitted in the Supreme Court. Why may not it be said, with the strictest propriety, when a writ of error is brought from an inferior to a superior court of law in this State, that the latter has jurisdiction of the fact as well as the law? It is true it cannot institute a new inquiry concerning the fact but it takes cognizance of it as it appears upon the record and pronounces the law arising upon it. This is jurisdiction of both fact and law; nor is it even possible to separate them. Though the common-law courts of this State ascertain disputed facts by a jury, yet they unquestionably have jurisdiction of both fact and law; and accordingly when the former is agreed in the pleadings they have no recourse to a jury but proceed at once to judgment. I contend therefore, on this ground, that the expressions, "appellate jurisdiction, both as to law and fact," do not necessarily imply a re-examination in the Supreme Court of facts decided by juries in the inferior courts. . . .

To avoid all inconveniences, it will be safest to declare generally that the Supreme Court shall possess appellate jurisdiction both as to law and *fact*, and that this jurisdiction shall be subject to such *exceptions* and regulations as the national legislature may prescribe. This will enable the government to modify it in such a manner as will best answer the ends of public justice and security.

This view of the matter, at any rate, puts it out of all doubt that the supposed *abolition* of the trial by jury, by the operation of this provision, is fallacious and untrue. The legislature of the United States would certainly have full power to provide that in appeals to the Supreme Court there should be no re-examination of facts where they.had been tried in the original causes by jury. This would certainly be an authorized exception; but if, for the reason already intimated, it should be thought too extensive, it might be qualified with a limitation to such causes only as are determinable at common law in that mode of trial.

The amount of the observations hitherto made on the authority of the judicial department is this: that it has been carefully restricted to those causes which are manifestly proper for the cognizance of the national judicature; that in the partition of this authority a very small portion of original jurisdiction has been reserved to the Supreme Court and the rest consigned to the subordinate tribunals; that the Supreme Court will possess an appellate jurisdiction, both as to law and fact, in all the cases referred to them, but subject to any *exceptions* and *regulations* which may be thought advisable; that this appelate jurisdiction does, in no case, *abolish* the trial by jury; and that an ordinary degree of prudence and integrity in the national councils will insure us solid advantages from the establishment of the proposed judiciary without exposing us to any of the inconveniences which have been predicted from that source.

No. 82: Hamilton

The erection of a new government, whatever care or wisdom may distinguish the work, cannot fail to originate questions of intricacy and nicety; and these may, in a particular manner, be expected to flow from the establishment of a constitution founded upon the total or partial incorporation of a number of distinct sovereignties. 'Tis time only that can mature and perfect so compound a system, can liquidate the meaning of all the parts, and can adjust them to each other in a harmonious and consistent WHOLE.

Such questions, accordingly, have arisen upon the plan proposed by the convention, and particularly concerning the judiciary department. The principal of these respect the situation of the State courts in regard to those causes which are to be submitted to federal jurisdiction. Is this to be exclusive, or are those courts to possess a concurrent jurisdiction? If the latter, in what relation will they stand to the national tribunals? These are inquiries which we meet with in the mouths of men of sense, and which are certainly entitled to attention.

The principles established in a former paper [No. 32] teach us that the States will retain all *pre-existing* authorities which may not be exclusively delegated to the federal head; and that this exclusive delegation can only exist in one of three cases: where an exclusive authority is, in express terms, granted to the Union; or where a particular authority is granted to the Union and the exercise of a like authority is prohibited to the States; or where an authority is granted to the Union with which a similar authority in the States would be utterly incompatible. Though these principles may not apply with the same force to the judiciary as to the legislative power, yet I am inclined to think that they are, in the main, just with respect to the former, as well as the latter. And under this impression, I shall lay it down as a rule that the State courts will *retain* the jurisdiction they now have, unless it appears to be taken away in one of the enumerated modes. . . .

But this doctrine of concurrent jurisdiction is only clearly applicable to those descriptions of causes of which the State courts have previous cognizance. It is not equally evident in relation to cases which may grow out of, and be *peculiar* to, the Constitution to be established; for not to allow the State courts a right of jurisdiction in such cases can hardly be considered as the abridgement of a pre-existing authority. I mean not therefore to contend that the United States, in the course of legislation upon the objects intrusted to their direction, may not commit the decision of causes arising upon a particular regulation to the federal courts solely, if such a measure should be deemed expedient; but I hold that the State courts will be divested of no part of their primitive jurisdiction further than may relate to an appeal; and I am even of opinion that in every case in which they were not expressly excluded by the future acts of the national legislature, they will of course take cognizance of the causes to which those acts may give birth. This I infer from the nature of judiciary power, and from the general genius of the system. The judiciary power of every government looks beyond its own local or municipal laws, and in civil cases lays hold of all subjects of litigation between parties within its jurisdiction, though the causes of dispute are relative to the laws of the most distant part of the globe. Those of Japan, not less than of New York, may furnish the objects of legal discussion to our courts. When in addition to this we consider the State governments and the national governments, as they truly are, in the light of kindred systems, and as parts of ONE WHOLE, the inference seems to be conclusive that the State courts would have a concurrent jurisdiction in all cases arising under the laws of the Union where it was not expressly prohibited.

Here another question occurs: What relation would subsist between the national and State courts in these instances of concurrent jurisdiction? I answer that an appeal would certainly lie from the latter to the Supreme Court of the United States. The Constitution in direct terms gives an appellate jurisdiction to the Supreme Court in all the enumerated cases of federal cognizance in which it is not to have an original one, without a single expression to confine its operation to the inferior federal courts. The objects of appeal, not the tribunals from which it is to be made, are alone contemplated. From this circumstance, and from the reason of the thing, it ought to be construed to extend to the State tribunals. Either this must be the case or the local courts must be excluded from a concurrent jurisdiction in matters of national concern, else the judiciary authority of the Union may be eluded at the pleasure of every plaintiff or prosecutor. Neither of these consequences ought, without evident necessity, to be involved; the latter would be entirely inadmissible, as it would defeat some of the most important and avowed purposes of the proposed government and would essentially embarrass its measures. . . .

But could an appeal be made to lie from the State courts to the subordinate federal judicatories? This is another of the questions which have been raised, and of greater difficulty than the former. The following considerations countenance the affirmative. The plan of the convention, in the first place, authorizes the national legislature "to constitute tribunals inferior to the Supreme Court." [Section 8, Article 1.] It declares, in the next place, that "the JUDICIAL POWER of the United States *shall be vested* in one Supreme Court, and in such inferior courts as Congress shall ordain and establish"; and it then proceeds to enumerate the cases to which this judicial power shall extend. It afterwards divides the jurisdiction of the Supreme Court into original and appellate, but gives no definition of that of the subordinate courts. The only outlines described for them are that they shall be "inferior to the Supreme Court," and that they shall not exceed the specified limits of the federal judiciary. Whether their authority shall be original or appellate, or both, is not declared. All this seems to be left to the discretion of the legislature. And this being the case, I perceive at present no impediment to the establishment of an appeal from the State courts to the subordinate national tribunals; and many advantages attending the power of doing it may be imagined. It would diminish the motives to the multiplication of federal courts and would admit of arrangements calculated to contract the appellate jurisdiction of the Supreme Court. The State tribunals may then be left with a more entire charge of federal causes; and appeals, in most cases in which they may be deemed proper, instead of being carried to the Supreme Court may be made to lie from the State courts to district courts of the Union.

Unfortunately, there is little evidence that the *Federalist Papers* had any notable influence on the citizens of the state for whom they were written. They did not create, in any event, a majority in favor of the Constitution. If they convinced or converted some, the balance, nonetheless, seemed clearly in favor of the anti-Constitutionalists. The opposition to the Constitution was more widespread and intractable than in any other state. That New York came belatedly to ratify the Constitution was the work essentially of Alexander Hamilton. Hamilton was a man of great personal charm, the most powerful and influential politician in the state, an astute and often ruthless adversary, a debater of unusual force and eloquence. He was also the most exotic of the "Fathers," a man who had as many bitter enemies as devoted followers. Born in the West Indies, of doubtful legitimacy— John Adams referred to him as "the bastard brat of a Scotch pedlar" —he had made himself indispensable to Washington as a member of the general's staff during the Revolution, had married advantageously, had squabbled with his commanding officer over some petty point of protocol, fought bravely at Yorktown and acquired a reputation as a relentless pursuer of women. Abigail Adams, who shared her husband's dislike of the New Yorker, called him a "cock sparrow," a bird notorious for its sexual appetites, and wrote to her husband that she had often observed Hamilton's "lewd, surveying eye" when he entered a drawing room.

The issue of ratification in New York became, among other things, a contest over who would control the complicated political machinery of the state. Hamilton had cast his lot with the Constitution, his political future rested on its ratification, and he left nothing undone to carry the day. Part of the strategy was to delay the New York convention until enough states had ratified to give formal effect to the Constitution. Even so, when the delegates convened on June 17 at Poughkeepsie, the enemies of the Constitution were confident of victory. Robert Yates and John Lansing, two of the New York delegates to the federal convention, were bitterly opposed to the Constitution. Allied with them was the most popular and successful political figure in the State, George Clinton, wartime hero and former governor, who was promptly elected "president" of the convention.

Robert Livingston, another veteran of New York politics, opened the debates with a discussion of the dangers of disunion and the vulnerability of the state to attacks from its neighbors or by foreign enemies. He was answered by Lansing, who staked out the grounds of his opposition by pointing out that since the new Constitution made no provision for the civil liberty of the people, he was bound to oppose it. Melancton Smith, of Dutchess County, employed biblical imagery: "We may wander . . . in the fields of fancy without end, and gather flowers as we go. It may be entertaining but it is of little service to the discovery of truth. We may, on one side, compare the scheme [the Constitution] advocated by our opponents to *golden images, with feet of iron* and parts of clay; and on the other, *to a beast dreadful and terrible, and strong exceedingly, having great iron teeth,—which devours, breaks in pieces, and stamps the residue with his feet*; and after all . . . we shall find that both these allusions are taken from the same *vision*; and their true meaning must be discovered by sober reasoning."

Hamilton undertook to rebut Smith. It was his first statement to the convention and it was in his best style. Finally, exhausted, he requested that he be allowed to continue the following day. It fell to Hamilton, as the only advocate of the Constitution who had also been a delegate to the Philadelphia convention, to respond to Yates and Lansing as well as the other principal opponents of the Constitution. He and Clinton clashed repeatedly. Melancton Smith stressed the danger that under the Constitution an aristocracy would take control of the government. "Aristocracy" was a sore point in New York. The great Dutch patronships constituted a native "aristocracy." The colony and later the state had been notorious in New England for its aristocratic tendencies. The Livingston family, powerful in the colony for generations, was part of this "aristocracy," and Robert Livingston replied testily to Smith that his arguments being weak, he had "recourse to the phantom aristocracy. . . . I have always considered it as the bugbear of the party. We are told that, in every country, there is a natural aristocracy, and that this aristocracy consists of the rich and the great: nay, the gentleman goes further, and ranks in this class of men the wise, the learned, and those eminent for their talents or great virtue. Does a man possess the confidence of his fellow citizens for having done them important services? He is an *aristocrat*. Has he great integrity? Such a man will be greatly trusted: he is an *aristocrat*. Indeed, to determine that one is an aristocrat, we need only be assured that he is a man of merit. But I hope we have many such. I hope, sir, we are all aristocrats."

Smith replied with some warmth that Livingston had tried to make his argument ridiculous by carrying it to an extreme. "All I said was, that mankind were influenced, in a great degree, by interests and prejudices; that men, in different ranks of life, were exposed to different temptations, and that ambition was more peculiarly the passion of the rich and great. . . . My argument was, that, in order to have a true and genuine representation, you must receive the middling class of people into your government. . . ."

As the debates wore on, they developed into an exchange between Melancton Smith, supported by Yates and Lansing, and Hamilton aided by Livingston. For Hamilton, who had been ailing, it was an especially grueling experience. Several times, as he had initially, he declared himself too exhausted to continue and asked for a recess. As in the Virginia debates, tempers grew short and arguments excessive. Thomas Tredwell from Suffolk County gave one of the convention's longest and most impassioned attacks on the Constitution, declaring that "it is founded on sin and reared up in iniquity; the foundations are laid in the most sinful breach of public trust, and the top-stone is a most iniquitous breach of public faith; and I fear, if it goes into operation we shall be justly punished with the total extinction of our civil liberties."

Finally on July 3, the delegates began debating each article and proposing amendments to each. The convention now became a battleground of parliamentary maneuvering, with the enemies of the Constitution resorting to tactics of delay and its proponents leaving no stone unturned or pressure unapplied to line up a majority in favor of ratification without amendments or conditions. Finally, after several weeks of uncertainty and intermittent meeting, the proponents of the Constitution, having presumably counted noses, were ready to put the issue to a test. There were several important defections from the anti-Constitutionalists' ranks, the most notable being Melancton Smith. Perhaps Smith was converted by Virginia's ratification. When the initial vote was taken on ratification *"in full confidence"* that the desired amendments on civil liberties would be made, the advocates of the Constitution triumphed 31 to 29. Two votes decided the issue. Thus in the three most important states, out of a total of 583 votes, the Constitution was approved by a margin of eighteen votes. That was the margin by which the Federal Constitution became the law of all the land.

Cicero wrote, *"Historica opus oratorium maxime—* history at its highest is oratory." It is an intriguing sentence. Did Cicero conceive of oratory as the highest form of dramatic expression and thus history as the highest form of drama? Or did he mean that "spoken history," words uttered at those critical moments of history that seem to change its course decisively, that these words constitute history "at its highest"? In any event it is clear that there are moments when speech commands the forces of history and these surely are the high points in the story of the human race. Since the days of Periclean Athens and the great debates of the Roman senate the power of speech had been sustained most conspicuously in the formal liturgies of the Roman Catholic Church and by the poets and bards of the Middle Ages. The Reformation had released speech in the form of the sermon and given new force to the Scriptural verse: "In the beginning was the Word. . . ." The *word* was manifest in the world with a strange new power. Protestant congregations sat for hours, infatuated to hear the word of God expounded. All the iconographic beauty and power contained in images was swept aside lest it interfere with the *word*. The tongue overcame the "lordship of the eye." With the spread of printing and books, and the rise of the sermon as the main feature of the reformed Christian faith, the written and spoken word came into their own. The debates of the federal convention and of the state conventions, more particularly those of Massachusetts, Virginia, and New York, were the culmination of that process. They referred back, in a thoroughly self-conscious way, to Republican Rome. But they articulated almost two millennia of subsequent Western history. They converted the Classical-Christian tradition into contemporary politics. And they did it in a magnificently sustained effort through the power of speech.

Reading the debates in their often tedious entirety, one discovers a curious poignance in the speeches of the opponents of the Constitution and probes in vain for the political, and, one suspects, more important, the psychological roots of their apprehensions. An unsympathetic historian has called them "men of little faith"—little faith in the potentialities and the future of their country—but somehow that seems too severe. They were, of course, the losers and thus it is difficult to give them their due. We only know how it turned out. With all the qualifications one must make today about "how it turned out" it was certainly an astonishing success story and it strains the imagination to conceive how it might have turned out had the anti-Constitutionalists carried the day. Yet despite their intractability and paranoia, they belong, as they themselves repeatedly insisted, to that tradition in America which has been most jealous of our liberties, most suspicious of power and of its abuse by the wealthy and powerful, and most solicitous for "the middling and lower orders," those without power and often without advocates.

CHAPTER

X

THE FEDERAL GOVERNMENT

THE EXPIRING CONGRESS, MEETING IN NEW YORK, VOTED TO "PUT in motion the new System of government." The new Congress was to convene in New York. Presidential electors were to be chosen on the first Wednesday in January, the President elected on the first Wednesday in February. "The first Wednesday in March is the time, and this city the place for commencing proceedings," Henry Lee wrote to Washington from New York. Washington of course was chosen president and John Adams vice-president and at the end of April the new government took up its duties.

Even with ratification there were shoal waters ahead for the new ship of state. Patrick Henry, still smarting from his defeat in the Virginia convention, managed to block the election of Madison to the Senate. Richard Henry Lee and William Grayson, two of the bitterest opponents of the Constitution, were chosen as senators. The word was spread that Madison was an enemy to amendments, and it was only a last-minute campaign by Madison to set the record straight that secured him a seat in the House when the new Congress met. Despite the fact that a number of states had, as we have seen, called for prompt amendment of the Constitution by a Bill of Rights, the members of Congress showed considerable reluctance to tackle the question. The most obvious reason was that the principal pressure for reform of the Articles of Confederation was economic. The Articles had seriously inhibited the growth of American commerce. The hope was that the new Constitution would facilitate trade by establishing laws regulating commerce. Congress was thus inclined to devote its energies primarily to raising federal revenues by taxation. But Madison and some of his fellow congressmen felt strongly that the good faith of the new government required that immediate attention be given to those amendments, essentially constituting a Bill of Rights, which the states had pressed for most strongly. This would do more, Madison argued, to reconcile the doubters and dissenters to the new government than any other measures Congress might adopt. Madison persevered and presented to Congress a list of amendments which were essentially the Virginia Declaration of Rights drafted by George Mason a decade earlier. He assured the delegates that the amendments could be passed "without endangering any part of the Constitution, which is considered as essential to the existence of the government by those who promoted its adoption."

Elbridge Gerry, who had opposed the Constitution in part because of the absence of a Bill of Rights, now argued that "the salvation of America depends on the establishment of the Government, whether amended or not." Another member supported Gerry, urging that the House give its time to more essential matters. What was needed most of all was to get the new government under way. It was a government in name only, "And how long it will remain in such a situation, if we enter upon amendments, God only knows. . . . We are not content with two revolutions in less than fourteen years; we must enter upon a third, without necessity or propriety."

The matter was referred to a committee made up of a representative from each state. When the committee reported to the House, the next question was whether the amendments be interwoven with the Constitution or simply appended to it as a block of amendments.

Vining of Delaware, chairman of the committee, was horrified at the thought of trying to inject the amendments into the Constitution as it stood. "He had seen an act entitled 'an act to amend a supplement to an act entitled an act for altering part of an act entitled an act for certain purposes therein mentioned.' If gentlemen were disposed to run into such jargon in amending and altering the Constitution, he could not help it; but he trusted they would adopt a plainness and simplicity of style . . . which should be easily understood."

Initially, debate proceeded on the assumption that the Constitution would be revised to include the proposed amendments. It was evident at once what a can of worms the members had opened. A proposal was made to alter the preamble by inserting the words: "Government being intended for the benefit of the people, and the rightful establishment thereof being derived from their authority alone." Gerry wanted to add "of right." Roger Sherman thought it redundant. The people, through their representatives, had established the Constitution. "Here we propose to come in and give them a right to do what they did on motives which appeared to them sufficient to warrant their determination."

Next came the idea of increasing the representation in the House, a bone of contention in some of the ratifying conventions. The House voted to raise the representation to two hundred (later defeated when the states refused to ratify it). Each proposed amendment produced prolonged debate. Should the representatives "consult" with their constitutents or be "instructed" by them? If free speech were protected, why not the right of a man to wear his hat, and get up and go to bed when he wished?

The members of the House became bored, distracted, irritable, and impatient. Thomas Burke of South Carolina denounced the House for not being more receptive to the amendments of his state. The amendments that they were discussing "are not those solid and substantial amendments which the people expect; they are little better than whip syllabub, frothy and full of wind, formed only to please the palate. . . ."

Baffled by the problems involved in trying to amend the Constitution as a whole, the committee confined its attention to the issues covered by the Bill of Rights. When the committee reported to the full House, Gerry pressed to have all the proposed amendments considered, but he was voted down two to one. A significant exchange took place over the wording of the clause which read, "The powers not delegated by the Constitution, nor prohibited to it by the States, are reserved to the states respectively." Thomas Tucker of South Carolina, a defender of state rights, wished the passage to read "all powers not expressly delegated." To this Madison replied that "it was impossible to confine the Government to the exercise of express powers; there must necessarily be powers admitted by implication, unless the Constitution descend to recount every minutia. He remembered the word 'expressly' had been moved in the convention of Virginia, by the opponents of the ratification, and, after full and fair discussion, was given up by them, and the system allowed to retain its present form." Tucker's motion was lost, and the Constitution, in consequence, enjoyed an important degree of flexibility. Interestingly enough, Madison moved that the amendments constituting a Bill of Rights be binding on the states as well as on the national government, but his motion was defeated, primarily on the ground that it would give too much power to the national government.

When the House in formal session took up the proposed amendments, Tucker and Gerry attempted once more to introduce other amendments designed to limit the powers of the federal government (Tucker proposed seventeen such amendments) but the members stood fast. It was another decisive moment. The opponents of the Constitution, defeated in their state conventions, had made another attempt to undo the work of the federal convention, but better judgment prevailed. Roger Sherman again pressed to have the amendments added in a block and this time carried the day.

On August 19, after a day of increasing futility, Madison urged the members to leave well enough alone. He was dismayed by the disposition of the House to rake over issues that had been debated dozens of times before. At this point Egbert Benson of New York, who had attended the Annapolis Convention three years earlier, moved that the amendments, when approved by two thirds of the Senate, be dispatched to the state legislatures and when ratified by three fourths of them be accepted as valid parts of the Constitution. The amendments were thus sent sent forward to the Senate, where William Grayson and Richard Henry Lee tried once more to effect there what they had been unable to accomplish in the Virginia Convention.

The Senate cut down the number of amendments to fourteen and then in conference with the House reduced them to twelve. They were then transmitted to President Washington to be dispatched to the states. During the period in which they were being ratified, Rhode Island, North Carolina, and Vermont entered the Union. Two of the amendments, one dealing with the number of members of the House of Representatives, the other with pay of the members of Congress, were not ratified.

The most crucial element in the success of the new government was undoubtedly the fact that Washington had accepted the presidency. He gave the entire government the sanction and authority that no one else could have. By being president he authenticated the Constitution. In his appointments to the Supreme Court he followed the principle of representing all sections. He appointed John Jay of

New York as Chief Justice. Jay was forty-four years of age, a leading proponent of the Constitution in New York, and formerly chief justice of the state. Virginia had an array of unusually able lawyers which included George Wythe, Edmund Pendleton, John Blair, and Edmund Randolph. Washington was determined, as he wrote Madison, to draw "the first characters of the Union into the Judiciary. . . ." He settled on Blair as an associate justice and offered Randolph the position of attorney general. Blair was fifty-seven. He had served ten years as chief justice of the Virginia Court of Appeals and as a judge of the High Court of Chancery.

From Massachusetts, Washington chose William Cushing, at fifty-seven the oldest judge appointed. Cushing had had a distinguished career as chief justice of the Massachusetts Supreme Judicial Court. From Pennsylvania Washington chose James Wilson, who, the reader will recall, had been one of the central figures in the federal convention and had carried the main burden in the Pennsylvania Ratifying Convention.

Washington chose John Rutledge from South Carolina and James Iredell from North Carolina. Rutledge we have encountered before in the federal convention. Iredell, who had served as attorney general of North Carolina, was, at thirty-eight, the youngest of the justices. Washington, by his initial appointments to the Court, indicated how seriously he regarded its function and its responsibilities. As Ralph Izard, a prominent South Carolinian, wrote to a friend, the justices "had been chosen from among the most eminent and distinguished characters in America, and I do not believe that any Judiciary in the world is better filled." Three of the justices had shared in drafting the Constitution and three others in securing its ratification in their respective states, and thus may be presumed to have had an excellent notion of the intentions of the framers.

The argument has sometimes been advanced that the framers of the Constitution had a very limited or nugatory concept of the Supreme Court and that certain strong justices, most conspicuously, of course, John Marshall, made it into a branch of government with far more power than the framers had envisioned. This misconception, as the reader will surely perceive it to be, is based largely on the fact that the text of the debates themselves was not published until the 1830s and the reasoning behind the establishment of the Court was therefore not known (as for example Madison's proposal to have it, with the president, constitute a Council of Revision to pass upon all laws *before* they took effect). In addition, since the Court was a special object of attack by the anti-Federalists, the defenders of the Constitution had gone out of their way in the state ratifying conventions to play down the role of the Court in order to reassure the champions of state sovereignty. The reader will recall that in the Virginia Convention, John Marshall scouted the notion that a private citizen could bring a state before the Court.

The Court met for the first time in New York, the temporary seat of the new government at the Royal Exchange at the foot of Broad Street. The justices wore black and red robes, on which a Philadelphia newspaper commented: "In their robes of justice, the elegance, gravity and neatness of which were the subject of remark and approbation with every spectator." Missing were the wigs worn by English judges. Jefferson had spoken for a number of his countrymen when he exclaimed, "For Heaven's sake, discard the monstrous wig which makes the English Judges look like rats peeping through bunches of oakum!"

The first session of the Court lasted ten days, days which, since there were no cases in the docket, were taken up in admitting lawyers to practice before the Court and in ceremonial activities, concluded by a feast put on by the grand jury of the New York District Court on which occasion thirteen toasts were drunk including one to "the National Judiciary" and the "Constitution of our Country, may it prove the solid fabrick of liberty, prosperity and glory."

The Court was the most novel branch of the new government and its functions were still shrouded in mystery, but America was a law-obsessed country and there was a widespread interest in it throughout the states. Although it had no important case brought before it in the first few years of its existence, the judges, riding circuit as they were required to do in three judicial districts, performed a valuable function by, in effect, lecturing to substantial audiences of lawyers and plain citizens on the function of the law and the role of the Court. When the Circuit Court for the District of Connecticut was opened at New Haven in April, 1790, the *Farmer's Weekly Museum* reported, "His Honor the Chief Justice delivered an eloquent and pertinent charge. . . . The good sense and candor of the Judges has left an impression on the minds of the people favorable to this new institution."

The "new institution" in its early years gave little indication that it would, in time, become the most striking and controversial feature of the Constitution. It lay, if not exactly dormant, quite inconspicuous. The first case of consequence that it considered concerned the pension claims of veterans of the Revolution. Congress, swamped by such cases, shifted the load to the Supreme Court justices on circuit. They would consider the claims subject to review by Congress. The first case under the new act of Congress rose in the New York Circuit Court, where it was heard by Jay and Cushing. In delivering their opinion they pointed out that the three branches of the government were separate and distinct under the Constitution. Each was obliged to resist encroachments by the others. The duties of the justices were exclusively judicial. To add others of an executive nature was against the express terms of the Constitution and therefore void. Having stated the legal position, the justices declared themselves willing to hear pension claims out of respect for Congress. Wilson and Blair took a more militant stand. Reiterating the position of the other justices, they refused to examine the petition of William Hayburn for a pension. Wilson added to the objections of his fellow justices the point that the decisions of justices might subsequently be reversed by the executive or legislative branches.

The reaction of the press and public was at first largely favorable, although cries arose in Congress for impeachment of the recalcitrant justices. Oddly enough, the Court found its principal supporters among the anti-Federalists. Benjamin Franklin Bache's *General Advertiser*, hostile to a predominantly Federalist Congress, wrote: "Never was the word 'impeachment' so hackneyed as it has been since the spirited sentence passed by our judges on an unconstitutional law. The high-fliers, in and out of Congress, and the very humblest of their humble retainers talk of nothing but impeachment! impeachment! impeachment! as if forsooth Congress were wrapped up in the cloak of infallibility, which had been torn from the shoulders of the Pope; and that it was damnable heresy and sacrilege to doubt the constitutional orthodoxy of any decision of theirs, once written on calf-skin."

Fenno's *Gazette of the United States*, thought to speak for Alexander Hamilton, regretted, on the other hand, that "the humanity of Congress has been thwarted by the actions of the judges." The anti-Federalists were delighted with any judicial decision that would have the effect of questioning or curtailing the powers of the legislative or executive branches, which they thought too powerful in any event. They would sing a different tune when the Court presumed to pass judgment on the states.

Attorney General Randolph perhaps made the shrewdest comment on the pension-claims case when he wrote that his only regret was "that the Judiciary in spite of their apparent firmness in annulling the pension law are not, what sometime hence they will be, a resource against infractions of the Constitution on the one hand, and a steady assertion of Federal [as opposed to state] rights on the other." "Many severe experiments, the result of which upon the public mind cannot be foreseen, await the Judiciary," he wrote Washington.

In the February, 1793, term of the Court there were two important cases facing the justices. *Oswald v. State of New York* involved a suit against a state by a citizen, just the kind of case that Marshall in the Virginia Ratifying Convention had insisted would not come before the Court or rather that the Court would not exercise jurisdiction over. The case was continued but the equally explosive case of *Chisholm v. Georgia* was on the docket. Again it was a suit by a citizen of one state, Chisholm, against another state. Georgia took the position that as a sovereign state she was immune to suit by an individual and refused to contest the case. Attorney General Edmund Randolph, who, of course, had been a member of the Virginia Convention, saw the case as one "which brings into question a constitutional right, supported by my own conviction, to surrender it would be in me official perfidy." Randolph talked for two and a half hours in presenting the case for Chisholm. The Court then adjourned until the following day. By that time word had spread of the case and the courtroom was crowded. The judges spent two weeks preparing their decision and finally presented it on February 18 before "a numerous and respectable audience," with Judge Iredell, of North Carolina, the lone dissenter.

The justices presented their opinions *seriatim* (serially), a practice that prevailed until Marshall persuaded them a decade later to present a common majority opinion (which he, of course, almost invariably wrote). Jay stated the implications of the case directly enough. They were "1st. In what sense is Georgia a sovereign State. 2nd. Whether suability is incompatible with such sovereignty. 3rd. Whether the Constitution, to which Georgia is a party, authorizes such action against her."

Jay's reply was emphatic: "The sovereignty of the nation is in the people of the nation, and the residuary sovereignty of each state is in the people of each State." Jay was equally emphatic that such sovereignty as Georgia might claim was still "suable." Such a right as Chisholm claimed "clearly falls not only within the spirit but the very words of the constitution."

James Wilson's decision is especially significant because of his leading role in the federal convention and the fact that as professor of law at what was formerly the College of Philadelphia and is now the University of Pennsylvania, he was recognized as a legal theorist of some standing.

Wilson, *Justice*:—This is a case of uncommon magnitude. One of the parties to it is a state; certainly respectable, claiming to be sovereign. The question to be determined, is, whether this state, so respectable, and whose claim soars so high, is amenable to the jurisdiction of the supreme court of the United States? This question, important in itself, will depend on others, more important still; and, may, perhaps, be ultimately resolved into one, no less radical than this—"do the people of the United States form a nation?" . . .

Man, fearfully and wonderfully made, is the workmanship of his all perfect creator: A state, useful and valuable as the contrivance is, is the inferior contrivance of man; and from his native dignity derives all its acquired importance. When I speak of a state as an inferior contrivance, I mean that it is a contrivance inferior only to that, which is divine: Of all human contrivances, it is certainly most transcendantly excellent. It is concerning this contrivance that Cicero says so sublimely, "Nothing, which is exhibited upon our globe, is more acceptable to that divinity, which governs the whole universe, than those communities and assemblages of men, which, lawfully associated, are denominated states."

Let a state be considered as subordinate to the people: But let everything else be subordinate to the state. The latter part of this position is equally necessary with the former. For in the practice, and even at length, in the science of politics there has very frequently been a strong current against the natural order of things, and an inconsiderate or an interested disposition to sacrifice the end to the means. As the state has claimed precedence of the people; so, in the same inverted course of things, the government has often claimed precedence of the state; and to this perversion in the second degree, many of the volumes of confusion concerning sovereignty owe their existence. The ministers, dignified very properly by the appelation of the magistrates, have wished, and have succeeded in their wish, to be considered as the sovereigns of the state. This second degree of perversion is confined to the old world, and begins to diminish even there: but the first degree is still too prevalent even in the several states, of which our union is composed. By a state I mean, a complete body of free persons united together for their common benefit, to enjoy peaceably what is their own, and to do justice to others. It is an artificial person. It has its affairs and its interests: It has its rules: It has its rights: And it has its obligations. It may acquire property distinct from that of its members. It may incur debts to be discharged out of the public stock, not out of the private fortunes of individuals. It may be bound by contracts; and for damages arising from the breach of those contracts. In all our contemplations, however, concerning this feigned and artificial person, we should never forget, that, in truth and nature, those who think and speak and act, are men.

Is the foregoing description of a state a true description? It will not be questioned, but it is. Is there any part of this description, which intimates in the remotest manner, that a state, any more than the men who compose it, ought not to do justice and fulfil engagements? It will not be pretended that there is. If justice is not done; if engagements are not fulfilled; is it upon general principles of right, less proper, in the case of a great number, than in the case of an individual, to secure, by compulsion, that, which will not be voluntarily performed? Less proper it surely cannot be. The only reason, I believe, why a free man is bound by human laws, is, that he binds himself. Upon the same principles, upon which he becomes bound by the laws, he becomes amenable to the courts of justice, which are formed and authorized by those laws. If one free man, an original sovereign, may do all this, why may not an aggregate of free men, a collection of original sovereigns, do this likewise? If the dignity of each singly, is undiminished, the dignity of all jointly must be unimpaired. A state, like a merchant, makes a contract: A dishonest state, like a dishonest merchant, wilfully refuses to discharge it: The latter is amenable to a court of justice: Upon general principles of right shall the former when summoned to answer the fair demands of its creditor, be permitted, proteus-like, to assume a new appearance, and to insult him and justice, by declaring, I am a sovereign state? Surely not. . . .

Concerning the prerogative of kings, and concerning the sovereignty of states, much has been said and written; but little has been said and written concerning a subject much more dignified and important, the majesty of the people. The mode of expression, which I would substitute in the place of that generally used, is, not only politically, but also (for between true liberty and true taste there is a close alliance) classically more correct. On the mention of Athens, a thousand refined and endearing associations rush at once into the memory of the scholar, the philosopher, and the patriot. When Homer, one of the most correct, as well as the oldest of human authorities, enumerates the other nations of Greece, whose forces acted at the siege of Troy, he arranges them under the names of their different kings or princes: But when he comes to the Athenians, he distinguishes them by the peculiar appellation of the people of Athens. The well known address used by Demosthenes, when he harangued and animated his assembled countrymen, was, "O men of Athens." With the strictest propriety, therefore, classical and political, our national scene opens with the most magnificent object which the nation could present. "The people of the United States" are the first personages introduced. Who were those people? They were the citizens of thirteen states, each of which had a separate constitution and government, and all of which were connected together by articles of confederation. To the purposes of public strength and felicity, that confederacy was totally inadequate. A requisition on the several states terminated its legislative authority: Executive or judicial authority it had none. In order, therefore, to form a more perfect union, to establish justice, to ensure domestic tranquillity, to provide for common defense, and to secure the blessings of liberty, those people among whom were the people of Georgia, ordained and established the present constitution. By that constitution legislative power is vested, executive power is vested, judicial power is vested.

The question now opens fairly to our view; could the people of those states, among whom were those of Georgia, bind those states, and Georgia among the others, by the legislative, executive, and judicial power so vested? If the principles, on which I have founded myself, are just and true, this question must unavoidably receive an affirmative answer. If those states were the work of those people; those people, and, that, I may apply the case closely, the people of Georgia, in particular, could alter, as they pleased, their former work: To any given degree, they could diminish as well as enlarge it. Any or all of the former state powers they could extinguish or transfer. The inference, which necessarily results, is, that the constitution ordained and established by those people; and, still closely to apply the case, in particular by the people of Georgia, could vest jurisdiction or judicial power over those states and over the state of Georgia in particular.

The next question under this head, is.—Has the constitution done so? Did those people mean to exercise this, their undoubted power?

These questions may be resolved, either by fair and conclusive deductions, or by direct and explicit declarations. In order, ultimately, to discover, whether the people of the United States intended to bind those states by the judicial power vested by the national constitution, a previous enquiry will naturally be: Did those people intend to bind those states by the legislative power vested by that constitution? The articles of confederation, it is well known, did not operate upon individual citizens; but operated only upon states. This defect was remedied by the national constitution, which, as all allow, has an operation on individual citizens. But if an opinion, which some seem to entertain, be just; the defect remedied, on one side, was balanced by a defect introduced on the other. For they seem to think, that the present constitution operates only on individual citizens, and not on states. This opinion, however, appears to be altogether unfounded. When certain laws of the states are declared to be "subject to the revision and control of the Congress," it cannot surely, be contended that the legislative power of the national government was meant to have no operation on the several states. The fact, uncontrovertibly established in one instance, proves the principle in all other instances, to which the facts will be found to apply. We may then infer, that the people of the United States intended to bind the several states, by the legislative power of the national government. . . .

Whoever considers, in a combined and comprehensive view, the general texture of the constitution, will be satisfied, that the people of the United States intended to form themselves into a nation for national purposes. They instituted for such purposes, a national government, complete in all its parts, with powers legislative, executive, and judiciary; and in all those powers extending over the whole nation. Is it congruous, that, with regard to such purposes, any man, or body of men, any person, natural or artificial, should be permitted to claim successfully an entire exemption from the jurisdiction of the national government? Would not such claims, crowned with success, be repugnant to our very existence as a nation? When so many trains of deduction coming from different quarters, converge and unite, at last, in the same point; we may safely conclude, as the legitimate result of this constitution, that the state of Georgia is amenable to the jurisdiction of this court. . . .

The decision of the Court in favor of the plaintiff stirred up a storm of protest. It seemed to confirm the deepest suspicions of the anti-Constitutionalists. It irritated and disconcerted many of the Federalists since it put them on the defensive and gave substance to the charges of their enemies that the Constitution was designed to obliterate the authority of the states. The public reaction also showed very clearly how vague and ill defined the understanding of the Constitution was even in the minds of the more knowledgeable. A violent newspaper controversy raged over the decision. To one editor, the decision "involved more danger to the liberties of America than the claims of the British Parliament to tax us without our consent." To another "the craft and subtilty of lawyers" had introduced the disputed clause into the Constitution as a Trojan horse within whose deceiving form the aristocrats plotted to reduce the states to mere corporations. Wilson's elaborate philosophically disposed decision was described by one indignant anti-Constitutionalist as "more like an epic poem than a Judge's argument . . . the rhapsody of some visionary theorist."

There was a practical, economic basis for much of the outcry and that was described, a touch cynically, by the editor of the Pennsylvania *Independent Chronicle,* who noted: "The numerous prosecutions that will immediately issue from the various claims of refugees, Tories, etc. . . . will introduce such a series of litigation as will throw every State in the Union into the greatest confusion." This of course was the nightmare of every patriot who had acquired, by fair means or foul, the property of Tory refugees, as well as that of American debtors to British merchants.

Two of the states most apt to be affected by such suits—Massachusetts and Virginia—responded by calling special sessions of their legislatures to urge an amendment to the Constitution. In Georgia, the lower house, with typical Southern truculence, passed a bill stating that any federal marshal or other agent of the national government who tried to execute the process served by the Court should be "declared guilty of felony and shall suffer death, without benefit of clergy, by being hanged."

The urgings of Massachusetts and Virginia were not needed. The day after the decision of the Court an amendment was introduced into Congress to make the states immune to suits by residents of another state or of a foreign state. It was ratified in 1798 as the Eleventh Amendment.

In the 1794 session of the Court the justices had before them two cases with important constitutional implications. First there was the case of *Georgia v. Brailsford.* The decision of the justices was unanimous—Georgia could not confiscate the debts due to citizens of another state or another country. The next case, Citizen *Gênet v. the Sloop Betsey*, involved the admiralty jurisdiction of the federal district courts. This was unanimously affirmed by the justices.

It was the 1796 session of the Court before another important constitutional issue was presented to the justices. This was the case of *Hylton v. the United States*, a case brought to test the powers of Congress. The Constitution, it will be recalled, forbade a direct tax except on a proportional basis. Congress had voted a tax on carriages, presumably to discourage luxury and ostentation. A Virginian, Daniel Hylton, owned 125 carriages and refused to pay the tax on the ground that it was unconstitutional. The controversy rested on the question of whether the fee was a tax or a duty. Alexander Hamilton was attorney for the government and so many of the legislators flocked to hear him that Congress was virtually deserted. The justices were unanimous in deciding that it was an indirect tax or duty and thus within the powers of Congress. *Hylton v. the United States* was followed by *Ware v. Hylton*, which concerned the issue of whether treaties were paramount over state law. The Treaty of Paris in 1783 called for (or it might be more accurate to say, "expressed a pious hope for . . .") the payment by Americans of debts owed the British prior to the war. This had been an especially hard provision for the states to swallow; most of them had confiscated British or loyalist property during the Revolution and wiped British debts off their books. The prospect of having to disgorge large sums after a victorious war, incident to which many debtors had suffered substantial losses, caused strong reactions in patriot bosoms. The case before the Court represented the first significant effort of British creditors to collect a prewar debt.

John Marshall appeared for Virginia, the defendant in the case, and argued that a verdict in favor of the creditors would "impair the sovereignty of Virginia." After two weeks of deliberation the justices brought in the verdict that the British treaty provisions, as the law of the land, must prevail over state laws. Cushing, in his opinion, stated: "The provision that 'creditors shall meet with no lawful impediment,' etc. is as absolute, unconditional, and preemptory, as words can well express, and made not to depend on the will and pleasure, or the optional conduct of any body of men whatever." Again one of the points most feared by the anti-Constitutionalists had been affirmed by the Court.

It was somewhat of a setback to the dignity and importance of the Court when Jay resigned to take the position of governor of the state of New York. When John Rutledge, Washington's first nominee, was rejected by the Senate, Washington appointed Oliver Ellsworth chief justice. Under Ellsworth the Court enjoyed a period of relative obscurity. No dramatic cases were brought before it but its verdicts continued the line already clearly marked out: the progressive assertion of the powers of the Court and the supremacy of the federal government over the state governments.

CHAPTER

XI

THE EXECUTIVE

THE COURT WAS, OF COURSE, NOT THE WHOLE STORY. PRECEDENTS were being established and constitutional powers explored in both the legislative and executive branches of the government. For the legislative it was often, with the notable exception of *Hylton v. the United States,* a matter of seeing limits set to their powers by the Court. With the executive it was more a question of developing nugatory or ill-defined powers, and in this it was the character and influence of Washington himself that was most decisive. Washington created, for example, the cabinet—nowhere provided for in the Constitution—by conferring with the heads or secretaries of the various executive departments—State, War, and Treasury most particularly. It is interesting to note that when he asked the Supreme Court for an advisory opinion on the constitutionality of such a procedure, the Court refused to give one on the grounds of the separation of powers and the fact that it was "a court in the last resort."

William Maclay, a Pennsylvania Democrat and a senator, was a watchdog against the development of any monarchial folderol gathering about the office of the president. He was stoutly opposed to John Adams' suggestion that the president be addressed as "Your Excellency" and that the members of Congress should stand in his presence and remove their hats.

As we know, the Constitution provided that the president had the power to make and conclude treaties with the advice and consent of the Senate. Washington, accompanied by his secretary of war, General Henry Knox, brought a treaty with the Southern Indians to the Senate. It was handed to the vice-president, as the presiding officer, and John Adams read the document, or, in Maclay's words, "hurried over the paper." The carriages driving past the senatorial chambers made such a noise that the senators, according to Maclay, could hear only an occasional word. It was read again, and then the first article of the treaty, following which, Adams asked, "Do you advise and consent, etc.?"

"There was a dead pause. Mr. Morris whispered to me, 'We will see who will venture to break the silence first.' "

Then as Adams started to call for a formal vote, Maclay "rose reluctantly . . . from the length of the pause, the hint given by Mr. Morris, and the proceeding of our Vice-President, it appeared to me that if I did not no other one would, and we should have these advices and consents ravished, in a degree, from us."

"Mr. President," Maclay declared, "the paper which you have now read to us appears to have for its basis sundry treaties and public transactions between the Southern Indians and the United States and the States of Georgia, North Carolina, and South Carolina. The business is new to the Senate. It is of importance. It is our duty to inform ourselves as well as possible on the subject. I therefore call for a reading of the treaties and other documents alluded to in the paper before us.

"I cast an eye on the President of the United States. I saw he wore an aspect of stern displeasure. General Knox turned up some of the acts of Congress and the protest of one Blount, agent for North Carolina. Mr. Lee rose and named a particular treaty which he wished read. The business labored with the Senate. There appeared an evident reluctance to proceed. . . ."

One by one the articles of the treaty were postponed to allow for the assembling of relevant papers for further consideration by the Senators. Maclay decided that the whole procedure was an impossible one. He saw no chance of a "fair investigation of subjects while the President of the United States sat there, with his secretary of war, to support his opinions and overawe the timid and neutral part of the Senate." A committee should be appointed, the relevant papers referred to it, the Senate to act upon the recommendations of the committee.

"As I sat down," Maclay noted, "the President of the United States started up in a violent fret. *This defeats every purpose of my coming here,*' were the first words that he said. . . . He cooled, however, by degrees." He was willing to have the matter postponed for a few days. "A pause for some time ensued. We waited for him to withdraw. He did so with a discontented air. Had it been any other man than the man whom I wish to regard as the first character in the world, I would have said, with sullen dignity.

"I cannot now be mistaken. The President wishes to tread on the necks of the Senate. . . . He wishes us to see with the eyes and hear with the ears of his Secretary only. The Secretary to advance the premises, the President to draw the conclusions, and to bear down our deliberations with his personal authority and presence. Form only will be left to us. This will not do with Americans. But let the matter work; it will soon cure itself."

The whole passage is marvelously evocative and instructive. It is appealing to speculate that Maclay's refusal to be overawed by Washington's majestic presence preserved for the Senate the right to give careful consideration to all treaties and, indeed, to all executive initiatives, but the fact is that, as Maclay said, "This will not do with Americans." If Maclay had not objected then and there, Washington or his successors would undoubtedly have encountered resistance to procedure so manifestly weighted in favor of the President. The incident nonetheless is an excellent demonstration of the inherent tension between the legislative and executive branches of the government. It was not even that Washington was deliberately trying to accumulate for the executive branch excessive powers. He was, in part, a commanding general going to his staff for advice and suggestions. In part, he was simply the presiding officer in a novel system and he was trying to find out how to make it work. He undoubtedly had in mind the image of the first minister of the king of Great Britain acting as the leader of the House of Commons. He was plainly disconcerted to find that model an inappropriate one. He soon stopped coming to the Senate to "ravish" their "advices and consents." He sent the papers, although there was an unending wrangle over what papers, a wrangle that centered on what came to be called "executive privilege." The question of what papers (or tapes) the president can legitimately withhold from Congress is one that may never be settled to the satisfaction of both parties.

It is also worth noting that Maclay displayed that pragmatic temper, that notion that if things are not forced hastily to some "principled" conclusion they will, given time, work themselves out, which has been characteristic of both British and American politics and which was, in fact, to mark, for many periods, the approach to complicated constitutional questions by the Supreme Court itself. "But let the matter work; it will soon cure itself."

The Constitution, as almost everyone was painfully aware, was, after all, only a piece, or several pieces, of paper. It fulfilled quite well Napoleon's axiom that "constitutions should be brief and obscure." Indeed, he may well have had the federal Constitution in mind. What is most dramatic in the early years of the new nation is the endlessly fascinating process by which theory became reality. It is the peculiar fortune of the nation that the development of the new government was left in the first formative years primarily in the solicitous hands of those who had devised it. If a strong national government was essential as the basis for a genuinely united nation, it was critical that its management be in the hands of individuals of that persuasion.

It is also important to keep in mind how embittered American politics became in the era immediately following the establishment of the new government. Parties revealed themselves divided roughly along the lines of Federalists and anti-Federalists, or anti-Constitutionalists, the supporters of a strong national government versus the supporters of state sovereignty, all of this complicated by attachments to England and attachments to the French Revolution. Class lines emerged as well. Gentlemen of fortune and respectability tended to the Federalist side, shopkeepers, artisans, mechanics, and small farmers to the anti-Federalist side, although such divisions varied greatly from section to section. The anti-Federalists, following the lead of Thomas Jefferson, began calling themselves Jeffersonian Democrats, or simply Democrats, and fired a relentless barrage of accusations against the Federalists, who were denounced in Democratic newspapers such as the poet Philip Freneau's (which was backed by Jefferson) as wishing to establish a monarchy and destroy the liberties of the people. Washington himself was accused of wishing to become a dictator.

The Federalists, who had never anticipated the development of such rancorous factions, or parties, were dismayed at the bitterness and hostility that appeared so promptly. To the Democrats the Supreme Court was the most blatantly antidemocratic element in the Constitution. Judges were appointed, not elected; they were thus beyond the control of the people at large. By sitting in judgment on laws passed by Congress they were in a position to thwart the will of the people as expressed through their representatives in Congress. The perception was accurate. As the reader will have noted frequently there was a definite opposition among the framers of the Constitution to unchecked democracy since the mass of the people were, as Elbridge Gerry put it, "neither wise nor good." This view was, of course, balanced by the opinion that the rich and powerful were, by and large, just as bad and by virtue of their wealth and power far more dangerous. While the Senate, as the smaller and more deliberative body, once removed by the manner of their selection from popular clamors and pressures, was counted on to moderate or "balance" the tendency of the popular branch to hasty and intemperate action, it was, in the final analysis, the Supreme Court that must reconcile congressional statutes with the Constitution, protect the rights of the minority from the greed or indifference of the majority, restrain the executive, and in other ways thwart, where necessary, "the will of the people."

In the December, 1791, session of Congress a resolution was introduced and debated that called for a constitutional amendment to abolish the system of federal courts, including, of course, the Supreme Court. The dissatisfaction was not confined to the Supreme Court. A Virginia friend wrote to Alexander Hamilton: "The operation of the Government has by no means been pleasing to the people of this country. On the contrary the friends to it are daily decreasing. Some of the highest in rank and ability among us and who supported it in our convention were now extremely dissatisfied and loud in abusing its measures; while some others of equal fame only express their chagrin in private."

Representative Theodore Sedgwick of Massachusetts wrote in the summer of 1792: "I fear the National Government has seen its best days. The distance at which it stands removed from the affections of the great bulk of the people; the opposition of so many great, proud, and jealous sovereignties; the undistinguished and indistinguishable boundary between National and State jurisdictions; the disposition which both may possess to encroach; and above all the rancorous jealousy that began with the infancy of the Government and grows with its growth, arising from an opposition, or supposed opposition of interests—produce in my mind serious doubts whether the machine will not soon have some of its wheels so disordered as to be incapable of regular progress."

Perhaps the emergence of parties, by turning attention to questions of how the Constitution was to be interpreted rather than to the more dangerous question of whether it should exist at all, helped to assure its existence.

The beleaguered Federalists, believing that the stability of the government was at stake, struck out at their opponents with the Alien and Sedition Acts, passed in 1798 and clearly designed to suppress political dissent. The Alien Act, which was directed primarily against Irish radicals, gave the president of the United States, then John Adams, the right "to *order* all such *aliens* as he shall judge dangerous to the peace and safety of the United States, or shall have reasonable grounds to suspect are concerned in any treasonable or secret machination against the government thereof, to depart out of the territory of the United States. . . ."

The Sedition Act, passed in the same session of Congress, was even more sweeping. It provided stiff fines ($5000, which in today's currency would be perhaps $50,000 or so) and jail terms of six months to five years for anyone who "shall unlawfully combine or conspire together, with intent to oppose any measure or measures of the government of the United States . . . or to impede the operation of any law of the United States . . . or counsel, advise or attempt to procure any insurrection, riot, unlawful assembly, or combination. . . ." It also provided for the prosecution in federal courts of anyone who "shall write, print, utter, or publish . . . any false, scandalous and malicious writing . . . against the government of the United States, or either house of the Congress . . . or the President of the United States . . . or to bring them, or either of them, into contempt or disrepute; or to excite against them . . . the hatred of the good people of the United States." The laws indicated a state of panic produced in Congress by the animosities stirred up primarily by the French Revolution. The acts were to last only for two years. They were thus clearly conceived of as, in effect, wartime emergency measures, what we call today "cold war," and they have to be understood against a background of the increasing aggressiveness of the French Directory and the activities of American proponents of the French Revolution, already entering a reactionary phase. England, allied with Russia in the so-called War of the Second Coalition, was engaged with the successful armies of Napoleon. In the United States the more fervent Francophiles were calling for the overthrow of the existing government and the establishment of one completely committed to the French cause.

If the Federalists overreacted to these events, their opponents, the Jeffersonian Democrats, led by Jefferson himself, overreacted even more drastically. Jefferson, who was John Adams' vice-president and thus presided over the Senate during the debate on and passage of the Alien and Sedition Acts, left Washington before the bills were actually passed and hurried home to Monticello, where he drafted the Virginia and Kentucky Resolutions, which, in effect, declared the acts unconstitutional and thereby null and void and threatened open rebellion if they were not at once repealed. His resolutions stated that the states were paramount to the federal Union. Perhaps the most mischievous portion of Jefferson's resolution was the statement that each state had "an equal right to judge for itself, as well of infractions [of the Constitution] as of the mode and measure of redress." If the tendency of Congress to encroach upon the rights of the states were not promptly checked, Jefferson stated, it would "necessarily drive these States into revolution and blood." Here Jefferson seemed to be calling for revolution.

What is perhaps most striking about the Virginia and Kentucky Resolutions is the fact it occurred to no one to take the issue to the Supreme Court. The Court, after all, had been established to adjudicate just such an issue. The anti-Constitutionalists had insisted on incorporating a Bill of Rights into the Constitution to guard against infringements of those rights by the federal government. Here was the perfect case in point. The Jeffersonian Democrats, now calling themselves Republicans, could not take their case to the Supreme Court because to do so would be to strengthen the Court which they wished to weaken or abolish.

In a sense, the whole brouhaha over the Alien and Sedition Acts and the Virginia and Kentucky Resolutions served to demonstrate as conclusively as possible that in the absence of a Court to adjudicate such conflicts, the only recourse was to disobedience, armed resistance, and disunion. Thus, although the Court was conspicuously uninvolved, the whole dangerous episode undoubtedly strengthened it indirectly by giving thoughtful observers a demonstration of the alternative to it.

By the same token it was necessary that Jefferson defeat Adams for the presidency, since Jefferson, by acceding to the first role in the government he was so suspicious of, was removed from the ranks of its adversaries. The presidential campaign was nonetheless an exceedingly acrimonious one. Jefferson was attacked as a man poisoned by French atheism; Adams as a friend to monarchy, an enemy to France, and an agent of repression. There were widespread predictions of armed uprising if the Federalists retained power and little old ladies were warned to hide their Bibles in the event of a Republican victory. Adams, burdened by the incubus of the Alien and Sedition Acts and deserted by the Hamiltonian faction of his own party, was narrowly defeated by Jefferson. But since the Constitution made no effective distinction between votes for the president and the vice-president, Aaron Burr, who had run as the ostensible vice-presidential candidate, received the same number of electoral votes as Jefferson. Burr and his adherents, not to mention the Federalist hard-liners, saw an opportunity to rob Jefferson of the presidency by throwing the election to Burr in the House of Representatives, still a Federalist stronghold. Again there was talk among infuriated Jeffersonians of an armed march on Washington. After weeks of uncertainty and backstage politicking, Jefferson mustered the votes to be declared president and soon after the Twelfth Amendment to the Constitution was introduced to prevent a recurrence of such a dangerous deadlock.

A measure of the prevailing spirit of factionalism was the end of the long and affectionate friendship between John Adams and Jefferson. They no longer spoke to each other and Adams, after Jefferson's inauguration, refused to welcome his successor. But Adams had an extraordinary revenge on his former friend. John Marshall had served as Adams' secretary of state in the waning days of his administration after he had fired Timothy Pickering for his pro-Hamilton activities. When Adams had lost the election of 1800 to Jefferson but before the latter had taken office, Adams gave his attention to the matter of filling the chair of chief justice of the Supreme Court, left vacant by the resignation of Oliver Ellsworth. He first offered the office to the former chief justice, John Jay. It had been his intention to offer it next to Associate Justice William Cushing, but Cushing was in his sixties and not in the best of health, so Adams had second thoughts. Next in line was William Paterson of New Jersey, author of the New Jersey plan in the federal convention and widely respected. Paterson, however, had the backing of the Hamilton faction of the Federalist party and Adams was determined to do nothing to advance that cause. He therefore passed over Paterson, to the indignation of the justice's supporters, and sent the name of John Marshall to the Senate on January 20, 1801.

There was substantial opposition to Marshall's appointment and Paterson's friends in the Senate delayed confirmation for a week while pressures were brought to bear on Adams to withdraw Marshall's name and substitute Paterson's. That was a lost cause. Adams was adamant. Jonathan Dayton, the senator from New Jersey, wrote to Paterson that it was "with grief, astonishment and almost indignation" that he sent him the news of Marshall's appointment "contrary to the hopes and expectations of us all." He offered his friend such consolation as he could, noting that Adams had shown "such debility or derangement of intellect" in his appointments as to console many Federalists for his defeat. In other words, he had not followed the advice of the Hamiltonians. "It must be gratifying to you," Dayton added, "to learn that all voices were united in favor of conferring this appointment upon you. The President alone was inflexible and declared he would never nominate you."

John Adams was a complex and secretive man. We do not know whether in fact he, by some kind of sixth sense, had discerned in Marshall the ideal person to defend the Constitution and strengthen the Court or whether the appointment was motivated, at least in part, by the understandable human impulse to plant a thorn in the side of his erstwhile friend and ally, Thomas Jefferson. Jefferson and Marshall, both Virginians, were political adversaries. Remarkably alike in style and appearance, they were the antithesis of each other in intellect and temperament. Adams was aware of Jefferson's hostility toward the Court. To place at the head of it a vigorous, able, comparatively young man already thoroughly identified with the Federalist cause was to combine the thorn with the stumbling block, so to speak. If that was its purpose, Adams' strategy was brilliantly successful, as we know. The appointment was indeed a thorn, a stumbling block, and, if excessive metaphors may be pardoned, a red flag, since the new president devoted a disproportionate amount of his time and energy attempting to destroy or at least seriously weaken the Court. And Marshall proved to be the president's nemesis.

If Adams wrought better than he knew, he soon came to understand the extent of his triumph and before his death wrote to Marshall's son: "My gift of John Marshall to the people of the United States was the proudest act of my life."

The stage was thus set, as though by a master dramatist, for a truly extraordinary play, a play which would do much to determine subsequent American history. The protagonists, Jefferson and Marshall, were, in a sense, successors to an earlier and equally compelling drama—Jefferson and Hamilton. As we have said, the two men affected much the same manner. Both were Virginia aristocrats, both stressed informality; Jefferson slopped about the White House in untidy clothes and old bedroom slippers. Marshall let his hair grow too long and often forgot to comb it. His boots were old and often caked with mud. The knee buckles of his britches were commonly loose. He was frequently observed doing menial tasks, carrying firewood or shopping for some food on his way home from a session of the Court. "In his whole appearance, and demeanour, dress, attitudes, gestures, sitting, standing, or walking, he is as far removed from the idolized graces of Lord Chesterfield, as any other gentleman on earth," wrote William Wirt.

We have similar descriptions of Jefferson. The two men had much the same physiognomy. They were tall and thin with small graceful heads and sharp features. But here the resemblance ended. Jefferson was passionate and headlong, quick to take offense, relentless in pursuit of an enemy, emotional, intuitive, a man of impulse. Hot. Marshall was firm but conciliatory, methodical, patient, undeviating in the pursuit of an idea or a goal. Cool. And, above all, of course, a brilliant expounder of the law.

Benjamin Latrobe, the architect and engineer, wrote that several Virginia lawyers surpassed Marshall as orators, "but for talent, he substitutes genius, and instead of talking *about* his subject, he talks upon it . . . he is superior to every other orator at the Bar of Virginia, in closeness of argument, in his most surprising talent of placing his case in that point of view suited to the purpose he aims at, throwing a blaze of light upon it, and of keeping the attention of his hearers fixed upon the object to which he originally directed it. He speaks like a man of plain common sense, while he delights and informs the acute."

All who knew Marshall commented on his sweetness of temper, his thoughtfulness, his equanimity, his courtesy. Albert Beveridge, his great biographer, professed to have searched in vain for some flaw in his hero which would make him seem somehow more human. But then biographers are notorious for having that difficulty, and it is safe to assume that Marshall had his share of human shortcomings.

Needless to say, the Jeffersonians had nothing good to say about Marshall. Benjamin Franklin Bache was Benjamin Franklin's grandson and editor of the Democratic newspaper, the *Aurora*. He characterized Marshall as "more distinguished as a rhetorician and sophist than as a lawyer and statesman, sufficiently pliant to succeed in a corrupt court, too insincere to command respect or confidence in the republic." Jefferson, in a letter to Madison in 1798, observed that his rival's "lax, lounging manners have made him popular with the bulk of the people of Richmond, and a profound hypocrisy, with many thinking men of our country." He had written to Monroe before Marshall's appointment that "nothing should be spared to eradicate this spirit of Marshallism." Marshall reciprocated. He wrote to Hamilton on January 1, 1801, when the election was still undecided: "To Mr. Jefferson . . . I have felt almost insuperable objections. His foreign prejudices [Jefferson's reputed sympathy for Napoleon and the Directory] seem to me to totally unfit him for the chief magistracy. . . . In addition to this solid and immovable objection, Mr. Jefferson appears to me to be a man who will embody himself with the House of Representatives. By weakening the office of President, he will increase his personal power. He will diminish his responsibility, sap the fundamental principles of the government. . . ."

Feeling as he did, Marshall may have given encouragement (as Jefferson certainly believed he had) to a Federalist scheme to resolve the Burr-Jefferson impasse by having Congress declare Marshall the new president.

Jefferson, who had threatened the government with the doctrine of nullification, which was to have a long and mischievous life, considered his election as marking a second revolution. The bad old Federalist administration, carrying the country rapidly to monarchy and repression, had been replaced by a republican-democratic administration committed to the ideals and principles of the original American Revolution, now twenty-five years old. Everything would now be different. In fact very little changed. The tone or temper changed certainly and the Federalists lapsed into gloomy mutterings and forebodings. But the Constitution proved impervious to Jefferson's sporadic attacks and he failed completely in his assault on the Court. It was vastly stronger at the end of his administration than it had been at the beginning. In a certain sense it was stronger *because* Jefferson had attacked it and thereby dramatized it and its function as nothing else could have.

CHAPTER

XII

MARBURY v. MADISON

WE MIGHT HERE ON THE EVE OF THIS FIERCE IF ULTIMATELY UN-
even contest review our progress thus far in this work. We have tried
to give an account of the development of the notion of a constitution
and how that notion finally crystallized in a particular document, the
federal Constitution of the United States, the first and certainly the
most important such document in modern times. And then a brief narrative of the earliest years of the new government with particular attention to the growth of the federal judicial system, a growth quite
unobtrusive on the whole, but one completely consistent with the
intentions of most of the framers of the Constitution. With the chief
justiceship of Marshall we now enter a new phase of our story. We
encounter, in a way that is perhaps unique to the history of the Court,
the manner in which personalities and various historical "forces" in-
teract to produce a particular history. The Court has proved, perhaps
even more than the presidency, the arena for dominant personalities
to affect our history in decisive ways. Out of all the justices who
have occupied the bench, only a half dozen, starting with Marshall,
have dominated the Court so completely as to give their name to the
period of their service as in the Marshall Court, the Taney Court,
or, more recently, the Warren Court. To make such an impression
the chief justice must hold office (one is tempted to say reign) for a
substantial number of years. Ideally, his tenure will run through two
or three presidencies. He will be himself not simply a powerful legal
thinker but, more important, a powerful personality. In some cases,
in the absence of dominating chief justices, associate justices have

exerted the most important influence—as with Holmes, Cardozo, Frankfurter. Our method will be to give close attention to these dominant personalities and at the same time to review systematically the most crucial cases in the evolution of the Constitution.

The first encounter between Jefferson and Marshall came over another judicial appointment in the waning days of Adams' administration. Adams had appointed William Marbury, a reliable Federalist, a justice of the peace. The commission, along with three others, had been approved by the Senate and signed by Adams. It was then sent to the secretary of state, John Marshall, but before it could be registered, the term of office of the Adams administration expired and Jefferson ordered all appointments and commissions made by Adams —he called them "an outrage on decency"—to be withheld. Marbury decided to test Jefferson's legal right to withhold the commissions.

Marbury's suit requested that the Court issue a mandamus, directing the new secretary of state, James Madison, to surrender the commission. Marbury's action put Marshall between a rock and a hard place. If he ordered Madison and thereby Jefferson, as head of the executive branch, to deliver the commission to Marbury, Jefferson would certainly refuse, thus insulting Marshall and diminishing the authority of the Court. Marshall's solution was remarkably ingenious. Marbury had based his plea on a provision in the Judiciary Act of 1789 which gave the federal judiciary authority to issue writs of mandamus "to persons holding office under the authority of the United States."

Just the fact that the Court expressed a willingness to consider Marbury's plea alarmed the Republicans. On December 24, 1801, John Breckinridge, senator from Kentucky and Jefferson's coadjutor in the matter of the Kentucky Resolutions, wrote to Monroe, a representative from Virginia: "What think you of the rule entered upon by the Federal Court last week against the Secretary of State to show cause? . . . I think it the most daring attack which the annals of Federalism have yet exhibited. I wish the subject of the Courts to be brought forward in the Senate next week." And another Republican congressman wrote that "the conduct of the Judges on this occasion has excited a very general indignation and will ensure the repeal of the Judiciary Law of the last session, about the propriety of which some of our Republican friends were hesitating."

There was a variety of implications in the Marbury case. The

Republicans made it clear that they intended to repeal the Circuit Court Act of 1801 just passed by the Federalist Congress on the ground that it represented an unwarranted extension of the powers of the federal courts (as well as creating a number of jobs which, as we have seen, Adams had hastened to fill with Federalists). A repeal, moreover, would be generally understood to be an indication of the determination as well as the authority of the legislative branch to clip the wings of the Court, which the Republicans believed had already accumulated dangerous and illegal powers. John Randolph, the Virginia firebrand, wrote that the ambitions of the justices "extend only to a complete exemption from Legislative control; to the exercise of an inquisitorial authority over the Cabinet of the Executive. . . . In their inquisitorial capacity, the Supreme Court . . . may easily direct the Executive by mandamus in what mode it is their pleasure that he should exercise his functions."

It was undoubtedly the case that Marshall, far from coveting the mandamus power for the Court, realized it was a troublesome power, one that was basically unenforceable and could well involve the Court in bitter political disputes. He was doubtless as eager to be rid of it as his Republican opponents.

While the justices debated the issue of the writ of mandamus to an officer of the executive branch, the bill to repeal the Circuit Court Act of 1801—which relieved the justices of the arduous labor of traveling on circuit and established six new circuit courts and sixteen judges—made its way through the Senate to the dismay of the Federalists. One of such persuasion wrote: "The passage of the bill to destroy the Judiciary may be much obstructed but it will pass. Mr. Jefferson has set his heart upon the measure. 'Tis his favorite measure and his party will (whatever scruples some of them may feel about the constitutionality of it) make this desired offering to his revengeful spirit." And when the bill, which in effect restored the *status quo ante*, that is to say the situation before the passage of the Circuit Court Act, was passed in the House by a substantial majority, a Federalist paper declared, "The sun of Federalism has set, indeed fallen like Lucifer, never to rise again." Another predicted that "the Constitution has received a wound it cannot long survive. The Jacobins [a reference to the supporters of the French Revolution] exult; the Federalists mourn; our country will weep, perhaps bleed." It was seen as "part of a systematic plan for the total subversion of the law itself . . .

operating in its consequence a complete destruction of the independence of an integral part of the Government, and introducing a system of corruption into the sanctuary of justice." It was "the death warrant of the Constitution."

Charles Cotesworth Pinckney, who had been a delegate to the federal convention, wrote to Alexander Hamilton, "It was natural to expect that persons who have been always hostile to the Constitution would, when they had power, endeavour to destroy a work whose adoption they opposed and whose execution they have constantly counteracted. But I do not imagine they will stop there; they will proceed in their mad and wicked career and the People's eyes will be opened." And Gouverneur Morris, who had written the final draft of the Constitution, wrote that "the repeal of the Judiciary Bill battered down the great outwork of the Constitution. The Judiciary has been overthrown."

One of the consequences of the bitter debate over the repeal of the Circuit Court Act was that its advocates were uneasy at the possibility that the Court might declare the *repeal* unconstitutional (as its Federalist opponents insisted it was). They thus went to considerable lengths to attack what they had recently defended, the right of the Court to judge the constitutionality of acts passed by Congress, thereby increasing the apprehensions of the opponents of repeal.

Given this climate a lesser man than Marshall might have panicked and either launched an all-out judicial war against the combined weight of the Republican legislature and executive or withdrawn into a protective shell and avoided any decisions likely to inflame the Court's enemies. That Marshall did neither, that he picked his way through the political thickets that confronted him without ever making a misstep, is the real measure of his profoundly political instincts, his "genius." At every point he discerned just what public opinion would tolerate and how to make his decisions most tolerable, while step by inevitable step strengthening the Court, *in the face of attack*, and doing so with a conspicuous lack of weapons.

On one issue there can be no serious question. There were prominent men in the Republican ranks who wished nothing more than the destruction of the power of the federal judiciary. As a Kentucky state legislator wrote the Kentucky senator, Breckinridge, the senator must never leave his post "till the Federal Courts and the Excise Law are both laid low in the grave with old Johnny Adams."

Having repealed the Circuit Court Act of 1801, Congress took the extraordinary and probably unconstitutional step of abolishing the June and December terms of the Court, presumably to delay the opportunity for the Court to issue a judgment on the constitutionality of the repeal. The case of *Marbury v. Madison* was also pending and in the long adjournment of the Court, some fourteen months, the anxieties of the Federalists increased and the hostility of Republicans toward the Court grew, if anything, more settled. William Plumer, congressman from New Hampshire, wrote: "The Judges of the Supreme Court must fall. They are denounced by the Executive, as well as the House. They must be removed; they are obnoxious, unyielding men, and why should they remain to awe and embarrass the Administration? Men of more flexible nerves can be found to succeed them." A Republican judge foresaw a less drastic course. He wrote to a friend, "Father Cushing and Uncle Chase [both associate justices] are on their last legs. When they go off the stage, the Supreme Tribunal which governs all things will be filled by those of the same cast of sentiment with the Executive. *Festina lente* should be his motto."

Caesar Rodney of Delaware won himself a modest measure of fame when he rode all night and arrived in Philadelphia on July 2, exhausted and covered with mud, to vote for the resolution declaring the United States independent of Great Britain, thereby swinging a reluctant Delaware to the ranks of those supporting independence. Now he breathed fire and damnation for the Court, writing to a friend that if the judges "assert unconstitutional powers, I confidently trust there will be wisdom and energy enough in the Legislative and Executive branches to resist their encroachments and to arraign them for the abuse of their authority at the proper tribunal. Such monstrous doctrines have been preached and such unlimited powers arrogated for them that I know not what they may possibly do. They should remember, however, that there is a boundary which they cannot pass with impunity. If they cross the Rubicon, they may repent when it will be too late to return. . . . We shall discover who is master of the ship."

When the Court assembled after its mandated recess, it was very evidently to render a decision in the case of *Marbury v. Madison*. "Most of the gentlemen of the Bar" were present and there was a keen air of expectancy.

As Marshall put the matter, "The following questions have been considered and decided.

"1st. Has the applicant a right to the commission he demands?

"2dly. If he has a right and that right has been violated, do the laws of his country afford him a remedy?

"3dly. If they afford him a remedy is it a *mandamus* issuing from this court?"

In the matter of appointments Marshall argued that where the appointee does not serve at the pleasure of the executive who appoints him but for good behavior, "the appointment is not revocable, and cannot be annulled. It has conferred legal rights which cannot be resumed. . . . The right to the office is then in the person appointed, and he has the absolute, unconditional power of accepting or rejecting it. . . ." It thus followed that "To withhold his commission . . . is an act deemed by the court not warranted by law, but violative of a vested legal right."

So far, so good for Marbury. Marshall seemed to be throwing down the gauntlet and challenging Jefferson directly. But not so fast. Well aware that he had no means of enforcing such a judgment, Marshall proceeded, with extraordinary intellectual agility, to extricate himself from the trap he appeared to have walked into.

"This," he noted, "brings us to the second inquiry: which is, If he has a right, and that right has been violated, do the laws of his country afford him a remedy?" Jefferson, as he read the decision, must have been puzzled at this point. Clearly the answer to the second question was also "yes." The Judiciary Act did give him a remedy. And if all was done with proper attention to the correct legal forms, the only question that remained was whether the Supreme Court had the power to render a judgment in the case. The Judiciary Act had indeed given the Court that authority and the Secretary of State was without question a person "holding office under the authority of the United States." It seemed that the trap that Marshall had been so patiently constructing for himself must now fall and ensnare him.

But Marshall had another arrow in his quiver. If the Court was not, in fact, "authorized to issue a writ of mandamus to such an officer, it must be because the law is unconstitutional, and therefore absolutely incapable of conferring the authority and assigning the duties which its words purport to confer and assign."

One can imagine at this point the startled looks that must have been exchanged among Marshall's auditors at this completely unpredictable turn in the chief justice's line of argument. Everyone waited entranced to hear how this conundrum was to be unraveled. It was simple as A, B, C. The Constitution gave the Supreme Court "original jurisdiction in all cases affecting ambassadors, other public ministers and consuls, and those in which a state shall be a party. In all other cases the supreme court shall have appellate jurisdiction. . . ."

"To enable this court, then, to issue a mandamus," Marshall continued, "it must be shown to be an exercise of appellate jurisdiction. . . ."

But had not Marshall already conceded that the Judiciary Act had, in fact, given the court that power? It had tried, to be sure, but since that article of the Act contravened the express words of the Constitution, it was unconstitutional and thus the Court could not act upon poor Marbury's plea. The authority upon which it was authorized to act—section 13 of the Judiciary Act—was unconstitutional and thus void.

There followed a careful explication of the point. The government of the United States was a government of set and specific limits. "The powers of the legislature are defined and limited; and that those limits may not be mistaken, or forgotten, the constitution is written. To what purpose are powers limited, and to what purpose is that limitation committed to writing, if these limits may, at any time, be passed by those intended to be restrained? The distinction between a government with limited and unlimited powers is abolished, if those limits do not confine the persons on whom they are imposed, and if acts prohibited and acts allowed are of equal obligation. It is a proposition too plain to be contested, that the constitution controls any legislative act repugnant to it; or, that legislature may alter the constitution by an ordinary act.

"Between these alternatives there is no middle ground. The constitution is either a superior, paramount law, unchangeable by ordinary means, or it is on a level with ordinary legislative acts. . . . So if a law be in opposition to the constitution; if both the law and the constitution apply to a particular case, so that the court must either decide that case conformably to the law, disregarding the constitution; or conformably to the constitution disregarding the law, the court must determine which of these conflicting rules governs the case.

This is of the very essence of judicial duty. . . .

"Thus, the particular phraseology of the constitution of the United States confirms and strengthens the principle . . . that a law repugnant to the constitution is void, and that *courts*, as well as other departments, are bound by that instrument.

"The rule must be discharged."

And poor Marbury, having been told that he was absolutely and entirely entitled to his commission as justice of the peace, was then told that the Court could do nothing to help him secure it. Even so he came out rather well. Marshall immortalized him. As long as constitutional law is studied Marbury's name will be green.

What is one to say of Marshall's decision? A piece of intellectual legerdemain? A sleight of hand, or rather of mind? A conjurer's trick? All great art may be said to contain something of the trickster, the magic illusionist. *Marbury v. Madison* is perhaps the most famous case in American constitutional history, rivaled only by the Dred Scott decision and, in modern times, *Brown v. Board of Education*. It was not that Marshall established some new constitutional principle. The Court had already in *Hayburn's Case* stated that laws passed by Congress contravening, in the opinion of the justices, the Constitution, were invalid. Ingenious as it was, the decision was not great law. Its importance lies primarily in the fact that the circumstances of the change of administrations from Federalist Adams to Republican Jefferson focused attention on the Court and gave to every clash between Jefferson and Marshall a vastly heightened dramatic effect.

Jefferson had triumphed in the election, and the Republicans had immediately set about reshaping the Constitution to fit their principles. But just at that instant the hero of Federalism rose from the dust of defeat to carry on the battle from the apparently impregnable citadel of the Supreme Court.

The reaction was as might have been anticipated. Republicans were enraged. Marshall had, in effect, accused Jefferson of an unjust and illegal act—withholding the commission. At the same time he had denied him the opportunity to retaliate by ignoring a decision of the Court. He had used an occasion which might have seriously weakened the Court to strengthen it.

Jefferson, needless to say, was furious at Marshall's decision and twenty years afterwards described it as "very irregular and very censurable." An anonymous writer in the *Virginia Argus* made a critical analysis. In his words, "three decisions are reported to have been decided. The last decision was that the Court had no jurisdiction to decide the other two, which they nevertheless decided. . . . To decide upon the merits of a cause without jurisdiction to entertain it, I affirm to be contrary to all law, precedent and principle."

That the decision did not arouse more Republican resentment was due, in large part, to the fact that its only direct consequence was that the objectionable mandamus was declared unconstitutional. Moreover, a few weeks later the Court handed down a decision declaring the Circuit Court Act a constitutional exercise of the powers of Congress. This keenly disappointed the Federalists, who wished to make the Court a political instrument with which to chastise the Republicans, and it disconcerted the Republicans, who, anticipating a negative decision, had hoped to use it to stir up popular animosity to the Court and thereby complete its destruction.

It is impossible to look into Marshall's mind, but one cannot help being impressed by the neatness of the sequence of events. In *Marbury v. Madison* Marshall had ruled an act, or a portion of an act, of Congress unconstitutional and then a week or so later he and the Court had turned around and ruled another act, very much to the disadvantage of the Court itself and of its principal supporters, the Federalists, constitutional. In both instances he had reasserted the right of the Court, already established in *Hayburn* and *Hylton v. U.S.*, to pass on the constitutionality of laws enacted by Congress. The fact is, there was surprisingly little discussion of or opposition to the power of judicial review. It was largely in retrospect that this aspect of the decision came to receive such great emphasis. It was clear in the wake of *Marbury v. Madison* that most of the opposition to the Court was based on apprehensions that the Court would overturn the decisions of state courts, especially in regard to the collection of the British debts and of land claims.

The Court's support of the constitutionality of the Circuit Court Act in *Stuart v. Laird* was hailed by the Republican press with praise as extravagant as its earlier criticism. The decision, Bache declared in the *Aurora*, "stands a living reproach to such as can believe . . . that you would surrender the chastity of the Court to the lust of envy. . . . The weight of your authority then calmed the tumult of action, and you stood, as you must continue to stand, a star of the first magnitude."

XIII

THE COURT UNDER FIRE

WITH *Marbury v. Madison* AND THE CIRCUIT COURTS CASE DECIDED
in their favor, the Republicans' clamor for impeachment of the judges
died down, but in the spring Justice Samuel Chase, a Marylander
and an intemperate Federalist who had enraged the Republicans by
his enthusiastic support of the Alien and Sedition Acts and his political activities on behalf of Adams during the presidential campaign,
undertook in a charge to a federal grand jury in Baltimore to denounce the act that had abolished the circuit courts and criticize the
state constitution of Maryland, stating that universal suffrage (provided for in the Maryland constitution) would "certainly and rapidly
destroy all protection to property and all security to personal liberty,
and our republican Constitution will sink into a mobocracy."

Chase's ill-advised charge provided Jefferson with grounds, in his
opinion, for initiating impeachment proceedings against Chase. If
Chase's impeachment were successful the ground would have been
prepared for the impeachment of other justices. At the very least the
prestige of the Court would be much diminished. "Ought this seditious
and official attack on the principles of our Constitution and on the
proceedings of the State to go unpunished?" Jefferson wrote a prominent congressman. The Federalist Timothy Pickering wrote to
Stephen Higginson in January, 1804: "I understand that it is the intention of the party to impeach every Judge, who in his charge has
given a political opinion. The Judges of the Supreme Court are all
Federalists. They stand in the way of the ruling power. . . . The
Judges, therefore, are, if possible, to be removed."

Early in 1804 the House brought in a bill of impeachment against

Chase. The *Connecticut Courant,* a Federalist paper, noted: "Behold this aged patriot, one of the pillars in our revolutionary struggle, rudely dragged by a Virginian stripling before the National tribunal." The issue was plainly and simply a partisan political issue. Around it swirled all the bitter factionalism that existed between two hostile camps of former allies in a revolutionary cause. Both claimed to be the legitimate heirs of the Revolution and both abused and reviled each other without respite. Fisher Ames, a Federalist, despaired of seeing justice done. The spirit of party was all-pervasive. "You may broil Judge Chase and eat him, or eat him raw," he wrote, "it shall stir up less anger or pity than the Six Nations would show if Cornplanter or Red Jacket was refused a belt of wampum."

Ames was excessively pessimistic. The trial of Chase opened in the Senate in January, 1805, at the beginning of Jefferson's second term as president. A group of Republican stalwarts were led by John Randolph of Roanoke and Caesar Rodney of Delaware, whose rancor toward the Court we have already taken note of. The Federalists, for their part, assembled five of the ablest lawyers of their own persuasion, among them Luther Martin of Maryland, one of the dissident members of the federal convention; Joseph Hopkinson, revolutionary poet and essayist; and Philip Barton Key of Maryland, father of the composer-to-be of "The Star-Spangled Banner." After a trial that lasted almost two months, impeachment was defeated. That the Senate transcended partisanship is indicated by the fact that of the thirty-four Senators hearing the impeachment, twenty-five were Republicans and nine Federalists. Twenty-three (a two-thirds majority) were required under the Constitution to convict. The largest number of votes that could be mustered on any of the eight articles of impeachment was nineteen.

The Federalist press was understandably jubilant, hailing the decision as a "triumph of reason and justice over the spirit of party." Jefferson, who had picked out a successor to Chase, was indignant at his exoneration and the Republican press was predictably critical. Henry St. George Tucker, a Virginia Republican, wrote a friend: "I regard the acquittal as a foul disgrace upon our country. . . . It really seems as if the People were afraid to touch this golden calf they have formed—this talisman, the fancied charm which is to preserve us through every danger." Ironically intended, there was much truth in Tucker's description of the Court. It was true that in a period of little more than a decade it had acquired an aura of sanctity; that it had come to represent a principle above the desperate partisanship that seemed continually about to tear the country apart. There is little doubt that beneath the surface of political attacks on the Court and equally political defenses of it, a sense had developed among the people of the states in general that it embodied, in some essential manner, the essence of the Revolution itself.

In any event Jefferson had failed. Chase was merely his target of opportunity. His real adversary had been and remained Marshall. The danger that lay in the impeachment proceedings was that Republicans, determined to find some rationale for impeachment short of high crimes and misdemeanors, had, in essence, argued that impeachment was a means of keeping the Court in line with the election returns, i.e., the popular will as expressed by the people in their election of a president and members of Congress. The Jeffersonian Republicans were certainly not the last party to see the Court as an obstacle to their plans and to try to devise some strategy to bend it to their will.

William Giles, a Virginia congressman, gave a classic statement of the position during the Chase impeachment proceedings, a statement copied down by John Quincy Adams. Giles undertook to convince the attorney general, Robert Smith, that not only Chase "but all the other Judges of the Supreme Court . . . must be impeached and removed . . . and if the Judges of the Supreme Court should dare, as they had done, to declare an Act of Congress unconstitutional, or to send a mandamus to the Secretary of State, as they had done, it was the undoubted right of the House of Representatives to impeach them, and of the Senate to remove them, for giving such opinions, however honest or sincere they may have been in entertaining them. . . . A removal by impeachment was nothing more than a declaration by Congress to this effect: you hold dangerous opinions, and if you are suffered to carry them into effect, you will work the destruction of the Union. We want your offices for the purpose of giving them to men who will fill them better."

The acquittal of Chase did not end the attacks on the Court. John Randolph denounced the Senate for the "mockery of a trial," and introduced a constitutional amendment to provide that: "The Judges of the Supreme Court and all other Courts of the United States shall be removed from office by the President on joint address of both Houses of Congress requesting the same."

Some of the Republican pressure on the Court was undoubtedly relieved by the retirement of one justice and the death of another, giving Jefferson two appointments to make. To one vacancy he appointed a thirty-two-year-old South Carolina Republican, William Johnson, and to the second, a New York judge, Henry Livingston, a member of the powerful Livingston clan. A new Western circuit was added, which meant another judge, and Jefferson appointed a Kentuckian, Thomas Todd, forty-one years old.

But the war between Jefferson and Marshall, or between the Republicans and the Court, was by no means over. Jefferson, who had never forgiven Aaron Burr for his effort to rob him of the presidency in the election of 1800, turned up evidence of treasonable doings by Burr in the Mississippi region. Burr was apparently planning an expedition against the Spanish at New Orleans. Jefferson saw an opportunity to even an old score and he ordered his attorney general to charge Burr with treason. In order to secure his victim Jefferson condoned a series of illegal acts which culminated in an acquiescent Senate voting to suspend habeas corpus in order to facilitate the president's pursuit of Burr.

Rufus King wrote of the Senate bill: "How the Senate could have passed an act which would have permitted such deeds of tyranny is strange and incomprehensible. That body, with all its weakness, meanness, and subserviency, contains men devoted to the freedom of their country, and worthy of its highest confidence." The House rejected the bill, thereby, in King's opinion, atoning "for much imbecility and folly that had before been exhibited."

Judge William Cranch, a nephew of ex-President Adams and compiler of the first set of Supreme Court opinions, wrote his father: "Never in my life have I been more anxious. You will see by the newspapers that I dared to differ from my brothers on the Bench. [Cranch had opposed the suspension of the writ of habeas corpus.] I have dared to set the law and the Constitution in opposition to the arm of Executive power, supported by popular clamor. I have dared to attempt to maintain principle at the expense of popularity. . . . When we reflect upon the extraordinary exertions made by all under the President's influence to exaggerate Burr's conspiracy into a horrid rebellion, so that the Administration may have the merit of quelling it without bloodshed—when they have so far succeeded as to excite the public mind almost to a frenzy in many parts of the country—

you may form some idea of the anxiety which attended my dissent from the majority of the Court." The case was appealed to the Supreme Court, where the district court was reversed and Cranch vindicated. The Court proved as determined to defend the law and the Constitution as Jefferson was to hunt down the wretched Burr. To the president it was further proof that the Court was interfering in the rights of the executive branch and trying to thwart him in his efforts as commander in chief to defend the country against its enemies.

If it had seemed that party bitterness had reached a level that could hardly be exceeded, the Court's ruling that sufficient evidence to support the charge of treason against Burr had not been presented further inflamed party feelings. The *New York Daily Advertiser* declared: "Now may the ensign of rebellion be once more unfurled, and *all* may hurry to its standard, fearless of the consequences." The *Aurora* was led to grave doubts, since the Court had condoned treason, "whether the existing Judiciary system and the English common law are exactly calculated for a free nation and a virtuous people." Angry as Jefferson was at the ruling of the Court in the matter of Burr's treason, he took consolation from the thought that the Court's protection of "that class of offenders [Burr and his allies] which endeavors to overturn the Constitution itself" would prepare the way for an amendment that placed the Court once for all under the authority of the president and Congress. He wrote in the same spirit to Giles that the decisions of the Court in the Burr case "will produce an Amendment to the Constitution which, keeping the Judges independent of the Executive, will not leave them so of the Nation."

The Republican campaign against the Court was renewed, as Jefferson had promised, two months after the Burr affair had been concluded. This time it was in the form of a proposed amendment providing for a limited term of office for the justices and their removal by the president on the request of two thirds of each house. When the amendment failed to get the necessary support in the House, Giles, at Jefferson's behest, brought in a bill to amend the law of treason, making it far more comprehensive. In the debate over the bill Giles attacked Marshall as "a miserable political intriguer, scrambling for power." A dismayed listener was Joseph Story, a Massachusetts lawyer who was to become a disciple of Marshall and a legal power in his own right. "Never," he wrote, "did I hear such all-unhinging and terrible doctrine. He laid the axe at the root of judicial power, and every stroke might be distinctly felt. . . . One of its objects was to prove the right of the Legislature to define treason."

The bitterness generated by the Court's decisions in the Burr trial lingered on. The Washington Fusiliers, a militia group, months later proposed a toast to "the Judiciary when they Marshall themselves on the side of treason, in opposition to law, justice and humanity, may they still hear 'the small still voice' of the Nation ordering them from their unhallowed seats into eternal political oblivion." A similar toast at a meeting of Republicans in Connecticut evoked an angry response from a Federalist paper: "The Chief Justice of the United States and a member of the Senate of the United States [Timothy Pickering] are associated with a murderer and a traitor [Burr], a wretch abandoned of his country and his God, and crucified with him in anticipation on the same tree. Look at the bloody annals of the French Revolution and you will find the same diabolical spirit which dictated this toast. . . ."

The Court, as we have seen, had become the symbolic enemy of the Republicans while the Federalists saw it as the ultimate defender of American liberties. The intractability with which Jefferson had sought to curtail the powers of the Court filled the Federalists, especially those of New England where the party still held power, with rage and despair. In the words of John Quincy Adams, "In the political creed of the Federalists, the independence of the Judiciary was the sheet-anchor of republican freedom. They thought they perceived in Mr. Jefferson's opinions and conduct a deliberate and systematic attempt to break it down! . . . These apprehensions were perhaps exaggerated; but there was too much foundation for them. Mr. Jefferson's radical animosities and prejudices against the Judiciary power have had an unwholesome influence upon the public opinions of the American people. . . ."

Those "radical animosities" were, indeed, one of the reasons that many New Englanders grew more and more preoccupied with the notion of New England breaking off from the United States and forming a "Northern Confederacy." In addition the Louisiana Purchase convinced the Federalists that Jefferson was a man without principle who interpreted the Constitution to suit himself. The president's policy of trying to force concessions from France and England by imposing an embargo on American shipping was, for many New Englanders, the last straw. Avowing pacificist doctrines, Jefferson was determined, in their view, to sacrifice the trade of New England in order to wring concessions from Great Britain and Napoleon. Northern New England became openly defiant and in May Jefferson declared Vermont to be in a state of insurrection. Revenue officers had been murdered in the performance of their duties and in September three militia men were killed. The Federalists were accused of "advocating British insults and murders and domestic insurrection, and in every corner." Joseph Story wrote from Congress in January, 1809, "If I may judge by the letters I have seen from the various districts of Massachusetts, it is a prevalent opinion there—and, in truth, many friends from the New England States write us—that there is great danger of resistance to the laws, and great probability that the Essex Junto [a group of hardcore Federalists] have resolved to attempt a separation of the Eastern States from the Union."

The *Boston Gazette* proclaimed: "We are ready for separation, if our independence cannot be maintained without it. We know and feel our strength, and we will not have our rights destroyed by the mad schemes of a Virginia philosopher." Jefferson's Virginia and Kentucky Resolutions came back to haunt him now in the mouths of Federalist extremists from Connecticut and Massachusetts. The *Richmond Enquirer* described the situation aptly. "Things turned Topsey-Turvy—Federalists turned Anti-Federalists—The Friends of Order turned Jacobin," its headlines announced. Jefferson's reaction to violations of the embargo was increasing repression. In defiance of the terms of the Embargo Act itself, he instructed the secretary of the treasury to order customs collectors to detain all vessels carrying provisions to a belligerent power. A Boston newspaper called the presidential order "wholly unconstitutional . . . an outrage on the dignity and sovereignty of a State, a violation of the sacred compact which unites these States."

Its legality was promptly tested in a suit brought in Baltimore and heard by Jefferson's new appointee, the young South Carolina Republican, William Johnson. Johnson declared the presidential order void, noting: "The officers of our government, from the highest to the lowest, are equally subject to legal restraint; and it is confidently believed that all of them feel themselves equally incapable, as well from law as inclination, to attempt an unsanctioned encroachment upon individual liberty."

The Federalists were delighted. One Federalist paper declared. "We are glad to find by the decision at Charleston that there is some tribunal to which an American citizen can resort to know whether a public officer is conforming to the law or not." A Baltimore paper observed that the opinion would, "add another ray to the lustre of the American Bench, that this gentleman who owes his elevation to Mr. Jefferson has not hesitated to maintain the predominancy of the law over Executive usurpations."

To the *Aurora*, however, it was only another example of "the profligacy of the Judiciary . . . and in violation of the most sacred rights and best policy of the Nation and Government. . . . An additional proof of the monstrous absurdity of what is called the independence of the Judges. . . . Unless their tenure of office is altered and that corps brought to some sort of responsibility, they must in the end destroy the government. If the laws and policy of the Nation are to be set aside upon a quibble, if the very principles of peace and war are to be involved in the wretched subterfuges and equivocations of this subtle class of men, what avails all the superiority of a representative government which cannot check or chastise the crimes of such a class?"

Jefferson, of course, was indignant. He urged his attorney general, Caesar Rodney, to rebut Johnson, which Rodney did, at some length, writing to Jefferson that it was high time the Court be checked: "The judicial power, if permitted, will swallow all the rest. They will become omnipotent. No other administration than yours could progress under such circumstances. It is high time for the people to apply some remedy to the disease. You can scarcely elevate a man to a seat in a Court of Justice before he catches the leprosy of the Bench."

Meantime the Court was confronted by the most explosive issue yet to come before it—the question of the constitutionality of the Embargo Laws themselves. The New England Federalists had been encouraging resistance to them on the grounds that they were unconstitutional. They were confident that the Court would decide so and anxious to see them tested. The Republicans, for their part, were as apprehensive of the outcome as the Federalists were confident. Certainly the Embargo Act went far beyond any congressional statutes yet passed in its infringement of the sovereignty of the states. Its first test was before a strongly Federalist judge, John Davis, in the United States District Court for the District of Massachusetts. The trial was one of those marvelous set pieces of the time with a formidable array of notable lawyers on each side of the question and a sense that a question vital to the integrity and indeed preservation of the Union was at issue. Joseph Story, twenty-nine years old and already one of the most brilliant lawyers before the Massachusetts Bar, argued in favor of the constitutionality of the Embargo Act.

Judge Davis, in effect, accepted Story's argument, thereby undoubtedly helping to assure him of a position on the Supreme Court, and extending substantially "the necessary and proper" clause of the Constitution. Ironically, it was the Republicans, strict constructionists, and enemies of the Court who hailed the decision, the Federalists who repined. To the Republicans the decision "was luminous, learned, and eloquent beyond anything we recollect of the kind." Charles Warren, the great historian of the Court, calls Davis's verdict "one of the most striking illustrations of judicial impartiality rising above partisan influence to be found in the history of the law. . . ."

There is certainly a remarkable appropriateness to the successive decisions by the two justices—Johnson and Davis—against the interests of their own parties, their friends, and their political patrons. One could hardly have asked for a more dramatic demonstration of the judicial principle. Moreover, both decisions had a moderating effect on party animosities! Johnson's decision, by giving Federalists hope that remedy to the harshest aspects of the Embargo Act might be found in the courts, and Davis's decision by notifying that party— the party of respect for law—that they could no longer oppose the Embargo Act on the grounds of unconstitutionality. If the decision had gone the other way, it is hard to imagine that a fatal breach between the Northern and Southern states could have been avoided. This thought could hardly have failed to be in Judge Davis's mind when he stretched the Constitution to affirm the constitutionality of the odious act.

CHAPTER

XIV

STRENGTHENING THE COURT

JEFFERSON RETIRED FROM OFFICE IN 1809, GIVING WAY TO HIS secretary of state and principal lieutenant, James Madison. Marshall remained behind to serve for another quarter of a century as chief justice and give the Court the irrevocable stamp of his mind and character. With Jefferson passing from the active political scene and the Federalists constantly losing ground politically, the bitterness of party was moderated though by no means extinguished. It turned out that the Court had weathered the most sustained assault that would ever be mounted against it. Here it might be well to try to account for the Republican opposition to the Court. Since the Constitution is the hero of this work and Jefferson the most conspicuous enemy of what the Federalists, at least, considered its keystone—the Court —we must needs say a word or two in Jefferson's defense.

First off, Jefferson, more than any of his contemporaries, was haunted by the perception, which had overwhelmed him at the beginning of the French Revolution when he was ambassador to France, that governments almost inevitably grow corrupt and repressive. When it is too late to reform them only a bloody and terrible upheaval (like the French Revolution) can give birth to a new and more humane political order. He was obsessed with the fear that the American government would rapidly become reactionary once the revolutionary ardor created by the fight for freedom had faded away. He believed, moreover, that the Federalists were the agents of this reaction and that "the people" were the only antidote. Thus any agency of government that interfered with the most direct expression of the will of the people was to be feared and resisted. In other words, Jefferson and his adherents broke sharply with the classic Christian notion of human depravity or original sin. The heart of man, far from being "desperately wicked," was good and benign. It was superstition in the form of priestly dogmas that warped man's natural reason. It was the rich and powerful, "the few," who had manipulated and exploited the "many," the people. In Jefferson's view we were entering, with the American and French Revolutions, a new era in which human reason would triumph over ignorance and superstition, an era in which, as one of Jefferson's favorite authors, Jean-Jacques Rousseau, had put it, "the voice of the people is the voice of God." Liberal political theorists, on the other hand, had yearned for centuries for "a government of laws not of men." That was because they saw all men, however situated, as equally inclined to "self-aggrandizement"—greed and exploitation. It was only through fair and equitable laws, properly administered, that the exploitation of one class or group or interest by another could be avoided. For men who held to such a conviction, the notion of a Supreme Court, a relatively impartial and independent power, charged with thwarting the popular will when that will was arbitrary and destructive of the legitimate rights of others, was one of the great political achievements in history.

There was much to be said for both views. Revolutions *do* become reactionary. The Supreme Court *was* the citadel of property interests and a bulwark for the most conservative elements in American life. But it was always fortunately something very considerably more. In any event the two views were irreconcilable. The best that could be hoped for was an armed truce. The ideology of the "age of reason," primarily French in origin and given great currency in America by the French Revolution, which to many Americans seemed a continuation or companion piece to their own revolution, gradually overwhelmed the "ideology" of the American Revolution. Faith in reason, in science, in education, in progress pervaded the American consciousness.

It would be going too far to say that the Constitution was an historical accident—after all, I have argued that it was, in a sense, the culmination of more than two thousand years of political thought (and thus much more than simply an American phenomenon). But it was clearly the product of a particular kind of consciousness, which I have chosen to call Classical-Christian, and that consciousness was almost immediately overwhelmed by what we might call the Secular-

Democratic Consciousness, given great stimulus in the United States by the French Revolution. The Federalist interlude of eleven years marked the twilight of the Classical-Christian Consciousness (many aspects of which, of course, persisted, and persist, because an old consciousness is remarkably tenacious and only gives way slowly and with the greatest reluctance). It was a critical twilight—the Federalist era—because it permitted that ripened form of the Classical-Christian Consciousness, the Constitution, to assume its basic character, especially that most original and essential aspect of it, "the third branch," the Supreme Court. And it left John Marshall as the explicator and defender of the third branch.

Jefferson was, of course, the theoretician and exemplar of the Secular-Democratic Consciousness. It would have been impossible after his "Democratic Revolution"—which he himself considered as important as the first revolution, since he believed his election saved the country from a monarchal or at least aristocratic form of government—to have devised any system of government with so "undemocratic" an element in it as the Supreme Court.

The depth of this discrepancy between the Classical-Christian and the Secular-Democratic Consciousness has been obscured in large part because it concealed itself behind the much more stridently argued states' rights/national government split. That division was certainly a real one, based partly on slavery but primarily on a profoundly parochial spirit that was closely if not directly related to the Secular-Democratic Consciousness. The old consciousness, acutely aware of being part of, or, as we have said, the culmination of, a world-historical process, was cosmopolitan and universalistic; the new consciousness was inherently provincial, witness Jefferson's hostility toward immigration and his desire to keep America uncontaminated by European influences.

It is not our purpose to argue that one was right and one was wrong but only to describe the way in which they combined to determine our history as a nation. The conflict between them (still unresolved), while it gives us a notion of the breathtakingly narrow margin by which we achieved a Constitution at all (and thereby a nation), also imparts to our history much of its inherent drama.

Put another way, throughout our subsequent history we could indulge our democratic fantasies to the utmost because the Constitution was always there, like a stern but benign parent, to restrain our excesses, which, after all, is precisely what the Founders intended it should do.

The next important case involving interpretation of the Constitution to come before the Court was the case of *Fletcher v. Peck.* In 1795, the Georgia legislature had sold 35,000,000 acres of land to four land companies at a cent and a half an acre. The whole deal was clouded by fraud and corruption, and the following year a new legislature repealed the contract. Fifteen years later the case was brought before the Court on the grounds that the subsequent legislature had no right to impair the original contract. The Court, in an opinion written and delivered by Marshall, supported the plaintiff on the grounds that the act of the Georgia legislature in repealing the original contract was unconstitutional.

The lands in controversy vested absolutely in James Gunn and others, the original grantees, by the conveyance of the governor, made in pursuance of an act of assembly to which the legislature was fully competent. Being thus in full possession of the legal estate, they, for a valuable consideration, conveyed portions of the land to those who were willing to purchase. If the original transaction was infected with fraud, these purchasers did not participate in it, and had no notice of it. They were innocent. Yet the legislature of Georgia has involved them in the fate of the first parties to the transaction, and, if the act be valid, has annihilated their rights also.

The legislature of Georgia was a party to this transaction; and for a party to pronounce its own deed invalid, whatever cause may be assigned for its invalidity, must be considered as a mere act of power which must find its vindication in a train of reasoning not often heard in courts of justice.

But the real party, it is said, are the people, and when their agents are unfaithful the acts of those agents cease to be obligatory.

It is, however, to be recollected that the people can act only by these agents, and that, while within the powers conferred on them, their acts must be considered as the acts of the people. If the agents be corrupt, others may be chosen, and, if their contracts be examinable, the common sentiment, as well as the common usage of mankind, points out a mode by which this examination may be made, and their validity determined.

If the legislature of Georgia was not bound to submit its pretentions to those tribunals which are established for the security of property, and to decide on human rights, if it might claim to itself the power of judging in its own case, yet there are certain great principles of justice, whose authority is universally acknowledged, that ought not to be entirely disregarded.

If the legislature be its own judge in its own case, it would seem equitable that its decision would be regulated by those rules which would have regulated the decision of a judicial tribunal. The question was, in its nature, a question of title, and the tribunal which decided it was either acting in the character of a court of justice, and performing a duty usually assigned to a court, or it was exerting a mere act of power in which it was controlled only by its own will.

If a suit be brought to set aside a conveyance obtained by fraud, and the fraud be clearly proved, the conveyance will be set aside, as between the parties; but the rights of third persons, who are purchasers without notice, for a valuable consideration, cannot be disregarded. Titles which, according to every legal test, are perfect, are acquired with that confidence which is inspired by the opinion that the purchaser is safe. If there be any concealed defect, arising from the conduct of those who had held the property long before he acquired it, of which he had no notice, that concealed defect cannot be set up against him. He has paid his money for a title good at law, he is innocent, whatever may be the guilt of others, and equity will not subject him to the penalties attached to that guilt. All titles would be insecure, and the intercourse between man and man would be very seriously obstructed, if this principle be overturned. . . .

If the legislature felt itself absolved from those rules of property which are common to all the citizens of the United States, and from those principles of equity which are acknowledged in all our courts, its act is to be supported by its power alone, and the same power may devest any other individual of his lands, if it shall be the will of the legislature so to exert it. . . .

The principle asserted is, that one legislature is competent to repeal any act which a former legislature was competent to pass; and that one legislature cannot abridge the powers of a succeeding legislature.

The correctness of this principle, so far as respects general legislation, can never be controverted. But, if an act be done under a law, a succeeding legislature cannot undo it. The past cannot be recalled by the most absolute power. Conveyances have been made; those conveyances have vested legal estates, and, if those estates may be seized by the sovereign authority, still, that they originally vested is a fact, and cannot cease to be a fact.

When, then, a law is in its nature a contract, when absolute rights have vested under that contract; a repeal of the law cannot devest those rights; and the act of annulling them, if legitimate, is rendered so by a power applicable to the case of every individual in the community.

It may well be doubted whether the nature of society and of government does not prescribe some limits to the legislative power; and, if any be prescribed, where are they to be found, if the property of an individual, fairly and honestly acquired, may be seized without compensation?

To the legislature all legislative power is granted; but the question, whether the act of transferring the property of an individual to the public, be in the nature of the legislative power, is well worthy of serious reflection.

It is the peculiar province of the legislature to prescribe general rules for the government of society; the application of those rules to individuals in society would seem to be the duty of other departments. How far the power of giving the law may involve every other power, in cases where the constitution is silent, never has been, and perhaps never can be, definitely stated.

The validity of this rescinding act, then, might well be doubted, were Georgia a single sovereign power. But Georgia cannot be viewed as a single, unconnected, sovereign power, on whose legislature no other restrictions are imposed than may be found in its own constitution. She is a part of a large empire; she is a member of the American Union; and that Union has a constitution the supremacy of which all acknowledge, and which imposes limits to the legislatures of the several states, which none claim a right to pass. The constitution of the United States declares that no state shall pass any bill of attainder, ex post facto law or law impairing the obligation of contracts.

Does the case now under consideration come within this prohibitory section of the constitution?

In considering this very interesting question, we immediately ask ourselves what is a contract? Is a grant a contract?

A contract is a compact between two or more parties, and is either executory or executed. An executory contract is one in which a party binds himself to do, or not to do, a particular thing; such was the law under which the conveyance was made by the governor. A contract executed is one in which the object of contract is performed; and this, says Blackstone, differs in nothing from a grant. The contract between Georgia and the purchasers was executed by the grant. A contract executed, as well as one which is executory, contains obligations binding on the parties. A grant, in its own nature, amounts to an extinguishment of the right of the grantor, and implies a contract not to re-assert that right. A party is, therefore, always estopped by his own grant.

Since, then, in fact, a grant is a contract executed, the obligation of which still continues, and since the constitution uses the general term contract, without distinguishing between those which are executory and those which are executed, it must be construed to comprehend the latter as well as the former. A law annulling conveyances between individuals, and declaring that the grantors should stand seized of their former estates, notwithstanding those grants, would be as repugnant to the constitution as a law discharging the vendors of property from the obligation of executing their contracts by conveyances. It would be strange if a contract to convey was secured by the constitution, while an absolute conveyance remained unprotected.

If, under a fair construction of the constitution, grants are comprehended under the term contracts, is a grant from the state excluded from the operation of the provision? Is the clause to be considered as inhibiting the state from impairing the obligation of contracts between two individuals, but as excluding from that inhibition contracts made with itself?

The words themselves contain no such distinction. They are general, and are applicable to contracts of every description. If contracts made with the state are to be exempted from their operation, the exception must arise from the character of the contracting party, not from the words which are employed.

Whatever respect might have been felt for the state sovereignties, it is not to be disguised that the framers of the constitution viewed, with some apprehension, the violent acts which might [have] grown out of the feelings of the moment; and that the people of the United States, in adopting that instrument, have manifested a determination to shield themselves and their property from the effects of those sudden and strong passions to which men are exposed. The restrictions on the legislative power of the states are obviously founded in this sentiment; and the constitution of the United States contains what may be deemed a bill of rights for the people of each state.

No state shall pass any bill of attainder, ex post factor law, or law impairing the obligation of contracts.

A bill of attainder may affect the life of an individual, or may confiscate his property, or may do both.

In this form the power of the legislature over the lives and fortunes of individuals is expressly restrained. What motive, then, for implying, in words which import a general prohibition to impair the obligation of contracts, an exception in favor of the right to impair the obligation of those contracts into which the state may enter?

The state legislatures can pass no ex post facto law. An ex post facto law is one which renders an act punishable in a manner in which it was not punishable when it was committed. Such a law may inflict penalties on the person, or may inflict pecuniary penalties which swell the public treasury. The legislature is then prohibited from passing a law by which a man's estate, or any part of it, shall be seized for a crime which was not declared, by some previous law, to render him liable to that punishment. Why, then, should violence be done to the natural meaning of words for the purpose of leaving to the legislature the power of seizing, for public use, the estate of an individual in the form of a law annulling the title by which he holds that estate? The court can perceive no sufficient grounds for making this distinction. This rescinding act would have the effect of an ex post facto law. It forfeits the estate of Fletcher for a crime not committed by himself, but by those from whom he purchased. This cannot be effected in the form of an ex post facto law, or bill of attainder; why, then, is it allowable in the form of a law annulling the original grant?

The argument in favor of presuming an intention to except a case, not excepted by the words of the constitution, is susceptible of some illustration from a principle originally ingrafted in that instrument, though no longer a part of it. The constitution, as passed, gave the courts of the United States jurisdiction in suits brought against individual states. A state, then, which violated its own contract was suable in the courts of the United States for that violation. Would it have been a defense in such a suit to say that a state had passed a law absolving itself from the contract? It is scarcely to be conceived that such a defense could be set up. And yet, if a state is neither restrained by the general principles of our political institutions, nor by the words of the constitution, from impairing the obligation of its own contracts, such a defense would be a valid one. This feature is no longer found in the constitution; but it aids in the construction of those clauses with which it was originally associated.

It is, then, the unanimous opinion of the court, that, in this case, the estate having passed into the hands of a purchaser for a valuable consideration, without notice, the state of Georgia was restrained, either by general principles, which are common to our free institutions, or by the particular provisions of the constitution of the United States, from passing a law whereby the estate of the plaintiff in the premises so purchased could be constitutionally and legally impaired and rendered null and void. . . .

While Georgians were furious at "this monstrous and abhorrent doctrine," the decision was accepted elsewhere with comparative equanimity.

The most notable addition to the Court during Madison's two administrations was Joseph Story, the young Massachusetts lawyer whom we have already encountered arguing before Judge Davis in support of the constitutionality of the Embargo Act. Although Story was a Republican and elected to Congress as such, he was also a New Englander and he irritated Jefferson by trying in the House to have the Embargo Act repealed. Story, disliked by Jefferson and viewed by Massachusetts Federalists as an enemy, was only thirty-two when he was appointed to the Court. He was a decided dark horse—the office was offered to three others before Madison, to everyone's surprise, nominated the young Massachusetts congressman. Story's appointment satisfied no one, but he proved to be one of the most outstanding justices in the history of the Court and a strong supporter of Marshall's nationalism.

In 1816, Virginia, in the case of *Martin v. Hunter's Lessee* challenged the right of the Supreme Court to receive cases on writs of error to the state courts; in other words, whether the Court could review a state court decision on the grounds that the state court might have been incorrect in its decision. What was at issue was a particular clause in the Judiciary Act of 1789 which gave such a right to the Court. Over a period of twenty-five years, the Court had taken jurisdiction of writs of error in sixteen cases without strong objection from the states. The Virginia case was the first direct challenge to this authority. The case had to do with English land claims dating back to the pre-Revolutionary period. Much land and much money was at stake and the case aroused intense feeling in Virginia. Since Marshall had been earlier involved in the case, he abstained and Judge Story gave the opinion of the Court, his first important opinion and a crucial one in the development of constitutional law.

Story, J., delivered the opinion of the court:
This is a writ of error from the Court of Appeals of Virginia, founded upon the refusal of that court to obey the mandate of this court, requiring the judgment rendered in this very cause, at February term, 1813, to be carried into due execution. The following is the judgment of the Court

of Appeals rendered on the mandate: "The court is unanimously of opinion that the appellate power of the Supreme Court of the United States does not extend to this court, under a sound construction of the constitution of the United States; that so much of the 25th section of the act of Congress to establish the judicial courts of the United States, as extends the appellate jurisdiction of the Supreme Court to this court, is not in pursuance of the constitution of the United States; that the writ of error, in this cause, was improvidently allowed under the authority of that act; that the proceedings thereon in the Supreme Court were, coram non judice, in relation to this court, and that obedience to its mandate be declined by the court."

The questions involved in this judgment are of great importance and delicacy. Perhaps it is not too much to affirm that, upon their right decision, rest some of the most solid principles which have hitherto been supposed to sustain and protect the constitution itself. The great respectability, too, of the court whose decisions we are called upon to review, and the entire deference which we entertain for the learning and ability of that court, add much to the difficulty of the task which has so unwelcomely fallen upon us. It is, however, a source of consolation that we have had the assistance of most able and learned arguments to aid our inquiries; and that the opinion which is now to be pronounced has been weighed with every solicitude to come to a correct result, and matured after solemn deliberation.

Before proceeding to the principal questions, it may not be unfit to dispose of some preliminary considerations which have grown out of the arguments at the bar.

The constitution of the United States was ordained and established, not by the states in their sovereign capacities, but emphatically, as the preamble of the constitution declares, by "the people of the United States." There can be no doubt that it was competent to the people to invest the general government with all the powers which they might deem proper and necessary; to extend or restrain these powers according to their own good pleasure, and to give them a paramount and supreme authority. As little doubt can there be that the people had a right to prohibit to the states the exercise of any powers which were, in their judgment, incompatible with the objects of the general compact; to make the powers of the state governments, in given cases, subordinate to those of the nation, or to reserve to themselves those sovereign authorities which they might not choose to delegate to either. The constitution was not, therefore, necessarily carved out of existing state sovereignties, nor a surrender of powers already existing in state institutions, for the powers of the states depend upon their own constitutions; and the people of every state had the right to modify and restrain them, according to their own views of policy or principle. On the other hand, it is perfectly clear that the sovereign powers vested in the state governments, by their respective constitutions, remained unaltered and unimpaired, except so far as they were granted to the government of the United States.

These deductions do not rest upon general reasoning, plain and obvious as they seem to be. They have been positively recognized by one of the articles in amendment of the constitution, which declares, that "the powers not delegated to the United States by the constitution, nor prohibited by it to the states, are reserved to the states respectively, or to the people."

The government, then, of the United States, can claim no powers which are not granted to it by the constitution, and the powers actually granted, must be such as are expressly given, or given by necessary implication. On the other hand, this instrument, like every other grant, is to have a reasonable construction, according to the import of its terms; and where a power is expressly given in general terms, it is not to be restrained to particular cases, unless that construction grow out of the context expressly, or by necessary implication. The words are to be taken in their natural and obvious sense, and not in a sense unreasonably restricted or enlarged.

The constitution unavoidably deals in general language. It did not suit the purposes of the people, in framing this great charter of our liberties, to provide for minute specifications of its powers, or to declare the means by which those powers should be carried into execution. It was foreseen that this would be a perilous and difficult, if not an impracticable, task. The instrument was not intended to provide merely for the exigencies of a few years, but was to endure through a long lapse of ages, the events of which were locked up in the inscrutable purposes of Providence. It could not be foreseen what new changes and modifications of power might be indispensable to effectuate the general objects of the charter; and restrictions and specifications which, at the present, might seem salutary, might, in the end, prove the overthrow of the system itself. Hence its powers are expressed in general terms, leaving to the legislature, from time to time, to adopt its own means to effectuate legitimate objects, and to mold and model the exercise of its powers, as its own wisdom and the public interests should require.

With these principles in view—principles in respect to which no difference of opinion ought to be indulged—let us now proceed to the interpretation of the constitution, so far as regards the great points in controversy.

The third article of the constitution is that which must principally attract our attention. The first section declares, "the judicial power of the United States shall be vested in one Supreme Court, and in such other inferior courts as the Congress may, from time to time, ordain and establish." The second section declares, that "the judicial power shall extend to all cases in law or equity, arising under this constitution, the laws of the United States, and the treaties made, or which shall be made, under their authority; to all cases affecting ambassadors, other public ministers and consuls; to all cases of admiralty and maritime jurisdiction; to controversies to which the United States shall be a party; to controversies between two or more states; between a state and citizens of another state; between citizens of different states; between citizens of the same state, claiming lands under the grants of different states; and between a state or the citizens thereof, and foreign states, citizens, or subjects." It then proceeds to declare, that "in all cases affecting ambassadors, other public ministers and consuls, and those in which a state shall be a party, the Supreme Court shall have original jurisdiction. In all the other cases before mentioned the Supreme Court shall have appellate jurisdiction, both as to law and fact, with such exceptions, and under such regulations, as the Congress shall make."

Such is the language of the article creating and defining the judicial power of the United States. It is the voice of the whole American people solemnly declared, in establishing one great department of that government which was, in many respects, national, and in all, supreme. It is a part of the very same instrument which was to act not merely upon individuals, but upon states; and to deprive them altogether of the exercise of some powers of sovereignty, and to restrain and regulate them in the exercise of others.

Let this article be carefully weighed and considered. The language of the article throughout is manifestly designed to be mandatory upon the legislature. Its obligatory force is so imperative that Congress could not, without a violation of its duty, have refused to carry it into operation. The judicial power of the United States shall be vested (not may be vested) in one supreme court, and in such inferior courts as Congress may, from time to time, ordain and establish. Could Congress have lawfully refused to create a supreme court, or to vest it in the constitutional jurisdiction? "The judges, both of the supreme and inferior courts, shall hold their offices during good behavior, and shall, at stated times, receive, for their services, a compensation which shall not be diminished during their continuance in office." Could Congress create or limit any other tenure of the judicial office? Could they refuse to pay, at stated times, the stipulated salary, or diminish it during the continuance in office? But one answer can be given to these questions: it must be in the negative. The object of the constitution was to establish three great departments of government; the legislative, the executive and the judicial departments. The first was to pass laws, the second to approve and execute them, and the third to expound and enforce them. Without the latter it would be impossible to carry into effect some of the express provisions of the constitution. How, otherwise, could crimes against the United States be tried and punished? How could causes between two states be heard and determined? The judicial power must, therefore, be vested in some court, by Congress; and to suppose that it was not an obligation binding on them, but might, at their pleasure, be omitted or declined, is to suppose that, under the sanction of the constitution they might defeat the constitution itself; a construction which would lead to such a result cannot be sound. . . .

There is an additional consideration, which is entitled to great weight. The constitution of the United States was designed for the common and equal benefit of all the people of the United States. The judicial power was granted for the same benign and salutary purposes. It was not to be exercised exclusively for the benefit of parties who might be plaintiffs, and would elect the national forum, but also for the protection of defendants who might be entitled to try their rights, or assert their privileges, before the same forum. Yet, if the construction contended for be correct, it will follow, that as the plaintiff may always elect the state court, the defendant, may be deprived of all the security which the constitution intended in aid of his rights. Such a state of things can in no respect be considered as giving equal rights. To obviate this difficulty, we are referred to the power which it is admitted Congress possess to remove suits from state courts to the national courts; and this forms the second ground upon which the argument we are considering has been attempted to be sustained.

This power of removal is not to be found in express terms in any part of the constitution; if it be given, it is only given by implication, as a power necessary and proper to carry into effect some express power. The power of removal is certainly not, in strictness of language an exercise of original jurisdiction; it presupposes an exercise of original jurisdiction to have attached elsewhere. The existence of this power of removal is familiar in courts acting according to the course of the common law in criminal as well as civil cases, and it is exercised before as well as after judgment. But this is always deemed in both cases an exercise of appellate, and not of original jurisdiction. If, then, the right of removal be included in the appellate jurisdiction, it is only because it is one mode of exercising that power, and as Congress is not limited by the constitution to any particular mode, or time of exercising it, it may authorize a removal either before or after judgment. The time, the process, and the manner, must be subject to its absolute legislative control. A writ of error is, indeed, but a process which removes the record of one court to the possession of another court, and enables the latter to inspect the proceedings, and give such judgment as its own opinion of the law and justice of the case may warrant. There is nothing in the nature of the process which forbids it from being applied by the legislature, to interlocutory as well as final judgments. And if the right of removal from state courts exist before judgment, because it is included in the appellate power, it must, for the same reason, exist after judgment. And if the appellate power by the constitution does not include cases pending in state courts, the right of removal, which is but a mode of exercising that power, cannot be applied to them. Precisely the same objections, therefore, exist as to the right of removal before judgment, as after, and both must stand or fall together. Nor, indeed, would the force of the arguments on either side materially vary if the right of removal were an exercise of original jurisdiction. It would equally trench upon the jurisdiction and independence of state tribunals.

The remedy, too, of removal of suits would be utterly inadequate to the purposes of the constitution, if it could act only on the parties, and not upon the state courts. In respect to criminal prosecutions, the difficulty seems admitted to be insurmountable; and in respect to civil suits, there would, in many cases, be rights without corresponding remedies. If state courts should deny the constitutionality of the authority to remove suits from their cognizance, in what manner could they be compelled to relinquish the jurisdiction? . . .

On the whole, the court are of opinion that the appellate power of the United States does extend to cases pending in the state courts; and that the 25th section of the judiciary act, which authorizes the exercise of this jurisdiction in the specified cases, by a writ of error, is supported by the letter and spirit of the constitution. We find no clause in that instrument which limits this power; and we dare not interpose a limitation where the people have not been disposed to create one. . . .

The next question which has been argued is, whether the case at bar be within the purview of the 25th section of the judiciary act, so that this court may rightfully sustain the present writ of error. This section, stripped of passages unimportant in this inquiry, enacts, in substance, that a final judgment or decree in any suit in the highest court of law or equity of a state, where is drawn in question the validity of a treaty or statute of, or an authority exercised under, the United States, and the decision is against their validity; or where is drawn in question the validity of a statute of, or an authority exercised under, any state, on the ground of their being repugnant to the constitution, treaties, or laws, of the United States, and the decision is in favor of such their validity; or of the constitution, or of a treaty or statute of, or commission held under, the United States, and the decision is against the title, right, privilege, or exemption, specially set up or claimed by either party under such clause of the said constitution, treaty, statute, or commission, may be re-examined and reversed or affirmed in the Supreme Court of the United States, upon a writ of error, in the same manner, and under the same regulations, and the writ shall have the same effect, as if the judgment or decree complained of had been rendered or passed in a circuit court, and the proceeding upon the reversal shall also be the same, except that the Supreme Court, instead of remanding the cause for a final decision, as before provided, may, at their discretion, if the cause shall have been once remanded before, proceed to a final decision of the same, and award execution. But no other error shall be assigned or regarded as a ground of reversal in any such case as aforesaid, than such as appears upon the face of the record, and immediately respects the before-mentioned question of validity or construction of the said constitution, treaties, statutes, commissions, or authorities in dispute.

That the present writ of error is founded upon a judgment of the court below, which drew in question and denied the validity of a statute of the United States, is incontrovertible, for it is apparent upon the face of the record. That this judgment is final upon the rights of the parties is equally true; for if well founded, the former judgment of that court was of conclusive authority, and the former judgment of this court utterly void. The decision was, therefore, equivalent to a perpetual stay of proceedings upon the mandate, and a perpetual denial of all the rights acquired under it. The case, then, falls directly within the terms of the act. It is a final judgment in a suit in a state court, denying the validity of a statute of the United States; and unless a distinction can be made between proceedings under a mandate, and proceedings in an original suit, a writ of error is the proper remedy to revise that judgment. In our opinion no legal distinction exists between the cases.

In causes remanded to the circuit courts, if the mandate be not correctly executed, a writ of error or appeal has always been supposed to be a proper remedy, and has been recognized as such in the former decisions of this court. The statute gives the same effect to writs of error from the judgments of state courts as of the circuit courts; and in its terms provides for proceeding where the same cause may be a second time brought up on writ of error before the Supreme Court. There is no limitation or description of the cases to which the second writ of error may be applied; and it ought, therefore, to be co-extensive with the cases which fall within the mischiefs of the statute. It will hardly be denied that this cause stands in that predicament; and if so, then the appellate jurisdiction of this court has rightfully attached.

But it is contended that the former judgment of this court was rendered upon a case not within the purview of this section of the judicial act, and that as it was pronounced by an incompetent jurisdiction, it was utterly void, and cannot be a sufficient foundation to sustain any subsequent proceedings. To this argument several answers may be given. In the first place, it is not admitted that, upon this writ of error, the former record is before us. The error now assigned is not in the former proceedings, but in the judgment rendered upon the mandate issued after the former judgment. The question now litigated is not upon the construction of a treaty, but upon the constitutionality of a statute of the United States, which is clearly within our jurisdiction. In the next place, in ordinary cases a second writ of error has never been supposed to draw in question the propriety of the first judgment, and it is difficult to perceive how such a proceeding could be sustained upon principle. A final judgment of this court is supposed to be conclusive upon the rights which it decides, and no statute has provided any process by which this court can revise its own judgments. In several cases which have been formerly adjudged in this court, the same point was argued by counsel, and expressly overruled. It was solemnly held that a final judgment of this court was conclusive upon the parties, and could not be re-examined. . . .

We have thus gone over all the principal questions in the cause, and we deliver our judgment with entire confidence, that it is consistent with the constitution and laws of the land.

We have not thought it incumbent on us to give any opinion upon the question, whether this court have authority to issue a writ of mandamus to the Court of Appeals to enforce the former judgments, as we do not think it necessarily involved in the decision of this cause.

It is the opinion of the whole court that the judgment of the Court of Appeals of Virginia, rendered on the mandate in this cause, be reversed, and the judgment of the District Court, held at Winchester, be, and the same is hereby affirmed.

Although Jefferson was no longer president, he continued to direct the Republican campaign against Marshall and the Court, encouraging his successors, Madison and, after Madison, James Monroe, to appoint strong Republicans to any vacancies on the Court and then watching as most of those Republican stalwarts turned into Marshall nationalists. He reminded Madison in 1810 of "the rancorous hatred which Marshall bears to the Government of his country" and spoke of "the cunning and sophistry within which he is able to enshroud himself." "His twistifications of the law in the case of Marbury, in that of Burr and the late Yazoo case [*Fletcher v. Peck*], show how dexterously he can reconcile law to his personal biases." To Gallatin, his former Secretary of the Treasury, he wrote of Marshall's "inveteracy . . . and his mind of that gloomy malignity which will never let him forego the opportunity of satiating it on a victim."

Ten years later he wrote to the most steadfast of the Republican justices: "The great object of my fear is the Federal Judiciary. That body like gravity, ever acting, with noiseless foot, and unalarming advance, gaining ground step by step, and holding what it gains, is ingulphing insidiously the special [state] governments into the jaws of that which feeds them. . . ."

Early in the 1818 term of the Court it was presented with a case (*Dartmouth College v. Woodward*) that was to have consequences as far-reaching as any ever decided by that body. Dartmouth College was a small private institution in the state of New Hampshire which had been founded by Eleazar Wheelock with the assistance of Lord Dartmouth to help in the education of the Indians. Never notably successful with the Indians, it had nonetheless survived as a modest regional institution whose most famous graduate was Daniel Webster, then thirty-six years old. The state of New Hampshire undertook to alter the charter granted Dartmouth College to bring it more under the control of the state. The college, thereupon, brought suit to preserve its charter intact, and when the case was carried on appeal to the Supreme Court, Dartmouth prevailed upon its alumnus Daniel Webster to argue its case. The issue before the Court was whether the state law altering the charter of the college was "an impairment of the obligation of a contract under the terms of the constitution." There was little general interest in the case and Webster, who took the first day in his argument, observed that there was a "small and unsympathetic" audience.

A reporter for the *Columbian Sentinel* noted, "Our friend Webster never made a happier effort. To a most elaborate and lucid argument he united a dignified and pathetic peroration which charmed and melted his hearers." It charmed and melted future generations of Dartmouth students as well for in the course of it he referred to the New Hampshire institution in these words: "It is a small college but there are those who love it."

The justices had difficulty coming to agreement on the case and it was carried over to the next term when the Court convened for the first time in a "splendid room provided for it in the Capitol."

Marshall for the Court: . . .

This court can be insensible neither to the magnitude nor delicacy of this question. The validity of a legislative act is to be examined; and the opinion of the highest law tribunal of a state is to be revised: an opinion which carries with it intrinsic evidence of the diligence, of the ability, and the integrity, with which it was formed. On more than one occasion this court has expressed the cautious circumspection with which it approaches the consideration of such questions; and has declared that, in no doubtful case would it pronounce a legislative act to be contrary to the constitution. But the American people have said, in the constitution of the United States, that "no state shall pass any bill of attainder, ex post facto law, or law impairing the obligation of contracts." In the same instrument they have also said, "that the judicial power shall extend to all cases in law and equity arising under the constitution." On the judges of this court, then, is imposed the high and solemn duty of protecting, from even legislative violation, those contracts which the constitution of our country has placed beyond legislative control; and, however irksome the task may be, this is a duty from which we dare not shrink. . . .

It can require no argument to prove that the circumstances of this case constitute a contract. An application is made to the crown for a charter to incorporate a religious and literary institution. In the application, it is stated that large contributions have been made for the object, which will be conferred on the corporation as soon as it shall be created. The charter is granted, and on its faith the property is conveyed. Surely in this transaction every ingredient of a complete and legitimate contract is to be found.

The points for consideration are:

1. Is this contract protected by the constitution of the United States?

2. Is it impaired by the acts under which the defendant holds? . . .

The origin of the institution was, undoubtedly, the Indian charity-school, established by Dr. Wheelock, at his own expense. It was at his instance, and to enlarge this school, that contributions were solicited in England. The person soliciting these contributions was his agent; and the trustees, who received the money, were appointed by, and act under, his authority. It is not too much to say that the funds were obtained by him, in trust, to be applied by him to the purposes of his enlarged school. The charter of incorporation was granted at his instance. . . .

Doctor Wheelock, as the keeper of his charity-school, instructing the Indians in the art of reading, and in our holy religion; sustaining them at his own expense, and on the voluntary contributions of the charitable, could scarcely be considered as a public officer, exercising any portion of those duties which belong to government; nor could the legislature have supposed that his private funds, or those given by others, were subject to legislative management, because they were applied to the purposes of education. When, afterwards, his school was enlarged, and the liberal contributions made in England, and in America, enabled him to extend his cares to the education of the youth of his own country, no change was wrought in his own character, or in the nature of his duties. Had he employed assistant tutors with the funds contributed by others, or had the trustees in England established a school with Dr. Wheelock at its head, and paid salaries to him and his assistants, they would still have been private tutors; and the fact that they were employed in the education of youth could not have converted them into public officers, concerned in the administration of public duties, or have given the legislature a right to interfere in the management of the fund. The trustees, in whose care that fund was placed by the contributors, would have been permitted to execute their trust uncontrolled by legislative authority.

Whence, then, can be derived the idea that Dartmouth College has become a public institution, and its trustees public officers, exercising powers conferred by the public for public objects? Not from the source whence its funds were drawn; for its foundation is purely private and eleemosynary. Not from the application of those funds; for money may be given for education, and the persons receiving it do not, by being employed in the education of youth, become members of the civil government. Is it from the act of incorporation? Let this subject be considered.

A corporation is an artificial being, invisible, intangible, and existing only in contemplation of law. Being the mere creature of law, it possesses only those properties which the charter of its creation confers upon it, either expressly or as incidental to its very existence. These are such as are supposed best calculated to effect the object for which it was created. Among the most important are immortality, and, if the expression may be allowed, individuality; properties by which a perpetual succession of many persons are considered as the same, and may act as a single individual. They enable a corporation to manage its own affairs, and to hold property without the perplexing intricacies, the hazardous and endless necessity, of perpetual conveyances for the purpose of transmitting it from hand to hand. It is chiefly for the purpose of clothing bodies of men, in succession, with these qualities and capacities, that corporations were invented, and are in use. By these means, a perpetual succession of individuals are capable of acting for the promotion of the particular object, like one immortal being. But this being does not share in the civil government of the country, unless that be the purpose for which it was created. Its immortality no more confers on it political power, or a political character, than immortality would confer such power or character on a natural person. It is no more a state instrument than a natural person exercising the same powers would be. If, then, a natural person, employed by individuals in the education of youth, or for the government of a seminary in which youth is educated, would not become a public officer, or be considered as a member of the civil government, how is it that this artificial being, created by law, for the purpose of being employed by the same individuals for the same purposes, should become a part of the civil government of the country? Is it because its existence, its capacities, its powers, are given by law? Because the government has given it the power to take and to hold property in a particular form, and for particular purposes, has the government a consequent right substantially to change that form, or to vary the purposes to which the property is to be applied? This principle has never been asserted or recognized, and is supported by no authority. Can it derive aid from reason? . . .

The particular interests of New Hampshire never entered into the mind of the donors, never constituted a motive for their donation. The propagation of the Christian religion among the savages, and the dissemination of useful knowledge among the youth of the country, were the avowed and the sole objects of their contributions. In these, New Hampshire would participate; but nothing particular or exclusive was intended for her. Even the site of the college was selected, not for the sake of New Hampshire, but because it was "most subservient to the great ends in view," and because liberal donations of land were offered by the proprietors, on condition that the institution should be there established. The real advantages from the location of the college, are, perhaps, not less considerable to those on the west than to those on the east

side of Connecticut River. The clause which constitutes the incorporation, and expresses the objects for which it was made, declares those
objects to be the instruction of the Indians, "and also of English youth,
and any others." So that the objects of the contributors, and the incorporating act, were the same; the promotion of Christianity, and of education generally, not the interests of New Hampshire particularly. . . .

The opinion of the court, after mature deliberation, is, that this is a
contract, the obligation of which cannot be impaired without violating
the constitution of the United States. This opinion appears to us to be
equally supported by reason, and by the former decisions of this court.

2. We next proceed to the inquiry whether its obligation has been
impaired by those acts of the legislature of New Hampshire to which the
special verdict refers. . . .

It is too clear to require the support of argument, that all contracts,
and rights, respecting property, remained unchanged by the revolution.
The obligations, then, which were created by the charter to Dartmouth
College, were the same in the new that they had been in the old government. The power of the government was also the same. A repeal of this
charter at any time prior to the adoption of the present constitution of
the United States, would have been an extraordinary and unprecedented
act of power, but one which could have been contested only by the restrictions upon the legislature, to be found in the constitution of the state.
But the constitution of the United States has imposed this additional
limitation, that the legislature of a state shall pass no act "impairing the
obligation of contracts." . . .

The will of the state is substituted for the will of the donors, in every
essential operation of the college. This is not an immaterial change. The
founders of the college contracted, not merely for the perpetual application of the funds which they gave, to the objects for which those funds
were given; they contracted also to secure that application by the constitution of the corporation. They contracted for a system which should,
as far as human foresight can provide, retain forever the government of
the literary institution they had formed, in the hands of persons approved
by themselves. This system is totally changed. The charter of 1769
exists no longer. It is re-organized; and re-organized in such a manner
as to convert a literary institution, moulded according to the will of its
founders, and placed under the control of private literary men, into a
machine entirely subservient to the will of government. This may be for
the advantage of this college in particular, and may be for the advantage
of literature in general, but it is not according to the will of the donors,
and is subversive of that contract, on the faith of which their property
was given. . . .

It results from this opinion, that the acts of the legislature of New Hampshire, which are stated in the special verdict found in this cause, are repugnant to the constitution of the United States; and that the judgment on this special verdict ought to have been for the plaintiffs. The judgment of the State Court must therefore be reversed.

The *Boston Daily Advertiser* hailed the decision as "calculated to ensure permanency to those numerous valuable institutions, so honorable to [the good people of New England], against the fluctuations of party and the rude attacks of rash innovators."

The Supreme Court perhaps never decided a case that had greater effect on subsequent American history. Jefferson and the Republican governor of New Hampshire, William Plumer, were predictably outraged. To Jefferson it was another example of the aristocratic disposition of the Court to defend the interests of property as opposed to the interests of the people of the states expressed through their elected representatives. But there was, considering the importance that decision would acquire in time, little said of it in the public prints. By upholding the unviolability of a private corporate charter, the Court gave protection to business from "the fluctuating policy which has directed the public councils." It also placed corporations for many years to come beyond the reach of state regulative agencies with decidedly ambiguous results.

Prior to the Dartmouth College case few corporations had been chartered in the United States. The Bank of North America had been chartered in 1780 by the state of Pennsylvania. By 1800 only eight manufacturing corporations had been chartered in the entire United States, three of these in Massachusetts and two in New York. Indeed, there had been only 213 corporations chartered in all, most of these banks, bridges, canals, and turnpikes. One factor was undoubtedly the uncertainty about whether legislatures might undo the work of their predecessors.

In 1819, during the administration of James Monroe, last of the so-called Virginia dynasty, a case came before the Court which aroused the strongest popular emotions. The Bank of the United States had been chartered in 1791, at the beginning of the Federalist Era. It was owned and controlled by the remnants of the Federalist party and by English investors and was thus doubly obnoxious to

Republicans. The core of opposition to the bank was in the agricultural South and in the West. To these regions the bank was a symbol of northeastern control of the money market. The Bank of the United States was often in conflict with state banks and its conservative fiscal policies were diametrically opposed to the easy-money inclinations of the state banks. Thus when its charter expired in 1811 it was not renewed. However, the general financial disarray that followed the end of the War of 1812 created pressure to revive the bank, and it was incorporated again in 1816. When numerous state banks failed in the following years the blame was laid at the door of the Bank of the United States. John Adams shared Jefferson's suspicion of banks in general and especially of the Bank of the United States, and he and Jefferson debated the question of which posed the greater danger to the liberties of the people—banks or a standing army in time of peace.

The strategy of the states was to place huge taxes on branches of the Bank of the United States. By 1819 seven Southern and Western states had imposed such taxes. The bank, meanwhile, increased its own vulnerability by speculation, bad management, and illegal loans. In this atmosphere a case, *McCulloch v. Maryland*, was brought to the Maryland District Court challenging the constitutionality of state taxes imposed on the Bank of the United States. When the case was carried on appeal to the Supreme Court an all-star cast of lawyers appeared to argue the matter: William Pinckney, Daniel Webster, and William Wirt, the attorney general, for the bank, and Luther Martin, Joseph Hopkinson, and Walter Jones for Maryland. Because of the emotionally heated atmosphere, the course of the trial was more closely attended than any other that had come before the Court. The arguments pro and con lasted for nine days and every day the courtroom was packed with spectators.

Luther Martin concluded his argument by stating that he had one final authority which he felt should be conclusive. He then read from Marshall's speech in the Virginia Ratifying Convention assuring the delegates that the Supreme Court would never call a sovereign state before it. The sentences were like a long-delayed time bomb to Marshall. He remembered the argument, if not the words, and he knew that the words had been recorded and would someday be exhumed and quoted against him. Story noticed that as Martin finished reading, Marshall draw a deep breath, with a sigh. Later when Story asked the chief justice the reason for the sigh, Marshall replied, "Why, to tell you the truth, I was afraid I had said some foolish things in the debate; but it was not so bad as I expected."

Pinckney gave the main argument against the right of the states to tax a corporation chartered by Congress. He spoke for three days to an entranced audience. Story wrote a Salem friend: "I never, in my whole life, heard a greater speech; it was worth a journey from Salem to hear it; his elocution was excessively vehement, but his eloquence was overwhelming. His language, his style, his figures, his arguments were most brilliant and sparkling. He spoke like a great statesman and patriot, and a sound constitutional lawyer. All the cobwebs of sophistry and metaphysics about State rights and State sovereignty he brushed away with a mighty besom. We have had a crowded audience of ladies and gentlemen; the hall was full almost to suffocation."

Although Bushrod Washington, nephew of the general, and Marshall himself were the only two Federalists left on the Court by this time, the Republicans nonetheless expected a decision upholding the power of the national government over those of the states. Three days after the close of arguments, Marshall read the unanimous decision of the Court, maintaining the authority of Congress to charter the bank and declaring the state laws impeding its operation invalid.

Marshall, Ch. J., delivered the opinion of the court:

In the case now to be determined, the defendant, a sovereign state, denies the obligation of a law enacted by the legislature of the Union, and the plaintiff, on his part, contests the validity of an act which has been passed by the legislature of that state. The constitution of our country, in its most interesting and vital parts, is to be considered; the conflicting powers of the government of the Union and of its members, as marked in that constitution, are to be discussed; and an opinion given, which may essentially influence the great operations of the government. No tribunal can approach such a question without a deep sense of its importance, and of the awful responsibilty involved in its decision. But it must be decided peacefully, or remain a source of hostile legislation, perhaps of hostility of a still more serious nature; and if it is to be so decided, by this tribunal alone can the decision be made. On the Supreme Court of the United States has the constitution of our country devolved this important duty.

The first question made in the cause is, has Congress power to incorporate a bank? . . .

The power now contested was exercised by the first Congress elected under the present constitution. The bill for incorporating the bank of the United States did not steal upon an unsuspecting legislature, and pass unobserved. Its principle was completely understood, and was opposed with equal zeal and ability. After being resisted, first in the fair and open field of debate, and afterwards in the executive cabinet, with as much persevering talent as any measure has ever experienced, and being supported by arguments which convinced minds as pure and as intelligent as this country can boast, it became a law. The original act was permitted to expire; but a short experience of the embarrassments to which the refusal to revive it exposed the government, convinced those who were most prejudiced against the measure of its necessity and induced the passage of the present law. It would require no ordinary share of intrepidity to assert that a measure adopted under these circumstances was a bold and plain usurpation, to which the constitution give no countenance.

These observations belong to the cause; but they are not made under the impression that, were the question entirely new, the law would be found irreconcilable with the constitution.

In discussing this question, the counsel for the state of Maryland have deemed it of some importance, in the construction of the constitution, to consider that instrument not as emanating from the people, but as the act of sovereign and independent states. The powers of the general government, it has been said, are delegated by the states, who alone are truly sovereign; and must be exercised in subordination to the states, who alone possess supreme dominion. . . .

This government is acknowledged by all to be one of enumerated powers. The principle, that it can exercise only the powers granted to it, would seem too apparent to have required to be enforced by all those arguments which its enlightened friends, while it was depending before the people, found it necessary to urge, that principle is now universally admitted. But the question respecting the extent of the powers actually granted, is perpetually arising, and will probably continue to arise, as long as our system shall exist.

In discussing these questions, the conflicting powers of the general and state governments must be brought into view, and the supremacy of their respective laws, when they are in opposition, must be settled.

If any one proposition could command the universal assent of mankind, we might expect it would be this—that the government of the

Union, though limited in its powers, is supreme within its sphere of action. This would seem to result necessarily from its nature. It is the government of all; its powers are delegated by all; it represents all, and acts for all. Though any one state may be willing to control its operations, no state is willing to allow others to control them. The nation, on those subjects on which it can act, must necessarily bind its component parts. But this question is not left to mere reason; the people have, in express terms, decided it by saying, "this constitution, and the laws of the United States, which shall be made in pursuance thereof," "shall be the supreme law of the land," and by requiring that the members of the state legislatures, and the officers of the executive and judicial departments of the states shall take the oath of fidelity to it.

The government of the United States, then, though limited in its powers, is supreme; and its laws, when made in pursuance of the constitution, form the supreme law of the land, "anything in the constitution or laws of any state to the contrary notwithstanding." . . .

Although, among the enumerated powers of government, we do not find the word "bank" or "incorporation," we find the great powers to lay and collect taxes; to borrow money; to regulate commerce; to declare and conduct a war; and to raise and support armies and navies. The sword and the purse, all the external relations, and no inconsiderable portion of the industry of the nation, are entrusted to its government. It can never be pretended that these vast powers draw after them others of inferior importance, merely because they are inferior. Such an idea can never be advanced. But it may with great reason be contended, that a government, entrusted with such ample powers, on the due execution of which the happiness and prosperity of the nation so vitally depends, must also be entrusted with ample means for their execution. The power being given, it is the interest of the nation to facilitate its execution. It can never be their interest, and cannot be presumed to have been their intention, to clog and embarrass its execution by withholding the most appropriate means. Throughout this vast republic, from the St. Croix to the Gulf of Mexico, from the Atlantic to the Pacific, revenue is to be collected and expended, armies are to be marched and supported. The exigencies of the nation may require that the treasure raised in the north should be transported to the south, that raised in the east conveyed to the west, or that this order should be reversed. Is that construction of the constitution to be preferred which would render these operations difficult, hazardous, and expensive? Can we adopt that construction (unless the words imperiously require it) which would impute to the framers of that instrument, when granting these powers for the public good, the intention of impeding their exercise by withholding a choice of means? If, indeed, such be the mandate of the constitution, we have only to obey; but that instrument does not profess to enumerate the means by which the powers it confers may be executed; nor does it prohibit the creation of a corporation, if the existence of such a being be essential to the beneficial exercise of those powers. It is, then, the subject of fair inquiry, how far such means may be employed. It is not denied that the powers given to the government imply the ordinary means of execution. That, for example, of raising revenue, and applying it to national purposes, is admitted to imply the power of conveying money from place to place, as the exigencies of the nation may require, and of employing the usual means of conveyance. But it is denied that the government has its choice of means; or, that it may employ the most convenient means, if, to employ them, it be necessary to erect a corporation. . . .

But the constitution of the United States has not left the right of Congress to employ the necessary means for the execution of the powers conferred on the government to general reasoning. To its enumeration of powers is added that of making "all laws which shall be necessary and proper, for carrying into execution the foregoing powers, and all other powers vested by this constitution, in the government of the United States, or in any department thereof." . . .

But the argument on which most reliance is placed, is drawn from the peculiar language of this clause. Congress is not empowered by it to make all laws, which may have relation to the powers conferred on the government, but such only as may be "necessary and proper" for carrying them into execution. The word "necessary" is considered as controlling the whole sentence, and as limiting the right to pass laws for the execution of the granted powers, to such as are indispensable, and without which the power would be nugatory. That it excludes the choice of means, and leaves to Congress, in each case, that only which is most direct and simple. . . .

. . . The subject is the execution of those great powers on which the welfare of a nation essentially depends. It must have been the intention of those who gave these powers, to insure, as far as human prudence could insure, their beneficial execution. This could not be done by confiding the choice of means to such narrow limits as not to leave it in the power of Congress to adopt any which might be appropriate, and which were conducive to the end. This provision is made in a constitution intended to endure for ages to come, and, consequently, to be adapted to the various crises of human affairs. To have prescribed the means by which government should, in all future time, execute its powers, would have been to change, entirely, the character of the instrument, and give it the properties of a legal code. It would have been an unwise attempt to provide, by immutable rules, for exigencies which, if foreseen at all, must have been seen dimly, and which can be best provided for as they occur. To have declared that the best means shall not be used, but those alone without which the power given would be nugatory, would have been to deprive the legislature of the capacity to avail itself of experience, to exercise its reason, and to accommodate its legislation to circumstances. . . .

Take, for example, the power "to establish post-offices and post-roads." This power is executed by the single act of making the establishment. But, from this has been inferred the power and duty of carrying the mail along the post-road, from one post-office to another. And, from this implied power, has again been inferred the right to punish those who steal letters from the post-office, or rob the mail. It may be said, with some plausibility, that the right to carry the mail, and to punish those who rob it, is not indispensably necessary to the establishment of a post-office and post-road. This right is indeed essential to the beneficial exercise of the power, but not indispensably necessary to its existence. So, of the punishment of the crimes of stealing or falsifying a record or process of a court of the United States, or of perjury in such court. To punish these offenses is certainly conducive to the due administration of justice. But courts may exist, and may decide the causes brought before them, though such crimes escape punishment.

The baneful influence of this narrow construction on all the operations of the government, and the absolute impracticability of maintaining it without rendering the government incompetent to its great objects, might be illustrated by numerous examples drawn from the constitution, and from our laws. The good sense of the public has pronounced, without hesitation, that the power of punishment appertains to sovereignty, and may be exercised whenever the sovereign has a right to act, as incidental to his constitutional powers. It is a means for carrying into execution all sovereign powers, and may be used, although not indispensably necessary. It is a right incidental to the power, and conducive to its beneficial exercise. . . .

But the argument which most conclusively demonstrates the error of the construction contended for by the counsel for the state of Maryland, is founded on the intention of the convention, as manifested in the whole clause. To waste time and argument in proving that without it Congress might carry its powers into execution, would be not much less idle than to hold a lighted taper to the sun. As little can it be required to prove, that in the absence of this clause, Congress would have some choice of means. That it might employ those which, in its judgment, would most advantageously effect the object to be accomplished. That any means adapted to the end, any means which tended directly to the execution of the constitutional powers of the government, were in themselves constitutional. This clause, as construed by the state of Maryland, would abridge, and almost annihilate this useful and necessary right of the legislature to select its means. That this could not be intended, is, we should think, had it not been already controverted, too apparent for controversy. . . .

The result of the most careful and attentive consideration bestowed upon this clause is, that if it does not enlarge, it cannot be construed to restrain the powers of Congress, or to impair the right of the legislature to exercise its best judgment in the selection of measures to carry into execution the constitutional powers of the government. If no other motive for its insertion can be suggested, a sufficient one is found in the desire to remove all doubts respecting the right to legislate on that vast mass of incidental powers which must be involved in the constitution, if that instrument be not a splendid bauble.

We admit, as all must admit, that the powers of the government are limited, and that its limits are not to be transcended. But we think the sound construction of the constitution must allow to the national legislature that discretion, with respect to the means by which the powers it confers are to be carried into execution, which will enable that body to perform the high duties assigned to it, in the manner most beneficial to the people. Let the end be legitimate, let it be within the scope of the constitution, and all means which are appropriate, which are plainly adapted to that end, which are not prohibited, but consist with the letter and spirit of the constitution, are constitutional. . . .

After the most deliberate consideration, it is the unanimous and decided opinion of this court that the act to incorporate the bank of the United States is a law made in pursuance of the constitution, and is a part of the supreme law of the land.

The branches, proceeding from the same stock, and being conducive to the complete accomplishment of the object, are equally constitutional. It would have been unwise to locate them in the charter, and it would be unnecessarily inconvenient to employ the legislative power in making those subordinate arrangements. The great duties of the bank are prescribed; those duties require branches; and the bank itself may, we think, be safely trusted with the selection of places where those branches shall be fixed; reserving always to the government the right to require that a branch shall be located where it may be deemed necessary.

It being the opinion of the court that the act incorporating the bank is constitutional, and that the power of establishing a branch in the state of Maryland might be properly exercised by the bank itself, we proceed to inquire:

2. Whether the state of Maryland may, without violating the constitution, tax that branch?

That the power of taxation is one of vital importance; that it is retained by the states; that it is not abridged by the grant of a similar power to the government of the Union; that it is to be concurrently exercised by the two governments: are truths which have never been denied. But, such is the paramount character of the constitution that its capacity to withdraw any subject from the action of even this power, is admitted. The states are expressly forbidden to lay any duties on imports or exports, except what may be absolutely necessary for executing their inspection laws. If the obligation of this prohibition must be conceded—if it may restrain a state from the exercise of its taxing power on imports and exports—the same paramount character would seem to restrain, as it certainly may restrain, a state from such other exercise of this power, as is in its nature incompatible with, and repugnant to, the constitutional laws of the Union. A law, absolutely repugnant to another, as entirely repeals that other as if express terms of repeal were used.

On this ground the counsel for the bank place its claim to be exempted from the power of a state to tax its operations. There is no express provision for the case, but the claim has been sustained on a principle which so entirely pervades the constitution, is so intermixed with the materials which compose it, so interwoven with its web, so blended with its texture, as to be incapable of being separated from it without rendering it into shreds.

This great principle is, that the constitution and the laws made in pursuance thereof are supreme; that they control the constitution and laws of the respective states, and cannot be controlled by them. From this, which may be almost termed an axiom, other propositions are deduced as corollaries, on the truth or error of which, and on their application to this case the cause has been supposed to depend. These are, 1st. that a power to create implies a power to preserve. 2d. That a power to destroy, if wielded by a different hand, is hostile to, and incompatible with these powers to create and to preserve. 3d. That where this repugnancy exists, that authority which is supreme must control, not yield to that over which it is supreme.

These propositions as abstract truths, would, perhaps, never be controverted. Their application to this case, however, has been denied; and, both in maintaining the affirmative and the negative, a splendor of eloquence, and strength of argument seldom, if ever, surpassed have been displayed.

The power of Congress to create, and of course to continue, the bank, was the subject of the preceding part of this opinion; and is no longer to be considered as questionable.

That the power of taxing it by the states may be exercised so as to destroy it, is too obvious to be denied. But taxation is said to be an absolute power, which acknowledges no other limits than those expressly prescribed in the constitution, and like sovereign power of every other description, is trusted to the discretion of those who use it. But the very terms of this argument admit that the sovereignty of the state, in the article of taxation itself, is subordinate to, and may be controlled by the constitution of the United States. How far it has been controlled by that instrument must be a question of construction. In making this construction, no principle not declared can be admissible, which would defeat the legitimate operations of a supreme government. It is of the very essence of supremacy to remove all obstacles to its action within its own sphere, and so to modify every power vested in subordinate governments as to exempt its own operations from their own influence. This effect need not be stated in terms. It is so involved in the declaration of supremacy, so necessarily implied in it, that the expression of it could not make it more certain. We must, therefore, keep it in view while construing the constitution. . . .

The sovereignty of a state extends to everything which exists by its own authority, or is introduced by its permission; but does it extend to those means which are employed by Congress to carry into execution—powers conferred on that body by the people of the United States? We think it demonstrable that it does not. Those powers are not given by the people of a single state. They are given by the people of the United States, to a government whose laws, made in pursuance of the constitution, are declared to be supreme. Consequently, the people of a single state cannot confer a sovereignty which will extend over them. . . .

We find, then, on just theory, a total failure of this original right to tax the means employed by the government of the Union, for the execution of its powers. The right never existed, and the question whether it has been surrendered, cannot arise. . . .

If we apply the principle for which the state of Maryland contends, to the constitution generally, we shall find it capable of changing totally the character of that instrument. We shall find it capable of arresting all the measures of the government, and of prostrating it at the foot of the states. The American people have declared their constitution, and the laws made in pursuance thereof, to be supreme; but this principle would transfer the supremacy, in fact, to the states.

If the states may tax one instrument, employed by the government in the execution of its powers, they may tax any and every other instrument. They may tax the mail; they may tax the mint; they may tax patent-rights; they may tax the papers of the custom-house; they may tax judi-cial process; they may tax all the means employed by the government, to an excess which would defeat all the ends of government. This was not intended by the American people. This did not design to make their government dependent on the states. . . .

. . . The people of all the states have created the general govern-ment, and have conferred upon it the general power of taxation. The people of all the states, and the states themselves, are represented in Congress, and, by their representatives, exercise this power. When they tax the chartered institutions of the states, they tax their constituents; and these taxes must be uniform. But, when a state taxes the operations of the government of the United States, it acts upon institutions created, not by their own constituents, but by people over whom they claim no control. It acts upon the measures of a government created by others as well as themselves, for the benefit of others in common with them-selves. The difference is that which always exists, and always must exist, between the action of the whole on a part, and the action of a part on the whole—between the laws of a government declared to be supreme, and those of a government which, when in opposition to those laws, is not supreme. . . .

The court has bestowed on this subject its most deliberate considera-tion. The result is a conviction that the states have no power, by taxation or otherwise, to retard, impede, burden, or in any manner control the operations of the constitutional laws enacted by Congress to carry into execution the powers vested in the general government. This is, we think, the unavoidable consequence of that supremacy which the constitution has declared.

We are unanimously of opinion that the law passed by the legislature of Maryland, imposing a tax on the Bank of the United States, is uncon-stitutional and void.

This opinion does not deprive the states of any resources which they originally possessed. It does not extend to a tax paid by the real property of the bank, in common with the other real property within the state, nor to a tax imposed on the interest which the citizens of Maryland may hold in this institution, in common with other property of the same description throughout the state. But this is a tax on the operations of the bank, and is, consequently, a tax on the operation of an instrument employed by the government of the Union to carry its powers into execution. Such a tax must be unconstitutional.

Justice Story wrote of the decision: "It excites great interest, and in a political view is of the deepest consequence to the Nation. It goes to establish the Constitution upon its great original principles." And Daniel Webster wrote to Story that the decision was "universally praised. Indeed, I think it admirable. Great things have been done at this session." Given all that we know about the intentions of the framers and the previous decisions of the Court, Marshall's comments in the Virginia Ratifying Convention to the contrary notwithstanding, the Court's decision in *McCulloch v. Maryland* appears inevitable. What is perhaps most worthy of comment is that despite an unbroken record of such decisions stretching back over a period of thirty years, they continued to produce bitter political reactions and dire warnings that the Court was destroying the Constitution. The answer, of course, was to be found in the political not the constitutional realm. In the years since the inauguration of the new government a bedrock of opposition to a strong national government had developed. Under the banner of states' rights marched a legion of Southerners and Westerners who were simply opposed to the federal government and the document which gave it its power. And since they could not, or chose not to, attack the Constitution itself, they concentrated their fire on that aspect of it which was, in fact, most crucial to its existence. The Court never deviated, but, fueled by the slavery issue, the Southern and Western states never flagged in their assaults upon it. The effect was to focus public attention on the Court to a degree hard to imagine today. The Court became the perpetual expounder of the Constitution, its explicator, defender, promoter, a kind of college of constitutional knowledge in which the greatest legal minds of the day were the instructors. If the decisions of the Court had been more or less taken for granted and largely ignored, if its interpretation of the Constitution had been the commonly accepted one, the Constitution might have quickly become what it is for most Americans today: a vague and remote document, honored in theory but superficially known and poorly understood.

Although Kentucky was a center of states' rights sentiment, the *Kentucky Gazette* in the aftermath of *McCulloch v. Maryland* wrote rather revealingly: "The mighty arm of the Judiciary has interposed its high and almost sacred functions for the purpose of giving effect to a provision of the Federal Constitution by which Congress are authorized to carry into execution expressly delegated powers—to preserve the supremacy of the Union over State encroachments . . .'' and the *Western Monitor,* another Kentucky paper, wrote to much the same effect of "the strong, lucid, masterly" arguments, the "strength and fairness of reasoning which we have seldom if ever seen surpassed. . . . At all events—whatever opinions may be entertained—we trust we shall have no forcible resistance to the laws of the United States —no contemptuous violations of judicial decisions—no acts of hostility to the government of the Union."

This time the opposition came primarily from those who deplored the failure of the Court to declare the right of Congress to take such actions as chartering banks unconstitutional, and many Southern and Western papers renewed the now familiar charges that the Court was subverting the Constitution by creating a "grand, consolidated government." James Madison's criticism was directed primarily at Marshall's practice of going beyond the immediate matter of law to speculate on broader constitutional issues, such reflections always having, in Madison's opinion, the tendency to reinforce the powers of the central government.

Virginia was, typically, the center of the protests against the decision, the legislature of that state going so far as to propose establishing a new tribunal to decide matters involving conflicts over state and federal authority. The *Niles Weekly Register* in Baltimore denounced the decision as a "total prostration of the States-Rights and the loss of the liberties of the Nation. . . . The principles established . . . are far more dangerous to the Union and happiness of the people of the United States than anything else that we ever had to fear from foreign invasion."

To the *General Intelligencer* of Philadelphia must go the palm for the most intemperate attack on the Court following *McCulloch v. Maryland.* "Never," it trumpeted, "was a bad case worse supported by constellated talents, learning and wisdom. . . . It seems as if nature had revolted from 'the debasing task assigned them' and that their reason and their judgment had forsaken them, upon an instinctive horror and disgust for the destructive purposes they were pledged to fulfil, in defiance of all human rights, human joys, and divine commandments. I feel a pang of despair for my country, when I think of the tyrannical purpose for which they pronounced their false judgment upon this subject. . . ."

Ohio took more drastic action. Declaring the decision in *McCulloch v. Maryland* to be the result of collusion in the suit, Osborn, the state auditor, directed his assistant to collect the tax the state legislature had levied on the Ohio branch of the Bank of the United States. Armed with a tax warrant, the assistant, John Harper, entered the bank, carried away $120,475, and, ignoring a federal court injunction, delivered the money to the state treasurer in Columbus. There was widespread criticism of the act. Many of the most partisan Republican papers refused to condone the action of the state. A Georgia paper denounced it as manifesting "a disregard for the union and harmony of the States, and a contemptuous defiance of the supreme constitutional authorities of the Republic." The governor of Ohio declared that he viewed "the transaction in the most odious light, and from my very soul I detest it. I am ashamed it happened in Ohio."

A court order was obtained requiring the state treasurer to return the money he had appropriated and when he refused, he was cited for contempt and placed in prison. The court designated commissioners, who took the key from the treasurer, entered the state treasury and retrieved the money in question. The Ohio legislature in reply expressed its support of the Virginia and Kentucky Resolutions and passed a statute outlawing the Bank of the United States in Ohio. Beyond that, it prepared a kind of reprise of those resolutions declaring a whole series of federal powers unconstitutional, and circulated these to all other states, soliciting their support in defying all federal statutes judged by the states to infringe upon their rights. Copies were also forwarded to the Senate and the House. Only Virginia and Kentucky endorsed the Ohio resolutions. Elsewhere they were ignored. When the case of *Osborn v. Bank of the United States* was finally decided in 1824 little notice was taken of it.

The "democratic" hostility to the Court was exacerbated by the question of admission of new states to the Union. The legislators from states north of the Mason-Dixon Line were determined to prevent the spread of slavery into the new states of the West. If new states were allowed to come into the Union as slave states, the Northerners feared that such an augmentation of the slave states would mean a decisive shift in power to the states of the South and West and with it the extension of slavery until the free states were an isolated minority. Since they held a narrow majority in Congress they insisted on the authority of Congress under the Constitution to prohibit slavery in states seeking admission to the Union. This enraged many Southerners. In their view it was the ultimate mark of federal despotism, a tyrannical exercise of unconstitutional and therefore arbitrary power. It turned out that there was to be no peaceable resolution of this issue. By 1820 the territory of Missouri, settled primarily by Southerners, many of them slaveholders, was seeking admission to the Union. There was in the Senate an equal division of slave and free states—eleven of each. To admit Missouri would swing the balance in the Senate to the proslavery side. This the Northern states would not accept. To resolve the impasse, Henry Clay came up with his famous Missouri Compromise. The northern portion of Massachusetts would be admitted as the twelfth free state of Maine, while Missouri would come in as the twelfth slave state and slavery in the Louisiana territory would be confined to a line south of 36 degrees, 30 minutes. The South consoled itself with the expectation that Florida and Arkansas would soon be admitted to the Union as slave states; the North with the fact that it had asserted the right of Congress under the Constitution to exclude slavery from the territories. Precarious as the compromise was—leaving nothing finally settled— it was to survive for another thirty years until it was undone by the Compromise of 1850 and, in 1854, the Kansas-Nebraska Act. John Quincy Adams called Clay's handiwork "a mere preamble—a title page to a great, tragic volume," and Jefferson denounced it as "a fire bell," sounding "the knell of the Union."

The best that can be said about the Missouri Compromise was that it delayed the Civil War for forty years and if, at the end of that time, slave and free states were no nearer a resolution of their conflict, the North at least had grown powerful enough economically, confident enough of its own strength, and sufficiently committed to the idea of union to fight to preserve it.

Meantime there was to be no peace and no reconciliation to the Court or to the Constitution as interpreted by the Court. All the springs of American life, political or social, were poisoned by conflict over slavery, indeed by the institution itself, by the revulsion against it on the part of the most liberal and enlightened sentiment in the North and the fierce defense of it by the South, a South which grew more bitter and paranoid with each passing decade.

The fact is that it is impossible to understand the continuing opposition to the Court as the consequence of a rational line of argument. The South was saddled with an institution which it could not rid itself of. Slavery, like a poisoned barb, worked its way deeper and deeper into the flesh of the South and the South, in its desperate efforts to halt the progress of that weapon in its vitals, grew wilder and more irrational until she raved like a patient in delirium.

XV

COMPLETING THE STRUCTURE

THE CASE OF *Cohens v. Virginia* CAME BEFORE THE COURT IN 1821. Cohens had been found guilty in a Virginia court of selling lottery tickets in the defiance of a state law prohibiting lotteries. The District of Columbia permitted lotteries and Cohens sued on the grounds that he was acting in accordance with a congressional statute. The issue, as it had been in the case of *Martin v. Hunter's Lessee*, was whether the Supreme Court could consider the case on a writ of error from the state court. Also at issue was the question of whether the Supreme Court had jurisdiction on a writ of error to a state court in a state criminal prosecution and whether Congress could authorize a lottery in a state whose laws forbade it. It was one of those cases that Marshall clearly relished, a case where a decision in favor of the state would substantially extend the powers of the Court.

The Virginia legislature had indiscreetly challenged the Court by passing a series of resolves denying that the Supreme Court had jurisdiction in the case (that, in the words of one of the resolves, it had "no rightful authority under the Constitution to examine and correct" the judgment of the state courts). The *Richmond Enquirer* strongly supported the Assembly's resolution, declaring the case to be "one of the most important questions in the whole range of the Judiciary Department. The principle which it asserts seems to be essential to the existence and preservation of States-Rights, and the true foundation of our political system."

Arguing before the Court, the counsel for Virginia, who was to become a justice of the Court, ended his argument opposing its jurisdiction by declaring, "Nothing can so much endanger [this government] as exciting the hostility of the State governments. With them it is, to determine how long this government shall endure."

William Pinckney, one of the great constitutional lawyers of his day, insisted that "this particular portion of the judicial power of the Union is indispensably necessary to the existence of the Union. The judicial control of the Union over State encroachments and usurpations was indispensable to the sovereignty of the Constitution—to its integrity—to its very existence. Take it away and the Union becomes a false foolish confidence—a delusion and a mockery!"

It might be said here that cases such as *Cohens v. Virginia* were in the nature of set pieces, legal dramas that held the attention of a wide audience. The most brilliant lawyers of the day contended in crowded courtrooms, and the arguments of the various counsels, as well as the decisions of the Court, were fully reported by newspapers in every state. Famous attorneys were admired rather as prominent athletes and entertainers are today and had their entourages who hung on their opinions and faithfully attended court when they pled a case. After the attorneys had completed their arguments in *Cohens v. Virginia,* Marshall delivered the opinion of the Court upholding—not surprisingly, considering the precedent of *Martin v. Hunter's Lessee,* the appellate authority of the Court in civil cases, and establishing the appellate authority of the Court in criminal cases.

Its jurisdiction asserted, the Court then proceeded to consider the actual verdict of the Virginia court. Since Virginia denied the jurisdiction of the Court, it refused to defend the verdict of the state court and Daniel Webster stepped forward in behalf of Virginia on the ground that he was already arguing a similar case in New York. Webster having been heard, the Court upheld the state court on the grounds that Congress had not intended to authorize the sale of lottery tickets in Virginia. No decision was rendered on whether, in fact, Congress had such powers.

The decision confirmed the *Richmond Enquirer*'s conviction that "The Judiciary power, with . . . a spirit as greedy as the grave, is sweeping to their destruction the rights of the States." The *Liberty Hall and Cincinnati Gazette* denounced the verdict as designed to destroy the federal principle in the Constitution and introduce "on their ruins a mightily consolidated empire fitted for the sceptre of a great monarch."

The next important constitutional case to come before the Court was in the 1824 term. Besides the issue of states' rights, the most controversial question of the day was that of "internal improvements." Should the building of turnpikes and canals be assisted with federal funds? The Constitution made no mention of such expenditures on the part of the national government, so the question revolved around the notion of implied powers. The broad constructionists argued that the phrase "necessary and proper" permitted the use of federal revenues for such purposes. The strict constructionists and states' righters denied it. In the case of *Gibbons v. Ogden* the Court for the first time dealt with the question of the power of the federal government over the internal commerce of the states. Like most other cases facing the Court, *Gibbons v. Ogden* had definite political overtones. The Livingston-Fulton steamboat company involved many of the most powerful Republicans in the state of New York. For almost twenty-five years the Livingstons and Fultons had enjoyed a monopoly on steamboat travel on the Hudson River and waters within the state under a charter from the New York state legislature. The monopoly was especially offensive to the states of Connecticut and New Jersey, whose waters were adjacent to or intermingled with those of New York. The legislatures of those states had passed laws forbidding any ships "operated by fire or steam" from traversing their waters. There had been exchanges of gunfire in some instances and threats of armed conflict between the contending states. An ex-governor of New Jersey, Aaron Ogden, himself the operator of a steamship line, brought a test suit. When the case reached the Supreme Court it enlisted, once again, a dazzling array of legal talent: Daniel Webster, William Wirt, former attorney general of the United States and one of the great lawyers of the day, and David Ogden, another luminary who had already appeared in a number of crucial cases before the Court.

A contemporary said of Wirt, "His presence is peculiarly imposing and all his manners graceful. His voice is powerful, his tones harmonious, and his enunciation clear and distinct. He never speaks without evincing ardor and feeling. . . . He delights and convinces, and no man hears him without understanding his arguments [which are] . . . constantly enlivened by classical allusions and flashes of wit. Many a dry cause, calculated to fatigue and weary, is thus rendered interesting to the spectator as well as the Court. . . ." Advising a friend to come and hear the steamship case argued, Wirt wrote: "Oakley [one of the attorneys for the monopoly] is said to be one of the first logicians of the age, as much a Phocion [the Great Athenian general and states-man] as Emmet [another of the monopoly lawyers] is a Themistocles, and Webster is as ambitious as Caesar. He will not be outdone by any man, if it is within the compass of his power to avoid it. It will be a combat worth witnessing."

The passage, with its classical references, is a revealing one. To the participants and to the spectators these were battles as dramatic and as resonant with history as the combat of Hector and Achilles at ancient Troy. Here the weapons were words instead of swords and vanquished warriors rose to fight another day, but Court and counsel still existed in the world of "history as oratory," which, as we have seen, gave such brilliant effect to the debates on the Constitution. The power of political speech, far from having diminished, seemed to rise on waves of more and more inspired eloquence.

In the beginning was the Word, politically as well as theologically. In this fashion was the country "spoken into existence." Other nations had risen out of custom and conquest, their origins often shrouded in myth. This one—the United States of America—took shape through the intoxicating power of inspired speech. Even if its elo-quence seems archaic or fails to move us today, we must make a conscious effort to enter imaginatively into that Ciceronian world of history as oratory—otherwise we can have no real insight into the intellectual and psychological origins of our nation.

In any event *Gibbons v. Ogden* presented the Court with a con-geries of constitutional issues. Was the New York legislature's grant of a monopoly in conflict with patents issued by Congress? Could it be said to involve commerce in any event? Was the right of Congress to regulate commerce a right that excluded state regulation? Webster was determined to argue the case on the broadest grounds: "the . . . novel question of the constitutional authority of Congress exclusively to regulate commerce in all its forms on all navigable waters of the United States . . . without any monopoly, restraint, or interference created by States' legislation."

On Wednesday, February 4, 1824, at eleven o'clock, the Court convened. Like a warrior preparing himself for battle, Webster had been up the entire night before. He had never had, on any occasion, he told his friend and biographer, George Ticknor Curtis, "so com-pletely the free use of his facilities. . . . At nine A.M., after eleven hours of continuous intellectual effort, his brief was completed. He sent for his barber and was shaved; he took a very slight breakfast of tea and crackers . . . he read the morning journals to amuse and change his thoughts, and then he went into Court and made that grand argument which, as Judge Wayne said about twenty years afterward, 'released every creek and river, every lake and harbor in our country from the interference of monopolies.' "

The room was "excessively crowded." Marshall, who still wrote with a quill, scorning that "barbarous invention" a steel pen, nibbed his quill with a pocket knife, and nodded to Webster to begin. Like a lover courting his mistress, Webster experienced an almost sensual satisfaction in performing before such a connoisseur. "I think I never experienced more intellectual pleasure," Webster wrote of the case, "than in arguing that novel question to a great man who could appreciate it, and take it in; and he did take it in, as a baby takes in its mother's milk."

Harriet Martineau, the English novelist, gave a vivid picture of Webster, noting, "It was amusing to see how the Court would fill after the entrance of Webster, and empty when he had gone back to the Senate Chamber. The chief interest to me in Webster's pleading, and also in his speaking in the Senate, was from seeing someone so dreamy and nonchalant, roused into strong excitement. Webster is a lover of ease and pleasure, and has an air of the most unaffected indolence and careless self-sufficiency. It is something to see him moved with anxiety, and the toil of intellectual conflict; to see his lips tremble, his nostrils expand, the perspiration start upon his brow, to hear his voice vary with emotion."

Justice Story described Webster's argument as amply demonstrating "his clearness and downright simplicity of statement, his vast comprehensiveness of topics, his fertility in illustrations drawn from practical sources; his keen analysis, and suggestion of difficulties; his power of disentangling a complicated proposition and resolving it in elements so plain as to reach the most common minds; his vigor in generalizations . . . his wariness and caution not to betray himself into untenable positions, or to spread his forces over useless ground. . . ."

Thomas Oakley, Wirt's Phocion, replied with one of "the most ingenious and able arguments ever made in this Court," one spectator noted, adding, "You can form no idea what interest this decision excites at Washington." The courtroom "was full to overflowing. So great," a reporter wrote, "was the assemblage of ladies that many of them were obliged to find seats within the bar." Many members of both houses of Congress were likewise in attendance.

Wirt concluded the case for the opponents of the monopoly and in the opinion of many eclipsed even Webster. The *Richmond Enquirer* called it "the finest effort of human genius ever exhibited in a Court of Justice . . . a powerful and splendid effusion, grand, tender, picturesque, and pathetic. The manner was lofty and touching; the fall of his voice towards the conclusion was truly thrilling and affecting, and I never witnessed such an effect from any burst of eloquence; every face was filled with the fine transport and prophetic fury of the oration, and all united in applauding the peroration, as affording for matter, diction, manner, happy application and striking effect the most powerful display of real oratory that they ever witnessed." All over a steamboat monopoly.

Anxious weeks passed while the judges considered their decision. Although Webster considered the outcome a foregone conclusion, others were not so certain since the Court now contained, as we have seen, only two strong Federalists, Marshall and Washington, the other members being considered, in one degree or another, states' rights advocates. That, at least, had been the basis on which they had been appointed to the Court by a succession of Republican presidents. But most had already shown a disconcerting tendency to turn into Federalists under the benign influence of Marshall. While all those interested awaited the Court's decision there was a delay due to an accident in which Marshall dislocated his shoulder. The task of completing the opinion was passed on to Story.

On March 2 the Court convened with Marshall present for the first time since his accident, obviously weak and in some pain. He read the Court's decision in a low voice, his listeners straining for every precious word. The decision was all that the advocates of a strong national government could have wished. Every point at dispute was resolved in favor of the supremacy of the federal government over the states. Webster was convinced that it was his brief that Marshall had principally relied on. Indeed, he declared that Marshall had told him so, not, Webster added, even mentioning Wirt, thus confirming Webster's judgment that Wirt, although "a great lawyer, and a great man" had missed the target or, in Webster's words "sometimes a man gets a kink and doesn't hit right."

Mr. Chief Justice Marshall delivered the opinion of the Court, and after stating the case, proceeded as follows:

The appellant contends that this decree is erroneous, because the laws which purport to give the exclusive privilege it sustains, are repugnant to the constitution and laws of the United States.

They are said to be repugnant:

1st. To that clause in the constitution which authorizes Congress to regulate commerce.

2nd. To that which authorizes Congress to promote the progress of science and useful arts.

The state of New York maintains the constitutionality of these laws; and their legislature, their Council of Revision, and their judges, have repeatedly concurred in this opinion. It is supported by great names—by names which have all the titles to consideration that virtue, intelligence, and office, can bestow. No tribunal can approach the decision of this question, without feeling a just and real respect for that opinion which is sustained by such authority; but it is the province of this Court, while it respects, not to bow to it implicitly; and the judges must exercise, in the examination of the subject, that understanding which Providence has bestowed upon them, with that independence which the people of the United States expect from this department of the government. . . .

This instrument contains an enumeration of powers expressly granted by the people to their government. It has been said that these powers ought to be construed strictly. But why ought they to be so construed? Is there one sentence in the constitution which gives countenance to this rule? In the last of the enumerated powers, that which grants, expressly, the means of carrying all others into execution, Congress is authorized "to make all laws which shall be necessary and proper" for the purpose. But this limitation on the means which may be used, is not extended to the powers which are conferred; nor is there one sentence in the constitution which has been pointed out by the gentlemen of the bar, or which we have been able to discern, that prescribes this rule. We do not, therefore, think ourselves justified in adopting it. What do gentlemen mean by a strict construction? If they contend only against that enlarged construction which would extend words beyond their natural and obvious import, we might question the application of the term, but should not controvert the principle. If they contend for that narrow construction which, in support of some theory not to be found in the constitution, would deny to the government those powers which the words of the grant, as usually understood, import, and which are consistent with the general views and objects of the instrument; for that narrow construction, which would cripple the government and render it unequal to the objects for which it is declared to be instituted, and to which the powers given, as fairly understood, render it competent; then we cannot perceive the propriety of this strict construction, nor adopt it as the rule by which the constitution is to be expounded. As men, whose intentions require no concealment, generally employ the words which most directly and aptly express the ideas they intend to convey, the enlightened patriots who framed our constitution, and the people who adopted it, must be understood to have employed words in their natural sense, and to have intended what they have said. . . .

The words are: "Congress shall have power to regulate commerce with foreign nations, and among the several states, and with the Indian tribes."

The subject to be regulated is commerce; and our constitution being, as was aptly said at the bar, one of enumeration, and not of definition, to ascertain the extent of the power it becomes necessary to settle the meaning of the word. The counsel for the appellee would limit it to traffic, to buying and selling, or the interchange of commodities, and do not admit that it comprehends navigation. This would restrict a general term, applicable to many objects, to one of its significations. Commerce, undoubtedly, is traffic, but it is something more; it is intercourse. It describes the commercial intercourse between nations, and parts of nations, in all its branches, and is regulated by prescribing rules for carrying on that intercourse. The mind can scarcely conceive a system for regulating commerce between nations, which shall exclude all laws concerning navigation, which shall be silent on the admission of the vessels of the one nation into the ports of the other, and be confined to prescribing rules for the conduct of individuals, in the actual employment of buying and selling, or of barter.

If commerce does not include navigation, the government of the Union has no direct power over that subject, and can make no law prescribing what shall constitute American vessels, or requiring that they shall be navigated by American seamen. Yet this power has been exercised from the commencement of the government, has been exercised with the consent of all, and has been understood by all to be a commercial regulation. All America understands, and has uniformly understood, the word "commerce" to comprehend navigation. It was so understood, and must have been so understood, when the constitution was framed. The power over commerce, including navigation, was one of the primary objects for which the people of America adopted their government, and must have been contemplated in forming it. The convention must have used the word in that sense; because all have understood it in that sense, and the attempt to restrict it comes too late. . . .

The word used in the constitution, then, comprehends, and has been always understood to comprehend, navigation within its meaning; and a power to regulate navigation is as expressly granted as if that term had been added to the word "commerce."

To what commerce does this power extend? The constitution informs us, to commerce "with foreign nations, and among the several states, and with the Indian tribes."

It has, we believe, been universally admitted that these words comprehend every species of commercial intercourse between the United States and foreign nations. No sort of trade can be carried on between this country and any other, to which this power does not extend. It has been truly said, that commerce, as the word is used in the constitution, is a unit, every part of which is indicated by the term.

If this be the admitted meaning of the word, in its application to foreign nations, it must carry the same meaning throughout the sentence, and remain a unit, unless there be some plain intelligible cause which alters it.

The subject to which the power is next applied, is to commerce "among the several states." The word "among" means intermingled with. A thing which is among others, is intermingled with them. Commerce among the states cannot stop at the external boundary line of each state, but may be introduced into the interior.

It is not intended to say that these words comprehend that commerce which is completely internal, which is carried on between man and man in a state, or between different parts of the same state, and which does not extend to or affect other states. Such a power would be inconvenient, and is certainly unnecessary.

Comprehensive as the word "among" is, it may very properly be restricted to that commerce which concerns more states than one. The phrase is not one which would probably have been selected to indicate the completely interior traffic of a state, because it is not an apt phrase for that purpose; and the enumeration of the particular classes of commerce to which the power was to be extended, would not have been made had the intention been to extend the power to every description. The enumeration presupposes something not enumerated; and that something, if we regard the language or the subject of the sentence, must be the exclusively internal commerce of a state. The genius and character of the whole government seems to be, that its action is to be applied to all the external concerns of the nation, and to those internal concerns which affect the states generally; but not to those which are completely within a particular state, which do not affect other states, and with which it is not necessary to interfere, for the purpose of executing some of the general powers of the government. The completely internal commerce of a state, then, may be considered as reserved for the state itself.

But, in regulating commerce with foreign nations, the power of Congress does not stop at the jurisdictional lines of the several states. It would be a very useless power if it could not pass those lines. The commerce of the United States with foreign nations, is that of the whole United States. Every district has a right to participate in it. The deep streams which penetrate our country in every direction, pass through the interior of almost every state in the Union, and furnish the means of exercising this right. If Congress has the power to regulate it, that power must be exercised whenever the subject exists. If it exists within the states, if a foreign voyage may commence or terminate at a port within a state, then the power of Congress may be exercised within a state.

This principle is, if possible, still more clear, when applied to commerce "among the several states." They either join each other, in which case they are separated by a mathematical line, or they are remote from each other, in which case other states lie between them. What is commerce "among" them; and how is it to be conducted? Can a trading expedition between two adjoining states commence and terminate outside of each? And if the trading intercourse be between two states remote from each other, must it not commence in one, terminate in the other, and probably pass through a third? Commerce among the states must, of necessity, be commerce with the states. In the regulation of trade with the Indian tribes, the action of the law, especially when the constitution was made, was chiefly within a state. The power of Congress, then, whatever it may be, must be exercised within the territorial jurisdiction of the several states. The sense of the nation, on this subject, is unequivocally manifested by the provisions made in the laws for transporting goods, by land, between Baltimore and Providence, between New York and Philadelphia, and between Philadelphia and Baltimore.

We are now arrived at the inquiry, What is this power?

It is the power to regulate; that is, to prescribe the rule by which commerce is to be governed. This power, like all others vested in Congress, is complete in itself, may be exercised to its utmost extent, and acknowledges no limitations, other than are prescribed in the constitution. These are expressed in plain terms, and do not affect the questions which arise in this case, or which have been discussed at the bar. If, as has always been understood, the sovereignty of Congress, though limited to specified objects, is plenary as to those objects, the power over commerce with foreign nations, and among the several States, is vested in Congress as absolutely as it would be in a single government, having in its constitution the same restrictions on the exercise of the power as are found in the constitution of the United States. The wisdom and the discretion of Congress, their identity with the people, and the influence which their constituents possess at election, are, in this, as in many other instances, as that, for example, of declaring war, the sole restraints on which they have relied, to secure them from its abuse. They are the restraints on which the people must often rely solely, in all representative governments.

The power of Congress, then, comprehends navigation within the limits of every state in the Union; so far as that navigation may be, in any manner, connected with "commerce with foreign nations, or among the several states, or with the Indian tribes." It may, of consequence, pass the jurisdictional line of New York, and act upon the very waters to which the prohibition now under consideration applies.

But it has been urged with great earnestness, that although the power of Congress to regulate commerce with foreign nations, and among the several states, be co-extensive with the subject itself, and have no other limits than are prescribed in the constitution, yet the states may severally exercise the same power within their respective jurisdictions. In support of this argument, it is said that they possessed it as an inseparable attribute of sovereignty, before the formation of the constitution, and still retain it, except so far as they have surrendered it by that instrument; that this principle results from the nature of the government, and is secured by the tenth amendment; that an affirmative grant of power is not exclusive, unless in its own nature it be such that the continued exercise of it by the former possessor is inconsistent with the grant, and that this is not of that description. . . .

Since, however, in exercising the power of regulating their own purely internal affairs, whether of trading or police, the states may sometimes enact laws, the validity of which depends on their interfering with, and being contrary to, an act of Congress passed in pursuance of the constitution, the court will enter upon the inquiry, whether the laws of New York, as expounded by the highest tribunal of that state, have, in their application to this case, come into collision with an act of Congress, and deprived a citizen of a right to which that act entitles him. Should this collision exist, it will be immaterial whether those laws were passed in virtue of a concurrent power "to regulate commerce with foreign nations and among the several states," or in virtue of a power to regulate their domestic trade and police. In one case and the other, the acts of New York must yield to the law of Congress; and the decision sustaining the privilege they confer, against a right given by a law of the Union, must be erroneous.

This opinion has been frequently expressed in this court, and is founded as well on the nature of the government as on the words of the constitution. In argument, however, it has been contended that if a law, passed by a state in the exercise of its acknowledged sovereignty, comes into conflict with a law passed by Congress in pursuance of the constitution, they affect the subject, and each other, like equal opposing powers.

But the framers of our constitution foresaw this state of things, and provided for it, by declaring the supremacy not only of itself, but of the laws made in pursuance of it. The nullity of any act, inconsistent with the constitution, is produced by the declaration that the constitution is the supreme law. The appropriate application of that part of the clause which confers the same supremacy on laws and treaties, is to such acts of the state legislatures as do not transcend their powers, but, though enacted in the execution of acknowledged state powers, interfere with, or are contrary to the laws of Congress, made in pursuance of the constitution, or some treaty made under the authority of the United States. In every such case, the act of Congress, or the treaty, is supreme; and the law of the state, though enacted in the exercise of powers not controverted, must yield to it.

In pursuing this inquiry at the bar, it has been said that the constitution does not confer the right of intercourse between state and state. That right derives its source from those laws whose authority is acknowledged by civilized man throughout the world. This is true. The constitution found it an existing right, and gave to Congress the power to regulate it. In the exercise of this power, Congress has passed "an act for enrolling or licensing ships or vessels to be employed in the coasting trade and fisheries, and for regulating the same." The counsel for the respondent contend that this act does not give the right to sail from port to port, but confines itself to regulating a preexisting right, so far only as to confer certain privileges on enrolled and licensed vessels in its exercise. . . .

If, as our whole course of legislation on this subject shows, the power of Congress has been universally understood in America to comprehend navigation, it is a very persuasive, if not a conclusive argument, to prove that the construction is correct; and, if it be correct, no clear distinction is perceived between the power to regulate vessels employed in transporting men for hire, and property for hire. The subject is transferred to Congress, and no exception to the grant can be admitted which is not proved by the words or the nature of the thing. A coasting vessel employed in the transportation of passengers, is as much a portion of the American marine as one employed in the transportation of a cargo; and no reason is perceived why such vessel should be withdrawn from the regulating power of that government, which has been thought best fitted for the purpose generally. The provisions of the law respecting native seamen, and respecting ownership, are as applicable to vessels carrying men as to vessels carrying manufactures; and no reason is perceived why the power over the subject should not be placed in the same hands. . . .

The court is aware that, in stating the train of reasoning by which we have been conducted to this result, much time has been consumed in the attempt to demonstrate propositions which may have been thought axioms. It is felt that the tediousness inseparable from the endeavor to prove that which is already clear, is imputable to a considerable part of this opinion. But it was unavoidable. The conclusion to which we have come, depends on a chain of principles which it was necessary to preserve unbroken; and, although some of them were thought nearly self-evident, the magnitude of the question, the weight of character belonging to those from whose judgment we dissent, and the argument at the bar, demanded that we should assume nothing.

Powerful and ingenious minds, taking, as postulates, that the powers expressly granted to the government of the Union are to be contracted, by construction, into the narrowest possible compass, and that the original powers of the States are retained, if any possible construction will retain them, may, by a course of well digested, but refined and metaphysical reasoning, founded on these premises, explain away the constitution of our country, and leave it a magnificent structure indeed, to look at, but totally unfit for use. They may so entangle and perplex the understanding, as to obscure principles which were before thought quite plain, and induce doubts where, if the mind were to pursue its own course, none would be perceived. In such a case, it is peculiarly necessary to recur to safe and fundamental principles to sustain those principles, and, when sustained, to make them the tests of the arguments to be examined.

For once a decision of the Court proved almost universally popular. Papers of all parties and all sections praised the decision, often in extravagant terms. It was called "one of the most solemn and able opinions that has ever been delivered in any Court," "probably the strongest document in support of the powers of the Federal Government that has ever issued from the same authority," "a masterpiece of judicial reasoning." Charles Warren, the great historian of the Supreme Court, called it "the emancipation proclamation of American commerce." A year after the decision the number of steamboats sailing from New York Harbor had increased from six to forty-three.

Perhaps even more significant than the assertion of the control of Congress over commerce, defined in the broadest sense, and the end of the steamboat and all other monopolies, was the encouragement that the decision gave to the broad constructionists, specifically the proponents of internal improvements and protective tariffs. For this reason the decision did not escape censure from the champions of states' rights although their protests were more muted than in earlier decisions whose effect had been to strengthen the powers of the federal government at the expense of the states.

Although the Court in the case of *Osborn v. Bank of the United States* had reaffirmed and somewhat extended the principles laid down in *McCulloch v. Maryland, Gibbons v. Ogden*, or, as it was more commonly called, *The Steamboat Case*, completed the "system" of the Marshall Court. The main lines of constitutional interpretation had been established. In the period prior to the Civil War important cases were to be heard, but there were remarkably few deviations from the lines laid down by Marshall and his fellow justices.

One of the most important cases decided by the Marshall Court came in these last years: *Barron v. Baltimore*. John Barron and his deceased partner had owned "an extensive and highly productive wharf." The city, in the course of paving, grading, and improving the sewerage disposal of the city, had diverted "certain streams" in such a manner as to cause the area around the wharf to silt up, making the wharf no longer accessible to ships. The plaintiff had sued the city for damages in the county court and won. The decision had been reversed on appeal and brought to the Supreme Court in the session of 1833 on the grounds that the plaintiff had been denied his constitutional rights under the Fifth Amendment to the Constitution, i.e., that he had been deprived of his property for public use without proper compensation. Barron insisted "that this amendment, being in favor of the liberty of the citizen ought to be so construed as to restrain the legislative power of a State, as well as that of the United States."

In Marshall's opinion the case was "of great importance but not much difficulty." He declared, "The Constitution was ordained and established by the people of the United States for themselves, for their own government, and not for the government of the individual States. Each State established a constitution for itself and in that constitution provided such limits and restrictions on the powers of its particular government as its judgment dictated." The Fifth Amendment (and all the rest) therefore were to be understood "as restraining the power of the general government, not as applicable to the States. . . . It is a subject on which they judge exclusively." Marshall rejected the argument of Barron's lawyer that "the Constitution was intended to secure the people of the several States against the undue exercise of power by their respective State governments; as well as against that which might be attempted by their general government. . . ." "Had the framers of these amendments intended them to be limitations on the powers of the State governments they would have imitated the framers of the original Constitution, and have expressed that intention. . . . We are of the opinion that the provision in the fifth amendment to the Constitution, declaring that private property shall not be taken for the public use without just compensation, is intended solely as a limitation on the exercise of power by the government of the United States, and is not applicable to the legislation of the States," Marshall concluded.

It is well to pause here to reflect upon the implications of Marshall's decision. *Barron v. Baltimore* makes two points clear: first, that citizens of particular states wished to place themselves under the Bill of Rights protection of the Constitution; and, second, that the Supreme Court resisted all such efforts on the undoubtedly accurate grounds that such had not been the intention of those who drafted the first ten amendments to the Constitution. As territories were organized to the west and grew gradually into states and as individual rights were often trampled on by state legislatures and state courts, it became apparent to a growing number of Americans that there was a striking disparity between the protection afforded to citizens of the United States from encroachments on their liberties by the federal government and those afforded them by the courts and legislatures of their own home states. But more than a century would pass before the rights of citizens of particular states would be "incorporated" under the Constitution's Bill of Rights.

CHAPTER

XVI

JACKSON AND THE COURT

THE MOST DIRECT CHALLENGE TO THE AUTHORITY OF THE COURT since Jefferson's presidency came early in the administration of Andrew Jackson. The Democrats' attack on the Court grew out of an incident involving the Cherokee Indians in Georgia. The state had ratified the Constitution and entered the Union with the proviso that the Cherokee Indians, who claimed eight million acres of land in Georgia and in what would become the states of Alabama and Mississippi, would remain under the jurisdiction of the state unless the federal government bought up the Indians' lands in question. The government failed to purchase any substantial portion of the land in question and although the Cherokees, under the terms of a treaty with the United States, had authority to goven themselves, Georgia insisted on exercising its own jurisdiction in opposition to the treaty. The issue was brought to a head when an Indian named Corn Tassel was seized by the Georgia authorities for murdering another Indian on Indian lands, sentenced by a Georgia court for murder, and hanged despite an injunction from the Supreme Court ordering a stay of execution. The attempted intervention of the Court provided the occasion for the Democratic majority in Congress to press legislation to deprive the Supreme Court of appellate jurisdiction over the state courts by repealing section 25 of the Judiciary Act of 1789. The *National Intelligencer* of New York took the gloomiest view of this development. The refusal of Georgia to submit her laws "to this learned, able, upright and respectable tribunal," its editor wrote, could be understood as nothing more than an attack on the Constitution itself. "Once deprive the Court of the power of determining constitutional questions and the Legislatures of the States will be let loose from all control, and as interest or passion may influence them, will reduce the National Government to a state of dependence and decrepitude. . . ." To revert to our earlier proposition, it might be said that with the election of Jackson, the Secular-Democratic Consciousness had triumphed finally and conclusively over the Classical-Christian Consciousness, at least in the political realm. This renewed assault, after years of comparative calm, demonstrated in the most dramatic fashion the vulnerability of the Court. If one state refused to obey a decision of the Court and was supported in its recalcitrance by the president, the entire authority of the Court was at once called in question. It was thus clearly the most fragile branch of the government. Put another way, in the face of such vulnerability it was in the nature of a miracle that the Court had survived.

The Judiciary Committee of the House reported out the bill to repeal section 25, accompanied by a report which stated that the power of the Court was "so vast and alarming that the constantly increasing evil of interference of Federal with State authorities must be checked." When debates on the bill began it turned out that the Court had a substantial number of supporters even among congressional Democrats. John C. Calhoun, author of the doctrine of nullification, wrote: "However strange it may seem, there are many who are violently opposed to Nullification."

At this stage James Madison, who knew better than any living man the intentions of the framers, spoke up in behalf of the beleaguered Court whose decisions he had so often deplored. With Jefferson dead it may well have been that Madison's original Federalist sympathies reasserted themselves. Or perhaps it was simply pride in a document to which he had contributed more than any other delegate to the federal convention of 1787. "The jurisdiction claimed for the Federal Judiciary," Madison wrote, "is truly the only defensive armor of the Federal Government, or rather for the Constitution and laws of the United States. Strip it of that armor, and the door is wide open for nullification, anarchy and convulsion." The defeat of the bill could be anticipated from the fact that the representatives of the Northern states, by virtue of their larger populations, dominated the House. The bill was rejected, 158 to 51, but its defeat could not protect the Court against the hostility of the president.

Having lost the drive to repeal section 25, the enemies of the Court proposed an amendment limiting the terms of the justices. This bill failed by a vote of 115 to 61.

Meanwhile the Cherokee Nation appealed to the federal courts for vindication of its treaty rights. The Cherokees were not without their friends and defenders, though few if any seem to have resided in Georgia. The Cherokee Nation sought an injunction from the Supreme Court "to restrain the State of Georgia, the Governor, Attorney General, Judges, justices of the peace, sheriffs, deputy sheriffs, constables and others, the officers, agents and servants of that State, from executing and enforcing the laws of Georgia, or any of these laws, or serving processes, or doing anything towards the execution or enforcement of those laws within the Cherokee territory, as designated by treaty between the United States and the Cherokee Nation." Georgia's leading newspaper probably spoke for the great majority of the citizens of the state when its editor stormed over the presumption of the Supreme Court in even taking account of "a few savages. . . . Unparalleled impudence!"

The Court decided the question on the narrow ground of whether the Cherokees constituted, in the terms of the Constitution, an independent nation and ruled that since they did, it had no jurisdiction in the case, though Marshall implied that the sympathies of the justices were with the Indians. The question that must arise in the mind of a modern reader is whether the justices, knowing that they could not count on the president to enforce a decision unacceptable to the state of Georgia and unwilling to place the Court in an untenable position, took the easy way out by disclaiming jurisdiction on what were largely technical grounds. This at least was the view in New England, where there was great sympathy for the plight of the Cherokees. Judge Story gave more than a clue to the feelings of the Court when he wrote a friend: "The subject touches the moral sense of all New England. It comes home to the religious feelings of our people; it moves their sensibilities, and strikes at the very bottom of their sense of justice. Depend upon it, there is a depth of degradation in our National conduct, which will irresistibly lead to better things. There will be, in God's Providence, a retribution for unholy deeds, first or last."

The *Baltimore Republican* said in March, 1832: "Frenzy or infatuation seems to have taken possession of the minds of many of the people of the North in relation to the Indian question. In indulging their sympathy for the Indians in Georgia they seem to lose sight of all other considerations and forget that the State has rights and feelings equal to their own."

It was reported that Marshall, seventy-five years old, was so disheartened by the decision and by the renewed attacks upon the Court that he planned to retire. He wrote a sad and bewildered letter to Story: "I cannot be insensible to the gloom which lours over us. I have a repugnance to abandoning you under such circumstances which is almost invincible. But the solemn convictions of my judgment, sustained by some pride of character, admonish me not to hazard the disgrace of continuing in office a mere inefficient pageant."

The rumor of Marshall's imminent retirement spread alarm through conservative circles. The *New York Daily Advertiser* declared him to be "beyond question, the most important public character of which the Union can now boast. . . . The safety of the very Union might be hazarded by the appointment of a successor. . . . The mischief which a nullifying Chief Justice might introduce into the execution of the laws and administration of justice would be boundless and in the highest degree fatal to the peace and safety of the Union." John Quincy Adams expressed his own concern in his diary: "Wirt spoke to me . . . in deep concern and alarm at the state of the Chief Justice Marshall's health. He is seventy-five years of age and has until lately enjoyed fine health, exercised great bodily agility and sustained an immense amount of bodily labor. . . . His mind remains unimpaired, but his body is breaking down. He has been thirty years Chief Justice, and has done more to establish the Constitution of the United States on sound construction than any other man living. The terror is that, if he should be now withdrawn, some shallow-pated wild-cat like Philip P. Barbour, fit for nothing but to tear the Union to rags and tatters, would be appointed in his place. Mr. Wirt's anticipations are gloomy, and I see no reasonable prospect of improvement."

The state of Georgia, dominated throughout most of its early history by intemperate politicians with whom, since the Yazoo Land case, hostility to the Court was a matter of principle, now became the Court's incubus. The legislature had passed a law in 1831 requiring all whites living in Cherokee country to take a loyalty oath to the state. Two missionaries who declined to comply were sentenced to four years' hard labor. The verdict was appealed to the Supreme

Court and the Court instructed the state to appear on the appeal, but again the Court was defied and the new governor of Georgia announced that "any attempt to infringe the evident right of the State to govern the entire population within its territorial limits . . . would be a usurpation of a power never granted by the States. Such an attempt, whenever made, will challenge the most determined resistance; and if persevered in, will inevitably eventuate in the annihilation of our beloved Union."

The case of the missionaries was argued before the Court in the absence of attorneys for the state of Georgia. It was certainly one of the most dramatic meetings of the Court. The room was so crowded with "gentlemen and ladies," as well as members of Congress, that the Court had to adjourn to a larger chamber. The presence of two Cherokee chiefs added to the drama of the occasion. As one reporter noted, "the deep solicitude depicted in their countenances must have moved the sympathy of everyone present whose heart was not hard as adamant." Justice Story wrote, during the course of the hearing, "I confess that I blush for my country when I perceive that such legislation, destructive of all faith and honor towards the Indians, is suffered to pass with the silent approbation of the present Government of the United States."

There was a double irony in the plight of the Cherokees. The framers of the Constitution had undertaken to devise a government in which the rights of any minority would be protected against abuse by the majority. As we have seen, it was their conviction that there was in human beings generally, regardless of class or caste, an ineradicable impulse toward "self-aggrandizement," to greed and selfishness. The science of government making was based on the candid recognition of man's fallen nature. In their view the Supreme Court was the most essential agency in protecting the rights of the powerless or the exploited. It was, as we have said, the "original sin" branch of the government, designed to check the excesses of democracy where prejudice and passion could so easily carry the day. That the policy of the new Jacksonian democracy had been to ruthlessly disregard the rights of the Cherokee Indians was a graphic demonstration, to those who still adhered to the old faith, of the soundness of the framers' "political science." Today, with an awakened concern for the rights of native Americans, it is well to remind ourselves that what was perhaps the most cruel abuse of their rights as human beings in our history was perpetrated under the banner of democracy.

Harriet Martineau, the English writer, visited the Court and observed "the Chief Justice . . . delivering judgment, the three Judges on either hand gazing at him more like learners than associates; Webster standing firm as a rock, his large, deep-set eyes wide awake, his lips compressed, and his whole countenance in that intent stillness which easily fixes the gaze of the stranger. Clay leaning against the desk in an attitude whose grace contrasts strangely with the slovenly make of his dress, his snuff box for the moment unopened in his hand, his small grey eye, and placid half-smile conveying an expression of pleasure which redeems his face from its usual unaccountable commonness . . . these men absorbed in what they were listening to, thinking neither of themselves nor of each other, while they were watched by the groups of idlers and listeners around them; the newspaper corps, the dark Cherokee chiefs, the stragglers from the far West, the gay ladies in their waving plumes, and the members of either House that have stepped in to listen; all these I have seen at one moment constitute one silent assemblage, while the mild voice of the aged Chief Justice sounded through the Court. . . ."

The Court ruled that the Georgia statute under which the missionaries had been convicted was unconstitutional on the basis that only the federal government had jurisdiction over the Cherokees "and that the State had no power to pass laws affecting them or their territory." The missionaries were ordered released. Story wrote, "Thanks be to God, the Court can wash their hands of the iniquity of oppressing the Indians and disregarding their rights." And to another friend he wrote, "The Court has done its duty. Let the nation now do theirs."

When the state of Georgia breathed fire and vengeance, flatly refusing to honor the orders of the Court, Marshall felt that his life's work in trying to establish the Constitution on firm ground was slipping rapidly away. He wrote another despairing letter to Story: "I yield slowly and reluctantly to the conviction that our Constitution cannot last. Our opinions are incompatible with a united government. . . . The Union has been prolonged thus far by miracles. I fear they cannot continue."

Fortunately another miracle was in the making. The South Carolina legislature, perhaps emboldened by Georgia's resistance to federal authority and confident that the president himself was on the side of states' rights, passed an ordinance in November of 1832 spelling out its notion of the doctrine of nullification. In addition to the ordinance, the legislature framed an *Address to the People of the United States* which solicited support in other states for the principle of nullification. As certainly as anything can be said of history, the South Carolina ordinance if unchallenged and subscribed to by other Southern states meant the end of the United States as the framers of the Constitution had envisioned it and as it had in fact functioned since 1789.

South Carolina Ordinance of Nullification, November 24, 1832

Whereas the Congress of the United States, by various acts, purporting to be acts laying duties and imposts on foreign imports, but in reality intended for the protection of domestic manufactures, and the giving of bounties to classes and individuals engaged in particular employments, at the expense and to the injury and oppression of other classes and individuals, and by wholly exempting from taxation certain foreign commodities, such as are not produced or manufactured in the United States, to afford a pretext for imposing higher and excessive duties on articles similar to those intended to be protected, hath exceeded its just powers under the Constitution, which confers on it no authority to afford such protection, and hath violated the true meaning and intent of the Constitution, which provides for equality in imposing the burthens of taxation upon the several States and portions of the confederacy: And whereas the said Congress, exceeding its just power to impose taxes and collect revenue for the purpose of effecting and accomplishing the specific objects and purposes which the Constitution of the United States authorizes it to effect and accomplish, hath raised and collected unnecessary revenue for objects unauthorized by the Constitution:

We, therefore, the people of the State of South Carolina in Convention assembled, do declare and ordain, . . . that the several acts and parts of acts of . . . Congress . . . purporting to be laws for the imposing of duties and imposts on the importation of foreign commodities, . . . and, more especially, . . . [the 1828 and 1832 tariffs] . . . are unauthorized by the Constitution of the United States, and violate the true meaning and intent thereof, and are null, void, and no law, nor binding upon this State, its officers or citizens; and all promises, contracts, and obligations, made or entered into, or to be made or entered into, with purpose to secure the duties imposed by the said acts, and all judicial proceedings which shall be hereafter had in affirmance thereof, are and shall be held utterly null and void.

And it is further ordained, that it shall not be lawful for any of the constituted authorities, whether of this State or of the United States, to enforce the payment of duties imposed by the said acts within the limits of this State; but it shall be the duty of the Legislature to adopt such measures and pass such acts as may be necessary to give full effect to this ordinance, and to prevent the enforcement and arrest the operation of said acts and parts of acts of the Congress of the United States within the limits of this State, from and after the 1st day of February next, and the duty of all other constituted authorities, and of all persons residing or being within the limits of this State, and they are hereby required and enjoined, to obey and give effect to this ordinance, and such acts and measures of the Legislature as may be passed or adopted in obedience thereto. . . .

And we, the people of South Carolina, to the end that it may be fully understood by the Government of the United States, and the people of the co-States, that we are determined to maintain this, our ordinance and declaration, at every hazard, do further declare that we will not submit to the application of force, on the part of the Federal Government, to reduce this State to obedience; but that we will consider the passage, by Congress, of any act authorizing the employment of a military or naval force against the State of South Carolina, her constituted authorities or citizens; or any act abolishing or closing the ports of this State, or any of them or otherwise obstructing the free ingress and egress of vessels to and from the said ports, or any other act on the part of the Federal Government, to coerce the State, shut up her ports, destroy or harass her commerce, or to enforce the acts hereby declared to be null and void, otherwise than through the civil tribunals of the country, as inconsistent with the longer continuance of South Carolina in the Union: and that the people of this State will thenceforth hold themselves absolved from all further obligation to maintain or preserve their political connexion with the people of the other States, and will forthwith proceed to organize a separate Government, and do all other acts and things which sovereign and independent States may of right do.

Jackson's response was prompt and firm, undoubtedly one of the most important presidential statements ever issued. South Carolina was put on notice that the president would use his power as chief executive to punish any such attempt.

The ordinance is founded, not on the indefeasible right of resisting acts which are plainly unconstitutional and too oppressive to be endured, but on the strange position that any one State may not only declare an act of Congress void, but prohibit its execution; that they may do this consistently with the Constitution; that the true construction of that instrument permits a State to retain its place in the Union and yet be bound by no other of its laws than those it may choose to consider as constitutional. It is true, they add, that to justify this abrogation of a law it must be palpably contrary to the Constitution; but it is evident that to give the right of resisting laws of that description, coupled with the uncontrolled right to decide what laws deserve that character, is to give the power of resisting all laws; for as by the theory there is no appeal, the reasons alleged by the State, good or bad, must prevail. If it should be said that public opinion is a sufficient check against the abuse of this power, it may be asked why it is not deemed a sufficient guard against the passage of an unconstitutional act by Congress? There is, however, a restraint in this last case which makes the assumed power of a State more indefensible, and which does not exist in the other. There are two appeals from an unconstitutional act passed by Congress—one to the judiciary, the other to the people and the States. There is no appeal from the State decision in theory, and the practical illustration shows that the courts are closed against an application to review it, both judges and jurors being sworn to decide in its favor. But reasoning on this subject is superfluous when our social compact, in express terms, declares that the laws of the United States, its Constitution, and treaties made under it are the supreme law of the land, and, for greater caution, adds "that the judges in every State shall be bound thereby, anything in the constitution or laws of any State to the contrary notwithstanding." And it may be asserted without fear of refutation that no federative government could exist without a similar provision. . . .

If this doctrine had been established at an earlier day, the Union would have been dissolved in its infancy. The excise law in Pennsylvania, the embargo and nonintercourse law in the Eastern States, the carriage tax in Virginia, were all deemed unconstitutional, and were more unequal in their operation than any of the laws now complained of; but, fortunately, none of those States discovered that they had the right now claimed by South Carolina. The war into which we were forced to support the dignity of the nation and the rights of our citizens might have ended in defeat and disgrace, instead of victory and honor, if the States who supposed it a ruinous and unconstitutional measure had thought they possessed the right of nullifying the act by which it was declared and denying supplies for its prosecution. Hardly and unequally as those measures bore upon several members of the Union, to the legislatures of none did this efficient and peaceable remedy, as it is called, suggest itself. The discovery of this important feature in our Constitution was reserved to the present day. To the statesmen of South Carolina belongs the invention, and upon the citizens of that State will unfortunately fall the evils of reducing it to practice.

If the doctrine of a State veto upon the laws of the Union carries with it internal evidence of its impracticable absurdity, our constitutional history will also afford abundant proof that it would have been repudiated with indignation had it been proposed to form a feature in our Government. . . .

I consider, then, the power to annul a law of the United States, assumed by one State, *incompatible with the existence of the Union, contradicted expressly by the letter of the Constitution, unauthorized by its spirit, inconsistent with every principle on which it was founded, and destructive of the great object for which it was formed.*

After this general view of the leading principle, we must examine the particular application of it which is made in the ordinance.

The preamble rests its justification on these grounds: It assumes as a fact that the obnoxious laws, although they purport to be laws for raising revenue, were in reality intended for the protection of manufactures, which purpose it asserts to be unconstitutional; that the operation of these laws is unequal; that the amount raised by them is greater than is required by the wants of the Government; and, finally, that the proceeds are to be applied to objects unauthorized by the Constitution. These are the only causes alleged to justify an open opposition to the laws of the country and a threat of seceding from the Union if any attempt should be made to enforce them. The first virtually acknowledges that the law in question was passed under a power expressly given by the Constitution to lay and collect imposts; but its constitutionality is drawn in question from the *motives* of those who passed it. However apparent this purpose may be in the present case, nothing can be more dangerous than to admit the position that an unconstitutional purpose entertained by the members who assent to a law enacted under a constitutional power shall make that law void. For how is that purpose to be ascertained? Who is to make the scrutiny? How often may bad purposes be falsely imputed, in how many cases are they concealed by false professions, in how many is no declaration of motive made? Admit this doctrine, and you give to the States an uncontrolled right to decide, and every law may be annulled under this pretext. If, therefore, the absurd and dangerous doctrine should be admitted that a State may annul an unconstitutional law, or one that it deems such, it will not apply to the present case.

The next objection is that the laws in question operate unequally. This objection may be made with truth to every law that has been or can be passed. The wisdom of man never yet contrived a system of taxation that would operate with perfect equality. If the unequal operation of a law makes it unconstitutional, and if all laws of that description may be abrogated by any State for that cause, then, indeed, is the Federal Constitution unworthy of the slightest effort for its preservation. . . .

The Constitution declares that the judicial powers of the United States extend to cases arising under the laws of the United States, and that such laws, the Constitution, and treaties shall be paramount to the State constitutions and laws. The judiciary act prescribes the mode by which the case may be brought before a court of the United States by appeal when a State tribunal shall decide against this provision of the Constitution. The ordinance declares there shall be no appeal—makes the State law paramount to the Constitution and laws of the United States, forces judges and jurors to swear that they will disregard their provisions, and even makes it penal in a suitor to attempt relief by appeal. It further declares that it shall not be lawful for the authorities of the United States or of that State to enforce the payment of duties imposed by the revenue laws within its limits.

Here is a law of the United States, not even pretended to be unconstitutional, repealed by the authority of a small majority of the voters of a single State. Here is a provision of the Constitution which is solemnly abrogated by the same authority.

On such expositions and reasonings the ordinance grounds not only an assertion of the right to annul the laws of which it complains, but to enforce it by a threat of seceding from the Union if any attempt is made to execute them.

This right to secede is deduced from the nature of the Constitution, which, they say, is a compact between sovereign States who have preserved their whole sovereignty and therefore are subject to no superior; that because they made the compact they can break it when in their opinion it has been departed from by the other States. Fallacious as this course of reasoning is, it enlists State pride and finds advocates in the honest prejudices of those who have not studied the nature of our Government sufficiently to see the radical error on which it rests. . . .

The Constitution of the United States, then, forms a *government*, not a league; and whether it be formed by compact between the States or in any other manner, its character is the same. It is a Government in which all the people are represented, which operates directly on the people individually, not upon the States; they retained all the power they did not grant. But each State, having expressly parted with so many powers as to constitute, jointly with the other States, a single nation, can not, from that period, possess any right to secede, because such secession does not break a league, but destroys the unity of a nation; and any injury to that unity is not only a breach which would result from the contravention of a compact, but it is an offense against the whole Union. To say that any State may at pleasure secede from the Union is to say that the United States are not a nation, because it would be a solecism to contend that any part of a nation might dissolve its connection with the other parts, to their injury or ruin, without committing any offense. Secession, like any other revolutionary act, may be morally justified by the extremity of oppression; but to call it a constitutional right is confounding the meaning of terms, and can only be done through gross error or to deceive those who are willing to assert a right, but would pause before they made a revolution or incur the penalties consequent on a failure. . . .

The laws of the United States must be executed. I have no discretionary power on the subject; my duty is emphatically pronounced in the Constitution. Those who told you that you might peaceably prevent their execution deceived you; they could not have been deceived themselves. They know that a forcible opposition could alone prevent the execution of the laws, and they know that such opposition must be repelled. Their object is disunion. But be not deceived by names. Disunion by armed force is *treason*. Are you really ready to incur its guilt? If you are, on the heads of the instigators of the act be the dreadful consequences; on their heads be the dishonor, but on yours may fall the punishment. . . .

Fellow-citizens of the United States, . . . I rely with equal confidence on your undivided support in my determination to execute the laws, to preserve the Union by all constitutional means, to arrest, if possible, by moderate and firm measures the necessity of a recourse to force; and if it be the will of Heaven that the recurrence of its primeval curse on man for the shedding of a brother's blood should fall upon our land, that it be not called down by any offensive act on the part of the United States.

On the heels of making his statement, Jackson persuaded his supporters in Congress to introduce a bill to give the federal courts and the executive branch powers to suppress any effort at nullification.

Known as the Force Bill, or Bloody Bill, it aroused the violent opposition of the dedicated states' righters who felt that Jackson had betrayed them. The *Richmond Enquirer* spoke for this faction when it declared that the Force Bill "constitutes Gen. Jackson Monarch of the American Empire, and must be resisted to the death." The *United States Telegraph* made much of the inconsistency of Jackson's seeming acquiescence in Georgia's actual defiance, and his angry reaction to South Carolina's anouncement of what was simply a docrine: "Georgia refused to obey the decisions of the Federal Judiciary. Not a word is said by the Executive or his minions, except that she is right in doing so. South Carolina says she will do so at a future period, and the Palace is in arms. Denunciations fall thick and heavy from its enraged occupant."

In addition to his reply to South Carolina, Jackson let it be known that "he would carry any decision the Supreme Court should make in the imprisonment of the missionaries into effect." Rather than put the matter to a test, the governor of Georgia agreed to pardon the missionaries if they would withdraw their suit. And, marvel of marvels, Jackson invited Story, whom it was said he had characterized as "the most dangerous man in America," to have a glass of wine with him. "But what is more remarkable," Story wrote a friend, "since his last Proclamation and message, the chief justice and myself have become his warmest supporters. . . . Who would have dreamed of such an occurrence?" More astonishing still, the high priest of Whig-Federalism, Daniel Webster, received marks of presidential favor and was rumored to be Jackson's choice to succeed Marshall. To cap it all, Story's *Commentaries on the Constitution of the United States* was published and widely acclaimed. One reviewer wrote: "Constitutional law, in our day, instead of being the calm occupation of the schools or the curious pursuit of the professional student, has become, as it were, an element of real life. The Constitution has been obliged to leave its temple, and come down into the forum and traverse the streets."

When Andrew Jackson, champion of democracy, embraced the constitutional principles of John Marshall and Daniel Webster, the bitter controversies that had raged around the Constitution since the first challenge of Thomas Jefferson's democratic revolution of 1800 could now be laid to rest. Charles Francis Adams, hearing of the death of his grandfather, John Adams, and Thomas Jefferson on July 4, 1826, fifty years after the Declaration of Independence, had declared, "There is no eloquence like the eloquence of facts." This strange denouement could hardly have been so well contrived by a dramatist. For the moment the Court was safe. It had done its best; the future of constitutional government would await the trial of arms almost a generation later.

Andrew Jackson had fought in a minor engagement of the Revolution as a boy of fourteen. He had been captured by the British and when he refused to shine the shoes of a British lieutenant, the officer had slashed his arm and head. Now, as president, he had, to the astonishment of friends and enemies alike, effected a reconciliation with the spirit of the Constitution, if not with the stalwarts among the declining Whig-Federalists, one of the most distinguished of whom, Chancellor Kent, the great New York jurist, wrote of Jackson "as a detestable, ignorant, reckless, vain and malignant tyrant."

The fact was that the future of the Court had become almost exclusively a political issue, and at the heart of that issue lay slavery. When Robert Hayne of South Carolina in January, 1830, advanced the notion in the Senate that a state had the right to veto laws as unconstitutional which had been passed by Congress and upheld by the Court, Daniel Webster replied to him, thus touching off the famous debates that came to bear the names of the two principal adversaries. Webster's speech defending the Constitution and declaring it to be the touchstone of the entire American system of government became a reference point for all subsequent discussions of Constitution and the Court. It might best be likened to the opening act of a great tragic drama, for it defined the issue in an irresistible way and fixed the attention of the nation on that issue more powerfully than any particular Court case or series of cases had been able to do. It was rather as though Webster had produced a distillation of all the cases that the Court had handed down decisions on since its inception. Union or disunion was quite simply the question, Webster insisted, going on to touch the deepest chords of memory.

Whatever his personal failings and weaknesses may have been, Webster more than any other man of his time gave form and substance to the ideal of the Union. In an age still susceptible to eloquence he exercised his remarkable oratorical powers to a very considerable effect. While the whole focus of the Court shifted after the death of Marshall from great constitutional matters to decisions favorable to the growing business and commercial spirit of the times, Webster wove around the Constitution, as the indispensable center of the Union, a kind of magic barricade of words.

CHAPTER

XVII

A NEW ERA

ON JULY 6, 1835, MARSHALL, WHO HAD BEEN IN FAILING HEALTH
for several years, died at the age of eighty after thirty-four years as
chief justice. Even middle-aged men could hardly recall a time when
Marshall had not been the dominating figure of the Court. No American, other than Washington himself, whom Marshall so much admired, has had such an influence on the development of American
institutions. Many of Marshall's decisions, or the decisions of the
Court which he presided over, were severely criticized during his
lifetime and have been criticized since. He was an old-style Federalist,
an ideal example of what we have called the Classical-Christian
Consciousness, who survived into a very different age carrying with
him always the principles he had absorbed in the Revolutionary era.
It is probably safe to say that Marshall's personal qualities, his un-
impeachable character, his lack of pretentiousness, his ability to win
the affection and loyalty of his associates, were as important as his
legal talents.

Marshall's death marked the end of an epoch. He was the last
conspicuous public tie with the Revolution and the early Republic,
the lonely survivor of a past that Americans struggled to retain some
hold on amid the increasingly bitter sectional disputes, amid the
hasty and reckless growing and the fever of sectional politics, above
all of slavery and the impending showdown between a quasi-feudal
South and an industrial North. The Court would continue to be a central element in American politics, its influence waxing and waning
according to the flow of events and whether the pressure points of
American life were susceptible of constitutional definition and reso-

lution. But the great days when history was, in the highest sense, oratory, were over. The great orators, on whose most extravagant flights of rhetoric hushed auditors hung, entranced at the illuminating, transporting power of the word, were a vanishing species. Quiet arguments, laboriously assembled precedents, fine points of interpretation, gradually took their places. There was no longer the sense that the future of the Union rested on a particular decision of the Court. But it had been a grievously protracted and in some ways profoundly mysterious struggle. The intentions of the framers of the Constitution were not, on the whole, obscure. From its earliest decisions, well prior to Marshall, the Court had declared those intentions as law. They had never substantially wavered or retreated, though they had always shown a nice concern for the political consequences of their decisions. And yet, decade after decade, the perilous battle had continued. The opponents of the Court had done their best to create the illusion that the primary purpose of the Constitution was to protect the sovereignty of the states rather than to create a strong national government.

Almost before the ink on the Constitution had dried, the Secular-Democratic Consciousness had begun its astonishing ascendancy, persevering through a third of a century in its unremitting effort to subdue the Classical-Christian Consciousness as represented by the Court. Its enemies had come remarkably near to success at times in their efforts to depict the Court as the innovator, the aggressor, the willful and aristocratic distorter of the *ur* document. Despite how much was articulated by those articulate generations, it was obvious that much remained hidden in the deeper recesses of the evolving American psyche.

The *New York Evening Post* spoke for the Secular-Democrats on the occasion of Marshall's death: "That a man so aristocratick in his views on Government as John Marshall should occupy a place where his opinions could be, and were, exercised so prejudicially to the cause of democratick principles, was necessarily an occasion of deep regret to us. We should have been pleased had he been removed long ago and are pleased that he is removed at last. But we never desired that he should be removed by death; and now that he is taken away in ripe old age, we regret his demise as that of 'an eminent and exemplary man' at the same time we view the circumstances, politically, as auspicious to the cause of those great principles of democratick government which furnish, in our judgment, the only stable foundation for the equal rights of mankind."

With Marshall's death the Court was virtually immobilized. The Senate, feuding with Jackson over his removal of the government deposits from the Bank of the United States, had already rejected his appointment of Roger Taney to fill one of the positions of associate justice and the angry Jackson, denouncing the senators to an aide as "damned scoundrels," had refused to send up another appointment.

The question of Marshall's successor was, of course, an extremely touchy one. Everyone anticipated a judge chosen from the ranks of Democratic lawyers or judges and the *New York Evening Post* declared: "There is no doubt that as yet the Democratick tendencies of the Nation have not yet been fairly represented in that tribunal. It has been the stronghold of the antiquated, strong-government, Federal ideas, which, in every other branch of the Government have been long since discarded," and the *Richmond Enquirer* anticipated: "The President will nominate a Democratic Chief Justice, and thus, we hope, give some opportunity for the good old State-Rights doctrines of Virginia of '98–'99 [the Virginia Resolutions] to be heard and weighed on the Federal Bench."

Jackson, strengthened by the outcome of the election of 1834, sent the name of Roger Taney once more to the Senate, this time as Chief Justice. Bitter partisan controversy followed, with the Whig-Federalists denouncing the appointment and predicting the dissolution of the Union while the Democrats praised Taney's "proud honesty and independence and his want of subserviency to the United States Bank and other 'monied monsters.' "

Taney was, in fact, an able and distinguished lawyer and under him the Court handed down a number of decisions which gave expression to the burgeoning commercial spirit of the age. The new Chief Justice was described by a contemporary as "a tall, square-shouldered man, flat-breasted, in a degree to be remarked upon, with a stoop that made his shoulders even more prominent, a face without one good feature, a mouth unusually large, in which were discolored and irregular teeth, the gums of which were visible when he smiled, dressed always in black, his clothes sitting ill upon him, his hands spare with projecting veins, in a word, a gaunt, ungainly man. His voice, too, was hollow, as the voice of one who was consumptive. And yet, when he began to speak, you never thought of his personal appearance, so clear, so simple, so admirably arranged were his low-voiced words. He used no gestures. He used even emphasis but sparely. There was an air of so much sincerity in all he said, that it was next to impossible to believe he could be wrong. Not a redundant syllable, not a phrase repeated, and, to repeat, so exquisitely simple. . . ."

Roger Taney proved to be an excellent Chief Justice but he belonged to that unfortunate company of historical characters destined to achieve fame not for his numerous virtues but for a single act to which great opprobrium came to be attached—the Dred Scott decision.

In addition to Taney, Jackson was able, during his eight years in office, to appoint six associate justices. While this did not, as the proponents of the Marshall Court feared, mark the end of constitutional government in the United States, it did mark a notable shift in the decisions of the Court from judgments which often, by their attention to the obligation of contracts and the sanctity of property rights, had the effect of supporting monopoly and suppressing free competition. It has been said that the decisions of the Supreme Court follow the election returns—the implication being that, whatever their commitment to the abstract principles of the law, the justices are inevitably swayed by strong expressions of popular sentiment.

What had been so remarkable about the Marshall Court was that the chief justice's powers of moral and juridical persuasion were so strong that decade after decade the election returns, consistently registering the rise of the democratic tide, failed to substantially influence the decisions of that Court, thereby, as we have seen, enraging a succession of presidents. It thus fell to the Court under Taney's guidance to adjust the Constitution, or the Court's interpretation of it, to a thirty-five-year accumulation of new forces and new politics that expressed those forces.

The first important case that Taney had to deal with—*Charles River Bridge v. Warren Bridge*—was a kind of replay of the Dartmouth College case. The bridge company, among whose stockholders were a substantial number of rich and influential Bostonians, argued that their original charter gave them virtually monopoly rights over the crossing of the river. Taney rejected their contention, pointing out that sacred as the rights of property might be, the public had rights that must be respected as well. One of the justices wrote fifteen years later, "No opinion of the Court more fully satisfied the legal judgment of the country, and consequently none has exerted more influence upon its legislation."

Much has been made of the case as marking the new direction of the Court, but the reader will remember that in the Dartmouth College case, the right of a state legislature to impair a contract had been successfully challenged. The difference in the *Charles River Bridge v. Warren Bridge* decision was that the Dartmouth College case dealt with the inviolability of a contract granted by the state while the bridge case revolved around the question of whether the original charter of the state to the company implied a monopoly. It was less that the decision broke new ground than that, as the first important decision of the Taney Court, it attracted widespread attention and was understood to be a blow against monopolistic practices which had been encouraged by the decision in the Dartmouth College case. The public reaction to the decision emphasizes once more the point we have made often before—the political climate in which a particular decision is made is quite as important as the decision itself, or, in some instances, more important. What drew particular attention was Taney's argument, which spoke emphatically of the importance of public or community interests as opposed to private interests.

Taney, C. J.: . . . Borrowing, as we have done, our system of jurisprudence from the English law . . . it would present a singular spectacle, if, while the courts in England are restraining, within the strictest limits, the spirit of monopoly, and exclusive privileges in nature of monopolies, and confining corporations to the privileges plainly given to them in their charter; the courts of this country should be found enlarging these privileges by implication; and construing a statute more unfavorably to the public, and to the rights of the community, than would be done in a like case in an English court of justice.

But we are not now left to determine for the first time the rules by which public grants are to be construed in this country. The subject has already been considered in this court, and the rules of construction above stated fully established. In the case of the *United States v. Arredondo* . . . the leading cases upon this subject are collected together by the learned judge who delivered the opinion of the court, and the principle recognized that, in grants by the public nothing passes by implication. . . .

The case now before the court, is, in principle, precisely the same.

It is a charter from a state; the act of incorporation is silent in relation to the contested power. The argument in favor of the proprietors of the Charles River bridge, is . . . that the power claimed by the state, if it exists, may be so used as to destroy the value of the franchise they have granted to the corporation. . . . The fact that the power has been already exercised, so as to destroy the value of the franchise, cannot in any degree affect the principle. The existence of the power does not, and cannot, depend upon the circumstance of its having been exercised or not. . . .

The object and end of all government is to promote the happiness and prosperity of the community by which it is established; and it can never be assumed, that the government intended to diminish its power of accomplishing the end for which it was created. And in a country like ours, free, active and enterprising, continually advancing in numbers and wealth, new channels of communication are daily found necessary, both for travel and trade, and are essential to the comfort, convenience and prosperity of the people. . . .

No one will question that the interests of the great body of the people of the state, would, in this instance, be affected by the surrender of this great line of travel to a single corporation, with the right to exact toll, and exclude competition, for seventy years. While the rights of private property are sacredly guarded, we must not forget that the community also have rights, and that the happiness and well-being of every citizen depends on their faithful preservation.

Adopting the rule of construction above stated as the settled one, we proceed to apply it to the charter of 1785 to the proprietors of the Charles River bridge. This act of incorporation is in the usual form, and the privileges such as are commonly given to corporations of that kind. It confers on them the ordinary faculties of a corporation, for the purpose of building the bridge; and establishes certain rates of toll, which the company are authorized to take. This is the whole grant. There is no exclusive privilege given to them over the waters of Charles river, above or below their bridge; no right to erect another bridge themselves, nor to prevent other persons from erecting one, no engagement from the State, that another shall not be erected; and no undertaking not to sanction competition, nor to make improvements that may diminish the amount of its income. Upon all these subjects the charter is silent; and nothing is said in it about a line of travel, so much insisted on in the argument, in which they are to have exclusive privileges. No words are used from which an intention to grant any of these rights can be inferred. If the plaintiff is entitled to them, it must be implied, simply from the nature of the grant, and cannot be inferred from the words by which the grant is made. . . .

The inquiry then is, does the charter contain such a contract on the part of the State? Is there any such stipulation to be found in that instrument? It must be admitted on all hands, that there is none—no words that even relate to another bridge, or to the diminution of their tolls, or to the line of travel. If a contract on that subject can be gathered from the charter, it must be by implication, and cannot be found in the words used. Can such an agreement be implied? The rule of construction before stated is an answer to the question. In charters of this description, no rights are taken from the public, or given to the corporation, beyond those which the words of the charter, by their natural and proper construction purport to convey. There are no words which import such a contract as the plaintiffs in error contend for, and none can be implied. . . . The whole community are interested in this inquiry, and they have a right to require that the power of promoting their comfort and convenience, and of advancing the public prosperity, by providing safe, convenient, and cheap ways for the transportation of produce and the purposes of travel, shall not be construed to have been surrendered or diminished by the State, unless it shall appear by plain words that it was intended to be done. . . .

And what would be the fruits of this doctrine of implied contracts on the part of the States, and of property in a line of travel by a corporation, if it should now be sanctioned by this court? To what results would it lead us? If it is to be found in the charter to this bridge, the same process of reasoning must discover it, in the various acts which have been passed, within the last forty years, for turnpike companies. . . . If this court should establish the principles now contended for, what is to become of the numerous railroads established on the same line of travel with turnpike companies, and which have rendered the franchises of the turnpike corporations of no value? Let it once be understood that such charters carry with them these implied contracts, and give this unknown and undefined property in a line of travelling, and you will soon find the old turnpike corporations awakening from their sleep and calling upon this court to put down the improvements which have taken their place. The millions of property which have been invested in railroads and canals upon lines of travel which had been before occupied by turnpike corporations will be put in jeopardy. We shall be thrown back to the improvements of the last century, and obliged to stand still until the claims of the old turnpike corporations shall be satisfied, and they shall consent to permit these States to avail themselves of the lights of modern science, and to partake of the benefit of those improvements which are now adding to the wealth and prosperity, and the convenience and comfort, of every other part of the civilized world. . . .

Taney's decision for the majority of the Court was highlighted by the dissenting opinion of Justice Story, the last holdout of the Marshall era, who wrote, "I can conceive of no surer plan to arrest all public improvements founded on private capital and enterprise, than to make the outlay of that capital uncertain and questionable. . . . The very agitation of a question of this sort is sufficient to alarm every stockholder in every public enterprise of this sort throughout the whole country."

The next important case that confronted the Taney Court was *Briscoe v. Bank of Kentucky*. The issue here was the right of the Bank of Kentucky to issue bank notes. The bank had been enjoined not to issue the notes on the grounds that they were in fact bills of credit and thus unconstitutional. The Court decided that the notes were not bills of credit and that the bank thus had the right to issue them. This decision, along with Jackson's destruction of the Bank of the United States, left the way open for the rapid development of state banks.

The notion that the Court had embarked on a course diametrically opposed to the Marshall Court and to the true principles of the Constitution was encouraged by the gloomy prophecies of the declining Whigs, one of whom wrote of the bank decision: "the tone and character . . . chime in with doctrines which tend . . . deplorably, to the subversion of the principles of law and property. . . . It is quite obvious that old things are passing away. The authority of former decisions, which had been set as landmarks in the law, is assailed and overthrown, by a steady, destructive aim. . . . Under the progressive genius of this new judicial administration, we can see the whole fair system of the Constitution beginning to dissolve like the baseless fabric of a vision."

All of this was much ado about very little. The Taney Court failed to fulfill the fears of its opponents and the expectations of its adherents. And this was probably its most significant achievement. While employing a new rhetoric, its decisions, in the main, supported, as well as Marshall himself could have wished, the doctrine of federal supremacy. The new democratic spirit proved as national, in essence, as had the old Federalist spirit. As we noted earlier, the presidency, under the influence of Jackson's powerful personality, became the focus of attention rather than the Court.

Taney was thoroughly imbued with the principles of Jacksonian democracy, which saw the enemy not as the states but as what were already called by this time "the vested interests," the controllers and manipulators of money, the bankers and corporate leaders of Boston, New York, and Philadelphia. He wrote to Jackson: "In large commercial cities the money power is, I fear irresistible. It is not by open corruption that it always, or even most generally operates. But when men, who have families to support who depend for bread on their exertions, are aware that on the one side they will be employed and enriched by those who have the power to distribute wealth, and that, if they take the other, they must struggle with many difficulties that can be thrown in their way, they are very apt to persuade themselves that that path is the best one in which they meet fewest difficulties and most favour, and surrender the last blessings of freedom and manly independence for pecuniary advantages. They forget the grinding oppression that awaits them from the power they are contributing to establish. . . . These attempts to destroy the spirit of freedom and manly independence in the working classes of society are new in this country. . . . But one thing is clear, that if the effort to render the laboring classes servile and corrupt and to destroy their independent spirit and self-respect shall be successful, that class of society who are striving to produce it, will be the first and most terrible victims of their own policy."

Five years later Taney wrote again to Jackson: "I remember your unshaken confidence in the virtue and intelligence of the people, and I trust they will yet, in due time, bring matters right. Nevertheless, I cannot conceal from myself that paper money and its necessary consequences—that is, speculation and the desire of growing rich suddenly and without labor, have made fearful inroads upon the patriotism and public spirit of what are called the higher classes. . . ."

Taney's reflections represent a high watermark of the Secular-Democratic Consciousness. He refers to the fact that both he and Jackson have a strong faith in the goodness and intelligence of the people and fear only that they will be corrupted by the money men. But the passion for cheap money and quick riches, far from being the exclusive preoccupation of the "monied class," revealed themselves as national characteristics. The point at which the Classical-Christian and the Secular-Democratic Consciousness could be most clearly distinguished was on just this matter of the inherent goodness of "the people" as contrasted to the dominant class. It was the conviction of most of the framers of the Constitution, as the reader will recall, that all men, of whatever class, were tainted with original sin and therefore, given the opportunity to exploit their fellows, would cheerfully do so. "The people" were, in essence, no better than their leaders (or rulers, or the dominant class). That did not mean, of course, that the rulers, having more power, would not abuse it more egregiously. The formula went something like this: original sin times power (most typically money) equals substantially greater wickedness than is commonly available to ordinary persons tainted by original sin but without the power to oppress or exploit others. It followed from this formula that all power must be restrained, diffused and, so far as possible, checked by other "powers." That was the art of government—the diffusion and control of power, which, in the United States, was most typically expressed by money (rather than by kinship or through an hereditary class). The men who framed the Constitution, far from having any sentimental illusions about the "goodness of the people," perceived them as another kind of power, a power disposed to hasty and intemperate actions, a power as ready to appropriate the property of the wealthy as the wealthy were to exploit them. These facts constituted, for the framers, the ultimate rationale for a republican-democratic form of government. Since no individual or class could be trusted with power, the power must be, as we have said, diffused; everyone must have a share, hence democracy. Because the individual was, in the last analysis, the only one capable of judging what his interests were, everyone must have a voice in the political affairs of the nation. What this difference between the Classical-Christian and the Secular-Democratic Consciousness boiled down to in terms of practical politics was that Federalists-Whigs placed somewhat more faith in the propertied classes while the Republicans-Democrats placed all their faith in the inherent goodness of "the people," and were, like Taney, puzzled and demoralized when "the people" seemed as greedy and self-seeking as those "money-mongering monsters," the bankers of New York and Boston.

Although it seems to me from all the evidence of history and from personal experience as well that the Classical-Christian Consciousness has all the better of the argument on an abstract level, in the practical political realm my sympathies lie quite unabashedly with the Secular-Democratic Consciousness. The reason for this is that, while acknowledging the intolerance, prejudice, and indifference to many of the most fundamental human rights that often characterize the Secular-Democratic Consciousness, my suspicion of all excessive concentrations of power in the hands of "the few" by far outweighs my ineradicable skepticism about the goodness of "the many." Thus I would recommend thinking like a Classical-Christian and acting like a Secular-Democrat, and this is, in a real sense, the system that the Constitution and its most original component, the Supreme Court, has fastened on us for better or worse. This formulation helps to explain, I believe, the constant friction between "the people," or their spokesmen, and the Court through the first almost a hundred years of the Court's existence. The Secular-Democratic Consciousness found itself saddled with the fruit of the Classical-Christian Consciousness and it kicked and bucked considerably in consequence. It wished to be free of this unnatural constraint on its natural "goodness."

If Taney suffered disillusionment with the goodness of the people, the decisions of his Court nonetheless steered a cautious line between concern for the general good and regard for the aggressive business interests that were so conspicuous a part of the American scene.

In the case of *Kendall v. Stokes* the Court upheld the right of circuit courts to issue mandamus writs to federal officials which was widely interpreted as a slap at President Van Buren and through him at his predecessor, Jackson. Another series of important cases established the right of a corporation to do business in other states than the one in which it had been chartered. Daniel Webster argued for the broadest rights of the corporation and discussed the question, "constitutionally, legally and socially." A decision of the lower court which had denied that a corporation chartered in one state could carry on its business in another, Webster declared to be "anti-commercial and anti-social, new and unheard of in our system, and calculated to break up the harmony which has so long prevailed among the States and people of this Union. . . ."

The champions of states' rights had been confident that the Taney

Court would administer "the *coup de grâce* on . . . *wandering* corporations," so that "vagabond banks" would be "chained up, to bite and bark only at their own houses." When the verdict of the Court in *Kendall v. Stokes* appeared to allow the "vagabond banks" to bark in other states' yards, a Whig paper exulted: "The decision will give great satisfaction to the business community at large. It will increase the confidence of the people in the purity and independence of the Court. The insolent organ of the Executive has found its attempts at dictation in this instance repelled." Another paper "rejoiced that the march of agrarianism which had reached the ermine, has been stayed by the Supreme Court." ("Agrarianism" was a reference to the *bête noire* of the propertied interests, laws passed in the period of the Roman Empire taking land from great landlords and redistributing it among the poor.)

On the other hand, a Democratic paper declared itself ready to "battle for the rights, the inalienable rights of the People; and the first blow that we strike is against the *Life Judiciary of the United States*—the judicial noblemen of America."

XVIII

SLAVERY

IN 1840 THE TWELVE-YEAR TENURE OF THE JACKSONIAN DEMOCRATS came to an end with the victory of the Whig candidate, William Henry Harrison, over Van Buren, and the Court had, in its first session under the new administration, *Groves v. Slaughter*, a case that involved what would be its major preoccupation for the next twenty years—the powers of the federal and state governments in the matter of bringing slaves into a state. The issue was a critical one, of course. If a state, or the federal government, could prohibit a slaveowner from bringing slaves into a state, the power of the slaveholding states would eventually, with the addition of new states, be overwhelmed. The argument of the slaveholders was that slaves were property and thus the slaveholder in the possession and transportation of his slaves enjoyed all the protections afforded property by the Constitution. As long as slavery existed and slaves were bought and sold as property, the argument of the slaveholders was a hard argument to refute in strictly legal terms. It was plainly a moral issue and one so complex and intractable that it could only be solved ultimately by a bitter and bloody war.

The question before the Court involved a statute passed by the state of Mississippi in 1832 prohibiting "the introduction of slaves into this State as merchandise or for sale." Did the state of Mississippi act unconstitutionally since the power to regulate interstate commerce was given by the Constitution to Congress? Henry Clay and Daniel Webster, the "Ajax and Achilles" of the federal bar, appeared in behalf of the plaintiff and against the state. The case attracted so much attention that the Senate was half deserted during the seven days it took for the Court to hear the arguments. Webster was, as usual, the star of the drama. "He spoke," a witness wrote, "about two hours, with a closeness of logic no other man in the country can equal. There was not the least attempt at display, and a child of ten years could have kept the run of the whole case. It is a curious case under our complex government."

While the Court avoided a decision on a technicality, one of the judges who were opposed to slavery insisted on including a statement on the right of individual states to protect themselves "against the avarice and intrusion of the slave dealer; to guard its citizens against the inconveniences and dangers of a slave population. The right to exercise this power is higher and deeper than the Constitution. The evil involves the prosperity and may endanger the existence of a State. Its power to guard against, or to remedy the evil, rest upon the law of self-preservation. . . ." Coming from a Supreme Court justice this sounded like states' rights doctrine of the most militant variety. Ironically, the slave states were pleased by the judge's statement since they argued that it clearly left it to the states to regulate slavery or the transportation of slaves. It also, in their view, validated state laws forbidding entrance to free blacks.

Even more dramatic than the case of *Groves v. Slaughter* was that of *United States v. Schooner Amistad.* In 1839 a ship carrying blacks illegally to the United States had been seized by its black cargo. After the officers had been killed the vessel was intercepted by a United States Navy frigate and brought to an American port. There the owners of the vessel claimed the blacks as their property. The case was brought to the Court, where John Quincy Adams, once president of the United States and now, in his seventy-fifth year, a member of the House of Representatives from Massachusetts, appeared to argue for the blacks. Adams, a determined foe of slavery, had not appeared before the Court for more than thirty years. Allied with Adams was Roger Baldwin of Connecticut, who opened the case by declaring that it presented, "for the first time, the question whether the United States government . . . can, consistently with the genius of our institutions, become a party to proceedings for the enslavement of human beings cast upon our shores, and found in the condition of freemen within the limits of a free and sovereign State."

John Quincy Adams' argument consumed twelve hours over three days and was certainly one of the most remarkable performances in the history of the Court. Justice Story wrote to his wife describing Adams' effort as "extraordinary. . . . Extraordinary, I say, for its power and bitter sarcasm, and its dealing with topics far beyond the records and points of discussion." A week after Adams concluded his argument the Court ruled that the blacks were free and should be returned to their homeland.

The slavery question, which had surfaced before the Court in the case of *Groves v. Slaughter* and *United States v. Schooner Amistad*, now became a persistent issue. As antislavery and abolitionist sentiment grew and hardened in the North, more and more slaves, encouraged by word of help and haven from Northern abolitionist whites, fled their masters and became "fugitives." The increase in runaways, and the fact that they were being harbored by Northerners and their return impeded, enraged Southerners. They pressed constantly for federal legislation that would facilitate the recovery of their lost property and they turned to the courts to uphold their rights. The courts thus became involved in perpetuating a system that seemed to many Northerners the epitome of injustice. In the case of *Prigg v. Pennsylvania*, a state law giving fugitive slaves the right of a jury trial in case of their being apprehended was ruled unconstitutional by the Court on the ground that it conflicted with the Fugitive Slave Law, requiring that captured slaves be promptly turned over to their owners.

In the cases involving slavery and the slave trade that came before the Court in increasing numbers, the justices adhered faithfully to the *Prigg v. Pennsylvania* decision, that is to say that the states could not pass laws in effect nullifying federal statutes, most particularly, of course, the federal Fugitive Slave Law. Though it is difficult to say what other course the Court could have followed, it now became the object of attack by the abolitionists, who charged that it was, in effect, upholding an unjust and pernicious system.

After the death of President Harrison and the succession of his vice-president, John Tyler, the Whigs in Congress introduced a series of bills, strongly opposed by the Democrats, which had the effect of substantially extending the powers of the federal government. The most important of these was perhaps the National Bankruptcy Act of 1841, which permitted all people to declare bankruptcy. Imprisonment for debt was still the law in some states, and it was said that over five hundred thousand individuals were insolvent largely as a consequence of the devastating depression of 1837. The law was thus a progressive and humane one, but it was attacked by the Democrats as a dangerous extension of the powers of the federal government. To Senator Thomas Benton it was more "glaringly unconstitutional" than the Alien and Sedition Laws, "the most daring attack on the State laws and the rights of property and on public morals which the history of Europe or America has exhibited."

A decision of the Court with far-reaching consequences was that of *Louisville etc. R.R. v. Letson,* in which the justices for the first time accepted the argument that a corporation could claim the rights of a citizen of the state in which it was chartered. As Justice Story wrote a friend after the decision, the Court "has at last come to the conclusion that a corporation is a citizen, an artificial citizen, I agree, but still a citizen." Another justice took a different view, writing, "It may be safely assumed that no offering could be made to the wealthy, powerful and ambitious corporations of the populous and commercial States of the Union so valuable."

The Letson case is especially significant as indicating the inclination of the Court, perhaps subconsciously, to go along with the prevailing mood of the country, which was one of hectic speculation and business activity. The railroads were in a period of remarkable expansion. The Northeast was becoming industrialized at a rapid pace and while the great majority of Americans were still engaged in agricultural pursuits, many rural communities were infected by land speculation and many small towns dreamed of becoming metropolises. As William Taft, later president of the United States and subsequently chief justice of the Supreme Court, put it: "The ruling was directly in the interest of the new States, who were thirsting for foreign capital. . . . Its more special purpose was to allay the fears of such injustice in the minds of those whose material aid was necessary in developing the commercial intercourse between the States, and thus to induce such intercourse and the investment of capital owned in one State in another."

Since it might be argued, and frequently is, that the business ethos has been the dominant spirit in the history of the Republic, it seems useless to lament the often unhappy consequences of the Letson decision and similar decisions of the Court followng in its path. Taft's comments remind us that "foreign" capital, that is to say capital from other states and from other countries as well (England in particular) was eagerly solicited by Americans anxious to exploit the resources of the territories and the new states which sought admission to the Union in every decade of the century. That the Court should have become the ally of the corporations seems in retrospect inevitable. If in its first fifty-odd years it persistently strengthened the powers of the federal government vis-à-vis the states, thus, in the opinion of this writer, enabling the Union to endure, in the next seventy-five years or so it entered into a kind of partnership with American corporations. This did not mean any retreat, of course, in the accumulation of national power but rather the reverse, since it was the states initially which were disposed to try to control the exploitive activities of business enterprise. The Court thus became in large measure a court of appeal for corporations seeking to avoid state regulation. But this Court, in its initial incarnation was, one must keep in mind, the Taney Court, a Court appointed by Democratic presidents and firmly committed to Democratic principles. Thus while the issue came in time to be seen as corporations versus the people, the first stage was one in which the dominant ethos, rural or urban, storekeeper or tycoon, was decidedly hospitable to entrepreneurial or business activity in a wide variety of forms.

In the words of an editor of the *Boston Post*, the Court had always been disposed to "sustain privilege and monopoly" and while protecting "the strictly legal rights of the poor man," they took care "never to extend those rights by construction, while they always favor the vested privileges of exclusive classes, even beyond the letter and spirit of the written law." One of the justices, John Catron, echoed the same theme, complaining of "the unparalleled increase of corporations throughout the Union within the last few years; the ease with which charters containing exclusive privileges and exemptions are obtained; the vast amount of property, power and exclusive benefits, prejudicial to other classes of society, that are vested in and held by these bodies of associated wealth."

In the Supreme Court session of 1848 an interesting case was decided striking down a Massachusetts law—the so-called Passenger Law—that attempted to check immigration into the state. It is worth noting that the North, while reprobating laws passed by Southern states to keep out free blacks, did not scruple to pass laws designed to bar undesirable immigrants. The Court was badly split on the decision and even the arguments of the majority varied widely. The practice of a single decision for the majority, established by Marshall, now gave way in a number of cases to individual opinions read by each justice. The effect was to blunt the force of the decisions and create considerable confusion among lawyers and in the lower courts. The practice also demonstrated the fact that under the pressure of the slavery issue, judicial opinion had itself become diffuse and often contradictory.

The end of the Mexico War in 1848 and the acquisition of the vast new areas of what were destined to become the states of Texas, California, Arizona, and New Mexico raised in the most acute form the question of the future of slavery. The Southern states were determined to have their proper share of the territory and the enemies of slavery were equally determined that the evil be confined to the states of the Old South. The stage was thus set for a decade of bitter animosity culminating in the fiercest struggle in our history.

John Calhoun of South Carolina became the champion in the Senate of the position that Congress had no authority to ban slavery in the territories. From this it was only a step to the argument that the Constitution in fact guaranteed protection of the institution of slavery in the territories. The question first argued in connection with the application of Oregon for admission to the Union acquired a fresh urgency in the matter of admission of California as a state and the organization of the territory of New Mexico, a huge area which included the greater part of the future states of Nevada, Utah, Colorado, and Wyoming. John Crittenden, senator from Kentucky, wrote a friend that it was important above all to keep "our tropical friends of the South, cool and temperate. . . . They must see that numbers are against them, and that they must be beaten on the question of the extension of slavery. . . . The right to carry slaves to New Mexico or California is no very great matter, whether granted or denied. And more especially when it seems to be agreed that no sensible man would carry his slaves there if he could. For the North or the South to talk about dissolving the Union for such a question, decided one way or the other, sounds to my ears like nonsense or something worse."

Since a majority of the justices on the Court were Southerners, it was assumed by the opponents of slavery, by the abolitionists, as we have seen, and by those who now came to call themselves Free-Soilers, that any decision by the Court would favor slavery. The antislavery groups prepared for this eventuality by trying to undermine public confidence in the Court. John Hale, a senator from New Hampshire, called it "the very citadel of American slavery. . . . Upon its decision rests the final hope of slavery." Meanwhile the Democrats, long enemies of the Court, now confident that the regional origins of the justices would dispose them to render verdicts favorable to their section, i.e., to the extension of slavery, took every occasion to praise the Court's wisdom and impartiality and to urge their countrymen to abide by its decisions in the matter of slavery. A Georgia senator declared sonorously, "The Supreme Court has been established for the very purpose of giving its authoritative interpretation, and as a lover of the Union, I am willing to abide by its solemn decisions."

One consequence of the rancorous debate over the extension of slavery was the repeated effort of Congress to try to find a way to shift the responsibility for deciding the issue to the Supreme Court. Cowardice and desperation were doubtless strong motivating factors as well as the conviction of many Southerners that the Court would decide in their favor. But beyond that, the move was evidence that the Court had come to enjoy great prestige and authority in the country as a whole. Many who wished to have the Court decide the question genuinely felt that it was above politics and that, whatever its decisions might be, they would have a much better chance of being accepted without open and violent resistance than enactments of Congress.

Against this background of increasing acrimony the Fugitive Slave Law became the object of particular resentment in the North. The radical antislavery forces, believing slavery an immoral, un-Christian abomination, considered it intolerable that a slave who had escaped from the South with great personal risk and hardship should, when apprehended, be returned to his master. This law, it appeared to them, made the citizens of free states accomplices in enforcing slavery by requiring them to return escaped slaves to their masters, whereupon of course they were usually severely punished. Thus everything that tended to support the Fugitive Slave Law was anathema to antislavery Northerners. This feeling strengthened the hands of the abolitionists, who, in the early years of their opposition to slavery, had been regarded as fanatics. For most Northerners, slavery, however morally objectionable, was remote. Nothing did more to bring home to those dwelling north of the Mason-Dixon Line the enormity of slavery than these terrible dramas enacted in their midst in which slaves, some of whom killed themselves rather than return to their home plantations, were denied the freedom they had risked so much to achieve and dragged off, frequently by a federal marshal.

A combination of dissatisfaction, especially in the Western states, with the tendency of the Court to uphold corporations in the face of state efforts to control their activities plus the resistance in the Northern states to the Fugitive Slave Law, led to an increasing number of incidents in which states openly defied the edicts of the Court. In 1854 Ohio, California, and Wisconsin all refused to abide by Court decisions affecting those respective states. This time the doctrine of nullification appeared most conspicuously among the opponents of slavery, and the new Republican Party, which had as one of its basic principles the checking of slavery, declared that "the Republican Party naturally stand on the State-Rights doctrine of Jefferson." While the *New York Tribune* declared: "It is high time that the insolence and tyranny of our Federal Judges should be rebuked and punished."

One of the justices expressed the resentment of himself and his colleagues at the constant attacks in the papers and in Congress on the wisdom and impartiality of the Court: "It cannot be doubted," he wrote, "that the position of the judges of the Supreme Court, at this time, is in high degree onerous; and that while it exposes them to attack, such as no honest judiciary, in any country within my knowledge have been subjected to, they have not the consideration and support to which they are entitled. Their salaries are so poor that not one Judge on the bench can live upon what the Government pays him, and the legislative branch of the Government are not friendly to them." The *American Law Register*, a respected law journal, noted that "every disorganizing agency in the country appears to be at work. . . . There is such exasperation on one side and determination on the other, as was never known before; and it will need the greatest caution and good sense, to prevent an explosion which would rend the Union into fragments." "The Court was daily assaulted," the writer continued, "yet it has been and is a vast agency for good; it has averted many a storm which threatened our peace, and has lent its powerful aid in uniting us together in the bonds of law and justice. Its very existence has proved a beacon of safety. And now, when the black cloud is again on the horizon, when the trembling of the earth and the stillness of the air are prophetic to our fears, and we turn to it instinctively for protection,—let us ask ourselves, with all its imagined faults, what is there that can replace it? Strip it of its power, and what shall we get in exchange? Discord and confusion, statutes without obedience, Courts without authority, an anarchy of principles and a chaos of decisions, till all law at last shall be extinguished by an appeal to arms."

Futile as appeals to the authority of the Court were to be, there was, in the effort, a profound poignance. The depth of the anxieties expressed by Americans of all sectors and all persuasions are hardly to be plumbed. The feeling had grown year by year and now month by month that the life of the Republic was in the direst jeopardy. All that had been fought and struggled for in the Revolution, now only a memory—but a memory nonetheless that had preserved the country—seemed about to slip away: the slow and difficult growth in comity and in a feeling for the Union of the states, the vast and imponderable growing of the nation westward, the titanic legislative battles, the accumulation of judicial decisions creating a body of law, the muscles and ligaments of the body politic. There was not to be and, in retrospect, it is hard to see how there could have been any peaceful resolution of the central issue—slavery. The Court could no more cope with the problem than could the executive or the legislative branches of government. Thus what one witnessed in the last half of the decade of the 1850's was the disintegration of a people. It was a fearful moment for there is no more terrible experience than the death throes of a nation.

Much is said today, and rightly said, of the sins of white Americans against blacks. The grim count can never be finally tallied. But it must be remembered that it was not just blacks who suffered from the "peculiar institution." One of the great tragedies of history engulfed white and black alike, and in the strange calculus of history—in that unthinkable cataclysm which engulfed the peoples of every state, an episode too desperate and terrible to ever adequately render—white Americans paid a very full accounting, as George Mason in the federal convention had predicted they must, for an evil which relatively few of them shared in directly.

So we move, with the inevitability of a Greek tragedy, to the Court's denouement, the case of the black man Dred Scott. The case appeared on the docket of the Court in the spring of 1856 as *Dred Scott v. Sandford*. The origins of the case lay in a suit brought ten years earlier by Scott against the widow of his owner, a doctor, who, he argued, by taking him into free territory had made him a free man even after he had returned to Missouri, a slave state.

While the case was making its laborious way through the state courts and the federal circuit courts, Congress passed the Kansas-Nebraska Act repealing the Missouri Compromise of twenty-five years' standing and in effect declaring itself unable to resolve the question of the status of slavery in the territories. In the words of the Kansas-Nebraska Act, Congress did not "legislate slavery into any Territory or State nor . . . exclude it therefrom."

The Kansas-Nebraska Act thus represented the abandonment by Congress of its responsibility for solving the slavery issue. Passed under the threat of secession by the Southern *and* the Northern states, it turned the question over to the people themselves, as though to say we, your representatives, are powerless to cut this Gordian knot. Try it yourselves. There remained one final hope, the Court. But that hope, as we have already observed, was groundless.

When the Dred Scott case finally reached the Court in 1856, the wound of slavery was beyond healing. The justices, well aware of the explosive implications of the case, delayed returning a verdict so long that the *New York Tribune* wrote, "The black gowns have come to be artful dodgers." And the *New York Courier* wrote that the question which confronted the Court was whether it was "a political body made up of political judges. . . . The Court in trying this case, is itself on trial—a trial as vitally involving its character before the American people. . . ."

The Court *was* divided in fact along sectional lines with a majority ruling that (1) Scott was not a citizen of the United States and thus could not sue in a federal court and (2) that Congress could not, in any event, bar slavery from the territories (a ruling that in effect held the Missouri Compromise to have been unconstitutional). Dred Scott was still a slave. His owner, Dr. Emerson's widow, had meanwhile married an abolitionist congressman from Massachusetts, and a few months after the decision of the Court she set Scott free.

Taney, C. J.: . . . There are two leading questions presented by the record:

1. Had the Circuit Court of the United States jurisdiction to hear and determine the case between these parties? And

2. If it had jurisdiction, is the judgment it has given erroneous or not? . . .

The question is simply this: Can a negro, whose ancestors were imported into this country, and sold as slaves, become a member of the political community formed and brought into existence by the Constitution of the United States, and as such become entitled to all the rights, privileges and immunities, guarantied by that instrument to the citizen? One of which rights is the privilege of suing in a court of the United States in the cases specified in the Constitution. . . .

It is true, every person, and every class and description of persons, who were at the time of the adoption of the Constitution recognized as citizens in the several States, became also citizens of this new political body; but none other; it was formed by them, and for them and their posterity, but for no one else. And the personal rights and privileges guarantied to citizens of this new sovereignty were intended to embrace those only who were then members of the several State communities, or who should afterwards, by birthright or otherwise, become members, according to the provisions of the Constitution and the principles on which it was founded. . . .

It becomes necessary, therefore, to determine who were citizens of the several States when the Constitution was adopted. And in order to do this, we must recur to the Governments and institutions of the thirteen colonies, when they separated from Great Britain and formed new sovereignties, and took their places in the family of independent nations. . . .

In the opinion of the court, the legislation and histories of the times, and the language used in the Declaration of Independence, show, that neither the class of persons who had been imported as slaves, nor their descendants, whether they had become free or not, were then acknowledged as a part of the people, nor intended to be included in the general words used in that memorable instrument. . . .

They had for more than a century before been regarded as beings of an inferior order, and altogether unfit to associate with the white race, either in social or political relations; and so far inferior, that they had no rights which the white man was bound to respect; and that the negro might justly and lawfully be reduced to slavery for his benefit. . . .

The legislation of the States therefore shows, in a manner not to be mistaken, the inferior and subject condition of that race at the time the Constitution was adopted, and long afterwards, throughout the thirteen States by which that instrument was framed; and it is hardly consistent with the respect due to these States, to suppose that they regarded at that time, as fellow-citizens and members of the sovereignty, a class of beings whom they had thus stigmatized; whom, as we are bound, out of respect to the State sovereignties, to assume they had deemed it just and necessary thus to stigmatize, and upon whom they had impressed such deep and enduring marks of inferiority and degradation; or, that when they met in convention to form the Constitution, they looked upon them as a portion of their constituents, or designed to include them in the provisions so carefully inserted for the security and protection of the liberties and rights of their citizens. It cannot be supposed that they intended to secure to them rights, and privileges, and rank, in the new political body throughout the Union, which every one of them denied within the limits of its own dominion. More especially, it cannot be believed that the large slave-holding States regarded them as included in the word citizens, or would have consented to a constitution which might compel them to receive them in that character from another State. . . .

To all this mass of proof we have still to add, that Congress has repeatedly legislated upon the same construction of the Constitution that we have given. . . .

The conduct of the Executive Department of the Government has been in perfect harmony upon this subject with this course of legislation. . . .

And upon a full and careful consideration of the subject, the court is of opinion, that, upon the facts stated in the plea in abatement, Dred Scott was not a citizen of Missouri within the meaning of the Constitution of the United States, and not entitled as such to sue in its courts; and, consequently, that the Circuit Court had no jurisdiction of the case, and that the judgment on the plea in abatement is erroneous. . . .

We proceed, therefore, to inquire whether the facts relied on by the plaintiff entitled him to his freedom. . . .

In considering this part of the controversy, two questions arise: 1. Was he, together with his family, free in Missouri by reason of the stay in the territory of the United States hereinbefore mentioned? And 2. If they were not, is Scott himself free by reason of his removal to Rock Island, in the State of Illinois, as stated in the above admissions?

We proceed to examine the first question.

The Act of Congress, upon which the plaintiff relies, declares that slavery and involuntary servitude, except as a punishment for crime, shall be forever prohibited . . . north of thirty-six degrees thirty minutes north latitude, and not included within the limits of Missouri. And the difficulty which meets us at the threshold of this part of the inquiry is, whether Congress was authorized to pass this law under any of the powers granted to it by the Constitution; for if the authority is not given by that instrument, it is the duty of this court to declare it void and inoperative, and incapable of conferring freedom upon any one who is held as a slave under the laws of any one of the States.

The counsel for the plaintiff has laid much stress upon that article in the Constitution which confers on Congress the power "to dispose of and make all needful rules and regulations respecting the territory or other property belonging to the United States"; but, in the judgment of the court, that provision has no bearing [but] is confined, and was intended to be confined, to the territory which at that time belonged to, or was claimed by, the United States, and was within their boundaries as settled by the treaty with Great Britain, and can have no influence upon a territory afterwards acquired from a foreign Government. It was a special provision for a known and particular territory, and to meet a present emergency, and nothing more. . . .

At the time when the territory in question was obtained by cession from France, it contained no population fit to be associated together and admitted as a State; and it therefore was absolutely necessary to hold possession of it, as a Territory belonging to the United States, until it was settled and inhabited by a civilized community capable of self-government, and in a condition to be admitted on equal terms with the other States as a member of the Union. But, as we have before said, it was acquired by the General Government, as the representative and trustee of the people of the United States, and it must therefore be held in that character for their common and equal benefit; for it was the people of the several States, acting through their agent and representative, the Federal Government, who in fact acquired the Territory in question, and the Government holds it for their common use until it shall be associated with the other States as a member of the Union.

But until that time arrives, it is undoubtedly necessary that some Government should be established, in order to organize society, and to protect the inhabitants in their persons and property; and as the people of the United States could act in this matter only through the Government which represented them, and through which they spoke and acted when the Territory was obtained, it was not only within the scope of its powers, but it was its duty to pass such laws and establish such a Government as would enable those by whose authority they acted to reap the advantages anticipated from its acquisition, and to gather there a population which would enable it to assume the position to which it was destined among the States of the Union. . . .

But the power of Congress over the person or property of a citizen can never be a mere discretionary power under our Constitution and form of Government. The powers of the Government and the rights and privileges of the citizen are regulated and plainly defined by the Constitution itself. . . .

Thus the rights of property are united with the rights of person, and placed on the same ground by the fifth amendment to the Constitution, which provides that no person shall be deprived of life, liberty, and property, without due process of law. And an act of Congress which deprives a citizen of the United States of his liberty or property, merely because he came himself or brought his property into a particular Territory of the United States, and who had committed no offense against the laws, could hardly be dignified with the name of due process of law. . . .

Now . . . the right of property in a slave is distinctly and expressly affirmed in the Constitution. The right to traffic in it, like an ordinary article of merchandise and property, was guaranteed to the citizens of the United States, in every State that might desire it, for twenty years. And the Government in express terms is pledged to protect it in all future time, if the slave escapes from his owner. This is done in plain words—too plain to be misunderstood. And no word can be found in the Constitution which gives Congress a greater power over slave property, or which entitles property of that kind to less protection than property of any other description. The only power conferred is the power coupled with the duty of guarding and protecting the owner in his rights.

Upon these considerations, it is the opinion of the court that the act of Congress which prohibited a citizen from holding or owning property of this kind in the territory of the United States north of the line therein mentioned, is not warranted by the Constitution, and is therefore void; and that neither Dred Scott himself, nor any of his family, were made free by being carried into this territory; even if they had been carried there by the owner, with the intention of becoming a permanent resident. . . .

But there is another point in the case which depends upon State power and State law. And it is contended, on the part of the plaintiff, that he is made free by being taken to Rock Island, in the State of Illinois, independently of his residence in the territory of the United States; and being so made free, he was not again reduced to a state of slavery by being brought back to Missouri.

Our notice of this part of the case will be very brief; for the principle on which it depends was decided in this court, upon much consideration, in the case of *Strader et al. v. Graham.* . . . In that case, the slaves had been taken from Kentucky to Ohio, with the consent of the owner, and afterwards brought back to Kentucky. And this court held that their status or condition, as free or slave, depended upon the laws of Kentucky, when they were brought back into that State, and not of Ohio; and that this court had no jurisdiction to revise the judgment of a State court upon its own laws. . . .

So in this case. As Scott was a slave when taken into the State of Illinois by his owner, and was there held as such, and brought back in that character, his *status*, as free or slave, depended on the laws of Missouri, and not of Illinois. . . .

Upon the whole, therefore, it is the judgment of this court, that it appears by the record before us, that the plaintiff in error is not a citizen of Missouri, in the sense in which that word is used in the Constitution; and that the Circuit Court of the United States, for that reason, had no jurisdiction in the case, and could give no judgment in it. Its judgment for the defendant must, consequently, be reversed and a mandate issued, directing the suit to be dismissed for want of jurisdiction.

Southerners were, of course, pleased with the decision and praised the wisdom and impartiality of the Justices. Northerners were furious and the *New York Tribune* led the way in vituperation. The verdict was referred to as being rendered by "five slaveholders and two doughfaces." One editorialist wrote, "If epithets and denunciation could sink a judicial body, the Supreme Court of the United States would never be heard of again. Chief Justice Taney's opinion was long, elaborate, able and Jesuitical. His arguments were based on gross historical falsehoods and bold assumptions and went the whole length of the Southern doctrine." To the *Tribune* the decision was worth as much "as the judgment of a majority of those congregated in any Washington bar-room."

The *New York Independent* declared in a headline, "The Decision of the Supreme Court is the Moral Assassination of a Race and Cannot be Obeyed," adding, "If the people obey this decision, they disobey God."

A Democratic paper in Pennsylvania announced hopefully that the decision settled "certain points . . . beyond the reach of the fanatics of the Nation. . . . The decision is a closing and clinching confirmation of the settlement of the issue. . . . Whoever now seeks to revive sectionalism arrays himself against the Constitution, and consequently against the Union." The *Daily Union* of Washington struck a similar note. "If the sectional question be not now settled, then we may despair of the Republic. We believe it settled and that henceforth sectionalism will cease to be a dangerous element in our political contests. . . ."

The storm aroused by the decision had little to do with the decision itself but much with the state of mind of the country. It was plainly a blow to Taney, then eighty years old and infirm of body, who was near the end of a long and distinguished career on the Court, a career in which, by upholding the powers of the federal government while interpreting them in a manner more congenial to the spirit of the times, he had served to extend and strengthen the tradition established by Marshall. The attacks on the Court following the Dred Scott decision revive the memory of its early years, when every case seemed to provoke a move by members of Congress to render the Court ineffectual and unleashed a torrent of abuse in the Democratic press.

One effect the Dred Scott decision may well have had. The new champion of the Republican Party was a relatively obscure congressman from Illinois, Abraham Lincoln. In his famous debates with Stephen Douglas, a prospective candidate for the presidential nomination on the Democratic ticket, Lincoln forced Douglas into the position of opposing that part of the Dred Scott decision which forbade the territorial governments from excluding slavery. Since Douglas had staked his political career on the notion of popular or "squatter" sovereignty, that is to say that the inhabitants of a territory could, in establishing territorial governments exclude slavery if they wished, the result was a split among the Democrats, with John C. Breckinridge of Kentucky adhering strictly to the implications of the Scott case and Douglas breaking off to lead the Northern and Western wing of the Democratic Party.

In addition the Constitutional Union Party, most of whose members were old Whigs who put the preservation of the Union ahead of the slavery issue, nominated John Bell as its candidate. The three-way split enabled Abraham Lincoln to become president with a decided minority of popular vote. His opponents together polled two-thirds of the more than four and a half million votes cast.

Lincoln's election and the secession of South Carolina, followed by the attack on Fort Sumter, carried the question of the authority of the federal government from the courts to the battlefield. But Taney had another decision to render in *Ex parte Merryman*. A Southern sympathizer named Merryman, living in Baltimore, had been arrested and charged with passing information to the confederated forces in Virginia. Jailed by the military in Fort McHenry, Merryman got a writ of habeas corpus from Taney. When the officer in charge of Merryman's confinement refused to release him on the ground that Lincoln had ordered the suspension of habeas corpus in such cases, Taney issued a citation against the officer for contempt. In addition Taney issued an opinion declaring the suspension of habeas corpus unconstitutional and so instructed the president.

Taney, C. J.: . . . A military officer residing in Pennsylvania issues an order to arrest a citizen of Maryland, upon vague and indefinite charges, without any proof, so far as appears. Under this order his house is entered in the night; he is seized as a prisoner, and conveyed to Fort McHenry, and there kept in close confinement. And when a *habeas corpus* is served on the commanding officer, requiring him to produce the prisoner before a justice of the Supreme Court, in order that he may examine into the legality of the imprisonment, the answer of the officer is that he is authorized by the President to suspend the writ of *habeas corpus* at his discretion, and, in the exercise of that discretion, suspends it in this case, and on that ground refuses obedience to the writ.

As the case comes before me, therefore, I understand that the President not only claims the right to suspend the writ of *habeas corpus* himself, at his discretion, but to delegate that discretionary power to a military officer, and to leave it to him to determine whether he will or will not obey judicial process that may be served upon him.

No official notice has been given to the Courts of Justice, or to the public, by proclamation or otherwise, that the President claimed this power and had exercised it in the matter stated in the return. And I certainly listened to it with some surprise, for I had supposed it to be one of those points of constitutional law upon which there was no difference of opinion, and that it was admitted on all hands that the privilege of the writ could not be suspended except by act of Congress. . . . The great importance which the framers of the Constitution attached to the privilege of the writ of *habeas corpus* to protect the liberty of the citizen, is proved by the fact that its suspension, except in cases of invasion and rebellion, is first in the list of prohibited power; and even in these cases the power is denied and its exercise prohibited unless the public safety shall require it. It is true that in the cases mentioned Congress is of necessity to judge whether the public safety does or does not require it; and its judgment is conclusive. But the introduction of these words is a standing admonition to the legislative body of the danger of suspending it and of the extreme caution they should exercise before they give the Government of the United States such power over the liberty of a citizen.

It is the second Article of the Constitution that provides for the organization of the Executive Department, and enumerates the powers conferred on it, and prescribes its duties. And if the high power over the liberty of the citizens now claimed was intended to be conferred on the President, it would undoubtedly be found in plain words in this article. But there is not a word in it that can furnish the slightest ground to justify the exercise of the power. . . .

And the only power, therefore, which the President possesses, where the "life, liberty and property" of a private citizen is concerned, is the power and duties prescribed in the third section of the Second Article which requires, "that he shall take care that the laws be faithfully executed." He is not authorized to execute them himself, or through agents or officers, civil or military, appointed by himself, but he is to take care that they be faithfully carried into execution as they are expounded and adjudged by the co-ordinate branch of the government, to which that duty is assigned by the Constitution. It is thus made his duty to come in aid of the judicial authority, if it shall be resisted by force too strong to be overcome without the assistance of the Executive arm. But in exercising this power, he acts in subordination to judicial authority, assisting it to execute its process and enforce its judgments.

With such provisions in the Constitution, expressed in language too clear to be misunderstood by anyone, I can see no ground whatever for supposing that the President in any emergency or in any state of things can authorize the suspension of the privilege of the writ of *habeas corpus*, or arrest a citizen except in aid of the judicial power. He certainly does not faithfully execute the laws if he takes upon himself legislative power by suspending the writ of *habeas corpus*—and the judicial power, also, by arresting and imprisoning a person without due process of law. Nor can any argument be drawn from the nature of sovereignty, or the necessities of government for self-defence, in times of tumult and danger. The Government of the United States is one of delegated and limited powers. It derives its existence and authority altogether from the Constitution, and neither of its branches— executive, legislative, or judicial—can exercise any of the powers of government beyond those specified and granted. . . . The documents before me show that the military authority in this case has gone far beyond the mere suspension of the privilege of the writ of *habeas corpus*. It has, by force of arms, thrust aside the judicial authorities and officers to whom the Constitution has confided the power and duty of interpreting and administering the laws, and substituted a military government in its place, to be administered and executed by military officers. . . .

The Constitution provides, as I have before said, that "no person shall be deprived of life, liberty, or property without due process of law." It declares that "the right of the people to be secure in their persons, houses, papers, and effects against unreasonable searches and seizures shall not be violated, and no warrant shall issue but upon probable cause, supported by oath or affirmation, and particularly describing the place to be searched and the persons or things to be seized." It provides that the party accused shall be entitled to a speedy trial in a court of justice.

And these great and fundamental laws, which Congress itself could not suspend, have been disregarded and suspended, like the writ of *habeas corpus*, by a military order, supported by force of arms. Such is the case now before me; and I can only say that if the authority which the Constitution has confided to the judiciary department and judicial officers may thus upon any pretext or under any circumstances be usurped by the military power at its discretion, the people of the United States are no longer living under a Government of laws, but every citizen holds life, liberty, and property at the will and pleasure of the army officer in whose military district he may happen to be found.

In such a case my duty was too plain to be mistaken. I have exercised all the power which the Constitution and laws confer on me, but that power has been resisted by a force too strong for me to overcome. It is possible that the officer who had incurred this grave responsibility may have misunderstood his instructions, and exceeded the authority intended to be given him. I shall therefore order all the proceedings in this case, with my opinion, to be filed and recorded in the Circuit Court of the United States for the District of Maryland, and direct the clerk to transmit a copy . . . to the President of the United States. It will then remain for that high officer, in fulfillment of his constitutional obligation to "take care that the laws be faithfully executed" to determine what measure he will take to cause the civil process of the United States to be respected and enforced.

The *New York Tribune*, so often the defender of the Court, accused Taney of treason, declaring: "No Judge whose heart was loyal to the Constitution would have given such aid and comfort to public enemies. . . ." The *Missouri Democrat* wrote "if the Government will follow up the suspension of the writ of habeas corpus with the dispension of . . . Taney it will be a good riddance for the country." The *Baltimore American*, on the other hand, supported the chief justice on the reasonable ground "that a Government which is fighting to maintain the integrity of the Constitution should impose no arbitrary action to suspend or interfere with rights plainly guaranteed under it, if it would have the support and countenance of its citizens."

Constitutional historians have subsequently upheld Taney's action as a proper one. If posterity upheld the justice, Lincoln was unimpressed and through the course of the war he took actions whose authority was nowhere to be found in the Constitution—among them rigorous censorship, military arrest and trial, and the continued suspension of habeas corpus. In his view the necessity of preserving the Union justified such measures. In his own words: "Thoroughly imbued with a reverence for the guaranteed rights of individuals, I was slow to adopt the strong measures which, by degrees, I have been forced to regard as being within the exceptions of the Constitution and as indispensable to the public safety. . . . I concede that the class of arrests complained of can be constitutional only when in cases of rebellion or invasion the public safety may require them. . . ."

It is difficult to quarrel with Lincoln's logic. The question that remains, however, was whether the public safety did indeed require such severe (or unconstitutional) measures. On this point historians have differed. Taney, for his part, believed that Lincoln had destroyed the dignity and authority of the Court. Shortly before his death he wrote gloomily that the Court would never again "be restored to the authority and rank which the Constitution intended to confer upon it. The supremacy of the military power over the civil seems to be established and the public mind has acquiesced in it and sanctioned it."

The situation of the Court during the war was, inevitably, an anomalous one. The Constitution had made little or no provision for the particular exigencies of war, certainly not a civil war. Lincoln took a number of actions of very uncertain constitutionality, as we have seen. However, if the courts had clipped Lincoln's wings by declaring his acts unconstitutional, the result might well have been the defeat of the Union or a sharp increase in the internal divisions in the North with crippling effects on its military efforts.

Chief Justice Taney died in October, 1864, at eighty-eight years of age. He had presided over the Court for twenty-eight years. George Ticknor Curtis, who had argued for Dred Scott before Taney, wrote,

"He was indeed a great magistrate, and a man of singular purity of life and character. That there should have been one mistake in a judicial career so long, so exalted, and so useful, is only proof of the imperfection of our natures. . . ." One of his fellow judges wrote of him: "He had inducted into office nine Presidents of the United States; and as he stood on that historic eastern front of the Capitol, the Republic's giant steps, in the lofty dignity of his great form and office, year after year witnessing and assisting at the rise and fall of parties, of administrations, of dynasties, all else seemed to be transitory as day and night, evanescent as dream-spectres, whilst he and it were stable and monumental alone in this government." It may well have been that in the formative years of the Republic Americans could tolerate the relative briefness of their leaders' terms of office—four or eight years—because Marshall and Taney served thirty-five and twenty-eight years successively, and those years gave to the federal government an appearance of continuity that it sorely needed. The fact is, the Supreme Court, in the American system, took the place of kings, popes, and priests in that it represented both continuity and authority. It passed judgment on the most profound theoretical and moral issues as well as on a host of thoroughly practical and mundane matters.

XIX

THE COURT AND
RECONSTRUCTION

WITH TANEY'S DEATH, FOLLOWED LESS THAN A YEAR LATER BY THE
surrender of the South and the reestablishment of the Union, the first
and most significant period of the Court's history came to an end.
Through the first sixty years of its life the decisions of the Court had
been given dramatic emphasis by the uncertain issue of states' rights
(nullification in its most extreme form) versus federal power. Hardly
an important case came before the Court that was not affected by this
basic division. The war settled it for all practical purposes. The Court
was thus able to turn its attention to other matters. By the same token,
while its decisions consistently favored the commercial and industrial
interests which, it might be argued, had most clearly triumphed in the
victory of the North and now intended to enjoy the spoils of war, they
attracted far less attention and created much less controversy. The
principal opposition to the Court had been Southern Democratic.

To the dominant Secular-Democratic Consciousness the Court, as
we have seen, was the antidemocratic element in the Constitution, the
branch which was perceived as persistently thwarting the popular will.
The defeat of the South and the destruction of its political power for
half a century or more, while it resulted in the freeing of the slaves,
meant also, paradoxically, a setback for democracy. A strong national
government was much to be preferred by the business interests to a
weak central government, provided always that they could dominate
the government.

Salmon P. Chase of Ohio was appointed by Lincoln to succeed

Taney. In the first session of the Court after the new chief justice took his seat, John S. Rock of Massachusetts was admitted to practice before the Court. The *New York Tribune* published an account of the event: "The black man was admitted. Jet black, with hair of an extra twist—let me have the pleasure of saying, by purpose and premeditation, of an aggravating 'kink'—unqualifiedly, obtrusively, defiantly 'Nigger'—with no palliation of complexion, no let-down in lip, no compromise in nose, no abatement whatever in any facial, cranial, osteological particular from the despised standard of humanity brutally set up in our politics and in our Judicatory by the Dred Scott decision—this inky-hued African stood, in the monarchial power of recognized American Manhood and American Citizenship, within the bar of the Court which had solemnly pronounced that black men have no rights which white men were bound to respect. . . . By Jupiter, the sight was grand! 'Twas dramatic, too." [The Court, incidentally, had never said that "black men have no rights which white men were bound to respect."]

The death of Lincoln in April, 1865, and the succession of Andrew Johnson, his vice-president, drew the Court, the executive branch of the government, and indeed the Constitution itself into a desperate struggle for survival. We have already taken note of the hostility of the infant Republican Party to the Court in the decade prior to the war, a hostility based in large part upon the Dred Scott decision. After the war the Radical Republicans undertook to punish the South. President Johnson was equally firm in his resolution to carry on the policies of Lincoln, to attempt to bind up the wounds caused by the war and to assist in reconstructing that devastated region. For the Republicans, firmly in control of Congress, the president and the Court were the principal obstacles to carrying out their punitive policies in the South. The issue was greatly complicated by the question of the freed slaves. The more extreme Republicans were determined to place political power in the hands of Southern blacks, who by and large were ill equipped to exercise it. These efforts at "black Reconstruction" produced a situation in many Southern states bordering on anarchy. Black consciousness could not overnight be converted by the simple act of emancipation into white consciousness. It was not a matter of racial inferiority on the one hand and superiority on the other, although the issue came ultimately to be cast in those terms; it was that white consciousness and black consciousness differed profoundly. The

South, facing the threat of rule by its former slaves, rallied all its resources to resist this imposition. A Republican Congress showed itself equally determined to effectuate it. The contest that ensued was almost as bitter and protracted as the war itself. The first target of Congress was the president.

The *New York Herald* declared: "The country is in the hands of Congress. The Congress is the Radical majority, and that Radical majority is old Thad Stevens. Government by the people has its glories!"

The uneasiness of the Republicans over the role of the Court in Reconstruction was confirmed when the Court in the case of *Ex parte Milligan* ruled that Lincoln had acted unconstitutionally when he ordered military courts in places where civil courts were functioning. The implications of the Milligan decision were plain. The Republicans anticipated continuing to occupy the South with military forces until the Southern states capitulated to the wishes of Congress. *Ex parte Milligan* threatened to put a serious crimp into such plans.

The decision was rendered by Justice Davis, who had been a close friend of Lincoln's. "No graver question was ever considered by this Court," he declared, "nor one which more nearly concerns the rights of every American citizen when charged with crime, to be tried and punished according to the law. The Constitution of the United States is a law for rulers and people, equally in war and peace, and covers with the shield of its protection all classes of men, at all times, and under all circumstances." It could not be suspended "during any of the great exigencies of government." To argue otherwise would be to invite "anarchy or despotism. . . . Martial rule can never exist when the Courts are open, and in the proper and unobstructed exercise of their jurisdiction."

> Davis, J.: . . . The controlling question in the case is this: Upon the *facts* stated in Milligan's petition, and the exhibits filed, had the military commission mentioned in its *jurisdiction*, legally, to try and sentence him? Milligan, not a resident of one of the rebellious states, or a prisoner of war, but a citizen of Indiana for twenty years past, and never in the military or naval service, is, while at his home, arrested by the military power of the United States, imprisoned, and, on certain criminal charges preferred against him, tried, convicted, and sentenced to be hanged by a military commission, organized under the direction of the military commander of the military district of Indiana.

Had this tribunal the *legal* power and authority to try and punish this man?

The Constitution of the United States is a law for rulers and people, equally in war and in peace, and covers with the shield of its protection all classes of men, at all times, and under all circumstances. No doctrine, involving more pernicious consequences, was ever invented by the wit of man than that any of its provisions can be suspended during any of the great exigencies of government. Such a doctrine leads directly to anarchy or despotism, but the theory of necessity on which it is based is false; for the government, within the Constitution, has all the powers granted to it which are necessary to preserve its existence; as has been happily proved by the result of the great effort to throw off its just authority.

Have any of the rights guaranteed by the Constitution been violated in the case of Milligan? and if so, what are they?

Every trial involves the exercise of judicial power; and from what source did the military commission that tried him derive their authority? Certainly no part of the judicial power of the country was conferred on them; because the Constitution expressly vests it "in one Supreme Court and such inferior courts as the Congress may from time to time ordain and establish," and it is not pretended that the commission was a court ordained and established by Congress. They cannot justify on the mandate of the President, because he is controlled by law, and has his appropriate sphere of duty, which is to execute, not to make, the laws; and there is "no unwritten criminal code to which resort can be had as a source of jurisdiction."

But it is said that the jurisdiction is complete under the "laws and usages of war."

It can serve no useful purpose to inquire what those laws and usages are, whence they originated, where found, and on whom they operate; they can never be applied to citizens in states which have upheld the authority of the government, and where the courts are open and their process unobstructed. This Court has judicial knowledge that in Indiana the federal authority was always unopposed, and its courts always open to hear criminal accusations and redress grievances; and no usage of war would sanction a military trial there for any offense whatever of a citizen in civil life, in nowise connected with the military service. Congress could grant no such power; and to the honor of our national legislature be it said, it has never been provoked by the state of the country even to attempt its exercise. One of the plainest constitutional provisions was, therefore, infringed when Milligan was tried by a court not ordained and established by Congress, and not composed of judges appointed during good behavior.

Why was he not delivered to the circuit court of Indiana to be proceeded against according to law? . . . If it was dangerous, in the distracted condition of affairs, to leave Milligan unrestrained of his liberty, because he "conspired against the government, afforded aid and comfort to rebels, and incited the people to insurrection," the *law* said, arrest him, confine him closely, render him powerless to do further mischief; and then present his case to the grand jury of the district, with proofs of his guilt, and, if indicted, try him according to the course of the common law. If this had been done, the Constitution would have been vindicated, the law of 1863 enforced, and the securities for personal liberty preserved and defended.

Another guarantee of freedom was broken when Milligan was denied a trial by jury. . . .

It is claimed that martial law covers with its broad mantle the proceedings of this military commission. The proposition is this: that in a time of war the commander of an armed force (if, in his opinion, the exigencies of the country demand it, and of which he is to judge) has the power, within the lines of his military district, to suspend all civil rights and their remedies, and subject citizens as well as soldiers to the rule of *his will*; and in the exercise of his lawful authority cannot be restrained, except by his superior officer or the President of the United States. . . .

The statement of this proposition shows its importance; for, if true, republican government is a failure, and there is an end of liberty regulated by law. Martial law, established on such a basis, destroys every guarantee of the Constitution, and effectually renders the "military independent of, and superior to, the civil power,"—the attempt to do which by the king of Great Britain was deemed by our fathers such an offense, that they assigned it to the world as one of the causes which impelled them to declare their independence. Civil liberty and this kind of martial law cannot endure together; the antagonism is irreconcilable; and, in the conflict, one or the other must perish. . . .

The necessities of the service, during the late rebellion, required that the loyal states should be placed within the limits of certain military districts and commanders appointed in them; and, it is urged, that this, in a military sense, constituted them the theatre of military operations; and, as in this case, Indiana had been and was again threatened with invasion by the enemy, the occasion was furnished to establish martial law. The conclusion does not follow from the premises. If armies were collected in Indiana, they were to be employed in another locality, where the laws were obstructed and the national authority disputed. On *her* soil there was no hostile foot; if once invaded, that invasion was at an end, and with it all pretext for martial law. Martial law cannot arise from a *threatened* invasion. The necessity must be actual and present; the invasion real, such as effectually closes the courts and deposes the civil administration. . . .

Martial rule can never exist where the courts are open, and in the proper and unobstructed exercise of their jurisdiction. It is also confined to the locality of actual war. Because, during the late rebellion it could have been enforced in Virginia, where the national authority was overturned and the courts driven out, it does not follow that it should obtain in Indiana, where that authority was never disputed, and justice was always administered. And so in the case of a foreign invasion, martial rule may become a necessity in one state, when, in another, it would be "mere lawless violence." . . .

Chase, in a concurring opinion, supported the power of Congress "to authorize trials for crimes against the security and safety of the National forces," while agreeing with his fellow justices that Milligan should go free. Such power, he noted, "may be derived from its constitutional authority to raise and support armies and to declare war. . . ." The *Cleveland Herald* spoke for a host of indignant Republicans when it declared: "A new and most mischievous weapon has been placed in the hands of those who oppose the great Union party," and another paper called it "the most dangerous opinion ever pronounced" by the Court, "a mere partisan harangue." The *New York Herald* called for the removal of "these antediluvian Judges" who "seem to forget that the war was an appeal from the Constitution to the sword."

The *National Intelligencer*, a Washington paper, expressed the view that "treason, vanquished upon the battlefield and hunted from every other retreat, has at last found a secure shelter in the bosom of the Supreme Court." Again one can hardly avoid reflecting on the irony of the situation: in the early years of the Court, it was Jefferson and the South which attacked the Court relentlessly. Now that same Court was the primary bulwark of the South against the vindictiveness of the North. Again the Court undertook to thwart "the will of the majority," a primary tenet of democracy, in the name of constitutional justice.

President Johnson, acting promptly upon the decision of the Court, ordered all trials by military commissions of civilians in Southern states terminated and the defendants dismissed. It must be admitted that while *Ex parte Milligan* was good law and has since been acclaimed as a landmark in decisions affecting civil rights, the fact was that by outlawing the military courts which had been used to supersede state courts, it made it very difficult to convict a white Southerner of depriving a black Southerner of *his* civil rights. Thus the principal sufferer was the freedman, who lost the protection afforded him by the intervention of military courts.

Thaddeus Stevens, leader of the Radical Republican faction, realizing that any project to impeach the justices would be full of pitfalls and dangers, decided to move for the impeachment of the president himself. Meanwhile, congressmen explored other ways to curtail the powers of the Court. *Harper's Weekly*, denouncing the Court for frustrating the will of the people, recommended that "it be swamped by a thorough reorganization and increased number of Judges. . . . The question . . . is . . . whether loyal men or rebels shall reorganize the Union." In the House a congressman from Pennsylvania called the Court "the main reliance of the intractable, ruling classes of the South." The demand for the reform of the Court was not a party issue but "the demands of a great revolution which cannot be resisted but which must run its course." The issue boiled down to whether the Court would in effect nullify the Reconstruction legislation passed by Congress.

Since *Ex parte Milligan*, and a series of decisions following it, were rendered by a sharply divided Court, the next strategy of the Republican Congress was to pass a statute requiring that on all decisions involving constitutional issues, the Court must have a two thirds majority in order for the decision to stand. This passed the House 116 to 39. The *Independent* applauded the bill, declaring, "The Supreme Court is at this hour the guilty confederate of Andrew Johnson. The country will rejoice to see it checkmated." The *Indianapolis Journal*, defending the Reconstruction Acts as "full of the rights and liberties of millions of men," deplored the possibility of their being "stricken down, by the decision of some old fossil on the Supreme Bench whose political opinion belongs to a past era. . . ."

Congress also passed the Tenure of Office Act withdrawing from the president the right of dismissing officers of the executive branch without the consent of Congress. The act was of doubtful constitutionality at best and when Johnson, in defiance of the act, fired Secretary of War Stanton, who had done his best to undermine Johnson's authority, his enemies were confident that they had grounds for impeachment. The end of Johnson's term as president was only seven or eight months away and it was evident that he could not be re-elected. The move to impeach him under such circumstances was clearly directed at curtailing the powers of the presidency and, along with the attack on the Court, had the manifest intention to destroy all checks on the powers of Congress.

Johnson was indicted by the House on the grounds of "high crimes and misdemeanors" and brilliantly defended by William Evarts, who made a shambles of the case against Johnson. To Salmon P. Chase, the chief justice, who presided over the proceedings in the Senate with notable fairness, must go a substantial portion of the credit for the failure of the impeachment. Seven Republican senators jeopardized their political future by voting against impeachment, the most dramatic case being that of William Fessenden of Maine, who had been one of the organizers of the Republican Party and Lincoln's secretary of the treasury. Fessenden, under intense pressure from Benjamin Wade, Thaddeus Stevens, and the leaders of the Radical Republican as well as from his own constituents, held out against impeachment, which failed by one vote of the necessary two thirds required for conviction.

While it is, of course, impossible to state with any certainty what the outcome would have been if Johnson had been convicted, it is hard to believe that it would not have represented a serious setback for the principle of constitutional government. At the very least it would have tipped the balance of power decisively toward Congress. It might well have been followed by the emasculation of the Court.

Despite the verdict in Johnson's favor, the Republicans did not abandon their assault on the Court. In December, 1869, after the election of Ulysses Grant but before Johnson's term was completed, Lyman Trumbull, senator from Illinois, introduced a bill which stated that since the Reconstruction Laws were political in character, "the propriety or validity of which no judicial tribunal was competent to question," the Court should not have "jurisdiction of any case growing out of the execution of said Acts." The *New York World* pointed out that Congress, by passing such a bill, would, in effect, be placing itself above the law. "The design," the paper declared, "is to emancipate Congress from all constitutional restraints which arise under any power that Congress chooses to assert is political in character." "If a majority of Congress is sure not to do wrong," asked a writer for the *Nation*, "why have any Constitution at all . . . Why not let them make their own Constitution, every session?"

The inclination of the Court to strengthen both the federal government and the corporate interests of the country was demonstrated in a series of cases following the conclusion of the war. Ironically, the Fourteenth Amendment, section 1 of which was designed to prevent freed slaves from being deprived of their rights without due process of law, became the basis for strengthening the rights of corporations. It read: "All persons born or naturalized in the United States, and subject to the jurisdiction thereof, are citizens of the United States and of the State wherein they reside. No State shall make or enforce any law which shall abridge the privileges or immunities of citizens of the United States; nor shall any State deprive any person of life, liberty, or property, without due process of law; nor deny any person within its jurisdiction the equal protection of the laws."

Two points might be made here. First the reader will recall the phrase "life, liberty, and property" as part of the Lockean trinity of rights so often invoked in pre-Revolutionary America and also recall that it was Jefferson's inspiration to substitute "pursuit of happiness" for "property" in the Declaration of Independence. Now "property" reasserted itself, and in so doing made it possible for corporations to claim rights under the Fourteenth Amendment in conflicts with states which sought to control their often greedy and exploitative activities. The corporation did this by the "fiction" of the Court that corporations enjoyed the same rights as "individuals." So it might be said that an amendment passed to protect the newly freed black, while it often failed in that respect, did advance the burgeoning interests of business. But that is only part of the story of the Fourteenth Amendment, the most significant of all those passed since the original eight, the Bill of Rights. The most important function of the Fourteenth Amendment was that it finally gave effect to the first eight. The reader will recall that the framers of the Constitution did not consider a Bill of Rights necessary since all the state constitutions had such bills and it seemed to them redundant to include one in the Constitution itself.

For the first seventy-five years of the country's history, the framers were vindicated. Marshall in *Barron v. Baltimore* had ruled that the first eight amendments did not extend to the legislation of particular states. Infringements of the bills of rights of the respective states were decided in state courts.

As we have already noted, the state courts, under greater political pressure than the federal courts, could not be relied upon to protect the rights of the citizens of the respective states, rights presumably guaranteed them under their own constitutions. The issue was brought to a head by the situation of the freed slaves. A number of Southern states passed laws after the war that severely limited the rights of free blacks. The Fourteenth Amendment was intended as a means of securing those rights. This could only be done, in the last analysis, if the Court was able to extend its jurisdiction over the state courts so that it could hear cases appealed to it from the state courts and even exert original jurisdiction where the rights of a freeman were impaired by a state. The need to give effect to the Fourteenth Amendment thus led to the doctrine of "incorporation." By extending the jurisdiction of the Federal Courts over certain cases having to do with the "rights" of individuals, primarily of course blacks in the post-Civil War era, the Court took a step toward making the Bill of Rights for the first time an effective part of the Constitution. The enemies of a strong central government who had insisted on appending a Bill of Rights to the Constitution because they feared the abuse of "national" power in the area of "rights" could hardly have anticipated that the first eight amendments to the Constitution would make possible the greatest, and in some ways the most important, extension of federal power in our history. If the Fourteenth Amendment failed of its noble purpose in the initial period of its history and was, in fact, egregiously abused, it certainly came, in time, to have its "day in court."

The *Slaughter-House Cases* came before the Court in 1873. These cases involved the right of the Reconstruction legislature of Louisiana to give a monopoly on slaughtering cattle to a single corporation. The plaintiffs retained John Archibald Campbell as their advocate. Campbell, an Alabaman, had served on the Court from 1853 to 1861. After Alabama left the Union, he resigned from the Court. Now he saw an opportunity to bring a case before it that might apply due process to lifting the federal military government over the

Southern states. He thus prepared a remarkable brief, a kind of mine of due process arguments drawn from history, philosophy, and law in almost equal proportions. It was one of the great legal briefs of the century and several of the justices pronounced themselves carried away by its logic and eloquence. The burden of his argument was, in the words of William Hamilton, that the Thirteenth and Fourteenth Amendments applied to all forms of servile and degrading work, thus they "ended not only slavery but involuntary servitude in every degree and form; [they] made forever unlawful throughout the whole land a servitude for a year, for an hour, or even for an occasion. A master could no longer command a servant to dance, to frolic, to make merry before him." White and black were equally entitled to their provisions. The amendments "brought the federal government into immediate contact with every person and gave to every citizen a claim upon its protecting power." Campbell's view was: the right to work was the only property the workingman had.

The justices split, four against the Louisiana statute granting the monopoly, five judging it a constitutional if unfortunate exercise of the authority of the state legislature. The crucial vote was that of Justice Samuel Miller, a Northerner, an abolitionist, a defender of the Union. "As the ex-Confederate [Campbell] asserted that whites and blacks were equal before the Constitution, the abolitionist on the bench refused to erase the color line. . . . The legislature had passed the statute as a health measure, and with the act of a sovereign state the Court would not interfere."

> The plantiffs in error . . . allege that the statute is a violation of the Constitution of the United States in these several particulars:
>
> That it creates an involuntary servitude forbidden by the 13th article of amendment;
>
> That it abridges the privileges and immunities of citizens of the United States;
>
> That it denies to the plaintiffs the equal protection of the laws; and,
>
> That it deprives them of their property without the process of law; contrary to the provisions of the 1st section of the 14th article of amendment.
>
> This court is . . . called upon for the first time to give construction to these articles [the 13th and 14th amendments].
>
> We do not conceal from ourselves the great responsibility which this duty devolves upon us. No questions so far reaching and pervading in

their consequences, so profoundly interesting to the people of this country, and so important in their bearing upon the relations of the United States and of the several states to each other, and to the citizens of the states, and of the United States, have been before this court during the official life of any of its present members. We have given every opportunity for a full hearing at the bar; we have discussed it freely and compared views among ourselves; we have taken ample time for careful deliberation, and we now propose to announce the judgments which we have formed in the construction of those articles, so far as we have found them necessary to the decision of the cases before us, and beyond that we have neither the inclination nor the right to go.

Twelve articles of amendment were added to the Federal Constitution soon after the original organization of the government under it in 1789. Of these all but the last were adopted so soon afterwards as to justify the statement that they were practically contemporaneous with the adoption of the original; and the twelfth, adopted in eighteen hundred and three, was so nearly so as to have become like the others, historical and of another age. But within the last eight years three other articles of amendment of vast importance have been added, by the voice of the people, to that now venerable instrument.

The most cursory glance at these articles discloses a unity of purpose, when taken in connection with the history of the times, which cannot fail to have an important bearing on any question of doubt concerning their true meaning. Nor can such doubts, when any reasonably exist, be safely and rationally solved without a reference to that history; for in it is found the occasion and the necessity for recurring again to the great source of power in this country, the people of the states, for additional guaranties of human rights; additional powers to the Federal government; additional restraints upon those of the states. Fortunately that history is fresh within the memory of us all, and its leading features, as they bear upon the matter before us, free from doubt.

The institution of African slavery, as it existed in about half the states of the Union, and the contests pervading the public mind for many years, between those who desired its curtailment and ultimate extinction and those who desired additional safeguards for its security and perpetuation, culminated in the effort on the part of most of the states in which slavery existed, to separate from the Federal government, and to resist its authority. This constituted the War of the Rebellion, and whatever auxiliary causes may have contributed to bring about this war, undoubtedly the overshadowing and efficient cause was African slavery.

In that struggle slavery, as a legalized social relation, perished. It perished as a necessity of the bitterness and force of the conflict. When the armies of freedom found themselves upon the soil of slavery they could do nothing less than free the poor victims whose enforced servitude was the foundation of the quarrel. And when hard pressed in the contest these men (for they proved themselves men in that terrible crisis) offered their services and were accepted by thousands to aid in suppressing the unlawful rebellion slavery was at an end wherever the Federal government succeeded in that purpose. The Proclamation of President Lincoln expressed an accomplished fact as to a large portion of the insurrectionary districts, when he declared slavery abolished in them all. But the war being over those who had succeeded in reestablishing the authority of the Federal government were not content to permit this great act of emancipation to rest on the actual results of the contest or the Proclamation of the Executive, both of which might have been questioned in after times, and they determined to place this main and most valuable result in the Constitution of the restored Union as one of its fundamental articles. Hence the 13th article of amendment of that instrument. Its two short sections seem hardly to admit of construction; so vigorous is their expression and so appropriate to the purpose we have indicated.

1. Neither slavery nor involuntary servitude, except as a punishment for crime, whereof the party shall have been duly convicted, shall exist within the United States or any place subject to their jurisdiction.

2. Congress shall have power to enforce this article by appropriate legislation.

To withdraw the mind from the contemplation of this grand yet simple declaration of the personal freedom of all the human race within the jurisdiction of this government—a declaration designed to establish the freedom of four millions of slaves—and with a microscopic search endeavor to find in it a reference to servitudes, which may have been attached to property in certain localities, requires an effort, to say the least of it.

That a personal servitude was meant, is proved by the use of the word "involuntary," which can only apply to human beings. The exception of servitude as a punishment for crime gives an idea of the class of servitude that is meant. The word "servitude" is of larger meaning than "slavery," as the latter is popularly understood in this country, and the obvious purpose was to forbid all shades and conditions of African slavery. It was very well understood that in the form of apprenticeship for long terms, as it had been practiced in the West India Islands, on the abolition of slavery by the English government, or by reducing the slaves to the condition of serfs attached to the plantation, the purpose of the article might have been evaded, if only the word "slavery" had been used. The case of the apprentice slave, held under a law of Maryland, liberated by Chief Justice Chase, on a writ of habeas corpus under this article, illustrates this course of observation. *Matter of Turner*, 1 Abb. (U.S.) 84. And it is all that we deem necessary to say on the application of that article to the statute of Louisiana now under consideration.

The process of restoring to their proper relations with the Federal government and with the other states those which had sided with the Rebellion, undertaken under the Proclamation of President Johnson in 1865, and before the assembling of Congress, developed the fact that, notwithstanding the formal recognition by those states of the abolition of slavery, the condition of the slave race would, without further protection of the Federal government, be almost as bad as it was before. Among the first acts of the legislation adopted by several of the states in the legislative bodies which claimed to be in their normal relations with the Federal government, were laws which imposed upon the colored race onerous disabilities and burdens, and curtained their rights in the pursuit of life, liberty, and property, to such an extent that their freedom was of little value, while they had lost the protection which they had received from their former owners from motives both of interest and humanity.

They were in some states forbidden to appear in the towns in any other character then menial servants. They were required to reside on and cultivate the soil without the right to purchase or own it. They were excluded from many occupations of gain, and were not permitted to give testimony in the courts in any case where a white man was a party. It was said that their lives were at the mercy of bad men, either because the laws for their protection were insufficient or were not enforced.

These circumstances, whatever of falsehood or misconception may have been mingled with their presentation, forced upon the statesmen who had conducted the Federal government in safety through the crisis of the Rebellion and who supposed that by the 13th article of amendment they had secured the result of their labors, the conviction that something more was necessary in the way of constitutional protection to the unfortunate race who had suffered so much. They accordingly passed through Congress the proposition for the 14th Amendment, and they declined to treat as restored to their full participation in the government of the Union the states which had been in insurrection, until they ratified that article by a formal vote of their legislative bodies.

Before we proceed to examine more critically the provisions of this amendment, on which the plaintiffs in error rely, let us complete and dismiss the history of the recent amendments, as that history relates to the general purpose which pervades them all. A few years' experience satisfied the thoughtful men who had been the authors of the other two Amendments that, notwithstanding the restraints of those articles on the states, and the laws passed under the additional powers granted to Congress, these were inadequate for the protection of life, liberty, and property, without which freedom to the slave was no boon. They were in all those states denied the right of suffrage. The laws were administered by the white man alone. It was urged that a race of men distinctively marked as was the negro, living in the midst of another and dominant race, could never be fully secured in their person and their property without the right of suffrage.

Hence the 15th Amendment, which declares that "the right of a citizen of the United States to vote shall not be denied or abridged by any state on account of race, color, or previous condition of servitude." The negro having, by the 14th Amendment, been declared to be a citizen of the United States, is thus made a voter in every state of the Union.

We repeat, then, in the light of this recapitulation of events, almost too recent to be called history, but which are familiar to us all; and on the most casual examination of the language of these amendments, no one can fail to be impressed with the one pervading purpose found in them all, lying at the foundation of each, and without which none of them would have been even suggested; we mean the freedom of the slave race, the security and firm establishment of that freedom, and the protection of the newly made freemen and citizen from the oppressions of those who had formerly exercised unlimited dominion over him. It is true that only the 15th Amendment, in terms, mentions the negro by speaking of his color and his slavery. But it is just as true that each of the other articles was addressed to the grievances of that race, and designed to remedy them as the fifteenth.

We do not say that no one else but the negro can share in this protection. Both the language and spirit of these articles are to have their fair and just weight in any question of construction. Undoubtedly, while negro slavery alone was in the mind of the Congress which proposed the 13th article, it forbids any other kind of slavery, now or hereafter. If Mexican peonage or the Chinese coolie labor system shall develop slavery of the Mexican or Chinese race within our territory, this Amendment may safely be trusted to make it void. And so, if other rights are assailed by the states which properly and necessarily fall within the protection of these articles, that protection will apply though the party interested may not be of African descent. But what we do say, and what we wish to be understood, is, that in any fair and just construction of any section or phrase of these amendments, it is necessary to look to the purpose which we have said was the pervading spirit of them all, the evil which they were designed to remedy, and the process of continued addition to the Constitution until that purpose was supposed to be accomplished, as far as constitutional law can accomplish it. . . .

The constitutional provision there alluded to did not create those rights, which it called privileges and immunities of citizens of the states. It threw around them in that clause no security for the citizens of the state in which they were claimed or exercised. Nor did it profess to control the power of the state governments over the rights of its own citizens.

Its sole purpose was to declare to the several states, that whatever those rights, as you grant or establish them to your own citizens, or as you limit or qualify, or impose restrictions on their exercise, the same, neither more nor less, shall be the measure of the rights of citizens of other states within your jurisdiction.

It would be the vainest show of learning to attempt to prove by citations of authority, that up to the adoption of the recent Amendments, no claim or pretense was set up that those rights depended on the Federal government for their existence or protection, beyond the very few express limitations which the Federal Constitution imposed upon the states—such, for instance, as the prohibition against *ex post facto* laws, bills of attainder and laws impairing the obligation of contracts. But with the exception of these and a few other restrictions, the entire domain of the privileges and immunities of citizens of the states, as above defined, lay within the constitutional and legislative power of the states, and without that of the Federal government. Was it the purpose of the 14th Amendment, by the simple declaration that no state should make or enforce any law which shall abridge the privileges and immunities of citizens of the United States, to transfer the security and protection of all the civil rights which we have mentioned, from the states to the Federal government? And where it is declared that Congress shall have the power to enforce that article, was it intended to bring within the power of Congress the entire domain of civil rights heretofore belonging exclusively to the states? . . .

The adoption of the first eleven amendments to the Constitution so soon after the original instrument was accepted shows a prevailing sense of danger at that time from the Federal power and it cannot be denied that such a jealousy continued to exist with many patriotic men until the breaking out of the late Civil War. It was then discovered that the true danger to the perpetuity of the Union was in the capacity of the state organizations to combine and concentrate all the powers of the state, and of contiguous states, for a determined resistance to the general government.

Unquestionably this has given great force to the argument, and added largely to the number of those who believe in the necessity of a strong national government.

But, however pervading this sentiment, and however it may have contributed to the adoption of the Amendments we have been considering, we do not see in those Amendments any purpose to destroy the main features of the general system. Under the pressure of all the excited feeling growing out of the war, our statesmen have still believed that the existence of the states with powers for domestic and local government, including the regulation of civil rights, the rights of person and of property, was essential to the perfect working of our complex form of government, though they have thought proper to impose additional limitations on the states, and to confer additional power on that of the nation.

But whatever fluctuations may be seen in the history of public opinion on this subject during the period of our national existence, we think it will be found that this court, so far as its functions required, has always held, with a steady and an even hand, the balance between state and Federal power, and we trust that such may continue to be the history of its relation to that subject so long as it shall have duties to perform which demand of it a construction of the Constitution, or of any of its parts.

The judgments of the Supreme Court of Louisiana in these cases are affirmed.

Mr. Justice Field, dissenting:

I am unable to agree with the majority of the courts in these cases, and will proceed to state the reasons of my dissent from their judgment. . . .

The act of Louisiana presents the naked case unaccompanied by any public considerations, where a right to pursue a lawful and necessary calling, previously enjoyed by every citizen, and in connection with which a thousand persons were daily employed, is taken away and vested exclusively for twenty-five years, for an extensive district and a large population, in a single corporation, or its exercise is for that period restricted to the establishments of the corporation, and there allowed only upon onerous conditions. . . .

The question presented is, therefore, one of the gravest importance, not merely to the parties here, but to the whole country. It is nothing less than the question whether the recent Amendments to the Federal Constitution protect the citizens of the United States against the deprivation of their common rights by state legislation. In my judgment the 14th Amendment does afford such protection, and was so intended by the Congress which framed and the states which adopted it.

The counsel for the plaintiffs in error have contended, with great force, that the act in question is also inhibited by the 13th Amendment.

That Amendment prohibits slavery and involuntary servitude, except as a punishment for crime, but I have not supposed it was susceptible of a construction which would cover the enactment in question. I have been so accustomed to regard it as intended to meet that form of slavery which had previously prevailed in this country, and to which the recent Civil War owed its existence, that I was not prepared, nor am I yet, to give to it the extent and force ascribed by counsel. Still it is evident that the language of the Amendment is not used in a restrictive sense. It is not confined to African slavery alone. It is general and universal in its application. Slavery of white men as well as of black men is prohibited, and not merely slavery in the strict sense of the term, but involuntary servitude in every form.

The words "involuntary servitude" have not been the subject of any judicial or legislative exposition, that I am aware of, in this country, except that which is found in the civil rights act, which will be hereafter noticed. It is, however, clear that they include something more than slavery in the strict sense of the term; they include also serfage, vassalage, villenage, peonage, and all other forms of compulsory service for the mere benefit or pleasure of others. Nor is this the full import of the terms. The abolition of slavery and involuntary servitude was intended to make everyone born in this country a freeman, and as such to give to him the right to pursue the ordinary avocations of life without other restraint than such as affects everyone, and to enjoy equally with others the fruits of his labor. A prohibition to him to pursue certain callings open to others of the same age, condition and sex, or to reside in places where others are permitted to live, would so far deprive him of the rights of a freeman, and would place him, as respects others, in a condition of servitude. A person allowed to pursue only one trade or calling, and only in one locality of the country, would not be, in the strict sense of the term, in a condition of slavery, but probably none would deny that he would be in a condition of servitude. He certainly would not possess the liberties nor enjoy the privileges of a freeman. The compulsion which would force him to labor even for his own benefit only in one direction, or in one place, would be almost as oppressive and nearly as great an invasion of his liberty as the compulsion which would force him to labor for the benefit or pleasure of another, and would equally constitute an element of servitude. The counsel of the plaintiffs in error therefore contend that "wherever a law of a state, or a law of the United States, makes a discrimination between classes of persons, which deprives the one class of their freedom or their property, or which makes a caste of them to subserve the power, pride, avarice, vanity, or vengeance of others," there involuntary servitude exists within the meaning of the 13th Amendment. . . .

This legislation was supported upon the theory that citizens of the United States as such were entitled to the rights and privileges enumerated, and that to deny to any such citizen equality in these rights and privileges with others was, to the extent of the denial, subjecting him to an involuntary servitude. Senator Trumbull, who drew the act, and who was its earnest advocate in the Senate, stated, on opening the discussion upon it in that body, that the measure was intended to give effect to the declaration of the Amendment, and to secure to all persons in the United States practical freedom. After referring to several statutes passed in some of the southern states, discriminating between the freedmen and white citizens, and after citing the definition of civil liberty given by Blackstone, the Senator said: "I take it that any statute which is not equal to all, and which deprives any citizen of civil rights, which are secured to other citizens, is an unjust encroachment upon his liberty; and it is in fact a badge of servitude which by the Constitution is prohibited." . . .

It is not necessary, however, as I have said, to rest my objections to the act in question upon the terms and meaning of the Thirteenth Amendment. The provisions of the Fourteenth Amendment, which is properly a supplement to the thirteenth, cover, in my judgment, the case before us, and inhibit any legislation which confers special and exclusive privileges like these under consideration. The Amendment was adopted to obviate objections which had been raised and pressed with great force to the validity of the civil rights act, and to place the common rights of the American citizens under the protection of the National government. It first declares that "all persons born or naturalized in the United States, and subject to the jurisdiction thereof, are citizens of the United States and of the state wherein they reside." It then declares that "No state shall make or enforce any law which shall abridge the privileges or immunities of citizens of the United States, nor shall any state deprive any person of life, liberty or property, without due process of law, nor deny to any person within its jurisdiction the equal protection of the laws." . . . .

[The] equality of right, with exemption from all disparaging and partial enactments, in the lawful pursuits of life, throughout the whole country, is the distinguishing privilege of citizens of the United States.

To them, everywhere, all pursuits, all professions, all avocations are open without other restrictions than such as are imposed equally upon all others of the same age, sex and condition. The state may prescribe such regulations for every pursuit and calling of life as will promote the public health, secure the good order and advance the general prosperity of society, but when once prescribed, the pursuit or calling must be free to be followed by every citizen who is within the conditions designated, and will conform to the regulations. This is the fundamental idea upon which our institutions rest, and unless adhered to in the legislation of the country our government will be a Republic only in name. The 14th Amendment, in my judgment, makes it essential to the validity of the legislation of every state that this equality of right should be respected. How widely this equality has been departed from, how entirely rejected and trampled upon by the act of Louisiana, I have already shown. And it is to me a matter of profound regret that its validity is recognized by a majority of this court, for by it the right of free labor, one of the most sacred and imprescriptible rights of man, is violated. As stated by the supreme court of Connecticut, in the case cited, grants of exclusive privileges, such as is made by the act in question, are opposed to the whole theory of free government, and it requires no aid from any bill of rights to render them void. That only is a free government, in the American sense of the term, under which the inalienable right of every citizen to pursue his happiness is unrestrained, except by just, equal, and impartial laws.

I am authorized by Mr. Chief Justice Chase, Mr. Justice Swayne and Mr. Justice Bradley, to state that they concur with me in this dissenting opinion.

It is hard to let go of the *Slaughter-House Cases*. For one thing, they dragged on for three years, and when they were finally decided and Justice Miller had given his opinion for the majority, he was followed by the dissents of Justice Field and two additional separate dissenting opinions. Thus one of the most important cases heard by the Court was decided by a 5 to 4 majority with the chief justice (Chase) among those in the minority. Since the Thirteenth and Fourteenth Amendments are clearly the two most important since the original ten, the justices' discussion of them as they bore on the *Slaughter-House Cases* makes fascinating reading. Together they make up one of those relatively infrequent opinions of the Court which a modern reader can read with the feeling that the arguments of the majority and of the minority are almost equally persuasive.

Especially impressive is Justice Miller's identification of the Court with the cause of the emancipated slaves. Justices Field and Bradley are equally convincing in arguing that it was the intention of the framers of the two amendments to extend the protection of the federal courts to all citizens whose civil rights were imperiled by states. It is certainly tantalizing to consider how close the Court came in 1873 to extending the Bill of Rights to all Americans without regard to state boundaries.

The *New York World*'s comments on the decision are revealing. The intention of the proponents of the Fourteenth Amendment, according to the *World*, was to "bleach the negro into a political white man, to raise the African to the level of the Caucasian in his civil and political rights [which the *World* plainly thought a ridiculous notion]. . . . Such suits would never have been thought of, if certain shallow people had not gone crazy about the scope of the Fourteenth Amendment. There is no limit to the follies which have clutched at that Amendment for support. The Women's-rights people have claimed that it ordains female suffrage. A Chicago she-attorney claims 'that it admits her to the Bar.' . . . But the Supreme Court has decided . . . that its only legal effect is to make full-fledged citizens of negroes, but leaving the government of the country in all other respects precisely the same as if the Constitution had stood as first adopted, and no negro had ever left his native Africa. . . ."

The *Chicago Tribune* hoped that the decision "will put a quietus upon the thousand and one follies seeking to be legalized by hanging on to the Fourteenth Amendment. . . . The decision has long been needed as a check upon the centralizing tendencies of the Government. . . ."

It is not difficult to read between the lines (or simply read the lines themselves). The sympathy with the plight of the freed slave had sharply diminished in the North. The defense of states' rights was motivated by a growing uneasiness over the movement of freed blacks to the North as well as by the rising tide of immigration and the intensified drive of women in the decades following the war for *their* rights. The fact was that Reconstruction was a failure. Republicans and Democrats would, of course, dispute the reasons. The Radical Republicans were convinced that reactionary forces had conspired to frustrate their efforts to diminish the powers of the presidency and the Court, to punish the white South and secure the civil rights of blacks beyond the encroachments of Southern legislatures.

The Democrats replied that the attempt to place power unconstitutionally in the hands of an alliance of predatory Northern "carpetbaggers" and inexperienced freed slaves had produced conditions bordering on anarchy in the South; that the doctrinaire and unrealistic policies of the Radical Republicans had, in the long run, done a disservice to blacks by placing upon them responsibilities that they were incapable of discharging.

Historians have continued to debate the question ever since the end of Reconstruction. For several generations the most commonly accepted view of Reconstruction was that while it had to its credit some notable achievements, especially in its efforts to enable slaves to make the difficult transition to freedom, its vindictive attitude toward the defeated Southern whites and its unrealistic expectations of the free blacks condemned its grand plan to failure.

More recently, with the civil rights movement, there has been a disposition to review the standard interpretation of the Reconstruction and to argue that the Radical Republicans were in the right, that they had made substantial progress in bringing former slaves into white society, protected their rights as citizens and as human beings and established the conditions for social and economic as well as political equality. By this interpretation, the reaction of Northern whites against Reconstruction was primarily an expression of racial hostility or, at the least, of growing indifference to the plight of Southern blacks. Certainly, the fate of the Fourteenth Amendment as a consequence of the *Slaughter-House Cases* marks the overthrow of the hopes of the liberals and reformers as well as the remnants of the Radical Republicans. But, as we shall see, the Fourteenth Amendment, comatose though it might be, was by no means dead.

Perhaps the best thing we can say about the postwar decade is that, like the decade preceding the war, it was so given over to bitter partisan conflicts centering on the issues of slavery and Union that it is difficult to summarize it in any ultimately satisfactory fashion. The anguish and agony of that fratricidal struggle reached, and still reaches, to the deepest levels of our collective psyche. To read the interminable discharges of rage and venom in journals, newspapers, and congressional debates is instructive and profoundly depressing. In the generally benign histories of our nation little of the ugliness of this unremitting conflict reveals itself, partly, I suspect, because in the vastness of the tragedy it is, quite literally incomprehensible. Yet it is the ultimate theme, the most tormenting and impenetrable essence of our experience as a people. For two hundred years it has clung to us like an evil spirit that could not be exorcised. Even when, with infinite blood and suffering, slavery appeared to be "solved," the Gordion knot cut, it refused to stay solved; it rose again in different guise to mock our most cherished illusions. The anthropologist Gregory Bateson has called our attention to the double bind, that situation in which individuals often find themselves, or put themselves, in which there is, literally, no solution. The efforts at a solution simply serve to increase the bind. I suspect nations, like individuals, not infrequently find themselves in such double binds. It might have been evident to a disinterested observer that the Southern states after the Civil War needed to be relieved of the heavy hand of the federal government in order to get their respective houses in order, to recover their morale and to reconstruct their shattered economies. At the same time, it is undoubtedly the case the civil rights of blacks were less apt to be adequately protected by state courts than by the Federal judiciary.

Charles Warren, writing his magisterial history of the Supreme Court in the early 1920's, had no misgivings about the effect of the *Slaughter-House Cases.* "Had the case been decided otherwise," he wrote, "the States would have largely lost their autonomy and become, as political entities, only of historical interest. If every civil right possessed by a citizen of a state was to receive the protection of the National Judiciary, and if every case involving such a right was to be subject to its review, the States would be placed in a hopelessly subordinate position. . . . The boundary lines between the States and the National Government would be practically abolished, and the rights of the citizens of each State would be irrevocably fixed as of the date of the Fourteenth Amendment. . . ." To him it was "one of the glorious landmarks of American law." Of course, the Fourteenth Amendment, within a few decades of the completion of Warren's book, came to play exactly the role that Warren warned against. Whether the consequences that he described as necessarily following from it are indeed taking place, it may be too early to say. Certainly the "public mind" seems presently little agitated by the question of states' rights versus federal authority. Rather there is a growing disenchantment with governmental bureaucracy at all levels.

There was to be yet another act in the drama of the *Slaughter-House Cases*. The dispossessed butchers bided their time. A new Louisiana state constitution nullified the obnoxious statute. The Crescent City Company, owner of the monopoly, sued in the federal court on the ground that the legislature had infringed the obligation of contract unconstitutionally and deprived the company of its property without due process of law. Again the powers of the state were upheld and this time Miller voted with the majority once more at some cost to his principles. The two of the concurring justices took the occasion to vindicate their earlier minority opinion by declaring that the Crescent City Company had never had a proper legal existence in the first place. It was not that the state had the power to abrogate the contract, but that the company's original charter had always been unconstitutional under the Thirteenth and Fourteenth Amendments, as the dissenting justices had earlier maintained.

What is most intriguing about the post-World War II dependence of the Court on the Fourteenth Amendment in the area of civil rights is that it is now being used as its authors intended and as the liberal reformers of the Reconstruction era hoped it might be used—for the protection of the rights of black people and minority groups in general.

Giving emphasis to the *Slaughter-House Cases*, the Court in the case of *Bradwell v. The State* held that the refusal of the Illinois Supreme Court to license a woman lawyer was not in violation of the Fourteenth Amendment. Three of the justices noted that "in view of the peculiar characteristics, destiny and mission of women, it is within the province of the Legislature to ordain what offices, positions and callings shall be filled and discharged by men, and shall receive the benefit of those energies and responsibilities, and that decision and firmness which are presumed to predominate in the sterner sex."

Chase died in May, 1873, having served eight years, and Grant, after considerable waffling, appointed Morrison R. Waite of Ohio to succeed him. Waite was chief justice for fourteen years, and "his" Court continued the new line of supporting the states against the federal government, especially in regard to the rights of corporations under the Fourteenth Amendment.

While we cherish the image of the Court as a group of high-minded men, above the fluctuating tides of partisan politics, deliberating in a kind of splendid legal vacuum and handing down decisions like edicts of the gods from Olympus, or tables of the law from Mount Sinai, and while, in fact, they often showed a striking and commendable capacity to rise above popular clamors, they were unarguably human. Thus, while they often resisted (though by no means always) gross political pressure, they were, understandably, far more susceptible to the shifting social moods of the country. This was both inevitable and, to a degree, desirable. To have operated in some pure empyrean region of abstract and immutable legal theory, if such a region had existed, would have been eventually to alienate all political parties and factions and drift off into irrelevance and oblivion.

If relics of the Revolution had deplored the money fever that possessed the country almost from its inception, they would have passed a far harsher judgment on the financial chicanery that characterized the post-Civil War period. The most marked difference between the financial activities of the two periods was that the "money fever" of the thirties was, in a sense, the expression of "the people." Wild speculation in land, in railroads, in small factories, in undercapitalized banks by ordinary citizens, was perhaps its most conspicuous feature.

After the Civil War that obnoxious type, the modern tycoon, emerged. This was the money manager, the individual capable of commanding large sums of money to launch vast enterprises, the continental railroads being the supreme symbol of this field of entrepreneurial activity. The so-called robber barons cornered commodity markets and made enormous profits virtually overnight. They watered stock and bilked thousands of the gullible. Wages were held down, unions were small and weak, and efforts at unionization were often ruthlessly suppressed as un-American. A Fisk and a Vanderbilt engaged in a titanic battle over possession of a railroad. In California, Collis Huntington and Leland Stanford amassed fortunes by dubious or illegal means. In every state beleaguered citizens banded together to try to control rampant capitalism and prevent themselves from being ruthlessly exploited. Denounced as radicals and socialists they persisted in their fight to impose legislative restraints on what appeared to them as dangerous and immoral enterprises. In many Midwestern and Southern states they emerged as an identifiable party —the Populists, sworn enemies of the Eastern money men. They marched to battle under the banners of Protestant Christianity and the principles of the Founding Fathers: their battle cry was "Raise less corn and more hell!"

The *Slaughter-House Cases* set limits to the Fourteenth Amendment in the area of civil rights while having the effect, if not the intention, of encouraging monopolies, or, as they came to be more commonly called, trusts.

From the *Slaughter-House Cases* the Court proceeded to the *Granger Cases*. The rallying points for opposition to the exploitative and monopolistic practices of the huge railroad companies were the local Grange Halls in small agricultural communities scattered throughout the Midwest, the meeting places of farmers who suffered most acutely from the railroads' control of transportation. It was through the Granges that a campaign was mounted to regulate and control the railroad magnates. It was the view of the Grangers that "the State must either absorb the railroads or the railroads will absorb the State."

The effects of the Granger campaign soon manifested themselves in legislation passed by a number of agricultural states regulating freight rates for railroads and storage rates for grain elevators, with stiff fines for companies which violated the laws. In the words of the *Chicago Tribune*: "The accommodation of the public was left out of sight altogether; and the monopoly, standing on high ground of irrepealable charters and vested privileges, was defiant and unyielding. The outraged popular feeling at last took form in the way of public meetings, conventions and organizations, which in due time resulted in legislative enactments."

Meantime the Panic of 1873 brought a number of railroads to the verge of bankruptcy and somewhat altered the picture. A great hue and cry was raised by the railroad directors and their stockholders against the various state laws which they insisted would complete their ruin. The restrictive state laws were promptly challenged by the railroads in the courts, and a writer in the *American Law Review* denounced them as an assault on private property. He could not believe "that a movement would succeed in America which was really directed not against abuses, but against the rights of property. . . . When the Grangers had once proclaimed that their object was to 'fix rates' . . . it was perfectly clear that the Granger movement was rank communism." The corporations based their defense primarily on the charge that the state regulations had the effect of depriving them and their stockholders of "life, liberty and property without due process of law." And thus violated the Fourteenth Amendment.

The Court, to its credit and to the surprise and alarm of the business community, ruled in the case of *Munn v. Illinois* that the state regulatory laws were valid and constitutional. In doing so the Court reasserted a crucially important doctrine which greatly limited the protection afforded to corporations by a long accumulation of Court decisions reaching back to the Marshall era. Chief Justice Morrison R. Waite declared for the Court: "Property does become clothed with a public interest when used in a manner to make it of public consequence, and affect the community at large. When, therefore, one devotes his property to a use in which the public has an interest, he, in effect, grants to the public an interest in that use, and must submit to be controlled by the public for the common good. . . ."

Mr. Chief Justice Waite delivered the opinion of the court:

The question to be determined in this case is whether the General Assembly of Illinois can, under the limitations upon the legislative power of the States imposed by the Constitution of the United States, fix by law the maximum of charges for the storage of grain in warehouses at Chicago and other places in the State having not less than one hundred thousand inhabitants, "in which grain is stored in bulk, and in which the grain of different owners is mixed together, or in which grain is stored in such a manner that the identity of different lots or parcels cannot be accurately preserved." It is claimed that such a law is repugnant:

1. To that part of section 8, article 1, of the Constitution of the United States which confers upon Congress the power "to regulate commerce with foreign nations and among the several States;"

2. To that part of section 9 of the same article which provides that "No preference shall be given by any regulation of commerce or revenue to the ports of one State over those of another;" and,

3. To that part of Amendment XIV, which ordains that no State shall "Deprive any person of life, liberty or property, without due process of law, nor deny to any person within its jurisdiction the equal protection of the laws."

We will consider the last of these objections first.

Every statute is presumed to be constitutional. The courts ought not to declare one to be unconstitutional, unless it is clearly so. If there is doubt, the expressed will of the Legislature should be sustained.

The Constitution contains no definition of the word "deprive," as used in the 14th Amendment. To determine its signification, therefore, it is necessary to ascertain the effect which usage has given it, when employed in the same or a like connection.

While this provision of the Amendment is new in the Constitution of the United States as a limitation upon the powers of the States, it is old as a principle of civilized government. It is found in Magna Charta, and, in substance if not in form, in nearly or quite all the constitutions that have been from time to time adopted by the several States of the Union. By the 5th Amendment, it was introduced into the Constitution of the United States as a limitation upon the powers of the National Government and by the 14th, as a guaranty against any encroachment upon an acknowledged right of citizenship by the Legislatures of the States. . . .

When one becomes a member of society, he necessarily parts with some rights or privileges which, as an individual not affected by his relations to others, he might retain. "A body politic," as aptly defined in the preamble of the Constitution of Massachusetts, "is a social compact by which the whole people covenants with each citizen, and each citizen with the whole people, that all shall be governed by certain laws for the common good." This does not confer power upon the whole people to control rights which are purely and exclusively private, . . . but it does authorize the establishment of laws requiring each citizen to so conduct himself, and so use his own property as not unnecessarily to injure another. This is the very essence of government. . . .

A mere common law regulation of trade or business may be changed by statute. A person has no property, no vested interest, in any rule of the common law. That is only one of the forms of municipal law, and is no more sacred than any other. Rights of property which have been created by the common law cannot be taken away without due process; but the law itself, as a rule of conduct, may be changed at the will, or even at the whim, of the Legislature, unless prevented by constitutional limitations. Indeed, the great office of statutes is to remedy defects in the common law as they are developed, and to adapt it to the changes of time and circumstances. To limit the rate of charge for services rendered in a public employment, or for the use of property in which the public has an interest, is only changing a regulation which existed before. It establishes no new principle in the law, but only gives a new effect to an old one.

We know that this is a power which may be abused; but that is no argument against its existence. For protection against abuses by Legislatures the people must resort to the polls, not to the courts. . . .

We conclude, therefore, that the statute in question is not repugnant to the Constitution of the United States, and that there is no error in the judgment. In passing upon this case we have not been unmindful of the vast importance of the questions involved. This and cases of a kindred character were argued before us more than a year ago by the most eminent counsel, and in a manner worthy of their well earned reputations. We have kept the cases long under advisement, in order that their decision might be the result of our mature deliberations.

The judgment is affirmed.

As the first of the so-called *Granger Cases*, the *Munn v. Illinois* decision ranks with the most important cases ever decided by the Court. The *Granger Cases* marked the decline, among other things, of the older notion of laissez-faire capitalism, the notion that businesses in pursuing their own best interests would inevitably advance the best interests of the community. These cases also recorded the decline of the notion of private property as an absolute right that must predominate over matters of public interest. The *New York Tribune*, commenting on the decisions called them "an advanced guard of a sort of enlightened socialism." The charge of socialism was indeed widely made. An authority on constitutional law spoke of the Granger decision as more dangerous than "the notorious Dred Scott Case," one that threatened "disastrous consequences to the future welfare and prosperity of the country. . . . By the demagogues who are conducting the agitation now going on throughout the country, it is confidently appealed to and relied upon to sustain the yet more communistic and destructive legislation which they demand."

It soon proved impractical, however, for the state legislatures to try to set rates for the railroads and similar public services and the practice of commissions appointed to control rates based on the principle of protection for the public interest and a fair rate of return for the corporation became a common one in most states. It is this commission system which today in most states controls prices in a wide range of industries from milk to various forms of fuel and energy. By the same token those rates on interstate commerce, which it became increasingly evident could not be wisely or uniformly controlled by individual states, came under the control of federal commissions.

As the century drew to a close, more and more cases were carried to the Supreme Court under the Fourteenth Amendment. The justices themselves began to protest that the amendment had become a kind of legal catchall. One of them wrote in 1885 that the hardship, impolicy, or injustice of state laws is not necessarily an objection to their constitutional validity. The protest was in vain, the number of cases under the Fourteenth Amendment grew yearly; in the period from 1889 to 1918, some 725 cases were decided by the Court under the amendment. Indeed, so ubiquitous did the amendment become that we can only wonder what strains the Constitution would have been subjected to if this almost "accidental" amendment, ostensibly directed toward much more limited purposes, had not been added to the Constitution.

We are again reminded of the degree to which the decisions of the Court are influenced by the general attitudes in the society when we review the history of the Fourteenth Amendment in the area that it was specifically designed to deal with—the civil rights of Southern blacks. We have already seen the Court in the *Slaughter-House Cases* deny the authority of the federal government to intervene in the states. In 1875 Congress passed the Civil Rights Act, one of the last gasps of Reconstruction, an act intended to prevent discrimination against blacks in schools, hotels, restaurants, and public transportation. The *Nation* expressed the opinion that the law would be promptly judged unconstitutional. "Deeply as we sympathize with [the blacks'] wrongs, we have no expectation or hope of seeing them righted, by hounding on his old masters to acts of violence and lawlessness by the passage of equally violent and lawless Acts of Congress. The Reconstruction period is ended, and the negro, in future, will occupy such a position as his industry and sobriety entitle him to. Such bills as the one we have been considering do nothing for him but turn his friends into enemies."

The next year the Court judged an earlier Civil Rights Enforcement Act, designed to protect the right of blacks to vote, unconstitutional. Abuse of the rights of blacks in Louisiana, particularly in regard to their right to vote, to assemble peaceably, and to petition for redress of grievances, led to an appeal to the Supreme Court. The Court ruled that the federal Bill of Rights did not apply to Louisiana. The rights being violated "were not rights which citizens enjoyed by virtue of, or which were secured to them by, the Constitution of the United States. . . . The right to vote was held to come from the States only. . . ." The *Independent,* approving the Court's decision, declared: "Southern questions, so far as they are purely State questions, must be left to the States themselves and to those moral influences which finally shape the course of legislation. The Central Government cannot authoritatively deal with them, without producing more evils than it will remedy."

Strange as such notions seem today, it may well have been the case that the federal government could not have protected the rights of freed slaves in the South in the 1870's and 1880's without reestablishing military government in the Southern states, a step the rest of the country would not have condoned. And the Court was wise to acknowledge the fact, however much it had to strain law and logic to do so. A case can be made that blacks and whites in the South had, at least initially, to work out their own relationship. Black "consciousness" had to discover the time and mode to assert itself and claim its rights. To try to force the time might well have been to create chaos. In any event it was a problem that plainly did not lend itself to any simple solution. What must be emphasized here is that in the *Slaughter-House Cases* and those that followed it dealing with civil rights and the powers of the federal government vis-à-vis the states, the Court imposed repeated barriers to the powers of Congress. Since Congress was at its nadir as a responsible body in this era, it is probably true that, the civil rights of blacks aside, the Court did the nation a service in those decisions that curtailed the powers of Congress. In the words of the *New York Tribune* after the war, "Greedy and malignant partisanship began to demand, as necessary to the public welfare, measures which were only needful for the maintenance of unworthy or corrupt men in power. . . ."

It must also be said that the record of the Court in regard to cases involving the civil rights of blacks was by no means all negative. A number of its decisions supported the right of blacks to serve on juries and to vote. In *Ex parte Virginia*, in 1880, the Court refused to release on a writ of habeas corpus a Virginia judge jailed on a federal indictment for refusing to accept blacks for jury duty.

For the rest of the century, the Court reversed its earlier rulings in the *Granger Cases* and similar cases, which had given the states practically unlimited control over corporate activities. In a long series of decisions, the Court, evoking the commerce clause of the Constitution, severely limited the right of states to regulate interstate commerce. Most notable were those cases dealing with railroad regulation. By virtually removing the railroads from state control the Courts paved the way for the establishment of such federal regulatory agencies as the Interstate Commerce Commission.

In *Butterfield v. Stranahan* in 1904 the Court declared that once Congress had passed regulatory legislation "as far as was reasonably practicable" it could "leave to Executive officials the duty of bringing about the result pointed out by the statute." Thus began a new species of executive agency which would proliferate like fruit flies until they pervaded every area of American life and became a kind of super-government in themselves.

In the case of *Juilliard v. Greenman* the Court rendered one of the most important decisions of the postwar era in supporting the right of Congress to pass laws making paper money legal tender. To accomplish this the Court invoked the "necessary and proper" clause of the Constitution. The decision was attacked by the advocates of hard money as tending to encourage speculation and inflation and by strict constructionists as opening the way for a dangerous centralization of power in the federal government through use of the necessary and proper clause. Democrats applauded the ruling as a blow against "the money power." It would, the *Cincinnati Enquirer* said, do more "for the good of those toiling millions than those of any other decision made by the Supreme Court." States' rights champions were further alarmed by two subsequent cases in 1886, *Van Brocklin v. Tennessee* (which forbade the states to tax federal property in a state) and *United States v. Kagama* (which upheld the jurisdiction of the federal government over Indian tribes living on reservations within a state).

Each year saw new accretions of federal power through decisions of the Court. The fact seems to be that the initial postwar encouragement of states' rights was almost entirely the consequence of the unwillingness of the Court to intervene in the states in behalf of blacks. There was, of course, also the fact that the states tried to control predatory corporate activities. But the whole movement of the country was toward greater and greater centralization as it became clear that the states could not cope with powerful national corporations. The Civil War had settled, apparently for good, the question of whether recalcitrant states could nullify federal statutes or, in an extreme case, contemplate secession. All social and economic trends in the country encouraged greater concentrations of federal power. The Spanish-American War carried the country into a period of imperialism which contributed to the growing spirit of nationalism. The change was reflected in the language. Politicians and journalists spoke and wrote of the "Nation" rather than the "Union." The change in words represented a profound change in national consciousness. It had taken almost a hundred years to decide the issue of whether the United States were simply that—united states—or a single unified nation.

Among the remaining obstacles to federal consolidation was the Eleventh Amendment, which declares that no state can be brought before the Supreme Court as a defendant. In 1886 the Court in the *Virginia Coupon Cases* discovered an ingenious way around the Eleventh Amendment. The United States, through its courts, could bring action against an official of a state, if not against the state itself. This was a point too fine for any but the most subtle legal minds but it worked and since the Eleventh Amendment had been used by the states to avoid payment of public debts, public opinion generally supported the Court's new interpretation of the amendment.

In the case of the *Wabash Railroad v. Illinois* in 1886, the Court retreated from its position in *Munn v. Illinois* and the *Granger Cases* by ruling that a statute of the Illinois legislature designed to prevent discriminatory freight rates and all rebates, drawbacks, "or other shift or evasion" was unconstitutional because it infringed the right of Congress to deal with all matters of commerce between states. Since the shipment on which the suit rested had originated in Illinois but been delivered in New York, the Court ruled that Illinois had no control over it. Justice Miller for the majority conceded the right of the state of Illinois to control commerce within its own boundaries, "but," he added, "when it is attempted to apply to transportation through an entire series of states a principle of this kind, and each one of the states shall attempt to establish its own rates of transportation, its own method to prevent discrimination in rates, or to permit it, the deleterious influence upon freedom of commerce among these states cannot be overestimated. . . . If it be a regulation of commerce, as we think we have demonstrated it is . . . it must be of . . . national character; and the regulation can only appropriately exist by general rules and principles, which demand that it should be done by the congress of the United States under the commerce clause of the constitution."

The decision in *Wabash v. Illinois* aroused considerable protest among embattled farmers and those who were enemies to corporate abuse of power. When it was followed by *Pollock v. Farmers' Loan*

& *Trust Co.*, which held a tax on income derived from real estate unconstitutional, attacks on the Court increased in rancor. The argument was made that the Court had become the handmaiden of the privileged.

In 1894 the bitter Pullman strike centered in Chicago broke out. Strikers sought to halt the movement of trains in order to force concessions from the railroads. When an injunction against the strikers was secured under the Sherman Anti-Trust Act (which in effect treated the unions as illegal conspiracies), Eugene Debs, the union leader, sued out a writ of habeas corpus in the Supreme Court. The Court upheld the injunction on the grounds that the government had authority over interstate commerce and transportation, especially in regard to ensuring the free passage of the mails. The practical effect of the Court's decision was to encourage employers threatened by strikes to seek injunctions against the strikers.

The decision also had the effect of upholding President Cleveland's use of the National Guard to restore order during the strike, an act which was perceived as unfriendly to their case by the strikers.

The use of the injunction issued by federal courts to prevent an action of uncertain legality or constitutionality came to be a prominent legal device in this period and again added substantially to the powers of the Supreme Court and the federal circuit courts. As might have been anticipated, the injunction came to be used far more often to restrain the efforts of labor to improve working conditions than to inhibit business enterprise. The use of the injunction in labor cases came to be so controversial that the Democratic platform in 1896 declared that "we especially object to government by injunction as a new and highly dangerous form of oppression by which Federal Judges, in contempt of the law of the States and the rights of citizens, become at once Legislators, Judges, and executioners. . . ."

In much the same spirit, the governor of Oregon attacked the Court for exercising excessive and unconstitutional powers as a consequence of "the plausible sophistries of John Marshall," adding that it had "usurped the legislative prerogative of declaring what laws shall not be." "Our constitutional government," he added, "has been supplanted by a judicial oligarchy." The remedy was for Congress to "impeach the nullifying Judges." For the first time in more than a generation a prominent political figure had called for the impeachment of Supreme Court justices.

The following year, in the case of *Plessy v. Ferguson*, the Court sounded the death knell for the civil rights movement, at least as it related to the rights of black people. Here the Court upheld a Louisiana law providing for racially segregated railroad cars and stations on the grounds that there was no discrimination under the Thirteenth and Fourteenth Amendments if the segregated facilities were "equal," hence "separate but equal." It ranks, as Justice Harlan declared, with the Dred Scott decision in its negative effect on the lives of black people, particularly in the South. The most that can be said for the Court was that its decision was undoubtedly in line with the sentiments of a great majority of white people in the South and in the nation as well. To have ruled the Louisiana statute unconstitutional might well have created racial turmoil in the Southern states.

Plessy, the plaintiff was, ironically, "seven-eighths Caucasian and one-eighth African blood." Justice Brown delivered the opinion of the majority. Justice Harlan's dissent, one of the most eloquent in the history of the Court, is included here.

Mr. Justice Brown, after stating the facts in the foregoing language, delivered the opinion of the court.

This case turns upon the constitutionality of an act of the general assembly of the state of Louisiana, passed in 1890 providing for separate railway carriages for the white and colored races. . . .

The first section of the statute enacts "that all railway companies carrying passengers in their coaches in this state, shall provide equal but separate accommodations for the white, and colored races, by providing two or more passenger coaches for each passenger train, or by dividing the passenger coaches by a partition so as to secure separate accommodations: provided, that this section shall not be construed to apply to street railroads. No person or persons shall be permitted to occupy seats in coaches, other than the ones assigned to them, on account of the race they belong to." . . .

The information filed in the criminal district court charged, in substance, that Plessy, being a passenger between two stations within the state of Louisiana, was assigned by officers of the company to the coach used for the race to which he belonged, but he insisted upon going into a coach used by the race to which he did not belong. Neither in the information nor plea was his particular race or color averred. . . .

The constitutionality of this act is attacked upon the ground that it conflicts both with the thirteenth amendment of the constitution, abolishing slavery, and the fourteenth amendment, which prohibits certain restrictive legislation on the part of the states. . . .

2. By the fourteenth amendment, all persons born or naturalized in the United States, and subject to the jurisdiction thereof, are made citizens of the United States and of the state wherein they reside and the states are forbidden from making or enforcing any law which shall abridge the privileges or immunities of citizens of the United States, or shall deprive any person of life, liberty, or property without due process of law, or deny to any person within their jurisdiction the equal protection of the laws.

The proper construction of this amendment was first called to the attention of this court in the Slaughter-House Cases, 16 Wall. 36, which involved, however, not a question of race, but one of exclusive privileges. The case did not call for any expression of opinion as to the exact rights it was intended to secure to the colored race, but it was said generally that its main purpose was to establish the citizenship of the negro, to give definitions of citizenship of the United States and of the states, and to protect from the hostile legislation of the states the privileges and immunities of citizens of the United States, as distinguished from those of citizens of the states.

The object of the amendment was undoubtedly to enforce the absolute equality of the two races before the law, but, in the nature of things, it could not have been intended to abolish distinctions based upon color, or to enforce social, as distinguished from political, equality, or a commingling of the two races upon terms unsatisfactory to either. Laws permitting, and even requiring, their separation, in places where they are liable to be brought into contact, do not necessarily imply the inferiority of either race to the other, and have been generally, if not universally, recognized as within the competency of the state legislatures in the exercise of their police power. The most common instance of this is connected with the establishment of separate schools for white and colored children, which have been held to be a valid exercise of the legislative power even by courts of states where the political rights of the colored race have been longest and most earnestly enforced. . . .

The distinction between laws interfering with the political equality of the negro and those requiring the separation of the two races in schools, theaters, and railway carriages has been frequently drawn by this court. . . .

Upon the other hand, where a statute of Louisiana required those engaged in the transportation of passengers among the states to give to all persons traveling within that state, upon vessels employed in that business, equal rights and privileges in all parts of the vessel, without distinction on account of race or color, and subjected to an action for damages the owner of such a vessel who excluded colored passengers on account of their color from the cabin set aside by him for the use of whites, it was held to be, so far as it applied to interstate commerce, unconstitutional and void. . . . The court in this case, however, expressly disclaimed that it had anything whatever to do with the statute as a regulation of internal commerce, or affecting anything else than commerce among the states. . . .

It is claimed by the plaintiff in error that in any mixed community, the reputation of belonging to the dominant race, in this instance the white race, is "property," in the same sense that a right of action or of inheritance is property. Conceding this to be so, for the purposes of this case, we are unable to see how this statute deprives him of, or in any way affects his right to, such property. If he be a white man, and assigned to a colored coach, he may have his action for damages against the company for being deprived of his so-called "property." Upon the other hand, if he be a colored man, and be so assigned, he has been deprived of no property, since he is not lawfully entitled to the reputation of being a white man. . . .

So far, then, as a conflict with the fourteenth amendment is concerned, the case reduces itself to the question whether the statute of Louisiana is a reasonable regulation, and with respect to this there must necessarily be a large discretion on the part of the legislature. In determining the question of reasonableness, it is at liberty to act with reference to the established usages, customs, and traditions of the people, and with a view to the promotion of their comfort, and the preservation of the public peace and good order. Gauged by this standard, we cannot say that a law which authorizes or even requires the separation of the two races in public conveyances is unreasonable, or more obnoxious to the fourteenth amendment than the acts of congress requiring separate schools for colored children in the District of Columbia, the constitutionality of which does not seem to have been questioned, or the corresponding acts of state legislatures.

We consider the underlying fallacy of the plaintiff's argument to consist in the assumption that the enforced separation of the two races stamps the colored race with a badge of inferiority. If this be so, it is not by reason of anything found in the act, but solely because the colored race chooses to put that construction upon it. The argument necessarily assumes that if, as has been more than once the case, and is not unlikely to be so again, the colored race should become the dominant power in the state legislature, and should enact a law in precisely similar terms, it would thereby relegate the white race to an inferior position. We imagine that the white race, at least, would not acquiesce in this assumption. The argument also assumes that social prejudices may be overcome by legislation, and that equal rights cannot be secured to the negro except by an enforced commingling of the two races. We cannot accept this proposition. If the two races are to meet upon terms of social equality, it must be the result of natural affinities, a mutual appreciation of each other's merits, and a voluntary consent of individuals. . . . Legislation is powerless to eradicate racial instincts, or to abolish distinctions based upon physical differences, and the attempt to do so can only result in accentuating the difficulties of the present situation. If the civil and political rights of both races be equal, one cannot be inferior to the other civilly or politically. If one race be inferior to the other socially, the constitution of the United States cannot put them upon the same plane. . . .

The judgment of the court below is therefore affirmed.

Mr. Justice Harlan dissenting. . . .

In respect of civil rights, common to all citizens, the constitution of the United States does not, I think, permit any public authority to know the race of those entitled to be protected in the enjoyment of such rights. Every true man has pride of race, and under appropriate circumstances, when the rights of others, his equals before the law, are not to be affected, it is his privilege to express such pride and to take such action based upon it as to him seems proper. But I deny that any legislative body or judicial tribunal may have regard to the race of citizens when the civil rights of those citizens are involved. Indeed, such legislation as that here "in question is inconsistent not only with that equality of rights which pertains to citizenship, national and state, but with the personal liberty enjoyed by every one within the United States. . . ."

If a white man and a black man choose to occupy the same public conveyance on a public highway, it is their right to do so; and no government, proceeding alone on grounds of race, can prevent it without infringing the personal liberty of each. . . .

The white race deems itself to be the dominant race in this country. And so it is, in prestige, in achievements, in education, in wealth, and in power. So, I doubt not, it will continue to be for all time, if it remains true to its great heritage, and holds fast to the principles of constitutional liberty. But in view of the constitution, in the eye of the law, there is in this country no superior, dominant, ruling class of citizens. There is no caste here. Our constitution is color-blind, and neither knows nor tolerates classes among citizens. In respect of civil rights, all citizens are equal before the law. The humblest is the peer of the most powerful. The law regards man as man, and takes no account of his surroundings or of his color when his civil rights as guaranteed by the supreme law of the land are involved. It is therefore to be regretted that this high tribunal, the final expositor of the fundamental law of the land, has reached the conclusion that it is competent for a state to regulate the enjoyment by citizens of their civil rights solely upon the basis of race.

In my opinion, the judgment this day rendered will, in time, prove to be quite as pernicious as the decision made by this tribunal in the Dred Scott Case.

It was adjudged in that case that the descendants of Africans who were imported into this country, and sold as slaves, were not included nor intended to be included under the word "citizens" in the constitution, and could not claim any of the rights and privileges which that instrument provided for and secured to citizens of the United States; that, at the time of the adoption of the constitution, they were "considered as a subordinate and inferior class of beings, who had been subjugated by the dominant race, and, whether emancipated or not, yet remained subject to their authority, and had no rights or privileges but such as those who held the power and the government might choose to grant them." . . . The recent amendments of the constitution, it was supposed, had eradicated these principles from our institutions. But it seems that we have yet, in some of the states, a dominant race—a superior class of citizens,—which assumes to regulate the enjoyment of civil rights, common to all citizens, upon the basis of race. The present decision, it may well be apprehended will not only stimulate aggressions, more or less brutal and irritating, upon the admitted rights of colored citizens, but will encourage the belief that it is possible, by means of state enactments, to defeat the beneficent purposes which the people of the United States had in view when they adopted the recent amendments of the constitution by one of which the blacks of this country were made citizens of the United States and of the states in which they respectively reside, and whose privileges and immunities, as citizens, the states are forbidden to abridge. Sixty millions of whites are in no danger from the presence here of eight millions of blacks. The destinies of the two races, in this country, are indissolubly linked together, and the interests of both require that the common government of all shall not permit the seeds of race hate to be planted under the sanction of law. What can more certainly arouse race hate, what more certainly create and perpetuate a feeling of distrust between these races, than state enactments which, in fact, proceed on the ground that colored citizens are so inferior and degraded that they cannot be allowed to sit in public coaches occupied by white citizens? That, as all will admit, is the real meaning of such legislation as was enacted in Louisiana.

The sure guaranty of the peace and security of each race is the clear, distinct, unconditional recognition by our governments, national and state, of every right that inheres in civil freedom, and of the equality before the law of all citizens of the United States, without regard to race. State enactments regulating the enjoyment of civil rights upon the basis of race, and cunningly devised to defeat legitimate results of the war, under the pretense of recognizing equality of rights, can have no other result than to render permanent peace impossible, and to keep alive a conflict of races, the continuance of which must do harm to all concerned. . . . That argument, if it can be properly regarded as one, is scarcely worthy of consideration; for social equality no more exists between two races when traveling in a passenger coach or a public highway than when members of the same races sit by each other in a street car or in the jury box, or stand or sit with each other in a political assembly, or when they use in common the streets of a city or town, or when they are in the same room for the purpose of having their names placed on the registry of voters, or when they approach the ballot box in order to exercise the high privilege of voting. . . .

The arbitrary separation of citizens, on the basis of race, while they are on a public highway, is a badge of servitude wholly inconsistent with the civil freedom and the equality before the law established by the constitution. It cannot be justified upon any legal grounds.

If evils will result from the commingling of the two races upon public highways established for the benefit of all, they will be infinitely less than those that will surely come from state legislation regulating the enjoyment of civil rights upon the basis of race. We boast of the freedom enjoyed by our people above all other peoples. But it is difficult to reconcile that boast with a state of the law which, practically, puts the brand of servitude and degradation upon a large class of our fellow citizens,—our equals before the law. The thin disguise of "equal" accommodations for passengers in railroad coaches will not mislead any one, nor atone for the wrong this day done. . . .

I am of opinion that the statute of Louisiana is inconsistent with the personal liberty of citizens, white and black, in that state, and hostile to both the spirit and letter of the constitution of the United States. If laws of like character should be enacted in the several states of the Union, the effect would be in the highest degree mischievous. Slavery, as an institution tolerated by law, would, it is true, have disappeared from our country; but there would remain a power in the states by sinister legislation to interfere with the full enjoyment of the blessings of freedom, to regulate civil rights common to all citizens, upon the basis of race, and to place in a condition of legal inferiority a large body of American citizens now constituting a part of the political community called the "People of the United States" for whom, and by whom through representatives, our government is administered. Such a system is inconsistent with the guaranty given by the constitution to each state of a republican form of government, and may be stricken down by congressional action, or by the courts in the discharge of their solemn duty to maintain the supreme law of the land, anything in the constitution or laws of any state to the contrary notwithstanding.

For the reason stated, I am constrained to withhold my assent from the opinion and judgment of the majority.

Another "landmark" decision of the Court was that of *Lochner v. New York*. The New York legislature had undertaken to limit the working hours of bakers to ten hours a day. A bakery owner who believed that the statute had the effect of depriving him of his property, i.e., profits, without due process of law, carried his case to the Supreme Court, which, in 1905, again by a five to four majority, declared that it did indeed so deprive him and was therefore invalid.

Mr. Justice Peckham, after making the foregoing statement of the facts, delivered the opinion of the court: . . .

The state, therefore, has power to prevent the individual from making certain kinds of contracts, and in regard to them the Federal Constitution offers no protection. If the contract be one which the state, in the legitimate exercise of its police power, has the right to prohibit, it is not prevented from prohibiting it by the 14th Amendment. Contracts in violation of a statute, either of the Federal or state government, or a contract to let one's property for immoral purposes, or to do any other unlawful act, could obtain no protection from the Federal Constitution, as coming under the liberty of person or of free contract. Therefore, when the state, by its legislature, in the assumed exercise of its police powers, has passed an act which seriously limits the right to labor or the right of contract in regard to their means of livelihood between persons who are *sui juris* (both employer and employee) it becomes of great importance to determine which shall prevail,—the right of the individual to labor for such time as he may choose, or the right of the state to prevent the individual from laboring, or from entering into any contract to labor, beyond a certain time prescribed by the state. . . .

This is not a question of substituting the judgment of the court for that of the legislature. If the act be within the power of the state it is valid, although the judgment of the court might be totally opposed to the enactment of such a law. But the question would still remain: Is it within the police power of the state? and that question must be answered by the court.

The question whether this act is valid as a labor law, pure and simple, may be dismissed in a few words. There is no reasonable ground for interfering with the liberty of person or the right of free contract, by determining the hours of labor, in the occupation of a baker. There is no contention that bakers as a class are not equal in intelligence and capacity to men in other trades or manual occupations, or that they are not able to assert their rights and care for themselves without the protecting arm of the state, interfering with their independence of judgment and of action. They are in no sense wards of the state. Viewed in the light of a purely labor law, with no reference whatever to the question of health, we think that a law like the one before us involves neither the safety, the morals, nor the welfare, of the public, and that the interest of the public is not in the slightest degree affected by such an act. The law must be upheld, if at all, as a law pertaining to the health of the individual engaged in the occupation of a baker. It does not affect any other portion of the public than those who are engaged in that occupation. Clean and wholesome bread does not depend upon whether the baker works but ten hours per day or only sixty hours a week. The limitation of the hours of labor does not come within the police power on that ground. . . .

We think the limit of the police power has been reached and passed in this case. There is, in our judgment, no reasonable foundation for holding this to be necessary or appropriate as a health law to safeguard the public health, or the health of the individuals who are following the trade of a baker. If this statute be valid, and if, therefore, a proper case is made out in which to deny the right of an individual, *sui juris*, as employer or employee, to make contracts for the labor of the latter under the protection of the provisions of the Federal Constitution, there would seem to be no length to which legislation of this nature might not go. . . .

We think that there can be no fair doubt that the trade of a baker, in and of itself, is not an unhealthy one to that degree which would authorize the legislature to interfere with the right to labor, and with the right of free contract on the part of the individual, either as employer or employee. . . . It is unfortunately true that labor, even in any department, may possibly carry with it the seeds of unhealthiness. But are we all, on that account, at the mercy of legislative majorities? A printer, a tinsmith, a locksmith, a carpenter, a cabinetmaker, a dry goods clerk, a bank's, a lawyer's, or a physician's clerk, or a clerk in almost any kind of business, would all come under the power of the legislature, on this assumption. No trade, no occupation, no mode of earning one's living, could escape this all-pervading power, and the acts of the legislature in limiting the hours of labor in all employments would be valid, although such limitation might seriously cripple the ability of the laborer to support himself and his family. . . .

It is also urged, pursuing the same line of argument, that it is to the interest of the state that its population should be strong and robust, and therefore any legislation which may be said to tend to make people healthy must be valid as health laws, enacted under the police power. If this be a valid argument and a justification for this kind of legislation, it follows that the protection of the Federal Constitution from undue interference with liberty of person and freedom of contract is visionary, wherever the law is sought to be justified as a valid exercise of the police power. Scarcely any law but might find shelter under such assumptions, and conduct, properly so called, as well as contract, would come under the restrictive sway of the legislature. Not only the hours of employees, but the hours of employers, could be regulated, and doctors, lawyers, scientists, all professional men, as well as athletes and artisans, could be forbidden to fatigue their brains and bodies by prolonged hours of exercise, lest the fighting strength of the state be impaired. We mention these extreme cases because the contention is extreme. We do not believe in the soundness of the views which uphold this law. On the contrary, we think that such a law as this, although passed in the assumed exercise of the police power, and as relating to the public health, or the health of the employees named, is not within that power, and is invalid. The act is not, within any fair meaning of the term, a health law, but is an illegal interference with the rights of individuals, both employers and employees, to make contracts regarding labor upon such terms as they may think best, or which they may agree upon with the other parties to such contracts. Statutes of the nature of that under review, limiting the hours in which grown and intelligent men may labor to earn their living, are mere meddlesome interferences with the rights of the individual, and they are not saved from condemnation by the claim that they are passed in the exercise of the police power and upon the subject of the health of the individual whose rights are interfered with, unless there be some fair ground, reasonable in and of itself, to say that there is material danger to the public health, or to the health of the employees, if the hours of labor are not curtailed. If this be not clearly the case, the individuals whose rights are thus made the subject of legislative interference are under the protection of the Federal Constitution regarding their liberty of contract as well as of person; and the legislature of the state has no power to limit their right as proposed in this statute. . . .

It is manifest to us that the limitation of the hours of labor as provided for in this section of the statute under which the indictment was found, and the plaintiff in error convicted, has no such direct relation to, and no such substantial effect upon, the health of the employee, as to justify us in regarding the section as really a health law. It seems to us that the real object and purpose were simply to regulate the hours of labor between the master and his employees (all being men, *sui juris*), in a private business, not dangerous in any degree to morals, or in any real and substantial degree to the health of the employees. Under such circumstances the freedom of master and employee to contract with each other in relation to their employment, and in defining the same, cannot be prohibited or interfered with, without violating the Federal Constitution. . . .

Mr. Justice Holmes dissenting:

I regret sincerely that I am unable to agree with the judgment in this case, and that I think it my duty to express my dissent.

This case is decided upon an economic theory which a large part of the country does not entertain. If it were a question whether I agreed with that theory, I should desire to study it further and long before making up my mind. But I do not conceive that to be my duty, because I strongly believe that my agreement or disagreement has nothing to do with the right of a majority to embody their opinions in law. It is settled by various decisions of this court that state constitutions and state laws may regulate life in many ways which we as legislators might think as injudicious, or if you like as tyrannical, as this, and which, equally with this, interfere with the liberty to contract. Sunday laws and usury laws are ancient examples. A more modern one is the prohibition of lotteries. The liberty of the citizen to do as he likes so long as he does not interfere with the liberty of others to do the same, which has been a shibboleth for some well-known writers, is interfered with by school laws, by the Postoffice, by every state or municipal institution which takes his money for purposes thought desirable, whether he likes it or not. The 14th Amendment does not enact Mr. Herbert Spencer's Social Statics. . . . Some . . . laws embody convictions or prejudices which judges are likely to share. Some may not. But a Constitution is not intended to embody a particular economic theory, whether of paternalism and the organic relation of the citizen to the state or of *laissez faire*. It is made for people of fundamentally differing views, and the accident of our finding certain opinions natural and familiar, or novel, and even shocking, ought not to conclude our judgment upon the question whether statutes embodying them conflict with the Constitution of the United States.

General propositions do not decide concrete cases. The decision will depend on a judgment or intuition more subtle than any articulate major premise. But I think that the proposition just stated, if it is accepted, will carry us far toward the end. Every opinion tends to become a law. I think that the word "liberty," in the 14th Amendment, is perverted when it is held to prevent the natural outcome of a dominant opinion, unless it can be said that a rational and fair man necessarily would admit that the statute proposed would infringe fundamental principles as they have been understood by the traditions of our people and our law. It does not need research to show that no such sweeping condemnation can be passed upon the statute before us. A reasonable man might think it a proper measure on the score of health. Men whom I certainly could not pronounce unreasonable would uphold it as a first instalment of a general regulation of the hours of work. Whether in the latter aspect it would be open to the charge of inequality I think it unnecessary to discuss.

The commerce clause became, as we have seen, the basis of a widening control by Congress over interstate commerce. Between 1903 and 1917 Congress passed a series of acts regulating interstate carriers and virtually all of these acts were subsequently upheld by the Court. Thus it might be said that Congress and the Court moved together to consolidate the power of the federal government over the states and, not incidentally, to greatly increase the power of Congress itself. Congress also claimed in these years—and the Court supported—"the right to regulate the manner of production, manufacture, sale and transportation of articles," all under authority of the commerce clause, and thereby infringed substantially on the police powers of the states. In the words of a United States attorney general, "Congress has the power to regulate commerce, including its instrumentalities, and *likewise* power to regulate the persons by whom articles of commerce are produced in respect to matters not connected with commerce, to prohibit the transportation of articles of value, which are in themselves innocuous and which are lawfully made or produced, for reasons not affecting interstate commerce." The last in reference to Congress undertaking to ban child labor by prohibiting interstate commerce in articles in whose manufacture children had been employed. However salutary the motive, such legislation certainly stretched the commerce clause of the Constitution to new limits and the Court, indeed, in 1918, in *Hammer v. Dagenhart* ruled the Child Labor Law of 1916 unconstitutional.

The Court, while extending its own powers and the powers of Congress, was inclined to uphold the police powers of the states in cases involving the rights of individuals. In the period from 1889 to

1918, the Court decided some 725 cases in which state statutes were questioned under the Fourteenth Amendment. Of these only fourteen concerned personal rights, indicating the disheartening effect of the *Slaughter-House Cases* and *Plessy v. Ferguson* on the issue of civil liberties.

What clearly had been happening in the latter years of the nineteenth century is that the Court had enlarged its notion of what might be called its social responsibilities. It came gradually to accept a concept of the law which saw it not as a fixed and immutable set of precepts or propositions but as a set of working postulates about the relation of individuals in a society to each other and to the principal institutions of that society. Law became "sociologized." Roscoe Pound, dean of the Harvard Law School, spoke for this new movement when he wrote, "One of the notable characteristics of our age is that in science, sociology, economics, psychology, philosophy, and religion, the movement is from the abstract to the concrete, from speculation to experience, from logic to life.

"The fact that our Supreme Court has grasped the deeper meaning of this movement, that it looks through technicalities and logical formulas to facts—to reality—has strengthened it in the confidence of the people and increased its effectiveness for the work properly belonging to it in our coordinate system of government." Another writer noted that the Court, far from being rigid, "had yielded somewhat unduly to public criticism in giving effect to legislation, which, however desirable from the standpoint of social reform, yet involves a measurable encroachment upon some of those individual rights to secure which the Fourteenth Amendment was adopted."

Such an observation as that of Dean Pound can be taken to measure how far the Court had come from the natural-law philosophy that underlay the Constitution itself and the framers' notion of how the Court should function in relation to it. If law was simply what the dominant interests in the society at any one time wished it to be, it was difficult to find a point at which it was not to be merely confirmatory of current attitudes. Yet clearly stubborn resistance on the part of the Court to the changing conditions of American life would have resulted in its powers being sharply curtailed or its decisions simply ignored.

It is interesting to note that Roscoe Pound himself in his later years came to have a great interest and respect for the idea of natural law, moving further away from "sociological" law with each decade.

The direction in which the Court should move was described by Louis Brandeis prior to his appointment to the Court: "In the last century, our democracy has deepened. Coincidentally, there has been a shifting of our longing from legal justice to social justice. . . . What we need is not to displace the Courts but to make them efficient instruments of justice."

When Charles Warren concluded his history of the Supreme Court in the early 1920's, his cautionary words were directed at what seemed to him the excessively liberal bent of the Court, a Court which, in his view, was too much influenced by majority opinion. He reminded his readers that the Founding Fathers had been at considerable pains to protect the interests of the minority. But the minority that Warren is speaking of is not the kind of minority we think of today when we use the word. It is the minority of the wealthy whose interests are in danger of being overridden by the impatient spirit of democracy, or "majority tyranny," as Warren called it. It is hard to quarrel with Warren's observation that "the majority must . . . prevail in the long run, and eventually a Court must harmonize its juristic conceptions with the conception of liberty and right which public opinion sustains; but a majority is not always right temporarily." The qualification is a revealing one. It is of course possible (and the framers of the Constitution recognized the fact) that the majority might be wrong in the long run as well as the short one. That Warren, who was in most respects a conservative legal theorist, could so cheerfully accept the majority as the ultimate arbiter of political, social, and, in the last analysis, constitutional questions demonstrates how far Americans had come from the intellectual climate or consciousness of the Revolutionary generation. Furthermore, there is no inkling in Warren's closing paragraphs that a vast unmapped region of constitutional law remained to be explored. That was to be the area of civil rights.

XX

THE AUGMENTATION OF THE EXECUTIVE POWER

IF THE PERIOD FROM THE END OF THE CIVIL WAR TO THE BEGINNING of the nineteenth century was a period in which Congress, and the Court as its coadjutor, increased its own power, in large part at the expense of the executive branch, the first three quarters of the new century were to be distinguished by a vast increase in the powers of the president. When William McKinley was assassinated and his vice-president, Theodore Roosevelt, succeeded to the presidency, the former governor of New York ushered in the new era of augmented presidential power. Haranguing his fellow citizens in his frenetic style, he brought a freshness and drama to the White House (along with a good measure of the absurd) that it had seldom, if ever, experienced before. He personalized the office as it had not been personalized since the days of Jackson and Lincoln. In constitutional terms, the new presidential style was expressed in his zest for battle. When the Court thwarted his trust-busting legislation, he announced that while he might not know much about the law, he knew how to intimidate a Supreme Court justice, an obscenity Warren clearly could not bring himself to repeat. The fact is that the Court, despite the presence on it of such luminaries as Oliver Wendell Holmes and Louis Brandeis, seemed to have seen its happiest days. Roosevelt's spectacular forays into foreign diplomacy "speaking softly and carrying a big stick" anticipated the increasingly important role future presidents would play in international affairs, thereby strengthening them vis-à-vis Congress.

Indeed, Theodore Roosevelt might be said to have inaugurated the "imperial presidency." Grinning his remorseless and inexorable grin that at times seemed to hover over the continent like the disembodied grin of the Cheshire cat, shouting "Bully" in his high-pitched voice, riding herd with cowboys, hunting elephants in Africa, digging the Panama Canal, making peace between nations at war, dispatching the marines in support of some beleaguered American national, straightening things out in banana republics, sending the fleet around the world, busting trusts, intimidating Supreme Court justices, "Teddy" Roosevelt treated the American public to a kind of extended vaudeville act, one dazzling turn following another. No young American of even mildly liberal persuasion ever forgot the excitement that Teddy suddenly projected in the role of president.

By the end of the nineteenth century the failure of William Jennings Bryan to become president, the defeat of the Populists, the apparently unbreakable stranglehold of the trusts on the American economy, left those reform-minded men and women who hoped for a better day dispirited. The reelection of McKinley seemed to put the seal on business-run America's indifference to the aspirations of labor and the hopes of reformers generally. To have a repressible McKinley succeeded by an irrepressible Roosevelt brought a whole new stream of energy flowing through the country like an extension of the president's own limitless exuberance. There is no question that Roosevelt was a wholly new kind of chief executive. Whether at Sagamore or the White House, romping with his children or attacking the vested interests, he was constantly in the public eye. He was probably slightly mad, but he was just what the American people seemed to need, and both in "style" and in content he changed the character of the presidency. There would never be another Teddy Roosevelt, but even Herbert Hoover was to be photographed trout fishing in a stiff collar and coat while Calvin Coolidge, as authentic a remnant of Calvinism as his name suggested, was photographed in an Indian headdress, one of the most remarkable juxtapositions of visual objects vouchsafed to the century. The Founding Fathers had fretted over the possibility that the powers allocated to the president in the realm of foreign affairs might, if America became a great and powerful nation, place in the hands of the chief executive more power than any one man should be trusted with. Teddy Roosevelt began to give substance to their anxieties.

Perhaps we can best trace the augmentation of presidential power through the writings and subsequent actions of one of Roosevelt's most distinguished successors. In 1884, when Woodrow Wilson was twenty-eight years old, he wrote a book entitled *Congressional Government*. His general argument was that the Constitution had proved defective since it had allowed the powers of Congress to develop at the expense of the other branches of government, until, with the president a cipher, all the effective power lay in the hands of Congress which exercised its power carelessly and irresponsibly through a host of committees whose work was conducted, for all practical purposes, in secrecy.

What Wilson yearned for was a form of parliamentary government where legislation and administration would be part of a single integrated process, where a strong executive would provide genuine leadership, and where open debate in Congress would inform the American people of the critical issues which required the attention of a coordinated legislative-executive. While Wilson was still a student at Princeton he formed a pact with a classmate "to school all our powers and passions for the work of establishing the principles we held in common; that we would acquire knowledge that we might have power; and that we would drill ourselves in all the arts of persuasion, but especially in oratory . . . that we might have facility in leading others into our ways of thinking and enlisting them in our purposes." He missed those great oratorical exchanges which had characterized Congress in the days of Clay and Webster and which, in his view, had educated the country by articulating and dramatizing the essential issues facing the Union.

For a time at least, Wilson looked to the model of the British Parliament. Under "Congressional Government," he wrote, "despotic authority [was] wielded . . . by our national Congress . . . a despotism which uses its power with all the caprice, all the scorn for settled policy, all the wild unrestraint which marked the methods of other tyrants as hateful to freedom." "Eight words," Wilson wrote, "contain the sum of the present degradation of our political parties, no leaders, no principles, no parties."

Barring a reform along the lines of the British system, the only remedy, in Wilson's view, was restoration of the presidency to that "first estate of dignity" from which it had fallen since the days of Washington, Adams and Jefferson. To the young Princeton scholar it seemed clear that the American president had become a figure of "irreproachable insignificance."

By the time Wilson himself was a candidate for the presidency the character of the office and the powers of the president had been so dramatically augmented by Theodore Roosevelt that Wilson wrote in a very different spirit: "The President is at liberty, both in law and conscience, to be as big a man as he can . . . he cannot escape being the leader of his party . . . he is also the political leader of the nation, or has it in his choice to be . . . his is the only national voice in affairs. Let him once win the admiration and confidence of the country, and no other single force can withstand him, no combination of forces will easily overpower him. . . . His office is anything he has the sagacity and force to make it." The reader need hardly be reminded that Wilson as president undertook to do just that—to become a president so powerful that he could dispose of destinies of numerous European nations, and create, by the force of his own will as chief executive of the most powerful nation in the world, a new international order to be known as the League of Nations. In this final and most ambitious project of his remarkable political career, Congress did indeed "create a combination of forces" that defeated him.

In 1900, twelve years before Wilson became president and sixteen years after the original publication of the book, Wilson wrote a new introduction and recanted a number of his earlier doctrines. He described in some detail the newly gained power of the speaker of the House, but his principal adjustment was in the vastly augmented powers of the presidency, the result, in Wilson's view, of the war with Spain. "The greatly increased power and opportunity for constructive leadership given the President, by the plunge into international politics and into the administration of distant dependencies, . . . has been the war's most striking and momentous consequence," he wrote. "When foreign affairs play a prominent part in the politics and policy of a nation, its Executives must of necessity be its guide: must utter every initial judgment, take every first step of action, supply the information upon which it is to act, suggest and in large measure control its conduct. . . . There is no trouble now about getting the President's speeches printed and read, every word. Upon his choice, his character his experience hang some of the most weighty issues of the future. The government of dependencies must be largely in his hands. Interesting things may come out of the singular change. For one thing, new prizes in public service may attract a new order of talent." More specifically, Woodrow Wilson; now that the presidency had collected new powers, Wilson was ready to reach for the office.

Woodrow Wilson, the professor-president who was inclined to regard the American nation as an extension of his Princeton classroom, gave his citizen-pupils (and the members of Congress who were generally less receptive) brilliant lectures on American history and referred to his program as the New Freedom (Roosevelt had preferred the New Nationalism), thus setting the stage for a succession of "News," and expressing the touchingly naïve optimism of Americans that "new" was the equivalent of "better." From the vaudevillian of Sagamore Hill to the rather priggish schoolmaster who wished to reform the world on the American model was a change of "style" so extreme as to beggar description but the final effect was to further the powers of the presidency. The belated but decisive entrance of the United States into World War I, the Versailles Treaty, which marked the intrusion of American utopianism into a war-weary and disillusioned Europe, described as the Crusade of the Star-Spangled Banner, and the League of Nations were Wilson's doing. It turned out the professor had expected too much of his students. They shirked their assignment—joining the League—and thereby failed their final examination. Wilson's inflexibility and his conviction that once he had won "the admiration and confidence of the country . . . no combination of forces" could "easily overpower him," proved his undoing. He was as much the victim of his own unyielding pride, or *hubris*, as the Greeks called it, as of hostile senators and representatives. If he did not exactly demonstrate the limits of presidential power, he demonstrated that the most eloquent appeals to the electorate were ultimately futile without proper attention to the sensibilities of congressmen.

It was perhaps indicative of the mood of the country that a president of striking oratorical and intellectual abilities who sounded a high moral call to the American people was succeeded in office by a handsome nonentity without strong convictions on any subject. Warren Harding drew almost twice as many popular votes as his Democratic rival, James M. Cox (sixteen million to nine million, one of the largest percentages for a winning presidential candidate in our history). Harding's presidential style consisted of an amiable passivity. The antithesis of Roosevelt and Wilson, he was content to exercise the formal duties of his office and hand over the reins of power to the Republicans in Congress.

When Harding died of a heart attack near the end of his first term of office he was succeeded by Vice-President Calvin Coolidge. Coolidge, in his initial message to Congress, made clear his allegiance to business, aided and abetted by government. The new president's physical meagerness represented quite accurately the meagerness of his intellectual and emotional life. He had, to be sure, a dry Yankee wit which he seldom indulged. Power had no attraction for him. Reelected by a margin again almost twice that of his Democratic adversary, John W. Davis, wtih nearly five million votes going to the Progressive candidate, Robert La Follette, Coolidge continued to emphasize economy in government and preferential treatment for corporations and left as his most famous public utterance: "I do not choose to run. . . ."

Herbert Hoover continued the Harding-Coolidge tradition of presidential nonleadership even in the face of the Wall Street collapse and the beginning of the Great Depression. It thus remained for Franklin Roosevelt to demonstrate the degree to which a dominating personality could exercise presidential leadership on the domestic scene given the imperative of a financial crisis.

One of the ironies of Roosevelt's administration was that Harding had appointed ex-President Taft as chief justice of the Supreme Court in 1921. In a manner rather reminiscent of an earlier Democratic president's confrontation with the Supreme Court, Roosevelt found himself blocked in many of his programs by one of the most conservative Courts in our history.

CHAPTER

XXI

THE FOUR HORSEMEN
OVERTHROWN

As president and then, quite improperly, as chief justice, Taft had filled the Supreme Court with judges of his own political persuasion. Although Taft himself died in 1930 before Roosevelt was elected president, he left "his" Court behind, a Court dominated by the so-called Four Horsemen, Pierce Butler, Willis Van Devanter, George Sutherland and James C. McReynolds. The justices in their unrelenting conservatism made up an ideological team that time and again struck down social legislation designed to curtail exploitative business activities or improve the lot of the workingman. In doing so they highlighted the image of the Court as a stubbornly reactionary body, a charge which, as we have seen, had been only intermittently true. The conservative temper of the Four Horsemen was, ironically, reinforced by a theory of the proper function of the Court developed in large part by Justice Holmes and espoused by several of the "liberal" justices on the Court, most conspicuously by Felix Frankfurter. The Holmes philosophy was that the proper role for the Court was primarily a passive one. It was not up to the justices to make law, to extrapolate freely from the Constitution, or to respond, in Holmes's phrase, to Herbert Spencer's *Social Ethics* or any other sociological interpretation of the law. These were areas better left to the legislative and executive branches. Holmes's formulation of the proper role of the Court came in the wake of a number of decisions in which a conservative Court blocked what appeared to many people to be desirable social legislation. It may have seemed easier to him to persuade his colleagues not to meddle in political and social problems than to change their outlook to one more favorable to social reform. In any event the effect was to abandon the ground to those justices whose social and political philosophy was quite different from that of Holmes.

What brought all this to a head, of course, was the election of Franklin Roosevelt as president and his initiation of a sweeping legislative program designed to alleviate the suffering caused by the Depression. In 1935 the Court was presented with a case under the National Industrial Recovery Act which gave the president the power to set quotas on interstate shipments of oil. The Court, in an exceptional display of unanimity, declared that section of the act unconstitutional on the grounds that Congress had exceeded its authority in making such a delegation. At the time the decision was generally denounced by liberals as a reactionary impediment to necessary social legislation. There then followed a series of cases ranging from the regulation of prices and wages to unemployment compensation in which the Four Horsemen, with the addition of one other justice, usually Roberts, struck down New Deal legislation at odds with their own rigorous interpretation of the Constitution. These decisions did not represent so much a continuing conservatism—we have seen the Court often employed considerable latitude in interpreting the Constitution to give support to novel social legislation—as a crystallization of all the small-government, sanctity-of-property strains in American history going back to the Jeffersonian Democrats. (The justices, incidentally, frequently invoked that intractable enemy of judicial power.) Every romantic memory of a simpler and more innocent age found its champions in the "Four Horsemen plus one." Not since the days of Jefferson and Marshall had the conflict between the judicial and executive branches of the government been so dramatically highlighted. The legislation in question was, to be sure, congressional legislation, but the adversary was unmistakably the president, who had used Congress as a largely pliant tool to effectuate his New Deal Program. There was an angry response in the halls of Congress and in the strongholds of liberalism directed against the "nine old men" who seemed to stand so resolutely in the path of progress or, more simply, of "getting the country back on its feet."

Roosevelt devised the strategy of adding liberal jurists to the Court. Since virtually all the decisions of the Court striking down New Deal legislation had been by five-to-four margins, the shift of a single vote from the "conservative" to the "liberal" column would give the president a pro-New Deal majority. The size of the Court, the reader will recall, had varied from five to nine. Early in the Court's history justices had been added and subtracted when federal circuit courts were added or consolidated. To add six justices would bring the members of the Court to the round number of fifteen. Roosevelt launched his campaign to "pack the Court" with characteristic energy and self-confidence. He had, after all, just received an overwhelming mandate from the electorate. He and his New Deal were in full and apparently irresistible sail. Congress and the people, he assumed, would sustain him in any reasonable strategy for completing his grand social plan. For one of the few times in his extended presidential career, Franklin Roosevelt seriously misjudged public opinion. When his Court-packing scheme became known a vast chorus of protest rose from around the country. Suddenly it was revealed that the Court, for all its faults, had become a sacred institution not to be tampered with, however severe the provocation. Meanwhile, the Court, undoubtedly hoping to stave off Roosevelt's assault, made an about-face on several important cases declaring that "economic conditions" called for a "fresh consideration" of legislation designed to alleviate the misery caused by the Depression.

Soon after, the retirement of one of the Four Horsemen, Van Devanter, and his replacement by Senator Hugo Black, changed the ideological composition of the Court decisively with the consequence that it proceeded to reverse most of its anti-New Deal decisions. The crisis passed, but the Court was not the same. What Edward White calls the "oracular" notion of the role of the justices—that is to say the propounding of the Constitution as an immutable and unchanging document infallibly interpreted by the Court—no longer seemed viable. To put the issue in these terms is, of course, to prejudge it. The "old Court," the pre-New Deal Court, with its "oracular" mythology, was, by White's interpretation, revealed as a brilliantly sustained illusion, a remarkable feat but nonetheless illusory. The new reality was that the Court had best find some other task for itself and scrupulously refrain from trying to curtail the rapidly expanding powers of the federal government, whether expressed through Congress or through the executive branch. Thus what appeared on the surface as simply the last of a long line of confrontations between the judicial branch of the government and one or both of the other branches, confrontations previously resolved by discreet withdrawal on the part of the Court; by a change in its majority through death or resignation; by compromise; or, as in the case of the Civil War, by events completely beyond the control of the Court (or indeed anyone else), appears, at least in some interpretations, to mark a wholly new phase in the history of the Court.

What clearly was happening was that the executive branch was accumulating powers at an unprecented and, to many Americans, alarming rate, powers considerably beyond any envisioned by the framers of the Constitution. It is probably safe to say that only under the intense pressures created by the economic breakdown of the thirties could the American "system" have been so radically altered. The stubborn resistance of the Court in the face of the sustained ideological assault upon it strengthens that premise. Without the Depression, the need for an expanded field of social legislation would doubtless have expressed itself and I see no reason to doubt that the justices would, in good time, have responded positively to what was perhaps in any event an irresistible trend toward the welfare state. But the disheartening consequence of the way in which the Court-executive conflict manifested itself in the thirties was that the issue of social legislation, which was certainly not new to the Court and which it had by no means uniformly resisted, got mixed up with the issue of vastly expanded executive and legislative powers. While it is true that they were, in large measure, inseparable, they were at least *distinguishable*, and the Court had shown considerable ingenuity making such distinctions.

If we can imagine a history without the disruptive effects of the Great Depression (which is admittedly difficult), we may at the same time imagine a scenario, as they say, where both necessary social legislation and augmented federal power proceeded at a more moderate pace and was subjected to a far greater degree of judicial scrutiny. The Court might then have retained a substantial portion of its "oracular" function which we have throughout this work been disposed to see as an indispensable mode for relating the present to the past and of articulating those grand themes that refresh the "mystic chords of memory" which Abraham Lincoln believed constituted the essential spirit of a people.

All this is redundant, of course, if in fact all the New Deal legislation was necessary and the wide and rapid extension of federal power inevitable and wholly positive in its effect. But if we once were confident that this was clearly the case, we are beginning to be less so. And it is in the light of these present and perhaps growing misgivings that we must view the Court-executive conflict of the 1930's.

The American Historical Association meeting in Philadelphia in 1937, on the 150th anniversary of the drafting of the federal Constitution, devoted one of its sessions to a discussion of "The Constitution Reconsidered." The book that resulted gives us a good fix on the dominant attitudes of professors of constitutional history toward the Constitution and especially toward the Supreme Court, which, because of its resistance to New Deal social legislation, was perhaps at the nadir of its reputation with the liberal community.

Henry Steele Commager, a young professor of history at Columbia, contributed a paper on the relation of the Court to what he called "higher law." Commager traced the evolution of natural law into constitutional law and argued that the notion of "higher law" was often in the minds of the justices of the Supreme Court and helped to explain many of the Court's decisions. "The appeal to higher law was valid," he wrote, "it was inevitable. And it was made on behalf of human rights rather than of property rights. . . . The function of the Courts, in importing higher law doctrine into the Constitution, has been constitutional rather than legislative merely, and it may be said that since the 1880's the Supreme Court sat as a continuous constitutional convention. For the laws which the Court has formulated are in very fact higher laws. . . . It may be suggested more specifically that every attempt by the judiciary to discover what property is clothed with a public interest, what action constitutes a public purpose, what occupations or what conditions are of a nature to justify state regulation, what constitutes liberty in the economic order, and what may be a reasonable and what may be a confiscatory return on investment is higher law legislation."

Commager's thesis has considerable trenchancy. From its first years in a vast number of decisions the Court had clearly to go beyond the letter of the Constitution. The justices could only do this if they had the conscious or subconscious conviction that there was, somewhere, a higher law that the Constitution itself was an imperfect or at the very least incomplete expression of.

An essay by Max Lerner—"Minority Rule and the Constitutional

Tradition"—from the same symposium deals with the perpetual problem of the Court as an elitist, antidemocratic body. Lerner, probably at that time the most radical of the essayists, took the position that the Court has functioned primarily to reinforce and support the economic status of a ruling business elite and done this, moreover, at the expense of "the people." In his words, "Judicial review has not flowed merely from the will-to-power of individual justices, but has been the convenient channel through which the driving forces of a developing business enterprise have found expression and achieved victory."

This view of the Court will not come as a surprise to the reader. We have noted the charge being leveled at the Court from its earliest days. Ironically, one perhaps heard less of it in the period when it might have been most accurately made—the post-Civil War era. By the 150th anniversary of the Constitution it had become a truism of virtually all radical and liberal critiques of the Court. Even those students of the Constitution who were reconciled to the Court as an indispensable coordinate branch of the government described it as the citadel of special interests. In Lerner's words: "Scratch a fervent believer in judicial supremacy, and like as not you will find someone with a bitterness about democracy. The two are as close as skin and skeleton." Lerner engages in the interesting exercise of trying to salvage the Constitution, recently depicted by Charles A. Beard as a basically antidemocratic document, from Beard's influential indictment by, in effect, throwing the Supreme Court to the liberal adversaries of the Constitution. To Lerner there was no "antithesis between the Constitution as such and the democratic impulse." Liberals had conspired with the Court to make it appear so. When vested interests have been on the verge of defeat by "the democratic impulse," after all their institutional defenses have been breached, "the anti-democratic forces retreat to their last barricade—judicial review. There, behind the safe earthworks of natural law, due process, minority rights, the judges can, in the plentitude of their virtue and sincerity, veto and outlaw the basic social program of the majority."

However true this may have been of the Taft-picked Court of the Four Horsemen, it was a considerable oversimplification of the history of the Court throughout the nineteenth century. What does appear to be the case is that the Court, if its members read the Constitution scrupulously, failed to read or understand the debates of the federal convention that provided the intellectual and moral context for the

Constitution itself. Or if they read the debates they suppressed those ideas which were uncongenial. We have characterized the Supreme Court as the "original-sin branch," or that branch of government which most clearly perpetuated the Classical-Christian Consciousness. To revert to that thesis, the problem with the Court's deification of property was that it marked the abandonment of the framers' notion of original sin. Madison, in the convention and in the Tenth Federalist, had argued that power must be so carefully distributed that no single class, group, party, or interest could follow its natural impulse to exploit the powerless or less powerful. It was, after all, Gouverneur Morris, one of the most conservative delegates at the convention, who declared: "The Rich will strive to establish their dominion and enslave the rest. They always did. They always will. The proper security against them is to form them into a separate interest. The two forces will then control each other. Let the rich mix with the poor in a Commercial Country, they will establish an Oligarchy. Take away commerce, and democracy will triumph."

The framers did not so much fear "the people" as they feared the wickedness of the human heart. A number of them were especially wary of the power of banks and large corporations or, as with Madison and Morris, the "rich," because in the moral calculus of the Revolutionary generation original sin times money equalled corruption and exploitation. History vindicated Gouverneur Morris. The late nineteenth century and the early twentieth saw in America the "rich," the "robber barons," in Matthew Josephson's telling phrase, do just what Morris had predicted—establish an oligarchy, the rule of the rich. The robber barons bought state legislators and congressmen with the same ruthlessness with which they cornered the wheat market or watered cattle. If the justices of the Supreme Court failed to remember the warnings of the framers they were certainly not alone. Had they shown the same attention to the dangers inherent in all concentrations of power as they showed to the property rights of large corporations, they might have restrained the excesses of the robber barons. Certainly, by most measures, they did better than the "democratic" branches—the Congress or the president. Congress in the period following the Civil War ran the country pretty much as it pleased and the "interests" ran Congress.

Curiously enough, in all the voluminous decisions of the Court, one searches in vain for any clear evocation of the framers' concept of original sin. To proclaim the virtues of "democracy," however one defined that often elusive word, and the basic goodness of "the people," an equally slippery notion, became the stock in trade of American political rhetoric down to the present incumbent of the White House. To the Founding Fathers such ideas would have appeared as simple sentimentality. They had a much more tough-minded analysis of the problem of government. That is not to say, of course, that they were right, but only that our history as a people has yet to prove them wrong. Much of the confusion and shifting of ground that has characterized the decisions of the Court in various periods of its history can be traced, I believe, to the fact that the institution to which the justices were charged with giving effect was based on premises which they not only did not accept but of which they were not conscious. The branch of government which bore most clearly the imprint of the Classical-Christian Consciousness was occupied, in successive generations, by men who, however "conservative" they might be in certain respects and however devout in their personal lives, had lost the connection to the basic philosophical assumptions which had given rise to the Court (or did not dare to mention them). They thus, by default so to speak, allowed their enemies to continually put them on the defensive by describing them as undemocratic elitists. The issue, as the Founding Fathers had insisted, was not aristocracy versus democracy. It was the propensity to selfishness and "self-aggrandisement" of both aristocrats and democrats. In this system, the rich and powerful were more to be feared than the poor or those in modest means because, in James Otis's words, "empire," or power, "follows property." The danger of unchecked democracy was roughly equivalent to the danger of unchecked oligarchy. Just as an oligarchy would rob and despoil the poor, "always had, always will," unchecked democracy would pass agrarian laws, taking property from those who had a fair and legitimate claim to it and distributing it among those who had less or none.

Jefferson, the most thoroughgoing radical among the Founding Fathers, endorsed periodic redistributions of property, apparently on the grounds that no government, however ingeniously devised, could, in the long run, prevent certain individuals and groups from accumulating a disproportionate share of the wealth of a society.

What the Founding Fathers could not foresee was that the word "democracy" would take on a kind of independent value; that it would accumulate "mythic" elements as potent in their own right as the myth that came ultimately to validate and sustain the judicial system. Or that the two myths would come to exist in a kind of perpetual tension. All this is not to say that if the justices had persistently enunciated the theory of original sin as the controlling assumption of judicial decisions the American people would have swallowed such doctrine. It is, in any event, idle speculation. The justices never put the issue to a test.

To express the matter as simply as possible: the Constitution was drafted on the assumption that "man" was naturally "wicked" but the country was run on the assumption that he was naturally good. That made for an odd kind of discontinuity almost from the beginning and it also seems to have encouraged, or been accompanied by the notion, that Americans were especially chosen by God, a notion incidentally, which the Founding Fathers were at pains to disclaim, often asserting that Americans were quite human and that, while the nation had achieved independence with God's help, it could, in the long run, expect no special dispensations from the Almighty.

CHAPTER

XXII

THE "NEW" COURT

THE ONSET OF WORLD WAR II ENDED THE GREAT DEPRESSION. IT
also enabled Franklin Roosevelt to reassert the powers of the president in the realm of foreign affairs that had first been clearly deline-
ated by his boisterous cousin, Theodore. Having blazed new trails in
the exercise of presidential powers in domestic affairs, Roosevelt
added to those powers the almost limitless authority conceded to a
United States president in time of war. The result was a vast extension
of presidential influence through a succession of crises, the severity
of which muted criticism and indeed obscured the true nature of the
process itself.

The office that devolved on a bewildered Harry Truman at Roosevelt's death brought with it greater power than that accorded to the
chief executive of any democratic-parliamentary nation. The powers
in the realm of foreign affairs that had been acquired by the first
Roosevelt and augmented by Wilson had been further enhanced by
the second Roosevelt's brand of personal diplomacy—"summit meetings" with Churchill and, finally, at Yalta with Stalin. The meeting
was understood to bring together "the three most powerful men in the
world"—the leader of the most authoritarian regime in the world and
the two principal leaders of the "free world." Such a gathering of
rulers to make decisions of such magnitude was inconsistent with any
existing theory of democratic government.

The fact that the augmented powers of the presidency had come to
inhere in the office rather than simply in the man was at once demonstrated by the fact that shortly after Roosevelt's death his successor
had to make, in secret, one of the most fateful decisions in history—

whether to drop the atomic bomb on Japan. The end of the war saw another exercise in summit diplomacy as the leaders of the communist and capitalist "worlds" mapped out their respective spheres of influence. No Byzantine emperor could have exerted greater power than that exercised by the former Missouri haberdasher in the name of democracy. The postwar era saw the Truman Doctrine, the Marshall Plan, the drafting of the charter of the United Nations, all perhaps exemplary enterprises and none, to be sure, undertaken without the support of Congress. But at least in the field of foreign policy, Congress seemed willing to follow the presidential lead with surprising docility. In the period from the humiliation of the Court in the thirties to the present, the Court has imposed only one substantial check on presidential power. In 1952 Harry Truman, to avert a strike in the steel industry, issued an executive order taking over the steel plants. The steel industry challenged the action in the Supreme Court. "A work stoppage," the president declared, "would immediately jeopardize and imperil our national defense and the defense of those joined with us in resisting aggression, and would add to the continuing danger of our soldiers, sailors, and air men engaged in combat in the field." American troops were fighting in Korea, and the president declared, "it is necessary that the United States take possession of and operate the plants, facilities, and other property of said companies."

To the assistant attorney general arguing the government's case, one of the justices directed a question: "So you contend the Executive has unlimited power in time of an emergency? . . . and that the Executive determines the emergencies and the Courts cannot even review whether it is an emergency."

The assistant attorney general: "That is correct."

Although six justices declared the seizure unconstitutional there was a wide divergence of opinion as to the grounds. The judge who heard the case in the district court referred to Theodore Roosevelt's theory that the president was the people's "steward" and in their name exercised virtually unlimited power. "With all due deference and respect for that great president . . . ," he declared, "I am obliged to say that his statements do not comport with our recognized theory of government, but with a theory with which our government of laws and not of men is constantly at war." For the Court itself Justice Black expressed the view that the president could not act on his own in an area where Congress had authority to grant him powers but had not seen fit to do so. Several other justices took the simpler line that Congress had, in fact, already passed legislation dealing with the adjudication of labor disputes and the president's action had been taken in defiance of the Taft-Hartley Act, which provided for definite procedures to be followed in such cases. In the words of one justice, "Congress authorized a procedure which the president declined to follow."

John F. Kennedy, the proponent of the New Frontier, removed any lingering doubts about presidential power by embarking on one of the most dubious undertakings in the history of United States foreign affairs—the Bay of Pigs—without a pretense of consultation with anyone but his own closest advisers within the executive branch of the government. The country had hardly absorbed the implications of this desperate venture when the Cuban missile crisis erupted. Once again the world was treated to the spectacle of the imperial president of the world's greatest democracy negotiating with his opposite number in Russia over an issue that involved war or peace probably for the better part of the world, and doing so with no more than a gesture to the coordinate branch of government.

On the domestic front, the steel companies, failing to pay attention to presidential price guidelines, were threatened by a governmental take-over and "jawboned" or, more plainly, bullied into retreating. Regardless of where the right or wrong of the matter lay, the technique was a revealing one. The only agency of government, it now seemed, capable of dealing with the giants of a particular industry, was a giant president, a president with powers swollen beyond any precise accounting.

Having initiated the fiasco of the Bay of Pigs and "eyeballed" the only "other man" whom the president of the United States acknowledged to be his "equal" in power, Kennedy must have felt it a matter of very small moment to send "advisers" and "technicians" to South Vietnam to assist this "outpost of democracy" in opposing the "unlawful aggression" of its northern sister. It seems safe to say that, among other things, the Vietnam War was an unconstitutional war if ever there can be such a thing. The morality of it aside, it was undeclared and it was waged essentially by Lyndon Johnson and Richard Nixon against the increasing opposition of a substantial portion of the American people and eventually of most of the young people of the country. Not only was the war itself unconstitutional (if it was not unconstitutional then we need an amendment to make it at least retroactively unconstitutional and thus, hopefully, unrepeatable), during the course of it any number of particular unconstitutional and unconscionable actions were taken by all three presidents who waged the war, actions which involved lying to and in other ways misleading and deceiving the Congress and the American people.

During the Vietnam War the other branches of government kept, as the saying goes, a low profile. Congress and the Supreme Court were willing to let a succession of presidents assume full responsibility for the second greatest disaster in American history (if we count the Civil War as number one). By the time the Vietnam "intervention" was over, it was harder than ever to discover a line at which presidential power could be clearly and incontestably drawn.

A leading authority on the Constitution, Bernard Schwartz, after having described in detail the extraordinarily broad powers that the president has assumed in the name of emergency or, more recently, "national security," asks, quite pointedly, "If this be true and the President does possess such broad inherent power, are we not back to the Stuart concept [of English monarchy] of absolute prerogative, under which the king might take whatever action he considered necessary for the good of the country." Schwartz then reminds us that the presidential prerogative is limited in four ways: by being subordinate to statute-law legislation passed by Congress; by being constrained against acts against private property or individual rights and being subject to judicial review. The framers intended Congress to act as the controlling factor in regard to misuse of presidential authority in the area of foreign affairs, and yet, as Schwartz notes, "in the world of the twentieth century, it is *power* in the field of foreign affairs that has waxed and *control* that has waned. The most important factor in American foreign policy in our day has been Presidential leadership; the Congressional check has at times seemed a mere shadow of that intended by the framers. . . . The Constitution may appear to leave open the question of who is to have the decisive voice in foreign affairs. In practice, it is the President and those appointed by him who are the architects of American foreign policy." It is thus no accident that by far the greater part of Schwartz's discussion of presidential power is given over to foreign affairs and to "war power," a section twice as long as any other in the book. At the end the author writes: "The effects of war under modern conditions may be felt in the economy for years and years and, if the war power can be used in days of peace to treat all the wounds which war inflicts on our society, the power is one which may abide with us forever. It is this indeterminate aspect of its duration that helps to make the war power the most dangerous one to constitutional government in the whole catalogue of powers." Schwartz wrote this in 1962, before the Vietnam War mushroomed.

To the accumulation of vast powers in the hands of the president must be added the technological innovation of television. The presidential powers, and the possibilities of abuse of them, are essentially personal in nature. The most powerful presidents have, with the notable exception of Richard Nixon, been figures of considerable personal charm or persuasiveness. While such persuasiveness may be necessary to strong leadership in a society such as ours it is also the stuff of which demagogues, dictators, and tyrants are made. Its most dangerous aspect is that of *immediacy*. Such a leader, by employing radio, and subsequently television, can appear in the living room of most citizens and in the most reasonable tones, or the most vivid and inflammatory ones, explain a decision already taken and appeal to the patriotism and loyalty of his countrymen to support him in the crisis declared, or created, by him. It is hard to imagine, under such circumstances, any strong opposition to his actions however inimical to the best interests of the country.

A striking recent example was the case of the seizure by the Cambodians of the ship *Mayaguez* and the subsequent United States assault to recapture the ship and its crew. President Ford presented himself to the American people as the initiator of a bold and courageous action to defend American honor and protect American rights. That it was a brutal and unnecessary move, and a badly bungled one in addition, was concealed by presidential rhetoric. There was no time for the country to collect its wits, reflect upon the full significance of the event, or even learn the facts.

In the post-World War II era while a succession of presidents from John F. Kennedy through Lyndon Johnson to Richard Nixon consolidated and extended presidential power, the Supreme Court, virtually abandoning its historic role of setting constitutional limits to the extension of power in the coordinate branches of government, discovered a new course for itself. The whole area covered by the first eight amendments to the Constitution—the Bill of Rights—had remained, as we have had more than one occasion to note, a largely unexplored territory. The Court, under the leadership of Earl Warren, set out to map that terrain, the civil rights of all Americans.

We have seen the Court become the victim of its own intransigence during the New Deal era. That it could ever again come to exert its influence in any decisive way in what was once its classic function—defining and setting limits to the powers of its sister branches—appeared doubtful in the extreme. The question that then arose was, If the critical social, political, and economic issues were, in effect, beyond the Court's purview, what was it in fact to do? What new role could it define that would allow it to once more assert itself as a branch of weight and respectability? If it could not impose restraints on the accumulation of unreasonable and often unconstitutional powers by its coordinate branches, it could perhaps establish itself as the guardian of the rights of those neglected individuals who appeared increasingly as the victims of a system which rewarded some of its members very handsomely and others very meagerly. Thus, for the first time in its long history, the Court addressed itself in a serious and sustained way to the question of those rights presumably guaranteed to all Americans by the first eight amendments to the Constitution. Many citizens of the United States were also residents of particular states. Their rights had been, in a series of decisions over the years, delivered to their states by the Court. (It is only fair to remind the reader that the framers thought that that was where they should in fact be lodged and that was why they had not bothered to include an enumeration of the classic rights in the main body of the Constitution.)

The Fourteenth Amendment was intended, as we have seen, to remedy this, especially in regard to the civil rights of freed slaves. But if states could not always be relied on to protect the civil rights of white citizens, they were positively aggressive in repressing the civil rights of blacks. The Court rendered the Fourteenth Amendment null and void in regard to the federal enforcement of civil rights, white or black, in the *Slaughter-House Cases*, but Justice Harlan retrieved something from the debacle by his dissent in the case of *Plessy v. Ferguson*. Once planted, the idea that the Fourteenth Amendment had had the effect of incorporating the rights of every citizen of every state under the Constitution's Bill of Rights grew. The federal government might, by this interpretation, reach into any particular state to protect the rights of a citizen of the United States. Needless to say this doctrine appeared horribly subversive to the champions of states' rights and those who wished to keep blacks in their place.

The Court, caught up, like the rest of the country, in the anticommunist hysteria that followed the end of World War II, did, to be sure, little to protect the rights of political dissidents, especially those denominated, in this cold war era, as communists or those affiliated with a long list of subversive organizations defined as such by the Attorney General of the United States. In the case of *Dennis v. United States* it upheld the constitutionality of the Smith Act, which imposed severe political and economic handicaps on communists. Indeed it was not until the destruction of McCarthy that the Court regained its morale in the general area of political dissent.

Increasingly, however, the Court began to express concern for the rights of racial minorities.

The "climate of opinion" in post-World War II America was favorable to the expansion of the rights of black people. Although no one had yet settled on an adequate name for the darker-skinned and generally less "advantaged" peoples of the world, it was clear that they had aspirations which must be recognized by the "Free World" if they were not to drift into the orbit of the "Communist World." While they had not yet been denominated the "Third World," their "emergence" highlighted the situation of dark-skinned citizens of the United States, more especially those called Negroes or, more genteelly, "colored people."

In 1950 in *Sweatt v. Painter* the Court had ruled that a Texas law school for Negroes was not "equal" to the University of Texas law school closed to black students. It was a straw in the wind. When *Brown v. Board of Education* came before the Court in 1953, Fred Vinson was chief justice. The Court was divided. Frankfurter, in keeping with his theory of the "passive" role of the Court, wished to avoid a decision on the case. Four justices were in favor of overruling *Plessy v. Ferguson*. The case was carried over to the next term. Meanwhile Vinson died and Eisenhower appointed Earl Warren, the highly successful Republican governor of California and a rival candidate for the Republican nomination for President as chief justice. Warren, aware of the importance of the case, took considerable pains to assure unanimity on the part of the Court. The issue was, in essence, whether "separate" was or could be "equal." To answer this question required that the Court do what Holmes had cautioned it not to do—go beyond the letter of the law into the realm of social morality or, as Holmes had put it, "ethics." In *Brown v. Board of Education* the Court entered into that realm with consequences almost beyond calculation.

Chief Justice Warren:

1. . . . . We must look . . . to the effect of segregation itself on public education.

In approaching this problem, we cannot turn the clock back to 1868 when the Amendment was adopted, or even to 1896 when *Plessy v. Ferguson* was written. We must consider public education in the light of its full development and its present place in American life throughout the Nation. Only in this way can it be determined if segregation in public schools deprives these plaintiffs of the equal protection of the laws.

2. Today, education is perhaps the most important function of state and local governments. Compulsory school attendance laws and the great expenditures for education both demonstrate our recognition of the importance of education to our democratic society. It is required in the performance of our most basic public responsibilities, even service in the armed forces. It is the very foundation of good citizenship. Today it is a principal instrument in awakening the child to cultural values, in preparing him for later professional training, and in helping him to adjust normally to his environment. In these days, it is doubtful that any child may reasonably be expected to succeed in life if he is denied the opportunity of an education. Such an opportunity, where the state has undertaken to provide it, is a right which must be made available to all on equal terms.

3. We come then to the question presented: Does segregation of children in public schools solely on the basis of race, even though the physical facilities and other "tangible" factors may be equal, deprive the children of the minority group of equal educational opportunities? We believe that it does.

In *Sweatt v. Painter* . . . in finding that a segregated law school for Negroes could not provide them equal educational opportunities, this Court relied in large part on "those qualities which are incapable of objective measurement but which make for greatness in a law school." In *McLaurin v. Oklahoma State Regents,* the Court, in requiring that a Negro admitted to a white graduate school be treated like all other students, again resorted to intangible considerations: ". . . his ability to study, to engage in discussion and exchange views with other students, and, in general, to learn his profession." Such considerations apply with added force to children in grade and high schools. To separate them from others of similar age and qualifications solely because of their race generates a feeling of inferiority as to their status in the community that may affect their hearts and minds in a way unlikely ever to be undone. The effect of this separation on their educational opportunities was well stated by a finding in the Kansas case by a court which nevertheless felt compelled to rule against the Negro plaintiffs:

"Segregation of white and colored children in public schools has a detrimental effect upon the colored children. The impact is greater when it has the sanction of the law; for the policy of separating the races is usually interpreted as denoting the inferiority of the negro group. A sense of inferiority affects the motivation of a child to learn. Segregation with the sanction of law, therefore, has a tendency to [retard] the educational and mental development of Negro children and to reprive them of some of the benefits they would receive in a racial[ly] integrated school system." Whatever may have been the extent of psychological knowledge at the time of *Plessy v. Ferguson,* this finding is amply supported by modern authority. Any language in *Plessy v. Ferguson* contrary to this finding is rejected.

4. We conclude that in the field of public education the doctrine of "separate but equal" has no place. Separate educational facilities are inherently unequal. Therefore, we hold that the plaintiffs and others similarly situated for whom the actions have been brought are, by reason of the segregation complained of, deprived of the equal protection of the laws guaranteed by the Fourteenth Amendment. This disposition makes unnecessary any discussion whether such segregation also violates the Due Process Clause of the Fourteenth Amendment.

5. Because these are class actions, because of the wide applicability of this decision, and because of the great variety of local conditions, the formulation of decrees in these cases presents problems of considerable complexity. On reargument, the consideration of appropriate relief was necessarily subordinated to the primary question—The constitutionality of segregation in public education. We have now announced that such segregation is a denial of the equal protection of the laws. In order that we may have the full assistance of the parties in formulating decrees, the cases will be restored to the docket, and the parties are requested to present further argument. . . .

Not only did Warren delay the decision of the Court until the justices were unanimous, he wrote a short and simple decision that could be printed in any newspaper or journal. Most Supreme Court decisions are lengthy, often excessively so to the mind of the layman. No case in this work, for instance, is printed in anything like its entirety. So it was a happy inspiration for Warren, knowing how far-reaching the consequences of the Court's decision must be, to make it accessible in length and style to any moderately literate person.

Brown v. Board of Education of Topeka was, of course, followed by a host of decisions strengthening and extending its influence, and in the area of civil rights generally the Warren Court handed down a series of notable and increasingly controversial decisions.

One of the most important areas in which the Warren Court blazed a new trail was in the matter of the rights of those accused of criminal acts. In *Mapp v. Ohio* (1961) the Court ruled under the unreasonable search and seizure provision of the Fourteenth Amendment that evidence obtained in violation of that amendment could not be used as evidence in legal proceedings. The importance of *Mapp v. Ohio* was that it clearly established that the Court was prepared to accept the doctrine of incorporation and henceforth rule on cases involving infringement of rights under the first nine amendments.

On May 23, 1957, three Cleveland police officers arrived at appellant's residence in that city pursuant to information that "a person [was] hiding out in the home, who was wanted for questioning in connection with a recent bombing and that there was a large amount of policy paraphernalia being hidden in the home." Miss Mapp and her daughter by a former marriage lived on the top floor of the two-family dwelling. Upon their arrival at that house, the officers knocked on the door and demanded entrance but appellant, after telephoning her attorney, refused to admit them without a search warrant. They advised their headquarters of the situation and undertook a surveillance of the house.

The officers again sought entrance some three hours later when four or more additional officers arrived on the scene. When Miss Mapp did not come to the door immediately, at least one of the several doors to the house was forcibly opened and the policemen gained admittance. Meanwhile Miss Mapp's attorney arrived, but the officers, having secured their own entry, and continuing in their defiance of the law, would permit him neither to see Miss Mapp nor to enter the house. It appears that Miss Mapp was halfway down the stairs from the upper floor to the front door when the officers, in this highhanded manner broke into the hall. She demanded to see the search warrant. A paper, claimed to be a warrant, was held up by one of the officers. She grabbed the "warrant" and placed it in her bosom. A struggle ensued in which the officers recovered the piece of paper and as a result of which they handcuffed appellant because she had been "belligerent" in resisting their official rescue of the "warrant" from her person. Running roughshod over appellant, a policeman "grabbed" her, "twisted [her] hand," and she "yelled [and] pleaded with him" because "it was hurting."Appellant, in handcuffs, was then forcibly taken upstairs to her bedroom where the officers searched a dresser, a chest of drawers, a closet and some suitcases. They also looked into a photo album and through personal papers belonging to the appellant. The search spread to the rest of the second floor including the child's bedroom, the living room, the kitchen and a dinette. The basement of the building and a trunk found therein were also searched. The obscene materials for possession of which she was ultimately convicted were discovered in the course of that widespread search. . . .

. . . We hold that all evidence obtained by searches and seizures in violation of the Constitution is, by that same authority, inadmissible in a state court.

Since the Fourth Amendment's right of privacy has been declared enforceable against the States through the Due Process Clause of the Fourteenth, it is enforceable against them by the same sanction of exclusion as is used against the Federal Government. Were it otherwise, then just as without the Weeks rule the assurance against unreasonable federal searches and seizures would be "a form of words," valueless and undeserving of mention in a perpetual charter of inestimable human liberties, so too, without that rule the freedom from state invasions of privacy would be so ephemeral and so neatly severed from its conceptual nexus with the freedom from all brutish means of coercing evidence as not to merit this Court's high regard as a freedom "implicit in 'the concept of ordered liberty.' " . . . Only last year the Court itself recognized that the purpose of the exclusionary rule "is to deter—to compel respect for the constitutional guaranty in the only effectively available way—by removing the incentive to disregard it." *Elkins v. United States.* . . .

Indeed, we are aware of no restraint, similar to that rejected today, conditioning the enforcement of any other basic constitutional right. The right to privacy, no less important than any other right carefully and particularly reserved to the people, would stand in marked contrast to all other rights declared as "basic to a free society." *Wolf v. People of State of Colorado.* . . . This Court has not hesitated to enforce as strictly against the States as it does against the Federal Government the rights of free speech and of a free press, the rights to notice and to a fair, public trial, including, as it does, the right not to be convicted by use of a coerced confession, however logically relevant it be, and without regard to its reliability. . . . And nothing could be more certain than that when a coerced confession is involved, "the relevant rules of evidence" are overridden without regard to "the incidence of such conduct by the police," slight or frequent. Why should not the same rule apply to what is tantamount to coerced testimony by way of unconstitutional seizure of goods, papers, effects, documents, etc.? We find that, as to the Federal Government, the Fourth and Fifth Amendments and, as to the States, the freedom from unconscionable invasions of privacy and the freedom from convictions based upon coerced confessions do enjoy an "intimate relation" in their perpetuation of "principles of humanity and civil liberty [secured] . . . only after years of struggle." . . . They express "supplementing phases of the same constitutional purpose—to maintain inviolate large areas of personal privacy." . . . The philosophy of each Amendment and of each freedom is complementary to, although not dependent upon, that of the other in its sphere of influence—the very least that together they assure in either sphere is that no man is to be convicted on unconstitutional evidence. . . .

Moreover, our holding that the exclusionary rule is an essential part of both the Fourth and Fourteenth Amendments is not only the logical dictate of prior cases, but it also makes very good sense. There is no war between the Constitution and common sense. Presently, a federal prosecutor may make no use of evidence illegally seized, but a State's attorney across the street may, although he supposedly is operating under the enforceable prohibitions of the same Amendment. Thus the State, by admitting evidence unlawfully seized, serves to encourage disobedience to the Federal Constitution which it is bound to uphold. Moreover, as was said in Elkins, "[t]he very essence of a healthy federalism depends upon the avoidance of needless conflict between state and federal courts." . . .

The ignoble shortcut to conviction left open to the State tends to destroy the entire system of constitutional restraints on which the liberties of the people rest. Having once recognized that the right to privacy embodied in the Fourth Amendment is enforceable against the States, and that the right to be secure against rude invasions of privacy by state officers is, therefore, constitutional in origin, we can no longer permit that right to remain an empty promise. Because it is enforceable in the same manner and to like effect as other basic rights secured by the Due Process Clause, we can no longer permit it to be revocable at the whim of any police officer who, in the name of law enforcement itself, chooses to suspend its enjoyment. Our decision, founded on reason and truth, gives to the individual no more than that which the

Constitution guarantees him, to the police officer no less than that to which honest law enforcement is entitled, and, to the courts, that judicial integrity so necessary in the true administration of justice.

The judgment of the Supreme Court of Ohio is reversed and the cause remanded for further proceedings not inconsistent with this opinion.

Reversed and remanded.

In *Malloy v. Hogan,* in 1964, the Warren Court invoked the Fifth Amendment's ban on self-incrimination against the states and in one of its most important and controversial decisions, *Escobedo v. Illinois,* the Court held by five to four that a person charged with a crime had a right to counsel.

Mr. Justice Goldberg delivered the opinion of the Court.

The critical question in this case is whether, under the circumstances, the refusal by the police to honor petitioner's request to consult with his lawyer during the course of an interrogation constitutes a denial of "the Assistance of Counsel" in violation of the Sixth Amendment to the Constitution as "made obligatory upon the States by the Fourteenth Amendment," . . . and thereby renders inadmissible in a state criminal trial any incriminating statement elicited by the police during the interrogation. . . .

Petitioner testified that during the course of the interrogation he repeatedly asked to speak to his lawyer and that the police said that his lawyer "didn't want to see" him. The testimony of the police officers confirmed these accounts in substantial detail.

Notwithstanding repeated requests by each, petitioner and his retained lawyer were afforded no opportunity to consult during the course of the entire interrogation. At one point, as previously noted, petitioner and his attorney came into each other's view for a few moments but the attorney was quickly ushered away. Petitioner testified "that he heard a detective telling the attorney the latter would not be allowed to talk to [him] 'until they were done' " and that he heard the attorney being refused permission to remain in the adjoining room. A police officer testified that he had told the lawyer that he could not see petitioner until "we were through interrogating" him. . . ."

It is argued that if the right to counsel is afforded prior to indictment, the number of confessions obtained by the police will diminish significantly, because most confessions are obtained during the period between arrest and indictment, and "any lawyer worth his salt will tell the suspect in no uncertain terms to make no statement to police under any circumstances." *Watts v. Indiana.* . . . This argument, of course, cuts two ways. The fact that many confessions are obtained during this period points up its critical nature as a "stage when legal aid and advice" are surely needed. . . . The right to counsel would indeed be hollow if it began at a period when few confessions were obtained. There is necessarily a direct relationship between the importance of a stage to the police in their quest for a confession and the criticalness of that stage to the accused in his need for legal advice. Our Constitution, unlike some others, strikes the balance in favor of the right of the accused to be advised by his lawyer of his privilege against self-incrimination.

We have learned the lesson of history, ancient and modern, that a system of criminal law enforcement which comes to depend on the "confession" will, in the long run, be less reliable and more subject to abuses than a system which depends on extrinsic evidence independently secured through skillful investigation. . . .

This Court also has recognized that "history amply shows that confessions have often been extorted to save law enforcement officials the trouble and effort of obtaining valid and independent evidence. . . ."

We have also learned the companion lesson of history that no system of criminal justice can, or should, survive if it comes to depend for its continued effectiveness on the citizens' abdication through unawareness of their constitutional rights. No system worth preserving should have to *fear* that if an accused is permitted to consult with a lawyer, he will become aware of, and exercise these rights. If the exercise of constitutional rights will thwart the effectiveness of a system of law enforcement, then there is something wrong with that system.

We hold, therefore, that where, as here, the investigation is no longer a general inquiry into an unsolved crime but has begun to focus on a particular suspect, the suspect has been taken into police custody, the police carry out a process of interrogations that lends itself to eliciting incriminating statements, the suspect has requested and been denied an opportunity to consult with his lawyer, and the police have not effectively warned him of his absolute constitutional right to remain silent, the accused has been denied "the Assistance of Counsel" in violation of the Sixth Amendment to the Constitution as "made obligatory upon the States by the Fourteenth Amendment," . . . and that no statement elicited by the police during the interrogation may be used against him at a criminal trial . . .

The judgment of the Illinois Supreme Court is reversed and the case remanded for proceedings not inconsistent with this opinion.

Reversed and remanded.

Mr. Justice Harlan, dissenting:

Supported by no stronger authority than its own rhetoric, the Court today converts a routine police investigation of an unsolved murder into a distorted analogue of a judicial trial. It imports into this investigation constitutional concepts historically applicable only after the onset of formal prosecutorial proceedings. By doing so, I think the Court perverts those precious constitutional guarantees, and frustrates the vital interests of society in preserving the legitimate and proper function of honest and purposeful police investigation.

Like my brother Clark, I cannot escape the logic of my brother White's conclusions as to the extraordinary implications which emanate from the Court's opinion in this case and I share their views as to the untold and highly unfortunate impact today's decision may have upon the fair administration of criminal justice. I can only hope we have completely misunderstood what the Court has said.

In another five-to-four decision in *Miranda v. Arizona,* 1965, these "rights" were substantially strengthened by specifying a series of procedures that arresting officers must follow in order to safeguard the rights of the suspect. Thus, we often see in the innumerable police shows on television a scene following the arrest of a suspect in which the triumphant criminal recites to a frustrated policeman his rights, drawing on the words of the *Miranda* decision. The moral of the scene is that the policeman is unduly hampered in the performance of his duties by the overscrupulous requirements of the Supreme Court.

Mr. Chief Justice Warren delivered the opinion of the Court.

The cases before us raise questions which go to the roots of our concepts of American criminal jurisprudence: the restraints society must observe consistent with the Federal Constitution in prosecuting individuals for crime. More specifically, we deal with the admissibility of statements obtained from an individual who is subjected to custodial police interrogation and the necessity for procedures which assume that the individual is accorded his privilege under the Fifth Amendment to the Constitution not to be compelled to incriminate himself.

We dealt with certain phases of this problem recently in *Escobedo v. State of Illinois.* . . . There, as in the four cases before us, law enforcement officials took the defendant into custody and interrogated him in a police station for the purpose of obtaining a confession. The police did not effectively advise him of his right to remain silent or of his right to consult with his attorney. Rather, they confronted him with an alleged accomplice who accused him of having perpetrated a murder. When the defendant denied the accusation and said "I didn't shoot Manuel, you did it," they handcuffed him and took him to an interrogation room. There, while handcuffed and standing, he was questioned for four hours until he confessed. During this interrogation, the police denied his request to speak to his attorney, and they prevented his retained attorney, who had come to the police station, from consulting with him. At his trial, the State, over his objection, introduced the confession against him. We held that the statements thus made were constitutionally inadmissible. . . .

We start here, as we did in *Escobedo*, with the premise that our holding is not an innovation in our jurisprudence, but is an application of principles long recognized and applied in other settings. We have undertaken a thorough re-examination of the *Escobedo* decision and the principles it announced, and we reaffirm it. That case was but an explication of basic rights that are enshrined in our Constitution—that "No person . . . shall be compelled in any criminal case to be a witness against himself," and that "the accused shall . . . have the Assistance of Counsel"—rights which were put in jeopardy in that case through official overbearing. These precious rights were fixed in our Constitution only after centuries of persecution and struggle. And in the words of Chief Justice Marshall, they were secured "for ages to come, and . . . designed to approach immortality as nearly as human institutions can approach it," . . .

Our holding will be spelled out with some specificity in the pages which follow but briefly stated it is this: the prosecution may not use statements, whether exculpatory or inculpatory, stemming from custodial interrogation of the defendant unless it demonstrates the use of procedural safeguards effective to secure the privilege against self-incrimination. By custodial interrogation, we mean questioning initiated by law enforcement officers after a person has been taken into custody or otherwise deprived of his freedom of action in any significant way. As for the procedural safeguards to be employed, unless other fully effective means are devised to inform accused persons of their right of silence and to assure a continuous opportunity to exercise it, the following measures are required. Prior to any questioning, the person must be warned that he has a right to remain silent, that any statement he does make may be used as evidence against him, and that he has a right to the presence of an attorney, either retained or appointed. The defendant may waive effectuation of these rights, provided the waiver is made voluntarily, knowingly and intelligently. If, however, he indicates in any manner and at any stage of the process that he wishes to consult with an attorney before speaking there can be no questioning. Likewise, if the individual is alone and indicates in any manner that he does not wish to be interrogated, the police may not question him. The mere fact that he may have answered some questions or volunteered some statements on his own does not deprive him of the right to refrain from answering any further inquiries until he has consulted with an attorney and thereafter consents to be questioned. . . .

The difficulty in depicting what transpires at such interrogations stems from the fact that in this country they have largely taken place incommunicado. From extensive factual studies undertaken in the early 1930's, including the famous Wickersham Report to Congress by a Presidential Commission, it is clear that police violence and the "third degree" flourished at that time.

In a series of cases decided by this Court long after these studies, the police resorted to physical brutality—beatings, hanging, whipping—and to sustained and protracted questioning incommunicado in order to extort confessions. The Commission on Civil Rights in 1961 found much evidence to indicate that "some policemen still resort to physical force to obtain confessions," . . . The use of physical brutality and violence is not, unfortunately, relegated to the past or to any part of the country. Only recently in Kings County, New York, the police brutally beat, kicked and placed lighted cigarette butts on the back of a potential witness under interrogation for the purpose of securing a statement incriminating a third party. . . .

The examples given above are undoubtedly the exception now, but they are sufficiently widespread to be the object of concern. Unless a proper limitation upon custodial interrogation is achieved—such as these decisions will advance—there can be no assurance that practices of this nature will be eradicated in the foreseeable future. The Conclusion of the Wickersham Commission Report, made over 30 years ago, is still pertinent:

"To the contention that the third degree is necessary to get the facts, the reporters aptly reply in the language of the present Lord Chancellor of England (Lord Sankey): 'It is not admissible to do a great right by doing a little wrong. . . . It is not sufficient to do justice by obtaining a proper result by irregular or improper means.' . . . We agree with the conclusion expressed in the report, that 'The third degree brutalizes the police, hardens the prisoner against society, and lowers the esteem in which the administration of justice is held by the public' " . . .

. . . Although confessions may play an important role in some convictions, the cases before us present graphic examples of the overstatement of the "need" for confessions. In each case authorities conducted interrogations ranging up to five days in duration despite the presence, through standard investigating practices, of considerable evidence against each defendant. . . .

Over the years the Federal Bureau of Investigation has compiled an exemplary record of effective law enforcement while advising any suspect or arrested person, at the outset of an interview, that he is not required to make a statement, that any statement may be used against him in court, that the individual may obtain the services of an attorney of his own choice and, more recently, that he has a right to free counsel if he is unable to pay. . . .

The practice of the FBI can readily be emulated by state and local enforcement agencies. The argument that the FBI deals with different crimes than are dealt with by state authorities does not mitigate the significance of the FBI experience. . . .

Mr. Justice White, with whom Mr. Justice Harlan and Mr. Justice Stewart join, dissenting. . . .

That the Court's holding today is neither compelled nor even strongly suggested by the language of the Fifth Amendment, is at odds with American and English legal history, and involves a departure from a long line of precedent does not prove either that the Court has exceeded its powers or that the Court is wrong or unwise in its present reinterpretation of the Fifth Amendment. It does, however, underscore the obvious —that the Court has not discovered or found the law in making today's decision, nor has it derived it from some irrefutable sources; what it has done is to make new law and new public policy in much the same way that it has in the course of interpreting other great clauses of the Constitution. This is what the Court historically has done. Indeed, it is what it must do and will continue to do until and unless there is some fundamental change in the constitutional distribution of government powers.

But if the Court is here and now to announce new and fundamental policy to govern certain aspects of our affairs, it is wholly legitimate to examine the mode of this or any other constitutional decision in this Court and to inquire into the advisability of its end product in terms of the long-range interest of the country. At the very least, the Court's text and reasoning should withstand analysis and be a fair exposition of the constitutional provision which its opinion interprets. Decisions like these cannot rest, alone on syllogism, metaphysics or some ill-defined notions of natural justice, although each will perhaps play its part. In proceeding to such constructions as it now announces, the Court should also duly consider all the factors and interests bearing upon the cases, at least insofar as the relevant materials are available; and if the necessary considerations are not treated in the record or obtainable from some other reliable source, the Court should not proceed to formulate fundamental policies based on speculation alone. . . .

The obvious underpinning of the Court's decision is a deep-seated distrust of all confessions. . . . the result adds up to a judicial judgment that evidence from the accused should not be used against him in any way, whether compelled or not. This is the not so subtle overtone of the opinion—that it is inherently wrong for the police to gather evidence from the accused himself. . . .

In some unknown number of cases the Court's rule will return a killer, a rapist or other criminal to the streets and to the environment which produced him, to repeat his crime whenever it pleases him. As a consequence, there will not be a gain, but a loss, in human dignity. The real concern is not the unfortunate consequences of this new decision on the criminal law as an abstract, disembodied series of authoritative proscriptions, but the impact on those who rely on the public authority for protection and who without it can only engage in violent self-help with guns, knives and the help of their neighbors similarly inclined. There is, of course, a saving factor: the next victims are uncertain, unnamed and unrepresented in this case.

Nor can this decision do other than have a corrosive effect on the criminal laws as an effective device to prevent crime. A major component in its effectiveness in this regard is its swift and sure enforcement. The easier it is to get away with rape and murder, the less the deterrent effect on those who are inclined to attempt it. This is still good common sense. If it were not, we should posthaste liquidate the whole law enforcement establishment as a useless, misguided effort to control human conduct. . . .

We cannot leave the Warren Court without some attention to one of its most important decisions, *Baker v. Carr. Baker v. Carr* involved the issue of reapportionment in the state of Tennessee. A suit was brought against the state on the grounds that certain counties were underrepresented in the state legislature and the inhabitants of those counties thereby deprived of "the full protection of the laws" under the Fourteenth Amendment. In one of the longest and most ambitious decisions, the Court decided that it had jurisdiction on the case and ordered Tennessee (and all other states where representation in the legislatures did not accurately reflect population distribution) to reapportion their legislative districts.

G. Edward White, a student of the Warren Court, sums up its accomplishments in these words: "It offered, in separate parts, the

Eighteenth-century linguistics of Marshall and his bold, creative use
of power; the subtle philosophic insights of Holmes, along with his
fatalistic acceptance of the dictates of legislative majorities; the hu-
manitarian impulses of modern liberalism in heaping doses. . . ."
Perhaps the most important of all, it discovered a new area for the
Court to explore and thereby greatly strengthened the rights of individuals, especially the most marginal individuals in our society. It is
not surprising that since its accomplishments came at a time when a
rapidly rising crime rate constituted one of the country's most alarming social problems, the decisions caused little joy among beleaguered
law-enforcement officials or in the mass of citizens who felt themselves
in imminent danger of being shot, stabbed, mugged, or robbed. Nor, it
seems clear, do most Americans care much for other people's civil
rights. Periodic street-corner surveys discover that most interviewees,
being given the Bill of Rights to read without identification, denounce
it as a commie plot to weaken national security by protecting freaks
and hippies from their just deserts. Right-wing groups made it an article of their political faith to call for the impeachment of Earl Warren,
and a future president of the United States went so far as to introduce
a bill into Congress to impeach Justice Douglas for extralegal writings offensive to him.

It is certainly too cynical to say that the civil rights issue was a
godsend to the Court, but the fact remains that attention to the rights
of individuals, important as it was, did more to point up the inequities
and breakdowns in our society than to remedy them. Unwilling or
unable to check the growth of centralized power in the legislative
and executive branches, the Court did the next best thing: it alleviated
some of the pressure on the individuals at the bottom of the pile.
That, ironically, may emerge as the essential and almost exclusive
concern of the Court—the protection of the individual from the
grosser forms of injustice bred by a sprawling and inhuman bureaucracy. But waffling over the constitutionality of the death penalty
and the precise definition of obscenity hardly seem adequate responses
to the major dilemmas of our society. Such concerns, while legitimate, are a far cry from the days when the decisions of the Court
affected the highest levels of governmental policy.

What must be said finally about the Warren Court is that by its
complete acceptance of incorporation, it gave us a very precious gift,
long withheld, the Bill of Rights, and in doing so erected what may

turn out to be the sturdiest defense of all for the sadly battered Constitution, which has given us our shape as a people and remains our guardian against anarchy. Perhaps it will become the primary function of the Court to ensure our most essential right, that of free speech, so that we may explore without inhibition or constraint the means of containing and redistributing those undue concentrations of power which threaten our sanity and our survival.

CHAPTER

XXIII

CONCLUSION

AMONG THE DISMAL CONSEQUENCES OF THE VIETNAM WAR WAS
Watergate. If we take Watergate as a kind of code word for the lawlessness of the executive branch of the government (the lawlessness
extended far beyond the president himself), we must, I believe, admit
that its roots lie in the terms of the "good presidents"—Roosevelt,
Eisenhower, Johnson, and Kennedy—who used such agencies of the
executive branch as the I.R.S., the F.B.I. and the C.I.A. to harass
their political opponents and enhance their own power. We may be
reminded again of those maxims to the effect that power corrupts
and unrestrained power will be used corruptly. The significance of
Watergate was that it dramatized, hopefully in an unforgettable way,
the truth of this ancient axiom.

Yet Watergate was plainly an accident, a wholly fortuitous combination of bizarre circumstances. Contrast it, for example, with the
duly appointed procedures of the Supreme Court in historic cases
rising from abuse of presidential powers. In those instances learned
lawyers assembled extensive briefs and argued them before fascinated
and attentive audiences—before, in a real sense, the whole country.
Watergate began with a bungled burglary. Gradually, in large part
because of the indefatigable efforts of two young investigative reporters, more and more of the facts behind the Watergate episode
began to come out, *but* if it had not been for the vanity and folly of
President Nixon in taping the discussions with the White House staff
there would have been no clear link between him and CREEP (the
Committee to Re-Elect the President) or the Plumbers unit.

The existence of the tapes was revealed almost inadvertently. If

Nixon had simply destroyed the tapes when their existence became known on the not unreasonable grounds that they contained confidential information, there would have been insufficient grounds to initiate impeachment proceedings against him. Thus the egregious abuse of presidential power and the involvement of the president himself in a conspiracy to obstruct justice came to light by a series of chance events. Even with all this, he might have escaped virtually unscathed if he had not repeatedly lied about the nature of his involvement. Every response of the president to the storm that rose over Watergate was ill conceived and bore the marks of that self-destructiveness that so often characterized his actions. There is considerable evidence that Nixon never really understood the peril that he was in. This was, one fears, in part at least because he perceived himself as simply doing more skillfully what other occupants of the White House had done before him. His whole demeanor expressed his chagrin over the unfairness of his being gigged for what the other fellows had all been doing with impunity. The impeachment proceedings strengthened his conviction that he was the victim of the malice of the liberal establishment and its pliant tool, the press.

Moreover, if Nixon had had the advantage of a strong Republican majority in Congress it is doubtful that the impeachment proceedings would ever have gotten off the ground. It was his particular misfortune to be the erring president of a party very much in the minority in both the House and the Senate. Party interests thus reinforced the public demand that justice be done. What followed was a drama of extraordinary potency enacted before a substantial portion of the American people. The electronic miracle of television turned the nation into a town meeting or a single vast hearing chamber. Newspapers and magazines hastened to inform the public about the nature of impeachment, how derived and when it had been used before (in the abortive effort of Jefferson to impeach Justice Samuel Chase and in the impeachment proceedings against Andrew Johnson following the Civil War). The Constitution, a direct knowledge and understanding of which had faded in the consciousness of the American people to a few textbook platitudes, was suddenly revealed as "a living document," a document in the name of which a president with markedly criminal inclinations could be removed from office. People were awed and impressed. Many Americans suddenly felt a need to know more about this rather obscure charter. How could it reach over all the intervening years to force a president out of office, a president who had just been elected by one of the largest majorities in our history?

This book was conceived in the aftermath of Watergate. Its purpose was to give the reader, through text and narrative, a handy reference work containing the essential documents and some helpful commentary. The task turned out to be more arduous and more interesting than I had anticipated. I discovered the Constitution myself for the first time. I had anticipated ending the book on a definite upbeat "Watergate" note. This is the Constitution. This is how it was created. It rose out of a strange conjunction of political and theological ideas several thousand years fermenting. It was brought off by the narrowest of margins, the greatest act of political prestidigitation in all recorded history. It found its essential focus in the Supreme Court, which defined it with, on the whole, remarkable skill and wisdom for the last two hundred years, making it the longest-lived and most serviceable written constitution in the world, a model for virtually every subsequent constitution. And now with the Constitution a far less immediate reality to us than it had been to our ancestors, Watergate reminded us, in most striking fashion, of the existence and the importance of the document that shaped us in our formative years.

But the book, discovering its own life and logic, stubbornly refused to come out that way. This would have been, I am sure, no surprise to a scholar in American constitutional history, but it was to me, an amateur of the Constitution. Watergate, for example, turned out to be a far more ambiguous event than I had at first imagined. What it pointed up was the fact that we no longer have properly functioning constitutional restraints on the powers of the president. The Supreme Court did, of course, behave in an exemplary manner in the Watergate episode. At every point the justices preferred the law to the president and forced him relentlessly to disgorge the tainted tapes. The justices reasserted the ancient principle, dating from Sir Edward Coke, that even the king is under the law ("the law doth command the king"), a principle which it was clear the president did not believe applied to him. He, it will be recalled, invoked something called "executive privilege," the effect of which, if accepted, would have been to place him beyond the law, or above it.

Still it is not clear by any means that, criminal activities aside, he was not "beyond" it, beyond at least the classic constraints of the Constitution. It has been said that the Constitution is what the Supreme Court says it is. It might now be said that the powers of the president are what the president *does*, sometimes hampered and sometimes aided by Congress. In trying to describe in rather summary fashion the powers of the executive branch of the government, I have found it increasingly difficult to do so in terms of the Constitution, or in terms of powers clearly granted to the president under the Constitution. It is ironic that the Founding Fathers, rejecting so emphatically the model of a king, created an office presently invested with authority far beyond that of any surviving king and only to be rivaled by the powers of absolute monarchs. Most Americans, in modern times at least, have watched that office grow in power, reassured by the conviction that, as John Adams put it, "only wise and honest men" would occupy it. Richard Nixon proved that hope illusory, or, more accurately, his stumbling revealed how susceptible the office had become to gross abuse of its powers and revealed also that his predecessors had, in many instances, been only slightly less arrogant and arbitrary in the misuse of that power, albeit considerably luckier in not being found out.

This excursion has converted my mild uneasiness over the powers accumulated by the president into outright alarm. I am not convinced that constitutional government can survive (or, indeed, that it has). There are quite clearly no simple remedies. Our society and the world are beset by large, more or less unmanageable concentrations of power. The criminal tendencies of huge corporations like ITT and Lockheed are matched or exceeded by those of Big Labor sometimes allied with Big Crime. Occasionally the criminal tendencies in Big Government combine with those in Big Business or Big Labor or Big Crime to carry out criminal activities on a global scale—ITT in Chile, the alleged Mafia-C.I.A. alliance to assassinate Castro, the seduction of labor unions, universities and the press by the C.I.A., and so on. We are told solemnly and repeatedly that a virtually omnipotent president and a ubiquitous bureaucracy are necessary in order to cope with the "realities of the modern world." It seems to me that that is tantamount to telling us that we have to accept the dismantling of the Constitution or the simple ignoring of it and condone criminal behavior in order to preserve our high standard of living and protect our "national security."

In *The Constitution Reconsidered*, the 1937 symposium volume, William Yandell Elliott, professor of government at Harvard, described the "myth" of the Constitution and its hold on the popular imagination as recently demonstrated by the public resistance to Franklin Roosevelt's efforts to pack the Court with new appointees. Could the myth be sustained? he asked. "How much skepticism can be tolerated in a period of new faiths that really clash? This is a problem of greater and more permanent import. Will it be possible to retain a form which places such emphasis on negative restraints on power through checks and balances—the federal principle, judicial review, etc.—in times when the national security and domestic tranquility, that is so-called social security, both seem to indicate a concentration of powers for planning that accomplish results without the possibilities of stalemate and indefinite delays?" It seemed to Elliott that the "corporate state," an uneasy alliance of business, government, and labor, already visible in England, was the coming form of social and economic order in the United States. He answered his rather pessimistic question by an ambiguous quotation from Alfred North Whitehead: "Those societies which cannot combine reverence to their symbols with freedom of revision, must ultimately decay either from anarchy, or from the slow atrophy of a life stifled by useless shadows."

Clearly, since Elliott wrote his gloomy if prophetic analysis, we have moved far down the path of the "corporate state." In its inordinate growth it has demonstrated the ancient principle that excessive concentrations of power are invariably abused. In addition they create countervailing concentrations of power, so that there is a multiplier effect in both inhumanity and inefficiency. The classic example is the growth of federal regulatory agencies, which if they are not unconstitutional are certainly aconstitutional in that the Constitution does not provide for them. The framers could not have imagined them, and, existing as semiautonomous entities with, in many cases, extraordinary powers, they are, by their nature, undemocratic. But it must be kept in mind that they grew up in order to check abuses and to regulate the irregular activities of large corporations. (I am informed that there are somewhere in the neighborhood of twenty-six agencies that have regulatory responsibilities in regard to the steel industry.) Businessmen howl in often justifiable rage at the arbitrary actions of such agencies and at the knots and tangles of red tape in which they entwine them. The liberal reformer listens with little sympathy, taking note of the fact that the regulatory agencies are often stacked with representatives of the industries that they are supposed to regulate, which, in his view, is like putting the wolves to guard the sheep.

It is difficult to imagine that the Supreme Court can find a way to reassert its classic role of limiting the powers of the coordinate branches of the government roughly within the confines of the Constitution. There is simply too much to be undone. On the other hand, it is madness, thinly glossed over, to trust the future of the world to one man—the president of the United States. So perhaps we have painted ourselves into an ideological corner from which there truly is no escape, and this work, which set out to be a handbook by means of which concerned citizens might come to understand and value the Constitution, becomes "academic," a "history" instead of a "handbook," an exercise in increasingly popular nostalgia.

I find the central focus of the constitutional epoch a story of great and inexhaustible drama and poignance, full of captivating if by no means perfect heroes and not-so-villainous villains. It has enough unexpected denouements, surprise endings, ironic turns of events, and intensely human subdramas to fill a hundred novels. It rushes, or lurches, from one crisis to another but always seems to survive and indeed emerge from each crisis stronger than before, but not always and not forever. The story even has a superficially happy ending (one that I had hoped would be a more or less unqualifiedly happy one)— that is to say, the modern Court has animated, almost literally for the first time, the great repository of individual human rights contained in the first eight amendments to the Constitution and thus given the Constitution itself a new life and prominence.

Rereading the decisions of the Court, one is impressed anew with the ingenuity of human reason in discovering rationales for declaring true what it wishes to be true (or constitutional). We have seen the Court, time after time, alter, by often curious and subtle arguments, the intention of earlier decisions which had become an impediment to "progress" or, perhaps more accurately, an impediment to the "popular will." On the other hand we have seen the Court, in many instances, cling stubbornly to its principles however unpopular or uncongenial those principles may have been to a majority of the citizens of the Republic. A cynic might echo Mr. Dooley's observation that the decisions of the Court follow the election returns. But, as Mr. Dooley might also say, "Not so fast." The most basic strength of the Court is that someone or some agency has to make ultimate judgments on all matters regarding our political life. It is thus better that a decision be made by which, right or wrong, people can abide rather than seek redress by a less orderly process. It follows that even if the decisions of the Court had been far more inconsistent or subject to challenge than they in fact have been, we might well have endured them in preference to the alternatives.

But the Court, of course, was far more than that. In the words of Alexis de Tocqueville writing in the 1830's: "The Supreme Court is placed at the head of all known tribunals, both by the nature of its rights and the class of justiciable parties which it controls. The peace, the prosperity and the very existence of the Union are placed in the hands of the Judges. Without their active cooperation the Constitution would be a dead letter; the Executive appeals to them for protection against the encroachment of the Legislative power; the Legislature demands their protection against the designs of the Executive; they defend the Union against the disobedience of the States; the States, from the exaggerated claims of the Union; the public interests against the interests of private citizens; and the conservative spirit of order against the innovations of an excited democracy."

I believe that the Classical-Christian Consciousness, as it was manifested in the minds of the Founding Fathers and in the debates of the federal convention, contains many ideas as valid today as when they were so strikingly articulated in the eighteenth century. The Secular-Democratic Consciousness, for all its indisputably positive elements, is comparatively superficial beside it. I can find no major flaw in the framers' view that since all people were tainted with original sin, i.e., disposed to pursue their own selfish interests rather than the common good, it was necessary to distribute power in such a way as to minimize the dangers of its being abused, and to protect all legitimate social and economic interests from appropriation or exploitation. If they overstated the degree of human depravity, that was certainly a far sounder approach than to overestimate man's natural goodness as the theoreticians of the French Revolution did. Our problem today is, more than ever, how to restrain and redistribute power. The Founders' formula—human selfishness times power equals corruption—has been verified thousands of times since they framed the Constitution.

Another of their doctrines was that when a people became confused and demoralized they should return to "first principles," the basic postulates from which their peoplehood had been derived, the controlling social and political assumptions which had determined their history as a nation. I believe in the soundness of that proposition as well. Those who tell us that the ideals and the philosophy of the Founding Fathers are irrelevant to our present "world posture" should have to prove their case before the bar of informed public opinion.

I trust it is clear by now that I am not excessively sanguine about a resolution of our present difficulties. I am, however, entirely persuaded that we cannot possibly find a way out of those difficulties without thoughtful attention to all that our past has to teach.

Mysterious and protean, the Constitution, accomplished by the narrowest of margins, expresses the essence of our reality as a people. In the federal debates and in the long succession of Supreme Court cases that were, in a sense, a continuation of the debates themselves, the American people were spoken into existence as a nation. There has been no comparable event in history. In those repeated and indefatigable explorations through *speech*, passion and logic fused and held auditors transfixed. By such means was the Union continually defined and redefined. The nation could not have survived without these dramatic enactments of our most basic reality. If we talk about the role of the Court in narrow legal terms—a series of decisions creating a body of constitutional law—we miss the most important function of the Court in the first century of our history. The Court was a theater, a stage, on which the greatest actors of the day *enacted* American history, a history which otherwise must have remained largely inaccessible to the average citizen. It was as though the great legal orators were constantly improvising scripts to explain us to ourselves. Other nations had taken their shape over centuries; the rise and fall of dynasties, the overthrow of feudalism, the gradual accumulation of history, of customs and forms that described and verified a people's common life, ultimately their nationhood.

In America some means had to be discovered that would telescope the slow, almost instinctual development of a nation into a few brief generations. The Court, in a way that none of the framers could have anticipated, performed this function marvelously well and thereby gave new potency to Cicero's maxim: "History at its highest is oratory." After the Civil War, with the issue of Union settled, the role of the Court changed. It was no longer necessary for it to function as dramatic representation, as a forum in which powerful orators created the consciousness of the nation. Its task became the more mundane —one of consolidating the power of the federal government, thereby creating a *national system,* the symbol and reality of which were the railroads which spanned the continent. It was evidently America's destiny to become a great industrial nation. The Court, for the most part, assiduously abetted what it doubtless could not have resisted in any event.

Then, rendered a cipher by unprecedented growth of presidential power supported by a pliant Congress, the Court found a new and creative role for itself in the area of civil rights and thereby entered, to most observers surprisingly, on one of its great creative eras.

We have seen that the Founding Fathers and the justices of the early Court believed that there was a discoverable order in the universe that governed, or should govern, in the affairs of men as it governed the movement of the planets and the world of nature. The source of this law was God. The duty of the faithful was to try, by reference to history and revelation (indeed history itself was a revelation of divine purpose) to understand the divine purpose and to assist that purpose by certain human contrivances, among them constitutions. It was also clear that the understanding of God's purpose was progressive. That is to say, it might and hopefully would be better understood in the future than it had been in the past. Thus while divine absolutes governed the universe, man's understanding of them was "relative," i.e., subject to continual refinement. Therefore any constitution must be subject to change, to improvement and modification as a consequence of a better understanding of God's law and his intentions for the race. This consciousness is, in essence, what I have chosen to call the Classical-Christian Consciousness. It should also be evident by now that the basic assumptions which formed this consciousness are no longer believed in or adhered to by the vast majority of Americans who live under the Constitution. In that sense it is, as its critics have charged, an archaic document. But it is equally clear that the Secular-Democratic Consciousness which has largely replaced it is incapable of constitution making and is, indeed, in such a state of confusion and demoralization that it has neither the will nor the energy to even undertake the task. That is, on the whole, fortunate, inasmuch as it would have little or no chance of improving on the present system, whatever its shortcomings. Quite the contrary, such an effort would simply demonstrate to what degree the "consensus" that made the creation of the United States possible has been eroded by abuse of power, greed, self-seeking, and materialism.

This is not, however, to end on a cynical or despairing note. While it is true that the consciousness that created the Constitution no longer exists, at least as a collective consciousness, the Constitution has developed, as we say, a life of its own. It has taken on a powerful symbolic and mythic quality that transcends the circumstances of its origin. It has proved so congenial to or adaptable to the democratic-capitalist temper that most of us cannot conceive of doing without it or imagine how it might be substantially improved. In simple fact, a major argument of this work is that far from needing to be changed "to more realistically reflect the changed times," it needs to be far more rigorously observed. If it is true, as I and certainly many others have contended, that the powers of the presidency are dangerously inflated, our best hope of restraining and pruning those powers rests with a more faithful observation of the spirit, as well as the letter, of the Constitution. The first step in that process is to recover the original meaning and intent of that famous but too little known document.

There is a further source of hope. The state of mind (or the consciousness) which disposed the Court to abandon its traditional role of trying to set limits to the powers of the other branches of government may be in the process of changing. Our rather simpleminded faith in the capacity of Big Government to solve all problems seems to have substantially diminished. A movement to recover local initiatives and a profound skepticism about overblown institutions and inefficient bureaucracies are manifest in many segments of our society. Suspicion of the "big" and a romantic attachment to the "small" are similarly evident. The Secular-Democratic Consciousness itself seems to be undergoing a crisis of the spirit. It is perhaps only necessary for the more creative and enduring elements of the Classical-Christian Consciousness to reassert themselves for a new intellectual climate to emerge in which much that presently seems irretrievably lost may be recovered.

History is, fortunately for the species, wiser than historians. No one can profess to know for a certainty how it will come out. The American people have displayed a remarkable resiliency. We have seen them confront, in constitutional terms, a series of problems that often seemed insoluble. Indeed, they were less solved than surmounted and the surmounting came to constitute the solution. The future of the Constitution, like the future of our country, is uncertain. Despite the enormous obstacles to the survival of the Constitution in anything like the form or spirit in which it was conceived, we have come to understand the inexhaustible creative resources and energies which mankind and womankind are capable of deploying against the most intractable of problems. If the Founding Fathers doubted the natural goodness of the race, they did not doubt its determination and resourcefulness. Nor, I believe, should we.

APPENDIX

AMENDMENTS TO THE CONSTITUTION

ARTICLES IN ADDITION TO, AND AMENDMENT OF THE CONSTITUTION of the United States of America, proposed by Congress, and ratified by the Legislatures of the several States, pursuant to the fifth Article of the original Constitution.

[The first ten articles proposed 25 Sept. 1789; declared in force 15 Dec. 1791]

ARTICLE I

Congress shall make no law respecting an establishment of religion, or prohibiting the free exercise thereof; or abridging the freedom of speech, or of the press; or the right of the people peaceably to assemble, and to petition the Government for a redress of grievances.

ARTICLE II

A well regulated Militia, being necessary to the security of a free State, the right of the people to keep and bear Arms, shall not be infringed.

ARTICLE III

No Soldier shall, in time of peace, be quartered in any house, without the consent of the Owner, nor in time of war, but in a manner to be prescribed by law.

ARTICLE IV

The right of the people to be secure in their persons, houses, papers, and effects, against unreasonable searches and seizures, shall not be violated, and no Warrants shall issue, but upon probable cause, supported by Oath or affirmation, and particularly describing the place to be searched, and the persons or things to be seized.

ARTICLE V

No person shall be held to answer for a capital, or otherwise infamous crime, unless on a presentment or indictment of a Grand Jury, except in cases arising in the land or naval forces, or in the Militia, when in actual service in time of War or public danger; nor shall any person be subject for the same offense to be twice put in jeopardy of life or limb; nor shall be compelled in any criminal case to be a witness against himself, nor be deprived of life, liberty, or property, without due process of law; nor shall private property be taken for public use, without just compensation.

ARTICLE VI

In all criminal prosecutions, the accused shall enjoy the right to a speedy and public trial, by an impartial jury of the State and district wherein the crime shall have been committed, which district shall have been previously ascertained by law, and to be informed of the nature and cause of the accusation; to be confronted with the witnesses against him; to have compulsory process for obtaining witnesses in his favor, and to have the Assistance of Counsel for his defense.

ARTICLE VII

In Suits at common law, where the value in controversy shall exceed twenty dollars, the right of trial by jury shall be preserved, and no fact tried by a jury, shall be otherwise re-examined in any Court of the United States, than according to the rules of the common law.

ARTICLE VIII

Excessive bail shall not be required, nor excessive fines imposed, nor cruel and unusual punishments inflicted.

ARTICLE IX

The enumeration in the Constitution, of certain rights, shall not be construed to deny or disparage others retained by the people.

ARTICLE X

The powers not delegated to the United States by the Constitution, nor prohibited by it to the States, are reserved to the States respectively, or to the people.

ARTICLE XI
[proposed 5 Mar. 1794;
declared ratified 8 Jan. 1798]

The Judicial power of the United States shall not be construed to extend to any suit in law or equity, commenced or prosecuted against one of the United States by Citizens of another State, or by Citizens or Subjects of any Foreign State.

ARTICLE XII
[proposed 12 Dec. 1803;
declared ratified 25 Sept. 1804]

The Electors shall meet in their respective states, and vote by ballot for President and Vice-President, one of whom, at least, shall not be an inhabitant of the same state with themselves; they shall name in their ballots the person voted for as President, and in distinct ballots the person voted for as Vice-President, and they shall make distinct lists of all persons voted for as President, and of all persons voted for as Vice-President, and of the number of votes for each, which lists they shall sign and certify, and transmit sealed to the seat of the government of the United States, directed to the President of the Senate; —The President of the Senate shall, in the presence of the Senate and House of Representatives, open all certificates and the votes shall then be counted;—The person having the greatest number of votes for

President, shall be the President, if such number be a majority of the whole number of Electors appointed; and if no person have such majority, then from the persons having the highest numbers not exceeding three on the list of those voted for as President, the House of Representatives shall choose immediately, by ballot, the President. But in choosing the President, the votes shall be taken by states, the representation from each state having one vote; a quorum for this purpose shall consist of a member or members from two-thirds of the states, and a majority of all the states shall be necessary to a choice. And if the House of Representatives shall not choose a President whenever the right of choice shall devolve upon them, before the fourth day of March next following, then the Vice-President shall act as President, as in the case of the death or other constitutional disability of the President.—The person having the greatest number of votes as Vice-President, shall be the Vice-President, if such number be a majority of the whole number of Electors appointed, and if no person have a majority, then from the two highest numbers on the list, the Senate shall choose the Vice-President; a quorum for the purpose shall consist of two-thirds of the whole number of Senators, and a majority of the whole number shall be necessary to a choice. But no person constitutionally ineligible to the office of President shall be eligible to that of Vice-President of the United States.

ARTICLE XIII
[proposed 1 Feb. 1865;
declared ratified 18 Dec. 1865]

Section 1. Neither slavery nor involuntary servitude, except as a punishment for crime whereof the party shall have been duly convicted, shall exist within the United States, or any place subject to their jurisdiction.

Section 2. Congress shall have power to enforce this article by appropriate legislation.

ARTICLE XIV
[proposed 16 June 1866;
declared ratified 28 July 1868]

Section 1. All persons born or naturalized in the United States, and subject to the jurisdiction thereof, are citizens of the United States and of the State wherein they reside. No State shall make or enforce any law which shall abridge the privileges or immunities of citizens of the United States; nor shall any State deprive any person of life, liberty, or property, without due process of law; nor deny to any person within its jurisdiction the equal protection of the laws.

Section 2. Representatives shall be apportioned among the several States according to their respective numbers, counting the whole number of persons in each State, excluding Indians not taxed. But when the right to vote at any election for the choice of electors for President and Vice-President of the United States, Representatives in Congress, the Executive and Judicial officers of a State, or the members of the Legislature thereof, is denied to any of the male inhabitants of such State, being twenty-one years of age, and citizens of the United States, or in any way abridged, except for participation in rebellion, or other crime, the basis of representation therein shall be reduced in the proportion which the number of such male citizens shall bear to the whole number of male citizens twenty-one years of age in such State.

Section 3. No person shall be a Senator or Representative in Congress, or elector of President and Vice-President, or hold any office, civil or military, under the United States, or under any State, who, having previously taken an oath, as a member of Congress, or as an officer of the United States, or as a member of any State legislature, or as an executive or judicial officer of any State, to support the Constitution of the United States, shall have engaged in insurrection or rebellion against the same, or given aid and comfort to the enemies thereof. But Congress may by a vote of two-thirds of each House, remove such disability.

Section 4. The validity of the public debt of the United States, authorized by law, including debts incurred for payment of pensions and bounties for services in suppressing insurrection or rebellion, shall not be questioned. But neither the United States nor any state shall assume or pay any debt or obligation incurred in aid of insurrection or rebellion against the United States, or any claim for the loss or emancipation of any slave; but all such debts, obligations, and claims shall be held illegal and void.

Section 5. The Congress shall have power to enforce, by appropriate legislation, the provisions of this article.

ARTICLE XV
[proposed 27 Feb. 1869;
declared ratified 30 Mar. 1870]

Section 1. The right of citizens of the United States to vote shall not be denied or abridged by the United States or by any State on account of race, color, or previous condition of servitude.

Section 2. The Congress shall have power to enforce this article by appropriate legislation.

ARTICLE XVI
[proposed 12 July 1909;
declared ratified 25 Feb. 1913]

The Congress shall have power to lay and collect taxes on incomes, from whatever source derived, without apportionment among the several States, and without regard to any census or enumeration.

ARTICLE XVII
[proposed 16 May 1912;
declared ratified 31 May 1913]

The Senate of the United States shall be composed of two Senators from each State, elected by the people thereof, for six years; and each Senator shall have one vote. The electors in each State shall have the qualifications requisite for electors of the most numerous branch of the State legislatures.

When vacancies happen in the representation of any State in the Senate, the executive authority of such State shall issue writs of election to fill such vacancies: *Provided,* That the legislature of any State may empower the executive thereof to make temporary appointments until the people fill the vacancies by election as the legislature may direct.

This amendment shall not be so construed as to affect the election or term of any Senator chosen before it becomes valid as part of the Constitution.

ARTICLE XVIII
[proposed 18 Dec. 1917;
declared ratified 29 Jan. 1919; repealed
by the 21st Amendment]

Section 1. After one year from the ratification of this article the manufacture, sale, or transportation of intoxicating liquors within, the importation thereof into, or the exportation thereof from the United States and all territory subject to the jurisdiction thereof for beverage purposes is hereby prohibited.

Section 2. The Congress and the several States shall have concurrent power to enforce this article by appropriate legislation.

Section 3. This article shall be inoperative unless it shall have been ratified as an amendment to the Constitution by the legislatures of the several States, as provided in the Constitution, within seven years from the date of the submission hereof to the States by the Congress.*

ARTICLE XIX
[proposed 4 June 1919;
declared ratified 26 Aug. 1920]

The right of citizens of the United States to vote shall not be denied or abridged by the United States or by any State on account of sex.

Congress shall have power to enforce this article by appropriate legislation.

ARTICLE XX
[proposed 2 Mar. 1932;
declared ratified 6 Feb. 1933]

Section 1. The terms of the President and Vice-President shall end at noon on the 20th day of January, and the terms of Senators and Representatives at noon on the 3d day of January, of the years in which such terms would have ended if this article had not been ratified; and the terms of their successors shall then begin.

Section 2. The Congress shall assemble at least once in every year,

---

* Superseded by the Twenty-first Amendment.

and such meeting shall begin at noon on the 3d day of January, unless they shall by law appoint a different day.

Section 3. If, at the time fixed for the beginning of the term of the President, the President elect shall have died, the Vice-President elect shall become President. If a President shall not have been chosen before the time fixed for the beginning of his term, or if the President elect shall have failed to qualify, then the Vice-President elect shall act as President until a President shall have qualified; and the Congress may by law provide for the case wherein neither a President elect nor a Vice-President elect shall have qualified, declaring who shall then act as President, or the manner in which one who is to act shall be selected, and such person shall act accordingly until a President or Vice-President shall have qualified.

Section 4. The Congress may by law provide for the case of the death of any of the persons from whom the House of Representatives may choose a President whenever the right of choice shall have devolved upon them, and for the case of the death of any of the persons from whom the Senate may choose a Vice-President whenever the right of choice shall have devolved upon them.

Section 5. Sections 1 and 2 shall take effect on the 15th day of October following the ratification of this article.

Section 6. This article shall be inoperative unless it shall have been ratified as an amendment to the Constitution by the legislatures of three-fourths of the several States within seven years from the date of its submission.

ARTICLE XXI
*[proposed 20 Feb. 1933;
declared ratified 5 Dec. 1933]*

Section 1. The Eighteenth article of amendment to the Constitution of the United States is hereby repealed.

Section 2. The transportation or importation into any State, Territory, or possession of the United States for delivery or use therein of intoxicating liquors, in violation of the laws thereof, is hereby prohibited.

Section 3. This article shall be inoperative unless it shall have been ratified as an amendment to the Constitution by conventions in the several States, as provided in the Constitution, within seven years from the date of the submission hereof to the States by the Congress.

ARTICLE XXII
[proposed 24 Mar. 1947;
declared ratified 26 Feb. 1951]

Section 1. No person shall be elected to the office of the President more than twice, and no person who has held the office of President, or acted as President, for more than two years of a term to which some other person was elected President shall be elected to the office of the President more than once. But this Article shall not apply to any person holding the office of President when this Article was proposed by the Congress, and shall not prevent any person who may be holding the office of President, or acting as President, during the term within which this article becomes operative from holding the office of President or acting as President during the remainder of such term.

Section 2. This article shall be inoperative unless it shall have been ratified as an amendment to the Constitution by the legislatures of three-fourths of the several States within seven years from the date of its submission to the States by the Congress.

ARTICLE XXIII
[proposed 16 June 1960;
declared ratified 3 April 1961]

Section 1. The District constituting the seat of Government of the United States shall appoint in such manner as the Congress may direct:

A number of electors of President and Vice-President equal to the whole number of Senators and Representatives in Congress to which the District would be entitled if it were a State, but in no event more than the least populous State; they shall be in addition to those appointed by the States, but they shall be considered, for the purposes of the election of President and Vice-President, to be electors appointed by a State; and they shall meet in the District and perform such duties as provided by the twelfth article of amendment.

Section 2. The Congress shall have power to enforce this article by appropriate legislation.

ARTICLE XXIV
[proposed 27 August 1962;
declared ratified 23 Jan. 1964]

Section 1. The right of citizens of the United States to vote in any primary or other election for President or Vice-President, for electors for President or Vice-President, or for Senator or Representative in Congress, shall not be denied or abridged by the United States or any State by reason of failure to pay any poll tax or other tax.

Section 2. The Congress shall have power to enforce this article by appropriate legislation.

ARTICLE XXV
[proposed 6 July 1965;
declared ratified 10 Feb. 1967]

Section 1. In case of the removal of the President from office or his death or resignation, the Vice-President shall become President.

Section 2. Whenever there is a vacancy in the office of the Vice-President, the President shall nominate a Vice-President who shall take the office upon confirmation by a majority vote of both houses of Congress.

Section 3. Whenever the President transmits to the President pro tempore of the Senate and the Speaker of the House of Representatives his written declaration that he is unable to discharge the powers and duties of his office, and until he transmits to them a written declaration to the contrary, such powers and duties shall be discharged by the Vice-President as Acting President.

Section 4. Whenever the Vice-President and a majority of either the principal officers of the executive departments or of such other body as Congress may by law provide, transmit to the President pro tempore of the Senate and the Speaker of the House of Representatives their written declaration that the President is unable to discharge the powers and duties of his office, the Vice-President shall immediately assume the powers and duties of the office as Acting President.

Thereafter, when the President transmits to the President pro tempore of the Senate and the Speaker of the House of Representatives his written declaration that no disability exists, he shall resume the powers and duties of his office unless the Vice-President and a majority of either the principal officers of the executive department or of any such body as Congress may by law provide, transmit within four days to the President pro tempore of the Senate and the Speaker of the House of Representatives their written declaration that the President is unable to discharge the powers and duties of his office. Thereupon Congress shall decide the issue, assembling within 48 hours for that purpose if not in session. If the Congress, within 21 days after receipt of the latter written declaration, or, if Congress is not in session, within 21 days after Congress is required to assemble, determines by two-thirds vote of both houses that the President is unable to discharge the powers and duties of his office, the Vice-President shall continue to discharge the same as Acting President; otherwise, the President shall resume the powers and duties of his office.

ARTICLE XXVI
[proposed 23 Mar. 1971;
declared ratified 30 June 1971]

Section 1. The right of citizens of the United States, who are 18 years of age or older, to vote shall not be denied or abridged by the United States or by any state on account of age.

Section 2. Congress shall have power to enforce this article by appropriate legislation.

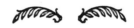

INDEX